Joseph P. Gillespie

The Powers of Psychiatry

BOOKS BY JONAS ROBITSCHER

Pursuit of Agreement: Psychiatry and the Law

Eugenic Sterilization (editor)

The Powers of Psychiatry

The Powers of Psychiatry

JONAS ROBITSCHER, J.D., M.D.

Boston
HOUGHTON MIFFLIN COMPANY
1980

Library of Congress Cataloging in Publication Data

Robitscher, Jonas B
The powers of psychiatry.

Includes bibliographical references and index.
1.Psychiatry—Social aspects. 2.Power (Social sciences)
3.Control (Psychology) 4.Forensic psychiatry.
I.Title. [DNLM: 1. Psychiatry. WM21R666P]
RC455.R57   616.89   79-27764
ISBN 0-395-28222-5

Printed in the United States of America

P 10 9 8 7 6 5 4 3 2 1

The author gratefully acknowledges permission to quote from the following works:

Words for Dr. Y: Uncollected Poems of Anne Sexton, edited by Linda Gray Sexton. Copyright © 1978 by Linda Gray Sexton and Loring Conant, Jr., Executors of the Will of Anne Sexton. Reprinted by permission of Houghton Mifflin Company.

"The Exception and the Rule," in *The Jewish Wife and Other Short Plays,* by Bertolt Brecht, translated by Eric Bentley. Copyright © 1965 by Bertolt Brecht. Reprinted by permission of Grove Press.

"Personal Politics and Psychoanalysis," by Jeffry Galper, in *Social Policy,* November/December 1973, pp. 35–36, 40–41. Copyright © 1973 Social Policy Corporation.Reprinted by permisson of Social Policy Corporation.

To Jan, Christine, and John

Acknowledgments

THIS BOOK REPRESENTS the accumulation of twenty years of work and thought on the extent of psychiatric power and the checks needed to control that power. During this period I have been stimulated by a host of legal psychiatrists and lawyers working and writing in the field, by law students at Villanova and Emory universities, and by other professional colleagues.

Some of the writers and workers in legal psychiatry who have influenced my views are Alan Stone, Loren Roth, Joel Klein, the late Browning Hoffman, Alexander Brooks, Ralph Slovenko, A. Louis McGarry, Robert Sadoff, Herbert Thomas, and Jonas Rappeport. Although I have benefited from them and they have influenced my thinking, they should not be considered responsible for my opinions, for we do not necessarily see eye to eye.

Jeffry Galper has required me to think about the implicit values of therapists, and I am grateful to him for this.

I owe particular debt to the law students who have taken my paper-writing courses; I have gained from their research, their questioning, their points of view.

Three persons who have had unusual experiences in the mental hospital system have been willing to share these, and I wish to acknowledge my debt to Roy Schuster, Peter Mayock, and the patient referred to in this book as "George Davis."

At long distance I was able to secure much help from June Strickland, Librarian of the Institute of the Pennsylvania Hospital, who was unfailingly cheerful in furnishing answers and material. Closer at hand, I relied on Claydean Cameron and Robert Coleman for research help and am in their debt. People too numerous to count have been kind enough to answer questions and furnish citations, and this has more than made up for the lack of response to some queries and the

vii

unavailability of statistics and information that would have been helpful. I am particularly grateful to Carol Kilroy, who typed this manuscript in its various versions and was able to turn almost illegible interlineated rough drafts into a neat product.

I have a special gratitude to three groups that have sponsored some of my work, although not specifically this book. The Center for Studies of Crime and Delinquency of the National Institute of Mental Health at one time supported a teaching program for residents at the University of Pennsylvania School of Medicine, and this helped me achieve a more complete immersion in the field of legal psychiatry. Later, the center also funded a project for the study and conceptualization of dangerousness of mental patients, and I owe thanks to PHS Research Grant #MH26092-02, NIMH (Center for Studies of Crime and Delinquency) for the opportunity to consider many of the ideas that appear in Chapter 12, and particularly to Saleem Shah, the chief of the center. The Henry Luce Foundation has funded my dual chair in the Schools of Law and Medicine at Emory University and this has given me the opportunity to develop professionally and find more time for writing. Finally, the Isaac Ray Award Board of the American Psychiatric Association gave me its annual award in 1976, and this obligated me to put my thoughts into shape for presentation as lectures; from these lectures this book evolved. My particular gratitude goes to Naomi Goldstein who headed that board and who gave me great encouragement.

Three people deserve special mention. My wife has always been ready to give me time to discuss my ideas and to review my manuscript. She has allowed my concerns to take precedence in what, even without them, would have been a busy schedule. John Ware, literary agent, encouraged me to set to work in earnest, and he has made me sharpen my writing skills. Jonathan Galassi has been, so it seems to me, a perfect editor—firm but diplomatic. If it had not been for him, this book would have been much longer. To all these people and to others unnamed go my sincerest thanks.

Contents

INTRODUCTION · xi

Part One

THE GROWTH OF PSYCHIATRIC AUTHORITY

Part Two

DILEMMAS OF PSYCHIATRIC POWER

Part Three

HOW PSYCHIATRISTS EXERCISE THEIR POWER

Part Four

THE LIMITS OF PSYCHIATRIC AUTHORITY

Introduction

WHEN OUR ANCESTORS were living in forests and in caves, hunting and being hunted, they knew that many of the everyday decisions they made were life or death, do or die. The point on the arrow, the location of the cave, the collection of firewood—any of these might determine if the individual and the family were to survive. Every person made decisions that were easily seen to be crucial.

Civilization brought with it a division of labor and a delegation of responsibility. Our immediate ancestors and we ourselves have lost control over the decision-making power as it affects us in the most major ways. In minor ways we have a greater decision-making power than ever before: We can decide to spend our money on a wider variety of products, we can decide to enjoy experiences that were not previously available to most people. But we have little control over the complicated decisions that have now become the province of the expert. The use of nuclear power, the plan for national defense, the allocation of energy resources, the use of chemical preservatives in food, these are all decisions that can profoundly affect the individual and the group—life-or-death decisions that are made by experts over whom we have little control.

Of course the experts are ourselves: They are selected or self-selected from us and they represent us. But as we are fallible they may be fallible. We uneasily delegate to them great responsibility, although we do not know their competence in dealing with this responsibility.

There are other, more personal decisions that are equally momentous for the individual, which at some distant time in the past were the responsibility of the individual but which later became the responsibility of a special group. Should I lie? Should I steal? To what extent do I want to follow tradition? What are my obligations to my fellow human beings and to myself ? Primitive man made his own altars and worshipped his own gods; he was the author of his own morality and he was responsible for it. Later this function was turned over to priests who had the power to direct behavior and to forgive transgressions. Later, philosophers, and more recently, behavioral scientists—psychologists, psychiatrists, sociologists, cultural anthropologists—have become the authorities who tell us what is right and wrong, moral and immoral, expedient and inexpedient.

It would be difficult and not very profitable to try to determine who is the most crucial of those delegated decision makers who now exercise such authority over us. The physicist who determines international nuclear needs and the diplomat who negotiates treaties regulating nuclear energy, the economist who determines money management strategy and the politician who puts this policy into effect—these are some of our crucial decision makers. The system of laws and law enforcers—courts and judges and police—makes the important decisions that affect the civil relationship of individuals and their relationship to the state; in the criminal justice process we are particularly aware of the power that the decision maker has over individuals. The argument can be made that high in the hierarchy of those in our society who enjoy major delegated decision-making authority are the behavioral scientists and psychiatrists who determine such fundamental issues as what is normal and abnormal, who should be controlled through confinement or medication and who should be allowed to be unconfined, what is "good" for people and what is "bad." These same behavioral scientists determine or help to determine at a crucial level the values by which society lives—or dies. This behavioral science authority (which is subsumed under the heading of "psychiatric authority" but includes the authority of many other behavioral scientists in addition to psychiatrists) has particular effect on the individual because profound decisions are made for individuals on the basis of a discipline that is not well understood, has a powerful mystique, and has not been subjected to nearly enough criticism and control.

Most of us go through our lives almost oblivious to the power of behavioral science and psychiatric authority. We read that a fifteen-year-old girl who may or may not be mentally retarded is eugenically sterilized without the authority of any state law or any procedural safeguards and that there is no recourse against this abuse of psychiatric authority, but very few of us are potentially subject to such a heavy-handed imposition of control. Very few of us are committed to mental hospitals against our will, very few of us are diagnosed as sexual psychopaths and as a result find that our legal rights are drastically curtailed. We are becoming aware that more and more people in our society are reaching the stage where, because of senility or some other failure of intellect, they may be declared incompetent to manage their own financial affairs, and that more and more divorcing parents are having their right to the custody of their own children determined by psychological and psychiatric evaluations, but we do not usually see this as an immediate threat, if we see it as a threat at all. The problem of coerced therapy—the court order for the individual to continue injections of medication regularly on penalty of involuntary hospitalization for lack of cooperation—is seen more as a boon than a threat by many, and in any case it applies to others, not ourselves. The power that behavioral scientists and psychiatrists enjoy because of their ability to impose values and value systems is so pervasive and so familiar that we do not stop to question these "scientists" or ask where they are leading us. We can and do ignore the power of psychiatric authority.

It is the thesis of this book that psychiatric authority is a recent addition to the scene, that it comes to us with the imprimatur of science although it is not always scientific, that it carries the weight of medical authority although it is only occasionally truly medical, and that its power and influence are constantly growing. The more complicated and the more out of control our lives become, the more we are willing to turn over responsibility to the experts, and these behavioral scientists and psychiatrists are the experts in human behavior. The process began only two centuries ago when English courts for the first time began to give credence to the special expertise of alienists, the first psychiatrists. It gained momentum in the nineteenth century with the development of psychiatry as a medical specialty. When Freud introduced the idea of a dynamic unconscious that controlled many of our actions and proposed that, through therapy designed to uncover the unconscious, irrationality could be brought under control, psychiatry took a major step in acquiring more authority. More recently, psychiatry has expanded its control over individual destinies by the application of psychological testing, profiling, and behavior modification techniques.

As society has lost many of its older sources of authority with the decline of religion, the shattering of legal precedents, and the weakening of traditional morality, the behavioral scientists and psychiatrists have become a source of guidance and direction. They have become the new authority that promises to give us more scientific, more practical, often more permissive and less burdensome guidelines than the demanding injunctions that had been imposed by tradition, by religion, and by law.

The history of the growth of psychiatry in this century shows mounting faith in, enthusiasm for, and extension of the power of psychiatry, and until very recently the psychiatric approach has been accepted uncritically. Psychiatrists operated in an area where there was much pain and suffering, and they were seen as healers and helpers. The psychologist, psychiatrist, psychiatric social worker, psychiatric nurse all describe themselves as members of the "helping professions."

Therapy and a behavioral science orientation to living have been helpful to many people; often they have been lifelines. Describing her analysis with Freud, H.D. (Hilda Doolittle), the poet, says she saw Freud as "the old Hermit" who lived on the edge of the vast domain of the unknown, the supernormal, the supernatural, who would help her put the pieces of her life together. They were involved in a mutual effort to bring her order and understanding. "Fragmentary ideas, apparently unrelated, were often found to be part of a special layer or stratum of thought and memory, therefore to belong together; these were sometimes skillfully pieced together like the exquisite Greek tear-jars and iridescent glass bowls and vases that gleamed in the dusk from the shelves of the cabinet that faced me where I stretched, propped up on the couch . . ."[1]

The help that psychiatry can give is described in thousands of books and ten thousands of articles, but psychiatric power also harms, and many of the hurting aspects of psychiatric authority are not given great attention.

In the past quarter of a century we have seen the first important criticisms of how psychiatrists use their powers, and this has resulted in the beginnings, in a few areas, of curbs on the exercise of these powers. But generally psychiatric authority continues to grow. Where it will find its appropriate limits, or the extent to which it will exercise moderate power, is not yet apparent; the scene is evolving. Because so many of the topics affected by psychiatric authority are either unpleasant to contemplate, or beyond the scope of ordinary experience, or too complicated for the ordinary citizen to feel comfortable with, there has been little effort to think about appropriate limits to the exercise of psychiatric authority. Yet if society is not to come under the sway of these new technologists and if individuals are to be left free to make decisions, the job of understanding the invasiveness of psychiatric decision making and of setting appropriate limits needs to be undertaken.

I came to psychiatry with a different perspective than most of my fellow psychiatrists. I had finished law school and had practiced law for three years before I started medical school and began a long process that continued through internship, psychiatric residency, and psychoanalytic training. All through this process some legal part of myself saw the psychiatrist-patient relationship through the eyes of a lawyer, and my particular concern became the powerlessness of the patient and the untrammeled power of the psychiatrist.

During my residency I worried about the inability of hospitalized patients to obtain legal assistance, although theoretically they had a right to counsel to help them gain their freedom. I also learned to look at the problem from the psychiatric point of view—that the ineffectiveness of the patient's attempt to contact a lawyer indicated either his inadequacy or his unconscious wish to remain in the hospital—and that in either case there was not a need to worry about the patient's rights. I am enough of a psychiatrist to see that there is some merit in this position, at least as it applies to most of those patients whose threats to leave the hospital are part of their struggle to deny the need for hospitalization. But I have come to see that ascribing a patient's inadequacy to his pathology is a dangerous game. The psychiatrist holds all the cards, the penalty for the patient is severe, and although most patients committed to hospitals need to be there, not all do.

During several years when I was a consulting psychiatrist for a prison, I learned the excitement and pleasure of wielding great power —the thrill that came with the ability to confer liberty, the thrill that came from knowing I could deny liberty by not recommending parole. It was a heady experience, but the responsibility was disturbing and I was glad in the end to turn over my decision-making power to a less conflicted, less ambivalent, less legally oriented successor. One particularly sobering part of the prison experience was my indoctrination as an institution-oriented rather than a patient-oriented psychiatrist. I learned that there were institutional rules that took precedence over clinical judgment. For instance, a patient should not be recommended for a parole too early, no matter how I saw his psychiatric status, since the parole board would not favorably consider such a request, and a refusal would prejudice the hearing of his application six months later. I learned to tailor my psychiatric evaluations to the facts of prison life.

Still later, teaching in law school, I discovered the wealth of psychiatric case material to be found, not in psychiatric texts, but in official reports of legal cases.

Most court decisions do not receive the dignity of a reported decision. Many of the injuries received by patients, occurring to relatively powerless people in an atmosphere removed from public scrutiny, will never become known, and when an injury does give rise to a legal action, often it continues to get little attention. Our main source of information about these cases comes from the small fraction that reach an appellate court, where decisions are reported. These reported cases give us our most detailed knowledge of the powers of psychiatrists. It is not through the self-searching of psychiatrists but through the opinions of judges that we learn how psychiatric patients are treated.

In *Kaimowitz* v. *Michigan Department of Mental Health*[2] we learn about an experimental program to perform psychosurgery on patients hospitalized as criminally insane, in which the patient is given the alternative of becoming part of a brain-altering surgical experiment or remaining in a maximum security hospital for the rest of his life. We learn in *Baxstrom* v. *Herold*[3] how prisoners diagnosed as insane and transferred to maximum security hospitals are held past the end of their sentences, presumed to be "dangerous" although there has been no proceeding to determine that they are dangerous. In *Painter* v. *Bannister*[4] we learn how the testimony of a psychologist that moving a child from the custody of his grandparents to the custody of his father will give the child "a ninety percent chance" of going "bad" (a largely subjective opinion, not based on hard data) keeps the father from regaining his child.

Legal case reports contain tremendously condensed but powerful portraits of psychiatric patients caught in an authoritarian and bureaucratic system where their legitimate pleas for freedom or relief can go completely unnoticed. My feeling is that these cases are the tip of an iceberg, but I have learned that no one is interested in collecting the data that would determine the size of the submerged portion of the iceberg. Statistics, of course, are not available, but we can assume on the basis of reported cases that similar examples of the misuse of psychiatric authority exist, are not reported, and outnumber the reported cases by an overwhelming ratio. We get the same impression from reading the newspaper stories, the studies of sociologists, and the personal accounts of patients and former patients that document some part of the abuses mental patients receive. It is only by going to these sources that we learn how psychiatric power is used, for there is nothing in the standard psychiatric texts to indicate psychiatric power is ever misused.

Teaching legal psychiatry has taught me that most psychiatrists are almost totally uninterested in questioning the legitimacy of their psychiatric power. Many lawyers are interested, but often their interest comes from a desire to wrest control of the psychiatric machinery from the psychiatrists and run it along lines they feel would be more appropriate, but which I feel would possibly not be helpful to patients. Neither psychiatrist nor lawyer has carefully addressed the problem of the proper limits of psychiatric authority. Yet I am convinced that psychiatric decision making has become so threatening, so invasive, that it deserves our serious attention now. Psychiatric intervention is producing rapid changes in our criminal-justice system, our methods of social control, the relationships between individuals, the values we live by. These are strange and troubling times. New kinds of behavioral science interventions come at us from a variety of directions, and they all involve added power for the behavioral scientists, more authority that can be imposed on patients. Like Bilbo Baggins, the hero of Tolkien's *The Hobbit,* who saw his ordered world change as new kinds of creatures came into his neighborhood, I have a feeling of disquiet as I see evidence of strange psychiatric innovations at our borders, and then within them. It gives rise to the feeling that all is not as it has been, all is not quite as it should be. As in the time when strangers began to come into Bilbo's shire, only a few pay heed to the signs, and those who do, like Bilbo, are not sure what they portend.

* * *

Psychiatry is a method of social control. It gives the power to confer exemptions and excuses; it gives the power to lock people up and throw away the key.

A daughter of a psychiatrist, herself a doctor (although not a psychiatrist), is visiting me. She asks me what work I am involved in. I tell her I am writing a book on the uses and abuses of psychiatry. Please, she says, stress the uses as well as the abuses. My father, she says, has treated so many college girls who are depressed and failing in school or are suicidal; no one will ever know how much good he, and psychiatrists like him, do. No one outside of psychiatry understands the reality of mental illness. She has a point. Psychiatrists do a great deal of good, and grateful patients are much quieter when they raise their voices in praise than ungrateful patients are when they protest the treatment they have received. Someone should speak up for psychiatrists.

I can always collect a handful or a sheaf or even a ream of stories of psychiatric atrocities—I can go to a file I keep with many instances —but my use of these anecdotes is very selective, and if I wanted, I could select an equal or greater number of stories showing the psychiatrist as benign and helpful. But there has been too much emphasis on the good that psychiatrists do. Few practitioners are concerned with psychiatric abuses. So, to answer the loyal daughter who is worried that psychiatrists like her father are not getting enough appreciation, I will recognize the uses of psychiatry, but I will try to stress even more the inequality of a situation in which psychiatrists control those who lack the authority to contest their control, in which psychiatrists can provide excuses for the fortunate people who can afford their services, while others less fortunate are denied the benefit of a psychiatric excuse and must pay a penalty.

Psychiatrists can make determinations that put people into institutions, force treatment on them, separate them from their jobs. They can make determinations that preserve a job that otherwise would be lost, that prevent an imprisonment or relieve a soldier of a dangerous duty. Whether the psychiatrist is exerting his authority to compel and control or whether he is using his power to confer benefits by excusing, he has the superior standing of *the* expert. It is difficult to contest his opinion. His decisions are usually made in an atmosphere of low visibility and the extent to which power has been delegated to him is not understood.

Psychiatrists are changing our concepts, our values, and our lives. Some of their powers are used helpfully, many are used injuriously. Only a quest for knowledge of the growing power of psychiatry and a determination to limit its harmful potential can prevent greater injuries in the time to come. The more passionately we believe in the usefulness of psychiatry, the more willing we should be to work against its abuses.

PART ONE

THE GROWTH OF
PSYCHIATRIC AUTHORITY

We must be aware of the dangers which lie in our most generous wishes. Some paradox of our nature leads us, when once we have made our fellow men the objects of our enlightened interests, to go on to make them the object of our pity, then of our wisdom, ultimately of our coercion.

—LIONEL TRILLING
The Liberal Imagination

The Scope of Psychiatric Power

PSYCHIATRY IS DIFFERENT things to different people. It is hard to define and it is controversial. Many of its claims that it is a cure for emotional illness are unproven. Yet in spite of the weakness of the arguments for the efficacy of psychiatry, psychiatry continues to prosper, and it increasingly extends its authority over every aspect of life. Individuals rely on it to work out complicated intrapsychic and interpersonal problems. Society relies on psychiatry to handle people who are disturbing.

A. has a weekly appointment with his psychiatrist who listens to his anxieties and fears, and offers him an opportunity to work up out of depression and confusion. For A. psychiatry is therapy—it offers hope and a prospect of change—and he feels a deep sense of relief as he verbalizes his thoughts and feelings to this member of the "helping professions" who seems interested and knowledgeable. A. may see psychiatry as a lifesaver.

For B. psychiatry is an occasional visit to a busy doctor who renews a prescription for Thorazine and warns her that if she fails to take the medication, in spite of the numb feeling it gives her, he will not be willing to treat her further. B. may feel that her therapy is necessary to protect her from the racing and confused thoughts, the feelings of persecution, the rages she experienced before she began her medication, but she does not look forward to her sessions with her psychiatrist. She continues with them because she feels she has no alternative.

When C. talks about his experience with psychiatry, he has in mind his evaluation by a court-appointed psychiatrist who asks for his cooperation but is not really his therapist. This psychiatrist is prepared to go into court and present evidence that C. is a threat to society and requires indefinite detention in a prison or a hospital.

D.'s encounter with psychiatry comes as a result of his company's requirement that before he can return to his job he must submit to psychiatric evaluation to see if he is equal to the demands of his work.

E. has no mental or emotional problems. She has the practical problem that her father disinherited her in his will. If she can find a psychiatrist who can prove to the satisfaction of the court that the dead father lacked the capacity to write a valid document at the time he signed his will, E. can inherit after all. The psychiatrist's function here is to allow legal flexibility, to provide testimony that will allow the court to refuse probate even though the will meets all other legal requirements.

The list can continue through a large variety of relationships and functions that are included in modern psychiatry. Some psychiatric interventions seem helpful to the individual, although they may not necessarily be in the best interest of society—as when a psychiatrist deals with the guilt of a patient who trustingly discusses a past crime. The psychiatrist is bound by professional strictures against revealing the confidence, and society may not benefit from the interchange, except to the extent that the patient thereafter functions better as a member of society.

Some psychiatric interventions seem much more oriented to the needs of society than to the individual, as when a psychiatrist testifies that an exhibitionist will continue to be dangerous and should be sent away. Some involve a specific decision on the part of the psychiatrist: Should this individual be committed? Others involve the setting of society's values: Is this kind of behavior a psychiatric illness, and should the person who commits this behavior be considered mentally ill; does a deviant life style or sexual preference represent mental illness, or criminality, or an acceptable variation from more average behavior?

The question of the normality of the individual is related to the definitions of normality that psychiatrists propose as social ideals. When psychiatrists make judgments, their own subjective attitudes play an important role in their decisions. An analytically oriented psychiatrist holds to a model of individual responsibility and autonomy. He sees the peculiar behavior of the person he is evaluating as something that that individual must control. Relying on the theoretical concept of a tripartite psyche composed of ego, superego, and id, he works to help the patient reduce conflict and secure a better alignment of the structures of the mind. Another psychiatrist sees pathological behavior as a natural response to society's stresses and advocates not individual, but social, change. Of course, the causes of peculiar or unacceptable behavior do not have to be either internal or external. Mental sickness (assuming that there is such a thing, an idea we will examine in more detail later) can have its roots in both the psyche of the individual and the structure of society. But to the extent that the fault is seen as the individual's, the aim in therapy is to promote individual change; to the extent that it is seen as the fault of society, the aim is to promote social change.

We can then have two different approaches in psychiatry and two different concepts of the role of psychiatry. If a psychiatrist helps a patient to adjust to stress, is he acting as an agent of conformity, as an upholder of the status quo? Is the real role of psychiatry to help the individual to free himself from societal constraints, to become less conforming and more creative? The argument can be made that one psychiatric approach is made on behalf of oppression and another is liberating. But the argument can also be made that the conservative approach is made in the interest of order and structure and the more liberal kind of psychiatry promotes a kind of permissive individualism that is socially destructive.

Since psychiatry means different things to different people, we are not sure what we are discussing when we discuss the role and the uses of psychiatry. Is psychiatry a force with a great untapped potential for usefulness and therefore something to be supported, supplied with more funding, and extended into new areas? Or do we want to restrict psychiatry because it perpetuates oppressive practice and is constantly becoming a more effective agent of social control?

To achieve the two possible goals of psychiatry—to liberate or to control—there are various schools of psychiatrists utilizing different approaches. Until we have a fairly clear concept of who does what to whom and for what purpose in modern psychiatry, we cannot even come to conceptualize the best role for psychiatry in our life.

Until a generation ago there were primarily two kinds of psychiatrists. The organic psychiatrist, or neuropsychiatrist, traced his roots back to the eighteenth- and nineteenth-century alienist who believed mental illness arose from physical causes and would respond to physical treatment. The organic psychiatrist is still with us. He prefers dispensing drugs to dealing with psychology. He gives directions to his patients, relies on drugs, and often uses electroconvulsive therapy freely. His aim is to eliminate symptoms and to restore the patient to his premorbid state.

The opposing school of psychiatric thought derived from Freud, with his ideas of functional illness, intrapsychic conflict, the efficacy of verbal therapy, and the use of treatment not only to remove symptoms but to change personalities.

With psychiatry divided into two opposing camps, it was easy to disparage both kinds of psychiatrist as unscientific and ineffectual. The neuropsychiatrist was a formidable figure, seeing many patients as suffering from "constitutional inferiority" or some other incurable organic deficit, distancing himself from his patients, and making authoritarian pronouncements about them. Before the era of tranquilizing drugs, his work in controlling violent patients in hospitals made him socially useful, but his scientific explanations often seemed inadequate.

The Freudian approach also could be disparaged. It emphasized speculative concepts—the Oedipus complex, infantile sexuality, stages of psychosexual development; it elevated the analyst into the position of the interpreter of the otherwise incomprehensible unconscious; it reconstructed childhood traumas—all of which appealed to some but left many others skeptical. Analytically oriented psychiatry found many adherents, and it had other kinds of impacts. Its concept of unconscious motivation and determinism has led to altered attitudes on criminality, addictions, and sexual deviations, and it has influenced art, literature, sociology, and anthropology. But the drugless, analytically oriented therapist was often seen as ineffectual and his ideas as overly fanciful.

Starting in the 1920s and 1930s in America, these two approaches began to be joined together. Organically oriented psychiatrists added psychoanalytic formulations to their therapy, and although they continued to rely primarily on drugs or other physical treatment methods they gained in authority by their ability to make dynamic formulations. Analysts made greater use of organic approaches. The modern psychiatrist, whichever position on the treatment spectrum he occupies, has become a person of extraordinary power, a shaman who knows the thoughts of the subject better than the subject himself, who is able to tell courts when punishment is appropriate, who can calm the agitated with drugs or shock or stimulate the depressed with antidepressants, and who is able to give help and advice on virtually every aspect of human behavior.

Both the organic and analytic schools of psychiatry remain with us, plus an eclectic school that endorses both approaches equally, and new variations of old schools. Adler, Horney, Rogers, Maslow, Perls, and many others developed psychological approaches based on Freud but deviating from him. Until very recently the popularity of a Freudian or a modified Freudian approach placed the older, more biological psychiatry on the defensive. But with new evidence of genetic susceptibility to some kinds of mental illness, the development and increasing popularity of new chemotherapeutic agents, and the renewed popularity of electroshock, more organic and less analytical methods of treatment have come to the fore again. During a period when more and more people are seen as needing psychiatric help, the probing methods of analytically oriented treatment are unable to prove their cost-effectiveness. In particular, the psychiatry furnished by the government stresses an organic approach, as well as behavior modification, rather than "depth psychology."

We have seen the development of behavior modification, which sprang from psychology rather than psychiatry, but which has become incorporated into the psychiatric approach, bringing with it entirely new concepts and new techniques of treatment. We have seen new therapies as well as modifications and elaborations of older treatment methods practiced by traditional therapists—psychiatrists and psychologists—and also by a variety of new mental health professionals. The list of therapeutic approaches now includes:

Psychoanalysis

Psychoanalytic psychotherapy

Existential analysis

Direct analysis

Milieu therapy

Rogerian therapy

Humanistic psychology as developed by Maslow

Gestalt therapy

Reichian bioenergetics

Primal therapy

Mystico-transcendental approaches

Group therapies, including psychodrama and transactional analysis

Family therapy

Network therapy

Crisis intervention therapy

Behavioral-directive approaches, including chemotherapy and other somatic therapies and the behavior therapies

Biofeedback

I am listing only primary therapies. There are a number of additional approaches—art therapy, occupational therapy, recreational therapy, dance therapy, vocational therapy, and more—that deserve mention as ancillary methods of treatment. Stanley Lesse, a psychiatrist, has said, "There are two hundred, more or less, varieties of treatment procedures that in the broadest definition of the term could be labeled as psychotherapy."[1]

Indeed, we have opened the boundaries of our discipline so wide that when we use the terms psychiatrist and psychiatric treatment we include practitioners who are not formal psychiatrists, clinical psychologists, or psychoanalysts. We include social workers, registered nurses, practical nurses, counselors, pastoral counselors, ex-addicts and ex-alcoholics and other indigenous workers, and a large category we term "mental health technicians" to indicate a lack of advanced professional training. All these people enjoy psychiatric authority, and they all make psychiatric decisions.[2]

Of these decision makers, however, psychiatrists and psychologists have the greatest power. They have the influence over patients that all "helpers" have, resulting from the patients' need and dependence. They also have coercive power because they can place a diagnostic label and a prediction of future dangerousness on an individual and thus justify an involuntary commitment. This coercive authority leads to a great range of other manipulations. If the patient does not voluntarily sign himself into a hospital, the psychiatrist may change his voluntary status to involuntary. If the patient refuses to take his medication, he can be threatened with electroshock therapy. Under such conditions, patients usually accede to the wishes of the psychiatrist. More than that, the psychiatrist's special place in society brings him stature and prestige, and even his noncoercive authority grows. His advice is followed because he is a psychiatrist, even though the scientific validity of his advice and recommendations has never been firmly established.[3]

Many other people in society have great authority accorded to them. The advice of the lawyer, for example—good or bad, correct or incorrect—may be followed by his client, and usually is. But very few people in society have coercive power except for agents of the government, particularly agents of the criminal-justice and corrections systems, and then the coercion cannot be applied unless a law or regulation has been disobeyed, and then strict procedural safeguards must be observed. The psychiatrist is the most important nongovernmental decision maker in modern life. He has more power than most government officials and he can apply it to people who have done nothing more than think in ways he sees as pathological. And the patient often has inadequate legal protection against this power.

There is also a distinction between those psychiatric decisions that bear on the individual—the voluntarily assumed and coercive authorities we have been discussing—and those that set norms or act on groups or on society generally. The psychiatrist who says that his patient is delusional and requires hospitalization is not only making a specific judgment of his patient, he is also implying that delusions are pathological and all those subject to delusions are at risk of hospitalization. Psychiatrists set up broad categories defining normality and abnormality. Homosexuality for most of the life of modern psychiatry has been abnormal; recently it has been declared normal. Many of our modern concepts of child rearing are the results of psychiatric theory: Sexual experimentation is healthy in childhood, and corporal punishment is bad. Permissiveness is on the whole good. It is harmful for a child to observe parental intercourse, but masturbation is normal and should not be guilt-provoking. It is better for a child to have his parents separate or divorce than to continue to see them united in a bad marriage. A whole host of ideas as to how we should bring up our children and how we should behave as adults, many of them undoubtedly with some basis but most of them not as capable of proof as the theorems of other scientific disciplines, are attributable to modern psychiatry.

*   *   *

Most people are not aware of the impact of psychiatry on modern life because they see it as dealing only with patients, but psychiatric values, whether they are Freudian and celebrate duty over sexuality or follow Norman Brown and celebrate sexuality over duty, influence the whole climate in which we live our lives. Recently Martin Gross, in *The Psychological Society,* attacked psychiatry for offering "mass belief, a promise of a better future" and for promoting a conformist society in which we "are taught not only what to think of ourselves and others, but how to feel."[4]

Psychiatry exerts its influence over all segments of the population. Those who patronize individual therapy are primarily the affluent and the educated, but the community mental health care system sponsored by the federal government has brought psychiatry into the experience of the remainder of the population. In addition, many people who have no mental problems, or if they do, resist consulting psychiatrists, find that such aspects of their lives as job promotions or disability pensions depend on psychiatric approval, and they raise their children in accordance with their interpretation of psychiatric thought. They absorb psychiatric points of view in their reading and television viewing. Our culture is permeated with psychiatric thought. Psychiatry, which had its beginnings in the care of the sick, has expanded its net to include everyone, and it exercises its authority over this total population by methods that range from enforced therapy and coerced control to the advancement of ideas and the promulgation of values.

Accepting the Psychiatrist's Authority:
The Cases of Virginia Woolf
and Janet Gotkin

PSYCHIATRIC PATIENTS can be divided into the voluntary and the coerced, but the division between the two categories is not always clear. In the first place, many patients, at the time they decide to see a psychiatrist, are so desperate—they have fears of losing control and hurting others, or of hurting themselves, or of death or dissolution, or of sinking into such a deep depression that they will never emerge—that they agree to the terms of treatment, the rules, and the directives of the psychiatrist, without much question. They do not feel they have alternatives. Secondly, when they continue in an analytically oriented type of treatment for an extended period, all patients develop a transference to the therapist. The transference may be positive, negative, or indifferent, but the patient makes the therapist the depository for unresolved feelings that arose in earlier relationships. Especially if the transference is positive it may be very hard for the patient to leave the relationship. Thirdly, even though the patient is seeing the therapist voluntarily, he does not know how "sick" he is or seems to the therapist, and in many cases there is the fear, often not dealt with in therapy, that the therapist may recommend hospitalization if the patient does not show his willingness to cooperate and conform.

Many patients feel extreme gratitude for the attention and the services of their psychiatrists, and often they should. Many psychiatrists provide help. Many of the interventions they make are well intentioned, at least on a conscious level, and many patients respond by losing their anxieties and gaining a new perspective on their problems. (On a less conscious level the therapist may be expressing his own pathology in the relationship. He may feel a need to control, may be using the patient to gratify his own unresolved unconscious needs, or he may perpetuate the relationship after it has outlived its usefulness by encouraging the patient to continue to be dependent. This therapist pathology may be perceived by the patient, only to be explained away with the interpretation that it is the patient's problem, not the therapist's.) There are statistics disquieting to the defenders of psychiatry that indicate much psychotherapy is not beneficial, and some recent contributions to psychiatric literature emphasize the negative effects of therapy. In spite of this, many patients continue to feel therapy is helpful, and they voluntarily submit to psychiatric treatment for long periods. Those patients who depend on chemotherapy or reassurance often wish to continue with these dependent adaptations, sometimes for life, and those who are in verbal therapy are often willing to spend years resolving conflicts and coming to terms with their own pathology.

Other patients do not like therapy, and they either avoid it or quit at the earliest opportunity and only come back to treatment if their anxiety or other symptoms prove unbearable.

Many patients are forced to stay in treatment because of their great needs, and this places them at the mercy of the authoritarian psychiatrist. Not all psychiatrists are authoritarian. The more analytically oriented a psychiatrist is, the more he tries to be nondirective and not to impose his sense of "should" upon the patient (although critics of psychoanalysis have pointed out that underneath the permissive facade of analysis there is a whole range of authoritarian demands, and the teacher-pupil relationship in even the least directive analysis puts the two on an unequal basis).

One of the means by which even the ostensibly permissive and nondirective analyst exerts his power is his threat to terminate treatment if the patient does not conform. The analyst at all times imposes a value system of his own, often sensible and meant to be helpful, but often one that has never been consciously conceptualized by the psychoanalyst and that frequently does not coincide with the values of the patient. Freud's patient known as the Wolf-man (because a previous neurosis of early childhood had centered on a fear of wolves) in recent years has written about Freud's directive to him in the early years of his analysis (around 1910). "I would have married Therese then and there, had this not been contrary to the rule Professor Freud had made that a patient should not make any decision which would irreversibly influence his later life. If I wanted to complete my treatment with Freud successfully, it was necessary for me to follow his rule whether I wanted to or not."[1]

Virginia Woolf has given us a description of the authority that psychiatrists impose on their patients. Woolf, at least in her essays, gives the appearance of being the most intellectual and rational of beings, but she was subject to manic-depressive mood swings in which she was sometimes wildly psychotic.

Shortly after the death of her mother, in the summer of 1895, when Virginia was thirteen, she had what has been called by her biographers her "first nervous breakdown." She heard what she called "those horrible voices," her pulse raced so fast that she could hardly bear it, she became excitable and nervous, and then deeply depressed. She became fearful of people and could not face strangers in the street. The family doctor ordered her to stop all her lessons and prescribed a simple life with much outdoor exercise. She was to be out of doors, walking or taking rides with her half sister on the tops of buses, for four hours a day.[2]

When she was twenty-two, in 1904, she had her second psychiatric episode. She tried to commit suicide by throwing herself from a window. Again she heard voices. She starved herself, and three nurses were required to keep her under control. This illness was prolonged and recovery was slow. Dr. George Savage, her specialist and a friend of the family, ordered her to lead a quiet life, if possible away from London.[3]

All her life Virginia Woolf was told, and she believed, that when the symptoms of an "impending breakdown" began to appear—excitability, persistent headaches, a rapid pulse, racing thoughts—the remedies were to be away from stimulation, especially London, to stay in bed for long periods, and to be fattened up on milk and wholesome foods, and she believed she saved herself from breakdowns by heeding these symptoms and taking the rest and isolation cure that she loathed. Whether her acceptance of the role of a semi-invalid was in her best interest, whether she could have worked through these symptoms and learned to tolerate greater quantities of stimulation and excitement is something that will never be known. Dr. Savage was giving the standard medical advice of the period. Directives such as "lead a quiet life," or "take a sea voyage," or advice to visit a spa were the usual psychiatric prescriptions of the time.

Six months after the start of the second psychotic period, Dr. Savage approved her plan to stay with her cousins. She would be accompanied by one nurse. Virginia wrote: "I have written to ask Madge to have me about the 16th, as Savage approves—really a doctor is worse than a husband! Oh how thankful I shall be to be my own mistress and throw their silly medicine down the slop pail! I never shall believe, or have believed, in any anything any doctor says—I learnt their utter help-lessness when Father was ill. They can guess at what's the matter, but they cant put it right."[4]

Dr. Savage continued his orders that she stay away from London and, for fear that she might try suicide again, cautioned that if she took walks she must be attended. Virginia fought for the right to take walks alone and won that battle, but she still was not allowed to return to London. She wrote,

> That silly old Nessa [her sister Vanessa] has been absorbing Savages theories as usual. I cant conceive how anybody can be fool enough to believe in a doctor. I know he will soon climb down and tell me what is the fact. That I am quicker and better in London than anywhere else—just as he had to give in about walking alone and being isolated. My life is a constant fight against Doctors follies, it seems to me. Of course I dont sleep better here, though I get quite a good amount and feel perfectly well. I think of my perfectly quiet room at home, where I need never talk or be disturbed with a pang. Lord what fools people are.[5]

Two months later she wrote: "I am discharged cured! Aint it a joke!"[6]

Five years later Vanessa told Savage that Virginia was in the depth of another depression. Vanessa wrote to Virginia that Savage said she should enter the nursing home at Twickenham, and this time Virginia agreed to follow his directive. She wrote to Vanessa: "Savages decision is of course, rather depressing; but not unexpected. I only feel cross that he didn't insist at once."[7]

Virginia was to remain at Burley, the private sanitarium for females, for a month. Her letters, reading, and visitors would all be restricted. She would be kept in bed in a darkened room. Wholesome foods would be pressed on her. After she recovered she wanted to return to London, but Dr. Savage thought she should be in the country, and once again she gave in to his wishes.

Virginia married an intellectual, Leonard Woolf, who is described by her biographers as a saint because he nursed her so carefully for the remainder of her life, but he may have contributed to the perpetuation of her illness by acquiescing in an almost sexless marriage and by not protesting her flirtations.[8] She discovered on her honeymoon that she was frigid and wrote a friend: "Why do you think people make such a fuss about marriage & copulation?"[9]

Virginia looked forward to having children. One of her wedding gifts was an antique cradle. She exulted, "My baby shall sleep in the cradle."[10] Soon after their marriage they discussed having children, but Leonard was concerned because of her history of mental illness.

Although Savage (now Sir George Savage) advised that it would do her a world of good, other doctors gave the opposite opinion. Eventually Leonard decided that they should not have children and persuaded Virginia that this was the best course. Quentin Bell, her nephew and biographer, says that this would be a permanent source of grief to Virginia and that in later years she never thought of her sister's children without misery and envy.[11] (Ten years after her marriage, Virginia wrote in her diary: ". . . Never pretend that the things you haven't got are not worth having; good advice, I think. . . . Never pretend that children, for instance, can be replaced by other things.")[12]

There were other illnesses, another suicide attempt, other encounters with doctors. In 1921 she was persuaded to see some Harley Street specialists, the third and last of these being the famous pathologist Dr. Saintsbury. Leonard Woolf wrote of that encounter,

> At our last interview with the famous Harley Street specialist to whom we paid our three guineas, the Great Dr Saintsbury, as he shook Virginia's hand, said to her: "Equanimity—equanimity—practice equanimity, Mrs Woolf." It was, no doubt, excellent advice and worth the three guineas, but, as the door closed behind us, I felt that he might just as usefully have said: "A normal temperature—ninety-eight point four—practice a normal temperature, Mrs Woolf."[13]

Virginia Woolf tells us what she thinks of her doctors and their directives in her 1925 novel *Mrs Dalloway.* She combines some of the qualities of Savage and Saintsbury in her character of the successful, assured, complacent psychiatrist, Sir William Bradshaw. Bradshaw invokes not equanimity but "proportion, divine proportion."

> To his patients he gave three-quarters of an hour; and if in this exacting science which has to do with what, after all, we know nothing about—the nervous system, the human brain—a doctor loses his sense of proportion, as a doctor he fails. Health we must have; and health is proportion; so that when a man comes into your room and says he is Christ (a common delusion), and has a message, as they mostly have, and threatens, as they often do, to kill himself, you invoke proportion; order rest in bed; rest in solitude; silence and rest; rest without friends, without books, without messages; six months' rest; until a man who went in weighing seven stone six comes out weighing twelve.
>
>   Proportion, divine proportion, Sir William's goddess, was acquired by Sir William walking hospitals, catching salmon, begetting one son in Harley Street by Lady Bradshaw, who caught salmon herself and took photographs scarcely to be distinguished from the work of professionals. Worshipping proportion, Sir William not only prospered himself but made England pros-

per, secluded her lunatics, forbade childbirth, penalised despair, made it impossible for the unfit to propagate their views until they, too, shared his sense of proportion . . .[14]

Virginia Woolf represents the voluntary patient, though not completely voluntary, because there is always the possibility that the psychiatrist will recommend further institutional care if treatment is broken or his recommendations are not followed. But nevertheless the relationship is as voluntary as is possible between any deeply disturbed patient and his or her psychiatrist, considering that the patient's life is determined by the concepts of the psychiatrist.

The power to commit is a major source of the psychiatrist's authority. Sociologist and anthropologist Erving Goffman, psychiatrist and psychoanalyst Thomas Szasz, law professor Alan Dershowitz, and many others have recommended that all involuntary commitments be done away with so that there can be a truly equal relationship between psychiatrist and patient. (The proposal is not very practical, as anyone who has dealt with acutely psychotic people knows. They are uncontrollable and unpredictable, and if we did not have an involuntary commitment mechanism, we would often be forced to hold them in jails.) But the power to commit (or more properly, to recommend commitment, since commitment often requires a judicial stamp of approval) is only a part of the power that psychiatrists have. The authority and status of the psychiatrist and the willingness of the patient to submit depend as much on attitudes and self-concepts of psychiatrist and patient as they do on legal power.

The best protection the patient can have against the excessive assumption of authority on the part of the psychiatrist is a healthy distrust of psychiatric expertise—a realization by both patient and therapist that the therapist's knowledge is limited, and that his authority must always be subject both to scrutiny from the patient and the self-scrutiny of the therapist to prevent misuse of psychiatric power. But this degree of independence is only available to patients who are not too "sick."

Janet Gotkin's case represents a more modern example of the force of psychiatric authority, and one with which it is possibly easier to identify. We all know people who categorize themselves as patients and for the next years, sometimes for the rest of their lives, live out the status of patienthood, letting themselves be defined by the therapist's concepts of normal and abnormal, not only living life physically according to the directives of the therapist but also accepting the therapist's version of how emotional life should be lived. Janet Gotkin

15

was a patient caught in a life-and-death struggle not only with her fears and anxieties and destructive urges but also with her therapist, who had a vested interest in making her conform to his concept of "the good patient," even if she was destroyed in the process.

She began to have symptoms that she thought were the symptoms of mental illness during the first days after she left home to attend college. She suffered through sessions of "therapy" with doctors toward whom she felt no closeness and who apparently were not able to recognize her pain or help her with it. She was forced to leave college after her freshman year, with the condition for her returning a year later that she be in treatment and secure the approval of her therapist. This time she was referred to a psychoanalyst and felt even more strongly the sense of isolation and lack of understanding that she had experienced in two previous therapeutic attempts. Much of what she expressed, she says, was interpreted to her by her analyst as pathological fantasy, and what she did not express was interpreted to her as an attempt to repress sexual material. When she made a suicidal gesture—a wrist-cutting that had many other meanings but certainly was not meant to end her life—her doctor refused to see her further, and she was persuaded to enter voluntarily a private hospital described as a "therapeutic community" for young adults. There she met a succession of doctors who tried to control her and did not understand her feelings, and one doctor with whom she had a good relationship, but who left without warning to take his third year of residency somewhere else. She was finally told that she could leave the hospital if she went into outpatient therapy, and she went into treatment with a doctor who had treated her brother. In the book in which she tells her story she gives this doctor the fictional name of Dr. Sternfeld.

She was in treatment with Dr. Sternfeld for eight years. During this time she had several hospitalizations at a private hospital in Brooklyn, and a long stay in a New York state hospital. She underwent electroshock therapy, both modified (in a private hospital) and unmodified (in the state hospital)—that is, with muscle relaxants and anesthesia and without. She was treated with huge doses of tranquilizers and antidepressants and received innumerable hours of outpatient verbal psychotherapy.

She depended on Dr. Sternfeld for interpretations, direction, reassurance. In spite of the fact that therapy often did not go well—at times she had terrors, delusions, hallucinations, and eventually there was a serious suicide attempt—she chose to continue with Dr. Sternfeld. She had accepted his conceptualization of her problem and she looked to him for help.

16

She fell in love with and married Paul Gotkin. Marriage was not the answer to her problem, although her husband's presence was enormously supportive. She continued to be bound by Dr. Sternfeld's view of her, and she depended on his advice. She had secured his approval before living with Paul and before marrying him, and she left to Dr. Sternfeld—as Virginia Woolf had left to her doctors—the decision on whether to have a baby.

On a trip to Paris with Paul, separated from Dr. Sternfeld, she had a change of feeling about Dr. Sternfeld. She felt he had defined her as a patient, called all her reactions pathological, kept her in a state of dependence. She says that for her whole adult life, for a period of ten years, psychiatrists had treated a suicidal thought as if it were an intention, had defined suicidal thoughts as pathological, had denied her the validity of all her feelings, and had drugged her and shocked her to keep these thoughts from her mind.

Janet Gotkin feels now that psychiatrists kept her from being herself. Although during most of her ten years in treatment she was free to terminate therapy or change doctors, she wanted only to continue with Dr. Sternfeld. She was impressed by his medical authority, and she saw herself as pathological because he saw her as pathological. After ten years she had come to the realization that anxieties and symptoms could not be banished by the authority of doctors; she would have to live with them and deal with them herself. Hannah Green's *I Never Promised You a Rose Garden*[15] gives an understanding of how helpful psychiatrists can be, how the same kind of acceptance of herself and her feelings that Janet Gotkin achieved by breaking away from her psychiatrist, Hannah Green achieved with the help of her psychiatrist. But we also know what Janet Gotkin means when she accuses psychiatrists of lying when they say, "We only want to help you."

In the book she and her husband wrote about her experience in therapy, she tells of her telephone call from Paris to Dr. Sternfeld, to ask him why he had not prepared her for the fact that even after her symptoms left she would have to struggle with anger, the sense of desolation, the terrors that go with everyday life.

> "I don't understand what you are asking me, Janet," she heard his calm guarded voice through the receiver.
> "What do you mean, you don't understand?" she said, her voice rising in anger. "I am asking you how you could treat me for eight years and not prepare me to live a normal life, how you could send me out into the world with *no* skill for survival. I am telling you you perpetrated a hoax, a farce on me—and I am asking you why."

"Are you drunk, Janet?"

"Yes. I am drunk, but I have never thought clearer in my life."

"You sound very upset, Janet. Why don't you take some Thorazine and calm down? You can call me again and we'll talk about it."[16]

Janet Gotkin writes that she believes she was lost, pained, suffering, troubled, and desperate but not that she was ever sick. "My so-called sickness was an invention of the psychiatric profession—of . . . Dr. Sternfeld, of all the doctors who treated me during my ten-year career as a mental patient. The fact that I—and my parents and my husband —believed in my sickness for so long attests to our own need to believe experts and to the effectiveness of the scare tactics, brainwashing, and public relations of the American psychiatric profession."[17]

Most patients do not end up as antipsychiatric as Janet Gotkin, who now devotes herself to Mental Patients' Resistance, an organization to combat established psychiatry. She makes some valid points about the authority that psychiatrists wield, but psychiatrists can be defended. If they are authoritarian and paternalistic, it is partly because patients often require doctors to treat them authoritatively and paternalistically. I am not unsympathetic with the plight of Dr. Sternfeld, forced by patients to take over and then resented for his domination. All therapists are to some extent Dr. Sternfelds. But the consciousness that psychiatry has some reason for being, some usefulness, does not negate the charges of Virginia Woolf and Janet Gotkin that psychiatrists exert too great authority over their patients. If the voluntary patients of private psychiatrists have this complaint, coerced patients —state hospital patients, prisoners sentenced to hospitals for the criminally insane—have much greater grievances against psychiatry, which in the name of therapy can force them to submit to treatment adverse to their interest and sometimes obliges them to spend the rest of their lives in institutions for little or no medical purpose.

The Law Begins Its Reliance
on Psychiatry

IF PSYCHIATRISTS were therapists only, they would be among the most powerful people in our society, but they are much more than therapists. Other doctors primarily treat sick people. Psychiatrists treat the "disease" known as "disordered behavior" and so they have great nontherapeutic authority. They report to courts about which defendants should get mild, and which harsh, treatment. They decide for courts that some defendants should not go to trial. They inform courts that some defendants should not be punished for what would otherwise, except for the psychiatric opinion that insanity was involved, have been considered a crime.

Psychiatrists have other legal functions, affecting civil as well as criminal matters. They can help break a will or they can help disavow a disadvantageous contract. The opinions of the psychiatrist are used to excuse all kinds of actions that otherwise would incur harsh treatment. A psychiatric opinion can also confer special benefits on individuals: He can decide that an air controller should be retired for disability at a high rate of pay or that an insurance contract should not be void after the insured commits suicide (although the policy expressly states it will not pay in cases of suicide), because the deceased did not have the ability to control his behavior.

Psychiatrists like myself who are involved in the interaction of law and psychiatry are forensic psychiatrists. Forensic psychiatry is the stepchild of psychiatry. It does not have the status of other psychiatric subspecialties—general psychiatry, psychoanalysis, child psychiatry—which are concerned more with treatment and less with evaluation and disposition. There are three distinct kinds of forensic psychiatrists, but generally we are all grouped together. One kind of forensic psychiatrist evaluates patients for legal or for court purposes and functions largely as a professional witness. Another is an employee of the courts or the correctional system, advising judges on disposition, sentencing, and rehabilitation programs, and advising parole boards.

The least frequently encountered forensic psychiatrist, the category in which I find myself now, is the law-psychiatry teacher in a law school or psychiatric residency program who attempts to introduce law students, medical students, or psychiatric residents to the complexities of forensic psychiatry. As this last kind of academic forensic psychiatrist, I have the privilege of being in a position to criticize what other forensic psychiatrists do.

All psychiatrists, however, exercise a forensic function when they commit patients to hospitals or persuade courts to commit. (Courts rely heavily on psychiatric opinion in commitment, and some commitment laws allow a patient to be involuntarily committed without any court proceeding, so in either instance the psychiatrist has great authority. Often this authority is exercised by physicians who are not primarily psychiatrists but who are considered knowledgeable enough about mental illness to recommend commitment or to commit—family doctors, general practitioners, internists, or surgeons.) Psychiatrists, other physicians, or clinical psychologists, all may have views about the competency of a person to fill a job, and their views may determine employment or disability. Whenever a medical decision is made that someone should be given special treatment—even such a relatively minor favor as a medical excuse to avoid taking an examination —on the grounds of emotional state, the physician is not treating but instead is changing the social and legal configuration in which the patient functions, changing the rules of the game.

The idea that some mental states should be used as the reason either to deprive people of some legal rights or to give them some extralegal benefits goes back to the earliest records of our legal system. Certainly as long ago as the ancient Romans, the estates of mentally ill persons were put in the hands of guardians to protect them from dissipation. The criminal law in particular long ago became an area where mental state justified different treatment.

It has been established in Anglo-Saxon law for at least a thousand years that certain people should not be punished for what would otherwise be criminal actions because they were insane at the time their acts were committed. The "Dooms of Alfred," which were probably promulgated in the ninth century, provided that if a man "be born dumb or deaf, so that he cannot acknowledge or confess his offences," his father must pay his forfeitures. The same kind of special treatment was probably also given to the mentally disordered who could not cooperate in their own defense. By the thirteenth century, as trial by ordeal was losing its authority and trial by jury becoming firmly established, it had probably also become established that a mad person who could not plead would be held at the king's pleasure until he had sufficiently recovered his senses to stand trial. We have the records of a discussion in 1353 between the itinerant justices of Edward III in which Justice Hill described a case of a man who had killed four people when he was "enrage." Hill decided not to try him, but instead to hold him in prison until he had recovered his senses. Eventually the prisoner was pardoned by the king.[1]

English courts recognized the effect of mental disorder, but they were not kind to most of the insane. A very severe degree of derangement had to be evident before mental state became the reason for deferring a trial or for escaping punishment. Originally, the decision to acquit the insane was made by the Crown. Nigel Walker, the criminological historian, gives as the earliest instance he can find of a jury verdict of unsound mind *(de non saine memoire)* leading to freedom without a decision of acquittal by the king, the case in 1505 of a man accused of murdering an infant.[2] If the court was persuaded a sufficient degree of derangement was present, great legal benefits might follow—the saving of a life when otherwise there would have been a sentence of death, the retention of the estate of a suicide that otherwise would have been forfeited to the Crown. Fitzherbert refers to a case in 1228 that held that "if a woman becomes demented and out of her wits and kill her lord, she does not forfeit any of her heritage or free property, but when she comes to her senses she possesses her property as before." However he also notes a case a century later in which a jury ruled that a woman known to be mad who had committed suicide by drowning had forfeited her chattels since she was only mad from time to time.[3]

In the eighteenth century, insanity as a criminal defense was increasingly common (although still infrequent according to modern standards) and for the first time psychiatrists were called in to help the courts as expert witnesses. These were the same determinations that courts had been making. The only difference was that now there was a recognized medical specialty of psychiatry, and a new kind of witness, the alienist, could be called in to court to help the judge and jury with their difficult decisions. Psychiatric opinions could be accepted or rejected by the courts. Theoretically they carried no more weight than other testimony, but unlike many other subjects of testimony, psychiatric condition is such a nebulous and strange issue

21

that the opinion of the expert often carried extraordinary weight.

The first recorded case that utilized expert psychiatric testimony was the trial in 1760 in the House of Lords of Earl Ferrers for the murder of his factor, Johnson. The physician superintendent of Bethlem Hospital, Dr. John Monro, was called in behalf of the defendant. Monro was the second in a line of four generations of Monros who superintended Bethlem for over a century. Because Ferrers was an earl, on trial in the House of Lords, he was obliged to undertake his own defense, although he was allowed to use counsel to argue points not of fact but of law. To paint a picture of familial insanity, Monro testified that he had treated the earl's uncle, the late Earl Ferrers, when he had been a patient at Bethlem "under the unhappy influence of lunacy." He described to the Lords the usual symptoms of lunacy, but when Ferrers asked him the most crucial question, "whether lunatics, when they are angered or without cause, know what they are doing," Monro gave the answer that may have served to hang Ferrers: "Sometimes, as well as I do now."

The solicitor general countered Ferrers' defense of insanity in his summing up by pointing out that all the symptoms that Ferrers and Monro had presented to prove lunacy, including common fury, jealousy, quarreling without a cause, and going armed when there was no apparent danger, might merely prove a bad heart and a vicious mind rather than lunacy. (Another of the earl's symptoms that had been presented as a part of the defense was his practice of drinking coffee hot out of the spout of the pot.) The solicitor general concluded with an argument that sounds modern indeed—that from a philosophical point of view all crime is perhaps pathological, but the legal system cannot afford to exempt criminals this freely.

> My lords, in some sense, every crime proceeds from insanity. All cruelty, all brutality, all revenge, all injustice is insanity. There were philosophers, in ancient times, who held this opinion . . .
>
> My lords, the opinion is right in philosophy but dangerous in judicature. It may have a useful and noble influence, to regulate the conduct of men; to control their important passions; to teach them that virtue is the perfection of reason, as reason itself is the perfection of human nature; but not to extenuate crimes, not to excuse those punishments, which the law adjudges to be their due.[4]

Each of the 117 peers present at the trial voted for Ferrers' guilt; at his hanging the newly invented device, the drop, failed to work and the executioner had to resort to the practice of jumping on the back of the slowly strangling earl to hurry his death.

During the remainder of the eighteenth century, medical witnesses were only called on in a handful of cases to give their opinions on the mental capacity of defendants. But starting with the trial in 1800 of William Hadfield for shooting at George III in the Drury Lane Theater, when for the first time a psychiatrist gave his opinion about the mental state of the defendant at the time the crime was committed on the basis of his examination after the crime, psychiatrists appeared often as witnesses.[5] Courts increasingly depended upon them for opinions on which defendants deserved or did not deserve to escape the consequences of their acts. In 1843, when Daniel M'Naghten was tried for the murder of Sir Robert Peel's private secretary, Edward Drummond (M'Naghten had put a pistol to Drummond's back and shot him under the mistaken impression that Drummond was Peel), four psychiatrists testified for the defense, two who had examined M'Naghten and two who testified on the basis of their observations of M'Naghten in the courtroom while the trial was in progress. In this trial, too, there was reliance by the defense on the theories of Isaac Ray, a general practitioner in Maine who five years earlier had published the first book on forensic psychiatry in English.[6]

Isaac Ray believed that the acts of the mentally ill were as much symptoms of their disease as the pocks were symptoms of smallpox. He believed that since disordered behavior was a symptom of disease, the established concept of partial responsibility—that a man might be demonstrably insane in some areas but still show enough mental ability to be held responsible in others—should give way to a greater emphasis on insanity as an organic disease that affected the total organism. The relationship of mental state and behavior, according to Ray, was understood by physicians and not by lay people—judges and juries. In modern times Ray's idea that more medical weight should be given to expert testimony has received the attention (at first very favorable, later, after experience with the concept in practice, very unfavorable) of Judge David Bazelon, who in his legal opinions has tried to deal with the difficult question of the importance that should be attributed to psychiatric authority.[7] M'Naghten was held not guilty by reason of insanity, but the trial led to the promulgation of new and more restrictive rules of criminal responsibility by Parliament, and the battle concerning the proper rule to follow continues to this day.

Because one psychiatric expert might have a very different attitude from another on the all-important questions of free will and the ability to control actions, psychiatrists could be found to testify persuasively for either the prosecution or the defense. In famous criminal cases we have been more aware of the psychiatrist for the defense, spinning out a theory by which the jury could, if it wished, find the defendant not guilty by reason of insanity, but in all but the most obvious cases, there is equal scope for the prosecution's psychiatrist to make a case for conviction. An example of the effectiveness of psychiatric testimony in shaping the result of a trial is the recent case of Robert Torsney, a policeman who shot and killed a fifteen-year-old black youth outside a New York housing project. Torsney claimed the youth had a gun, but in fact he was unarmed. A psychiatrist for the defense testified that a rare form of psychomotor epilepsy had caused this delusion and that the killing was thus justified because the officer believed he was acting in self-defense. The psychomotor epilepsy, according to the defense psychiatrist, was difficult to diagnose, and no symptoms associated with it had surfaced between the killing and the trial a year later. (After another year there had still been no recurrence of disease symptoms.) The testimony of the psychiatrist enabled the jury to bring in a verdict of not guilty by reason of insanity. Sent for evaluation to a hospital for the criminally insane, the officer was found by psychiatrists to be not dangerous and eligible for release. In the meantime, his attorney had proceeded with an action to secure for him a $15,000-a-year pension for a "service-related disability."[8]

Because a skillful defense often makes good use of psychiatric testimony, and also because we have seen pitched "battles of the experts" in some famous trials—particularly those with political implications, such as Jack Ruby's, Sirhan Sirhan's, and Patty Hearst's—we conclude that psychiatrists are either used for helping defendants escape justice or that psychiatrists cannot agree. The truth is that in less publicized cases, particularly when the defense lawyer is not psychiatrically knowledgeable or when the defendant is indigent, it is easy to find an expert witness for the prosecution to state that, in spite of previous symptoms or hospitalizations, the defendant knew what he was doing at the time of the crime and could have controlled his actions if he wished; and there is often no witness for the defense to give the opposite, equally plausible opinion.

Many testifying psychiatrists are prosecution-minded. A Canadian psychiatrist who served for two years on a commission to consider the use of the defense of criminal irresponsibility and who had heard the opinions of psychiatric experts across the country concluded that "lawyers are not always tough, demanding vengeance; psychiatrists are not always merciful with the feeling that everyone should be treated and no one should be punished. There are hanging judges, and there are hanging psychiatrists. On a number of occasions, psychiatrists who devoted a good deal of their professional life to the examination of criminals, and who usually appeared for the prosecution in any such trials that happen in a particular geographical area, frequently seemed to have lost their 'therapeutic orientation' and had it replaced by a 'punishment orientation.' "9

Criminal courts have relied on psychiatrists for another kind of determination: whether a defendant is sufficiently sane to receive a fair trial. The capability of the defendant is crucial to the fairness of the trial, for a defendant who does not understand the consequences of his plea or is not able to work with his lawyer runs the risk of imprisonment or death without the chance to put his best foot forward during the trial. In 1765 Blackstone wrote in his *Commentaries* that "as a matter of fairness and humanity" the trial of the insane defendant must be postponed until he is able to appreciate the significance of his legal predicament and work with his lawyers, otherwise "how can he make his own defense."10

He emphasized a related right, that a condemned man may not be executed if he appears to be insane. Coke and Hale, other early legal authorities, also said a madman could not be executed. Among their reasons were that the purpose of punishment was to strike terror into others and the execution of a madman would not have this effect, and that if the condemned man were not mad, he might be able to give some reason to change the sentence even at the last moment.11

After a condemned man has been saved from death because of his insanity, he will be examined periodically to see if he is sufficiently recovered to be put to death. It is a strange function for a physician, who is bound by the Hippocratic oath and tradition to use his medical art to preserve life, to treat a patient in order to help him reach the competency to be executed. The eclipse of capital punishment for fifteen years relieved psychiatrists of the need to deal with incompetency for execution. The issue of incompetency to stand trial is raised increasingly.

The decision of the psychiatrist that a defendant was not able to stand trial has until very recently been, and in many cases still is, made out of public sight, in the preliminary phase of the criminal-trial process. In this century this kind of evaluation, which was once made by judges and lawyers on the basis of their observation of the defendant, became entrusted to psychiatrists, who were usually ignorant of the fact that the law desired defendants to come to trial and only wanted to delay the trials of those who clearly could not meet the simple standards of trial competency. Judges, juries, and even psychiatrists can comfortably see a defendant who has been found incompetent to stand trial go off to a hospital, heedless of the fact that the institution the defendant goes to is not an ordinary mental hospital but a security-oriented special hospital for the criminally insane, where until very recently the defendant might spend the rest of his life without ever having his chance to come to trial and without therapy.

Many such defendants are innocent. Others have been charged with minor offenses or might have escaped conviction because of lack of evidence. Many cannot be civilly committed because they have not been shown to be dangerous. Nevertheless, they could be held in mental institutions for the rest of their lives, with never a chance to present their side of the case to the court. They could be, and often have been, literally forgotten on the chronic wards of hospitals for the criminally insane.

The determination of incompetency to stand trial puts an accused into a legal limbo where no one can act in his behalf; all legal proceedings are postponed until the ruling that competency has been restored.

When four soldiers convicted of murder and held for ten years by the army were found to have been improperly tried, three were set free, but the fourth, who had been declared incompetent to stand trial, was held in a hospital for the criminally insane because he did not have the capacity to participate in the proceeding to have his indictment dismissed.[12]

By the 1960s in the United States, 6000 defendants a year were being sent to hospitals for the criminally insane as incompetent to stand trial.[13] Although the power to keep defendants from trial did great injury to many people, only a few psychiatrists recognized the problem or showed concern. The first of the modern texts in legal psychiatry, published in 1952, does not even mention competency to stand trial.[14] Neither does a contemporary standard reference on legal medicine, although it deals in detail with tests of criminal responsibility.[15] In 1972 the Supreme Court finally took action and held that defendants found incompetent to stand trial could only be held without trial for a "reasonable period of time" to determine whether they can ever come to trial, and to help them reach the capacity to stand trial.[16] If they cannot attain competency, they must be treated in a civil hospital, not a hospital for the criminally insane, provided they are committable, and released if they are not. Most hospitals for the criminally insane, which are maximum security hospitals run like prisons, are so much worse than the poorest civil hospitals that this ruling is meaningful even for defendants who will never be released into society. One major abuse of psychiatric power had been eliminated.

Although matters of criminal justice attract more attention, more people are affected by civil law determinations. The alliance between law and psychiatry forged in the nineteenth century gave psychiatrists great credence in civil matters. Of course commitment, and whether a committed person should be released, were matters where courts relied on psychiatric testimony. They also used psychiatrists to help them come to conclusions about financial responsibility, about when a guardian should be appointed or when a contract should be abrogated. The old English law held that a person could not relieve himself of the obligation of a contract by pleading his own insanity, but in the United States some jurisdictions by statute and some by precedent allowed disadvantageous contracts to be abrogated when there was testimony to show the judge or jury that the person lacked capacity to make the contract. Psychiatric testimony led to many other kinds of legal determinations. On the testimony of psychiatrists, wills are broken; the marriage contract is affected by psychiatric state. Marriages are declared invalid and divorces are declared unobtainable if psychiatric testimony shows that one of the marriage partners is not competent to understand the obligations of a marriage or to consent to the details of a divorce.

Some psychiatrists have argued that not much power accrued to the profession as courts began to rely on its expert advice. After all, so this argument runs, courts only seek psychiatric expert opinions, they are not obliged to follow them. Juries and judges often overrule the opinions of psychiatrists.

The argument is superficially plausible. The testimony of the psychiatrist does not determine the issue. Courts have been comfortable in going against the weight of psychiatric testimony. In cases involving a psychiatric expert who reconstructs the state of mind of someone at an earlier period of time (as in determining criminal responsibility or testamentary capacity), courts have frequently instructed juries that the testimony of the expert should not be given as much weight as a lay person who was a witness at the event. In the case of criminal responsibility, one reason for disregarding the psychiatrist is that the courts often suspect the defendant of manufacturing symptoms, in spite of the protests of the psychiatrist who says that on the basis of his clinical experience he can determine if the defendant is acting or lying.

But the argument of psychiatrists that decisions are made by courts, not psychiatrists, does not stand up. In fact, courts do not understand psychiatry; they rely on psychiatrists to interpret psychiatric issues in legal terms, and in very many cases they accept psychiatric testimony uncritically.

One reason that psychiatrists are found useful in the legal process is that their testimony allows courts to achieve flexibility, sometimes to temper justice with mercy, sometimes to bend the law to conform to popular opinion. One example is the situation of a daughter trying to commit a mother to a mental hospital and not succeeding, and the mother then retaliating by writing the daughter out of her will. After the mother's death, when the will is presented for probate, the daughter can use the testimony of psychiatrists to show that her mother misconstrued the attempt to commit as persecution and that therefore she did not have the state of mind to write a valid will. The court can thus reward an apparently dutiful daughter and overrule the mother who did not feel that she was dutiful.[17]

In another case, a dedicated spinster leaves all her money to a feminist group. Slight evidence of mental illness is furnished not by a psychiatrist but by a general practitioner. This is enough to persuade the judge, who is male, that the testator's antimale animus resulted from an insane delusion concerning the untrustworthiness of men, which deprived her of the ability to write a valid will.[18]

*   *   *

The reliance of the law on psychiatry gave psychiatrists power and influence far greater than that of other doctors. Psychiatrists were accepted as experts on all disordered behavior. They not only filled medical functions such as running mental hospitals and prescribing for and treating patients, but their advice was sought in legal, and later in social, decision making. By the late nineteenth century, the psychiatrist took responsibility for maintaining a well-ordered society as well as for care of patients. He possessed medical authority, including the extraordinary power to commit, and legal and social authority.

In the twentieth century the advent of Freudian thought and new and more effective methods of treatment would make psychiatry even more useful to the legal system. Freud's theory of unconscious determination would make the psychiatrist the expert who alone could explain inexplicable actions. The talking therapies and new somatic methods of treatment would be used to treat the "sick" individual and also to deal with the gamut of social problems starting with crime and corrections and extending to vocational adjustment and family life. The alliance with law that began when Sir John Monro testified in the case of Earl Ferrers had brought psychiatrists a unique authority that had a basis both in medicine and law.

Psychoanalysis and the Broadening
of Psychiatric Power

IN 1900 Freud published his "dreambook," and in it for the first time he presented a full description of principles of unconscious functioning. In the famous final chapter of *The Interpretation of Dreams,*[1] he described primary- and secondary-process thinking, the differentiation of the unconscious and the conscious. The psychic process, said Freud, effortlessly and regularly avoids the memory of anything that has once been sufficiently distressing. This is relegated to the unconscious, where it continues to work on the conscious mind and becomes evident in dreams (as well as in slips of the tongue, mistakes of everyday life, neurotic symptoms, character deviations, and irrational acts that otherwise would defy explanation).

Psychoanalysis and psychoanalytically oriented psychiatry originated with Freud. He was the fecund genius who produced one after another all of the early concepts and most of the major concepts of psychoanalysis that have influenced thought and culture increasingly from 1900 to the present. The contributions of Freud have been incorporated into modern thought and life, and they have served to give psychiatrists and psychologists and other behavioral scientists, even those who profess themselves antianalytic, greatly enhanced authority.

First and foremost among Freud's contributions is the idea of a dynamic unconscious operating according to its own rules. Henri Ellenberger, the psychoanalytic historian, has said that society has been guilty of a collective forgetfulness, that the idea of an unconscious mind had developed through a long line of European thinkers including Mesmer, Leibniz, Schopenhauer, von Hartmann, Maudsley, and many more. He attributes the identification of Freud with the discovery of the unconscious to Freud's own belligerent personality, his organization of a group of enthusiastic and aggressive followers, and the development of that movement into a guild. And he attributes the acceptance of Freudian thought to its timely emergence when society was tending toward, and seeking justification for, mass consumption and hedonism (for although Freud emphasizes the contest between the pleasure principle and the reality principle, he indicates that the pleasure principle has the upper hand).[2]

Whether or not the unconscious mind is Freud's original contribution, the elaboration and popularization of the theory, the couching of it in scientific terms, and the development of a special technique to probe its depths—the psychoanalytic method—do belong to Freud. We associate Freud with the concept of a dynamic unconscious containing repressed material striving for consciousness and making itself manifest in disguised and symbolic ways, always facing the opposition of the forces of repression, which works to keep anxiety-provoking material away from consciousness.

The technique of psychoanalysis depended not only on the use of the couch and the positioning of the analyst away from the view of the analysand but on the observation of the primary rule of free association. The patient was instructed to try to reveal everything that crossed his mind without censorship and, it was hoped, without fear. A chain of associations would thus carry the analysand eventually into deeper and deeper layers of the mind. Freud saw this technique as the equivalent in the study of psychological life to the development of the microscope in relation to biological processes. The concept of finding the solution to conflict by coming into contact with the unconscious part of mental functioning has fostered a host of so-called regressive therapies, designed to bring the patient into touch with earlier and more primitive stages of himself.

Psychoanalysis was to be three things: a scientific method of studying the human mind and personality, a method of cure for psychological conditions that previously had not had any systematic treatment approach, and a body of theory that, on the basis of the laws of unconscious functioning, explained the courses of action and the fates of both individuals and societies.

There were a multitude of other Freudian contributions:

• The concept of sexual energy—libido—and aggression as the driving force for human activity.

• The concept of infantile sexuality with its stages of development, and the accompanying idea of psychic trauma and fixations in, and regressions to, the various stages. Only those who had escaped from developmental trauma or who could surmount or work through them, usually through psychoanalysis, could reach the stage of mature functioning.

• The central place of anxiety in psychological functioning.

• The concept of complexes—the Oedipus complex, the castration complex. Later, Freud's disciples and neo-Freudians emphasized other earlier and more primitive complex-fears—the separation of child from mother, the fear of disintegration and dissolution.

• The idea of the defensive use of certain mental mechanisms—rationalization, projection, displacement, and a host of others—and the relationship of the characteristic use of specific mechanisms with specific types of mental illness or character distortion.

• The meaning of symptoms, dreams, omissions, slips of the tongue, and the way that unconscious determinants brought these into being, and the related concept that professional help, preferably from a practitioner who has himself been analyzed, can facilitate the interpretation of these.

• The compulsion to repeat as a way of dealing with unresolved trauma.

• The need for punishment to atone for unconscious guilt.

Eventually Freud developed a companion theory to his original division of the mind into conscious and unconscious. This new structural theory gave us the concept of the mind divided into ego, id, and superego, each working against the others to find its own most comfortable accommodation.

Many of the complaints that patients brought to the early analysts had traditionally been treated medically—loss of appetite or libido, gastrointestinal symptoms, insomnia. The doctor had always had purgatives or tonics or sedatives to deal with such conditions. Other conditions treated by analysts had also been treated by doctors, not because they felt they had any competency to deal with them, but only because no one else had any therapy to offer for obsessions, compulsions, phobias, uncontrollable anxiety, and hysteria. Before analysis, doctors often dealt with such conditions, recommending an effort of will or prescribing a sea voyage or a stay at a spa. Now a host of neurotic and psychosomatic complaints were accepted as medical. Freud's followers further developed the scope of analysis (and eventually of analytically oriented treatment that did not necessarily use the couch or involve multiweekly appointments) to deal with conditions that had never been considered medical: people with such character misadaptations as passive-aggressive personalities, defective moral sense, histories of criminal behavior, or with such feeling states as alienation or loneliness. There is no deviation from "normal" and acceptable social functioning that some psychiatrists have not promised to cure, although in the course of time the hope for curing certain conditions, among them transvestism, transsexuality, criminal recidivism, has proved to be largely illusory or overly optimistic.

Depression has always been considered a psychiatric disease, but now unhappiness, loneliness, and alienation have become "diseases"; and from now on a suicide attempt would be seen not as morally wrong but as a product of sickness.

Before Freud, mental disease was an infrequently recognized occurrence; it was hidden from the world because it was stigmatizing and unusual. Now it is ubiquitous. President Carter's Commission on Mental Health has estimated (on the basis of insubstantial data) that at any one time the number of Americans who need mental health service is close to 33 million and that another 55 million suffer from mild to moderate depression, anxiety, and other symptoms of mental disorder that may not represent conventionally diagnosable mental illness but still might benefit from assistance. Mental health now has political dimensions: a huge army of "professionals" with a vested interest in "giving help" and a population to be served—if the commission's figures are to be believed—of half the country.[3]

The Freudian concepts of stages of psychosexual development and the effect of traumas in preventing optimal development and progression through these stages implied an important premise and a major promise. The premise was that people who grew up without trauma and with proper psychological support would almost inevitably end up well adjusted. This has given rise to most of our modern concepts of child rearing and early education. The promise was that people who had experienced deficits or wounds that prevented optimal psychological growth could undo these harms by psychoanalytic regression, interpretation of the patient's material, and working through the unresolved affects that worked against growth and adjustment. This has resulted in the development and wide use of many forms of non-somatic therapy, that is, therapy that does not depend on drugs or shock.

Freud saw analytic treatment as thoroughgoing and intensive and advocated daily analysis. When present-day patients ask how long an analysis will take, the standard response of many psychoanalysts is "a minimum of two years." Figures collected in one study by the American Psychoanalytic Association indicate that the average analysis takes four years and five months.[4] Freud himself came to see analysis as always being a matter of long periods of time—"of half a year, or whole years—or longer periods than the patient expects."[5]

Psychoanalysis is a meaningful experience for many of those who have experienced it. Because of its expense and the requirement of daily hours, only the affluent (and some low-fee analysands who serve as control cases for analysts in training) and those who plan to use analysis professionally (including prospective analysts who must go through a "training analysis") have the experience. The scientific value of analysis is difficult to prove. When people change greatly during the course of an analysis it is impossible to know if the same change would have occurred with the passage of time alone or with a different kind of treatment. Analysts claim psychoanalysis is a science and point out the expressions of satisfied analysands (although analytic success has been ascribed to brainwashing and the wish to believe and other phenomena that are the results of the relationship between analyst and analysand, rather than to the science of analysis). They also point out that analysts can make accurate predictions, put otherwise inexplicable behavior in perspective, and point out meaningful patterns of behavior that would be meaningless without the analytic framework.

But even those analysts who most emphasize the scientific nature of analysis believe that analytic "truth," the making of correct analytic interpretations, the securing of analytic understanding, only result from the confirmation of tentative hypotheses advanced during the course of the analysis. As the analysis develops, interpretations are made that are then confirmed or denied by succeeding material; the analytic explanation of behavior results from a collaborative effort in a process involving analyst and analysand.

Defending the scientific validity of psychoanalysis, Robert Waelder has said that "psychoanalytic interpretations of single events, or a psychoanalytic chart of an individual person, or general psychoanalytic propositions can hardly be proved on the basis of external, physical, measurable data alone." But he asserts that

> the combinations of such data with the data of a patient's self-observations (including the self-observations pursuant to the tentatively proposed interpretation) and with the data of our observations of his behavior, including his verbal behavior, viewed as expressions of psychic processes, each of these sets of data viewed critically in the light of other data, form a kind of evidence which is just as convincing as the evidence found in the study

of a single variable in such fields where single variables can be meaningfully studied in isolation.[6]

He adds that this is true only if the analyst has learned, as Freud expressed it, to "restrain speculative tendencies."

In spite of criticisms of psychoanalysis for its deficiencies as science and in spite of the opposition aroused by analysts who interpreted all behavior as sexually motivated, the theories of analysis grew increasingly influential. Eventually followers of Freud such as Adler, Horney, Sullivan, and Melanie Klein modified analytic theory to stress social and interpersonal and early mother-child relationships rather than the Oedipal triangle (seen popularly as the child's wish to possess the parent of the opposite sex and destroy the parent of the same sex), and analytic ideas became more palatable. Psychoanalysis became able to reach many more people through Franz Alexander's popularization of analysis. Alexander's psychoanalytically oriented psychotherapy involved a more active analyst with a patient seen weekly or twice weekly instead of daily. The couch was made optional. It was hoped that therapy would be shortened from years to months.

Alexandrian therapy raised the promise of treatment for all, and treatment became the recommended means of solving problems formerly dealt with by the family, the legal system, and religion. Philip Rieff has coined the phrase "the triumph of the therapeutic" to describe the allegiance of modern man to the Freudian concept of the achievement of personal well-being.[7]

The Alexandrian psychiatrist was more public than the more classical Freudian, who saw the maintenance of his anonymous and neutral position as a prerequisite for the full revelations of his patient's inner life, which would be projected onto this "blank screen." Freudians do not want to contaminate the transference by becoming a real person in the life of the patient and they ostensibly try not to make decisions for the patient. The more Freudian the analyst, the less is he willing to make diagnoses, prognoses, and to exert his psychiatric authority outside the office. Analysts rarely appear in courtrooms to testify. They believe that psychopathology becomes understandable only after a long uncovering process, so they do not make definitive diagnoses after brief encounters.

But all the psychoanalytic terms and dynamic explanations have been adopted by nonanalysts. Freudian concepts appear in the courtroom. They become a part of social decision making not because the subject of the decisions has been in analysis, but because some mental health professional, who may or may not be a psychiatrist and who sometimes has had some experience of his own as an analysand, but usually has not, is willing to apply the Freudian concept of the unconscious to an individual who has not been studied thoroughly, sometimes to a person who has only been seen briefly, and sometimes to one who has not been seen at all.

Psychiatric reports and evaluations are used for many purposes. In the criminal-justice process they often make the difference between no sentence, a short sentence, or a long sentence. Many of these reports and evaluations contain dynamic formulations about the cause of behavior based on as little as twenty minutes spent with the subject of the report. Even when the report contains no psychodynamic formulation it carries the authority of psychiatry, which in turn carries the authority of the understanding of the unconscious. Some Texas psychiatrists have recommended the death penalty for convicted first-degree murderers with no more meaningful information in their reports than that the convicted man showed no remorse and that they regard him as a sociopath.

Medical psychology (Freud's term for psychoanalysis) has embraced a much larger field than traditional psychiatry; psychiatry has expanded its concepts of who are patients and what are treatable conditions.

Following the dissemination of Freudian theory, many conditions that psychiatrists had not previously taken seriously or that they had thought represented malingering were now dignified and given the status of real illnesses. "Combat fatigue" would no longer be seen as a way to evade the battle through feigned illness. In particular, neurotic illness would from this time on be as worthy of serious consideration as any other illness.

So the incorporation of Freudian thought into medical practice increased the scope of psychiatry in a number of ways. It enlarged the definition of mental illness to the point where almost every personality could be seen as having at least some neurotic aspects. It had given status to all these conditions—they could henceforth be seen as worthy of treatment and as treatable.

But psychiatry gained even more from the Freudian infusion. The psychiatrist had received from Freud a new kind of power, different from, and greater than, any he had wielded before. Psychiatrists and psychologists could now claim to understand what was going on in the unconscious. They could do this not only with the cooperation of the patient who spoke in free associations but also without the aid of the patient, by interpreting behavior, inadvertent help of slips of the tongue, and mistakes. They could read patients' minds through the use of projective testing, a new kind of intrusion into the mind. In 1921 Hermann Rorschach published his *Psychodiagnostik*,[8] in which he described his method of comprehending the contents of the unconscious mind through the use of the reaction to inkblots. Earlier Carl Jung had developed a projective method, the testing of the length of the hesitation in response to a word stimulus ("Red?" "Green." "Mother?" . . . "Father."), that would indicate pathological complexes. Now the behavioral scientist could enter the mind without permission.

Psychoanalysis began as a branch of medicine, although in many ways it was not at all medical. Freud did not want his movement to become the captive of medicine—his first pupils comprised some doctors, but also school teachers, musicologists, and other intellectuals. In the 1930s the American branch of his movement succeeded in making a medical degree a requirement for psychoanalytic training, and this rule is generally observed, although psychoanalysts in other countries, including England and France, are often not physicians. Psychoanalysis did not need to go the medical route. It could have remained a separate discipline of its own, but then it would have lacked the status of its medical affiliation and its practitioners would not have had the medical powers to commit, treat involuntarily, physically restrain, and prescribe medicines that give it such great authority. There are a few psychoanalysts who would prefer to have psychoanalysis accepted as a psychological and educational nonmedical discipline, but most psychoanalysts enjoy their medical affiliation, its power and prestige, and the insurance coverage that the medical affiliation allows some of their patients.

As heirs of the traditions of both medical psychiatry and Freudian psychology, modern psychiatrists have truly exceptional power—to read what is in a person's mind, to predict what he will do in the future, and to treat him with a talking therapy, drugs, or some other somatic treatment. A patient can be treated for problems of which he is unaware or for thoughts he never knew he was thinking. The practice of committing people to mental hospitals involuntarily, based on such subjective criteria as ominous Rorschach responses or disturbing results on the many other projective tests now in use, has been prohibited by law in a few states. There, the basis for a psychiatric commitment must be more than a surmise concerning what is going on in the patient's head, and there must be objective evidence of danger. But most psychiatric decisions are not based simply or even largely on objective criteria. At most they are determined by a combination of observations of the behavior of the patient, the results of testing, and surmise on the part of the psychiatrist as to what is going on in the patient's mind. At the least, surmise alone often suffices to make the diagnosis and prognosis.

A curious thing happened as psychiatry developed. At first psychiatry was a medical discipline, and psychiatrists had all the considerable power of doctors. Then Freudian psychology gave increased power both to doctors who were psychoanalysts, relying on psychoanalytic concepts in their work, and to neuropsychiatrists, who were not analytic adherents, but who benefited from the increased stature of psychiatry after the infusion of psychoanalytic theory. In time there was so much work for psychiatrists to do that psychologists and many other kinds of professionals invaded the field. Decisions came frequently to be made not by psychiatrists and psychologists but by social workers and by new professionals with much less training, such as mental health technicians and pastoral counselors. The present situation is that at a case conference to decide whether a patient is to be released from the mental hospital, the major determinant may not be the psychiatrist but the vote of other "treatment team" members—social worker, nurse, practical nurse, aide, attendant, psychiatric resident, psychology or social work intern, medical student, or whoever else has become part of the patient's team or had contact with the patient. The psychiatrist puts his signature to the report and recommendation, taking responsibility but it is often a group decision and sometimes made by a split vote. Mental health workers with less training and those in the field with no training at all have great psychiatric power. All doctors are entitled to consider themselves psychiatrically knowledgeable because psychiatry is one of their medical-school subjects and because they are able to use psychiatric and psychoanalytic concepts and treatment methods as part of any kind of medical practice. Much psychiatric testimony and many psychiatric decisions come from family practitioners, internists, and surgeons.

The post-Freudian emphasis on social factors in mental and emotional malfunctioning gave psychiatry other kinds of influence. Psychiatrists became the experts on education, child rearing, family relationships, the attitudes society should take toward the aging, juvenile delinquency, adolescent maladjustment, and so on, until alienation in modern society, unemployment, economic stresses, and the distribution of wealth had become part of the psychiatrist's field of interest. The psychiatrist had become the universal expert.

Freudian thought infiltrated the popular mind. James Joyce and Tennessee Williams and others have introduced the concept of the dynamic unconscious to the common reader or playgoer. Eventually television situation comedies and soap operas came to appropriate watered-down analytic concepts, and Woody Allen was able to build a comedy career on jokes concerning his neurotic pathology and the ineffectiveness of its interminable treatment.

In short, psychiatry and psychoanalysis have redefined all problems of human life, all aspects of behavior, as medical problems and brought them within the medical model.[9] The medical model proposes that conditions have discoverable causes and scientific cures, that experts should exercise authority in the application of these cures, and that the nonexperts, the rest of the population, should submit to the authority of these experts. Such legal considerations as procedurally protected rights need not be given major consideration since the experts will presumably only be operating in the interests of those they serve.

The Psychiatrist and the Prisoner

PSYCHIATRY HAS TWO entirely different functions: to give help to individuals and to help society run more smoothly. As psychiatry developed in the twentieth century, it extended its control over new groups of people for whom it functioned more to control behavior in the interest of society than to provide therapy for the individual.

The first application of this widened scope was helping the military to function in wartime. British army doctors gave the names "soldier's heart" and "irritable heart" to the cluster of symptoms complained of by Crimean War soldiers—rapid pulse, digestive upset, headache, disturbed sleep. A similar condition in Civil War soldiers was known as Da Costa's syndrome. In the late 1880s and the 1890s, neurologists became interested in the phenomenon of traumatic neurosis. At first they attributed the anxiety, agitation, insomnia, and depression of people who had been subjected to stress to physical trauma suffered by the body, and particularly the head. One theory was that the symptoms resulted from the molecular disturbance of neurons, another that it resulted from inflammation of nerves and nerve sheaths. In the early years of World War I, neurologists and neuropsychiatrists thought shellshock, also called "combat fatigue" and "effort syndrome," was caused by the physical effect of shocks acting either through the aural apparatus or by a concussing effect on the structure of the brain. French and British psychiatric hospitals were quickly overloaded with cases of shellshock. By 1916, Allied medical services had recognized that shellshock was a psychological disorder, often present when there had been no exposure to concussion, and the term "war neurosis" was adopted. These conditions had achieved legitimacy as a disease or diseases, although doctors often found it difficult to distinguish between neurotics and the malingerers who complained of symptoms to escape dangerous assignments. During World War I psychiatrists showed great inconsistency in their handling of this complaint. They had characterized a war neurosis as a legitimate psychiatric disability, but they labeled many soldiers with its symptoms as malingerers and dissemblers. By treating wartime psychic disorganization as conscious and cowardly, the psychiatrists discouraged the disease, and they used psychological techniques to return the soldiers to their posts as quickly as possible.

The wartime psychiatrist has a dual function: to treat the ill soldier and to keep the military machine intact. Most psychiatrists working for the military do not see any conflict between these two goals. It was not until the Vietnam War that psychiatrists began to see that remotivating a soldier to go back to a frontline assignment might be serving the interest of the state more than the individual.

By treating wartime anxieties as conscious and cowardly failures in a soldier's obligations, World War I psychiatrists kept an epidemic of neurotic illness from overwhelming the military. A medical historian has said that in Germany between 1914 and 1918 war neurosis and war hysteria were so widespread that it constituted a danger to the German nation. "It was an act of national self-protection to refuse to regard war neurotics and war hysterics as sick people. This was done by applying psychological arguments. As hysteria was psychogenic, it was not a disease."[1] A neuropsychiatrist had little difficulty in denying the validity of this kind of mental illness or planning a therapeutic regimen so unpleasant and degrading for the soldier that he was forced and shamed into "recovering." In Germany one method of treating neurotics was to administer painful electric shocks. The application of an electrogalvanic current was an old and accepted psychiatric treatment method. Early in his career Freud had bought an electric treatment machine, but he soon gave it up when he concluded that the successes of electrotherapy were due to the power of suggestion. (This was before the introduction of electroconvulsive therapy.) The current was meant to be stimulating, but it could be increased to the point of pain, and this in wartime had become a common method to treat "malingerers." Like many aversive stimulus therapies before and since, the painful shock was not thought of by the doctors who administered it as a torture to induce conforming behavior but as a treatment to suppress conflicts, to promote a healthy attitude.

"More-enlightened" psychiatrists, influenced by Freud's concept of unconscious motivation, gave neurosis the dignity of a real disease—as real as somatic disease—and advocated analytically oriented therapy, but the purpose was much the same as shame or electric shock: to get the soldier in shape to return to the front as soon as possible.

After the war Freud testified before the Austrian Commission for Enquiry into Violations of Military Duty, which wanted his expert opinion on the electrical treatment of war neurotics. Freud told the commission that war neurosis was caused by "an unconscious inclination in the soldier to withdraw from the demands, dangerous or outrageous to his feelings, made upon him by active service." He deplored the assumption that war neurotics were malingerers and saw this as an example of the deficiency of the psychological education of physicians. He expressed ignorance of whether the German practice of continuing to increase the current when the patient did not respond had also been the practice in Austria. He had no doubt that in Germany there had been deaths as the result of the treatment and suicides because of fear of it. He made a strong attack on the psychiatrist who serves two masters, ostensibly as the physician of the patient, actually as the agent of the state. He did not seem to realize that his psychoanalytic method of dealing with war neurosis might be used (with less-obvious cruelty) to uphold the state's notions of duty and patriotism. He said of the "other physicians," but not of psychoanalysts, "Here Medicine was serving purposes foreign to its essence. The physician himself was under military command and had his own personal dangers to fear—loss of seniority or a charge of neglecting his duty— if he allowed himself to be led by considerations other than those prescribed for him. The insoluble conflict between the claims of humanity, which normally carry decisive weight for a physician, and the demands of a national war was bound to confuse his activity."[2]

Freud was seemingly unaware that the same criticism could be made of his new approach to war neuroses, the use of the psychoanalytic method to produce abreaction, the relieving of repressed traumas so that the feelings connected with them could be discharged, which might also serve the purpose of the state better than that of the patient.

The wartime military found other uses for psychiatrists and psychologists. When the United States entered World War I, the problem of mentally deficient and mentally unstable recruits plagued the armed forces. Psychiatrists and psychologists were given the job of deciding who would serve effectively and in what capacity. The United States Army's Surgeon General's Office created a section in psychology in its Division of Neurology and Psychiatry. Eventually this section was made a division in its own right, and a school of psychology was established in the army to train more testers in the new art of military classification. The purposes of the testing were both to eliminate severe mental defectives and to classify soldiers for special services on the basis of their aptitudes. By the time of the Armistice, 1,151,552 men had been examined and classified and, according to a historian of the World War I Medical Department, "the jargon of psychology had become slang."[3]

The success of psychiatry in dealing with the classification and control of military personnel made it natural for it to turn its attention to another group of segregated and controlled individuals, prisoners. Psychiatry began to claim that it understood the psychology of the criminal and could help in his rehabilitation.

The correctional system had always had a mixture of objectives—to hold the criminal in a place where he could be temporarily immobilized and so unable to commit more crimes, to be a deterrent to future criminality, to exact the retribution of society, and to promote behavioral change in the direction of lawfulness. The promotion of behavioral change was an honored penal aim. Some of the earliest American prisons were designed as "penitentiaries" to encourage remorse in the interest of change. Early prisons emphasized solitude in which the inmate could be forced to study his Bible, meditate, and work through a reformation process. In the first quarter of this century, as a result of the spread of Freudian thought, the idea emerged that behavioral science rather than religion and conscience could be the source of rehabilitation.

The goal of rehabilitation instead of punishment and the application of psychiatry to accomplish this are at first glance benign. It has taken fifty years for even some behavioral scientists—a small minority—to see that the rehabilitative model has dangers. A danger that seems obvious, but that has not been sufficiently recognized, is that courts and psychiatrists feel comfortable holding people for years in situations where they can be contained and coerced if the rationale is cure. Even an indeterminate sentence, which may be for life, does not seem excessive, and does not have to be related to the severity of the crime, if the purpose is cure. Mild-mannered exhibitionists have spent their lives waiting for their "cures" in hospitals for the criminally insane after being diverted from the criminal justice system. Psychiatrists justified long-term or lifetime detention by their inaccurately optimistic belief that cures could be obtained through "insight." The lengthy sentence for rehabilitation and the indeterminate sentence for cure became accepted in the American penal system. The procedural protections that had developed to prevent the oppression of criminal defendants were seen as obstructions to therapy, and they were minimized or eliminated in the new rehabilitative model.

All these dangers can seem unimportant to the psychiatrist who is convinced that crime is irrational, that it is motivated by pathology that is largely unconscious, and that therapy can cure crime.

Freudian theory is largely responsible for the widespread acceptance of the belief that the causes of crime are psychological and environmental. Emil Kraepelin, Freud's contemporary, took the approach that criminal behavior was the result of an inherited criminality and low intelligence. Kraepelin was the great classifier of psychiatric conditions, but he had no psychological theory to explain abnormal behavior and did not offer the hope of a psychological cure. In his lectures to students, published in 1904, he attributed the transvestism of a twenty-one-year-old waiter to "congenital feeble-mindedness" with a resulting perversion of the sexual inclinations resulting from the "imbecility." Kraepelin describes another patient with a history of chronic conflicts with the law and with his family as intellectually gifted but morally insane, in the class of born criminal for whom the only remedy is "to isolate them as being unfit for society, and as far as possible to find them occupations." A third patient Kraepelin described as "a born swindler," and added that although the alienist might see such a person as a "morbid personality" it was not probable that a judge would ever regard him as anything but a crafty and dangerous impostor.[4] (The ideal of therapeutic reform has gone through a full cycle in less than a century and Kraepelin's "old-fashioned" and "unhumanitarian" views are now the new wave of correctional theory. The "new" ideas of Samuel Yochelson and Stanton Samenow, like the recommendations of Norval Morris and Ernest van den Haag,[5] stress a correctional rather than a psychological approach.)

Freud did not show great interest in the problem of crime, and he probably had as little sympathy for common criminals as Kraepelin— although when neuroticism was expressed as sexual deviancy it did arouse his special sympathy and understanding.

Freud apparently took the view that although the therapist or the patient himself might understand the unconscious determinants of criminal behavior, nevertheless the patient could be expected to conform to the law or accept the consequences. But Freud's followers found a new use for psychiatry: to excuse the lawbreaker on the ground that his offense was unconsciously motivated.

Forensic psychiatrists readily accepted the concept that crime could have its root in the unconscious and they found striking examples of psychopathology in criminals. Unfortunately, their dynamic formulations were simplistic, and the promise of a quick cure through understanding was illusory. A typical early case history, published in 1916 by Bernard Glueck, a psychiatrist at St. Elizabeths Hospital in Washington, D.C., concerns a twenty-three-year-old black man who had repeatedly stolen. The stealing was accompanied by panting, perspiration, and excitement, and after every incident of stealing, the need to have a bowel movement. Glueck concluded that the man was anally and homosexually fixated and, because the idea of homosexual gratification was unacceptable to him, was forced to repeatedly commit crimes to gain substitute satisfaction. "The process of sublimation . . . took an asocial turn in this individual, with the resultant pathological stealing."[6]

This new approach to criminal behavior stressed deviance as pathology. The criminal was to be seen not as "bad" but as "mad," and he was to be given the benefit of the medical approach to madness. He should be helped to understand his unconscious motivation and to go through a process of psychoanalytic change. From today's viewpoint, we may feel not that the emphasis on dynamics was necessarily wrong, but that the belief that this new knowledge would answer the problem of crime was wrong.

Glueck, William Healy, who pioneered in the psychological approach to juvenile delinquents, and the few other American psychiatrists who became involved with criminal behavior were, from any perspective, enlightened and courageous; they spent their professional lives with unpromising patients who provided little financial reward. It would be unfair to attribute bad motives to these pioneers in the field of psychiatric criminology. But in spite of good motives and, indeed, some basis for their belief in rehabilitation through therapy (though few criminals have received adequate therapy, some criminals can be greatly helped by thoroughgoing psychiatric efforts to promote self-understanding), the major result was to give society a new tool for controlling deviant behavior and to give psychiatrists new authority. A huge new group in society was now converted into patients. The only people who understood their illness, who could advise on their disposition and could cure them, were psychoanalytically oriented psychiatrists who could plumb the depths of the unconscious.

Therapy in prisons and in hospitals for the criminally insane was generally characterized by inadequate staffing and the use of poorly trained psychiatrists. Work with criminals only attracted a minute fraction of psychiatrists. Most psychiatrists did not become involved. But the therapeutic model replaced the punitive model, and psychiatric concepts, misapplied or used for social ends that did not necessarily coincide with the individual's needs, influenced all phases of criminal justice and corrections.

Psychiatrists and psychologists have increasingly been called upon to prepare presentence reports to advise on what crimes should not be prosecuted and what crimes deserve severe treatment. They also testify at trials on conscious and unconscious motivation. Only the courtroom appearance—and this only when the trial has received much publicity—gives the psychiatrist much visibility. The pretrial and presentence evaluations are done out of the limelight, and they are not subject to debate and discussion.

The merger of the concept of social deviancy and mental illness is now being reconsidered, and determinate sentences are again being advocated. "Liberals" in the corrections field are promoting a punitive rather than a rehabilitative philosophy, on the grounds that the therapy orientation incarcerates too many people for too long and has not proven its effectiveness. (A newspaper tells us that "a startling new theory suggests criminals are born, not made . . .")[7]

A formal structure arose, the court clinic, through which psychiatrists participated in criminal-justice and correctional decisions. The first American court clinic was initiated in the Chicago Municipal Court in 1914. The movement progressed slowly, but by 1966 there were at least twenty-six American cities where courts employed psychiatrists to help make determinations. Of course psychiatrists are called in on an intermittent basis in places where there is no regular court clinic. Juvenile courts have relied heavily on psychiatric services, a result of the legal concept that a determination of delinquency is not punitive but part of a therapeutic or rehabilitative approach to the minor. Evaluations for competency to stand trial are made frequently. Court clinics and private psychiatrists have defendants referred to them for outpatient therapy, which is often vastly preferable to a prison sentence even though therapy under the threat of a prison term, if it is unsuccessful (or if the patient incurs the wrath of the therapist), has disadvantages.

The examinations are often done by psychiatrists and psychologists who are seen by their colleagues as less well trained or less competent than the average practitioner. Reports are often liable to criticism (although they are rarely criticized) on the grounds that they are conclusory and not factual. Judge Justine Wise Polier, writing about the court-employed psychiatrist, "the civil servant-psychiatrist," who "sometimes becomes more moralistic in his judgments than scientific in his evaluations," has said, "Like many of the children sent to them for study, these physicians have lost their sense of identity. No longer part of the mainstream of psychiatric thought, they seem to draw strength from the law's power to pass judgment and from a moralistic application of value judgments."[8] Other critics of the evaluations being done for court purposes stress the inadequacy of the examination—often only a few minutes—and the "boiler plate" quality of the reports themselves, which often describe very different individuals in almost identical terms. The reports tend to be skimpy; they may consist only of a diagnosis and a recommended disposition with no supporting data. They often obscure the legal issues, as when they recommend that a defendant be held incompetent to stand trial because he is a schizophrenic, although the test for competency to stand trial depends not on any diagnostic category but on the severity of the disability as it affects the criminal-trial process.

The psychoanalytic concept of unconscious motivation for criminal behavior gave the psychiatric expert a much larger scope for courtroom testimony. Before Freud, the insanity defense involved much testimony on the effects of mental disease, but now the testimony became more speculative and often much more fantastic. In 1924 Clarence Darrow, in his defense of Leopold and Loeb, the educated, well-to-do young killers of Bobby Franks, produced a battery of psychoanalytically oriented psychiatrists to testify to such then-novel notions as the emotional warping of the defendants from childhood and their delusion that they were supermen entitled to disregard the laws of society. The testimony was aimed not at the question of guilt or innocence but at the question of punishment. It was credited (perhaps incorrectly, since no killers as young as these defendants had ever been executed in Illinois) with saving Leopold and Loeb from execution. This use of analytically oriented explanations of criminal behavior set off a storm of protest and much antipsychiatric sentiment. Nevertheless the history of courtroom testimony from that time to this shows an increasing dependence on the psychiatric explanation of the unconscious dynamics of behavior.

In the late 1930s a new and important power was given to psychiatrists. Society did not know what to do with the offender who repeatedly committed sexual offenses and could not be induced by prison sentences to give up his perverse or aggressive sexual behavior. Some sexual offenders were guilty of minor crimes—exhibitionism, making obscene phone calls. Others were rapists and child molesters and sexual murderers. If these offenders could be entrusted to psychiatrists for treatment and cure, these conditions would be recognized as illnesses—seemingly a humane step—and the offenders would be held in hospitals where they could no longer threaten the public. Sexual-offender laws and defective-delinquency laws, designed to deal with other types of offenders with defective intelligence, or even a "defective moral sense" that kept them embroiled with the law, were passed in most states. They allowed criminal defendants to be diverted from the criminal-justice system into the mental health system on the certification of psychiatrists that they met the criteria for "sexual psychopathy" or "defective delinquency." The psychiatric diagnoses were necessary for the diversion to take place, but the categories did not fit the traditional psychiatric nosology, and there was only vague statutory language to guide the psychiatrist in his determination. If a psychiatrist was satisfied that a person accused of a crime had "criminal propensities to the commission of sex offenses" or "demonstrated persistent aggravated antisocial or criminal behavior" he could find him a psychopath or delinquent. The term "quasi criminal" has been applied to offenders like these who are diverted from the criminal-justice to the mental health system.

Sexual-psychopath and defective-delinquency laws were eventually adopted in a majority of states. They are still in use in some, although they have fallen into disrepute, and in others they have been repealed or are not being utilized. Under the authority of these laws, exhibitionists and other minor offenders have been held in mental hospitals, usually in hospitals for the criminally insane, for long periods of time (or even for life) for offenses that carry a short maximum sentence in the conventional criminal-justice system.

Judge Morris Ploscowe has described the rationale for the detention of the quasi criminal. It was an outgrowth of the familiar way of dealing with the insane and the mentally defective. Insane people had traditionally been committed to hospitals, and in recent years psychiatrists had been given authority in many states to commit by notarized certificates without the need for any courtroom adjudication of the issue of insanity. Defendants who successfully pleaded not guilty by reason of insanity were sent to hospitals for the criminally insane to be held until the staff found them safe to be released. Prisoners serving time were transferred to hospitals for the criminally insane if they exhibited signs of mental illness. From there it was only a step to devising a scheme for holding sexual psychopaths and defective delinquents. The reasoning of society, which Ploscowe described but did not agree with, was these people, though not in a condition of legal insanity that would allow their commitment, were mentally abnormal, and their abnormality made them dangerous. The laws were designed to "permit such offenders to be kept in custody indefinitely as long as the abnormality and the state of danger persists."[9]

Ploscowe has also described some of the shortcomings of such laws: They do not distinguish dangerous and nondangerous sexual offenders, they lack adequate procedural safeguards, they do not have criteria that indicate when the person deserves to be released, and they do not require that the hospital for the criminally insane have any real treatment program.

One of the great defects of the sexual psychopathy laws was its dependence on maximum security hospitals, hospitals for the criminally insane, to produce cures. The hospital for the criminally insane is a cross between a prison and a hospital for the most severely disturbed mental patients. It has a long history. In the 1850s, hospital superintendents began to express the need for specialized institutions so that insane criminals, and also those "noncriminals" who had been hospitalized after a verdict of not guilty by reason of insanity, would not disrupt normal hospital routine. In 1859, New York opened America's first hospital for the criminally insane, the State Lunatic Asylum for Insane Convicts at Auburn. When, after a generation, this became full to overflowing, new facilities were provided at Matteawan State Hospital, and in 1900 a special institution was opened at Dannemora for felons who became insane while serving prison sentences.

In many states large institutions were built, often in isolated regions where mental health professionals were unavailable. Sometimes a wing of the state hospital was declared a hospital for the criminally insane. In these institutions innocent and guilty, mild and dangerous, tried and untried, felons and misdemeanants live side by side. These may include defendants picked up for a crime, possibly a minor offense, and very possibly a crime of which they are not guilty, who have been sent by the court for an examination for competency to stand trial; patients who may have been adjudged incompetent to stand trial after a court hearing; incompetents who may be innocent or guilty of an alleged offense, and who hospitals have traditionally retained long after they regained sanity. In 1972 the Supreme Court belatedly recognized that grave injustices were being done to those ruled incompetent to stand trial, that minor offenders were being held for much longer than their maximum potential prison sentence, and that some defendants were being held for life because they never regained competency to stand trial. Accordingly, in *Jackson* v. *Indiana* the Court ruled that this kind of psychiatric holding could only be for a "reasonable time" in order for competency to be regained or for a decision that it could never be regained.[10]

Hospitals for the criminally insane also hold patients who have pleaded criminal irresponsibility and been found not guilty by reason of insanity; they are held until the hospital staff decides they are safe to be released. There are patients diagnosed as sexual psychopaths who are held until "cured" or safe to be released. There are also

48

convicted criminals who have become psychotic during the course of imprisonment and are transferred to the hospital for the criminally insane until they are mentally healthy enough to return to prison. (Until recently these transferees from the prison system were not given credit on their sentences for time spent in such maximum security hospitals.) Finally, there are involuntarily committed patients from other mental hospitals who are so dangerous that they needed to be placed in the most secure type of hospital.

The most striking thing about this mixed bag of patients is that many of them are not psychotic. Most of the untried defendants being evaluated for competency to stand trial are not psychotic. Most of the defendants found not guilty by reason of insanity are no longer psychotic, if they ever were. Almost none of the sexual psychopaths meet conventional criteria for insanity when they enter the hospitals, although they can easily develop a more clear-cut psychosis after being hospitalized for a long period. These are strange "hospitals," where most of the patients are not sick and most of the staff are administrators or guards, not therapists.

The psychiatrist who acts as evaluator and administrator in such a hospital has extraordinary powers, the most striking of these being the ability to detain the patient for as long as the psychiatrist feels necessary, with few or no procedural safeguards, no obligation to prove the necessity of continued hospitalization, and little chance for the patient to demonstrate that he is ready to be released.

One of my first experiences with the authority that psychiatrists have over sexual psychopaths came in the early 1960s when I was serving as the psychiatric consultant for a Pennsylvania medium security prison. The law in Pennsylvania, later declared unconstitutional, allowed the judge to sentence a sexual psychopath to serve his sentence either in a prison or in a mental hospital. The consulting psychiatrist to the prison had the job of evaluating every six months all those sentenced to one day to life to see if they were "cured."

An elderly prisoner was serving an indeterminate sentence for a homosexual offense committed against his eight-year-old nephew. He had served a previous prison sentence for a similar offense with another boy and had been out on parole. Part of his parole plan had been for him to live with his sister. Neither the parole officer nor his sister had seemed to think it remarkable that he would have to share a double bed with his nephew. The sister was horrified to learn that her son had been molested. She had her brother rearrested, and this time he was sent to prison under the sexual psychopath statute.

There were two psychologists at the prison, which had a population of more than 1000. When the patient continued to deny that he was sick and maintained that homosexuality was beneficial and normal, he was designated as unsuitable for treatment.

Every six months I would interview this amiable old gentleman, who would involve me in philosophical arguments about the sexual practices of the Greeks and his theory that boys attained optimal heterosexuality only after experiencing an overt homosexual phase. Because I had so many prisoners to evaluate and treat in my one day a week at the prison, these interviews were usually compressed into only a few minutes. My stock question was to ask him if he would resume his homosexual practices were he to be released. His stock response was that in good conscience he could not be persuaded to recant. I would tell him that until I got a more appropriate response I could not write a favorable report. When I left the service of the prison he was still serving his sentence. If the law under which he had been sentenced had not been declared unconstitutional, on the ground that the statute was deficient in due process,[11] he might be in prison still.

When defendants who are subject to this kind of authority have differed or disagreed with their psychiatrists, they have usually found that they were powerless. When they have successfully fought psychiatric authority, it has often taken years and years of legal maneuvering and repeated court cases.

We have very little information about what goes on in most hospitals for the criminally insane. Occasionally there are legislative investigations, and serious and widespread abuse of patients and grossly inadequate care have been documented in New York, Massachusetts, Alabama, Florida, Pennsylvania, and other states. Psychiatrists in private practice have no interest in these patients. They do not see them as their problem. Often they do not see these as psychiatric cases, and they certainly do not see them as amenable to conventional psychiatric therapies. The American Psychiatric Association has not given much attention to the use of psychiatric power in such institutions; only one small underfunded and understaffed division of the National Institute of Mental Health, the Center for Studies of Crime and Delinquency, has been concerned with the plight of the criminally insane. But we do get a glimpse, through legal cases, of what can happen to a person subject to the control of the psychiatrist. We also see how authoritarian psychiatrists can be.

In 1952 a Michigan defendant, Embra Maddox, was charged with committing sexual offenses. He denied the charge. Before the trial he was diagnosed as a sexual psychopath and committed to a state hospital. In the hospital he continued to deny that he had committed the offenses. The staff decided he was not amenable to therapy and recommended transfer to a state prison, in spite of the fact that he had never been tried on the charge. At a hearing, four psychiatrists from the state hospital testified that for this kind of resistant patient who denies the reality of his actions, incarceration in a state prison would be the best kind of treatment. It might make Maddox admit his guilt. It could make him more amenable to therapy, and when this breakthrough occurred he could be returned to the state hospital for treatment.

The court accepted the recommendations of the four psychiatrists and Maddox was transferred to prison. He was given no special treatment and was dealt with like any other prisoner. The only difference between Maddox and other prisoners was that every six months he was given an interview and review by a state hospital psychiatrist. For six years these reports recommended that Maddox be continued to be held in the prison because he had not yet been able to admit his offenses.

Maddox sued on the ground that he was being improperly held, but the lower court ruled that Maddox was "getting treatment" and was "properly being confined in . . . prison." On appeal, the Supreme Court of Michigan found that he was being improperly held because he had been denied the due process safeguards of a criminal trial before going to prison. But the decision did not free him, because he was still classified as a criminal sexual psychopath, subject to involuntary hospitalization, if not to imprisonment. The Supreme Court of Michigan did point out that Maddox had been committed under legislation designed to be remedial and corrective, not punitive, but had ended up serving a potential life sentence in prison. It commented that "incarceration in a penitentiary designed and used for the confinement of convicted criminals is not a prescription available upon medical diagnosis and order to any administrative branch of the government."[12] The case is sometimes given as an example of the proclivity of psychiatrists to label as "treatment," detention situations that do not appear even slightly therapeutic.

During the 1950s the use of psychiatry in the criminal-justice process received much support from liberals who were convinced that the traditional correctional approach to prisoners was inhuman and unproductive. The same decade saw civil commitment of individuals reach an all-time high of five hundred and fifty thousand in 1955. This was the culmination of a steady growth in civilly committed inpatients —two hundred thousand in 1915, three hundred thousand in 1930, and over four hundred and fifty thousand in 1945. More and more patients were being crowded into increasingly inadequate hospitals. Psychiatrists were controlling the lives and destinies of more and more citizens, both traditional mental patients and such new categories as juvenile delinquents and the quasi-criminal psychopaths and defective delinquents.

Psychiatric power grew, but very few psychiatrists were concerned that they might have an excess of authority. Indeed, many were concerned that courts and correctional officials were not relying enough on psychiatric advice. Karl Menninger wrote in 1945: "The scientific method as shown in psychiatry must sooner or later totally displace existing legal methods." Menninger asked if lawyers must "still continue solemnly to apply medieval stupidities in the name of 'established precedent,' 'public policy,' and other mouthy archaisms?"[13] As psychiatrists were given more status, liberals such as Justice William O. Douglas, Abe Fortas, and Judge David Bazelon, who wrote for the Circuit Court of Appeals for the District of Columbia a series of opinions that increased the power of psychiatrists, asked for an even greater acceptance of psychiatric authority.

America's most famous psychiatrist-lawyer team, Dr. Manfred Guttmacher and law professor Henry Weihofen, hailed the accelerating pace of legal change that had led to such advances as legally less protected commitment procedures (so that many courts no longer even required the presence of the patient), the adoption of sexual-psychopath laws, and the use of psychiatric clinics in adult and juvenile courts. With increased cooperation between psychiatrists and lawyers, they wrote, "still more rapid progress could be achieved."[14] Guttmacher and Weihofen expressed pride in the growing reliance of the criminal courts on psychiatrists who served as officers of the court and felt that this reliance had already demonstrated its effectiveness in juvenile rehabilitation and in adult psychiatric probation. They were pleased that "in the more progressive states" psychiatrists were delegated to separate incorrigible prisoners from those for whom a different kind of detention was more appropriate. They quoted a leading penologist who felt that a psychiatrist should not only be on, but should preside over, every prison classification board. They felt psychiatrists were the appropriate decision makers concerning parole and recommended that impartial psychiatric experts should resolve their differences out of court to prevent the battle of court experts (although cross-examination and the ability to challenge witnesses had always been the main safeguard against excessive reliance on scientific authority). Because they found psychiatry so scientific, they did not see that criminals needed protection from it, although they did express some concern about the use of the new criminal-sexual-psychopath laws.[15]

Guttmacher and Weihofen were not concerned that psychiatrists were being given the power to commit patients to mental hospitals without legal procedural protections. "If through error or malice a sane person should be committed, the hospital authorities would release him as soon as the fact became apparent. State mental hospitals, like most public institutions, are overcrowded; they are not anxious to hold anyone who can safely be released."[16]

They gave particular approval to a new Maryland statute that would set up a unique kind of hospital-prison, unlike the traditional hospital for the criminally insane because it would be run by therapy-minded psychiatrists and would be treatment-oriented.[17] This law created a class of patients, to be known as "defective delinquents," whose entire psychiatric pathology might be no more than a diagnosed "predisposition to commit crime." The institution that was developed as a result of the new law is known as Patuxent. It was planned by humanistic reformers who wanted to attack the problem of crime through a modern psychiatric approach. Because the therapists were entitled to keep the patients in the institution until they demonstrated progress through therapy, and because so many inmates spent such excessively long periods working their way through the four tiers of the treatment program—or never worked their way through them to graduation and freedom—the law has become the target of a newer wave of reformers who see it as coercive and authoritarian. Recently the Maryland legislature, after years of agitation, repealed the one-day-to-life sentences to Patuxent, and patients there can no longer be held for longer than the maximum sentences for the crime of which they have been found guilty.

The movement to give psychiatrists more power was considered liberal in the 1950s. Conservatives deplored the increase of psychiatric authority, not because of its coercion and the powerlessness of the individual to combat it, not because it was anti–civil rights, but because it was believed that psychiatrists were too ready to excuse crime and too soft on criminals.

Psychiatrists outdid each other in making extravagant claims for the use of psychiatric authority over criminals, relying on the medical model to justify their interventions. One psychiatrist said he was satisfied that all juveniles who were in repeated trouble with the law were "mentally ill." Another said that "every criminal has a defective personality." Another that "the 'normal' offender is a myth."[18] Benjamin Karpman, in a classic statement of the rehabilitative position, proposed that we treat rather than penalize all criminal defendants, because the criminal is led into his behavior by irrational impulses over which he has no control, and thus there is no more reason to punish an individual for his crime than "to punish an individual for breathing through his mouth because of enlarged adenoids . . ."[19]

Judge David Bazelon rewrote the law of criminal responsibility for the District of Columbia in the *Durham* case so that persons with behavioral or personality disorders—who are far less overtly disturbed than the traditional irresponsible criminal—could also be excused from the consequences of criminal behavior.[20] His stated objective was to give more weight to psychiatric testimony and expand the group of defendants who would be covered by the insanity defense. If he had tried to rewrite any other aspect of the criminal code he would have been seen as overstepping his judicial authority, but because he made this change on the advice of psychiatric experts, and because the mysteries of psychiatry were impenetrable to the average journalist, legislator, or man in the street, he was allowed to put this change into operation. The American Psychiatric Association later gave him a Certificate of Commendation for his friendship to psychiatry.[21] Abe Fortas, the lawyer for the defense in the *Durham* case who would become a Supreme Court justice, hailed the decision as "a charter, a bill of rights, for psychiatry . . ."[22] Justice Douglas, when he gave the commencement address at the William Alanson White Institute of Psychiatry, Psychoanalysis, and Psychology, told the graduating class and other guests that "recent developments in the law should hearten psychiatrists that their pleas do not always fall on deaf ears."[23]

In the midst of all the congratulations psychiatry was receiving (and giving itself) for its enlarged role, some critics spoke up, saying that psychiatry was too soft on, or too inconsistent toward, criminals, that clever defendants could manipulate the insanity defense for their own ends, that the rich benefited more from psychiatric excuses than the poor. Many of the criticisms were discounted because they came from conservatives or the unenlightened. Psychiatry was seen as the hope for progress in criminal justice and corrections. More serious defects in the psychiatry-law-corrections approach were not even recognized. Little attention was paid to the fate of those subjected to psychiatric authority who were deprived of procedural safeguards because they were being treated instead of punished. The assumption was that psychiatrists as physicians would only use their power to help their patients.

Extreme Psychiatric Authority:
The Cases of Roy Schuster and George Davis

VIRGINIA WOOLF and Janet Gotkin saw themselves as mentally or emotionally ill. Though they were very unhappy with the way psychiatrists treated them, they had some control over their relationship with psychiatry. If they were not too needy and dependent, if they did not exhibit characteristics that could lead to commitment, they were free to walk away from the psychiatrist and declare themselves independent of his control.

When patients are diverted from the criminal-justice system to the mental health system, they frequently do not see themselves as ill and often do not have the symptoms that usually indicate mental illness. If they are unhappy with the way psychiatrists treat them, they have no opportunity to leave therapy. Their insistence that they do not need therapy may intensify the conviction of the psychiatrist that they lack insight and need further treatment. These are public patients in the control of public psychiatrists, and they feel the authority of psychiatry even more than private patients. Private-practice psychiatrists, who make up the majority of the profession, and official psychiatric groups, such as the American Psychiatric Association and the Group for the Advancement of Psychiatry, ignore the problem of the domination that public psychiatrists exercise over public patients.

Critics of psychiatry describe flagrant cases of patients who have suffered under the massive force of public psychiatric authority, but the public psychiatrists who are in charge of these patients are satisfied that they are fulfilling a useful social function, and private psychiatrists do not meddle.

*   *   *

In 1968 I received a letter from a young Canadian, whom I will call George Davis, who was in a provincial psychiatric hospital. He wrote that he had read my book on legal psychiatry. He asked if I would "take a private case involving a person in an institution after you were informed of the circumstances surrounding that person's confinement?" I wrote back that I practiced psychiatry, not law, that I was not familiar with Canadian commitment laws, but that I would be glad to give my opinion if he would send me more information. He wrote back that he had been in the provincial mental hospital for five years after pleading not guilty by reason of insanity to a charge of murdering a young girl by stabbing. He was being held under a lieutenant governor-in-council's warrant. (Although the situation involves Canadian law, this case is not substantially different from many American cases that result in a verdict of not guilty by reason of insanity.)

The patient was an adopted child; he was brought up by strict, but apparently interested, parents. From an early age he showed evidences of tantrums and emotional storms. When he was fourteen he was sent to a mental hospital after three incidents in which he allegedly enticed young girls to remove their clothes (according to official records, "without any certain sexual interference but maybe an intention of frightening them, besides primitive exploratory efforts"). He was examined by psychiatrists, who found no evidence of any specific mental disease. After he committed two more similar offenses he was sent to an institution for disturbed youth. He was kept there for almost two years. He was then returned to his home so he could continue his schooling, after he had satisfied the institution staff that he had achieved an ability to control his tantrums and "acting out."

He did not do well at school, and a job was found for him working in a department store. There he lured a ten-year-old girl into a stockroom, apparently attempted sexual intimacy, and repeatedly stabbed her when she made an outcry. He was persuaded by his father and his lawyer to plead not guilty by reason of insanity. On the evidence of one psychiatrist he was held to have committed the crime in a state of insanity, and he was put under a lieutenant governor's warrant, which authorized his detention in a mental hospital until the lieutenant governor would sign an order for his release. This is a potential lifetime hospitalization.

His case had been diverted from the criminal-justice system into the mental health system because of the testimony of one psychiatrist that he was a psychopath. "Psychopath" (sometimes called "sociopath") is an imprecise psychiatric diagnostic category. The condition is described as characterized by lack of conscience, lack of compassion, lack

of remorse, egocentricity, and an inability to enter into feeling interpersonal relationships. The controversy concerning this diagnosis is
enormous. It is a frequently used label in correctional institutions, and
in many prisons a large percentage of the inmates are considered
psychopaths, although some experienced psychiatrists deny that there
is any such condition or state, or say that if there is, it is so rare as to
be almost nonexistent. It is very easy for the same individual to be seen
by some psychiatrists and psychologists as psychopathic and by others
as not.

As the years went by the patient learned that the opinion of the
psychiatrists was that his psychopathy was incurable, and that he could
never be released if society was to be protected. His good behavior in
the institution did not affect this diagnosis and prognosis. The nature
of his crime, rather than his current mental status, determined the
results of the psychiatric and psychological evaluations. He learned
that some psychiatrists feel that no psychopath is amenable to change
and that none of the psychiatrists working for the province's mental
health service would be willing to take the responsibility for saying he
had improved. He also discovered that if he had not elected to plead
the insanity defense, he would have spent twelve or thirteen years in
a prison and then, assuming he received credit on his sentence for
good behavior, been freed. He began to see that the advice he had
received to plead insanity had not been good. He had exchanged the
status of a criminal defendant for that of a mental patient, but he
had accepted the possibility of a lifetime, instead of a time-limited,
detention.

One of his problems in the hospital was that he was considered more
of a security risk than the other patients (because of his offense, not
his current mental state) and was not allowed to receive the gradually
increasing range of privileges that were part of the therapeutic program for civilly committed patients. When he had been in a hospital
for almost three years he complained to the psychiatrist-superin-
tendent about the prohibition that kept him, alone of all the patients,
from attending hospital dances, and the long hours he was required
to spend on a locked ward.

The superintendent's reply called attention to the bargain he had
made. It addressed him familiarly by his first name.

I don't know whether or not you realize the gravity of your position. You
were very pleased at one time in Court, when it was pronounced that you
were "not guilty" by reason of insanity. Had you been found "guilty" at that
time you would have had to serve approximately 12 to 13 years at the

penitentiary, that is if your behaviour were satisfactory, after which you would have been quite free and during which time you would have been able to have more freedom of movement within that institution—the chance to work and a chance to have recreation. These things would be possible because the penitentiary is an institution of maximum security.

The nature of the crime of which you were found "not guilty" but which act you did admit, was such that you were condemned to this institution for the rest of your natural life or at the will and pleasure of the Lieutenant Governor. With such a verdict and such a ghastly act, I doubt if the pleasure of any Lieutenant Governor would be that you live in the outside world.

Since this is a place which is not of maximum security, I have to be more strict and this I have been told to do by the Attorney General's Department. In other words, at one and the same time you are both a patient and a prisoner. The deed you have committed certainly demands more security in your case than in others. I have gone my limit by allowing you to walk outside unshackled along with an attendant, also in letting you go to the shows (movies) under the same regulation. I cannot and will not allow you to attend dances where girls and women are present. Two reasons should be quite obvious to you, one is security. I trust you can understand my position.

The patient began to communicate with anyone who he thought could help him prove that he was not insane or that he had improved, or that he should not be locked up for a lifetime because he had followed bad legal advice. In our correspondence I made it clear that I would not be able to help him with his legal problems and was not prepared to state that he was improved or no longer dangerous. One reason was my lack of belief in the credibility of most such psychiatric evaluations, including my own. Another was my unwillingness to take this much responsibility, which belonged to the court or the correctional system, on my own shoulders. He had been declared a mental patient, and only a psychiatrist could decide if he was well enough to be released, but the evidence of mental disease was so thin and his presence in the hospital so obviously a political expedient that it would be difficult for a psychiatrist to say precisely what disease it was that he had recovered from. We continued to correspond. He sent me tapes describing some of the stress and trauma that he went through in adolescence, and I gained a complete picture of the frustration and hopelessness caused by his peculiar twilight status as a prisoner-patient. During most of the fifteen years following his commitment he was considered too much a prisoner to merit a therapeutic program involving increasing responsibility and privileges; yet he was not a prisoner and did not have the prisoner's advantage of a time-limited sentence.

Over the years he was examined by a host of psychologists and psychiatrists to see whether he continued to be a "psychopath." Most of the examiners found him a psychopath who was potentially extremely dangerous to the community. It was said in these reports that he "must be institutionalized for the rest of his natural life." One evaluator noted that he was "unfortunately quite intelligent," and care would have to be taken so that he did not in the future persuade the authorities that he should be released as cured. After he had been in institutions for eleven years, one psychologist reported that on the basis of more than fifteen hours of testing (Rorschach, an intelligence test, a Thematic Apperception Test, a Minnesota Multiphasic Personality Inventory Test, and several more), Davis was "an immature person with lack of anxiety, unable to profit or learn from experience, with weak control over emotionality and impulses and inability to experiment or engage in a deep emotional relationship." This was typical of the conclusions of many psychological evaluations. On the other hand, at roughly the same period another psychologist found that he showed definite signs of improvement concerning anxiety level and in self-control over sexual impulses, and that "his ways of coping with his present environment are more appropriate now as compared to when he was first hospitalized which suggests that when needed he is capable of acquiring still more progress if proper training is made available."

In 1970, in accordance with a new Canadian law, a Review Board had been appointed to review the case at six-month intervals. Sometimes, at the insistence of the patient, the board had returned to the hospital for a second review. Its sole functions were to determine if the patient had "recovered" and if so, to decide whether it was in his interest and in the interest of the public for him to be discharged. At the first review the board made the finding that he had not yet recovered from the condition "under which he laboured at the time the crime was committed" and in subsequent reviews it stated it could find no reason to alter the opinion. The patient continued to maintain that he had changed, that he did indeed have feelings, in spite of the opinion of the psychologists and psychiatrists that he lacked them, and that he did indeed have insight into his behavior, contrary to the opinion of the psychologists and psychiatrists. It was his word against theirs.

He had the burden of proving that expert psychiatric opinion was wrong. In 1973, a doctor at the provincial hospital, who was not his ward doctor and not intimately concerned with him, reported that he had interviewed him for a half an hour in order to provide a progress note for the Review Board.

On Interview patient is quiet, cooperative and relates easily to the interviewer, but only on an intellectual level. His speech is spontaneous, coherent. He is well oriented in all spheres and presents no thought disorder.
    ... Patient speaks abundantly about the fact that contrary to the opinion of other people, he thinks that he has changed a lot since the beginning of his commitment. He thinks he is more mature and has a better control of his impulses. It is noteworthy that in verbalization of this patient there is a lack of emotional tone and he seems to function on a purely intellectual level.

This doctor diagnosed him in his evaluation as an "Anti-Social Personality." The doctor appeared before the Review Board. He testified that "it is well known" that for this particular kind of case and crime "this is the worst prognosis," that "it is well known that there is no known treatment for anti-social personality," that it was doubtful that an anti-social personality would change in the span of time that the patient had been in the hospital. (He had been in the hospital for ten years.)

The board asked the doctor how he could testify on such matters as the patient's incapacity to love when the ward situation made it impossible for him to establish normal human relationships. The doctor explained how he assessed such patients. "If he is very bright and very intelligent, he is going to give you an answer to make you feel that he does not have these characteristics and in this kind of interview, you are not going to get anything from him. During these interviews, you just let this patient talk and from his talking I will get the feeling that the patient has these characteristics by his talk. You just let him talk . . ."

The doctor concluded his testimony by repeating that there was no known treatment for anti-social personality. He said that in his opinion the patient should be kept at the hospital for life. Psychotherapy might be helpful as a treatment method but "in this particular setting of this hospital, I don't think it's possible to give him this kind of treatment." He added: "I would be very hesitant of leaving Mr. Davis going back to society. Perhaps it's because he is trying so hard to do the right thing here, it gives me the impression that he could still be considered dangerous. I get the feeling that all the time he is trying to impress as to how good he is, and this to me is not normal."

In the first years of his hospitalization when he had been allowed no privileges, Davis had made several attempts to escape. On one occasion he succeeded in escaping but turned himself in. Now and for many years his behavior had been excellent and there were no further black marks on his record. This was evidence that was used against him. A psychiatric nurse told the board: "His behavior has been extremely good since he came to [our] ward . . . Sometimes he could be classed as a model patient—sometimes giving the impression that he is much too model a patient, always trying to impress that he is, indeed, abiding by the rules and regulations." The nurse testified that he had such characteristics of a sociopath as "constant charm" and "superficial charm" (but he also testified that since he had known the patient he had not known him to show evidence of such other characteristics of a sociopath as untruthfulness, insincerity, or unreliability).

In the course of the review, the board interviewed the patient. The questions are worthy of a Grand Inquisitor: "Is it true that you do not profit from experience? What about the observation regarding your sense of responsibility? What about moral sense? How would you comment on the criticism that you are anti-social? Emotionally immature? That you exhibit the sociopathic quality of bold, direct behavior? That you lack insight?"

Davis answered these questions as best he could. "I try not to react so hot-headedly now . . . I have more respect for other people's feelings . . . I think here that I have found more meaningful relationships with the other patients . . . I don't think my emotions are immature as they were when I was younger . . ." How does one demonstrate moral sense and ability to take criticism? How does one prove that one has acquired insight? When one has a sometimes "model" record, has taken responsible positions in patient self-government, and done useful work around the hospital, what in addition can be adduced to show growth and change?

The psychiatrist's testimony against Davis counted for more than his testimony in his own behalf, and he was again refused a transfer to a hospital with a more active treatment program or a program of increasing responsibilities. The patient was caught in a never-never land between the mental health and the criminal-justice systems. No amount of normal functioning could persuade most of his evaluators that he was safe to be released. No amount of time spent in the institution would count as the repayment of a debt owed to society.

At last, in 1974, a psychiatrist was willing to stand up for him. A doctor who had become his ward psychiatrist wrote in his report to the board that he was not able to find any decisive symptoms to show that the patient was still a psychopath, that he had found genuine remorse and emotions in the patient, although previous psychiatric evaluators had always found him lacking in "affection, love and emotions," and that he should be given an opportunity to move from the maximum security ward to a less restrictive ward where "he would be able to prove that he can adjust himself to new surroundings." This psychiatrist continued in his report,

> I have tried in all respects to trace symptoms of psychopathia in this patient, but all in vain and I can only state that this patient has totally changed his attitude and behavior to the best during the years since he was taken to the hospital.
>
> In my opinion he is a fully normal and mature man and should according to this be discharged.

He added, "I would like to obtain for the patient . . . an opportunity for him to take the first step giving him possibilities to prove that he is no longer dangerous for the public." The Review Board was not influenced by the report.

The patient carried on an unending battle to challenge the legal basis for his indefinite hospitalization. He was in constant communication with every major forensic psychiatrist in Canada and the United States. Many of them expressed their best wishes and encouragement, but none could suggest any solution to the problem except to keep on fighting for a chance for eventual freedom.

Law professors and lawyers to whom he wrote were more practically helpful, and he received competent legal representation. He had now been diagnosed by one psychiatrist as being without psychiatric disease. Others had called him a psychopath or a sociopath, something very different from the psychotic defendants who at an earlier time had been excused from criminal responsibility. He raised the question of whether he had ever been "insane" and asked for a determination by the supreme court of the province on whether it would be correct to keep him under a lieutenant governor's warrant if he were not insane. He wanted a clearer legal definition of "recovery," the legal criterion for release. He asked for a court decision that medical testimony in his case showed he merited release and that the Review Board had disregarded testimony in his favor and been biased against him. None of these legal attacks on his detention were successful.

By 1975 the administration of the hospital and the doctors directly responsible for Davis (although not other doctors who did not know him so well) had come around to the view that Davis was continuing to be held, not because he demonstrated mental illness, but for political reasons, because of the outcry that might be raised if he were to be released. From then on, the hospital and his doctors consistently recommended to the Review Board that he should be discharged because he was not mentally ill. The board responded by having Davis evaluated by government doctors, who interviewed him and reported back to the board that he still displayed psychopathic characteristics. The hospital administration decided it would be almost impossible for him to secure a hospital setting with more opportunity to progress toward freedom and almost impossible for him to be freed from his present hospital, but if he were transferred to a hospital in another province, the political climate might allow him to work toward freedom. A hospital director who interviewed him recommended transfer to his hospital, but before this could take place this doctor had a heart attack, and the transfer was postponed. Six months later he was again getting ready for transfer when he received word that the doctor had died and the new hospital was no longer willing to receive him. In the spring of 1977, another year later, a hospital had been found that would accept him and the Review Board agreed to the change.

In the new hospital, removed from the area where he had committed his crime (for in spite of the not-guilty verdict, the act can hardly be described except as a crime), he was begun on a program of gradually increasing freedom and responsibilities. He was allowed to take a driving education course. He was allowed to take a job outside the hospital and return to the hospital after work hours. He was moved to a boarding home. He wrote me: "As you can see, I am doing really good and continue to move ahead." Finally he was given permission to live in a place of his own. But many people diverted from the criminal-justice system to the mental health system have been allowed to spend their lifetime in hospitals even when there were no clear-cut indications of mental disease, with the role of the doctor not to treat, but to justify, preventive detention. If Davis had not been brighter than the average such patient, and if he had not pursued his freedom boldly and directly, he would probably still be in his original provincial hospital carrying the diagnosis of an incorrigible permanent psychopath.

His case is a classic example of the fate of the defendant who is found not guilty by reason of insanity. At one time this was a defense relied on only in capital punishment cases. A lifetime in a mental hospital did not seem like a bad trade for certain execution by hanging or electrocution. More recently the plea has become more of a calculated risk: A long prison sentence may be avoided, but the tradeoff is that of giving the psychiatrist absolute control over the period of detention, which can be for longer than the criminal sentence. Very recently, psychiatrists have allowed some patients who have been judged not guilty by reason of insanity to leave hospitals after short stays. Sometimes the psychiatrist seems to be relying on case law, which justifies confinement in a mental hospital only if continued dangerousness is obvious. Sometimes the early release of the patient seems motivated more by a lack of interest on the part of the psychiatrist in the treatment of an individual who does not have a conventional mental illness. Sometimes it seems to be the result of administrative sloppiness. Many "irresponsible" defendants face a lifetime of detention. Others, depending on a host of factors, not the least important of which is the political climate, may get an early release. Whether the length of detention is excessively long or excessively short, it seems to have no correlation with disease, although the fiction continues that these are mental patients hospitalized for treatment. No one would deny that the state has the right to detain a murderer. Does the state have the right to play a cat-and-mouse game down through the years, offering "treatment" and speaking of "cures," but denying freedom?

Whether the patient is kept for a long period, or life, or is let go early, there are common features in many of these cases. The diagnosis is not precise, and many evaluators would not find any psychiatric illness present. The evaluators predict future dangerousness without proof that they have good criteria for making such predictions. The psychiatrist exercises great authority in an area where he has never clearly demonstrated his competence. Political factors and emotions in the community are important in the decision to hold or release. And because the defendant has been classified as a patient rather than as a criminal, he has lost most of the procedural rights that protect people caught up in the criminal justice and correctional systems.

No national agency keeps good figures on defendants found not guilty by reason of insanity. We do not know how many are serving time in mental hospitals, how long they stay, or how many remain there after any evidence of psychopathology has disappeared. Occasionally a law case surfaces or a vocal patient manages to make his situation known.

One solution proposed for the problem is the elimination of the insanity defense. Although dissatisfaction with the insanity defense and with the disposition of patients who are not guilty by reason of insanity is widespread, the problem cannot be eliminated merely by not allowing the plea. One of the oldest principles of our criminal law is that crime is dependent on intent. If we were to punish the insane and those who are mental defectives for unintended acts, we would have returned to primitive law. As long as there are people who commit crimes whom we want to treat instead of punish, psychiatry will have a use in the field of criminal justice. This is a legitimate field for psychiatry, but psychiatry has often overstepped its bounds and imposed its authority carelessly and wrongfully.

Psychiatrists and other behavioral scientists will have to define the limits of their expertise. They should concede that many conditions now perceived as mental illness are considered so for social reasons, not as a result of accurate medical diagnosis, and will have to see that being classified a patient does not cause harm to the defendant.

* * *

The case of Roy Schuster has some of the same stark qualities as Davis' case, but it is an even more clear-cut example of the effect of unbridled psychiatric power. Davis spent only a few more years in hospitals than he would have spent in prison if he had not been classified mentally ill, but Schuster's classification as a mental patient cost him twenty-eight extra years of detention.

Roy Schuster was a tap dancer and a vaudeville performer who was persuaded by his wife to give up the stage and become a dance instructor, and eventually head instructor, at Ned Wayburn's Dancing School in New York. He later accused her of unfaithfulness, but while they were separated she secured a court order through her lawyer requiring him to pay for her support. When he did not pay (he claimed he could not; this was early in the Depression), she threatened to have him held in alimony jail for contempt of court. He carried a pistol to a meeting at her lawyer's office, threatened suicide, and then fired several shots, killing her and injuring the lawyer.[1]

Schuster claimed he fired the shots in a state of panic and that he had not been aware of what he was doing. The state of New York presented psychiatric testimony to rebut the claim that he was suffering from any form of delusion or mental disease. He was convicted of second degree murder and sentenced to Sing Sing Prison for the term of twenty-five years to life. The year was 1931, and Schuster was twenty-seven years old.

He was considered a good prisoner at Sing Sing and at Clinton State Prison, where he was transferred in 1935. He taught a "cell-study" course that enabled prisoners to earn high-school equivalency degrees, and has a letter from the New York State Board of Corrections commending him for his work.

In 1941, when he had served ten years of his sentence and was seven years away from eligibility for parole, he began to charge that the prison was corrupt, both because inmates received high-school equivalency degrees on the basis of favoritism and bribery and because money that had been appropriated for prison purposes was being misspent. He decided to make these accusations public, tried through his family to hire a lawyer, and was preparing to swear to a deposition concerning these allegations when he was visited by the prison physician, Dr. Leaman Caswell. This doctor made out a certificate providing for his prompt transfer, without any hearing or any other kind of procedural safeguard, to Dannemora State Hospital, the New York facility for prisoners who had become psychotic during the course of their sentences. Dannemora was ostensibly a mental hospital, but like many forensic psychiatric units in other states, it was run not by the Department of Mental Hygiene but by the Department of Corrections. New York law at that time allowed a prisoner to be transferred upon the certification of one prison doctor that in his opinion the prisoner was "insane." Twenty-two years later, when Schuster was able for the first time to bring up in court the question of the legality and appropriateness of his transfer, it was not possible to determine Dr. Caswell's training, qualifications, or psychiatric experience.

The reasons for the transfer, as detailed by Dr. Caswell, were that Schuster "was circumstantial in his conversation, very talkative, complained bitterly. He was paranoid and suspicious. . . . This man was reported for writing letters regarding cowardly attacks made against him by the personnel and requested that something be done about it. In his letters he has shown the paranoid idea that members of the personnel are against him." According to law, Caswell's certificate should have given indications that the patient was violent, dangerous, excited, homicidal, or suicidal. Caswell included no information about the presence or absence of any of these emotional states or symptoms.

Schuster has since testified, without being contradicted, that several years later, evidence of the improper diversion of funds that had deprived the inmates of basic supplies, like soap and toilet paper, led to the firing of the warden, chief clerk, and controller of the prison.

Schuster was admitted to the entry ward at Dannemora. All his books and papers were taken from him. The incoming ward consisted of only a dayroom and a dormitory for the forty patients. There was no toilet in the dormitory. The toilet was on the far side of the dayroom and at night the door between the dormitory and the dayroom was locked. He has described the situation to me: "Now the door is locked, and you'd have to pound on the door for the nightman if you wanted to go to the toilet. The nightman would open the door and let you out, but he resented getting up from his newspaper or from his sleep and he's often beat the inmates up when they came back in. He'd bang them a couple and kick them."

He remembers one inmate who defecated on newspaper and hid

66

this under his bed because he was afraid of the nightman. He adds, "And they beat him up for that."[2]

He spent six months on the incoming ward and was then transferred to another ward. Every three or six months a psychiatrist would see him for "perhaps between two and five minutes." He continued to maintain that he had been improperly transferred, and that the purpose of his transfer had been political. The psychiatrists continued to maintain that he could not show his recovery from paranoia or that he had acquired "insight" from his hospital stay until he could admit that his transfer had been appropriate and his accusations had been based on delusional ideas. They recommended his retention.

For the first three years he was not allowed to send out letters requesting a lawyer. Finally his sister secured a lawyer for him, but the lawyer advised him that there was nothing he could do. "Most lawyers didn't want to mess in it," he says. "I did so much of my work *pro se* because after a while I wouldn't trust a lawyer." He asked for law books to help prepare his own appeals, but was refused them.

He reports no program of therapy. He describes nothing during his years at Dannemora that could be considered therapeutic. A Dannemora psychiatrist later testified that the reason for the lack of treatment was that Schuster's paranoia was so "deeply rooted" that it would not respond to treatment.

During much of the time he had nothing to do all day except to sit in the dayroom in a straight-backed wooden chair and "twiddle his thumbs." For a long period of time he was not allowed to have pencil and paper, and he had to secrete scraps for writing. He was not allowed access to his own books, which were stored for him. The library, he says, consisted only of books written for boys, and the books were so musty and moldy that he recoiled from their smell when he tried to read them.[3]

In 1948 Schuster was eligible for parole, but as he had continued to claim that he had been the object of a political persecution, he continued to be diagnosed as paranoid. According to the policy of the parole board, parole could only be granted to prisoners in a hospital for the criminally insane if they demonstrated their recovery from mental illness and could be returned to the regular prison system for release. He later testified in 1963, about his hearing before the parole board:

SCHUSTER: I entered the room, sat down on a chair before a desk at which the chairman of the Parole Board was presiding, and he asked me how I was getting along. I said, "All right." He said, "We will see you again when you are returned to prison." That is all. I said, "Please, may I have the opportunity to show cause why you should parole me at this time." His response was, "Will you wait outside." So I waited outside and was never called back in the room, and I have never seen him since.

FAITH SEIDENBERG [Schuster's attorney]: Now you say you have never seen them since. Do you mean by that that you never had another parole hearing?

SCHUSTER: No, I never had one. That is what I mean.

SEIDENBERG: Before nobody?

SCHUSTER: Before nobody.

SEIDENBERG: And this hearing where you were asked to wait outside, were you at any time permitted to go back to finish that hearing?

SCHUSTER: No, I was not called back. That was the finish of it.

SEIDENBERG: To your knowledge are other patients-prisoners paroled from Dannemora Hospital?

SCHUSTER: It is a regular policy [not to grant parole until after a transfer back to prison]. The inmates are all talking when they come back, they tell what happened. They say the same thing—that the Board said it would see them again when they are returned to prison. And that is all it amounts to.[4]

In 1950 Schuster brought his own legal action to secure his release. A series of hearings was held, after several postponements, before Judge F. Claude O'Connell in Plattsburgh. Schuster says that the judge ruled against him but advised him to continue to appeal the case on a constitutional question, that of whether there had been safeguards to protect him during the process of transfer to Dannemora, and the judge ordered his secretary to secure for Schuster a copy of the transcript of the hearings and all other papers that would be necessary for an appeal. Schuster claims he never received these.

In 1960 Schuster again sought a writ of habeas corpus on the grounds he was being improperly held. The court refused him a hearing. In 1962 he again petitioned for a writ. On the day before the hearing on the writ, Schuster was examined by Dr. Ludwig Fink, director of the Diagnostic Clinic and Center of Clinton Prison, who said he wanted to talk to him with regard to the hearing. Schuster took the position that he would be happy to answer all questions on the record, where they would be available for public inspection and possible appeal. The psychiatrist apparently reported to Judge Robert Main that Schuster had not been cooperative, and Judge Main dismissed Schuster's petition without a hearing. Judge Main probably assumed that since his original sentence had been for twenty-five years to life, he had no right to liberty and that the question of whether he should be detained in a prison or a hospital for the criminally insane was only an administrative matter in which the court should not interfere. The court did not recognize that although in prison he would be eligible for parole, as long as he was detained in Dannemora he could not be paroled.

Later in 1962 Schuster again petitioned for a writ of habeas corpus, his fourth attempt. This petition was granted, and the hearing was held in March of the following year. Schuster wanted his own psychiatric expert. But because he was indigent, he was forced to agree that the results of the examination of the court-appointed psychiatrist, Dr. William Carson, would be made available for the trial whether it was for or against him. An affluent plaintiff who could hire his own psychiatrist could have prevented the introduction of unfavorable testimony. Because Carson was the only psychiatrist and because he was acting as an impartial witness, his testimony carried great weight. Carson testified that Schuster was "an individual whose conduct in general is correct, who uses impeccable logic," and "who shows no sign of obvious mental illness such as deterioration, untidiness, hallucinatory experiences, bizarre ideas or bizarre behavior." In spite of this, Carson felt that Schuster had a paranoid condition and so was mentally ill. He told the court, "This is the type of illness in which an entire delusional but logical belief is based on a single false premise, and if one allows the truth of the false premise the patient's behavior no longer appears abnormal." Since Schuster continued to maintain that his detention was political, he could not be seen as recovered, and therefore his hospitalization was appropriate. Carson did concede that some of Schuster's allegations about graft and cheating at Clinton Prison in 1941 might have had some factual basis, but he labeled as proof of mental illness Schuster's belief that state authorities would commit a man to a mental hospital and hold him there for wanting to expose such practices.

Dr. Carson said such a paranoid illness was unfortunate because there was little chance of improvement and because such patients tend to resort to litigation (certainly true of Schuster) and violent action (never true of Schuster).

Carson testified, "Mr. Schuster, like many of these patients, is an amiable, intelligent, friendly man. I think anyone would be sorry for him. I certainly feel sympathetic to him and sorry for his plight, but in my professional opinion, he is mentally ill within the meaning of the statute, he is in need of care and treatment in a mental institution. I don't think he should be allowed to leave the hospital at the present time."[5]

On cross-examination Schuster's attorney tried to elicit a purpose for the hospitalization. Schuster was not and never had been on medication. Was he receiving any "mental therapy" for his illness? Carson replied, "As far as mental therapy is concerned, of course, he is in a mental hospital where he is under the care of psychiatrists and trained attendants and is seen, at least the record would indicate, seen at intervals, which is a form of therapy."[6]

At the end of the hearing Schuster asked Judge Harold Soden to hear his rebuttal to Carson's testimony, not to accept it as true merely because it was the testimony of an expert. "He may be honestly mistaken . . . and I would like to show what I believe to be reasonable proof that Dr. Carson is mistaken . . ."

The judge replied with the kind of cruelty that judges often show to the indigent and troublesome, who are easy targets for irony and a show of superiority.

> JUDGE SODEN: May I ask you this, Mr. Schuster, do you claim that you are a qualified psychiatrist, licensed to practice in the State of New York, a qualified doctor?
>
> SCHUSTER: No, I do not claim that I am a qualified psychiatrist, but I do claim—
>
> JUDGE SODEN: Wait a minute, now, you have asked this court to appoint a qualified doctor, a psychiatrist, to testify in your behalf . . . Now, as your witness, you can't impeach him.
>
> SCHUSTER: I don't understand, in the first place, that he was my witness, I understood that it was a formality of the court, that there must be a psychiatrist to examine, and that he was impartially a witness of both sides, but that his testimony was not to be taken—[7]

Judge Soden cut Schuster off and he was never allowed to give his answer to Carson. The question was raised that Schuster had never had legal help in 1941 when he was transferred from the prison to the hospital. This was not considered important. Assistant Attorney General Charles Lewis told Judge Soden, "This man apparently has waited now some twenty years to bring this point up, he could have done it by way of appeal, at the time, and we feel that this was the method available to him had he exercised it."[8]

Judge Soden dismissed the petition for the writ, ruling that Schuster was still insane and in need of treatment at Dannemora. Schuster appealed. It took one year for the appeal to be denied by the appellate division. He appealed this denial, and again it took a year before Judge Soden's decision against him was once more affirmed without an opinion.

Because he had pursued his appeals as far as he could through the state court system and exhausted his legal remedies there, and because he had raised a constitutional issue, he could now proceed through the federal courts. So in 1965 Schuster was able to initiate a new petition for a writ of habeas corpus to the federal district court. In 1966, while this petition was pending, the Supreme Court issued a ruling on the legality of the detention of another prisoner who had been transferred to Dannemora, Johnnie Baxstrom.[9]

Johnnie Baxstrom had come to Dannemora under much the same circumstances and procedures that Schuster had. He had been convicted in 1959 of second-degree assault and been sentenced to two and one-half to three years in a New York prison. When his term had almost expired, he was transferred to Dannemora on a certification of insanity by a prison psychiatrist. After his sentence expired, the superintendent of Dannemora secured a certificate, based on examinations by two physicians, that he needed continued hospital care. Instead of being sent to another mental hospital run by the Department of Mental Hygiene, Baxstrom was retained at Dannemora, the mental hospital run by the Department of Corrections. This was in accordance with the policy of the Department of Corrections that end-of-sentence men (prisoners who had been classified as insane, transferred to Dannemora, and while at Dannemora had served out the full term of their sentences) could be retained at Dannemora as presumably dangerous, although others could only be committed to Dannemora after a court determination that their presence in a "civil hospital" was a danger to the safety of other patients or employees or the community.

The *Baxstrom* case is one of the handful of cases in which the Supreme Court has been willing to consider the rights of mental patients (in contrast to its thousands of cases having to do with the rights of insurance companies, labor unions, banks, and utilities and other corporations). The Supreme Court held that before a determination that justified a holding at Dannemora, Baxstrom had the right to the same procedural safeguards as those patients who had not had a criminal detention.

The *Baxstrom* case is famous in legal psychiatry. Henry Steadman, a sociologist, has done a series of follow-up studies on the 967 patients who were released from Dannemora because, like Baxstrom, they were end-of-sentence men. He has shown that although the Dannemora staff psychiatrists had seen them all as dangerous, they were rarely dangerous.[10] Roy Schuster was not an end-of-sentence man (his term was potentially for life), so he was not one of the 967 Dannemora men released because of Baxstrom. But the following year, 1967, the United States District Court for the Northern District of New York ruled favorably on his petition of two years earlier and remanded the case for a hearing to consider evidence on whether the 1941 transfer from Clinton State to Dannemora had been proper.

District court Judge Edmund Port dismissed Schuster's petition after hearing the evidence. There was a question about whether he would be allowed to appeal this ruling, since he had not requested a certificate of probable cause before filing his appeal, but it was finally decided that because he had made an oral request the appeal could be heard.

In 1969 Judge Irving Kaufman for the United States Circuit Court of Appeals for the Second Circuit handed down an important decision in favor of Schuster.[11] It establishes a constitutional principle concerning due process in the transfer of a patient from a prison to a mental hospital. "... Before a prisoner may be transferred to a state institution for insane criminals, he must be afforded substantially the same procedural safeguards as are provided in civil commitment proceedings ..." Schuster's 1941 transfer from Clinton State Prison to Dannemora had been improper.

Judge Kaufman pointed out that the deficiencies and inequities of Dannemora and Matteawan had been fully documented in a thorough study by a committee of the Association of the Bar of the City of New York. A transferred prisoner may not be mentally ill at all, but he may be confined with men "who are not only mad but dangerously so," and "exposed to physical, emotional and general mental agony."

Kaufman said that there "always lurks the grisly possibility" that a prisoner sent to Dannemora will be forgotten. At Matteawan there were 4 patients who had been there for more than fifty years, 29 for more than forty, and 119 for more than thirty. The Bar Association study revealed that one eighty-three-year-old inmate had been at Matteawan since he was nineteen. Another inmate, who had been accused of stealing a horse and buggy in 1905 and pleaded not guilty, had been found to be suffering from "acute delusional insanity" and was retained for fifty-nine years. He was released at the age of eighty-nine when he was found to be no longer "a menace to society or to other patients." Kaufman also cited the case of *Dennison* v. *State,* which concerned a sixteen-year-old who had stolen candy valued at $5. He spent twenty-four years at Dannemora and was awarded $115,000 when he sued the state for improper confinement.[12] (Dennison was later deprived of his award. The ruling in his favor was reversed on the ground that the state was immune to such a suit.)[13] Schuster, said Kaufman, "is simply a forgotten man in a mental institution which has nothing to offer him."

Kaufman also noted that studies on the 967 *Baxstrom* case patients showed that 176 had received their liberty, 454 were able to get the better care available at civil hospitals, and only 7 had been returned to a hospital for the criminally insane after a judicial determination that they continued to be dangerous. Kaufman reversed the lower court ruling by Judge Port against Schuster and remanded the case to the district court for a sanity hearing to be held within sixty days to determine if Schuster was sane enough to be transferred back to prison, the necessary step in the process toward parole.

It appeared that Schuster, now sixty-five years old, was about to secure his liberty. But Schuster was kept in Dannemora while still more legal battles were fought. The state of New York decided to appeal. It petitioned the United States Supreme Court for a review of the decision. The Supreme Court allowed Kaufman's ruling to stand, deciding not to grant the writ of certiorari that would lead to review.[14] Then the state of New York raised a technical legal point as to whether Schuster had brought his case in the proper court.

While this issue was winding its way through a series of courts, another legal issue emerged. Schuster had a lifetime savings of $75, most of it representing the remnants of $420 he had received from his mother's estate. He wanted to have $40 of this used to buy legal books that he thought would help him in working for his release. The hospital superintendent wrote Judge Port that Dannemora had an "extensive legal library" and the money would not be released. Judge Port again found against Schuster. This too was appealed to Judge Kaufman's court, where the decision in favor of Schuster noted that the "extensive legal library" at Dannemora consisted of six volumes, only four of which could be removed from the supervisor's office. Although the issue of Schuster's continued hospitalization was not properly before the circuit court of appeals, the court took advantage of the occasion to express wonder that in view of the special circumstances surrounding Schuster's long detention, the state had not waived the issue of venue, of the appropriateness of the legal forum.[15]

The state did not waive the venue issue, in spite of Kaufman's suggestion. It took three years for this issue to be resolved. In 1972 the sanity hearing that Schuster desired was finally scheduled. A week before the hearing Schuster was suddenly told that Dannemora no longer considered him insane, that it was ready to return him to the prison system.

Schuster later testified,

> They called me up and said, "We are thinking about sending you back to prison, what prison would you like to go to?" I told him, "I have a hearing coming up, I would not want to be transferred until I have had the hearing with a jury trial," which I was entitled to there, and he said, "in that case I'll have to take out a retention action against you." I said, "Go ahead, I have

no objection." He said, "You have no objection?" I said, "No, none whatsoever." Then he thought a while and said, "No, I am determined to transfer you."

Schuster did not see this as a helpful move. He wanted his day in court to prove he had not been insane, and he wanted the federal court to continue to have jurisdiction over his case. By this move, all his legal issues had been mooted and he was once again entirely in the power of the parole board. Schuster filed a motion to enforce the order for the sanity hearing, but the court ruled that since he was no longer at Dannemora—after the determination of sanity he had been sent to Green Haven Correctional Facility—and since he had been diagnosed as well, there was no reason for a sanity hearing.

He had a new parole board hearing. At the beginning of the hearing he handed the board his written statement that the board was "not morally fit to supervise anyone, certainly not me." Schuster told the board he was twenty-five years past his parole eligibility time and he thought he deserved unconditional release rather than parole with continued supervision. The board felt that he could be released only with parole conditions.

> BOARD: We are in a position to talk to you about possible parole, but by your own statement you are not interested.
> SCHUSTER: I would not accept parole. Absolutely not. I am 25 years over my parole time. I would regard even an offer of parole as a gratuitous insult . . .
> BOARD: By reason of your own statement, and apparently your own attitude, you do not want parole. Is that correct?
> SCHUSTER: That's correct . . .
> BOARD: Now, are you steadfast—as you have heard me say to you what we can and can't do, are you steadfast that this is the way you want it? That you do not want to be considered for parole?
> SCHUSTER: That's right. Now if you'll excuse me, I'll go.
> BOARD: All right. We'll make this a matter of the record.[16]

Schuster's parole was denied. In a subsequent trial Judge Joseph Hawkins would describe the questioning of the board as "Socratic" and say that its purpose was to induce Schuster "to re-enter the maze from which he would be unable to extricate himself."[17]

Some psychiatrists may want to argue that Schuster's insistence on this "point of honor" is evidence of mental illness, in the same way Russian psychiatrists have asserted that the refusal of dissidents to concede a political point is evidence of mental illness. But the pertinent issue here should never have been mental illness, but dangerousness, and there was no evidence during the thirty-one years that Schuster had been in institutions that he had ever been dangerous. And in any case no one any longer asserted that he was mentally ill.

Schuster appealed the denial of the parole. A New York State court did not order his absolute release but instructed the parole board to hold another hearing promptly and at that hearing to "give due weight to the existing unusual and extraordinary facts which . . . appear to compel unencumbered parole."[18] Release for Schuster seemed near, but the state of New York appealed this decision and secured a reversal of the order for a new hearing, on the grounds that the discretion of the parole board within its statutory limits was absolute and beyond court review and the court had exceeded its authority when it ordered the new hearing.[19] Schuster sought to appeal this denial of hearing, but the New York Court of Appeals said he did not have a basis for appeal.[20]

Once again he had exhausted all his state remedies; once again he had earned the right to resort to the federal courts. The federal district court ordered that a hearing be held with Schuster and a representative of the parole board present. At the urging of district court Judge Richard Owen, the parole board offered Schuster a special release agreement that would have relieved him of most of the ordinary conditions of parole, such as making periodic reports. The parole board would not have the power to return him to prison for parole violations.[21] Schuster, a determined old man, continued to demand unconditional release. The judge ruled he could not give Schuster the freedom from the authority of the parole board that he wanted and reluctantly dismissed Schuster's habeas corpus petition. He suggested that a pardon from the governor would solve the impasse, but no one followed up on this suggestion.

Now, for the final time, Schuster appealed. Six years had gone by since the famous case that he had won and that he had expected would give him his freedom. When Judge Kaufman heard this appeal, he was indignant. He began his decision: "Although we are reasonably certain that the shocking story revealed in the Gulag Archipelago could not take place in this country, the facts of Roy Schuster's case are reminiscent of Solzhenitsyn's treatise."[22]

Said Kaufman, "We can no longer sit by and permit the State to continue toying with Roy Schuster's freedom. . . . The inference is virtually inescapable that Schuster's entire 31-year confinement in the hospital for the criminally insane was improper." He ruled that Schuster had constructively been paroled by his 1969 decision, that he had more than completed the five-year parole period that the parole board required, and that the parole board no longer had jurisdiction over Schuster, who was "to be discharged from the State's custody forthwith."

The famous 1969 Schuster case stands for the proposition that the transfer of a prisoner to a hospital for the criminally insane must be procedurally safeguarded. The less well known 1975 case stands for the more important proposition that America has its own Gulag Archipelago. A system of hospitals for the criminally insane had grown up that could swallow up a man and keep him forever. A literate and litigious patient may be heard from again, but many more sink from public view without a trace.

We do not know how many cases there are like those of George Davis and Roy Schuster. We know that people diagnosed as criminally insane are held in such places as Bryce Hospital in Tuscaloosa, Alabama; Atascadero State Hospital in California; the Forensic Unit at Chattahoochee State Hospital in Florida (described by Kenneth Donaldson in *Insanity Inside Out*);[23] the Forensic Unit of the East Louisiana State Hospital at Jackson; the Forensic Hospital of the Perkins Hospital Center in Maryland; Bridgewater State Hospital in Massachusetts (scene of Frederick Wiseman's film *Titicut Follies*); the Forensic Unit of Trenton Psychiatric Hospital in New Jersey; and Farview State Hospital in Pennsylvania. Every now and then there is a legislative inquiry or a newspaper exposé of one of these hospitals. A civil-liberties-minded lawyer moves to stop experimental psychosurgery from being performed on a patient at Ionia State Hospital in Michigan.[24] A Philadelphia newspaper headlines a story on Farview Hospital: "Where the state treats patients with drugs, brutality and death."[25] Patients at the California Medical Facility at Vacaville are put on a behavior modification program in which a drug that paralyzes respiration is used as an aversive stimulus.[26] A patient diagnosed a sexual psychopath is discharged as cured after long years of treatment and then sentenced for his original crime.[27]

Here and there we get a glimpse of activities that usually take place out of sight and that involve the detention and the treatment of the criminally insane, the sexual psychopath, the criminal recidivist, and others who have recently been embraced in the population considered suitable for therapy. Psychiatry has widened its circle. These new patients are almost invisible. No official agency keeps any kind of complete records on how many patients there are and where they are held. Some are held in hospitals for the criminally insane, and others are held in prison medical facilities. Some are held in ordinary prisons, and others are allowed to be free as long as they return for injections of a long-acting tranquilizer or some other kind of therapy. As outpatients they may feel that therapy is an oppression, but often they have hanging over them some possible punishment that coerces them into going along with the treatment. They are rarely verbal or aggressive enough to secure newspaper notice or legal help. We have only a vague idea of what kind of treatment they receive and who the behavioral scientists are who treat them. The injustices multiply and continue for long periods of time.

(7)

Controlling Patients: Somatic Therapies
and Behavior Modification

WHILE FREUDIAN UNDERSTANDING of the unconscious was giving
psychiatry new scope and added stature, and while Freudian concepts
of neurosis and character disorders were enlarging the definition of
the patient, more-traditional psychiatrists and neuropsychiatrists (organic and directive therapists) were developing new methods of
somatic treatment, and behavioral psychologists were introducing
their own method of change, based on conditioning theory, which also
became integrated into psychiatry.

At the start of the twentieth century, psychiatrists were grasping
for effective methods of treatment. In its several-hundred-year history, psychiatry had treated patients by purging, dosing, exciting,
frightening, and isolating, but none of these approaches was so
effective that it was not easily displaced when newer ideas
emerged. In the mid twentieth century new physical treatment
methods gave powerful new tools to the therapist. Shock therapies,
and in particular electroshock therapy, and more effective chemotherapy were developed and found quick acceptance. More-drastic
physical treatment methods involved implanting electrodes and
cutting into the brain. The behavior modification techniques introduced by psychologists used not only traditional rewards like candy
and money for improved behavior, but also such bizarre methods
of influencing behavior as inducing vomiting or causing pain
through electric currents.

The psychiatrist has always been ready to try anything to combat
mental illness. The early psychiatrist experimented with and advocated mercurials and purges to "expel" disease and opium prepara-
tions to change mood. Herbs, extracts, oils, tartar emetic, camphor,

78

copper sulphate, and hundreds of other remedies were administered or applied.

Doctors have always believed in the efficacy of such mechanical methods as purging, dosing and cutting. At the time of the American Revolution, Benjamin Rush, the father of American psychiatry, who was himself the father of a psychotic son, became the chief advocate of bloodletting as a cure for many human ailments, including mental illness. No one knows how many patients died from the enthusiastic treatment of Rush and his followers, who saw a worsening of the patient's condition as a reason to let still more blood. Zilboorg, the psychiatric historian, describes Rush as swearing "by the psychiatric 'trinity' of emetics, purgatives, and bloodletting." Rush also recommended "ingenious intimidation"—clever ways of psychologically shocking the patient—as a therapeutic method. One method of intimidation was "ducking," throwing the patient into water and keeping him under as long as he could survive without being "quite stifled." Rush also used the twirling chair, which spun the patient to the point of unconsciousness and, it was hoped, rearranged the brain and restored it to normal balance in the process. Mercury was administered to patients orally, and the soreness it caused to the patient's mouth became part of the therapeutic action, by focusing the patient's complaints on a new site. The main therapeutic benefit was to convey "morbid action out of the body by the mouth."

Another Rush remedy was a "caustic applied to the back of the neck, or between the shoulders, and kept open for months or years. The remedy acts by the permanent discharge it induces from the neighborhood of the brain."[1]

For a century bloodletting was one of the psychiatrist's preferred remedies. By the time of the Civil War this method was losing favor, but a modified form of bloodletting—"cupping"—and the application of leeches was still advocated. For women with pelvic symptoms, leeches were applied to the genital area.[2]

Tartar emetic was a popular therapy. This irritating substance made of antimony and potassium tartrate had been used in small doses as an expectorant, in larger doses as an irritant, and in even larger doses as an emetic. For psychiatric patients it was given internally as medicine and applied externally as a poultice. In the early nineteenth century in Germany, one psychiatrist advocated shaving the scalp, painting on tartar emetic, and while the skin sloughed and new skin formed on the scalp, confining the patient to a diet of water, soup, milk, and white bread.[3]

Psychiatric ingenuity produced a variety of somatic treatment methods. Psychiatrists congratulated themselves on the progress of psychiatry and humanity because the mentally ill were no longer burned at the stake as witches or persecuted by the Inquisition, but they themselves found ingenious methods of torturing patients: flagellation, firing of cannons to cure by fright, revolving and swinging chairs, sudden immersion in cold water, exposure to high pressure streams of water (the "Scotch douche" played alternating streams of very hot and very cold water on the patient), laxatives, and irritant plasters and poultices. Above all, seclusion, isolation, and forced rest were a favorite treatment method. The idea became generally accepted that the "insane asylum," a place where the patient could be removed from all the influences that had helped precipitate his illness, was the most important factor in the regimen.

The insane asylum contained many violent patients because methods of controlling violence—opium, alcohol, continuous warm tubs, wet sheet "packs"—were primitive, and there was enough confusion and coercion on the wards that those who were not violent when they arrived had ample cause to become so. Methods like seclusion, shackling, placing in a straitjacket, handcuffing, and binding with belts or tying to a "restraining chair" were always available. But the stated purpose of the asylum was to promote rest and freedom from harmful excitement, and in the best asylums the coercive restraints were kept in the background. (A few hospitals tried to dispense with them and rely on a more humane interpersonal approach.) Wilhelm Griesinger, a leading German psychiatrist and neurologist of the mid nineteenth century, wrote that the removal of the patient into a "good lunatic asylum" was in most cases "the treatment which is most prominently indicated." Here the patient could get a regulated diet, exercise in the open air, baths, and medicines, and the sight of other patients in the process of convalescence would be an encouragement to the patient. Some of the treatments Griesinger discussed were: cupping, leeching, douching, cold plunge baths (a method he deplored), cold compresses and the application of ice to the head, cold baths (in particular river baths), tepid baths, footbaths, poultices and plasters, opium, digitalis, and other diuretics, ether and chloroform, belladonna, quinine, purgatives (including rhubarb), emetics, bitters and tonics, and the application of galvanic electrical current (which, again, he did not advocate). Then there was diet, outdoor exercise or carriage rides, and gymnastic exercise.[4]

During the nineteenth century in some asylums the concept of moral treatment replaced the traditional practice of isolation and shackling. The moral approach was psychological. The treatment consisted of making the patient comfortable, arousing his interest, inviting his friendship, encouraging discussion of his troubles, and helping him find useful ways to spend his time.

Among all the variety of remedies that were prescribed, there were some that did have the effect of changing moods, quieting anxieties, calming thoughts. Laudanum and paregoric, solutions of opium in alcohol, were two of the most popular remedies. "Brunonianism" (named after a seventeenth-century Scotch physician, John Brown) taught that disease came from an improper relationship between excitation and lethargy or depression—too much or too little stimulus—and the proper administration of alcohol and opium could balance out these states. The problem, which was not generally recognized, was that these remedies were extremely addicting.

Primitive psychological approaches coexisted with primitive somatic remedies. Medical interest in hypnotism dates back to the French Revolution, when Anton Mesmer developed his therapy, aimed at establishing the magnetic equilibrium of the body, but which was eventually labeled as suggestive rather than biologic. Benjamin Franklin was a member of a committee in France that failed to find a scientific basis for Mesmer's "cures," but mesmerism and hypnosis continued to find a place in psychiatric treatment, and even such a confirmed neuropsychiatrist as Kraepelin, who resisted the concept of psychological causation of emotional and mental disturbed states, advocated hypnosis as a treatment method.

About the time of Mesmer, Franz Joseph Gall organized a "scientific psychiatry" based on the idea that functions of body and mind were localized in the brain and could be assessed by "reading" the skull, which was a "faithful cast" of more deep-seated anatomical structures. Gall has been credited with focusing medical attention on the brain rather than on the liver, the bile, other organs, or the proportions of the various humors, which earlier theories had seen as the cause of mental symptoms.

The beginning of modern somatic therapy and of psychopharmacology came with the introduction of bromide salts in the 1850s by Sir Charles Locock. Locock believed that epilepsy was caused by masturbation—in contrast to one of his contemporaries who gave overcrowded teeth as the cause—and he mistakenly believed bromides were antiaphrodisiacs. As a result of these two incorrect assumptions, he became a famous psychopharmacological pioneer. He reported a series of fourteen cases of epilepsy he had treated with bromides, out of which good results were achieved in thirteen. His success record has never been duplicated, but bromides were recognized as a drug to calm and quiet. Bromides soon became a preferred remedy for epilepsy, but they also became popular for a variety of nervous and emotional complaints. They were ingredients in many of the popular patent medicine "nerve tonics," and they became so popular that the tonnage sold each year outweighed that of any other drug.[5]

The established opium derivatives and the new bromides became the most used psychiatric drugs. Emil Kraepelin, the most famous European psychiatrist of his day, recommended for "maniacal-depressive insanity," a combination of "moderate doses of opium and bromides."[6]

About ten years after the introduction of bromides, a German physician, searching for a drug that would release chloroform slowly in the body to produce tranquility without sleep, decided to utilize chloral hydrate, a drug that had been synthesized thirty years earlier but had not been used for mental patients. This innovation was also based on a mistaken concept. Although chloral hydrate did produce chloroform in the test tube, in the human there were other degradation steps and no chloroform was produced. Nevertheless the patients were made sleepy and tranquil. Chloral hydrate was a hypnotic-sedative. In larger doses it produced sleep; in smaller doses it controlled agitation.

The bromides and chloral hydrate soon turned out to have their drawbacks. Bromides gave rise to bromide intoxication, and the condition became so common that a special diagnostic label, "bromism," was introduced. Before the phenothiazine era, initiated by the introduction of Thorazine in the early 1950s, an appreciable percentage of patients admitted to mental hospitals—variously estimated at from 2 to 10 percent—was suffering from bromism.[7] A much larger group suffered from subclinical bromide toxicity. They had enough bromide in their systems to exacerbate the symptoms of emotional illness or to create new symptoms, but not to the point where bromide toxicity was implicated as the cause. (A similar problem with subclinical toxicity has occurred with many of the newer drugs that have since been introduced, the barbiturates and Librium and Valium being outstanding examples of drugs that have caused perhaps as much symptomatology as they have cured.) Chloral hydrate soon turned out to be habit-forming, and it was found that it led to liver and kidney damage. A variety of new mental symptoms could be produced in the patient by chronic use of both chloral and bromides. In 1882, paraldehyde, said to be less toxic than chloral because it did not contain chlorine, was introduced. Paraldehyde, like chloral, is disagreeable to the taste. It has been served with shaved ice as a "paraldehyde cocktail" to generations of hospitalized alcoholics, but one of its problems is a distinctive, lingering, unpleasant odor that permeates the room. Yet in spite of all the drawbacks of these drugs, they curbed agitation and reduced violence, and they were rapidly adopted as principal therapies.

In the late 1800s the first of a family of hypnotic-sedatives, the barbiturates, was synthesized in Germany. The goal of a nontoxic drug that can reduce anxiety and tension is so alluring that hundreds of researchers have spent their lives working with barbiturates. Eventually, 2500 barbiturates were synthesized, over 200 developed to the stage of animal experimentation, and 50 or more introduced clinically. About a dozen are still currently manufactured and listed in *The Physician's Desk Reference.* The barbiturates were widely used to produce sleep, to calm the symptoms of mental patients, and to relieve everyday anxieties in the general public. They were dispensed freely by psychiatrists and family doctors and largely replaced the psychiatric hospital regimen of bromides and opium derivatives. But the barbiturates, too, turned out to be toxic and habit-forming, and their overuse not infrequently led to death. A combination of alcohol and barbiturates was particularly dangerous. Another problem was that the sleepy patient might inadvertently continue to take repeated doses past the limit of tolerance.

With the popularization of barbiturates, psychiatrists had more to offer their patients, although many patients would pay dearly for their relief from anxiety. The pill-dispensing psychiatrist, family doctor, and internist soon gained new power over patients. The ability to write prescriptions for these drugs kept patients who became dependent on them, as many did, returning for new supplies over long periods of time, often for a lifetime. The barbiturate phenomenon became so widespread that doctors used them to treat emotions that hitherto had been considered normal—the grief of bereavement, the anxiety of stage fright, stress during examinations. Doctors treated emotional states by prescribing alternate dosages of amphetamines and barbiturates, to elevate depressed moods and then to calm down the keyed-up mood. (The amphetamines also proved to be addicting.) The age of medically mediated moods had arrived. No really accurate statistics are available on the incidence of barbiturate use, and we do not know how many patients became habitual users.

For a half-century the barbiturates were the chief drugs used for psychiatric patients. Many of these probably remained psychiatric patients because of barbiturates. A vicious cycle was set up. Patients took barbiturates because they could not sleep, but the quality of their sleep under barbiturates was not normal and relaxing, and the patient thus experienced tension during the next day, more insomnia, and more need for barbiturates to produce sleep. Many violent and anxiety-ridden patients in hospitals were sedated by barbiturates, which helped them fight off their personal demons and maintain stability, but many became needlessly addicted to barbiturates. In hospitals the use of injected barbiturates made it easy to sedate even unwilling patients, and the threat of a hypodermic could persuade them to take their sedation orally.

The fact that the drug approach to psychiatric patients was so unsatisfactory was a main cause for the rapid spread of Freudian thought. The promise of an effective verbal therapy based on a sophisticated theory of mental functioning seemed vastly preferable to a mechanistic application of drugs that were either not very therapeutic or were definitely harmful. Freud had advocated his verbal therapy for patients willing and capable of undergoing psychoanalysis, but Franz Alexander pioneered a sit-up modification of psychoanalysis, "psychoanalytically oriented psychotherapy," for a larger range of patients, and John Rosen even used a modified psychoanalytic technique, "direct analysis," for psychotic patients. Analytically oriented private psychiatric hospitals, like Chestnut Lodge outside Washington, D.C. (the site of *I Never Promised You a Rose Garden*),[8] relied on verbal therapy in preference to medication. Many other private hospitals catered to patients' wishes and relied heavily on barbiturates and chloral hydrate. Public hospitals relied on medication if the patient exhibited symptoms, and custodial care when the symptoms had burned out or become quiescent and the patient did not cause any disturbance.

Psychiatrists also pursued more drastic somatic approaches to mental illness. Some psychiatrists have always preferred physical to psychological approaches to mental disease. Until fifty years ago psychiatric patients and the mentally deficient who could not restrain impulses to masturbate in society were "cured" of their symptom by "removing the cause of irritation"—circumcision in the male, clitoridectomy in the female. This was only one kind of surgical approach. Diseased organs were often thought to be the cause of insanity, and surgical procedures were performed on a variety of organs in the hope that removal of a "focus of infection" would be therapeutic. Gynecological surgery was often expected to cure the mental symptoms of women. Numberless uteruses have been removed for mental symptoms as well as for complaints as vague as tiredness and backache. In the 1920s in the United States, Henry Cotton popularized the focal infection theory, and thousands of patients had their teeth and tonsils removed as psychiatric "therapy." Eventually Cotton came to believe that mental symptoms were caused by an overly long colon that allowed food to remain undigested and become a source of poisons in the system, and a multitude of state hospital patients—the exact numbers are not known since psychiatric statistics have always been (and continue to be) neglected—had portions of their colons removed.

One of the most intrusive and drastic of these somatic treatments was used on mentally deficient girls and women, not in an attempt to relieve them of symptoms but to prevent the consequences of out-of-control behavior. Eugenic sterilization was advocated by psychiatrists and became popular as a means of keeping retarded women from having children. Under the authority of eugenic sterilization laws in thirty-two states, more than sixty thousand women in the United States had hysterectomies or salpingectomies after a psychiatrist or psychologist had determined that they were likely to have illegitimate children or not be good mothers.[9] In 1927 the Supreme Court upheld the constitutionality of the practice when authorized by state law,[10] and in 1978 held that a judge who authorized a eugenic sterilization without the authority of any state law was protected under a doctrine of judicial immunity from suit by the woman who had been sterilized without her consent.[11]

The problem of informed consent—an especially difficult problem when dealing with the retarded—was ignored in almost all of these cases. Either consent was never secured, or was secured without an inquiry into the competency of the retarded person to give consent. Many retarded women who were sterilized without consent or with the substituted consent of a parent were only mildly retarded and were probably able to give (or refuse) consent on their own, but their promiscuity made it seem expedient to social workers or their families that they be either institutionalized or sterilized. In the 1978 Supreme Court case, the unsuccessful plaintiff was diagnosed as only mildly retarded, but her mother wanted her sterilized because she kept company with disreputable boys and men and at the age of fifteen had stayed out overnight on several occasions. She had always gone to a regular public school and had never been held back. She was not aware that an order for her sterilization was being secured, and went to the hospital for her operation after a doctor told her that she had a bad appendix that required surgery.

In addition to drugs and surgery, there were other somatic approaches. Fever therapy was introduced in 1909. Many psychiatric patients were suffering from syphilis. Fever—sometimes induced by giving the patient malaria, sometimes by such medicines as sodium salts—was therapeutic for syphilitics, although it had no benefit for many nonsyphilitics who were also given the treatment. Eventually hot boxes and other mechanical means of inducing fever replaced chemical induction. Julius Wagner von Jauregg, the only psychiatrist ever to have been awarded the Nobel Prize, received it in 1927 for his malarial treatment of syphilis.

Attention turned to other somatic methods of treatment. A Hungarian, Laszlo Meduna, working with two theories, that epilepsy and schizophrenia were mutually exclusive disease processes and that some mental patients after a convulsion showed a remission of psychiatric symptoms, induced convulsions in patients by giving them camphor in oil orally. He later developed an improved convulsive method, by injecting them with another camphor preparation, Metrazol. Still later, Indoklon, an ether used as an inhalant, was employed to produce convulsions. In 1938 Cerletti and Bini demonstrated that an alternating electric current passed between the temples produced the same kind of convulsion. The electroshock machines were easy to build, the treatment was easy to administer, and electroshock soon replaced chemically induced shock. Electroshock therapy does not have to be given in a hospital; some neuropsychiatrists have shock machines in their offices.

The convulsions produced by Metrazol or electroshock were identical to the grand mal convulsions of epilepsy. The convulsive treatment turned out to be ineffective against schizophrenia, for which it was first advocated, but to have a remarkable effect on some psychotic depressions. The use of convulsive therapy for depression became the first great score of the organicists in their battle with the psychoanalysts over a somatic versus a psychological approach to mental illness. Electroshock therapy has a miraculous effect on some patients caught in the grip of retarded and agitated depressions. It has saved the lives of some patients whose depressive illness has brought them close to suicide or death from starvation. It has shortened the course of psychotic depression, the natural history of which is self-limited but lengthy. On the other hand, convulsive therapy turned out to have serious drawbacks, including memory loss, fractures, and occasional cardiac deaths, and it was ineffective in treating many conditions. It did not work for schizophrenia, neurosis, or character disorders, although it has been widely used for these conditions. (Some psychiatrists continue to claim it has a use in the treatment of schizophrenia of recent onset, although many others, myself among them, feel that nothing could be more harmful. An American Psychiatric Association Task Force has called it "probably effective" in "some types" of schizophrenia,[12] a not very certain appraisal of a treatment that has been used for forty years.) For reasons that are not easy to explain—a lack of scientific rigor in psychiatry? the indifference of most psychiatrists to what other psychiatrists do?—it has continued to be used for conditions in which it has no known effectiveness.

Convulsive therapy is the antithesis of interpersonal relationship therapy; it is mechanical, impersonal, and very frightening. Even though a combination of anesthesia and muscle relaxants have modified the convulsions into slight tremors and there are no longer broken bones and chipped teeth, patients continue to have a dread, not easily explained, of the treatment. The memory loss and the progressive infantalization of the patient, although only temporary, are disturbing to patients, and the memory-erasing approach means that no verbal therapeutic approach to dredge up the unconscious can be used. Some therapists, myself included, feel that treatment by convulsive therapy usually makes it much more difficult, even at some future time, for the patient to become involved in verbal therapy. And patients who apparently have benefited from shock therapy often appear to have lost the ability to relate closely to a therapist.

At the same time that convulsive therapies were developing, Manfred Sakel in Vienna was popularizing another kind of shock therapy. He administered insulin to the patient in large enough doses to cause hypoglycemia, convulsions, and then shock. Patients were maintained in a hypoglycemic state. During an initial hour, they felt fatigue and perspired profusely. In the second hour they were somnolent and showed speech and orientation disturbances and frequently had convulsions, and in the third stage of fifteen minutes to an hour they were in a deep coma. Then a sugar solution was administered to end the shock. These shock treatments were usually continued for thirty to fifty days. The treatment is dangerous; it has caused deaths. Used in the 1940s and early 1950s, especially in expensive private mental hospitals, it has since been supplanted by other therapies.

An ancient physical approach to the mind was its direct invasion, by cutting holes in the skull. Primitive man apparently thought intrapsychic pressures could be relieved by this kind of "ventilation," that the evil within the mind should be given a means of escape. Prehistoric skulls in Europe, Britain, and Peru show evidence of trepanning. Until recently primitive people have continued to use trepanning to treat psychiatric illness in British Columbia, Algeria, and Melanesia.

In the Netherlands in the sixteenth century, one popular theory of the cause of insanity was that it was the result of a stone in the head. Charlatans would make an incision in the skin of the forehead and a stone would be produced to show to the patient. The first attempts at modern psychosurgery were performed by a Swiss psychiatrist in the 1880s. He operated on the cerebral cortex to treat symptoms of mental disease; his work was soon forgotten. But modern neurosurgery has found ways to operate on the brain to deal with focal epilepsy, intractable pain, Parkinson's disease, and the effects of stroke. (The term "brain surgery" is reserved for surgery to remove a symptom with an organic cause. "Psychosurgery" refers to the kind of brain surgery, often very similar, performed to deal with emotional symptoms, such as the repetitious acts of severe compulsives or the disorganized behavior of schizophrenics, in conditions that do not have a clearly organic basis. Some cases fall in the gray area between the organic and the psychological.)[13]

The most invasive of all therapies, a modern form of surgery on the brain to alter behavior and feelings was first described in 1936 by Egas Moniz, a Portuguese neurologist, as a treatment for schizophrenia. Moniz used a blunt instrument to sever the fibers of the frontal lobes of the brain. The operation, called the leucotomy or prefrontal lobotomy, was supposed to reduce anxiety and eliminate mental symptoms without impairing intellect. Moniz received the Nobel Prize for this contribution.

In time the operation was refined so that burrholes in the skull were not needed. The leucotome, an icepicklike instrument, could be inserted into the margin of the eye and pushed upward into the frontal lobes and then moved back and forth to sever the frontal fibers. The patient would have black eyes to show for his ordeal but no holes in his head. Psychiatrists found that they could do this simple operation themselves without the necessity of a referral to a neurosurgeon. No one had any precise knowledge of how much of the frontal lobe fibers should be leucotomized, and no special neurosurgical skill was needed. In place of other anesthetics that might require the assistance of an anesthesiologist, electroshock could be used, so the procedure could be performed by a psychiatrist or neurologist with only an attendant to assist. Electroshock anesthesia not only made the patient unconscious but also gave him a retrograde amnesia so that he would not recall the events just before the operation.

From the time the first lobotomy was done in the United States in the early 1940s until it went out of vogue in the 1950s, an estimated 40,000 to 50,000 such operations were performed. Again, no one has reliable statistics, but one of the chief proponents of the procedure, Walter Freeman—who kept on doing this operation long after almost everyone else had given it up—has given 50,000 as his estimate. Freeman has said that he himself has done 4000. The operation was especially popular in Central and Latin America and the Caribbean. The popularity of the lobotomy declined in the United States after the introduction of tranquilizers, but the cost/efficiency ratio of a single simple surgical procedure versus a lengthy, and possibly lifelong, course of expensive drugs led to the continuation of the lobotomy in many poorer countries. There is no source of information on how widely practiced the lobotomy is today.

* * *

This, then, was the situation at the middle of the twentieth century, just before the introduction of phenothiazines upset the whole balance of verbal and somatic therapies. Patients who could afford and had available the "best" psychotherapy tended to go to verbal therapists. Patients who were "sicker" and needed hospital care often could not work in a verbal therapy approach (or found doctors not willing to work with them), and they were often subjected to physical control when drug therapy did not keep them quiet—handcuffs, straitjackets, seclusion rooms. A host of drugs and other somatic treatments were used: electroconvulsive therapy for outpatients as well as inpatients, forced intramuscular injections of drugs, insulin coma therapy, and, infrequently, brain surgery. If these did not prove too effective in helping patients, at least they gave comfort to the staff. Two British psychiatric historians write,

> Came the era of metrazol, modified insulin therapy, deep insulin therapy, psychosurgery, and electroconvulsive therapy. Each form of treatment was adopted with the same lack of discrimination with which it was abandoned. But while discrimination was lacking, enthusiasm was not. Thus the very impetus of the therapeutic movement opened doors, threw down railings, and gave enormous help and encouragement to both staff and patients—but particularly to staff. The most therapeutic element in this therapeutic programme was enthusiasm harnessed to the belief in the possibility of change.[14]

Psychiatry has always had this in abundance: enthusiasm harnessed to a belief, often without rational basis, in the possibility and imminence of change.

In the early 1950s Thorazine was introduced, the first of the phenothiazines, a new class of drugs that not only sedated but actually curbed psychotic thoughts. The phenothiazines and other more recently introduced mood-altering drugs have swung the balance toward somatic and away from verbal treatment. The analytically oriented psychotherapist does not prescribe drugs readily. In classical analysis the goal is not to relieve anxiety but to explore fears, and medication is usually not employed at all. But in the main it is educated and motivated patients and only some of these, who look to verbal treatment for the eventual relief of symptoms and character change. Increasingly, short-term treatment, relying heavily on drugs and on such approximations of verbal therapy as crisis intervention, or time-limited, therapy, or for hospitalized patients, milieu therapy, has replaced the analytically oriented treatment that uses the doctor-patient relationship as the main therapeutic tool.

Thorazine turned out to be a tremendous financial bonanza for the drug company that introduced it to the United States. The search was on for other tranquilizers and for other mood-altering drugs; Thorazine was followed by other phenothiazines, nonphenothiazine tranquilizers, minor tranquilizers (Miltown was the first to be widely used), trycyclic antidepressants, monamine oxidase–inhibitor antidepressants, and lithium (a specific for the mania of manic-depressive psychosis).

The modern drug era in psychiatry has produced a revolution. Hospital wards that were once noisy and disorganized are now quiet and orderly. The average length of hospital stay has decreased, and the censuses of mental hospitals have been cut enormously. Many more mental patients are treated in the community. Many of the effects of the drug revolution have been positive; many patients maintained free of psychosis on drugs show symptoms of psychosis when they go off their drugs. (Patients frequently are resistant to taking drugs, particularly tranquilizers; they often complain that they feel dead or "like a zombie." They may not regret losing the terrors of psychosis, but they often miss the expansive and megalomanic feelings that can accompany psychosis.) But a large price has been paid. The model of drug intervention for emotional symptomatology has led to a widespread use of drugs and other chemical substances throughout the population to maintain optimistic and stable moods. The use of marijuana and of other drugs on a wholesale basis was facilitated by the reliance many Americans had developed on chemical sources of well-being. The concept of chemical maintenance of mood supplanted the psychoanalytic ideal of "working through" conflicts. Valium, a minor tranquilizer, was prescribed in particular for almost any complaint or symptom and became the most widely prescribed drug in the United States. It too turned out to be habit-forming.

Until recently psychiatric outpatients could refuse drugs; only inpatients could be forced to take them. But eventually a phenothiazine was developed that could be forced on outpatients as well as inpatients. Because many patients with psychotic symptoms refused to take their medications once they were out of the hospital, the research psychopharmacologists set to work and developed a depot, or long-acting, phenothiazine, injectable fluphenazine. When injected into muscle it was absorbed slowly. Initial reports indicated it needed to be given only once in two weeks to control psychotic symptoms. Later reports showed that it can be given much less frequently, and some older patients can be maintained free of symptoms with doses at five- to six-week intervals. Psychiatrists now had a method of continuing their chemical control over patients whom they saw very infrequently and only for short periods of time after they had discharged them from the hospital, with the assurance that they would not deviate from their medication schedule. The patient can be coerced into coming back for his medication by effective threats. Some patients are discharged from the hospital or are treated initially as outpatients on their promise that they will continue to come in for their injections. If they do not show up for medication on the appointed day, they can be returned to the hospital. Other patients, those involved with the criminal-justice system, are sometimes not prosecuted or are given a suspended sentence on their promise to keep medication appointments. If they fail to do so, they can be sent to prison.

The injectable tranquilizer is one of the most powerful methods of control that psychiatrists employ, but the ethics and the legal safeguards surrounding its use have received almost no attention. When a judge sees a patient he does not clearly consider committable, he may order him to go for outpatient depot phenothiazine treatment, although a judge's authority to take control of patients who do not meet the involuntary-commitment criteria is extremely questionable. (Thanks to the judicial-immunity doctrine, judges do not have to worry about the niceties of due process in such cases.) More and more patients are being put on obligatory medication schedules as a condition for release or by a judge's ruling. Again, there are no statistics to show how many patients are affected or how rapidly the practice is growing.

*   *   *

In the 1950s a new kind of approach to treatment, behavior modification, was advanced by psychologists. It has since been adopted wholeheartedly by some psychiatrists, particularly those who administer large institutions, largely because it has the great advantage of using objective data that can be quantified. Behavior modification was hailed as a great advance over dynamic (psychoanalytically oriented) psychiatry in the treatment of sexual psychopaths and other quasi criminals because improvement could be accurately measured. The release of the patient did not depend merely on the subjective opinion of the therapist but on hard data—goals achieved, points earned.

Various kinds of behavior modification programs were developed, all with the goal of changing behavior through a process of relearning. Although they are described in the literature as distinct methods, the categories overlap and in actual practice are often hard to distinguish. There is classical conditioning, in the tradition of Pavlov. The first classical conditioning procedures used in psychiatry were with alcoholics and homosexuals. The attempt was to produce an unpleasant reaction in the patient to what had once been seen as pleasurable. First, painful electric shocks, later, emetics to cause nausea and vomiting, succinylcholine to cause respiratory paralysis, and other unpleasant stimuli were administered to the patient at the same time that he was indulging in homosexual fantasies (in response to erotic pictures) or enjoying alcoholic beverages or transvestic, fetishistic, or sadistic gratification. Eventually the patient learned that what he had once thought was enjoyable has disagreeable connotations.

One method for the "cure" of alcoholism is to have the patient take daily doses of disulfiram (Antabuse), a drug that is innocuous unless alcohol is consumed, at which point it produces flushing, throbbing in the head and neck, throbbing headache, respiratory difficulty, nausea and vomiting, sweating, thirst, chest pain, and additional symptoms. The alcoholic learns that while disulfiram is in his system he would do better to avoid alcohol. (It is hard to say if this is classical conditioning or an aversive stimulus.)

There is operant conditioning, in which a reinforcer or reward is given for a response that the conditioner feels is appropriate. There is systematic desensitization, in which reactions to situations are "counterconditioned." Most methods of conditioning require a motivator, either a reward or a punishment.

Token economies are widely used in mental hospitals, institutions for the retarded, juvenile homes, and prisons. Originally they were not recognized as having many of the same legal and ethical problems that beset aversive-stimulus conditioning. What could be wrong with having the patient earn privileges? In practice it turned out that the best motivation for the patient to earn privileges was a state of deprivation. Mental patients learned to clean their rooms if they were not allowed to sleep in a bed unless they did. They learned to brush their teeth if they were deprived of a meal when they did not. Prisoners were thus deprived of meals and clothing and the usual amenities so that they could earn them back. Eventually legal action halted some of these programs, as well as aversive-stimulus programs in which sexual psychopaths were administered electric shock to the inside of the thigh and prisoners were paralyzed in order to prevent voluntary respiration and thus induce fear as a stimulus to curb violence.

But behavior modification has rarely been questioned, and since it is a cheap and practical approach to behavior change that can be applied by therapists with minimal training, it has been widely used.

Behavior modification can gain in effectiveness when it is combined with the monitoring of physiological functions—biofeedback. Electrical read-out monitors to keep track of such signs as blood pressure and brain-wave frequencies had the goal of enabling the subject to gain more control over his physiological processes. Research in progress on determining more sensitive and accurate body responses promises to give the tester-technician new powers, not only to help the subject gain control over his physiological responses, but to be forced to reveal thoughts and feelings. We shall consider this more closely later.[15]

* * *

Many of the methods to control and change behavior were obviously coercive and intrusive. Verbal therapy has always seemed less so than somatic treatment and behavior modification. Now new therapies developed outside of the medical tradition that emphasized that they were not directive and that they had as a goal the facilitation of the potential of the patient (now called a "client") without pressuring him to conform or fit a preexisting ideal. Although these new therapy methods were aimed at making therapy less coercive, the authority of the therapist still placed him in a position to exert much control. Carl Rogers' Client Centered Therapy, or self-therapy, emphasized giving reassurance, letting the client know that the therapist understands and sympathizes. The client finds his own way back to health through interaction with a reassuring but nondirecting presence. Abraham Maslow developed Humanistic Psychology, which emphasized potential and capacity for growth and aspirations for love, esteem, knowledge, and beauty.

Two psychiatrists developed therapeutic models that combined aspects of psychiatry with contributions from other fields. Eric Berne introduced Transactional Analysis, using group therapy as its basis and combining psychodynamic psychiatry with sociological-anthropological analysis. Fritz Perls's Gestalt Therapy emphasized the here and now rather than the past, not asking why things happened, but focusing on personal growth and avoiding thinking in favor of feeling.

A whole new cadre of members of "the helping professions" appeared. Its members called themselves counselors but were in fact nonmedical therapists using techniques developed from both psychology and psychiatry. Some psychiatrists also used these newer and less conventional methods. Counseling began as a subdiscipline in psychology, but it soon became a field in its own right. Psychoanalysis and dynamic psychotherapy also developed new modifications—family therapy, group therapy, and marital therapy.

The press of business at the community health centers led to a decision that psychiatric intervention and counseling could be most cost-efficient, and sometimes most effective, when it was offered at times of family crisis; crisis intervention therapy and other time-limited treatments joined the list. Marital therapy was not able to take care of all the problems of marriage, so sex therapy, conjoint sex therapy (a couples therapy), and surrogate partner sex therapy (a singles therapy) were added to the list of treatment methods. Cognitive therapy appealed to the aspect of the mind that could absorb and process information, and it dispensed with the unconscious. Reality therapy dealt with current real-life problems.

Some therapy, like the Janovian primal-scream therapy, emphasized regression. One California psychiatrist provided nude marathon group therapy conducted in a swimming pool. The body therapies of Wilhelm Reich, Alexander Lowen, and Ida Rolf combined aspects of massage, chiropractic, breathing and relaxation therapy, and psychotherapy.

Some of the new therapies represented combinations of encounter group and consciousness-raising methods, derived from psychology and designed to improve the well-being of "normal" people, with the traditional verbal therapies that had been designed for "sick" people. Some therapies, such as assertiveness training, relaxation therapy, and transcendental meditation, were advocated both for those who were and those who were not psychiatric patients.

Martin Gross, a critic of modern psychiatry, estimates in his *Psychological Society* that, starting a count with classical Freudian psychoanalysis, there are over one hundred varieties of nonsomatic therapies, with more added to the number each year.[16] A four-day seminar offers, for $250, instruction in fifteen new verbal and physiological therapeutic modalities: transcendental meditation, marital therapy, marathon therapy, encounter therapy, nude therapy, crisis therapy, primal-scream therapy, electric sleep therapy, body-image therapy, deprivation therapy, expectation therapy, alpha-wave therapy, "art of living" therapy, "art of loving" therapy, and "do it now" therapy.[17]

Any psychiatrist who wants to invent a new therapy has the privilege. One psychiatrist has developed "Contra Technique" for use with adolescents. It consists of interjecting non sequiturs into conversations with argumentative teenagers in order to take the wind out of their sails. The author of this technique claims he has achieved "limited success."[18] A psychiatrist has integrated astrology into his psychotherapeutic technique and calls it a "very useful diagnostic tool."[19] No matter how ridiculous the therapeutic method is, if it is performed by a doctor or under his direction, it is eligible for medical reimbursement under insurance policies. But if a well-trained nonpsychiatrist applies traditional psychiatric techniques, there is usually no reimbursement. Every therapy done on a psychiatrist's recommendation qualifies as *medical* treatment.

Eventually a field that once had had only three kinds of practitioners —neuropsychiatrists, dynamic psychiatrists, and psychologists— broadened out to include dozens of kinds of therapists applying a bewildering offering of psychiatric methods. Self-improvement courses on audio cassettes using "psychological principles" were developed and sold to prisons, juvenile homes, and institutions for the retarded for mass treatment of inmates. Another commercial venture was Erhard Seminars Training (est), which promised to change one's life for the better in two successive weekend sessions. Art therapy, dance therapy, work therapy (sometimes called industrial therapy), were offered by "ancillary therapists." Then there were self-awareness therapy, self-assertiveness training, projection therapy, and more. But the most effective kind of psychiatric authority remained in the hands of psychiatrists and psychologists, who continued to emphasize a few treatments: dynamic psychotherapy, individual or group; behavior modification; and chemotherapy and other forms of somatic treatment.

Psychiatry had come of age. There was now a wealth of treatment approaches, and all sorts of things could be done to all kinds of people. Much therapy was nonmedical, but a medical model had achieved wide acceptance and many nonphysicians made use of the authority it bestowed.

Much of what went on in the name of treatment was silly and faddish. Much of it required cooperation and was not easily imposed upon unwilling subjects. But much was imbued with the authority of traditional psychiatry and medicine and had the potential of being used on coerced subjects.

Those who enjoyed the authority of the medical model had almost no limit on what they could do. The medical model justified doing unpleasant things to people against their will in the name of therapy or rehabilitation. Many of the most heavy-handed impositions of psychiatric authority took place in mental hospitals and other closed institutions out of sight and also out of mind. Psychiatry had developed so many treatment methods that almost anything could be done in the name of therapy. A great many opportunities had developed for the abuse of psychiatric authority, but this was usually ignored in psychiatry's self-congratulations about how far it had come, how much it had accomplished, and how many treatment methods it had produced.

Critics of Psychiatry

BY THE 1950s the psychiatrist was enjoying unprecedented power—to diagnose, treat, and commit mental patients and to intervene in the criminal-justice process. The answer to the problems of disordered behavior in society and of crime was seen to be more application of psychiatry in more situations and the ceding to psychiatrists of even more authority.

The movement toward psychiatric control was usually regarded as progressive: It was based on "scientific theory," on the medical model, which stated disordered behavior and crime were the symptoms of a disease process and required the care and control of a physician. In the field of criminal justice, the medical model, which had the welfare of the patient as its professed paramount goal, was replacing the traditional social deviancy model, which dealt punitively with disordered behavior. The medical model, in contrast, was rehabilitative.

As psychiatric stature and authority grew, psychiatrists were aware that they were not universally loved, and that severe criticisms were often made of psychiatry, but such criticisms were easy to defend against and discount. Since the early days of psychiatry the psychiatrist had been seen as an authoritarian figure who had acquired unprecedented control over people and could use this power unwisely and dishonestly. Charles Reade, Wilkie Collins, and other Victorian authors had exploited the dramatic situation of the mental patient improperly committed for malign reasons. The psychiatrists answered that some abuses had existed in the past, but now psychiatry had become more scientific. Even in the commitment process—an extreme demonstration of the power that psychiatrists could exert—psychiatrists argued that judicial review was not necessary, that psychiatry had become so scientific and so well accepted that the decision to commit could be left to doctors alone, without benefit of judicial review. Newspapers and magazines often printed exposés of neglect and overcrowding in state hospitals. This, however, was not the responsibility of psychiatrists, but of the legislators, who did not appropriate enough money for better-staffed, more therapeutically oriented hospitals; and even if patients were not well taken care of, the providing of free or almost free care could still be seen as a gift and as commendable. Certainly the trouble-ridden state hospital system seemed preferable to the alternative, which was not to provide care at all.

A second criticism of psychiatrists resulted from an antipathy to Freudian concepts, which stressed the ubiquity of sexual motivation, the early awakening of sexual feelings in infancy, the universality of the Oedipus complex, the presence of hostile and murderous impulses in even the most apparently benign person, and the central role of a dynamic unconscious. One defense the psychiatrists used against charges that their theories were too sex-oriented, too fanciful, or too unprovable was that it was only natural for people to refuse to accept these ideas, that they were defended against because it was too anxiety-provoking to deal with them and their consequences and implications. If people could not accept Freud, it only proved how correct he was about the inability of the psyche to come to terms with its own unconscious contents. Even if Freudian ideas were discounted, psychiatrists could turn to other theoretical concepts—those of Adler, Horney, Sullivan—or to theories of chemical and hormonal imbalance, or pragmatic applications of somatic therapies, so that the discipline did not lose viability and credibility. Behavioral scientists and psychiatrists of various schools made serious charges against each other. Some psychiatrists dismissed cognitive and learning-theory psychology as being simplistic and mechanical; J. M. Eysenck, a British psychologist, accused Freud of being not a scientist but "a novelist." But these criticisms did not impede the advance of psychiatry itself. There were enough theories of the causation of behavior and the treatment of disordered behavior so that some approach could be seen as useful even if Freudian theory were to be discounted.

A third frequent criticism of psychiatry was that psychiatrists were eccentric or peculiar. It was alleged that many of them might have gone into psychiatry because of their own problems and that they were sometimes as sick as their patients. This criticism got a hearing, but when patients were out of control, when disordered behavior caused tension in society, the psychiatrist was welcomed as the authority who defined normality and dealt with abnormality.

The critic of psychiatry was himself subject to the criticisms that he could not understand this humane approach, that because of his own defensiveness or inadequacy he could not open his mind to a new kind of truth. The defenders of psychiatry became identified with a liberal point of view, the attackers with a conservative or reactionary position.

In spite of these criticisms psychiatry prospered. More people felt the need for therapy. Laws were changed to give committing psychiatrists more power. Courts ordered more consultations, and criminal law relied more and more on psychiatric diagnosis and disposition.

Beginning in the 1950s the claim was frequently made by such prominent liberals as Justice William O. Douglas and Judge David Bazelon that society did not lean heavily enough on psychiatric authority, that psychiatrists should be entrusted with more authority than they had.

Anthony Crosland, the British Labor Party ideologue and later foreign secretary, predicted that as material want and poverty cease to be a problem, we shall increasingly need to focus attention "on the social and psychological causes of distress" and "we shall want the advice not of the economists but of psychiatrists, sociologists and social psychiatrists."[1] In the early 1960s Attorney General Ramsey Clark called for a more scientific and more technological approach to criminal behavior. Clark asked, "What can medicine, psychiatry, psychology, and sociology bring to corrections?" and proceeded to give his answer.

In crime prevention, behavioral science can offer techniques that will reduce crime . . .

Rudimentary studies indicate that murder could be deterred by early counseling . . . Preschool and grammar school guidance for children in high-crime areas and special counseling for youths who manifested poor social adjustment would have helped others beyond those given their chance—they would have spared the victims of the troubled youngsters . . .

Behavioral scientists can tell us how to condition violence from our personal capability. Psychiatry, psychology, anthropology and sociology hold the key.[2]

The constant theme in the forensic psychiatric literature of the 1950s and 1960s is that courts and the legal system and legislatures were being regressive, or unfair to criminals, or disrespectful to modern psychiatry because they were not seeking more help from behavioral scientists. The psychiatric literature is full of self-congratulation and self-advertisement on the part of psychiatrists, who write of the help they have given to criminal justice and corrections when given the opportunity, the good that could result if they were relied on more.

Over and over, the emphasis is that the behavioral sciences must be used for social purposes. The related theme is that psychiatrists could be more useful as witnesses and judicial advisers if they were removed from the adversary system, with its reliance on cross-examination, and given a protected status as an arm of the court, and that they could deal with patients more efficiently and get them into treatment more easily if the system of strict procedural protection for patients were discarded. Then psychiatrists would function as physicians, with a widened scope of authority. Manfred Guttmacher, the leading forensic psychiatrist of the 1950s, wrote,

> It is my belief that the time has arrived, or had I better say, is fast approaching, when the psychiatrist would be of more assistance to the court, in all cases in which psychiatric issues are pertinent, if he were more closely related to the judge. Perhaps something along the lines suggested by Judge Hand . . . could be developed. This psychiatrist, as I envisage him, would be a sworn court official, specially trained for his task, who would sit in the particular court room in which he was needed, free to give and even offer advice to the judge on psychiatric issues . . . Such a sworn court official could be available for consultation with any of the trial judges—even perhaps with judges at the appellate court level.[3]

At the time, Guttmacher's ideas were seen as progressive. Now it has become apparent that when the psychiatric expert is taken out of the adversary system and made an agent of the court, his opinions become almost impossible to attack. Even in the adversary process, where an individual is represented by a lawyer and has the right to give sworn testimony and to cross-examine, many psychiatric conclusions that should be challenged are not.

In 1952 Henry Davidson, in his *Forensic Psychiatry,* the first modern forensic psychiatric text, called for revised commitment laws with "a maximum reliance on medical judgment." Said Davidson, "The basic question in deciding whether a person should be hospitalized is his health and his medical needs," and focusing on this would reinforce the trend "of placing major emphasis in any admission procedure on the conclusions of qualified physicians who have examined the patient."[4]

The first major questioning of the growing authority of psychiatrists came from three Yale professors—a law professor, a psychoanalytically minded political scientist, and a psychiatrist. They were participants in a 1953 symposium of the American Psychopathological Association on the role of psychiatry in criminal justice. The symposium proceedings were published under the title *Psychiatry and the Law* in 1954.[5]

Most of the participants in the meeting were psychiatrists who described with a good deal of self-satisfaction the growing utilization of psychiatry in the criminal-justice system and who saw a great unfilled potential for psychiatry to be even more helpful in decision making and rehabilitation. The three Yale professors, on the other hand, were concerned with the growing popularity of sexual-psychopath legislation, with its categorization of sexual crimes as manifestations of illness and its reliance on one-day-to-life sentences, both as a motivation for the cure of the illness and as a protection for society in case the illness could not be cured.

The lawyer George Dession raised the question of the evaluating psychiatrist who interviews a patient and diagnoses him as a potentially dangerous and aggressive psychopathic sex offender, even though there is no indication that up to this time the offender has committed any offense more serious than indecent exposure. Dession asked if value judgments were not involved, and if the various diagnostic categories, prognoses, and formulations of treatment plans did not deviate from legal standards of proof that were required in the ordinary criminal-justice proceeding. The "psychopathic sexual offender," he said, "may thus far have committed no offense for which he could be imprisoned for more than a short term, or under some of the statutes, no offense at all," but if the examining psychiatrists saw him as falling into the psychopathic sexual-offender category and likely to continue to commit acts that the evaluators saw as dangerous, he could spend the rest of his life in an institution.[6]

Political scientist Harold Lasswell pointed out that the problem concerning therapeutic intervention to prevent criminal acts "is to protect against excessive zeal, to prevent an excess of prevention."[7] Psychiatrist Lawrence Z. Freedman, of the Yale Study Unit in Psychiatry and Law, brought out very clearly the value-laden and subjective nature of psychiatric opinion. Freedman said that the psychiatrist talks the language of the scientific method and has a need to consider his own social preference as resulting from scientific observation, but that he ran the danger of replacing the concepts of social morality with that of psychological morality without having changed the substance.[8] He pointed out that the predictions that psychiatrists make that are believed in so readily only apply to specific conditions—"if a man is sent to prison, can the doctor give a valid opinion as to how he will behave if he is paroled back into the community?"[9] Freedman was presaging the literature on the unreliability of the psychiatric prediction of dangerousness.

These three raised important questions about the direction of psychiatry, but their concern was largely for the future. The first thoroughgoing attack on psychiatric authority as it was being exercised in the criminal-justice system came in 1958 when Michael Hakeem, a sociologist at the University of Wisconsin, published a law review article titled "A Critique of the Psychiatric Approach to Crime and Correction."[10] Hakeem had a great distrust of psychiatrists and psychiatry. He said Freudian psychoanalytic theory was unscientific and unprovable. He described psychiatry as a "propagandistic discipline, clamoring for power" to make decisions, to establish new facilities. He said that psychiatry persuades us that it is useful by making that claim on an emotional basis; people who oppose psychiatry are categorized as unprogressive, unfeeling, unsophisticated.

The immediate stimulus for Hakeem's attack was Judge David Bazelon's decision to liberalize the law of criminal irresponsibility in the District of Columbia so as to make this plea available to more defendants and to give psychiatrists more authority to determine that a particular defendant was "mad" rather than "bad." That case was the famous *Durham* v. *United States,*[11] which was the law of the District of Columbia from 1954 to 1972 and which opened the way to a whole series of other attempts to find better and more scientific methods of distinguishing responsible from irresponsible defendants. (What Bazelon and the authors of the other new tests always ignored was that a decision on how much insanity is necessary to excuse a defendant from a crime is not medical or psychiatric, but instead is social and political, and that psychiatrists who state they can define the categories of "responsible" and "irresponsible" by resorting to medical or psychiatric principles are merely introducing their own subjective moral attitudes into the law under the guise of science.). Wrote Hakeem of *Durham,*

> There can be no doubt that the basic motivation of this decision was to "recognize" psychiatry. This is precisely what [Abe] Fortas, who was the court-appointed attorney representing Durham before the Court of Appeals and who advocated the adoption of the new test, sees as its chief significance. . . . An examination of the *Durham* decision itself leaves no doubt that it was designed to overcome psychiatric objections to the prevailing legal views on criminal responsibility.
>
> Anyone familiar with the psychiatric journals and the literature on forensic psychiatry does not need to have documented the wild elation with which the *Durham* decision was acclaimed . . .

But lawyers for the most part were very dubious about the *Durham* decision, for a variety of reasons. Its test of criminal responsibility was thoroughly vague and almost completely dependent on psychiatric testimony. (Originally the test of criminal responsibility had been decided by a jury, with some guidance from psychiatric experts.) The new test was broad enough to include almost all criminals. It could cover not only psychotic conditions but also any condition a psychiatrist declared was a personality disorder or a character disorder, including the common category of sociopath. What seemed very disturbing to some lawyers was that the court had invaded an area that was a matter for legislative control. Drawing the boundary line between the crimes that society did or did not want to punish had been historically a matter of social determination, but Judge Bazelon had said it was a matter of medical opinion, and therefore law could take it upon itself to liberalize the standards. (The *Durham* case is an example of a movement that has come to be called "judicial imperialism" or, in Raoul Berger's phrase, "government by judiciary.")[12] But although lawyers found some important reasons for disquietude with the liberalization of the responsibility tests, psychiatrists were enthusiastic about this decision to excuse all crime that could be considered to be the product of disease and that left it to psychiatrists to inform the jury whether or not the crime was the product of the disease.

Judge Bazelon went on in other cases to develop new "principles of law" affecting other phases of mental health. He devised a doctrine of the right to treatment that justified placing the administration of state hospitals under the control of the judiciary. This doctrine too, like the *Durham* test, did not have legal precedent. When first suggested by Morton Birnbaum in 1960,[13] it was designed to give state hospitals a hard choice—either to improve their treatment of involuntary patients so that they could be restored to society at the earliest moment or to free their patients. Birnbaum was seeking a legal lever to force state legislatures to provide more funds for hospitals.

Bazelon modified Birnbaum's idea. Instead of courts ordering untreated patients to be freed, the courts would decide on appropriate treatment, and they would take authority over the hospitals to see that it was provided.[14] (Like *Durham*, this Bazelon innovation has belatedly also been seen to rest on dubious legal grounds, and his concept of the right to treatment has been superseded by other theories designed to secure better care for mental patients: the theory that mental patients cannot legally be compelled to undergo cruel and unusual punishment and the theory—also emanating from Bazelon—that patients deserved to have their liberties curtailed only in the "least restrictive alternative" environment.[15]

Bazelon stands for all that Hakeem deplores. He has been willing to enlarge the law to expand the definition of mental illness and mental patient, and to expand the authority of the courts to make decisions affecting the treatment of patients.

Hakeem was writing in 1958, before the aggrandizing tendency of psychiatry and the political implications of its application had received recognition. He pointed out how psychiatric expertise had recently been uncritically accepted by the courts in spite of the fact that psychiatrists disagreed with each other, and he printed example after example of the overreaching claims that psychiatrists had been making on how psychiatry could be useful to the criminal-justice system. No one has assembled a finer collection of psychiatric grandiosity. Hakeem quoted Karl Menninger's recommendation for "permanent legal detention" of offenders found to be "inadequate, incompetent, and anti-social . . . irrespective of the particular offense committed . . ." He quoted Guttmacher and Weihofen: ". . . If analysis of the convict's personality indicates that he cannot safely be released, he may have to spend the rest of his life under legal supervision of some kind, even though the only crime he has actually committed was a minor one." He cited psychiatrist after psychiatrist who saw crime as a disease or a symptom of a disease and believed it should be treated therapeutically instead of punitively.

Even more devastatingly, Hakeem quoted various psychiatrists on varying definitions of psychopathy or sociopathy, and he demonstrated how this diagnostic category is considered scientific by some psychiatrists, without any scientific foundation by others. He demonstrated the difference of opinion among psychiatrists on the reliability of diagnosis, on the usefulness of psychological testing, on the treatability of various psychiatric conditions. He found a few psychiatrists —Jerome Hall, Fredric Wertham, and the still little known Thomas Szasz—who saw forensic psychiatry as unscientific or misleading and asked their colleagues to exert more self-control. But most of the authorities he quoted were enthusiastic about including more offenders in the category of "psychiatrically ill," giving more control over them to psychiatrists, and giving more credence to psychiatric testimony.

Hakeem's article foreshadowed current writings on the problem of defining mental disease, the problems of stating whether a particular individual fits within a diagnostic category, and the unreliability of both psychological testing and psychiatric predictions—and in spite of all this, the increasing delegation to psychiatrists of power to detain individuals for limitless periods of time.

The article was published in a respected law journal and contained much material that deserved thought. But the tide was flowing in favor of psychiatry, and the article was little noticed. Guttmacher dismissed it as an "intemperate diatribe."

Early critics of the use of psychiatric authority gained ammunition in the postwar period from two legal prosecutions that revealed psychiatry gone awry, the perjury trial of Alger Hiss and the hospitalization of Ezra Pound. Both of these cases were colored by politics, both received wide newspaper attention, and in both instances the "helpful" psychiatrists were ultimately criticized as authoritarian and unscientific. (A third political use of psychiatry, dating back to the 1950s, the experiments by the Central Intelligence Agency and the armed forces in the use of LSD and other mind-altering substances, and in methods of brainwashing and resistance to brainwashing, was a deep secret that, amazingly, did not become known until twenty years later.)

At the perjury trial of Alger Hiss,[16] the head of the Carnegie Endowment for International Peace, it was Whittaker Chambers, writer and former Communist, who was the chief witness for the prosecution. Hiss secured the services of Dr. Carl Binger, a respected psychiatrist and psychoanalyst, as expert witness to discredit Chambers on the grounds that he was a psychopath and therefore his word was not to be trusted. Binger never examined Chambers, but based his testimony, as psychiatrists are allowed to do, on his courtroom observations of Chambers and his knowledge from newspapers and other sources. He testified that in his opinion Chambers was "suffering from a condition known as psychopathic personality, which is a disorder of character, of which the outstanding features are behavior of what we call an amoral or an asocial and delinquent nature." Binger gave as one basis for that conclusion his observations that Chambers on the witness stand had not looked at the cross-examining lawyer directly, and frequently looked up at the ceiling "as if trying to recall something that he had previously said." The prosecuting attorney, Thomas Murphy, in a demolition of a witness that has been recommended to law students as a "superb" example of cross-examination,[17] asked Binger if the number of times he had looked at the ceiling (fifty-nine times in fifty minutes) was symptomatic of a psychopathic personality. Replied Binger: "Not alone." Murphy pressed the point: "Not alone?" Binger replied lamely: "No."

Hiss was convicted, and Binger's testimony has been cited as a use of psychiatry for partisan and political ends.

The second case to raise questions on the political use of psychiatry and the reliability of psychiatric opinion was the diversion from the criminal-justice system of Ezra Pound, who had been accused of treason. Pound, the expatriate American poet, has been called "the most morally, aesthetically, and culturally controversial figure of this century."[18] He settled in Italy in 1925 and became an enthusiastic supporter of Mussolini. In his book *Jefferson and/or Mussolini* he suggested that both the American founding fathers and Mussolini were interested in the praiseworthy attributes of order and discipline and that they had many resemblances. As he grew older he became increasingly querulous and often expressed his violent animosity against Jews, American corporations, and bankers.

When war broke out in 1939, Pound made regular broadcasts on Radio Rome denouncing the British and the Jews and expressing hope for an Axis victory. After Pearl Harbor, Pound and his wife made two attempts to return to the United States, but he was first refused permission to use his previously booked air passage, and then prevented from taking the diplomatic train that carried other Americans from Rome to Lisbon. He then offered his services to the Italian government to continue his broadcasts. He was still an American citizen, and his wartime broadcasts were unquestionably treasonous. When the Allies invaded Italy, he was arrested, held in a military prison camp, and then flown to Washington and indicted for treason. He faced a possible death sentence.[19]

On the eve of his trial in 1945 he was examined by a medical board composed of four psychiatrists, three employed by the government and one in his defense, which unanimously determined that he was incompetent to stand trial. The report said,

> The defendant . . . has long been recognized as eccentric, querulous, and egocentric. At the present time, he exhibits extremely poor judgment as to his situation. He insists that his broadcasts were not treasonable but that all his radio activities have stemmed from his self-appointed mission to "save the Constitution." He is abnormally grandiose, is expansive and exuberant in manner, exhibiting pressure of speech, discursiveness, and distractability.
>
> In our opinion, with advancing years his personality, for many years abnormal, has undergone further distortion to the extent that he is now suffering from a paranoid state which renders him mentally unfit to advise properly with counsel or to participate reasonably and intelligently in his own defence. He is . . . insane and mentally unfit for trial, and in need of care in a mental hospital.

Pound's lawyer was happy with this result. Pound would not be tried for treason; perhaps he could be released on bail. There would be a

better chance of a lighter sentence after time had elapsed and wartime emotions had died down.

Pound apparently had suffered a "nervous collapse" while being
held in custody by the military government in Italy, but he had never
been diagnosed as psychotic, and since the standards for competency
to stand trial are simple and provide a low threshold for entrance into
the criminal-justice system—requiring only the ability to know the
significance of the legal proceedings and to work with one's lawyer—
he probably at all times was competent to stand trial. But it was more
convenient to consider him incompetent.

Pound's lawyers were not able to obtain bail. Pound was sent to St.
Elizabeths Hospital, the federal mental hospital for the District of
Columbia. He spent his first months there in a large concrete dormitory without furniture or windows in which many of the patients were
in straitjackets or shackled. This was the Howard Pavilion, the forensic
services unit of St. Elizabeths, where patients were confined in connection with a criminal charge, before trial or after trial, when found
not guilty by reason of insanity. Pound was identified as Criminal No.
76028. In this most Kafkaesque of all possible worlds, it should be
noted that his psychiatrist was Dr. Jerome Kavka.[20]

At a hearing initiated by the attorney general in February 1946,
which was a formal inquiry into Pound's mental state, psychiatrists
testified to Pound's feeling that he would be greeted with gratitude
for his efforts to save "the Constitution of the United States for the
people of the United States," a belief which might have antagonized
a jury and hurt his case. The transcript of the hearing shows that
psychiatrists were ready to label what many would call political beliefs
—for example, that with himself as a leader, intellectuals and poets
could have kept World War II from occurring—as evidence of delusional thinking. One testifying psychiatrist was asked if that belief
indicated insanity. The answer was "No, one is entitled to some queer
ideas without being called insane," but that this sort of belief, when
combined with other irrational beliefs and when it "gets out of
bounds," indicates the mental disease of paranoia. Pound was held to
be continuingly incompetent.

Pound was eventually given a small cubicle in the hospital with a
table and a typewriter, and he continued his writing. His wife was
allowed to see him daily and he also had some of the most distinguished visitors who have ever graced St. Elizabeths—among them,
T. S. Eliot, E. E. Cummings, William Carlos Williams, Hemingway,
Frost, John Dos Passos, and Kay Boyle. In 1947 Dorothy Pound
brought a petition for a writ of habeas corpus to have the matter of

the legality of his continued detention thoroughly aired in court; the petition was denied. Mrs. Pound did not pursue an appeal—appearing in court "shakes his nerves up terribly" she told her lawyer, and it was decided it would be better to wait "until the November elections are over."

While he was in St. Elizabeths, Pound received the 1949 Bollingen Prize in Poetry, established by the Library of Congress through a gift from the Bollingen Foundation, for a book of verse that represented "the highest achievement of American poetry" for that year. The book was *The Pisan Cantos,* begun in Italy after his arrest and finished in St. Elizabeths. The award was controversial, both on political and esthetic grounds, and there was so much protest that the first literary prize ever awarded by an agency of the United States government also turned out to be the last.

Pound spent thirteen years in St. Elizabeths. In 1958, after conferring with the attorney general and finding the government was no longer intent on prosecuting Pound and would go along with the motion, Pound's attorney, Thurman Arnold, a leading and influential Washington lawyer who had replaced his former counsel, moved to dismiss the indictment. Eisenhower's Attorney General, William Rogers, joined him in the motion to dismiss, which the government described as in the interests of justice. Again there was psychiatric testimony. It was alleged that Pound remained incompetent to stand trial, that he was "still insane" (although his distinguished visitors had not found him any different from the irascible and eccentric Pound they had always known), that his insanity was incurable and could not ever respond to treatment. Other reasons for dismissal that were given were that in the fifteen years since the events of the indictment "memories have faded," and it would be difficult to secure witnesses to the alleged acts of treason (although recordings and transcripts of the broadcast existed), and that if he were ever brought to trial, there would be psychiatric testimony that the commission of the charges was excusable because of Pound's insanity at the time the broadcasts were made (which would have been a particularly dubious psychiatric opinion).

The indictment was dismissed. At the age of seventy-three Pound was free. The American Civil Liberties Union issued a statement commending the government decision not to oppose release, but went on to express the hope that other "persons of lesser or no prominence" who were still subject to incarceration for life by a criminal court without any conviction for a crime would also be helped. A multitude of others held as incompetent to stand trial, who were deprived of a right to a speedy trial just as certainly as Pound was, received no support until psychiatric studies of the 1960s indicated that psychiatrists were being overly diligent in keeping from trial defendants who might well meet the criteria for triability.[21] And they received no help until the Supreme Court in 1972 finally placed a "reasonable period of time" limitation on detention pending restoration to competency for trial.[22]

Everyone feels that something went seriously wrong with the administration of justice in Pound's case, but there is no agreement on what went wrong. Some thought the government had used psychiatry in order to avoid the embarrassment of a trial that would have led to a long jail sentence or death for an important intellectual. Some thought that the government had wanted to be punitive toward Pound by holding him in the equivalent of a prison when he had not been tried and found guilty. Some thought Pound had benefited by the maneuver because he had been allowed to evade the criminal-justice process. Everyone agreed that political considerations had been important in the decisions and their timing.

There were many other cases during this period that demonstrated the power of psychiatrists and the use of that power to achieve legal ends, but the Hiss and Pound cases (unlike those of indigent and uneducated offenders) were highly visible, and they became symbols of the misuse of psychiatric authority.

Legal psychiatry took its greatest step toward rational self-examination in 1961 when the American Bar Foundation published a monumental study, *The Mentally Disabled and the Law.*[23] This pulled together the statutory law and the case law of all our jurisdictions and presented them in tabular form, along with an enlightened text that explained some of the difficulties and some of the tensions in the field. This volume and the updated second edition, which came out ten years later, made it possible for writers on legal psychiatric subjects to deal with topics in a knowledgeable way without spending weary hours trying to discover the laws and statutes of fifty states, plus those of additional jurisdictions.

Two other extremely important works in legal psychiatry also appeared in 1961. Thomas Szasz published his *The Myth of Mental Illness,*[24] which for the first time brought the questions of the imprecisions of the diagnosis and the irrationality of the treatment of mental illness into the national consciousness. Psychiatry would never again be the same. Its practitioners could no longer claim without fear of rejoinder that their authority was used entirely for good (even though they were not forced to admit, as Szasz claimed, that psychiatry is akin to astrology and alchemy). And Erving Goffman published his *Asylums,* [25] in which for the first time the interaction between hospitalized patients and staff was described to reveal the ritualization, the stigmatization, the role definitions, and the other dehumanizing aspects of inpatient treatment.

These three books, all appearing in one year, focused unprecedented attention on how psychiatrists used their authority. Szasz was widely quoted by lawyers. Goffman started a trend of sociological investigations into what went on in mental hospitals. Soon there was a growing literature on the assignment of roles, stigmatization, discrimination, and the development and elaboration of a "labeling theory" of mental illness, which explained the relationship of the person designated as "doctor" with the person designated as "patient" on the basis of the mutual expectations that accompanied the imposing of names on the parties and a diagnosis on the "patient."

Szasz's work in particular has led to the examination of many psychiatric practices, although not by psychiatrists. His criticisms carry authority because he has the proper credentials—he is both a psychiatrist and a psychoanalyst.

Szasz has always been an advocate of freedom and responsibility, advocating that these be extended to their limits—complete freedom, total responsibility. He would allow drug addicts to pursue their addiction and potential suicides to act out their intentions. He is the Ayn Rand of psychiatry: Everyone can do what he wants, but he must take the consequences of his actions. No one will be excused from responsibility, regardless of his mental status or capacity. Szasz is also the Solzhenitsyn of psychiatry. He sees the demise of our civilization in an encroaching psychiatric authority that we do not have the energy or moral fiber to oppose. His position has often been called fanatical—he is compared to the Old Testament prophets—but he somehow appears less of a fanatic when the legitimacy of some of his criticisms of psychiatry is perceived.

Szasz feels that we take members of society who are deviant or nonconformist or who make us feel uncomfortable and turn them over to the psychiatrist for "safekeeping" and for thought control. He argues that the decision of the psychiatrist to hospitalize is based on socioeconomic and cultural grounds, not on the diagnosis of identifiable illness in the sense that "illness" has been used in traditional medicine. The authority of the medical model has been used to control emotional states and manifestations of behavior that would formerly have been considered nonmedical.

Manfred Guttmacher accused Szasz of calumnies, vituperations, and a wanton distortion of facts. It was suggested that Szasz be censured by the American Psychiatric Association because he had accepted an award from the Founding Church of Scientology, and thus he had "not chosen to limit his discussion to professional circles." Guttmacher accused Szasz of having "gone so far in associating himself with the extreme rightists as to publish one of his papers in the journal of their adherents, *The National Review.*"[26] (Psychiatrists can be guilty of imputing guilt by association.) Although Szasz is perhaps America's most famous psychiatrist, he has received no rewards or recognition from the American Psychiatric Association or other mainstream professional groups. In spite of his exposure of a multitude of psychiatric abuses and his recording of case histories demonstrating the dangers of too great reliance on psychiatric authority (for which attention psychiatrists could be grateful because it has kept psychiatry from even greater abuses of authority), he is usually denigrated or ignored. He has antagonized psychiatrists beyond redemption by his insistence that there is no such thing as mental disease.

Some of the issues to which Szasz brought attention are:

• The nebulous nature of psychiatric classification.

• The use of labels to confer authority.

• The unscientific quality of psychiatric predictions of future behavior.

• The injustice done to defendants declared incompetent to stand trial and sometimes forced to spend the remainder of their lives in hospitals for the criminally insane without the opportunity to prove either that they are competent to stand trial or that they are innocent of the charges against them.

• The "double agent" aspect of the psychiatrist who works for a third party such as the court, police department, or school health service as well as for his "patient."

• The involuntary nature of the so-called voluntary commitment, since by its terms it allows the hospital to retain the patient after he has expressed his desire to leave.

• The use of psychiatric testimony in testamentary cases to break wills that violate notions of public morality or welfare, although the testator's "incompetence" may be very dubious.

Szasz has called the defense of lack of criminal responsibility and other psychiatric interventions into the legal process, methods of "bootlegging" humanistic values into law. He has labeled the commitment system "a crime against humanity" and has helped found a group to abolish involuntary commitment. He called attention to the role of the government in the psychiatric detention of Major General Edwin Walker, which was accomplished by means of an affidavit signed by a federally employed psychiatrist who had never seen Walker. (This was motivated by the desire of then Attorney General Robert Kennedy to have the integration of the University of Mississippi proceed without any opposition incited by Walker.)[27] Szasz has written about Ezra Pound, and he has compared that case with the use of psychiatry in the service of the state in the Soviet Union. He says, "To Russian 'scientific psychiatry,' Valery Tarsis was mentally ill; to American 'scientific psychiatry' Ezra Pound was mentally ill."[28] He has also presented case histories of unknowns who have been injured by psychiatry. Psychiatrists, Szasz says, enjoy their roles as policemen and judges. They get satisfaction out of being able to apply coercive psychiatry under the authority of the court that forces the "patient" to be in "treatment." He has called for "liberty against psychiatry" because he feels that the legal system is threatened by the increasing use of therapy as a method of social control and because he sees a progressive "psychiatric dehumanization" of man.

Szasz sees the real role of the psychiatrist or the psychoanalyst as that of a teacher who will help a motivated patient (or "student," perhaps, since one is not a "patient" unless one is ill) communicate more directly and achieve greater self-knowledge and greater satisfaction in living. He says the modern psychiatrist is not satisfied with this role; he wishes to be the arbiter of human behavior.

Szasz's attack on psychiatrists complements another kind of antipsychiatric criticism, made by the British psychiatrist and psychoanalyst R. D. Laing.[29] Laing argues not that mental illness is a myth, but that it has a meaning that has escaped psychiatrists. Laing is opposed to the usual practice of psychiatry because he feels it is doing exactly the wrong job. He sees psychosis as a reparative process, in contrast to the common psychiatric view that psychosis is an overwhelming eruption of primitive impulses that have to be returned to control so that the person can function once again as before. Laing says, with some reason, that psychotic symptoms are an indication of adaptations, made under stress, that have become intolerable; the psychotic symptoms are the first signs that an unhealthy way of life is being rejected, that more healthy and workable adaptations are being sought and that a growth process is underway. He finds it hard to detect what others describe as the "signs and symptoms" of mental illness, since the behavior appears to him to be meaningful and appropriate rather than odd or irrelevant.

Szasz and Laing differ in their attitudes on the reality of mental illness, but they agree that the psychiatrist-patient relationship should be egalitarian rather than authoritarian. Most psychiatrists, myself included, disagree with Szasz and Laing. Mental illness does seem to be more than a concept used to achieve social control. Mentally ill people often appear to be out of control, and it seems more helpful than harmful to recognize the depth of the individual's plight, to attempt to halt the process of psychiatric decompensation, and to exert some authority in the process. But Szasz's criticisms point up the weaknesses of psychiatric theory and the injustices that have been perpetrated in its name. Mental illness can be too terrifying an experience for the patient for us to want to side with Laing in encouraging the patient to feel the experience to the utmost. Nevertheless his recognition of both the value of symptoms as warning signals and the potentially reparative function of the psychotic process should lead us to want to do more than merely stamp out symptoms. Psychiatrists have rejected Szasz's and Laing's criticisms almost completely; some lawyers have accepted them as if they represent proven truth.

Other psychiatrists have contributed to the antipsychiatric literature, but their books and articles are not taken seriously by psychiatrists, and they have not found the popular acceptance of Laing and Szasz. The articles usually appear in nonpsychiatric publications, and they are not read by mental health professionals. E. Fuller Torrey, who wrote "The Psychiatrist Has No Clothes,"[30] is also the author of *The Death of Psychiatry*[31] (he is not among the mourners). J. Herbert Fill has written of his five years as New York City commissioner of mental health in an article, "An Epidemic of Madness: The Confessions of a Perpetrator."[32] Lee Coleman, in a number of articles and speeches, has proposed an entirely nonauthoritarian and noncoercive psychiatry in which the therapist and patient would always be equals. The title of one of his articles—far from promoting the rapprochement of psychiatry and law that Guttmacher and Karpman proposed —is "Toward the Divorce of Psychiatry and Law."[33] Peter Breggin is the author of "Psychiatry and Psychotherapy as Political Processes."[34]

One of the most quoted criticisms of psychiatry is by a psychologist, D. L. Rosenhan, whose study of commitment and retention policies at eight mental hospitals was published in a leading journal under the title "On Being Sane in Insane Places."[35] Rosenhan uses data concerning the willingness of psychiatrists to admit to their hospitals experimenters with feigned symptoms of insanity as evidence of the inability of psychiatrists to make proper diagnoses (but the refusal to admit the same "patients" would have been seen as evidence of psychiatric inhumanity). Nevertheless, the article is often cited as "proof" that psychiatrists cannot diagnose psychosis.

Articles and books by journalists, lawyers, sociologists, and psychologists have added to the antipsychiatric literature. Lawyer Bruce Ennis and sociologist Henry Steadman have effectively demonstrated psychiatrists' overprediction of dangerousness and their obliviousness to the question of civil rights.[36]

Another main source is the writings of former patients and of patient-liberation groups and radical-therapy communes. Kenneth Donaldson has written of his fifteen years as a public-hospital patient in Chattahoochee State Hospital in Florida.[37] As noted in Chapter 2, Janet and Paul Gotkin have described Janet's experience as a mental patient for ten years in *Too Much Anger, Too Many Tears.*[38] In his *Reality Police,* Anthony Brandt has described a simulated-patient experience and also included the narrative accounts of ex-patients who were members of the Mental Patients' Liberation Project.[39]

The radical therapy movement wants to deprofessionalize psychiatry and expose the "misuses" of psychiatric knowledge, psychiatric theory, and psychiatric roles. An article by John Talbott on radical therapy in the *American Journal of Psychiatry* notes that in spite of psychiatric interest in radicalism in politics, campus life, and new life styles, there has been little psychiatric examination of radicals within the mental health field, and that the most widely read psychiatric journals have devoted little space to the issues raised by proponents of radical therapy.[40] Talbott studied twelve issues of the *Radical Therapist* (later named *Rough Times* and now called *RT: A Journal of Radical Therapy*) published over a two-year period. He says that the authors "without exception saw the goal of traditional psychiatry as the maintenance of personal and professional power and prestige, economic well-being, and control over others." Similar antipsychiatric expressions from the point of view of the patient are found in *Issues in Radical Therapy* and in *Madness Network News,* which has as its slogan, "All the Fits That's News to Print."

It is easy to dismiss these publications as simplistic, doctrinaire, or naive, but they also contain the firsthand reports of patients who express their belief that they have been treated badly by the mental health system, and they challenge the psychiatrist to come out of his consulting room and meet his constituency face to face.

One charge frequently made against psychiatry is that it bolsters the status quo, oblivious that "therapy is change . . . not adjustment." The writers in these publications reject the sickness label, saying instead that "paranoia is heightened awareness." In her "Open Letter to My

Former Shrink" a patient tells her psychiatrist that she is "ten years older and considerably poorer than I would have been without your ministrations. I am forty pounds heavier, and two academic degrees richer, not to mention, much, much wiser than when I began. I want to give credit where credit is due (though I suspect you would prefer cash) . . ."[41] Another patient describes the doctor who decided she needed electroshock therapy: "He was only 32 years old at the time, well-meaning but inexperienced, and he had been sent out like a time bomb by the psychiatric educational system to learn what electric shock is all about by ruining one good brain."[42] An article documents the use of tranquilizers in prisons to control the behavior of resistant prisoners.[43]

Law professor Nicholas Kittrie, in a book entitled *The Right to Be Different: Deviance and Enforced Therapy*,[44] emphasized the concept of divestment—the gradual relinquishment of authority by the criminal law over many traditional areas—sexual deviancy, juvenile delinquency, alcoholism, addiction, social deviancy—and the transfer of these areas to the authority of the psychiatrist. He suggested that considering the number of minors, mentally ill, mentally defective, and others who were routed to a therapeutic rather than a criminal justice process, only 46 percent of the American public is still subject to the criminal law; the other 54 percent is subject to therapeutic intervention. He pointed out statements of "irrepressible therapists" who wanted to define more and more conditions as mental illnesses. (For example, The National Institute of Mental Health's Joint Commission on Mental Health of Children has concluded that racism is the number one public-health problem facing America.) Kittrie concluded that we give too much power to those who wish to operate a therapeutic state.

Criticism of psychiatry has gained popular attention in the novels of Joseph Heller, Ken Kesey, and Kurt Vonnegut, Jr., where psychiatrists are portrayed either as irrational or as demonic wielders of power. Earlier, Mary Jane Ward's novel *The Snake Pit*,[45] which became a well-known movie, had exposed the conditions of public mental hospitals. But the criticisms by such novelists as Kesey go much deeper and question the moral integrity and even the sanity (by comparison with the patients) of the staff. *One Flew Over the Cuckoo's Nest*,[46] Kesey's story of the antagonism of McMurphy, who is not willing to be controlled, and Big Nurse, who finally succeeds in subduing McMurphy through the ultimate weapon, surgery on the brain to eradicate his deviant thoughts, brought the devastating power of the psychiatrist home to the public, particularly in its powerful movie version starring

Jack Nicholson. Frederick Wiseman's documentary on Bridgewater State Hospital, *Titicut Follies,* gave an intimate view of the character of a hospital for the criminally insane and of the decision-making process that goes on there.

But the public seeking help with emotional or mental problems, or merely with "problems of living," has not been turned away from psychiatry by its critics. Bertram Brown, former director of the National Institute of Mental Health, has said that in spite of the criticisms of psychiatry, the demand for psychiatric services has shown no evidence of decline, and he predicts that the demand will continue to grow for another decade.[47] The criticisms of psychiatry have led to greater scrutiny of the role of psychiatrists in commitment and in determinations of incompetency to stand trial, but in most legal areas —ranging from evaluating the suitability of a parent to have custody of his own child to the length of time a prisoner should serve—judges and courts are willing to rely more heavily on psychiatrists, to cede more authority to them.

The criticisms of psychiatry and the complaints of dissatisfied customers fall on generally deaf ears. The psychiatric profession has continued to be complacent, to ignore its deficiencies, to stress its usefulness, and to overlook its potential for abuse and harm. Because there are always people in pain and in trouble and because legal questions involving psychiatry are so difficult for nonpsychiatrists to address, it has by and large been able to prosper and to discount the strong segment of opinion that says it has not used its great authority well.

The Politicalization of Psychiatry

PSYCHIATRY HAD GROWN powerful. It had assumed many of the functions of religion, law, and education, and it had more authority than any of these because it not only provided guidelines and standards but it was also medical or therapeutic. Although a literature critical of psychiatry had developed, the adverse side of psychiatry was given less attention than its values. In this climate, inequality in the distribution of psychiatric care—its availability primarily to the affluent and to teaching-hospital clinic patients—came to be seen as an urgent social problem.

In the 1950s and 1960s there began to be the demand for more psychiatric services for more people, and before the end stage of hospitalization. This was a commendable aim, but in the process of trying to achieve it, psychiatry went through a transformation that led to even more abuses and also made it more political. Better mental health services, and therefore presumably better mental health, became a glib campaign promise that eventually led to the concept that mental health—never really defined—was a right of the individual and that there was a corresponding obligation for the government to provide care.

Traditionally, government has not seen as its function the curing of the sick unless some public health problem, as in the case of contagious disease, or some police problem, as in the case of the violent mental patient, forced community action. Government has traditionally limited its financing of care of mental hospital patients, relying on cheap state hospitals—institutions comparable to nineteenth-century almshouses and workhouses and old people's homes—to give custodial care to mental patients. The level of care was far below that of the private mental hospital, but it was offered free or for a low cost, and in the period before welfare and social security it put a roof over the heads of mental patients and kept them from starvation. When the government assumed the responsibility of providing health care for the poor or elderly, who were threatened with a disproportionate share of illness, it limited Medicare and Medicaid benefits for psychiatric inpatient hospitalization on the ground that this care can be so lengthy and the criteria for continued treatment are often so nebulous that providing inpatient care in private hospitals could bankrupt or at least excessively strain the financial resources of the health care system.

The state hospitals did not have many patients in the intensive treatment that might speed their return to the outside world at the earliest point of time. Many patients deteriorated and became chronic hospital inmates. If and when they could be discharged, they were not given follow-up services to support them and forestall another hospitalization. They were sent out to the situations in which they had already experienced flagrant symptoms, without any kind of psychiatric care.

When patients could afford private care, they went to an institution like Chestnut Lodge near Washington, D.C., or the Institute of the Pennsylvania Hospital, where a large staff was available to work with them. A patient at one of these hospitals might see his therapist—an attending doctor, staff doctor, or resident—for verbal therapy five times a week for thirty minutes to an hour each time. Some private hospitals, though not all, avoided or minimized the use of electroshock therapy.

Patients in public hospitals sometimes only saw their doctors once in six months or a year and then only for a few minutes. Many state hospitals believed in electroshock treatment and gave long courses of it routinely, as many as forty treatments in a course. Some patients received more than 300 shocks, in spite of the fact that some psychiatrists believe it causes organic damage to the brain.

Psychiatry had developed a two-tier system—one kind of care for the affluent and another for the state hospital patient—and there was no care at all for a vast number of people who could not afford private outpatient psychiatry and were not decompensated (or ill) enough for a hospital.

In reality, the better tier of the system was often not as beneficial for patients as it was generally believed to be. Some private hospitals used electroshock even more extensively than state hospitals did. They became known as "shock factories," and affluent patients who believed they were purchasing the best psychiatric care often received unnecessary electroshock therapy. Even when hospitals were considered progressive, patients often ended up with excessive medication or dependency on an interpersonal therapist. But though it was not all good, certainly many affluent people received what seemed to them real help and support from psychiatry, much of it accomplished without hospitalization, and the failure to provide this for others was seen as a blot.

The public hospitals had little to recommend them. Some hospitals, by using patient labor and patient-grown produce and by having almost no therapists—sometimes as few as one psychiatrist to 2000 patients—brought the cost down to as little as ten dollars per day per patient.[1] It was cheaper to commit a person who was a social nuisance than to try to cope with him in the community. Old men, clothed in inadequate hospital gowns or unclothed, spent their lives huddled on benches in dayrooms smelling of disinfectant or on screened porches. Women in shapeless housedresses spent their days serving food from dining room steamtables, and cooking and cleaning with no pay and no holidays.

Psychiatry concentrated on the office patient and ignored the state hospital patient. The American Psychiatric Association had been founded in the mid nineteenth century as an organization of hospital superintendents, but the psychiatric establishment had become primarily focused on private outpatient practice.

Until the 1920s and 1930s, the best psychiatric residency programs had been in state hospitals. Residency training required working with psychotic patients, and these were to be found by the thousands in the state hospitals. Eventually, teaching-hospital psychiatry departments developed residency programs with more prestige and greater opportunities to work with educated and verbal neurotic, rather than psychotic, patients. The psychoanalytically oriented therapies worked best with socially competent and affluent outpatients. The psychiatrist now could complete his training without exposure to the state hospital patients. Then he could go into private practice and could comfortably ignore the realities of state hospital life—that these hospitals were accumulating more and more patients and that they were providing almost nothing more than bare custodial care.

In the general disregard of the problem, there was occasionally a strong note of protest. In his presidential address to the APA in 1958, Harry Solomon called attention to the terrible condition of the state hospital system. He referred to published standards for private care and pointed out how far state hospitals were from providing adequate care. "I do not see how any reasonably objective view of our mental hospitals today can fail to conclude that they are bankrupt beyond remedy . . . In many of our hospitals about the best that can be done is to give a physical examination and make a mental note once a year, and often there is not enough staff to do this much."[2]

Occasionally there was this kind of taking of notice. There were sporadic newspaper exposés. From time to time there would be a sensational photographic essay in a magazine like *Life*. But no one showed any great continued interest or enthusiasm in trying to bring the standard of state hospital care closer to that of private psychiatric hospitals.

When I took my psychiatric residency in the 1950s there seemed to be very simple and straightforward ways to improve the state hospital system. Many more doctors and staff members were needed. It had been a disservice to patients to divert psychiatric residents to the more fashionable teaching hospital programs. It was also a disservice to psychiatric residents, who graduated into psychiatrists unaware of the range of psychiatric pathology and the varieties of social experience that play on patients, and who were now indoctrinated with the idea of practicing psychiatry for financial return and status.

State hospital buildings were ugly and uncomfortable, but patients needed good care more than they needed pleasant surroundings. Here and there a hospital demonstrated that with a better personnel-patient ratio and an enlightened treatment program—less neglect, less utilization of electroshock, more attempt to treat the patient as a person and provide him with a constructive milieu—hospitals could be improved. One obvious need was for follow-up care after the hospital. Many old hospitals had been put in out-of-the-way places, not only because established centers did not want mental patients in their midst but, probably more important, because the concept of a central state hospital required that the state's only mental hospital be established in its geographical center. These central state hospitals sometimes housed more than ten thousand patients. Patients were being treated far from family and friends, and after their discharge from the hospital they would be far from psychiatrists and medication.

The public mental hospital system is our oldest example of socialized medicine. I can think of three important reasons why the state was willing to do for mental patients what it did not do for most other patients (although state care was also provided in tuberculosis sanitariums, leprosariums, and hospitals for contagious diseases).

First, many mental patients who can be managed only in institutions require such long-term care (and this was particularly true before the introduction of tranquilizers in 1952) that few families could afford the expense involved. Mental illness is often chronic, rarely fatal. Private care was an impossibility for all except the affluent.

Secondly, domestic tranquility depended on the detention of at least some mental patients. They disturbed the peace, committed acts that, except for their disordered mental states, would have been considered criminal, went out publicly in their nightclothes or otherwise outraged their fellow citizens. State mental hospitals and institutions for the retarded have been called vacuum cleaners that swept up the undesirable and the deviant, but they were only part of a rudimentary welfare system that conducted the same kind of housecleaning operation to put away orphans, old people, vagrants, and the poor. The state hospital system, like orphanages, almshouses, and old people's homes, kept society neat.

Perhaps the most important reason that the state provided free health care for mental patients was that some people in society needed, or appeared to need, to be deprived of their liberty for their own protection, or for the protection of society. These were not patients who recognized their need for help. They were patients involuntarily. Once we decide to lock up patients against their will and over their protests, we are no longer in a position to say that if they do not want to pay for their hospitalization they can go free. The mental hospital serves as a civil counterpart to the criminal-law system. We lock people up in prisons under the police power of the state if they have done wrong. We lock up in mental hospitals people to whom we do not attribute wrong, at least in a legal sense, under the paternalistic authority of the state to care for its citizens, the so-called *parens patriae* power.

When historians write about the rise of the mental hospital system and they ascribe malign motives to society for providing such poor care for so many people, they overlook such facts as the lack of effective methods of treatment until well into this century and the lack of welfare and social security systems that could maintain people unable to work outside of hospitals. Patients had little reason to complain if their care was poor. It was free, and it had been given even though there was no obligation to provide it. (This does not mean that malign motives were not present, too. The caretakers of the mentally ill had often been relegated to their roles by economic need or psychological preference, and this often resulted in punitive and sadistic treatment of those in their charge.)

The federal government had always maintained that it had no responsibility to try to improve state hospital care. Under a federal system, this was a state concern, not subject to federal intervention. The same policy was followed concerning the running of orphanages, prisons, and other state-run institutions. The reluctance of the federal government, even during the administrations of such liberal presidents as Roosevelt, Truman, and Kennedy, is in contrast to the alacrity with which the government entered into almost every other phase of state activity. Only St. Elizabeths Hospital in Washington, hospitals run by the Veterans Administration and the armed services, and a hospital for the criminally insane in Springfield, Missouri (run as part of the Federal Bureau of Prisons), were of concern to the United States government.

The federal government would not even make surveys or reports on how state hospitals were run. When a Senate subcommittee of the Committee on the Judiciary, headed by Senator Sam Ervin, held hearings on appropriate commitment policy, President Kennedy's attorney general, his brother Robert, was asked if civil-rights legislation could not be used to improve the status of the state hospital patients. In his testimony the attorney general thought not.

> Primary responsibility and jurisdiction with respect to persons committed and treated in State mental institutions rests with the several States. The [Justice] Department's jurisdiction in this connection is limited . . .
>
> The Department . . . makes no surveys or investigations of State mental institutions to determine general conditions therein. It has no authority with respect to the manner in which patients are admitted or in connection with the quality of care and treatment accorded them. Such matters are within the exclusive jurisdiction of the States.[3]

Private psychiatry and the American Psychiatric Association had abdicated responsibility for improving the state hospitals. The federal government had said it was powerless (although subsequent Department of Justice policy has taken a completely opposite turn, and the Civil Rights Division of the Department of Justice now takes an activist role in attempting to force states to improve their standards of care). State legislatures had consistently shown they were unable to come to an understanding of the problem and to appropriate the money necessary to improve the state hospital system. The problems were easy to pinpoint—overcrowding, understaffing, outmoded facilities—but no one was prepared to try to improve them.

Behind the scenes however, outside the awareness of even most mental health professionals, a major change was in the making. The same Kennedy administration that had denied it had the power even to survey state hospitals for inadequacy was planning a revolutionary new system of mental health care that would not only bring the federal government into the field of mental health but would make it the chief provider of outpatient as well as inpatient services. In 1955, during the Eisenhower presidency, a resolution of House and Senate had called for the appointment of a Joint Commission on Mental Illness and Health to plan new methods of mental health service delivery. The act calling this commission into being noted that there were "seven hundred and fifty thousand mentally ill and retarded patients . . . hospitalized on any given day," that the cost of mental illness to taxpayers, including the cost of veterans on mental health disability pensions, was over $1 billion a year, and that "there is strong justification for believing that the constantly growing burden may well be due primarily to an outmoded reliance on simple custodial care in mental hospitals as the chief method of dealing with mental illness." The act stated that early intensive treatment was needed in mental hospitals to prevent a backlog of deteriorated patients, that "experience with certain community out-patient clinics and rehabilitation centers would seem to indicate that many mental patients could be better treated on an out-patient basis at much lower cost than by a hospital," and that many elderly hospitalized patients could be better cared for in another kind of facility.[4]

A total of fifty-two individuals served as members of the commission —psychiatrists, psychologists, educators, citizen representatives, and lawyers. There were thirty-six participating agencies that included the American Psychiatric Association, the American Psychoanalytic Association, the American Psychological Association, the Department of Defense, the National Association for Mental Health, and the Department of Justice. Five years later, having spent $1,548,000 to collect and write up its information, the commission returned with its report. Most of the psychiatric members of the commission were leaders of establishment psychiatry and conservative.[5] Nevertheless they agreed to a report recommending that psychiatry be deprofessionalized, that the definition of mental illness be broadened, that the range of outpatient service be enlarged to include much that had not been considered medical or psychiatric, and that these goals be made the responsibility of the federal government. Part of the explanation for this recommendation by conservatives that psychiatry extend its borders and take on a new character is that they thought psychiatry had only a beneficial effect and was applicable to all social ills. Another part is that private psychiatry, which these psychiatrists represented, was being criticized for not providing for the less affluent and the indigent; shifting the responsibility for providing care to the government would get the critics off psychiatry's back.

The commission came up with a revolutionary report.[6] It proposed a socialized medicine approach to mental health, embracing whole new categories of patients, accepting many new kinds of therapists, projecting a network of government-funded community care establishments to blanket the country. The need to improve care for state hospital patients was subordinated to the provision of new services for other segments of the population who had never been included in the mental health system, in the hopes that this preventive approach would deal with patients before they reached the extremity of hospitalization.

The report that the commission published in 1961 was the blueprint for an entirely new kind of mental health delivery system. The federal government would not only take a role in, but would sponsor and control, the health care delivery system. States would give service not only to the hospitalized but to all others with mental and emotional problems. It is doubtful that the members of the commission realized the implications of their report. Most of the psychiatrists on the commission were analytically oriented and at least paid lip service to the concept of interpersonal therapy based on "dynamic" principles. At their hospitals—the Institute of Living, in Hartford, the Institute of the Pennsylvania Hospital, the University of Pennsylvania Hospital, Seton Institute in Baltimore, Mount Sinai Hospital in New York—verbal methods of treatment were emphasized. But the commission called for innovations in delivery of mental health care that would eventually lead to deprofessionalized, impersonal, "nondynamic" care. It called for a "broad, liberal philosophy of what constitutes" treatment and "who can do treatment."[7] This has led to the present "biopsychosocial approach" that stresses chemotherapy and social-service-oriented treatment, the chemotherapy under the ostensible direction of a psychiatrist, the other services provided by a variety of new mental health care providers.

The report had some recommendations directed to state hospital care, and these were made without reference to what they would cost. No patients should be admitted to any hospital that already had 1000 patients in residence. No new facilities should be built for chronic care, but only for intensive short-term care.[8] Theoretically, mental hospitals would be relieved of strain because people treated in a network of community care centers would be spared a trip to the hospital. (In actual practice as the system has developed, the majority of the patients seen in community care have not been as seriously disturbed as traditional state hospital patients, and these less difficult patients have received most of the community care. As state hospitals reduced their patient populations and emphasized short-term stays, there eventually proved to be no place at all for the state hospital patients, the least capable and most chronic patients.)

The commission advocated that some patients receive the same kind of treatment currently rendered at "good" psychiatric hospitals by psychiatrists, psychoanalysts, and neurologists, but that other patients should be treated by "non-medical mental health workers" who would do "general short-term psychotherapy." This short-term psychotherapy would combine "some elements of psychiatric treatment, client counseling," "someone to tell one's troubles to," and "love for one's fellow man."[9]

Everyone would be eligible to be a therapist. The report said that "clergymen, family physicians, teachers, probation officers, public health nurses, sheriffs, judges, public welfare workers, scoutmasters, county farm agents, and others [are] already trying to help and to treat the mentally ill in the absence of professional resources. With a moderate amount of training through short courses and consultation on the job, such persons can be fully equipped with an additional skill as mental health counselors."[10]

Then too, services should be extended out into the community to schools and other institutions at second hand through the use of mental health consultants. These consultants would be recruited from the ranks of psychologists, social workers, nurses, family physicians, pediatricians, and psychiatrists, and they would provide "general professional supervision of subprofessional activities."[11]

The other recommendations in the report were similarly based on the concept, then popular in many areas of medicine, that huge infusions of money and manpower would solve the problem of disease. They included large expenditures of funds in basic research, with federal support for a string of research institutes and the building of new research facilities in regions where no research institutions existed.

The most striking recommendation was that "persons who are emotionally disturbed"—and this was defined as having "intolerable psychological stress"—"should have skilled attention and helpful counseling available to them in their community."[12] Said the report, "The objective of modern treatment of persons with major mental illness is to enable the patient to maintain himself in the community in a normal manner."[13] To this end there should be established a network of community care centers, one for every fifty thousand of the population, which would have meant the formation of 4400 community centers.[14] Since each of these should provide a variety of services for outpatients and inpatients and could easily cost $2 million a year to operate, the commission was talking in terms of perhaps $9 billion a year for community care, with additional sums for residence homes for children, hospital facilities, and long-term care facilities. The commission recommended that expenditures for public mental patients should be doubled in five years and tripled in ten, but the program as outlined would have raised the cost by much larger multiples. Eventually the plan was scaled down to 1500, which was only one-third the recommended number of community centers, and only 650 of these have been put into operation. Much of the research was never funded. Nevertheless the direct cost of mental health care has risen from $1 billion a year to $17 billion a year.

Funds for programs would come from a variety of sources—county, town, and municipal taxes, state funds, and federal funds. ". . . Any national program against mental illness adopted by Congress and the States must be scaled to the size of the problem, imaginative in the course it pursues, and energetic in overcoming both psychological and economic resistances to progress in this direction."[15] This was a swing from one extreme in public mental health to another, from neglect to a profusion of services.

The recommendations went off in so many different directions and asked for so many services in each area that inevitably attention would be diverted from what had been the problem that had prompted the appointment of the commission, the plight of acute and chronic publicly hospitalized patients. When recommendations are made concerning manpower, training, research, deprofessionalization, community treatment, and mechanisms to produce changes in social attitudes concerning mental illness, there is a guarantee that attention will not be left over to invest in reforming the state hospital system.

In 1963 President Kennedy sent to Congress the first presidential message to deal with mental health, recommending a network of federally funded mental health community centers and research institutes. The message led to the passage of the Community Mental Health Centers Act of October 1963 and the start of the community mental health center system. Kennedy's message was the first of a whole series of presidential interventions into the health area, and eventually cancer, stroke, heart disease, renal disease, and sickle cell anemia programs would all be promoted as evidence of concern of the New Frontier and the Great Society. All of these programs would be presented as necessary on the basis of simple justice for those unable to pay for medical care, but they would all ultimately become controversial, usually because the problem under attack did not respond to the expenditure of federal funds. The mental health program, unlike the others, had tremendous potential for intervention into all phases of the lives of individuals: It had as its target all human behavior that could be considered a result of mental illness, and this was never defined. Unlike other programs, it also had the ultimate authority of coercive therapy, since the patient could not always be considered competent to make the "medical" decisions about whether or not he wanted to accept treatment.

The community mental health center system did not aim to set up a therapeutic state, but as it has developed it has led to increased ability of the state to control behavior. Many people with little professional training or experience now share in psychiatric authority. Counselors have extended this authority into the schools, where large numbers of children who have never been properly evaluated are maintained on drugs because of their "hyperactivity," and many other children are given "guidance" or "counseling" by "counselors" with little experience or training. The combination of psychiatry, social work, and vocational rehabilitation makes the community health center a powerful influence on the family. Great quantities of drugs are dispensed in the system, with most of the patients receiving this treatment not under the direct care of any trained psychiatrists. Many of the psychiatrists work only part-time, often after hours. Psychiatric residents who are engaged in a full-time education program are at the same time the senior staff members of some community care centers as "moonlighters." They write prescriptions for patients they have never seen and renew or increase medications at the suggestion of the mental health technician who is the therapist. Other psychiatrists are foreign medical-school graduates with poor English-language skills who cannot qualify for a state medical license but are allowed to practice under special institutional licenses. Medical students, early in their exposure to psychiatry, are considered capable of "doing" therapy; in some programs medical students on their first rotation in psychiatry are assigned therapy patients. As inadequate as this training seems, it is far better than the two years of community-college training that qualifies some mental health technician therapists.

The community mental health movement has resulted in a spotty provision of services. Since only a fraction of the number of community centers that were originally projected have been funded and made operational, many parts of the country do not have community centers or have inadequate services, and many centers pay little attention to former state hospital patients. Only 40 percent of the country is covered by the community mental health center network. In spite of this, the thrust of recent state policy, motivated as much by a desire to save money as by interest in patient care, is to move patients out of hospitals into the community. The original commission report may have contemplated—the report is vague and often contradictory—that "dynamic" or "insight" therapy would be provided to many patients. Present programs, however, depend on chemotherapy, social-welfare help, time-limited brief treatment (hot lines, crisis intervention therapy) and directive therapy (rational and emotive therapy, gestalt therapy), and almost no patients get therapy from highly professional, analytically oriented psychiatrists or psychologists. Therapists increasingly are not psychiatrists, psychologists, social workers, or even psychiatric residents, but mental health technicians, pastoral and other counselors, teachers, and trainees such as psychology interns and medical students.

Stratagems have been devised so that third parties—insurance plans and Social Security—pay for these treatments as if they were "medical treatments," on the pretext that psychiatrists and Ph.D.-level clinical psychologists supervise the treatments, although the supervision is usually minimal or nonexistent. (Psychiatric therapy stresses personal integrity, uncompromising self-examination, confrontation, but many of the financial practices of psychotherapists are at deviance from the kind of wholesomeness or integrity that they would try to develop in their patients.)

Since much of what is being treated in the community health center is said to be a "disability defined in a situational context," it is proposed that the duty of the mental health professional is to change the situation, to eliminate poverty, joblessness, ghettos, poor housing, racism, drug traffic, and other causes of emotional distress. A great debate has gone on among the personnel of mental health centers concerning proper role definitions. Some see mental health as a restricted and well-defined field, but many mental health professionals believe they must work on the roots of mental problems, and a new term, "boundary busting," has been given to this kind of activism that involves mental health professionals in efforts to improve the economic lot and the political power of the underprivileged, to increase welfare supports, to improve schools and communities, and to secure better housing.[16]

Good cost figures on community treatment are almost impossible to secure. Figures I have seen indicate that for many centers the cost per client contact (not per patient visit) is $40 or $50 or more, and some centers go much higher. A knowledgeable psychiatrist recently estimated that the cost may be as high as $150 a patient visit. In contrast to the private practitioner, who can function with only a part-time secretary or with no office help, the community centers have a large proportion of personnel who do not see patients: administrators, coordinators, facilitators, and staff who do "in-house" education or perform other services that are primarily for the agency, not for the patient or client. Those people who do work with patients operate as members of a team, with much of their time spent in team meetings and in communicating with each other rather than with the patient. In order to be reimbursed by Medicare and Medicaid, there is complicated record keeping, which the same knowledgeable psychiatrist estimates can fully occupy one-fourth or more of the centers' personnel.

Private and community costs are not comparable, however, because the centers provide ancillary aid that is outside the professional competency of the private health practitioner—social work rather than psychiatric, such as securing welfare benefits, arranging for transportation, education, housing, vocational rehabilitation, employment, and in other ways straightening out lives. The services provided, which are more social than psychological, may be very useful to the patient (although one study shows "poor prognosis" schizophrenics do better without "major role therapy," a program to help one to become a student, employee, or housewife, than with this help), but they are so far from traditional medical therapies that their inclusion as treatment raises problems of defining psychiatric care and controlling its limits.

Some critics have suggested that the main beneficiaries of the community mental health system are the middle-class people who staff them and that the recipients of services would do better if they were given the money that the services cost instead of the services. A huge number of job opportunities for middle-class Americans have opened up, and a popular bumper sticker says ambiguously, "Mental Health . . . Is the Good Life!" Mental health care providers have become an important political constituency, and their unions exert power on decisions concerning deployment of resources.

The 1974 Nader Study Group Report on the community mental health movement declared that "the short life of the community mental health centers program already bears the familiar pattern of past mental health reforms that were initiated amid great moral fervor, raised false hopes of imminent solutions, and would end up only recapitulating the problems they were to solve . . . They were initiated as a reaction to the scandalous degeneration of state hospitals," but, the Nader report says, they have slighted the small minority of people whose problems do fall within the province of legitimate mental health concerns in favor of placing an "ever-greater number of categories of 'sick' people and 'behavioral problems' within the province of mental health care . . . The growing tendency to attach medical labels to (and thus presumably to seek medical solutions for) a range of social problems . . . enhances the possibility that mental health professionals will be used to legitimize subtle methods of control and retribution by making them appear to be instruments of treatment."[17]

The inflated goals of the commission members were incapable of being fulfilled. The number of centers has been scaled down. They have, as I have indicated, increasingly provided a more and more diluted and less and less professional kind of care to problems that are only remotely connected to mental health. But although the community center system has not proven itself, it has led to the acceptance of the concept of governmental responsibility for psychic well-being, the principle that the state must not only enable the pursuit of happiness but ensure that happiness.

Many of the people who take their problems to the community mental health centers have serious problems—psychoses, extreme anxiety, extreme depression—that traditionally have received mental health care. Others use the service as an entry into vocational rehabilitation, as a substitute for social work, as an alternative to criminal-justice processing, or for dealing with the problems of everyday life. The availability of help, or at least listeners, draws people into the mental health ambit who might have been able to cope on their own without help, and although in some cases this may result in benefit, in others it aggravates tensions and dependency and casts the person into the patient role. Free mental health services, particularly when other meaningful forms of help are absent, are seductive; more and more people are drawn into the system. The demand grows with supply. Cities where suicide prevention services are offered, for example, show a rise and not a fall in suicides, and although there is no evidence that the relationship is causal, there is equally no evidence that the help is effective, and there is the possibility—not sufficiently studied—that the services do actually engender pathology.

The community system is far from the private practice dynamic therapy model of a one-to-one patient-therapist relationship. Freud's concentration on the Oedipal complex has been supplanted by an emphasis on pre-Oedipal development; Freudian theory, as it has evolved through the work of Melanie Klein, Winnicott, Bion, Jacobson, and others, has emphasized the traumatic effects of a distorted mother-child relationship in very early years. The indispensable element for this kind of therapy is a close enough therapist-patient relationship so that early training and deprivation can be reexperienced, understood, come to terms with, and compensated for by adult coping mechanisms. The community care system often ignores the interpersonal aspects of the therapist-patient relationship, and the verbal therapy it does offer is usually provided by workers with less training and experience. It relies on shortcut treatment methods that are insufficient for the traditional severely disturbed psychiatric patient, many of whom have become "revolving-door patients."

The community health care system is usually given credit for the dramatic emptying of state hospitals. In 1955 inpatient populations of state and county mental hospitals reached their peak of five hundred sixty thousand (and in addition there were perhaps seventy-five thousand patients in private and federal hospitals). The drop in the inpatient census has been constant since that time, and the introduction of phenothiazines and financial aid to the mentally disabled, both of which antedated and were independent of the community health care system, is probably the major factor in the decline by 1975 to one hundred ninety-three thousand (plus the same seventy-five thousand in private and federal hospitals), a 65 percent decrease.

The extension of welfare assistance, the Aid to the Disabled program, to the mentally ill in 1963 provided the financial support to maintain patients in the community. (The abbreviation ATD originally stood for Aid to the Totally Disabled, but when it embraced the mentally ill, the concept of total disability was dropped.) In 1974 the program was transferred to the Social Security Administration and renamed the Supplemental Security Income (SSI) program. When the change was made to Social Security administration of the program, any stigma connected with the idea of disability was removed—now the recipients were merely "on Social Security." Many of the mentally ill, not able to support themselves by work and with no other income, were now able to be maintained in the community, with living arrangements including independent housing, board and care homes, and convalescent hospitals. Having a source of funds sometimes made patients more acceptable to their own families. Since there is only a perfunctory yearly review, many of the people who become eligible for the SSI program remain on it for years, or even life. Sometimes merely the fact that a person continues in psychiatric treatment is enough to justify the "disabled" designation that allows the support payments to continue.[18] In 1978, benefits of $1.1 billion were paid to 325,000 people classified as mentally disabled.[19] Inmates of federal and state prisons are eligible for disability payments (for physical as well as mental causes). While serving time, they may receive from $166 to $418 a month.[20]

All authorities agree that patients who formerly would have been in the category of the chronically hospitalized have not been well served by the community mental health care system. They live secluded and lonely lives in the community, and they are exploited financially and in other ways. The business of providing them with board and care has made entrepreneurs wealthy. Community mental health professionals have neglected them, preferring to focus on "preventive" programs such as school counseling and on treating more attractive, verbal neurotics and character disorders—the nonpsychotic.

Recently the community health care system has become more interested in these neglected people because other sources of funding have dried up and this population has been identified as a source of Medicare and Medicaid reimbursements. When this happens, the patient does not necessarily receive meaningful treatment, although he is encouraged to have frequent appointments at his neighborhood community health care center.

One study of "clients and patients" at community centers concludes that less than one-sixth of those utilizing the services are "sick and very sick people." The others come to the center "to seek compensation for the absence of traditional social supports: family and religion." These "less sick" patients utilize a wide range of services that have been provided for short-term care—walk-in clinics, crisis centers, "hot lines," and "other forms of institutionalized encounters with people in acute distress." Their utilization of the clinic is often limited to one or two interviews,[21] and the benefits of these brief encounters remain unproven. (Often the service does not meet the expectations of the client. A patient recalls: "I called Suicide Prevention though I was sure I wasn't going to kill myself. I just wanted somebody to tell me it was worthwhile not to. But I was placed on 'Hold' and they never came back to the phone so I laughed and thought, 'That's the end of that.' ")[22]

One psychiatrist, who works on a ward for "multiple recidivists" (people who have had many hospital admissions) in an "intensive short-term psychiatric institute," writes: ". . . Most such patients are no better off after the 4th or 5th or 10th relapse than before they originally came to this or other such hospitals. The current approach, directed at crisis resolution or used as an expedient, does not even attempt to be definitive for the illness. The hope that the community would serve to rehabilitate the seriously ill after a brief hospitalization has not generally been realized . . ."[23]

The kind of help offered is much more geared to so-called problems in living for those patients who have domestic problems, are in trouble with the law, have lost their jobs, have never had steady jobs, or have suffered other adjustment problems. These patients represent a new class, and a vast expansion numerically, of mental patients. Many are former social-work clients, now redefined as mental patients and forced to accept this classification if they want Social Security disability benefits or other social-work intervention. Many would not have sought help when psychiatric treatment was for mental and emotional disease but can accept it when it is pointed out to them that it is only for problems of living. They see adjustment as a right.

Other therapy services provided by the community center are related more to education, consciousness raising, sensitivity training, encounter experiences, or other forms of "pop psychology" than they are to serious therapy. Recently I found that someone had posted a sign advertising a community mental health center in the waiting room my patients use. It offered "assertiveness training, parent power, new beginnings for singles, Beyond Divorce, Relaxation Techniques, and other educational and personal growth experiences . . ."

The community mental health center is often accused of being ineffective. It fails to follow up many patients. But at the same time it is not innocucus, and it can extend great authority that can change lives. A social worker may suggest that parents file delinquency proceedings against their intransigent child, and an intrafamily quarrel may escalate into a matter of state interest. Social workers may advise that girls who are borderline mentally retarded and have a potential of growing up to be promiscuous be surgically sterilized.

For an example of the changes that can come about after a person becomes involved in the mental health care system, consider the case of Pauline Perez, a New York City woman with two children who decided she needed mental health help. She left her two children, Danny, aged seven and Marisal, aged six months, with a neighbor with whom she had shared baby-sitting chores. She went to the outpatient department of Bellevue Hospital, expecting to be back home that same day. Instead, it was decided to admit her, and she was in the hospital for six days. The neighbor could not continue to care for the children, and they were taken by the New York City Bureau of Child Welfare. Mrs. Perez refused to sign the form allowing the bureau to have custody, although she was assured that if she signed the form she could have the children back when she was out of the hospital. The bureau decided her signature was not needed and took custody.

When Mrs. Perez got out of the hospital she repeatedly demanded the return of her children, but she was not allowed to have them back. There was never a hearing to document the reasons for the refusal, and there was never a court order to give legality to the change of custody. The institution that had one of her children made a note in its record that the mother was "sweet" but "not mother material." The children were put into the more permanent foster care, instead of in temporary emergency placement, on the grounds of "mental illness of the person caring for the child," although there had never been any official proceeding to determine if the mother was mentally ill. After two years of efforts to get her children back, Mrs. Perez secured legal help; she filed a writ of habeas corpus petition to secure a ruling on the legality of her being deprived of her children. The bureau promptly initiated a proceeding charging Mrs. Perez with child neglect. The family court judge consolidated the two proceedings, dismissed the petition for the habeas corpus hearing, and found Mrs. Perez guilty of child neglect. Mrs. Perez appealed the decision. Three years later an appeals court reversed the finding of neglect because Mrs. Perez had not been allowed to present her side of the case in court, and it found that the removal and continued detention of the children was in violation of state law. But it still would not return the children, who had now been separated from their mother for six years, pending a new hearing on the question of whether Mrs. Perez had been guilty of neglect. In 1972 Mrs. Perez's attorney had also started a civil-rights action asking for money damages from two child-care institutions and four welfare workers. In 1976 Mrs. Perez died. A few months later her civil-rights action finally came to trial. The United States District Court for the Southern District of New York dismissed the case; this was appealed, with the grandmother of the children, Josephina Duchesne, as the plaintiff. In 1977 the United States Court of Appeals for the Second Circuit found that Mrs. Perez should not have had her children taken away from her, eight years after she had gone to Bellevue Hospital for help with her emotional problems, seven years after she had been judged to be "not mother material," and one year after her death.[24] Becoming involved with the mental health system can bring losses as well as gains.

*　　*　　*

Some politicians eagerly embraced the concept of the community mental health system as a means of providing adjustment or mental health to the electorate. In Georgia, Governor Jimmy Carter appointed a committee of four to plan for the future of mental health in his state, stressing the new approach. He appointed his wife, Rosalynn, as one of the members. (The others were two lawyers and a member of the Georgia State Senate.) The commission's entire staff was a twenty-two-year-old Harvard student (when he started work he was one month short of graduation), who also lacked mental health experience. He was the main author of the final report, which was produced in only five months. The philosophy of treatment developed in the report would affect the national mental health scene when Carter became president.

The report gave as reasons for an expanded mental health program a wide range of social factors, including decreased employment in the aircraft industry, the termination of the school lunch program, racial strife, and poor citizen-police relations. The commission also gave "personal examples" of the problems that made an expanded mental health program necessary: A family sees four to six outreach workers, each dealing with a different problem, all related to the lack of a job for the head of the family. The mother of a retarded child does not have a large enough welfare check to cover her food expenses, and the county does not have food stamps. A policeman is shot in the park. A liquor store charges five dollars to cash a welfare check. These were all given as examples of the kinds of problems with "emotional or mental components or which may lead to severe emotional distress" that demand community mental health attention.

The recommendation of the governor's commission was that "Georgia develop programs in the community that will solve the problems that citizens have." The recommendation was unequivocal: "Henceforth, no citizen should be told that an agency cannot help him. It is the responsibility of Georgia to help a citizen solve problems he cannot deal with alone . . . He should be told, 'We have you and your family to help; we stand ready to find some help for you; we will call the appropriate place and arrange for transportation for you to it; we will follow up to see that you do receive that help; if you have any difficulty in obtaining help, please call me . . . or come see me again.' "[25]

The resulting new mental health program, supervised by a new director of the Division of Mental Health, produced many changes and much upheaval, but the program did not in any way prove itself. The number of community centers was increased from one to fourteen. Hospitalizations were reduced to very short stays, patients were subjected to brief and repeated hospitalizations, many phases of the recommended program were never funded, and large numbers of former hospital patients went untended in the community. Without having ever proved itself, the program was nevertheless declared a success and an accomplishment of the administration.

When Carter became president, he appointed a similar commission on a much larger scale, with his wife as its head, to plan mental health strategy for the nation. The membership of the commission was planned to represent consumers of mental health services, and it comprised few experienced clinicians. The executive director, Thomas Bryant, a Georgian whose experience has been entirely in drugs and alcohol, was a doctor-lawyer who was not a psychiatrist.

Without waiting for her commission to make its recommendations and without regard to potential cost, Rosalynn Carter stated that she believed mental health care should be given full coverage under Medicare and Medicaid. "Mental illness is no different from other kinds of illnesses," she said. "It is very bad that mental illness is not included in those programs." (Not surprisingly, the commission's final recommendations followed this lead.)

Predictably, the commission report calls for government support for a great expansion of "mental health care." Like the previous plan for community mental health, it is both grandiose and simplistic. It starts out with the confession that the commission has not been able to come to terms with the definition of mental illness. Then it proceeds to include almost everyone under the classification of "mentally or emotionally ill" or in need of mental health services.[26] (According to the "Washington Report" in the *New England Journal of Medicine*, ". . . The curious fact is that, though the starting premise is that mental health in this nation is appreciably short of some desirable state, nowhere does the Commission favor us with a definition of its ultimate goal, though it offers many recommendations on how to get there."[27]

The president's commission greatly expanded the estimated number of the mentally ill. The report says that the established "popular" estimate that 10 percent of the population at one time needs psychiatric help is too low, and "new evidence" shows that the figure is nearer 15 percent, but that even this figure is too low because mental problems are underreported. Another 25 percent of the population suffers from mild to moderate depression, anxiety, and other symptoms of emotional disorder with which they cope outside of established mental health care; it is not specified how many of these people do need mental health help, but there is a suggestion that many of them do. Then there are 6 million retarded, 10 million with alcohol-related problems, an unspecified number with drug-related problems, plus learning-disability cases and those physically handicapped who also have emotional problems.[28] But even this huge aggregate, about one-half of the population, does not include all those who need help.

America's mental health problems cannot be defined only in terms of disabling mental illnesses and identified psychiatric disorders. This must include the damage to mental health associated with unrelenting poverty and unemployment and the institutionalized discrimination that occurs on the basis of race, sex, class, age, and mental or physical handicaps. They must also include conditions that involve emotional and psychological distress which do not fit in conventional categories of classification or service.

The answer to this massive problem is to develop more community services, utilizing and expanding the community care system and also providing other kinds of services not associated with centers. The report recommends that we "fulfill the national commitment to develop a network of accessible community mental health services." (It indicates that there has been serious criticism of the way already established centers function, but attributes this to excessive demand for services and inadequate funding. Not considered is the more basic question of whether this has been a good model for service delivery or whether what is being provided is "second-tier" diluted and deprofessionalized services—not the kind of care that even workers in these centers seek when they themselves have emotional or mental problems.)

The commission asks that the Department of Health, Education, and Welfare develop a plan for the continued phasing down and closing of large state mental hospitals, even though most of the once-large hospitals have shrunk to a very small size and there is much more criticism of uncared-for mental patients left to wander in the community or to cope in board-and-care homes than there is of mental patients unnecessarily hospitalized.

The commission recommends a further dilution of the old-fashioned concept of a therapist by advocating a new key mental health person, "the case manager." By maintaining a continued interest in cases and attempting to prevent too much discontinuity, the case manager will make up for the depersonalized and deprofessionalized care that is offered. A new administrative layer is added to the structure. One recommendation is that the National Institute of Mental Health fund programs not to train people but to develop programs on how to train people in case management.

One of the controversial and intrusive recommendations is that every child be given "a periodic, comprehensive, developmental assessment." This is a reflection of the recommendation in the 1971 state of Georgia commission report that before children would be allowed to start in school, they would be required to have completed testing and evaluation for emotional disturbance and mental illness (a measure similar to the one requiring proof that they have been immunized). This plan would make evaluation, including that of areas where test results are notably unreliable, an entrenched part of the educational process at a time when even intelligence testing has been criticized for being unreliable and harmful to many of those tested, who are afterward diverted to special programs that may hamper normal development.

Many of the proposals appear beneficent at first until the extent of their intrusiveness, their cost, their uncertain results, and the difficulties of administering them are considered. Many of the 117 recommendations in the report would undoubtedly lead to more intrusion of the government into the affairs of the individual.

The report does not deal with the major community center moral issue of the so-called supervision by psychiatrists and psychologists who do not actually supervise. Instead, it advocates an expansion of the supervision system so that more funds can be secured from insurance companies and other third-party payers, even if the treatment has no relationship to traditional medical or psychiatric treatment, and even if it is provided by personnel with little or no training: "In the case of care provided in organized settings or systems of care, reimbursement should be made to the system rather than to the practitioner providing the care. All covered services must be . . . rendered by, or be under the clinical supervision of a physician, psychologist, social worker, or nurse . . ."

Finally, the commission wants a program to change community attitudes toward the mentally ill. Few would argue in favor of discrimination against the mentally ill, but there remains the question of what kind of a public relations approach can change basic attitudes. At some points in its report the commission takes the position that mental problems are serious problems. At others it indicates that basically the mentally ill are the victims of misunderstanding and fear, which can respond to a "better quality of information available to the American people" and to representations of the mentally ill in the media that portray "the everyday lives and problems of people who struggle with a whole range of mental and emotional problems."

One of the claims for the innovations proposed by the president's commission is that they would be economical. The plan calls for government expenditures of only $650 million—over and above present expenditures—to be applied over a period of one year for some programs, three and five years for others.

The report achieves the appearance of relative "economy" by resorting to financial legerdemain. The cost of renewed programs for future years is often ignored, and a great effort is made to have mental health funded by many branches of the government, not just the Department of Health, Education, and Welfare, with funds from these new sources not included in the cost totals.

Two weeks after the report was issued, the Department of Housing and Urban Development announced an $18 million demonstration program to provide housing, at $18,000 per person, for 1000 mental patients. The director of Housing and Urban Development would also make rental assistance available for halfway houses. The recommendations are that HUD and other agencies would contribute unspecified amounts of money for mental health care. Social Security would increase its benefits to enable more people to live in group settings. Medicare and Medicaid benefits would be increased and ostensibly decreased government funding for community centers would thereby actually become a huge increase. Education funds would be tapped. New training programs are recommended, with no mention of the source of funding, but the Department of Labor would be expected to become a major source of health care funding. A new computer system for research is recommended, with no mention of cost. Legal advocacy systems to represent patients are to be provided in every state; no costs are given. The program, presented as a low-cost program, in reality would lead to a huge increase in mental health funding and a great expansion of mental health personnel. (According to Executive Director Bryant, the program is not meant to be a grandiose philosophical statement or a blueprint for long-range policy making, but rather a practical short-range guide to building upon the existing system.) The implementation of the program, which was to be the responsibility of Peter Bourne, the president's medical advisor, was taken up by Rosalynn Carter when Bourne was forced to resign after he was accused of writing an illegal prescription. Rosalynn Carter's influence led to recommendations for an increased mental health program during a period when many other health programs were being sharply curtailed.[29] A mental health newsletter headlines its story: "CMHCs Emerging in Strengthened Form from Budgetary Armageddon."[30]

*   *   *

More recently, it has appeared that many of the recommendations of the report will not be fully implemented; budgetary constraints felt in other fields have also begun to affect mental health. Some community centers have had budget decreases; others have not been funded on a scale to compensate for inflation.[31] But direct federal funding does not mirror true mental health expenditures, since funds come from many sources not formerly drawn on to support mental health. The Carter administration continues to press for expansion of mental health services.

How much does the community care system increase the authority of psychiatrists? It promulgates a policy of government responsibility for emotional well-being. It gives a government stamp and government funding to treatment methods that have not proved themselves or even become established. Most significant of all, it grafts psychiatry to social work and gives psychiatric authority to a host of new care providers.

In some ways the system is not very authoritarian. So many patients are lost between its cracks, and there is so little follow-up and so much disorganizaton, that the system only exercises its power intermittently and often irrationally. Some aspects of community care—particularly its use as an alternative to the criminal-justice system and the increasing practice of forcing outpatients to continue on their medication by injection of long-acting phenothiazines as a coerced alternative to hospitalization—represent the most effective kind of exercise of psychiatric authority. More than anything else, the new government care system and the acceptance of the idea that the government has a responsibility for the mental well-being of its citizens open every aspect of personal and family life to government interest, and in some cases government control. François Bondy has said, "The drive of the state to identify itself with the whole of society, and to be responsible for the happiness of all citizens, is a fearful trend . . ."[32] The all-encompassing concept of mental illness and mental health care turns everyone into a therapist or a patient, and everything into therapy. A state prevention coordinator of a Chemical Dependency Program Division writes not in alarm but matter-of-factly, not to warn against but to advocate, this kind of intrusion: ". . . An effective prevention program must affect the individual on all cognitive, affective, and behavioral levels and in all phases and settings of his/her life (school, church, job, friends, family, neighborhood, media and so forth). The prevention support program system offers this opportunity . . ."[33]

The commission's recommendations have been called by an experienced Washington observer "at least potentially, the most qualitatively and quantitatively significant breakthrough American mental health professionals have been able to score . . . at the rock-bottom materialistic level, an opportunity for expansion beyond our wildest recent dreams; at the moral and societal level, an opportunity to

140

'establish' mental health as a national value and goal" on a par with our interest in traditional medicine.[34]

Up to this point, the community mental health center is not so much a use or an abuse of psychiatry, although it has aspects of both, as it is a misuse. It diverts people from the opportunity of a meaningful kind of therapeutic experience—one where trust and hope are built up in an interpersonal relationship that later can be extended to a trust "not in a particular person, a particular relationship, a particular situation—but in life."[35] It directs them instead to a bureaucratic, impersonal system with a vastly widened scope, causing many people to fall into easy dependency. These are not drastic abuses, as in the cases of Ezra Pound or Roy Schuster, but the potential is great for future abuse as the system continues to grow and intrude itself into every variety of life activity.

Mental health has joined the ranks of a citizen's rights. Once it was maintained by the effort of the individual; now it is the responsibility of the state. A psychiatry that has never conceptualized its role and never entirely proven its usefulness, that according to its critics has harmed as many people as it has helped, or possibly more, and that has steadily increased its authority, developing powerful new methods to control behavior, with more developments in the process, now has the impetus of the government to advance it to new heights of control.

Two hundred years ago, psychiatry was a rudimentary specialty of medicine, dealing only with the most disordered mental states, affecting only a few people. It was ceded legal authority to make determinations of committability, criminal responsibility and competency to stand trial, and testamentary capacity. It developed the concept of the unconscious mind, and gained authority to tell what went on in its depths, and so became the interpreter of irrational behavior. It was given power to rehabilitate prisoners and to hold until "cured" certain offenders who were not clearly either criminals or mental patients but fell somewhere in between. It developed a range of methods to change behavior—verbal, chemical, electrical, and psychological. Now psychiatry has formed an alliance with social work and been granted huge infusions of government funding, and both psychiatric care and mental health have been accepted as rights. It exercises formidable, largely hidden powers over, and influence on, our society, and it promises to exercise even more in the future.

PART TWO

DILEMMAS OF
PSYCHIATRIC POWER

Who in the rainbow can draw the line where the violet tint ends and the orange tint begins? Distinctly we see the difference of the colors, but where exactly does the one first blendingly enter into the other? So with sanity and insanity. In pronounced cases there is no question about them. But in some supposed cases, in various degrees supposedly less pronounced, to draw the exact line of demarcation few will undertake, though for a fee becoming considerate some professional experts will. There is nothing namable but that some men will, or undertake to, do it for pay.

—HERMAN MELVILLE
Billy Budd, Sailor

The Problem of Defining Mental Illness

PSYCHIATRISTS ARE generally convinced that they act benignly and therapeutically and are genuinely puzzled when they are accused of being overly authoritarian. They do not see that some criticisms of psychiatry are meaningful and worthy of serious consideration. They spend very little time and effort to try to understand their critics and are not open to the suggestion that they pay serious attention to the source and extent of their power.

Psychiatrists can comfortably maintain this position as long as they are convinced that mental illness is a disease, that they have a special skill at diagnosing mentally ill people, and that they have effective treatment methods. But particularly since the beginning of the 1960s when major works of Erving Goffman and Thomas Szasz used sociological and psychiatric perspectives to question psychiatric assumptions, many critics have said that these assumptions are either incorrect or unprovable.

The most devastating attack that can be made on psychiatry is that there is no such thing as mental disease, that we label as mentally ill those in our society who make us feel anxious or uncomfortable, social deviants—those who are out of step. Another kind of criticism concedes that mental illness represents a truly pathological process but claims it is a reparative, not a disintegrative, process, or that if it is disintegrative, this is in the interest of eventual repair. According to this view, when psychiatrists try to stamp out mental illness by attacking its symptoms, they are interfering with the potential for growth.

A more influential critique of psychiatry concedes that there is such a thing as mental illness but says our diagnostic classification scheme is inadequate and that psychiatrists do a poor job in deciding who is mentally ill and in what classification of mental illness they should be placed. This position would allow psychiatrists authority when they

145

can prove their credibility, but finds them often not credible. A similar attack has to do not with diagnosis but prognosis. It points out that psychiatrists derive much of their authority from the accepted belief that they can predict future behavior and correctly assess who needs to be hospitalized. Many sociologists and lawyers have attacked the legitimacy of such predictions of future behavior, and particularly of the predictions of dangerousness that psychiatrists make to justify commitment and the continued holding of patients.

A less devastating criticism of psychiatry finds it credible, but that its interventions are often more harmful than helping. It emphasizes the detrimental uses to which even correct diagnoses can be put and says that psychiatric diagnoses may be accurate, but the act of diagnosing places a person in an inferior position and threatens his job security, family relationships, and self-concept. The labeling can become a self-fulfilling prophecy: Predicting school failure leads to school failure. Often the labeling accomplishes no real benefit; the "patient" could have been given as much help without a specific diagnosis.

Psychoanalytic psychiatrists, much more than nondynamic psychiatrists, are willing to refrain from diagnosing. They see the therapeutic process as a continuing exploration in which a patient at times may be in touch with very irrational feelings and thoughts and even appear psychotic, but at other times may reveal important strengths and ability to cooperate in the therapeutic process. Calling a patient by some label such as "schizophrenic" or "hysterical" or "borderline" does not do justice either to the complexity of human thought and emotion or the potential of the patient for change. One psychoanalyst has said that in analysis the diagnosis cannot be made until the final session. (Insurance companies and other third-party reimbursers for psychiatric treatment demand a diagnosis, but psychiatrists always have the option of placing a fairly innocuous label on a patient, such as "anxiety reaction" or "adjustment reaction," if they do not know the diagnosis or want to protect the patient by obscuring it.) Nondynamic psychiatrists are horrified by the thought of working with unlabeled patients, for they rely largely on drugs, and the right prescription depends on a proper diagnosis. Forensic psychiatrists need labels to inform the courts.

Psychiatrists have not responded to the barrage of attacks. They generally see themselves as useful, and indeed as indispensable, in the age-old struggle of reason against irrationality. They have not given deep thought to these criticisms. Lawyers have dealt more seriously with the problem of conceptualizing and defining mental disease. Since important legal consequences flow from psychiatric determinations and predictions—including personal freedom and answerability to the law—lawyers want psychiatrists either to be precise or to be less accepted as diagnosticians and predictors. Lawyers are nonplussed by the inconsistency of psychiatrists, who change their minds on diagnoses, give multiple diagnoses, and disagree with each other.

When a a judge or lawyer tries to pin psychiatrists down on the definition of mental illness, he finds he has entered the labyrinth. The official glossary of the American Psychiatric Association, published in 1973,[1] has no definition of mental disease or mental illness, and it has only the most amorphous kind of definition of mental health. If you look up "mental illness" or "mental disease," you will be referred in each case to "mental disorder," but mental disorder is not defined. Instead there is a declaration that a mental disorder is anything that is included as a mental disorder in classification schemes of the World Health Organization and the American Psychiatric Association. And the APA has admitted that both its own scheme and the WHO scheme are unsatisfactory. (The APA recently approved a new classification manual.) "Psychiatrist" is unsatisfactorily defined in the glossary as a licensed physician who specializes in the diagnosis, treatment, and prevention of mental and emotional disorders and whose training generally, but not invariably, includes three or more years of approved residency after a medical degree. The glossary's definition of "mental health" is equally vague: It is a "relative rather than absolute" state in which a person has achieved "a reasonably satisfactory integration of his instinctual drives."

In 1973, the same year that the glossary containing these nondefining definitions was published, the APA moved to appoint a task force to define officially the terms "mental illness" and "psychiatrist." Six years later the speaker of the APA declared that the question "What is a psychiatrist?" still remained unanswered. President Carter's Commission on Mental Health held public hearings across the country and had the assistance of "hundreds of individuals who comprised special fact-finding panels" that included, according to the commission, "the Nation's foremost mental health authorities," but it was not able to come up with a definition of mental health. It finally concluded that "opinions vary on how mental health and mental illness should be defined" and that "the available data" of the incidence of mental illness "are often inadequate or misleading." It also concluded that, in the absence of a good definition of mental illness, it could adopt its own expanded definition and that a definition must include the effects of poverty, unemployment, and discrimination.[2]

Faced with the task of defining mental illness, many psychiatrists and community mental health care advocates have concluded that all mental pain signifies mental illness. So for certain purposes—particularly to secure authority over the patient or to have his treatment covered by a reimbursement plan—almost any condition can be considered a mental disease. Sometimes the patient resists being labeled. Paradoxically, patients whom doctors see as "very sick"—psychotic patients—often deny illness, and patients who seem much less, or not at all, "sick"—neurotics—often welcome the designation of illness.

Another problem is that mental illness is usually attributed on the basis of behavior, whereas most other medical conditions are concerned with pathological physiological processes and are diagnosed by physical signs or abnormal laboratory results.

There is no doubt that some psychiatric conditions are organic and are truly medical. Other psychiatric conditions that are not assuredly organic, which have no clearly defined physiological cause (although they may be accompanied by a number of biochemical and hormonal aberrations), may have symptoms that resemble those of organic patients and may require the same kind of protective and supportive care. Because some psychiatric conditions almost assuredly belong to medicine, do all psychiatric conditions belong to medicine? The problem of the interrelationship of the mind and the body has always defied acceptable solutions. If strange thoughts and behavior are the results of altered body physiology, then we should not blame the people who exhibit this altered behavior (except possibly for those, like drinking drivers, who may be responsible for getting themselves into such a state). The early nineteenth-century leaders of psychiatry, men such as Phillipe Pinel and Isaac Ray, saw mentally abnormal behavior as symptoms of a disease—just as a runny nose is the symptom of a cold—and therefore saw psychiatrists as supremely qualified to tell who should be excused for his actions because he was diseased and who should be held responsible.

Eventually a number of psychiatric conditions were discovered to be truly medical—the result of syphilis and other neurological degeneration, hormonal imbalance, as in thyrotoxicosis, or malnutrition and vitamin deficiency, as in pellagra. Many psychiatrists had the hope that all mental illness would eventually be found to have a physical cause. As the definition of the mentally ill was broadened to include people formerly classified as criminal or immoral—pedophiles, exhibitionists, kleptomaniacs—it became more difficult to claim that all these people were physically ill. With Freud's contribution of the concept of the unconscious mind, psychiatrists were able to extend freedom from responsibility to this additional population. Even if the cause was psychological, it was outside of consciousness and not capable of being controlled. More recently, psychological causation has given ground to physiological theories. Genetic factors have been given a larger part in the predisposition to schizophrenia and other psychiatric disorders, and the remarkable effect of lithium on manic-depressive psychosis has given renewed credence to a physiological etiological theory. Alcoholism and addiction have been divested in part from the criminal-justice process and given the designation of illnesses.

A philosopher and biomedical ethicist, Robert Neville, points out that how we conceptualize the mind-body problem determines how far we are willing to try to change behavior by such somatic methods as drugs and psychosurgery. He says, "Because we need to establish moral limits and rationales for such interventions, there is an immediate practical problem now of understanding the relation between mental and physical functions."[3]

In trying to emphasize their affiliation with medicine, psychiatrists stress the body aspect of the body-mind dichotomy. They are fearful of the trend away from medicine in psychiatry that allows nonphysicians to deal with patients on an equal basis with physicians, and would prevent psychiatric services from being covered by medical insurance. (Huge amounts of money are available for psychiatric treatment when it is furnished under the sponsorship of a physician, but with the exception of the community mental health center system and school counseling programs, there is little money available for identical services provided by a nonphysician.)

There is no agreement on how medical psychiatry should be. The more medical we consider it, the more authority is exercised by psychiatrists. The more psychological we consider it, the less authority there is, and this authority must be shared with psychologists, psychiatric social workers, and counselors.

The medical identification is disputed by anthropologists, who assert that much of mental illness is defined culturally and behavior that is within normal limits in some societies at certain times is outside normality when seen in a different context. From the anthropological point of view, cure is hard to assess. In psychotherapy we often do not know if we have cured the patient (or, better phrased, have helped the patient to attain a cure) or merely taught him conformity.

Thomas Hackett, chief of psychiatry at Massachusetts General Hospital, has recalled regretfully how psychiatrists there stopped carrying stethoscopes in 1945, stopped wearing white coats around 1950, and stopped going to medical grand rounds in 1955. Says Dr. Hackett, "I predict that psychiatrists, should they continue winging their way through the heady atmosphere of nonmedical conceptual and therapeutic models, will soon find themselves an endangered species."[4] On the other hand, Gerald Grob, an intellectual historian, in *The State and the Mentally Ill,* published in 1966, wrote that the continued identification of psychiatry with medical science has exerted a profound negative effect on the mental hospital, leading to the assumption that nothing could be done because the cause of the illness still awaited discovery, and thus discouraging psychological and other nonsomatic approaches.[5]

Because mental disease is so vaguely defined, political considerations such as available funding can alter diagnoses. Most people, if they live long enough, develop some measure of organic brain disease—there are changes in the structure of the brain and a decreased supply of blood. Formerly many of these people were diagnosed as organically mentally ill, as having a chronic brain syndrome associated with senile brain disease or arteriosclerosis, and sent to the back wards of mental hospitals. Now they are diagnosed as not mentally ill and sent to nursing homes, where their care is not necessarily better than state hospital care, but where the money spent on it can go to private partnerships and corporations. The decision to see these people, and many others, as mentally ill or not so is entirely arbitrary, related not to the patient but to political and economic factors.

In spite of the fact that it is so difficult to define mental illness, psychiatrists characteristically say that they know it when they see it. What they mean is that some psychotic people are so tense and anxious, so irrational, so out of control or apparently close to being out of control, or so provoking of fear or anxiety in the evaluator, that there can be general agreement, even without hard medical factual data, that they are abnormal or need help. Most hallucinating, severely delusional, unceasingly active, or seriously apathetic patients seem so different and so troubled that there can be a societal consensus to call them sick.

The Szaszian denial of the reality of mental illness represents an effective method of guarding civil liberties, but it requires us to allow suicidal people to do away with themselves without our labeling and intervention, and it permits deranged patients to come into the hospital only when they see the need and desirability of their own hospitalization and will enter voluntarily. Society is not ready to go this far in the name of a nonmedical, nonpaternalistic, civil-liberties-oriented psychiatry. Laing's concept of mental breakdown as part of a reparative process receives more serious attention and has more potential for helping to build a less authoritarian psychiatry. There is much truth in his position that we perhaps do a good deal of harm to many patients by showing our fear of their thoughts and forcing them to repress them rather than by accepting their primitive emotions and reactions and working with them, but the associated Laingian concept that patients involved in a reparative process must be treated as if they are competent adults is not acceptable to many therapists.

Most of us can see that many ascriptions of psychiatric illness are culture-bound, and if we can use our imaginations to go beyond our culture, we will then see that some people that have been considered sick are well. The opposite may also be true: Some people we see as successful—for example, certain politicians, business tycoons, or movie and rock stars—may be so obsessional, driving, and self-occupied that they might easily be seen from the view of different cultures as mentally ill. Other successes in our society might be seen as mentally ill because they lack conscience and remorse and human feelings. Although I doubt the legitimacy of the psychiatric diagnosis of sociopath, I do not doubt that many successful people, including some of the most successful, could fit into this category just as easily as many of the apprehended, less successful corner-cutters who now carry the label. Hitler and Nixon are obvious examples of people who went to inordinate lengths to get and hold power, but if we label them as mentally ill we find that many other leaders also deserve to be in the same category, and the designation "mentally ill" rapidly becomes meaningless.

Because mental illness has had such flexible boundaries, it has been used, as Szasz has pointed out, to bootleg humanistic values into our legal system and into our social structure.[6] We have such a flexible concept of disease that it is easy for psychiatrists in their role of excuse-giver to secure special treatment for patients. The battle to determine the correct rule of criminal responsibility was not so much an effort to make the test more scientific as an effort to broaden the rule to allow more people to escape the consequences of their actions. When society decided to deal more kindly with alcoholics and addicts, it did this by redefining public drunkenness as a disease symptom, and chronic alcoholism and drug addiction as sickness.

Much of what goes on in this process of redefining socially deviant activities as psychiatric is for strategic rather than scientific reasons. Public drunkenness, chronic alcoholism, and drug addiction were labeled as disease symptoms, as was homosexuality, in order to help the people charged with these offenses escape criminal punishment. Physicians and behavioral scientists publicly campaigned for a more humane approach to these and other conditions "in the name of mental health." When the battle was won—when public sympathy finally favored the alcoholic or homosexual, when the social deviancy had been accepted as related to illness rather than as antisocial—then the strategy took a turn: The deviant had escaped criminal penalty but now was faced with the possibility of coerced psychiatric treatment. This could easily lead to hospitalization for a longer period than a prison sentence. The effort of the protectors of these people then was directed toward narrowing the boundaries of the definition of mental illness to exclude these conditions so they would not be considered either criminal or sick, much to the surprise of the psychiatrists who had been persuaded to give them the sickness label.

In the years after Judge David Bazelon had promulgated his new rule of criminal responsibility, the *Durham* rule, which was designed to give more evidentiary weight to psychiatric testimony, he concluded that the psychiatrists were not giving the courts the answers he had expected from them. Bazelon said, "We assumed that the expert could separate the medical judgments which he was supposed to make from the legal and moral judgments which he was not supposed to make. It has become abundantly clear that this theory has not worked out. Too often conclusory labels—both medical and legal— have substituted, albeit unwittingly, for the facts and analysis which underlie them . . ."[7]

Bazelon gave an example of the freedom of psychiatrists to testify as they desired, without regard to any scientific principles. The case, from another jurisdiction, was unreported (that is, it does not appear in official volumes of court decisions). It is the kind of case that rarely comes to public notice.

An air force enlisted man was accused of murder. He was examined by a psychiatrist, who concluded in his report that he was not criminally responsible and deserved to be acquitted on the ground of insanity. Before the court martial, however, the psychiatrist became concerned about his duty to society. (There was also some testimony that indicated he might have been concerned about his military advancement. His superior officers were anxious to obtain a verdict against the defendant.) He decided that if the defendant was found not guilty by reason of insanity and sent to a mental hospital, it was possible that he would soon appear sane to the hospital staff and would then be released prematurely and would kill again. The psychiatrist therefore testified, without giving the basis for his change of opinion, that the defendant was responsible for his criminal act. The defendant was found guilty and sentenced. Ten years later the prisoner successfully petitioned for a habeas corpus proceeding to review the appropriateness of his conviction. At the proceeding the psychiatrist was questioned on his change of opinion. He admitted that he had tailored his testimony to achieve a desirable social end. The court criticized the psychiatrist for his reliance on "socio-moral considerations of his own devising" and the sentence was set aside.[8] If the psychiatrist had not changed his opinion, if he had from the start seen the defendant as responsible, relying on the same "socio-moral considerations of his own devising," there would have been no basis to challenge his testimony.

Such free-wheeling psychiatric testimony is probably not unusual, but we have no way of knowing this, for there is no way of evaluating psychiatric testimony to determine its basis in fact.

Civil as well as criminal court cases deal with the definition of mental illness. Often large reimbursement sums for treatment, disability payments, or damage awards depend on a finding of a mental disease. One whole field of personal-injury law, the law of traumatic neurosis, depends on psychiatric testimony that a medical disease has resulted from some accident or injury. If the injured person is merely passingly anxious or upset, there is little prospect of recovering damages, but if a psychiatrist can testify that as the result of the accident or injury a "traumatic neurosis" has resulted, the award can be very large.

When one of two young girls jogging along a road in Bismarck, North Dakota, was killed by an auto, the other girl sued the driver. Though not physically injured, she claimed the shock had induced continuing nightmares and a personality change. A psychiatrist testified she needed therapy, and the jury awarded $26,000.[9]

A twenty-nine-year-old woman who claimed a cable car accident in San Francisco caused her to become a nymphomaniac was awarded $50,000 in damages by a California state court. A psychiatrist testified that although she sustained only bruises, the crash had triggered a reaction to a traumatic sex experience in childhood, resulting in nymphomania. According to newspaper reports, psychological injury from the accident, which had occurred six years earlier, led her to have sexual intercourse with 100 men in the most recent year.[10]

Mary Alice Firestone, divorced wife of millionaire Russell A. Firestone, Jr., was awarded $100,000 in compensatory damages for an article published in *Time* magazine. A six-member jury in Palm Beach, Florida, ordered *Time* to pay after hearings in circuit court. The final judgment stemmed from Mrs. Firestone's charge that she suffered mental anguish because of a story concerning her divorce from Firestone, heir to the Firestone rubber fortune.[11]

Mrs. Mary Pugliese, thirty-four, drove to a resort in the Cuyamaca Mountains near San Diego, California, to relax. Instead, without warning, she found herself in the middle of a pitched mock battle between opposing teams of U.S. Navy commandos in full combat gear. One group, apparently thinking they had given the others the slip, sneaked into the small resort area, stacked their rifles, and began playing pool in the lodge. As Mrs. Pugliese and her ten-year-old daughter, Mary, entered the lodge to rent a room, the opposing assault team charged into the establishment, blasting the enemy at short range. Shots were fired at point-blank range and people were running around with their hands up, yelling and screaming. Because of the experience Mrs. Pugliese suffered "severe anguish and shock," according to psychiatric testimony. Judge William Murray awarded Mrs. Pugliese $57,754 in damages, part of which was to pay for continuing psychiatric treatment.[12]

The Supreme Court, which has tried, for the most part successfully, to avoid mental health cases (there are less than ten significant Supreme Court decisions on mental health, in contrast to thousands on corporation law, banking, insurance, and other aspects of business life), has been forced to become involved in the question of the definition of mental disease in cases dealing with drug addiction and alcoholism. If these conditions represent mental disease, their symptoms should not be considered criminal activity. If they are not medical conditions, the symptoms can be criminally prosecuted. In 1962 the Court ruled in *Robinson* v. *California*[13] that the Eighth Amendment prohibition against cruel and unusual punishment prevented the imposition of any criminal sentence on a California man who had been charged under a statute that made it a misdemeanor to be addicted to the use of narcotics. (This was not a statute dealing with possession or sale, but with the status of drug addicts.) Lawrence Robinson was arrested when a policeman noticed scar tissue, needle marks, and a scab on his arms. Under questioning he admitted to the use of narcotics, but not within the previous eight days. Tests did not reveal drugs in his body; he had no withdrawal symptoms in jail. He was convicted as a drug addict under the statute. On appeal, the Supreme Court reversed the conviction, ruling that states can regulate drug traffic under their police power, but they cannot make it a criminal offense to be addicted to the use of narcotics. The reason for this, according to the Court, was that the status of addict was the symptom of the disease of drug addiction, and any punishment for a symptom of a disease would be a violation of the Eighth Amendment prohibition against cruel and unusual punishment. But the Court noted that psychiatrists have great power to deal with such conditions as if they were illnesses.

> It is unlikely that any State at this moment in history would attempt to make it a criminal offense for a person to be mentally ill, or a leper, or to be afflicted with a venereal disease. A State might determine that the general health and welfare require that the victims of these and other human afflictions be dealt with by compulsory treatment, involving quarantine, confinement, or sequestration. But in the light of contemporary human knowledge, a law which made a criminal offense of such a disease would doubtless be universally thought to be an infliction of cruel and unusual punishment . . . Even one day in prison would be a cruel and unusual punishment for the "crime" of having a common cold.

Justice Douglas, in a concurring opinion, noted that addiction can be present at birth, or it can be innocently acquired from medical prescriptions. He quoted the American Medical Association's Council of Mental Health: Criminal sentences for addicts interfered "with the possible treatment and rehabilitation of addicts and therefore should be abolished." Justice Douglas recommended a civil commitment rather than a criminal punishment for addiction, with words that should cause terror in addicts, civil-liberties-minded lawyers, and those who, like Thomas Szasz, Ronald Leifer, and Nicholas Kittrie, have been concerned that our emphasis on coerced therapy and our enlarging definition of mental disease can lead to the therapeutic state. Said Douglas: "The addict is a sick person. He may, of course, be confined for treatment or for the protection of society. Cruel and unusual punishment results not from confinement but from convicting the addict of a crime. . . . A prosecution for addiction, with its resulting stigma and irreparable damage to the good name of the accused, cannot be justified as a means of protecting society, where a civil commitment would do as well."

The literature on the subject is confusing, and many people would not characterize the initial stages of addiction, only the later physiologically dependent or organically deteriorated stages, as a medical condition. When the Court said that drug addiction was a disease, there was some thought that it might drop the other shoe and say that if addiction was a disease, then the compulsion of an addict to buy drugs or use drugs or sell drugs or make money illegally to pay for his drugs was also the symptom of a disease and equally exempt from criminal prosecution. Of course the Court never has taken that step, although it is hard to see the jurisprudential (in contrast to the pragmatic) reason for dealing with the addiction as a medical condition and the acts of addicts as criminal deviations. A major question raised by *Robinson* was whether the decision applied to other "status" crimes where the doer presumably is unable to control himself, such as child battering, indecent exposure, prostitution, pedophilia, and public solicitation for homosexuality. In particular, the suggestion was made that if the status of addiction was a disease, then the status of chronic alcoholism was equally a disease and symptoms like public drunkenness or creating a public nuisance should no longer be considered criminal. The Supreme Court attempted to settle this question six years later but the 5-4 decision, with Justice White acting as the swing vote, seemed both to declare alcoholism a disease and also say that the acts of alcoholics should not be exempt from criminal penalties.[14] Leroy Powell, a shoeshine "boy" of mature years, had over 100 arrests for public drunkenness, most of them in Austin, Texas. In December 1966 he was arrested again and fined $20. The Texas statute under which he was arrested provided only for a fine not to exceed $100 for public drunkenness, but convicted defendants who could not pay their fines—and Powell was often in this situation—were imprisoned and paid their debt to society at the statutory rate of one day in jail for every $5 of the fine that was not paid. He appealed and was given a new trial in the county court. His counsel argued that appellant was "afflicted with the disease of chronic alcoholism" and that "his appearance in public" while drunk was "not of his own volition." It was a symptom of a disease, and punishing Powell as if the symptoms of a disease were a crime would be a cruel and unusual punishment and unconstitutional. His principal witness was a psychiatrist who testified that there was debate in medicine about whether alcohol was physically addicting or merely psychologically habituating, but in any case by the time someone became a chronic alcoholic he was an "involuntary drinker" who was "powerless not to drink." The judge ruled that as a matter of fact chronic alcoholism was a disease that destroys the will to resist alcohol, that a chronic alcoholic does not appear drunk in public by his own volition but under a compulsion that is a symptom of the disease, and that Powell was "a chronic alcoholic who is afflicted with the disease of chronic alcoholism." After finding all these facts in Powell's favor, the judge went ahead and found him guilty as a result of a conclusion of law that the fact that a person "is a chronic alcoholic afflicted with the disease of chronic alcoholism" is not a legal defense to the charge of public drunkenness. He raised the fine to $50.

The case was appealed to the United States Supreme Court. Four members of the Supreme Court would have overturned Powell's conviction on the ground that Powell's offense was a symptom of the disease of chronic alcoholism and a "person may not be punished if the condition essential to constitute the defined crime is part of the pattern of his disease and is occasioned by a compulsion symptomatic of the disease." This more "liberal" four-man bloc was headed by the same Abe Fortas who as a lawyer had defended Monte Durham and, with the help of Judge Bazelon, devised and secured a greatly expanded definition of mental illness. Four other members of the Court, including Chief Justice Earl Warren, took a more "conservative" view and held that there was not enough knowledge about alcoholism and not enough evidence in the record to come to the conclusion that alcoholism is a disease or that Powell was suffering from it.

This conservative four-man bloc also pointed out that there is no agreement among doctors and social workers concerning a large-scale treatment approach to the problem of drinking.

> It would be tragic to return large numbers of helpless, sometimes dangerous and frequently unsanitary inebriates to the streets of our cities without even the opportunity to sober up adequately which a brief jail term provides. Presumably no State or city will tolerate such a state of affairs. Yet the medical profession cannot, and does not, tell us with any assurance that, even if the buildings, equipment and trained personnel were made available, it could provide anything more than slightly higher class jails for our indigent habitual inebriates. Thus we run the grave risk that nothing will be accomplished beyond the hanging of a new sign—reading "hospital"— over one wing of the jailhouse.
>
> One virtue of the criminal process is, at least, that the duration of penal incarceration typically has some outside statutory limit; this is universally true in the case of petty offenses, such as public drunkenness, where jail terms are quite short on the whole. "Therapeutic civil commitment" lacks this feature; one is typically committed until one is "cured."

The vote of Justice White was the swing vote that determined whether alcoholism was a disease and whether Powell should be punished. White voted with the liberal bloc that alcoholism was a disease, and so by a 5-4 vote the Supreme Court found alcoholism a disease. White also voted with the conservative bloc that the conviction should be affirmed, on the ground that even if it was a disease, it is the kind of disease that only compels homeless people, not married men with homes and families, to be drunk in public. For these destitute alcoholics for whom the public streets are home, said White, there is no other place for them to go and no place else for them to be when they are drinking and they must drink *somewhere*. He would find that for these alcoholics public drunkenness was a symptom of disease and not a crime. But Powell had not been shown to fit into this category.

The decision did not clarify the relationship of disordered behavior to mental disease, and the Supreme Court in the intervening years has not again tackled the question of defining mental illness. The debate still rages as to whether alcoholism is a disease. Certainly when people have been drinking for a long enough time to damage their liver, alter their enzymatic patterns, kill off brain cells, and damage nerve conduction, they have a disease that has resulted from alcoholism. But is alcoholism alone, without major physiological changes, a disease? The American Medical Association and the American Psychiatric Association insist that it is, but they admit that part of their desire to include alcoholism in the disease category is to see that doctors deal with the problem seriously. By that criterion, marital infidelity or antisocial attitudes could also be classified as diseases. Alcoholics Anonymous insists that alcoholism is a disease. Its belief is that alcoholics are genetically different from other people and have a different reaction to alcohol. The proposition is very helpful in keeping many alcoholics abstinent, but it is not scientific. Thomas Dawber of the Boston University School of Medicine has argued against the approach that calls alcoholism a disease. "The hypothesis has received wide acceptance, possibly because of its constant repetition in print and on radio and television. This attitude persists in spite of numerous studies that find no differences in the handling of alcohol by so-called alcoholics as compared to those not so classed."[15]

Psychiatrists have called many other behavioral manifestations symptoms of disease. Homosexuality until recently was classified as a psychiatric disease. Researchers have found that prostitutes who were encouraged to give up their trade and were given vocational retraining in four out of five cases soon were "addictively" drawn back into prostitution by such psychological factors as the need for excitement, courtship with danger, and the chance to outwit a client or the law. These researchers concluded that prostitution was "not an option, but . . . an addiction."[16] Juvenile delinquency has frequently also been called a disease.

Freud did not see most of his patients as suffering from diseases in the strict medical sense of the word. He saw them merely as suffering from arrests in the process of sexual adjustment. Jung saw much more disturbed psychotics as struggling with normal "complexes" that the "normal" individual had been able to master.[17] These conceptions of psychiatric conditions as developmental lags are far from the disease theory. Harry Stack Sullivan saw what we call mental illnesses as disorders of the "process of living."

The legal system essentially looks to psychiatrists to define disease and accepts as disease what psychiatrists say is such (although courts have pointed out that for some legal purposes there is a distinction between legal and medical disease definitions, and, for example, it has been common in law to have someone medically diagnosed as psychotic but ruled legally sane for a specific purpose, such as criminal responsibility or testamentary capacity). Psychiatrists have not been able to come to terms with the disease concept, but the legal system and society remain largely unaware of the difference between the use of that concept in psychiatry and in the rest of medicine, and the disease concept of mental illness and the medical model continue to prevail. Psychiatrists have a large stake in maintaining the disease concept of mental disorder. If psychiatrists conceded that these cases represent emotional and social maladjustment that cause pain and disability but fall short of disease, they would not have medical authority, their decisions would be open to more questioning, their treatment would not qualify for insurance reimbursement, and it would be obvious that legal safeguards to protect patients from excessive authority were essential.

A few psychiatrists want the disease concept narrowed so that only the organic and the most serious of functional conditions are characterized as diseases, and psychiatry can therefore assert its identification with medicine. Other psychiatrists, particularly if they advocate the community mental health center approach, want to see the definition of disease stretched to the utmost. Except when antipsychiatrists and the civil-liberties-minded attack psychiatric authority and psychiatrists unite to defend it, psychiatrists do not agree on the scope of the definition of mental illness and the proper role for psychiatrists.

Almost all psychiatrists see psychoses, whether caused by organic conditions or with no apparent organic causation, as true diseases. There is no agreement, however, on whether a formerly psychotic patient continues to be a sick person.

Psychiatrists are not generally agreed on whether character and personality disorders, transient situational disorders, psychoneurotic disorders and subclassifications of some of these categories (including sociopathic personality, alcoholism, drug addiction, and sexual deviation) are really diseases. They generally wish to see them included as diseases for purposes of health insurance and third-party payment of reimbursement for care, but many psychiatrists admit that these are far from the model of traditional medical diseases. Many conditions that they treat—marital disharmony, school and job maladjustment, inadequacy in job performance, and other "symptoms" that send people to consult a psychiatrist or to get help from a mental health center

—are not diseases in any sense except that they qualify for medical reimbursement.

The dispute about what constitutes disease spreads into other areas of government. Questions of disability for payment of Social Security and veterans benefits depend on the definition of disease. The Internal Revenue Service rules that alcoholism is a disease, and people hospitalized for it are entitled to a sick-pay exclusion when they file their returns.[18] The Department of Health, Education, and Welfare, in response to a congressional bill, spent years devising regulations to protect the handicapped against discrimination. The final regulations prevent recipients of federal funds from discriminating against "qualified handicapped persons" in employment and the operation of programs and activities. The definition of a handicapped person is one who "has a physical or mental impairment" that substantially limits one or more major life activity, or one who has a record of such an impairment, or who is regarded as having an impairment.[19] Are alcoholics handicapped? Are addicts? Are homosexuals? The regulations include alcoholics and addicts as handicapped and to be protected from discrimination, but not homosexuals. Secretary of Health, Education, and Welfare Joseph Califano issued a clarifying statement to allow those handicapped alcoholics and addicts whose disabilities interfere with their job performance to be separated from their jobs, and to clarify that the protection against discrimination only applies to alcoholics and addicts who are not so handicapped that their work performance is affected in any way.[20] The protection for alcoholics and addicts thus becomes meaningless (assuming it ever had meaning), because job performance can always be given as the rationale for job loss. ("We didn't fire him because he was an alcoholic but because his work is not up to standard.") The job protection for mental patients becomes equally meaningless, since to prove that they are entitled to their jobs, the "mentally ill" must show that they have or have had a major physical or mental impairment and must also rebut the testimony that their mental state affects job performance.

Psychiatry continues to wrestle with the problem of disease. Articles constantly appear with such titles as "Is Alcoholism Really a Disease?"[21] and "Is Homosexuality an Illness?"[22] A psychoanalyst writes an article, "All Dis-Ease Is Not Disease."[23] Szasz entitles an article, "Bad Habits Are Not Diseases."[24] A Yale psychiatrist writes that treating alcoholism as an illness only convinces the alcoholic he cannot be treated, and that only when medicine recognizes that it is not an illness will it become more effective in treating alcoholics.[25]

Challenged to support the position that mental illness is really illness, psychiatrists have recently been redefining health not as an absolute but as a range. A psychiatrist on a television program explains the growing acceptance of indefinite standards of disease in a rationale of the American Psychiatric Association's decision to delist homosexuality as a disease. "If 90 percent of the people have cavities you can say it is normal to have cavities. Or you may say that perfect health is what is normal and any deviation from it is illness. Either position is wrong. The American Psychiatric Association says that health is a range. For people to be labeled mentally abnormal, they should be out of the range and they should have subjective distress."[26] The "subjective distress" qualification is new to psychiatry. The traditional view is that people who lack subjective distress in situations where distress might be expected are ill.

The concept of mental disease remains vague, but the pragmatics of social functioning dictate that psychiatrists will continue to deal with people as if they are diseased whether or not the disease concept makes good sense. People need help and control. Psychiatrists are appointed by society to give this help and control, and they will call any condition a disease that will enable them to go about their business most efficiently. If in the process psychiatrists enjoy medical authority that should not really belong to them, the issue is so complex and the need for psychiatrists to function so great that mental illness is accepted as an illness in spite of its differences from other illnesses.

Psychiatrists are forced to exert authority because some people in society run out of control and demand that authority be imposed upon them. But psychiatrists should keep in mind that they are not truly medical; at most they are "medico-social." Since psychiatry has never been able to define mental disease, the medical basis for psychiatric authority must continue to be questioned, and psychiatric decisions that rely on medical authority must always be scrutinized.

Problems of Diagnosing Mental Illness

WHETHER OR NOT mental illness is really illness, we by convention treat it as a medical condition because this allows us to deal with it in an authoritarian fashion. When someone threatens suicide, or manifests frightening behavior, or has parted company with reality, we need to have the power to isolate him, and we gain this power by declaring him mentally ill and in need of care. The potential suicide may have motives for doing away with himself that would make good sense to anyone; at any rate he has reasons that make sense to himself. The frightening behavior of the psychotic may be a manifestation of our anxiety rather than the need of the patient to be hospitalized to protect himself or others. The hostile, out-of-control, threatening person may or may not turn out to be a danger. In all these situations, we are uncomfortable enough to assume that the person needs to be controlled, and we use the label of mentally ill to justify the imposition of control.

In Brian Clark's play *Whose Life Is It Anyway?* a paralyzed automobile accident victim asks for withdrawal of life-prolonging medical devices and then goes to the law to force it. This causes the doctor, who has saved his life, to decide to tranquilize him and to call in a psychiatrist. The wish to die is seen as a symptom of insanity. Antidepressants are the medical answer to the problem of the patient's loss of the will to live. The point of view of the patient is very different. He says, "I'd be insane if I weren't depressed."[1]

We also label people as mentally ill for social reasons that have nothing to do with concepts of health and disease. We label people mentally ill to give them the benefit of a psychiatric excuse: so a student can continue in college even though he has not taken his examinations, or so a woman will not be sent to prison even though she has murdered her baby. Whether these people are mentally ill or not does not seem very important; the label of mental illness is needed to justify what we feel needs to be done.

Other people who we feel are mentally ill we may decide not to label as such. Sometimes we ignore their strange behavior and refrain from giving it a name because we do not want to harm them with the stigma of the mentally ill label. At other times we want to deny them the excuse of mental illness. For example, we minimize the mental illness of some defendants because we want them to be dealt with by the criminal-justice system, held in prisons rather than hospitals. We were happy that David Berkowitz, the "Son of Sam," pleaded guilty so we did not have to deal with him as a mental patient. Whether or not mental illness represents real illness, we often conveniently act as if it is—although sometimes it is more convenient to act as if it is not.

The power to diagnose people as mentally ill that we give to psychiatrists and other health professionals in turn leads to other powers. In the case of the patient diagnosed as ill enough to be committed it gives the committing doctor the power to inject, invade, subdue, shackle, shock, and call into play any number of powerful treatment modalities.

Shakespeare has told us that some are born great, some achieve greatness, and some have greatness thrust upon them. So too with the diminished status that results from the label of mental disability. One can be born into the status, or it can be earned by the efforts of the patient as he seeks help and proclaims himself to be sick, or, in the case of the involuntary patient who denies his sickness, the doctor has the power to impose the label and in this way to gain power over the patient.

Szasz was the first psychiatrist to pick up and run with a theme that had been advanced by sociologists and semanticists: that psychiatrists acquire power over people by putting the label of mentally ill or mentally disabled on them, that labeling is in fact the source of psychiatric power. Psychiatrists have great discretionary power over whether or not to label, and they have great latitude about what label to apply.

Physicians, since they are accepted as authorities on disease, are in the enviable position of setting up classifications that are accepted as valid just because they have set them up and of having recognized as diseases whatever they declare to be diseases. When they are caused by organisms, wounds, breaks, cancerous growths, or the alteration of physiological function, they are easier to define, but when the causative agent is less obvious—when it may be psychological rather than physiological—when the entity called a disease is manifested entirely by a behavioral disturbance, then there is a great subjective element in the decision that a disease is present. No one has doubts about typhoid fever, but back pain and fatigue may or may not be considered evidence of an illness or disease, and at the purely psychological end of the spectrum, check kiting or exhibitionism or sexual sadism may or may not be seen as diseases, depending on the point of view and the goal of the person with the authority to label.

The fact that we label some people as mentally ill is not remarkable. The lack of precision and the hasty way that labels are bestowed and the inability of the patient to protest the label is much more worthy of notice.

Psychiatrists are at a great advantage in their role as labelers. In the first place, mental illness (or some other circumlocution that would help us avoid the word "disease") is relatively unknown territory where psychiatrists have had experience and others have not. Occasionally someone challenges the authority of the psychiatrist, but for the most part his assertion that he is an expert in the diagnosis of mental illness goes unchallenged. Someone is needed in society to label people as mentally ill. Families with a disturbed member, the police with a suspect showing strange behavior, courts dealing with commitment or criminal responsibility, insurance companies asked to reimburse for psychiatric treatment—all depend on the psychiatrist to tell them whether or not someone is sick, and they are by and large sufficiently grateful to and impressed by psychiatrists to accept them as credible labelers.

Secondly, under the peculiar rules of the game a patient cannot challenge his diagnosis. A patient who protests the diagnosis is labeled as lacking insight at the least, and he can be also seen as negativistic or paranoid or a troublemaker or as litigious. Joseph Heller has helped us to understand "Catch-22"—in some circumstances the doctor may label the patient well because he insists he is sick or sick because he insists he is well.[2]

Thirdly, the psychiatrist can manipulate the symbols and labels so that a person is sometimes sick, sometimes not sick. In doing so he can sometimes be of great service to his patient. A psychiatrist calls his patient sick so that medical insurance will pay for his treatment, but he informs the patient's employer that he is not sick and should be retained on his job. Psychiatrists can also use this kind of alternating diagnosis to harm patients. Sexual psychopaths under laws in some states are considered so sick that they have to be hospitalized for life, but they are not sick in the sense they deserve hospital treatment. They are held, rather than treated, in hospitals for the criminally insane, with no insurance reimbursement for treatment.

A leading textbook states, "diagnosis is, more or less, an arbitrary matter . . ."[3] The Supreme Court has said, "The subtleties and nuances of psychiatric diagnosis render certainties virtually beyond reach in most situations . . . Psychiatric diagnosis . . . is to a large extent based on medical 'impressions' drawn from subjective analysis and filtered through the experience of the diagnostician. This process often makes it very difficult for the expert physician to offer definite conclusions about any particular patient."[4] The ability to play with labels gives a special benefit to the middle-class or affluent person involved in some delinquency who can afford to see a private psychiatrist and who can elicit his interest and sympathy. The psychiatrist can excuse matters that would otherwise be felonies (for instance, embezzlement by writing false checks) by stating that this behavior is the result of psychopathology, but the diagnosis can be couched to imply that the sickness does not disqualify the patient from being able to carry on the duties of running a large corporation. The psychiatrist treating a disturbed adolescent can find him sick enough to justify long years of treatment but label him with an inconsequential diagnosis—such as "adjustment reaction of adolescence"—so as not to interfere with admission to college. Unlike doctors in other fields of medicine, the psychiatrist has great freedom to shift diagnostic labels, to apply them at one time and not another, or for one purpose and not another.

Fourth, the concepts that underlie the psychiatric labels are vague and ambiguous, and even a well-meaning and concerned psychiatrist trying to be objective and scientific will have trouble differentiating the well from the sick and conferring the proper label. There are cultural biases present here: Many cases that are diagnosed as schizophrenia in the United States would be diagnosed as manic-depressive illness in England or Western Europe. Many criminal acts of poor delinquents are seen as pathological acts if done by well-to-do delinquents. Many recovered schizophrenics are seen by psychiatrists as still ill on the basis of minor quirks in thinking or the psychiatrist's conviction of the patient's "fragility," whereas others in the population equally peculiar who have never had a schizophrenic break are not seen as ill. When a patient who has been acutely disorganized recovers, psychiatrists have trouble in saying when the patient has passed the dividing line and is back again into a state of health. A difference in emphasis makes it possible to see the recovered patient either as still sick or as well. Most psychiatrists would see schizophrenia as the classic example of psychiatric illness, but a British psychiatrist says schizophrenia is possibly only exaggerations of normal cogni-

tive and personality characteristics found in the general well population, not a qualitatively different mental state.[5] Because the subjective
bias of the evaluator helps determine the diagnosis, the patient is at
a disadvantage when he states that the diagnosis is wrong.

The vagueness of the diagnosis of schizophrenia is demonstrated by
a comparison of the usual rate of the diagnosis and the rate when
rigorous diagnostic criteria are used. The national range of incidence
of schizophrenia in patients admitted to mental hospitals is 24 percent,
but a research study that applied rigorous criteria that included formal
thought disorder, emotional blunting, hallucinations or delusions, and
the absence of depressive or manic-depressive disorder found only a
6 percent rate.[6] The authors of the study say that there was a fivefold
overdiagnosis of schizophrenia in the hospitals and clinics where their
research was conducted. One reason for the wide difference is the
diverse standards that are used. This study insisted on rigorous criteria, but in contrast, other researchers have said that "even a trace of
schizophrenia is schizophrenia."[7]

The overdiagnosis of schizophrenia does not necessarily mean that
too many people are being hospitalized. The same patients might have
been hospitalized, but with a different diagnostic label, if stricter criteria had been observed. But the schizophrenic label implies a bad
prognosis and carries more stigma than other psychiatric conditions,
and it dictates treatment plans and leads to the prescription of tranquilizers that may make a misdiagnosed depressed condition worse.

The dividing line between normality and mental illness is tenuous,
and it depends, as we have said, on the bias of the observer. Perhaps
psychiatric diagnoses are only reliable in acute or classical or extreme
cases. Certainly the social context in which the behavior is exhibited
and the frame of reference of the psychiatrist affect the labeling process.

The psychiatrist has a great advantage when he wants to diagnose
pathology because by his definitions great numbers of people (by some
definitions almost everyone) have serious psychiatric maladjustment.
Older statistics had it that 10 percent of the United States required
psychiatric help at any one time. The Carter Commission placed the
figure much higher, and some psychiatrists have raised the estimate
of the incidence of neurosis in our society to 95 percent or more. In
some prisons nearly every inmate is diagnosed as having a sociopathic
personality, although in other prisons the figure is placed at a low
level. Since symptoms of less than optimal behavior are exhibited by
almost everyone, almost everyone can be seen as having at least some
kind of psychiatric problem, and if someone showed no neurotic or

characterological disturbances at all, that in itself would raise the suspicions of some psychiatrists.

The psychiatric classification scheme does represent the accumulation of centuries of observations and the refinement of criteria, and it is a useful scheme for therapists, who must conceptualize what is wrong if they want to help to make it right. Psychiatric disease classification has a long history. The intellectual concepts of our ancestors do not bind us—we are not required to believe in witches because they believed in witches—but the developmental history of psychiatric nosology gives some credibility to the system. The distinction between mental disease present at birth and later, acquired mental disease is ancient. The effect of situational factors in the production of and the recovery from mental disorder was described in the *Odyssey* and the earliest books of the Old Testament. Hysteria, depression, mania, delerium, hallucinations, delusions, and other psychopathology were familiar to the populace as well as to physicians in the times of Shakespeare and Cervantes. Gradually a system of nomenclature developed that focused on the main conditions of disordered mental functioning: idiocy or mental deficiency, schizophrenia (once called dementia praecox), depression, mania, the insanities resulting from such neurological conditions as syphilis, and the organic deterioration resulting from senility. Emil Kraepelin, Freud's contemporary, gave authority to psychiatric labeling when he developed a classification system that was regarded as complete and scientific. Kraepelin stated three-quarters of a century ago that he tried at all times to keep the diagnostic point of view in the foreground because he was convinced of its fundamental importance, not only to the scientific advancement of psychiatry but also so that patients would receive the proper advice and be given the proper treatment.[8] Eugen Bleuler refined some of Kraepelin's concepts of dementia praecox and gave the condition the name of schizophrenia. Freud expanded the boundaries of psychiatric diagnosis by dignifying minor mental illnesses, the neuroses, and raising them to the status of recognized medical entities. Since then the trend has been to expand continuously the definition of psychiatric illness, and in this century psychosomatic disorders, personality disorders (patterns of maladaptive behavior that are often not characterized by anxiety or distress), alcoholism, addiction, and many kinds of deviant behavior have been included in the psychiatric nosology, as well as such transitory conditions as adjustment reactions and brief situational disturbances. Since the chemotherapeutic era, diagnosis has received extra attention in the interest of prescribing the "proper" medication.

In 1917 the American Medico-Psychological Association, as the

American Psychiatric Association was then known, adopted a system of nomenclature that was based, with modifications, on Kraepelin's scheme. In 1934 a version of this was issued as the first official APA Standard Nomenclature of Disease. Because of dissatisfactions with the system during the period of psychiatry's great growth in World War II, Dr. William Menninger, who was in charge of psychiatry in the armed services, simplified and revised the nosology, and his scheme seemed so satisfactory that it was adopted by the army and navy, and later by the Veterans Administration. It was the basis for the revised version published in 1952. In the 1952 revision the American Psychiatric Association adopted a scheme relying heavily on the Veterans Administration's version, and this was published as the *Diagnostic and Statistical Manual of Mental Disorders of the APA,* known as *DSM-I.* In 1968 it was revised again. This is the nomenclature now in official use, and it is called *DSM-II.* [9] In 1979 the APA approved the adoption and publication of a new manual, *DSM-III.* [10]

In spite of the fact that the nomenclature has evolved over centuries and has gone through many revisions, it lacks the precision of diagnostic classifications in other branches of medicine. In addition, in recent years psychiatrists have adopted new names for conditions that do not seem to be covered by the nosology. A large percentage of patients are being given these new labels—pseudoneurotic schizophrenia, borderline state, narcissistic personality. There has been a tendency to blame the classification scheme for what is perhaps an ambiguity inherent in psychiatry, for psychiatry deals with behavior rather than with more definite disease symptoms and the causes of psychiatric upset are multifactoral. Mental patients are square pegs and psychiatry provides round holes to accommodate them.

It is not only the psychiatrist who pins the label on the patient; patients label themselves. Patients characterize themselves as sick, they suffer, and if what they are going through is not a disease, they see it at least as some kind of severe aberration. They complain that they feel they are out of control or that they cannot stir themselves, that their thoughts are racing and unmanageable or that they have no thoughts, that they are overactive or apathetic, that they feel toxic and physically ill or that they feel dead. We can criticize the classification scheme as inexact, but we cannot decide not to classify.

*　　*　　*

In recent years we have seen three great diagnostic turnabouts that have brought into question the psychiatrists' use of labels. One was a much-cited case in which psychiatrists made what has been called a "celebrated 'big switch' or 'flip-flop.' "[11] The others were two official actions of the American Psychiatric Association, first to delist homosexuality as a disease label, then to abandon much of the traditional classification scheme.

Comer Blocker was tried in the District of Columbia for the 1957 murder of his common-law wife. The District three years earlier had adopted Judge Bazelon's "liberal" *Durham* rule of criminal irresponsibility, which for the first time had made it possible to save people who were labeled sociopaths and who did not have the obvious symptoms of mental disease from criminal conviction.[12] Although this liberalization of the law of criminal responsibility pleased most psychiatrists, some psychiatrists, particularly those who ran forensic services units and were responsible for the continued detention of people found not guilty by reason of insanity, and most lawyers were fearful of Bazelon's *Durham* case rule. There could be a huge increase in the number of people found not guilty by reason of insanity and forensic units might be overburdened with patients who seemed more like convicts than like sick people.

When the *Durham* decision was announced, the staff of St. Elizabeths Hospital, the federally run public hospital for the District of Columbia, reacted to this grant of increased authority by changing its definition of sociopathy in order to keep from being overwhelmed by newly defined mental patients. This change took place, as many psychiatric decisions do, in a conference behind hospital walls, outside of public consciousness. The official manual then in use, *DSM-I*, listed five categories of sociopathic personality disturbance: antisocial reaction, dyssocial reaction, sexual deviation, alcoholism (addiction), and drug addiction. The staff decided it should no longer consider sociopathy a disease, that sociopaths should be considered as "without mental disorder." From that time, the policy of the hospital was to insert the words "without mental disorder" after the diagnosis of sociopathic personality in the hospital records and to report to the courts that patients sent for evaluation concerning competency to stand trial, criminal irresponsibility, or disposition and who were diagnosed as sociopaths were without mental disorder.[13]

Blocker pleaded not guilty by reason of insanity, but two of the three psychiatrists who examined him at St. Elizabeths testified that he represented a "sociopathic personality disturbance" with chronic alcoholism at the time the murder was committed. The third doctor found that he had no diagnosable mental condition. All three psychiatrists conformed to the hospital policy and testified that a sociopathic personality disturbance was not a mental disease or defect. (The doctors were not entirely irrational; they were only ahead of their time. Nearly ten years later, when *DSM-II* was published, the term "sociopathic personality disturbance" was dropped, and the five conditions listed under it were included as subgroups under a category called "personality disorders and certain other non-psychotic mental disorders." The term "sociopath" since then has had no official standing, although it continues to be heavily utilized.) The jury, as might be anticipated, found Blocker guilty of murder.

Shortly afterward there occurred a flip-flop of the St. Elizabeths psychiatrists.[14] Dr. Addison Duval, assistant superintendent, testified in another case that he and the superintendent of the hospital had come to an agreement that people diagnosed as sociopathic personalities should henceforth be considered as mentally ill, suffering from mental disease. When the testimony in this case revealed a change of position, Blocker's attorney moved for and won a new trial.[15] The new trial did not win Blocker a not-guilty verdict. He was again found guilty, but the practice of the psychiatrists arbitrarily changing classifications had become a matter of public record and notice. When this case was appealed and the conviction again overturned (on other grounds not related to the change of classification), Judge Warren Burger, then of the District of Columbia Circuit Court of Appeals, used the occasion to express his dissatisfaction with psychiatric testimony. Commenting on the difficulty psychiatrists have in diagnosing mental disease or defect, he said, "Not being judicially defined, these terms mean in any given case whatever the expert witnesses say they mean. We know also that psychiatrists are in disagreement on what is a 'mental disease' and even whether there exists such a definable and classifiable condition . . . No rule of law can possibly be sound or workable which is dependent upon the terms of another discipline whose members are in profound disagreement about what those terms mean."[16]

A much more publicized instance of the variability of psychiatric diagnosis occurred in 1973 when the American Psychiatric Association dropped homosexuality from its classification of diseases. This was done largely through the efforts of one psychiatrist who was dedicated to achieving the change and who pushed it through as his own project without much input from the mass of psychiatrists or much debate. Many people who favored the result on humanitarian grounds still saw the sudden change and the manner in which it was produced as an illustration of the precarious nature of the psychiatric classificatory method.

Homosexuality was an official disease classification, listed under "personality disorders and certain other non-psychotic mental disorders" in *DSM-II*. The manual described how the classification should be applied. "This category is for individuals whose sexual interests are directed primarily toward objects other than people of the opposite sex, toward sexual acts not usually associated with coitus, or toward coitus performed under bizarre circumstances as in necrophilia, pedophilia, sexual sadism, and fetishism. Even though many find their practices distasteful, they remain unable to substitute normal sexual behavior for them." The manual exempted adolescent, boarding school, armed services, prison, and desert-island-castaway homosexuality.

Before homosexuality was considered a disease, it had been a crime, with penalties ranging from one year in jail in some states to life imprisonment in others. The arguments made by those who want homosexuality decriminalized have two main focuses: that society should show greater toleration for a variety of sexual practices, and, an alternative argument, that it is not abnormal, but merely represents one end of a normal continuum of sexual preferences, occupied by an appreciable percentage of the population at any time. Homosexuals found themselves in opposition to psychiatrists who considered homosexuals emotionally crippled.

Starting with Illinois in 1961, thirteen states have repealed their criminal sanctions against the private homosexual acts of consenting adults.[17] In many other jurisdictions, the laws on the books are not enforced unless flagrant public solicitation or relations with minors are involved, although in a few places police continue the practice of the entrapment of homosexuals in parks, restrooms, and homosexual bookshops and movie theaters. When criminal sanctions are repealed or not enforced, the disease label loses much of its advantage for most homosexuals, who resent the implication that their sexual preference represents disease and who feel stigmatized enough by the sexual-deviancy label without the additional imposition of a mental illness label.

Psychiatrists had seen themselves as humane. Homosexuality had been considered a crime, and they thought instead it should be treated as a disease. They saw themselves as benefactors of homosexuals, saving them from prison through the simple mechanism of diagnosing them as sick, helping them achieve public toleration, and in some cases using therapy to resolve the conflicts that had produced the sickness and offering the opportunity of heterosexuality. There was very little disagreement among psychiatrists concerning the disease status of homosexuality. They have always considered homosexuality to represent a seriously restricted sexual choice conditioned by severe pathology—childhood and adolescent anxiety, phobias, and primitive fears—that may or may not be conflictual and associated with anxiety, regret, or remorse on the part of the adult homosexual, but nevertheless represents a "crippling."

Freud consistently saw homosexuality as pathological. He felt that there was an organic factor in homosexuality, but he said this did not relieve psychoanalysts of the obligation of studying the psychical processes connected with its origin. He described as the "typical process" a young man a few years after the termination of puberty who "until this time has been strongly fixated to his mother, changes his attitude; he identifies himself with his mother, and looks about for love-objects in whom he can re-discover himself, and whom he might then love as his mother loved him." Freud lists as causative factors the fixation on the mother, which makes it difficult to pass on to another woman; identification with the mother; the inclination toward a narcissistic object-choice; the high value put on the penis and the inability to tolerate its absence in a love-object; renunciation of rivalry with the father out of respect or fear; and hostile and death wishes toward older brothers.[18]

Other psychoanalytic theories emphasize in male homosexuality the phobic reaction to the female genital and an ambivalent love-hate relationship with women. According to still other theorists (the various theories are not incompatible), the homosexual has a special sensitivity to castration that prevents him from acting like an adult male and penetrating a woman, or he is too concerned with a sense of inadequacy as a male to perform the traditional male role with women. Female homosexuals are said to be seeking maternal care and closeness. A general theme in all these formulations is that the homosexual has been fixated at, or regressed to, a less-than-mature stage of psychosexual development and is incapable of maintaining the kind of relationship that characterizes maturity. Charles Socarides, who has protested the declassification of homosexuality, writes, "It is my belief that in all homosexuals there has been an inability to make progression from the mother-child unity of earliest infancy to individuation. As a result, there exists in homosexuals a fixation, with the concomitant tendency to regression to the earliest mother-child relationship. This is manifested as a threat of personal annihilation, loss of ego boundaries and sense of fragmentation."[19]

Most psychiatrists treating homosexuals had found them deeply disturbed—close to depression and, in the case of most male homosexuals, forced to seek new male conquests compulsively as a defense against either depression or overwhelming anxiety. (As a counter to this view, the argument is made that psychiatrists do not have a chance to observe "healthy" homosexuals.)

Most psychiatrists would not want to treat homosexuals against their will, feeling that this would be fruitless and cruel, but until recently almost all psychiatrists had seen this obligatory restriction of sexual choice to one's own sex as pathological. (Prohomosexuals make the counterargument that heterosexuals are abnormal because they are forced to restrict their sexual activities to the opposite sex.)

Seeing homosexuality as sickness can lead to varied results. Affluent and respectable homosexuals charged with the offense of homosexuality could use the "sick" label to win psychiatric probation and could have outpatient treatment in lieu of a sentence. Other homosexuals were found to be sexual psychopaths by psychiatrists under laws that allowed them to be held in mental hospitals, almost always the notorious hospitals for the criminally insane, until the psychiatric staff judges them cured or safe to be released, which may be never.

It is hard for psychiatrists to understand that their desire to be helpful is seen by the objects of that help as menacing. Psychiatrists were more conscious of homosexuals who had benefited from the disease label than the sexual psychopaths who had been sent to a hospital to be cured. So psychiatrists were genuinely puzzled when, beginning in the late 1960s, gay activist groups demonstrated at psychiatric meetings and disrupted sessions on treatment, especially those on behavior modification, which was seen as treatment that could be imposed on an unwilling subject. In 1969, *Psychiatric News,* the American Psychiatric Association's newspaper, carried the headline: "Annual Meeting Rocked by Protest Disruptions." The story reported that demonstrators had forced the adjournment of a session on sexuality. At the 1971 meeting, protests culminated in pushing and shoving matches. In 1972, at the meeting in Dallas, a masked homosexual psychiatrist spoke on a panel to defend the thesis that homosexuality was normal behavior for some people. That same year, at the annual meeting of the American Association for Behavior Therapy in New York, the Gay Activist Alliance, a coalition of homosexual rights advocates, secured the floor at the session on aversion therapy as a treatment for homosexuality, and its spokesman, Ronald Gold, turned the meeting into a discussion of discrimination against homosexuals.[20] After the meeting Gold continued the discussion with Dr. Robert Spitzer, a member of the American Psychiatric Association's Task Force on Nomenclature and Statistics. After further discussions a meeting was arranged between a delegation representing homosexuals and the task force to discuss and demand a change in the official diagnostic classification to exclude homosexuality. Following that meeting Dr. Henry Brill, chairman of the task force, said that some changes in the official diagnostic scheme certainly seemed called for. Spitzer became the main mover for a change, and he was the author of the resolution and the position paper that were guided through the committee and eventually approved by the APA trustees. Malcolm Spector, a sociologist who has written on the campaign to remove homosexuality from the disease category, says that Spitzer was not an authority on homosexuality and did not claim to follow closely the voluminous literature on the subject, and he had not had any systematic or extensive therapeutic contact with homosexuals. Spitzer says that in his clinical practice he had treated eight homosexuals.[21] Two of the opponents of any change in the classification were Socarides and Irving Bieber, both of whom had had extensive clinical experience with homosexuals, had written on the subject, and believed there were reasons rooted in psychodynamics for the retention of homosexuality as a disease. Other psychiatrists with a psychoanalytic orientation who were not opposed to the dropping of homosexuality from the disease category wondered why it should be selectively dropped when other conditions with a similar psychodynamic derivation—alcoholism, drug addiction, compulsive gambling, kleptomania and more, all rooted in early deprivation, a need to combat depressive affect, and an inability to achieve psychosexual maturity—were still considered pathological.

Spitzer has described in an interview his initial involvement with the homosexual cause. "I went to this conference on behavioral modification which the gay lib group broke up. I found myself talking to a very angry young man. At that time I was convinced homosexuality was a disorder and that it belonged in the classification. I told him so."

Gold has described his part in the meeting with Spitzer: "He said he believed the illness theory. I said, alright who do you believe? And he hadn't read any of it . . . But he happened to know Socarides and thought he was a nut. Whom do you believe? Bieber? [Gold demanded]. Well, I don't know [Spitzer replied]. Have you read it? No. But they all believed it."[22]

After the 1973 APA convention, Spitzer circulated a draft of a paper to high APA officers in which he described homosexuality as not a disease but as "a form of irregular sexual behavior": The homosexual might be undisturbed by his sexual preference and would then be well, or might be disturbed, in which case he would fit into a new category to be called "sexual orientation disturbance." Judd Marmor, described by Spector as the most prominent liberal spokesman in the APA, then a member of the board of trustees and more recently an APA president, wrote to Spitzer criticizing his use of the term "irregular" as pejorative, indicating a bias against homosexuality. He proposed an alternative description of homosexual behavior as a "variant form of sexual development." The text finally approved by the trustees solved this difference by referring to homosexuality as "one form" of sexual behavior.

Spitzer's change was adopted in December 1973 when the trustees voted to remove homosexuality from the *DSM-II* category of diseases. The official decision of the association eliminated "homosexuality" and put in a new category, "sexual orientation disturbance (homosexuality)." The sting was taken out of the new diagnosis by stating that it did not apply to people who did not have present conflict about homosexuality or a desire to change. The subject's evaluation of his own condition thus became the criterion for inclusion in the disease or nondisease category, a major change from the traditional method of evaluating psychiatric conditions, in which the feeling of the subject about the degree of pathology he possesses is not taken at face value. A homosexual who has a conflict (disturbance) is ill; without the conflict, he is not.

The APA showed the importance it attached to this change by making it in the interim between the various editions of the nomenclature and printing a special new version of *DSM-II* to reflect the change.

In the accompanying "Position Statement on Homosexuality and Civil Rights," the board of trustees deplored all public and private discrimination against homosexuals and urged the enactment of civil-rights legislation to protect homosexuals and the repeal of all discriminatory legislation against homosexual behavior. It further deplored the use of "pejorative connotations derived from diagnostic or descriptive terminology used in psychiatry" as the basis for such discrimination.

Critics of psychiatry have argued since this change that if diseases can be created and eliminated by a vote of APA trustees, if a condition that had almost been considered pathological by almost all psychiatrists can by a stroke of the pen be made unpathological, then the underpinning of psychiatric classification had come dangerously loose. (The change was later endorsed, in a special referendum initiated by opponents, by 58 percent of voting members.)

Ever since the change, Spitzer and his Task Force on Nomenclature have been busy trying to find a definition of mental disease that will justify the exclusion of homosexuality while many related conditions that can be equally free of conflict are retained. They have done this by saying that homosexuality is not a medical disease but that the other conditions are medical. They have formulated a new and complicated definition of medical disease designed to achieve this end. But this in turn raised other issues of definition and classification, and the change regarding homosexuality eventually led to the formulation of a whole new revised system of psychiatric classification.

The declassification of homosexuality did not convince everybody. Dr. John Spiegel, as president of the APA, in 1974 requested the Immigration and Naturalization Service to change its policies on the exclusion of, and refusal of citizenship to, homosexuals "in view of the actions of the Board of Trustees of the American Psychiatric Association" in removing homosexuality "from the category of psychopathic personality." The Immigration Service replied that naturalization is a judicial function and that, although some courts have admitted homosexuals as citizens, the policy of the Immigration Service would continue to oppose admission. Five years later, the Immigration Service issued a directive ordering agents to cease preventing foreign visitors suspected of homosexuality from being deported. Instead, the agents were ordered to place such visitors on a "temporary parole station" while the question of the authority of the service to exclude or deport receives further clarification.[23] The APA did not protest the continuation of the policy of the State Department and the Central Intelligence Agency not to employ homosexuals,[24] although it did protest the Dade County, Florida, vote that rescinded a law providing for nondiscrimination against homosexuals.

David Rosenhan, the author of "On Being Sane in Insane Places," has pointed to the change as proof of his thesis that psychiatric classification corresponds not to real disease entities but only to psychiatrists' subjective perceptions, largely culturally determined. Spitzer had attacked Rosenhan's 1973 study utilizing pseudopatients as not relevant to the problem of the validity and reliability of psychiatric diagnosis. Rosenhan counterclaimed that psychiatric diagnoses are strongly influenced by contexts that color the perception of psychiatric patients: "Changes in informed public attitudes toward homosexuality have brought about corresponding changes in the psychiatric perception of it."[25] Bruce Ennis and Thomas Litwack, in a thorough and biting review that marshals all the evidence of psychiatry's inability to diagnose and predict, said,

For years "homosexuality" was listed in DSM-II as a subcategory of personality disorders. Recently, however, the American Psychiatric Association decided by vote that homosexuality should no longer be considered a mental illness. If all that is needed to remove large numbers of individuals from the ranks of the mentally ill and grant them the status enjoyed by the rest of society is a vote by the American Psychiatric Association, then surely other diagnostic labels are also highly suspect.

It should be obvious, then, that psychiatric diagnoses do not convey much meaningful information . . .[26]

The controversy about the disease status of homosexuality refuses to die. It is not only an important issue in itself but it represents a philosophical divide that is more significant than the individual question. Five years after the APA action to delist homosexuality, the debate continued. When *Medical Aspects of Human Sexuality* surveyed ten thousand physicians who were members of the American Medical Association, 69 percent said they still considered homosexuality to be "usually a pathological adaptation, as opposed to a normal variation," and only 18 percent considered homosexuality a normal variation. Harold Lief, a psychiatrist, in his introduction to the survey results, called the responses "surprising" in view of the 1974 poll in which APA members had endorsed the change, and he suggested, as many others had, that the APA had been influenced by "political and social considerations."[27]

The third of the great diagnostic turnabouts promises to be the most significant. It stems directly from the decision to delist homosexuality.

The psychiatric establishment had played into the hands of critics and had given them all the ammunition they needed for a demolishing attack on psychiatric classification. Psychiatry had said that for one condition, homosexuality, a novel criterion—the presence or absence of subjective distress—determined whether or not it was a disease. Now it had either to discard this new theory or revise the entire psychiatric classification system to be consistent with it. In the short run, revision could deflect some of the criticism of the delisting action because uniformity could once again be achieved. In the long run, it would, of course, only make the whole procedure of psychiatric diagnosis more subject to question.

The new criterion was dubious. If it was to be set forth as a principle, a new distinction must be constructed so that other similar nonconflictual conditions—exhibitionism, addictive gambling, and many more—would not also have to be dropped from the nomenclature and thus provide another example of the variability of psychiatric diagnosis and the political nature of the construction of the classification scheme.

The APA decided to take the course of developing an entirely revised nomenclature, throwing out old disease categories, introducing new ones. The stated goal was to produce a more medical and more "scientific" system.

The result is a proposed new classification scheme, scheduled for adoption and known as *DSM-III,*[28] that is much more complicated than *DSM-II.*

Spitzer apparently bases his new classification on his theory that psychiatric disease entities are real, very specific, and very discrete from each other. Once again the claim is made—as it was by Benjamin Rush and Isaac Ray and Philippe Pinel in the seventeenth and early eighteenth centuries and as authoritarian psychiatrists have always tried to maintain—that psychiatric conditions are truly medical and that psychiatrists should therefore have all the authority (and presumably all the financial reimbursement) that goes with treating medical conditions. Spitzer says his task force "eventually came to believe" that mental disorder was "merely a subset of medical disorder." It then redefined medical disorder as a condition that causes some type of disadvantage that may be physical, perceptual, sexual, or interpersonal. According to the task force, homosexuality does not meet the criteria because it does not carry with it a disadvantage. Fetishism, on the other hand, is a disability, and so the task force has included it as a disease. Transvestism, exhibitionism, and voyeurism remain diseases, whether or not conflict is present, as do sexual sadism and masochism.

Some of the categories in the new scheme, such as schizophrenia and affective organic mental disorders, result from scientific studies in the psychiatric literature, but other categories, such as personality disorders and sexual disorders, are to be included "on the basis of tradition with the hope that by defining them with greater precision than was previously done, further validity studies will justify their inclusion."[29]

The new DSM that Spitzer and his coworkers are constructing will be ten times larger than the present manual (it has been described as a "minitextbook") and it has been based on a new "multiaxial" approach to the patient. The diagnostic label should not only describe the patient according to psychiatric syndrome, personality disorders, and physical disorders but also according to "psychological stressers" and "highest level of adaptive functioning." (How a person uses his leisure time is one of the three major factors in assessing level of adaptive functioning.) Later the task force decided that only the first three of its five axes should be used for diagnosis.[30]

One of the great efforts of the task force was to dissociate psychiatry from psychoanalytic formulations and theories, since these are considered unscientific and not sufficiently grounded in medicine. Therefore the concept of neurosis was dropped. Spitzer writes: "Because intrapsychic conflict exists in so many psychiatric disorders as well as in persons without psychiatric disorders, it is not used in *DSM-III* as a basis for class formation; hence the absence of the traditional category, 'the neuroses.' " A spokesman for the American Psychoanalytic Association protested: "We think the term 'neurosis' has attained a certain clinical use over the years and don't think the image of psychiatry is improved by dropping it."[31] What formerly were described as neuroses would now appear as "disorders"—and so there were to be an anxiety disorder, a factitious disorder, a somatoform disorder, and a dissociative disorder.

The term "neurotic disorders," with various subclassifications, was later reinstated in the proposed *DSM-III,* and to further conciliate those who see psychiatry more as a psychological than a medical science, the APA Board of Trustees voted to include an introduction in the new classification book to explain how the new scheme might be used by dynamically oriented psychiatrists. Spitzer commented: "The Task Force feels that the inclusion of neurosis is a scientifically sound compromise." APA President Jules Masserman expressed reservations about *DSM-III:* "We will be saddled with it for the next ten years, and it can be improved." Past President Judd Marmor commented that *DSM-III* was not perfect but *DSM-II* also had not been perfect, and he expected the new scheme would "evolve over time." He said that the nomenclature dispute "has become a political issue more than a scientific issue . . ."[32]

Spitzer, in promoting his huge new classification manual, has said confusingly that *DSM-III* is not intended to provide a comprehensive definition of what is and what is not a mental disorder, and that to attempt to do so could be viewed as more harmful than helpful.

In the past, diagnostic classifications have been seen as an attempt to classify objectively what is and what is not a mental disorder without regard to the subjective bias of the patient or the attitude of society. Now categories are included in *DSM-III* because of criteria that describe a condition as causing subjective distress, impairing social functioning, or putting the individual at some intrinsic disadvantage compared to individuals who do not have the condition.[33] The task force has, however, decided to exclude "those conditions which have strong cultural or subcultural supports or sanctions."[34] The criteria are designed to keep homosexuality from reentering the classification by specifying that "the condition must be directly associated with distress, disadvantage, disability, or death of an individual," but in spite of this statement, compulsive gambling, alcohol abuse, cocaine abuse, and a whole variety of sexual dysfunctional conditions never before listed as psychiatric disease (premature ejaculation, inhibited sexual excitement) were included in the draft of the new classification.[35] Caffeinism is now to be a psychiatric disease, as are a marijuana-induced "high," stuttering, and "emancipation disorder of adolescence," although child abuse is a "condition not attributable to a mental disorder."[36]

Among the oddities of the draft of the new classification were the elimination of the traditional psychiatric category of "hysteria," the inclusion of the traditionally nonpsychiatric condition of "tobacco withdrawal," the creation of the new personality disorder "histrionic" and the new disease of childhood or adolescence called "the shyness disorder," and the dropping of the distinction between acute (or reversible) and chronic (or irreversible) organic brain syndromes. In addition, questionnaires were mailed to members of the American Psychiatric Association to ask for help in developing the criteria for the new diagnosis of "borderline personality disorder."

The classification changes and the new terminology led to other revisions. The APA's official glossary, defining psychiatric terms, had been published in 1975. Now it also had to be revised to add new terms, drop others, and rewrite definitions.

When changes are made in psychiatric classifications and concepts, the textbooks must be rewritten to accommodate the new position. The section on homosexuality in the 1967 edition of the *Comprehensive Textbook of Psychiatry* had been written by Irving Bieber, the leader, with Socarides, of the unsuccessful movement to have the delisting vote of the trustees rescinded. This has been discarded and a new section written by Judd Marmor, Spitzer's strongest supporter on the board of trustees.[37]

But the *Comprehensive Textbook* is not ideologically firm, and it is willing to leave the subject of psychiatric diagnosis fluid, making it dependent on what society wants and what psychiatrists think. The book declares its definition of mental disorder "may need to be changed in future years to correspond with a change in the attitude of society and the psychiatric profession toward certain conditions."[38]

The new concepts have been subject to sporadic criticism, although most psychiatrists find this subject so complex that they have not become involved. Few psychiatrists have been willing to delve to the bottom of the problem, to admit that psychiatric diagnoses are and have always been far less exact than diagnoses in the rest of medicine, that in many cases they describe processes or cover conditions bearing no resemblance to traditional medical disease, and that, in the interest of buttressing up their authority, psychiatrists have been content to live with their diagnostic classification schemes—and now are proposing to expand them—without a thorough discussion of either their scientific basis or their social-legal consequences. Very few psychiatrists are willing to say, as has Victor Adebimpe of Pittsburgh's Western Psychiatric Institute and Clinic, that in some psychiatric situations "you have no way of knowing whether your diagnosis is better than anyone else's . . . until you see if the treatment works."[39] (And even that would not be a scientific proof that the diagnosis had been correct.)

When psychiatrists do discuss diagnosis, they are often superficial in approach. One common answer to critics of psychiatry is that medical diagnoses are only precise when laboratory tests are available and in their absence medical diagnosis would be equally subject to criticisms. Lorrin Koran, writing on "Controversies in Medicine and Psychiatry" in the *American Journal of Psychiatry,* has said that "both medicine and psychiatry lack explicit diagnostic criteria and decision rules for diagnosing many diseases."

> Unfortunately, psychiatric diagnosis depends largely on the psychiatrist's ability to perceive evanescent behaviors . . . On the other hand, even well trained internists show a surprising degree of disagreement in diagnosing cardiac disease from electrocardiograms or physical examination, in diagnosing pulmonary emphysema from a physical examination, and in differentiating benign from malignant gastric ulcers on the basis of clinical, X-ray, and laboratory data.[40]

But apologists for the inexactitude of psychiatric diagnosis do not stress that not only life and health, but also liberty, can depend on the psychiatrist's diagnostic label and that the opinions of psychiatrists are used for many legal purposes that have little to do with health.

The present system of diagnosis has not worked, says Robert Stoller, a UCLA psychiatrist, because psychiatrists have tried to make it do too much, have claimed for themselves more scientific precision than they possess. If psychiatrists had come to agreement about the conditions they label—had agreed as to their clinical features, knew what dynamics produced those features, and had discovered the causes that start those dynamics in action—use of the classifications would be fine, says Stoller. But in the present state of diagnostic accuracy, the classification systems serve not only as labels for psychiatric conditions but also as "subtle public relations documents issued by psychiatry to the rest of medicine and the world at large," designed to convey the message that psychiatrists know more than they do in fact know. Says Stoller, "We pay an increasing price as our misrepresentation is discovered" that as psychiatrists continue to use these diagnostic systems they will have to take additional criticism, including "anger from the public, scorn from our medical colleagues, flawed treatment, flawed research, and delayed understanding of the nature of the mind and the causes of its pathology." He recommends a shift in classification that is opposite to the direction of *DSM-III,* away from absolutes and denotation and toward descriptions. He finds adjectives are useful when they simply describe; when they are transformed into nouns, which are then magically to be accepted as "things" and used to label, they confer too much authority on the labeling person.[41]

Like a number of other observers, I feel that the APA's new diagnostic system does not represent an improvement and that it does demonstrate publicly the inconsistencies of psychiatric thought and the increasingly unscientific and pragmatic nature of diagnostic classification. Ironically, one obvious purpose for the new scheme was to forestall the mounting criticism that psychiatric diagnosis was not sufficiently scientific, and Spitzer claims that research findings since 1968 have been used to increase the scientific validity of the scheme. But the scheme does not rise to the scientific level of the remainder of medicine, the studies used to support the changes are often far from scientifically precise, and the fact that changes can be made at will and that social, political, and economic reasons are involved in the change all weaken psychiatry's claim to a scientific nomenclature. The two new principles of designating disease that the task force has imparted to psychiatry—that absence of guilt or feeling of conflict can determine that no illness is present, as does general social approval of a condition—justify the deletion of homosexuality, but they destroy the pretension that the nomenclature is objective.

Practicing psychotherapists who are not medical doctors—psychologists, social workers, and others—see the proposed scheme as an effort by psychiatry to monopolize the reimbursement for therapy from third-party payers. They charge that the proposed manual tends to look at every problem as organic, and it has been called "a power play by psychiatrists to preempt their territory."[42] George Albee, a past president of the American Psychological Association, has written: "The unvarnished fact is that most of the emotional problems of living do not belong in the category of disease. To attribute marital conflict, or delinquency, or dehumanization, or depression, to a biological defect, to biochemical, nutritional, neurological, or other organic conditions, in the absence of compelling evidence, is to sell our psychological birthright for short-term gain."[43] Writing in *Psychology Today*, Daniel Goleman, an associate editor of the magazine and a psychologist, says, *"DSM-III* widens the orbit of psychiatry, staking claims to a wide new territory of human problems . . . The unwitting encroachment of psychiatry on domains not normally within its jurisdiction suggests *DSM-III* should be given even more scrutiny before it becomes official."[44]

* * *

Labels are used to denigrate people. They give the person imposing the label control over the person who is labeled. A labeled person loses legal rights. Nevertheless it is necessary to differentiate the sane from the insane, the "sick" from the "well," in an ordered society. All labelers are faced with the knowledge (although they often defend against it and do not permit themselves to feel this deeply) that they are operating in an ambiguous area where mistakes are common, and in psychiatry their wrong decision can have powerful effects. John Spiegel, in the 1975 presidential address to the American Psychiatric Association, recognized that psychiatry is a "high-risk profession." He admitted that psychiatrists "may never come up with the testable theory and replicated findings of the hard sciences. Because of the large number of variables underlying any type of human behavior, our therapeutic decisions are always taken in the context of a certain amount of ambiguity. Since the data available are never sufficient, we have to learn to live with uncertainty. Clinical judgment, based on training and experience, makes the uncertainty manageable, but *every decision we make is a risky decision.*"[45]

The psychiatrist would be a more acceptable and useful person if he could more frequently bring himself to admit that there is the possibility that he is wrong. The infuriating quality of psychiatrists—Spiegel's statement represents a rare exception—is their insistence that they are scientific and correct and that their detractors, therefore, must be wrong. Psychiatrists have the power not only to judge what is right but to label as uneducated, uninformed, malignant, perverse, or worse those who disagree with them.

Problems of Prediction

WHEN A PSYCHIATRIST labels someone as mentally ill he gains power over that person, but when he is able to label him not only mentally ill but dangerous—and, in particular, likely to continue to be dangerous—he gains the ultimate in power: the power to take away liberty, the power to keep confined, possibly for a lifetime, and, under new laws that have not received enough attention, even the power to determine that a person convicted of a capital crime can never cease to be dangerous and must be executed as a protection for society.

No one except psychiatrists and juvenile-court judges has the right to lock up people who have not been charged with any crime. In psychiatric commitment and juvenile-delinquency detention the rationale for the detention is the same—that it is for a therapeutic purpose and not as a punishment, and that therefore procedural safeguards are not important and the methods and the biases of the evaluators need not be scrutinized too closely. But courts and civil-liberties-minded lawyers have attempted in recent years to give greater procedural protection and have pointed out that patients and juveniles do not need this kind of therapy, or that in fact therapy will not be available in the institution and detention will be custodial or punitive.

Psychiatrists have a way of giving ammunition to their critics. In the interest of decreasing the stigma of being mentally ill, they have spent a great deal of energy trying to popularize the view that psychiatric patients are no more dangerous than anyone else. But when sued for failing to restrain their patients from committing harm, psychiatrists defended themselves by denying that they had any special expertise in predicting dangerousness. Both positions were expedient; both have come back to haunt them.

In 1922 a psychiatric study showed, or purported to show, that according to current records, mental patients after release from hospitals did not become involved in a high incidence of criminal behavior. Other studies followed, all showing lower-than-expected arrest rates. From the skimpy evidence derived from those studies, psychiatrists proceeded to claim that psychiatric patients were no more dangerous than anyone else—a good argument for welcoming former patients back into the community, hiring them, and not discriminating against them. The conclusion of one of the most comprehensive of these studies, done on male ex-patients released from New York State mental hospitals in 1946–1948, was that the arrests of former mental patients were concentrated in a relatively small, rather well demarcated group with previous criminal records. Crime rates were lower among former mental patients than among corresponding groups in the general population.[1]

In their desire to integrate psychiatric patients into the community, psychiatrists ignored a number of considerations that might have cast doubt on the notion that psychiatric patients were really not dangerous. First and foremost, the studies were done on former patients after discharge from what was usually a long period of hospitalization. Whether these patients had been dangerous at the time of commitment was not studied. Many of these patients were old, apathetic, chronic schizophrenics whose violence had long since burned out, and the fact that they were not violent did not indicate their potential dangerousness at an earlier point in their illness. Another flaw was that dangerousness was measured by subsequent arrest rates, but the majority of the dangerous acts of former mental patients are either not included in arrestable offenses, or the former patient escapes arrest by virtue of the fact that he is recognized as a mental case. In more recent years, new studies by Zitrin, Mullen, Sosowsky, Logos, and others indicate that the older studies are misleading, that former mental patients do have a higher than normal arrest rate, although often for such relatively minor offenses as drunken driving, and not usually for major criminal activity.[2] In addition, anecdotal evidence is accumulating, during a period when it has become more difficult to get patients committed, that some patients who are not committed do go on to commit dangerous acts. The United Press International reports that for the second time in two weeks firemen persuaded a nineteen-year-old not to leap from the thirty-third floor of a San Francisco hotel.[3] The Associated Press reports that a mental patient being returned to a Michigan hospital from Puerto Rico "beat a 7-year-old boy unconscious in the restroom of an airborne jetliner, then shot a policeman who tried to remove him" when the plane returned to the airport; two years earlier the same mental patient had been shot while brandishing a knife in the basement of his church.[4] United Press International reports that a mental patient who had checked himself out of the hospital the previous day, enraged by a domestic argument, tossed two of his children off a second-floor apartment balcony onto an asphalt parking lot, killing one child and seriously injuring the other.[5] The involvement of mental patients in family violence, crime, skyjacking, and political threats and assassination attempts attests to a relationship between mental disease and violence, although anecdotal evidence does not have the value of more thorough studies. Darold Treffert, a leading exponent of the position that psychiatrists need their authority to commit in order to protect patients from harming themselves and others, has described the phenomenon of patients released from care to "die with their rights on."[6] Our concept of the psychiatric patient as dangerous or nondangerous affects our attitude about exerting authority over him.

In 1960 Morton Birnbaum devised a novel legal theory, that the deprivation of liberty brought with it a right to be treated, and in the absence of treatment the patient deserved to be released. In support of this concept of "the right to treatment," Birnbaum advanced the argument that psychiatrists do not do a good job of predicting dangerousness. He showed that states that do not have many inpatient beds and that commit few patients do not as a result have high rates of suicide, homicide, and manslaughter, although some people might expect that would be the consequence; instead, they have low rates of such destructive acts. Birnbaum's argument is not entirely convincing. He is comparing states like Utah with New York City and the District of Columbia, and he ignores many factors such as population pressures. But he did open for discussion the question of the dangerousness of psychiatric patients.

In 1966, as the result of a Supreme Court decision, sociologists had an opportunity to test the predictive accuracy of psychiatrists in a fascinating *in vivo* experiment. Johnnie Baxstrom had been convicted of second-degree assault in 1959 and had been sentenced to a term of two and one-half to three years in a New York prison. While he was serving this sentence he was certified insane and transferred to Dannemora State Hospital for the criminally insane. In 1961 the head of Dannemora filed a petition—routine for end-of-sentence men—stating that Baxstrom's criminal sentence was about to terminate and requesting, under provision of state law, his civil commitment to Dannemora. Baxstrom continued to be detained there until the Supreme Court five years later ordered that Baxstrom and almost 1000 other end-of-sentence men either be released or, if they met commitment criteria, be committed to a regular state hospital.

Here was a chance for a sociologist to find out if these men were as dangerous as the psychiatrists had said. Henry Steadman, who followed up these men in a series of studies, found that after four years less than 3 percent had acted dangerously and were in a correctional facility or a hospital for the criminally insane. Most of the others had adjusted to less security-oriented hospitals, and over one-fourth were in the community.[7] (A surprisingly large group, 14 percent, were dead, perhaps indicating that these men had been dangerous to themselves if not to others; this aspect of the follow-up has not received much attention.)

Once we question the dangerousness of psychiatric patients we are led to ask a series of related questions: Are most of the patients considered dangerous by psychiatrists really dangerous? Are psychiatrists any better at predicting dangerousness than they are at labeling? Are psychiatrists better than other people at predicting dangerousness? How much leeway should psychiatrists be allowed in making errors concerning predictions of dangerousness?

Society wants to impute to psychiatrists the ability to predict danger. Someone is needed to impose social control on people who run around making threats and creating disturbances and who may or may not be dangerous.

Abraham Blumberg has written:

> Often the judge is confronted with a situation that offers too few or too weak criteria for decision. He will then deliberately involve probation and psychiatric reports or a district attorney's recommendations to diffuse responsibility or to mitigate his own anxieties.
>
> . . . The bureaucratic admonition to cover yourself applies as well to the judge as to any other individual in the organizational world.[8]

Prison administrators like to have behavioral scientists make predictions of future behavior so that they will not be blamed for recommending parole for an inmate who turns out badly. One study shows that prisoners who were transferred for observation and evaluation for parole eligibility to a security hospital (a hospital for the criminally insane) were usually dangerous offenders who had committed violent crimes before their convictions, or who had shown aggressive tendencies in prison, or who were sex offenders;[9] previous dangerous behavior, not previous psychiatric illness, prompted the request for a psychiatric opinion. In spite of the fact that psychiatrists have not proven their competence in predicting dangerousness, more and more people, particularly pretrial detainees and incarcerated offenders, are being referred for psychiatric evaluation.[10]

Since the middle 1960s psychiatrists have increasingly been challenged to prove that they are good predictors of dangerousness. This is the third prong in the three-prong attack on psychiatry, which had previously questioned the validity of both the concept of mental disease and of the disease categories that psychiatrists utilize.

In spite of attacks, psychiatrists proceed happily to make their predictions, and their predictions are relied on and become the basis for major decisions. Possibly psychiatrists are less capable of predicting danger than others in society. Studies show that ward attendants, who have a greater familiarity with patients, may be better at predicting than more highly trained psychiatrists and psychologists, who spend less time with the subjects. But society finds it expedient to continue to utilize psychiatrists and to assume that they are able to pierce the veil and predict the future.

The most frequent use of prediction of dangerousness is to justify commitment. Psychiatrists have always talked about a dangerousness standard as the basis for a decision to commit, but they have not usually seen the standard as rigorous. They have used dangerousness as a "term of art" to simplify the psychiatric desirability of hospitalization, rather than actual danger. Patients have never had to have been very dangerous to be committed. They could be committed for such reasons as eccentricity and nonconformity and tensions that they stir up in the family or the community, and these could be considered to be dangerous.

The law has always taken the word of psychiatrists that this eccentric person presents potential danger—and who is there to say that he does not? For the essence of mental or emotional illness, or even eccentricity, is nonconformity and irrationality, and when one is nonconforming and irrational, who is to say how this will be expressed? Even the best-behaved eccentric may lose control. Everyone knows that mental patients are unpredictable, so a psychiatrist cannot be blamed for anticipating the worst.

For many centuries the law has asked for some indication of dangerousness to justify commitment. English common law allowed for the arrest of a "furiously insane person," or one considered "dangerous to be permitted at large," and confinement for the duration of this condition.[11] Although the determination of dangerousness was not precise, until the middle of the nineteenth century there were not many hospital beds, and even after the rise of the modern mental hospital there was little incentive for the state to provide free care for people who did not need it. Only the most disturbed tended to be given the "benefit" of hospitalization, and for these people it often was better than the alternative—trying to get along in a society that provided no supports. Disordered people who were not hospitalized could die in neglect or could starve to death. Overprediction of dangerousness was seen as helpful to patient and to society, and there was little talk about abuse of civil rights.

Another problem was that before the era of tranquilizers, out-of-control people required physical restraint and handling by trained professionals. Their yells, shrieks, and unrestrained outbursts could not be dealt with except by trained nurses and attendants, who used a variety of specialized methods, such as shackles, restraints, wet packs, continuous tubs, and seclusion rooms. Whether or not the deranged were dangerous, they could be so hard to control that the prospect of caring for them outside the hospital would be frightening to their relatives. The prospect of having to manage a patient out of the hospital was more fearsome than it is today, when chemotherapy and outpatient care is available, so there was little incentive to question psychiatric authority.

After all, if commitment was not a carefully protected procedure, there was one great and time-honored legal institution that was designed to be an ultimate protection. Habeas corpus, the "great Writ," characterized by Dr. Samuel Johnson as "the single advantage which our government has over that of other countries,"[12] was to ensure that no person could be subjected to arrest, imprisonment, or other physical coercion without legal justification. Whenever a court grants the petition for the writ, there follows a full review of the appropriateness of detention and the propriety of the procedures involved in the detention. In the late nineteenth century the Supreme Court made it clear that effective use of the writ required access to a lawyer, and this too became a part of the right.

Although habeas corpus is a basic right, many committed mental patients trying to secure their release have found that the right is more theoretical than actual. Kenneth Donaldson, the patient in a civil commitment case decided by the Supreme Court, was refused writs of habeas corpus eighteen times during his fifteen years of hospitalization before he finally won his chance to have a court hear his case. When his case was heard, the court decided Donaldson had not been dangerous for years.[13] Courts have increasingly refused to grant the petition and have denied the petitioner his review in court. They have done this readily, on the showing by a hospital administrator that the person has been put through an administrative procedure in the hospital, and an additional assurance that he still suffers from a dangerous condition. Many patients in hospitals have great difficulty in finding lawyers to represent them, and even though there was the rise in the 1960s of a new kind of lawyer for the mentally ill, the public-interest, or *pro bono publico,* lawyer, most patients still do not have access to good legal help. The problem of excessive and unnecessary commitment has been ameliorated not through exercise of the writ of habeas corpus and effective legal help, but through government policies reducing the number of hospital beds, making it harder to get a patient committed, and making short hospital stays the norm.

The writ was less helpful than it appeared, but on paper, at least, it seemed to assure that only dangerous people would be committed or that nondangerous people would be readily released.

Dangerousness is most used as a criterion for commitment. The most important nineteenth-century American commitment case was heard in Massachusetts in 1845. This was the *Matter of Josiah Oakes.* [14] Oakes, an elderly and ordinarily prudent man, surprised his family by becoming engaged to a young woman of unsavory character a few days after the death of his wife. He did not evidence any violence or destructiveness. Oakes's children had him sent to McLean Asylum on the grounds that he suffered from hallucinations and that he displayed unsoundness of mind in conducting his business affairs. For these reasons, according to testimony of the doctors, he would be dangerous if released. In its decision the court paid lip service to the concept that only dangerousness is the justification for a deprivation of liberty. "The right to restrain an insane person of his liberty is found in that great law of humanity, which makes it necessary to confine those whose going at large would be dangerous to themselves or others . . . And the necessity which creates the law, creates the limitation of the law. The question must then arise in each particular case, whether a patient's own safety, or that of others, requires that he should be restrained for a certain time, and whether restraint is necessary for restoration, or will be conducive thereto. The restraint can continue as long as the necessity continues. This is the limitation, and the proper limitation." The case has often been cited for its insistence on the dangerousness standard. The fact that Oakes was held to be dangerous but may not have been dangerous is ignored.

Since that time, although the civil-rights pendulum has swung several times and there have been periods of emphasis on procedural rights of mental patients, the same attitude has been shown by courts. Relying either on statute or common law, courts called attention to the deprivation of liberty involved in commitment and the seriousness of the step being taken. They may have endorsed the concept of adherence to stringent standards, but they gave the committing doctor much latitude in interpreting the statute and fitting the patient within its definition. Many statutes gave a third criterion: In addition to safety of self and others, they allowed commitment for those "in need of care," and this put the patient at an even greater disadvantage in trying to prove that he should be free. It is only in the last decade that dangerousness in the context of some commitment laws has come to mean overt or recent dangerousness.

Judges accepted evidence of dangerousness not shown by any overt acts. Fantasies expressed in therapy or subjective responses revealed on Rorschach tests were enough to justify commitment. (In spite of recent statutes and cases that require evidence of overt dangerousness to justify commitment, sociologists report that judges still rely on the word of psychiatrists that patients who have not overtly evidenced dangerousness are dangerous.)[15]

Part of the problem is that psychiatrists are utilizing the medical model, and they see getting a patient into a hospital quickly and conveniently, without a great expenditure of their own time, as a sound therapeutic procedure. Civil-liberties-minded lawyers see psychiatry as nonmedical. They know—as psychiatrists do not know—that starting in 1968, courts in some "progressive" jurisdictions have called detention in a mental hospital as great a deprivation of liberty as imprisonment. These lawyers fight for strict procedural protections when loss of liberty is threatened.

I have argued that the legal attack on commitment policy represents focusing on the wrong issue. There are multitudes of abuses of psychiatric authority, and many people are detained in mental hospitals too long, but almost all people who are committed deserve evaluation, a protected place of custody, and at least some treatment. In recent years the tendency in many states is to insist on high standards of proof of danger, and many patients who could use hospitalization are not considered committable. Today we commit primarily people who have created major disturbances repeatedly over a period of time, and in this group it is hard to differentiate those who may be from those who will be dangerous. When lawyers and sociologists pinpoint the prediction of dangerousness as one of the vulnerable areas of psychiatry, they force the psychiatrist to allow people to be in the community who need more structured care, and they leave many more important issues of improper use of psychiatric authority neglected.

Even psychiatrists who consider themselves liberal oppose the new stricter commitment policies and laws. Psychiatrists who must prove overt dangerousness in a courtroom procedure spend a great deal of time in the process. They often have great difficulty in proving a real threat of danger, even though the person who is subject to the commitment procedure seems grossly disturbed.

Rigorous commitment laws that deprive psychiatrists of their authority make state hospital work difficult and unsatisfactory for psychiatrists; they drive them into private practice. Alan Stone has said that the logical force of the analogy of commitment to a criminal procedure leads to the conclusion that predictive judgments should be abandoned and all confinement be based on past dangerous acts that have been proved beyond a reasonable doubt.

> The basic premise, of course, is not based on helping people, it is based on a professed fair balancing of individual freedom against protecting the public. In fact, since there is no valid method for predicting dangerousness, reform that moves toward making the prediction of dangerousness the sole criterion for civil commitment is not reform; rather, it is abolition disguised as reform . . . If there are in fact reasons for society to provide treatment to people whose mental illness prevents them from accepting such treatment, then there may yet be a role for civil commitment in a free society.[16]

In *Addington* v. *Texas,* the Supreme Court endorsed that view, saying that although civil commitment "constitutes a significant deprivation of liberty that requires due process protection," nevertheless commitment cannot be equated with a criminal prosecution and therefore not all the criminal justice safeguards need be observed.[17]

Psychiatrists and other behavioral scientists predict dangerousness for many other purposes besides commitment, and many more people are hurt in the process. The criminal-justice system uses psychiatrists to predict dangerousness for sentencing, prison assignment, and parole, and gives the psychiatrists great unchecked power.

Sexual-psychopath laws, less popular than they were twenty years ago but still found in many states, allow the indeterminate diversion to a mental hospital, possibly for life, of certain sexual offenders if it is determined that they will continue to be dangerous. Homosexuality with consenting adults is no longer considered sexual psychopathy, but five categories of sexual offenses continue to be grounds for this diversion from the criminal-justice to the mental health system—rape (and attempted rape and assault with attempt to rape), child molestation, incest, exhibitionism and voyeurism, and such miscellaneous offenses as breaking and entering (to steal objects used as fetishes) and arson (when used for sexual excitement). In some jurisdictions (Maryland, for example) repeated criminality, not sexual in character, can lead to a diagnosis of defective delinquency, to be similarly treated with an indeterminate hospitalization.

A sexual-psychopath act was enacted for the District of Columbia in 1948 as "a humane and practical approach to the problem of persons unable to control their sexual emotions." People picked up for sexual offenses could be hospitalized as sexual psychopaths before or after trial or even when there had been no criminal charge. Congress defined a sexual psychopath as a person who was not insane but who showed by a course of repeated misconduct in sexual matters that he was dangerous to other persons, likely to "attack or otherwise inflict injury, loss, pain or other evil on the objects of his desire." Under the terms of the act, Maurice Millard was sent to St. Elizabeths Hospital in 1962. He had been charged in municipal court with indecent exposure, exhibiting himself and masturbating in public, the maximum punishment for which was imprisonment for ninety days or a fine of $300 or both. Two psychiatrists who examined Millard diagnosed him as a sexual psychopath according to the terms of the statute, so he was diverted from the criminal-justice system to the mental health system and sent to St. Elizabeths Hospital.

When Millard was admitted to the hospital he was diagnosed as not psychotic but suffering from a personality disorder, "passive-aggressive personality, passive-dependent type, exhibitionism." Six years later he was still in the hospital seeking his release. According to his hospital record, a social worker had been told by his wife that he had walked around naked in his house in the presence of his small children holding his penis in his hand. He had denied this. Neither the wife nor the social worker ever testified in any proceeding about this behavior, but the allegation of the incident—amounting only to hearsay—was part of the data that led to psychiatric judgments that Millard continued to be dangerous. During the six years at St. Elizabeths there had been no reports of further exhibitionism.

Millard attempted to secure his liberty through a writ of habeas corpus. The District of Columbia Circuit Court of Appeals ordered an evidentiary hearing to determine, among other issues, whether the sexual misconduct that the petitioner had indulged in, or was likely to indulge in, was sufficiently serious to justify further detention. Five psychiatrists testified at the hearing. None of them disagreed with the diagnosis; all of them testified that he was unable to enter into a mature relationship with women. According to the weight of the psychiatric testimony, he still suffered from the personality disorder and if released he would be likely to exhibit himself in public at times of stress. The fact that he had had no problems during six years in the hospital was readily explainable: He had been under supervision and there had not been opportunity. He had been shielded from the tension-producing situations involving women in general and his wife in particular that had precipitated his previous exhibiting behavior.

How dangerous was the behavior? The psychiatrists testified that the effect would vary with the viewer. Most women would find the act repulsive, but their distress would be brief. The consensus of the five psychiatric experts was that a highly sensitive woman would be more shocked and that a "very seclusive, withdrawn, shy, sensitive, suspicious" woman might become "quite upset" for a period of several days. For these reasons, the psychiatrists found Millard a continuing danger and in need of further hospitalization, and the court agreed. On appeal, Judge Bazelon ordered a reversal of the opinion on the ground that the likelihood of someone so sensitive or so immature that she could be damaged by the sight of Millard exposing himself was too remote to justify a permanent loss of liberty.[18] But Judge Bazelon is considered an enlightened judge and the District of Columbia a progressive jurisdiction. In most jurisdictions the psychiatrists' determination that Millard continued to be dangerous would not have been overruled, and in many he would not even have been granted an evidentiary hearing. Psychiatrists find nonpsychotic criminal defendants dangerous—sometimes sexually dangerous, sometimes criminally dangerous in nonsexual ways (the definition of sexual psychopath or defective delinquent varies in different jurisdictions)—and thus divert them from the criminal-justice system to an indeterminate psychiatric commitment in a hospital for the criminally insane. We have seen that they have also found end-of-sentence men like Johnnie Baxstrom and "mentally abnormal offenders" such as Roy Schuster continuingly dangerous and therefore ineligible for release. When a defendant successfully evades a criminal penalty by pleading not guilty by reason of insanity, psychiatrists can evaluate him as continuingly dangerous and hold him for the rest of his life.

Psychiatrists and other behavioral scientists make many other predictions having to do with dangerousness. They write pretrial reports, and often the allegation of dangerousness means that, instead of charges being dropped, a prosecution will continue. If the pretrial report states the defendant is dangerous, he is denied bail. On conviction, there is a presentence report, and the attribution of dangerousness in this can lead to a long sentence instead of a short or suspended sentence. The future course of a prison inmate is related entirely to an assessment of his dangerousness. If he has been seen as dangerous, he is sent to a maximum security institution, where he is under constant scrutiny, lacks good vocational programs and has less chance of an early parole.

No one knows how dangerous a person should be to justify a deprivation of his liberty. We routinely release dangerous people from prisons when they have served their sentences, so obviously dangerousness by itself is not the justification for detention. We hold people indefinitely as patients when there is dangerousness plus a diagnosed mental illness or equivalent—sexual psychopathy, defective delinquency, or a mental defect.

How long should we hold dangerous people to treat them? Szasz answers the question by saying that no amount of danger justifies any deprivation of liberty under a rationale of illness and treatment. If someone has broken a law, he can be imprisoned; if no law has been broken he should be free. At the opposite extreme, authoritarian and paternalistic psychiatrists and psychiatrists in totalitarian regimes diagnose any departure from psychiatric definitions of normality as a dangerous kind of mental illness. The definitions often depend on state policy. A disinclination to work can be seen as a danger to society and can lead to a diagnosis of mental illness. In our society, "takeover" psychiatrists who see almost all deviation as the result of disease do not think of themselves as totalitarians. Instead they consider their position humanistic. They have no doubt of the reality of mental illness, and they do not see the forcible detention of the mentally ill as a deprivation, but as a therapeutic opportunity. Between these extremes we have the mass of decision makers—inconsistent psychiatrists and bewildered judges—who utilize the nebulous concept of dangerousness flexibly and pragmatically, that is, differently at different times.

In some general hospital emergency rooms, anyone who has attempted suicide is considered potentially dangerous and is given a psychiatric evaluation. However, in some of the busiest municipal hospital emergency rooms, when psychiatric consultations are not readily available, it is assumed that by the time the would-be suicide has been treated, the danger of suicide is usually past. If evaluations are done, the personality and philosophy of the evaluator will affect whether more or fewer of these people are held for further observation. The availability of hospital beds in some cases is the chief determinant of the decision.

Like other psychiatric phenomena, suicide is hard to predict. One study showed that psychiatric patients committed suicide five times as frequently as the general population but much less frequently than those people with no history of psychiatric hospitalization who had made previous suicide attempts. Even in this most susceptible group, it was hard to predict suicide; a large majority did not go on to commit suicide. To save some lives it would have been necessary to lock up in preventive custody a much larger number of people who were members of the same "at risk" group but who were in fact not dangerous.[19] There is no way to pick out potential suicides except when there is acute obvious danger, and in that case no special psychiatric expertise is needed. Judges, juries, and the general public do not realize that many of the statements made by psychiatrists are based on common sense applied to data available to everyone. Because the opinion is expressed by an expert and because it is couched in an elaborate scientific vocabulary, its fallibility and its lack of special probative value are obscured.

The judges and psychiatrists who control behavior are themselves victims of a system, caught up in their own version of "catch-22." If they move to protect people, they will damage many who do not need protection. If they do not move to protect people, they will allow people who need protection to hurt themselves or to hurt others. There is no way to secure a perfect combination of protection of the patient *and* protection of his liberties. If the patient is at one of the extremes of a continuum, either greatly disturbed or hardly disturbed at all, the predictions are easier; if the psychiatrist is conscientious and spends more time on the evaluation, he can have a better rate of successful predictions; if he has read enough in the literature to know the fallibility of his ability to predict, he will apply his forecasts with more caution. But he will still either focus on liberty and put too many people at risk, or focus on therapy and safety and deprive too many people of liberty.

In 1943 Peter Mayock[20] was committed to the Connecticut State Hospital at Norwich, where he was held for three months and then released. Six months later Mayock removed his right eye in response to a demand by God. He was recommitted to the hospital; eventually, after treatment, he was released on probation. (Mental patients as well as prisoners are given their liberty dependent upon good behavior.) In 1947, on the last day of his probation period, he was examined by a psychiatrist who found him safe to be given unconditional liberty. Three days later he cut off his right hand. He was recommitted. He said he had reasoned from reading the Scriptures that he could keep mankind from being destroyed by obeying the precept of the Sermon on the Mount—"And if thy right eye offend thee, pluck it out, and cast it from thee; for it is profitable for thee that one of thy members should perish, and not that thy whole body should be cast into hell. And if thy right hand offend thee, cut it off, and cast it from thee for it is profitable for thee that one of thy members should perish, and not that thy whole body should be cast into hell."[21] Twenty-one years later Mayock still in the hospital, applied for a writ of habeas corpus on the ground that his detention was unnecessary. He had done no further injury to himself. He ran the newsstand in the hospital's administration building and he was active in patient recreational programs. He continued to maintain that he was a prophet with a divine message, that God had intended for one man to make a peace offering to Him, that it is far better for one man to sacrifice an eye or a hand for a divine purpose than for the world to continue on its present violent and destructive course. Mayock told his psychiatrist-evaluators that he had no plan to cut off any other part of his body, but when asked whether he would obey a divine revelation to cut off his foot, he replied that he would. The question at issue was his continuing dangerousness. The psychiatrists focused on the unremitting character of his beliefs, and they thought he should not be released. On the other hand, it was incontrovertible that he had not injured anyone except himself and that he had not injured himself in more than twenty years. A trial court found that the state had the right to continue to hold him for his own protection; an appeals court affirmed the decision. Mayock could not gain his freedom. One judge dissented: "As between the possibility that the plaintiff may amputate his foot and the certainty that, under this judgment, he must remain incarcerated against his will indefinitely, I choose the former."[22]

Mayock brought an action in the federal court, but here the psychiatric testimony was given with more certainty. The psychiatrists had learned from their experience in the first case that their testimony was not as compelling when they indicated their uncertainties (although it was sufficiently compelling to keep Mayock in the hospital), and this time they expressed fewer doubts that Mayock required hospital protection.

Ten years later I wrote to the superintendent of Norwich State Hospital to find out what had become of Mayock. My letter was referred to Mayock for his answer, and he wrote to me. He was still in the hospital. He had the privilege of signing himself out of the hospital until 10 P.M. on any day. He spent four or five hours off the hospital grounds visiting with his brother and friends about three days a week. He continued to run the hospital magazine stand, and he also fixed watches and clocks as a hobby. He had not brought any further legal action to win his freedom but instead had decided to "wait on time," to let "developments . . . mature" that were "contained in the reasoning" based on Holy Writ that he had not had a chance to discuss in previous trials. He wrote, "The crux of the matter in law is whether a person who has all the use of his faculties should be confined for what is presumed he may do in the future."

The most striking example of psychiatric prediction affecting the disposition of "dangerous people" is in recent capital punishment cases. Psychiatrists have traditionally given testimony that someone should or should not be held responsible for his actions, but under new statutes they sometimes testify further that the person will continue to be dangerous and should therefore receive the death penalty.

In 1972 the Supreme Court in *Furman* v. *Georgia,* [23] outlawed death penalties that were applied irrationally or unfairly, but left the option open for states to devise fairer death penalty statutes. In the years that have followed, eighteen states adopted a new kind of "guided discretion" death penalty act, which has been held by the Supreme Court to be constitutional. In most of these states the jury can find that any of a dozen specified "aggravating circumstances" is present in the case and can impose the death sentence, but in the Texas statute and also in the statutes of Mississippi, Oklahoma, Virginia, and Washington, an important consideration for the jury is evidence of continuing dangerousness.

In Texas the jury makes two determinations. The first is guilt or innocence on the capital offense charge. If the defendant is found guilty, then the jury considers whether the defendant will commit further antisocial dangerous acts in the future if he is not put to death.

The question the jury must decide, with the help of expert and other evidence, is: "whether there is a probability that the defendant would commit criminal acts of violence that would constitute a continuing threat to society . . ."[24] The jury can be guided by any kind of testimony from anyone who has data that may be useful, but often the predictions of a psychiatrist concerning the future dangerousness of the defendant are the most convincing testimony for the jury. Sometimes a psychiatrist is the sole prosecution witness at this second stage of the trial, and he usually has no difficulty in persuading the jury that the death penalty is appropriate. This was something new for psychiatry, recommending that death is the best solution for a behavioral problem.

One of the trials under the Texas guided discretion law concerned Ernest Benjamin Smith who, with Howie Ray Robinson, had robbed a Schepps Grocery Store in Dallas, Texas, in September 1973. When the cashier moved as if to reach for something, Smith yelled a warning to Robinson and Robinson fatally shot the cashier. Smith and Robinson were arrested and charged with murder with malice aforethought. The grand jury returned a bill of indictment against Smith, and the state gave notice that it intended to seek the death penalty. The judge ordered a psychiatric examination by Dr. James Grigson to determine whether Smith was competent to stand trial. There seems to have been no real reason for the examination, for there was no indication that Smith was not competent. But judges frequently order this evaluation, even though it is expensive for the state and sometimes subjects the defendant to sixty or ninety days in a psychiatric hospital and delays the trial, merely because they want to forestall the chance of a reversal if it turns out later that the defendant was incompetent to be tried. Most psychiatrists do not enjoy participating in what seems more like a charade than a purposeful evaluative procedure, but those in the employ of the state have no alternative, and some private practitioners, invite this kind of work. These few psychiatrists often evaluate huge numbers of patients, and they are often willing to evaluate a man as competent to stand trial on the basis of an examination as brief as thirty minutes.

Grigson does not give the most cursory kind of examination. He prides himself on his forensic ability. He is a main source of expert opinion for Texas prosecution in criminal cases where psychiatric testimony is needed. He has examined more than 8000 accused felons. Since the passage of the guided discretion death act, he has found all of the 30 defendants that he has examined for a death determination to be sociopaths and deserving to be executed. Of the 86 men awaiting execution in Texas at least 26 have been diagnosed by him as sociopaths.[25]

Grigson is not unique. In every state there are several psychiatrists who enjoy testifying, who are known to be "law-and-order-minded," who can be counted on to give good testimony for the prosecution, and who show confidence in their predictive ability and so are very persuasive in the courtroom. Robert Jones, a Canadian psychiatrist who has told us there are "hanging judges and there are hanging psychiatrists," went on to say: ". . . Psychiatrists who devoted a good deal of their professional life to the examination of criminals, and who usually appeared for the prosecution . . . frequently seemed to have lost their 'therapeutic orientation' and had it replaced by a 'punishment orientation.' "[26] An American psychiatrist wrote, "At times I have been embarrassed by my profession. My community, like most others, has a few psychiatrists who find all defendants not guilty by reason of mental disease or defect. There is another small group which finds everyone guilty."[27] Defense attorneys have called Grigson a "hired gun for prosecutors" and "the killer shrink," but he is no different from some other Texas psychiatrists and from psychiatrists in other jurisdictions who are known as reliable witnesses for the prosecution. George Dix, a law professor, has said of the Texas death cases, "... Mental health professional involvement has been substantial, and primarily on behalf of the prosecution."[28]

Grigson, with a few other Texas psychiatrists, is outstanding only because the determinations he has made under the new statute lead to the imposition of the death penalty. Usually when psychiatrists make predictions as a part of the sentencing procedure, the penalty is less severe and the cases receive less notice, and then the quality of psychiatric testimony is not questioned.

The defendant is at great disadvantage if he is indigent. An affluent defendant can hire his own psychiatric expert, and if the report is helpful to his case can use this psychiatrist as a defense expert; if it is not helpful the evaluation need not be brought into the trial process. An indigent defendant does not have this option. He can secure a court-appointed psychiatrist to evaluate him, possibly to counter the testimony of the prosecution, but the report is used in the trial no matter how adverse it is. Of the men awaiting death in Texas, the prosecution used a psychiatrist—often Grigson—for dangerousness testimony in more than 60 percent of the cases, and the defense used psychiatric testimony in less than 20 percent of the cases.[29]

In Smith's case there was no reason to suspect a lack of competency to come to trial and no evaluation was needed. Later the judge would defend his having ordered the psychiatric examination for competency: "In all cases where the State has sought the death penalty, I have ordered a mental evaluation of the defendant to determine his competency to stand trial. I have done this for my benefit because I do not intend to be a participant in a case where the defendant receives the death penalty and his mental competency remains in doubt." The accused is—in spite of the judge's high-minded sentiments—being done an injustice here because, as it will turn out, Grigson will be doing more than merely evaluating competency to stand trial. Without informing the accused, he will at the same time be making up his mind about the desirability of his execution. Dr. Grigson will interview the defendant, tell him he is a psychiatrist (and will let him know he is the psychiatrist for the state, not for the defense), and politely and affably proceed with his questioning. If the defendant responds to this show of courteous treatment by also being polite and well-mannered, Grigson will interpret this as an inappropriate lack of affect, a failure to display anxiety, an omission of expressions of contrition. The defendant does not understand the rules of this particular catch. If he cries and shakes and says he will burn in hell and shows instability, he can be seen as not dangerous, but if he shows good behavior, he is a sociopath, which is the worst kind of sickness because it is not amenable to therapy, and is thus best dealt with by execution. If the defendant refuses to participate in the evaluation, the psychiatrist may nevertheless diagnose him as an incurable sociopath who will present a continuing threat to members of society, on the basis of interviews with, among others, the officers who arrested and interrogated him.

After a ninety-minute evaluation conducted in the jail, Grigson concluded, predictably, that Smith was competent to stand trial. (The two defense attorneys appointed to represent Smith were not notified that the psychiatric examination was going to be done. No formal order of appointment of Grigson was entered, and Grigson never filed a written report. He did write a letter to the judge, but the defense attorneys did not learn that the examination had taken place until they found a copy of the letter in the court papers after the trial had commenced.)

Smith was convicted, which raised the question of disposition. The prosecution called Grigson, and he was allowed to testify over the objections of the defense about his conclusion on whether Smith should be executed. Grigson was the only prosecution witness in this punishment phase of the trial. The jury was informed that Grigson was the court-appointed psychiatrist, but not that he had been appointed only to evaluate Smith's competency to stand trial. Dr. Grigson testified about his procedure of psychiatric examination—much more about this than about Smith specifically—and went on to give his opinion. He characterized Smith as having a very severe sociopathic personality disturbance. His prognosis was that Smith would continue his previous behavior or get worse. There was no treatment that would improve Smith's sociopathy. Smith would commit criminal acts of violence that would constitute a continuing threat to society if he were not put to death. On cross-examination, Grigson testified that he was certain that Smith was a severe sociopath, that his diagnosis of sociopathic personality was based on Smith's failure to show guilt or remorse during the psychiatric examination, that he had not interviewed anyone else besides the codefendant, and that Smith during the examination had been pleasant, cooperative, polite, intelligent, rational, courteous, and had not tried to fake insanity.

Grigson was asked his prognosis by the prosecuting attorney.

GRIGSON: Oh, he will continue his previous behavior—that which he has done in the past. He will again do it in the future.

QUESTION: All right. So, were he released into society, I take it, then, you would not expect his behavior to differ from what it has been?

GRIGSON: No. If anything it would only get worse.

QUESTION: Now, Dr. Grigson, this sociopathic personality that Smith has —is this a condition that will improve with time? I guess—what I'm asking you is this: Is this a stage that he is passing through that he will grow out of?

GRIGSON: No. This is not what you would consider a stage. This is a way of life. Just as you work every day, well his personality comes out in his behavior, but it is not a stage he is going through. It's only something he will continue.

QUESTION: You said get worse?

GRIGSON: Yes.

QUESTION: If it can?

GRIGSON: Right.

The cross-examination was not sophisticated. Most lawyers are not aware enough of psychiatric practice and the limitations of psychiatric expertise to do a competent cross-examination of psychiatric witnesses. The fact that the diagnosis completely lacked substantiation was not brought out. The pattern of past maladaptive behavior that is necessary for a diagnosis of sociopath—conceding what should not be conceded, that this is a justifiable diagnostic classification—had not been shown. The diagnosis had been based on the criminal act, on Smith's failure to call an ambulance after his codefendant shot the victim, and the lack of expression of remorse. Once the diagnosis was made, the prognosis is also given: Sociopaths, by a definition Grigson gave, do not respond to therapy. (If he had chosen, Grigson could have brought out the evidence that much deviant behavior is modified by time alone.)

Grigson suggested how Smith could have shown remorse to him. "I think that his telling me this story and not saying, you know, 'Man, I would do anything to have that man back alive. I wish I hadn't just stepped over the body.' Or you know, 'I wish I had checked to see if he was all right' would indicate a concern, guilt or remorse. But I didn't get any of these."

Everything the defendant does becomes grist for the psychiatrist's diagnostic and prognostic mill. The fact that during the interview he is cooperative, pleasant, and polite can be seen as manipulative. The fact that there is not a record of previous problems with the law does not indicate that possibly this is not a case of sociopathy—which is usually manifested early and by repeated antisocial activity—but that this is such an extreme sociopath that he has escaped detection until this time.[30] A Texas lawyer who unsuccessfully defended another death case says, "I don't think I have ever seen any effective way to handle Grigson. You can tell your man not to talk to him, but Grigson will still look at him, ask him questions, then testify that his very silence means he's a sociopath and shows no remorse. It's a 'can't win' situation."[31]

Grigson's views, although not unusual for prosecution psychiatric experts, do not represent current psychiatric thinking. He seems unconcerned that there is a developing literature on the unreliability of psychiatric predictions of dangerousness and the elimination from the *Diagnostic and Statistical Manual* in its second edition of the diagnostic category of sociopath. "I have been doing this since 1960," he told an interviewer, "and in that time I've examined more murderers and more rapists than the combined number examined by the people who wrote the APA diagnostic manual. And based on my experience, here's *my* definition of sociopath. First, a sociopath doesn't have a conscience. He feels no remorse about his crime. I say to him, 'Hey, how did you feel about killing these people?' and he doesn't hang his head, his cheeks don't flush, he doesn't have any of the normal reactions you and I would have. Two, he repeatedly breaks the rules of society. Three, he cons and manipulates, lies, steals, and cheats for the pleasure of it.

"Most of the district attorneys only prosecute a very specific type of person for these death cases. They put it on the meanest, baddest guys, for the very *worst* type of offenses. If they prosecute a death case on a guy who's held up a Seven-Eleven store and shot the clerk, then that guy has already been identified as bad, bad, bad. I think you could do away with the psychiatrist in these cases. Just take any man off the street, show him what the guy's done, and most of these things are so clearcut he would say the same things I do. But I think the jurors feel a little better when a psychiatrist says it—somebody that's supposed to know more than they know."[32]

Smith produced several lay witnesses to testify that he had always had a good character and a good reputation. He had no history of dangerous crimes before the capital offense for which he had been convicted; his only other conviction had been for possession of marijuana.[33] The jury believed Grigson and gave Smith a death sentence.

In another of the Texas death cases, Grigson testified that James Livingston was sane but that he had an antisocial personality disorder, which, he explained to the jury, was not an illness or a sickness. (This kind of psychiatric testimony has to be tailored very carefully. If psychopathology is emphasized, the jury may become sympathetic or see the defendant as sick and not responsible, so the task of the prosecution expert is to pin a label on the defendant that will indicate that he is incapable of improvement but at the same time make the jury understand the label does not indicate any lack of responsibility on the part of the defendant.) The term antisocial personality disorder, Grigson said, is a term descriptive of mental characteristics. "It would be about like one way of describing, say, somebody that is six foot tall, 200 pounds."

Commenting on the *Smith* and *Livingston* cases, Alan Stone, the vice president (and more recently president) of the American Psychiatric Association, wrote that he had had "the rather chilling experience of reading trial records," that such testimony "raises formidable questions about the basic morality of our calling as physicians." Stone asks whether the examining psychiatrists warned the defendants that their responses to them may mean the difference between execution or not. He suggests that such a warning is required by personal ethics and possibly by law.[34]

An attack against the new Texas death act began, based on its effectiveness as a deterrent and its possible selective use against racial minorities or the economically deprived, but also based on the impossibility of predicting future dangerousness and the unreliability of expert psychiatric testimony in which future dangerousness is predicted.

When a United States District Court judge vacated Smith's death sentence, some of the reasons were the state's conduct in springing Dr. Grigson's testimony on unsuspecting defense attorneys and the unreliability of psychiatric testimony. The court cited eighteen cases, some of them involving numerous appeals, where Grigson's testimony against the defendant had been at issue in an appeal. It also noted a peculiarity of psychiatric testimony, not involved in Smith's case, since he had confessed, but arising in many others. The psychiatrist bases his diagnosis of sociopathy on the lack of remorse the defendant shows, but often the defendant denies he is guilty and the lack of remorse only assumes significance if the psychiatrist proceeds on the assumption, not proven at law, that the denial of guilt is false.[35]

The judge also pointed out that a psychiatric examination concerning the appropriateness of the death penalty does not have the same possibility of benefit to the defendant as the examination for competency to stand trial, and the defendant who does not raise the issue of dangerousness—and thereby waive his privilege against self-incrimination—cannot be compelled to participate in a psychiatric examination concerning dangerousness. Defendants must be notified that they have a right to remain silent.

Legal activism and judicial scrutiny will probably keep psychiatrists from playing a powerful role in determining appropriateness of execution, but it is obvious that without this activism and scrutiny psychiatrists would have been happy to send murderers to their deaths on the basis of psychiatric testimony colored by value judgments and with no scientific basis. Few psychiatrists have been aware that their fellow psychiatrists were playing this role; of the few who were knowledgeable, only four or five have publicly protested this misuse of psychiatry.

At a state habeas corpus proceeding in *Livingston* v. *State,* [36] Loren Roth, a psychiatrist speaking under American Psychiatric Association auspices, testified as to the unreliability of long-range predictions of future dangerousness and the dubious nature of the diagnostic category of sociopath. In the *Smith* case appeal from the district court to the circuit court, the APA trustees authorized the preparation and filing of an *amicus curiae* brief siding with the American Civil Liberties Union's attack on the Texas death cases.[37] The only point argued by the APA in its brief was that "due process requires that when psychiatric testimony is to be used at the penalty phase of a capital case, the defendant must be so advised before the psychiatrist examines him." The brief distinguished use of psychiatry in the punishment phase from the traditional use of psychiatry in determinations of trial competency and the insanity defense, where the issue of mental state is usually raised by the defendant. In the course of the argument the APA said, "In the view of *amicus,* this kind of inquiry about long-term future violence essentially does not involve medical analysis, and is not within the realm of established psychiatric expertise . . . The psychiatrist's medical training and experience do not qualify him to provide reliable testimony about the likelihood of long-term future harmful acts."

Psychiatrists cannot predict the probability of future violence with a high degree of accuracy. Studies show that, in the process of trying to identify a small number of people who will commit future dangerous acts, they will in the process make a few false negatives (identify as not dangerous people who are actually dangerous) and will also make many false positives (identify as dangerous people who are not dangerous). The problem of overprediction relates to the frequency of occurrence, and dangerousness is an infrequent occurrence, even in the mentally ill. For example, if we say that 5 percent of murderers will commit another murder in the future (a much higher figure than the actual figure), and we say that psychiatrists evaluating murderers have a 50 percent accuracy rate in predicting future violence (a much higher rate of accuracy than psychiatrists claim), there would be a great injustice involved in the attempt to differentiate in a group of 100 people who had committed murder the 5 who will kill again from the 95 others. The 50 percent accuracy rate would result in only 2.5 true future murderers being identified, and 47.5 nondangerous defendants would have been falsely identified as dangerous, and 2.5 future murderers would not have been picked out. This would not necessarily be a reflection on the psychiatrists, whose 50 percent accuracy rate might represent a higher degree of evaluative skill than the rate of accuracy of nonpsychiatrists (although no better than coin flipping or picking every second person).

The American Psychiatric Association is on record concerning the inadequacy of the psychiatric prediction of dangerousness. In an entirely different kind of case, when a psychiatrist was being sued for not having given a warning that might have saved the life of his violent patient's former girl friend, the APA filed an *amicus curiae* brief stating that "study after study has shown" that the psychiatrist "is ill-equipped to undertake . . . the prediction of his patient's potential dangerousness."[38]

One of the horrors of the kind of prediction made in the Texas cases is that the judgment that future crimes will be committed is based on the psychiatric diagnosis of sociopathy, which is a most inexact and subjective diagnosis. Most psychiatrists believe that there is a psychiatric entity characterized by complete amorality, total lack of an ability to sympathize and empathize, a total need to manipulate other people, and a total incapacity to serve any other purpose except the gratification of the self, which constitutes sociopathy (or, a former term for the same condition, "psychopathy"). A Danish forensic psychiatrist with a great deal of experience in evaluating offenders says he has seen only a handful of cases he would call sociopaths, but many psychiatrists diagnose this condition frequently, and some call a majority of criminals sociopaths.

In addition to the subjective bias of the evaluator, there are built-in biases when standardized tests are used to determine sociopathy. Some group classification tests, done with pen and paper and without the intervention of a psychologist, show that a large percentage of prisoners are sociopaths, but the questions could be changed so that few prisoners would test out as sociopaths. The category is so nebulous that the rate of case finding can vary according to the institution and the testing method used. In one Illinois prison 95 percent of the inmates were labeled sociopaths, but at the same time in another prison in the state only 5 percent were so labeled. At New York's Bellevue Hospital 52 percent of all sexual offenders received this diagnosis, but at the same period in a psychiatric facility set up to work with the New York City criminal courts, only 15 percent of sexual offenders were so labeled.[39] The activities of the staff of St. Elizabeths Hospital in calling sociopathy a mental disease, then striking it from the disease list, then deciding once again that it is a disease, have been described.[40]

Some critics of the use of the label of sociopathy have pointed out that people with this diagnosis vary widely and that most of them are not violent. Many are embezzlers, con artists, manipulators, check kiters, and other varieties of tricksters and cheaters who have no history of violent behavior. One flaw in the testimony of the prosecution experts in the Texas cases is their failure to refer to studies showing that people diagnosed as sociopaths tend to end their criminal careers at the age of thirty-five or forty. When juices have dried up or passions died down, the rate of criminal repeat convictions drops off dramatically, and some psychiatrists see sociopathy as a condition difficult or impossible to cure but which in time may cure itself.

Sociopathy is a catchall or wastebasket diagnosis, often used against a person disapproved of or disliked by the evaluator. Patients who are especially uncooperative in therapy are often diagnosed as sociopaths, particularly if their lack of cooperation is evidenced by failing to pay their therapy bills. Few of the frequently made determinations of sociopathy receive the public attention that the Grigson and Holbrook determinations finally secured.

But it is one thing to say that psychiatrists cannot predict dangerousness over long periods of future time and that their testimony in such cases is unreliable, and it is another to say that they should not have the power to commit patients to mental hospitals because they are not precise predictors, or because there must be recent overt acts of dangerousness, or because illness and danger must be proved beyond a reasonable doubt before a patient can be hospitalized.

Psychiatrists continue to want to hospitalize patients whom they think would benefit from hospitalization, and they want to hospitalize them whether or not they appear to be dangerous. More than on any other standard, psychiatrists probably rely on a "do unto others standard." The test they use, without ever verbalizing it, is: If I were this person, or if this person were a member of my family, would I see

207

hospitalization as the best alternative? Other psychiatrists admit they work on a "gut reaction test"; certain people give them such a sensation of disquiet or apprehension when they examine them that they feel they need hospitalization. Lawyers scorn such subjective criteria, but psychiatrists state that their feelings are the result of their training and experience and so represent the best authority of all, "clinical judgment."

Psychiatrists get tired of fighting with lawyers. Sometimes they allow patients to remain out of the hospital who they think should be committed, merely to avoid a court fight. Often they stop working in the state hospital and community mental health care system because their time is consumed by legal maneuvers. The public sector of psychiatry is providing fewer and fewer inducements. It is an easy decision to concentrate on private patients, who rarely require hospitalization, in the setting of "the oriental rugs and leather chair of the suburban psychotherapist's office."[41]

In the past the too easy commitment of mental patients has been an abuse, but now the pendulum has swung, and more patients suffer from lack of hospitalization than from too easy commitment.

The psychiatrist walks a fine line that has excessive risk-taking for the person and the community on one side and excessive loss of liberty on the other. No matter how carefully he walks it, how aware he is of the dangers on the one side and the other and of his own deficiencies in knowledge and skill, he will still be criticized. If he is aware, he will be critical of himself. The line can be moved in favor of individual liberty and risk-taking or in favor of authoritarianism and a protected society; no matter where the line is located, the psychiatrist will be criticized because the line is not somewhere else. Most psychiatrists see their role as paternalistic. They are forced by temperament and training and their perception of patients' needs to emphasize control of patients and community protection. The lawyer will continue to assert that the psychiatrist's subjective perceptions of the needs of patients is not a sufficient ground for loss of liberty.

Psychiatrists should be given more leeway when they use predictions of dangerousness to hold out-of-control patients than when they predict dangerousness to certify people as worthy only of execution. We can scrutinize the predictions of psychiatrists more carefully, and especially as they are used in the criminal-justice system, where they have caused particular harm, but we cannot dispense altogether with their predictions.

Recent headlines tell us that "Market Forecasts Show a Staggering Unreliability" and that earthquake predictions are proving elusive.[42]

We act on the advice of these experts even though we know they do not have a perfect prediction record. It is not very good, but it is the best we can do. If we need authority for our practice in civil commitment of relying on a weak classification scheme and a poor record of predicting future behavior, we can quote Justice Oliver Wendell Holmes: "Every year, if not every day, we have to wage our salvation upon some prophecy based upon imperfect knowledge."[43]

Testing, Tracking, and Profiling

PSYCHIATRISTS EXERCISE their most direct and most obvious power through the diagnosis of mental illness and the prediction of its course. Their judgments are readily accepted by courts and relied on by administrative agencies. But larger numbers of people are influenced, although in less obvious ways, by other kinds of power that have been assumed by psychiatrists, and particularly by psychologists and other new breeds of behavioral scientists who devise tests and schemes to put people into categories and classes based on psychological attributes. Power is exerted over people who take tests to see if they fit within certain "profiles" that qualify them for employment, job advancement, termination, or other penalties or benefits.

The subjects of these evaluations do not suffer anything as visibly traumatic as commitment to a mental hospital or subjection to electroshock therapy, but the more subtle manipulations they undergo—failure to advance at work, failure to be selected for graduate school, inexplicable rejections and disappointments—add up to strong influences on their lives.

Like the more medical interventions, these behavioral science interventions in the interest of "profiling" and "tracking" and categorizing are often beneficial. They can help people advance at work and can eliminate mismatching and waste, but when someone is maligned there is never an opportunity to prove that the scientific basis of the determination may not be truly scientific. There is usually only a Kafkaesque notification that one is deficient, without any specifics of the deficit even being disclosed and without a chance to respond to the charges.

At a time when labeling and predictions of future dangerousness are receiving so much attention and criticism, this more subtle kind of categorizing continues to enjoy increasing popularity. Business and government are looking for ways to weed out incompetent employees and identify future successful executives. The military relies heavily on aptitude testing and profiling. The prison system is looking for ways to separate good and bad prisoners, even before there is a record of behavior in prison on which to make an assessment, and is particularly interested in finding objective ways to test for appropriateness of parole. Schools and universities, which test for personality factors and adjustment as well as for school aptitude, are constantly trying to improve their testing methods in order to rely even more heavily on them.

A society that is increasingly enlarging and becoming depersonalized relies more and more on these scientific methods of assessing personality and characteristics. If we do not know a person well enough to know his aptitudes or do not trust our own judgment, we can give the behavioral scientist the responsibility to assess him for us.

When psychological testing originated, it was recognized that testing was a combination of science and art and that the subjective attitudes of the tester entered into the determination. One of the pioneers of testing, Sir Cyril Burt, working in the 1920s, decided that the Intelligence Quotient was an imperfect measure of "innate intelligence," and he adjusted the scores of his subjects to compensate upward for poor upbringing, bad schooling, and deprivation, and downward for superior advantages and better-than-average schooling. He never published the details of the factors he used in adjusting his scores.[1]

In more modern times, the intelligence tests that were intended to be an objective way to determine some innate qualities of the subject (there has always been controversy about just what exactly is being tested, but everyone agrees that these are meant to be objective tests of *something*) have been called into double duty as tests of personality, and there is much more room for interpretation and bias on the part of the evaluator. Projective tests, designed to display inner thoughts and repressed impulses, are very subject to interpretation. The validity (whether the test succeeds in testing what it is intended to test) and the reliability (whether the test can produce consistent results when given by different testers) of the famous Rorschach inkblot test has always been, and continues to be, a matter of controversy.

Psychiatrists and psychologists do not object to the subjective element in testing. Psychiatrists know that if they send a patient to be tested, the testing psychologist will usually want background information, a clinical judgment, and a possible diagnosis to focus him in on the subject—though if the tests were truly objective, they should be

211

able to give equally useful results without advance information. The final opinion results from test data, other data that have been furnished, and observations, all filtered through the tester according to his own experience and intuitions.

But this degree of complexity and subjectivity makes the results of the testing too dependent on who is conducting it, and too subject to criticism, and the search has always been for more quantifiable and more precise testing and evaluating methods.

The idea of testing for intelligence had its beginnings in the nineteenth-century eugenics movement, the effort to improve the human stock. Francis Galton's *Hereditary Genius*[2] was one of the first attempts to deal scientifically with individual differences in intelligence. Galton devised measures of intelligence that could be used to demonstrate the differences he saw in races and castes and to differentiate the fit to procreate from those who were unfit. For all his high-mindedness, he foreshadowed and contributed to Nazi theories of racial purity and superiority. He hoped that, as a result of his studies, the naturally gifted would form rural communities of people bearing children of purer blood than the inferior people who overpopulated the cities. The selected race would eventually become a power and gain control. Then, it was hoped, they would treat the lower-caste people "with all kindness" as "long as they maintained celibacy."[3]

The psychologists who have succeeded Galton are less obviously elitist, but their testing has the potential of separating out people on an equally unscientific basis, sentencing them to play roles in life preordained by those who devise the tests.

The concept of testing for school and vocational placement was developed in the last two decades of the nineteenth century and the first two decades of the twentieth. It received its first great impetus in World War I, when the American army wanted quick methods of weeding out potentially less useful recruits.

James Cattell, who had studied with Galton devised some of the first tests of intellectual functioning and promoted the scientific study of individual differences. In 1895 in France, Alfred Binet and Victor Henri published an article entitled "Individual Psychology," in which they proposed a type of testing more sophisticated than Cattell's tests of various areas of performance. They felt that the real measures of intelligence related to complex phenomena such as memory, reason, cognition, and judgment. In 1905 Binet devised the first intelligence scale to help screen out unpromising Paris school children, and a few years later he related the scale to chronological age to devise an intelligence quotient.

No one has ever been quite sure what is being tested in a test of intelligence. One theory is that every specialized ability relates back to a common general ability—that the capacity to perform is a function both of the specialized and the general ability—and according to this approach, it is valid to sum up the intelligence capacity of a person by summing up his individual performances on specialized subtests. Some writers doubt that the specialized abilities are quite so closely related to general ability. Some theorists have maintained that only tests of special performance, like verbal recognition, reasoning, rote memory, and perception of spatial configurations, have validity, and it is misleading to estimate general intelligence.

Much of the British and French work in intelligence testing has been based on the theory that intelligence was genetically determined. Weeding out people with superior performance potential or those who would not be able to perform, and devising special programs in order to "track" them on more demanding or less demanding courses of study would maximize the learning opportunities for both the intelligent and the unintelligent. American psychologists have seen intelligence as much more socially and culturally related, more capable of change, more susceptible to improvement by such interventions as Head Start programs and other changes of environment. (The Supreme Court's decision on busing in 1954 was based, at least in part, on psychological testimony that segregation led to psychological damage.)[4]

By World War II, it was accepted that psychiatry and psychology would take over the role of decision maker, differentiating those who should from those who should not be inducted, then classifying inductees and assigning them to the different branches of service. Testing procedures and psychiatric screening eliminated almost 2 million draftees as unacceptable for induction because of mental disorder or deficiency. The military was astounded that young American males had this much mental disability, and it was thankful that it had been spared these misfits. Brigadier General William Menninger, head of army psychiatry, hailed the army record, and his concept was accepted that the idea of early detection by screening methods had been "proven effective." David Musto, a Yale psychiatrist and historian, has questioned "these accomplishments that both psychiatrists and the military accepted so unreservedly." Musto sees the high rejection rate as the result of the oversensitivity of the psychiatrist to any hint of mental disorder (in the Vietnam War potential draftees would capitalize on this to manipulate their rejections), and he points out that although America rejected six times as many men as Britain did, the

British rate of discharge from active duty for psychological reasons was no higher than the American rate.[5]

We do know that intelligence testing gives an appreciable number of false negative results—people who are considered incapable when they are not—and that job and educational placements done by psychological testing have a high margin of error.

The apparent success of tests to indicate intelligence and the sub-components of intelligence raised the hope that testing methods could be used for other attributes such as ambition, drive, and motivation, and tests for these and other functions were developed. One problem here is that the human personality comprises so many traits (one list of attributes consists of 17,953 English adjectives used to describe specific modes of personality and thought, each adjective representing a potential trait for examination by the personality psychologist), and there is an infinite number of combinations and permutations of these traits, so the tester necessarily has to focus arbitrarily on what he decides are the important ones. One early list included twelve "primary" trait dimensions of personality: for example, cyclothymic (voluble and expressive) and schizothymic (withdrawn and reserved). Another attempt classified personality traits on the basis of needs: to achieve, to excel, to avoid hospitalization, to have sensual experiences, and many more. Other tests attempt to place the subject in such psychiatric diagnostic categories as hypochondriasis, paranoia, hysteria, and psychopathic deviation. The accuracy of a test based on psychiatric diagnostic classification would be related to the accuracy of the original classifications, which always have been subject to question but nevertheless have achieved great acceptance. Variations of personality inventory tests are used to discover if an individual has the temperament to become a mailman or a corporation executive.

Galton, in his studies at the London Anthropometric Laboratory, became interested in testing another entirely different kind of phenomenon, the relationship of ideas, or "associations." Finding what stimuli elicited what responses could lead to an understanding of the important unconscious determinants of motives and interests. Along with Carl Jung, who later elaborated his method, Galton used emotionally suggestive words. In the simplest versions of association tests, unusual associations, too facile associations, or difficulty in finding an association could be seen as evidence of inner conflict. As the method was elaborated, other, less measurable factors began to be seen as indicating "charged" stimuli, including facial expressions, changes of skin color, and signs of anxiety. Eventually physiological responses that can be recorded by instruments were used, and such devices as the polygraph test for truthfulness were devised. Now the tester could assess unconscious as well as conscious functioning, and he could appeal to graphs and read-outs and other hard data as proof of the correctness of his evaluation.

Word-association tests are objective—the time lag between responses can be measured and compared and other quantitative data recorded—but the interpretation of the meaning of the time lags is subjective, varying according to the psychological theories of the tester. Jung was influenced by Freud, and he developed the concept of the "complex," a term that denoted a group of interlinked repressed ideas affecting the individual, requiring him to think along certain channels and to make certain choices. Jung devised his association test method, in which responses to neutral and to emotionally charged stimulus words were timed to locate sensitive areas for further in-depth probing, and in particular to discover complexes. Sometime before 1910, Hermann Rorschach began his studies of the responses to ambiguous inkblots. Galton had pioneered in the use of the inkblot, and William James had developed a projective test based on ambiguous drawings, and Rorschach standardized the blots and the responses.

Eventually a variety of tests involving reactions to ambiguous stimuli was developed. By the 1970s more than 6000 methods of testing intelligence and personality had been described in the testing literature. Most of these have been of only passing interest, but scores continue to be used. Many of these tests are categorized as "objective personality tests" because the tester does not use his judgment. The answers are fixed responses to standard questions, forced choices with little room for shading and tester discretion, but the structure of the tests, their verification, and their validation have all involved much subjective input from the test developers.

Psychiatrists working in specialized fields like child psychiatry or forensic psychiatry often order testing done routinely (a clinic policy will call for every child to have a battery of tests, a court clinic will require every accused sexual criminal to be given projective personality testing). Psychiatrists working in a multidisciplinary setting, such as a clinic or community mental health center or hospital, may make routine referrals for psychological testing. Some psychiatrists order testing in order to protect themselves when they testify in court regarding a diagnosis.

Particularly when courts are involved, testing is done, not necessarily because the evaluator feels the need for, or even has much confidence in, the test results, but because this is the kind of objective evidence that courts accept uncritically and even demand.

Good testing often reveals a great deal of interesting information about the subject in a short period of time, and testers who are familiar with the elaboration of psychodynamics on the basis of their study of test results often produce reports that seem remarkably illuminating. But test reliability varies with the training and orientation of the tester, and although these tests are usually believed to be objective and they serve as objective tests for court purposes, they are often misleading or wrong. Nearly always in the courtroom situation, if the cross-examiner wanted to fly in the face of general opinion and make a detailed attack on the tests, he could demonstrate that they are more controversial and less exact than has been represented. The obvious example is the simplest and most objective kind of testing, intelligence testing. It has been criticized for cultural bias, for causing premature closure (which determines that certain children will be diverted into educational and training programs that may not be appropriate), and for not testing the intelligence that it is alleged to be testing, but instead measuring the ability to take a particular kind of examination.

The criticisms of personality testing are even more severe than the criticisms of intelligence testing. Ross Stagner of Wayne State University once performed a behavioral science experiment that involved some deception, an experiment of questionable ethical propriety but nevertheless of interest. Sixty-eight personnel men who utilized personality testing to evaluate others were given a personality test, and each was then supplied with an identical, "personal," trumped-up "Personality Analysis Report." The statements in the report were taken from astrology charts, including the "finding" that "your sexual adjustment has presented problems to you." Nine out of ten of the personnel men said their reports were "good" or were "amazingly accurate."[6]

But classification and predicting remain popular activities, and psychological testing has developed into a major American industry. Vocational testing alone is a profitable subspecialty in psychology, although we have very little information about how many of those tested utilize the test results. Are they more successful than nontested individuals if they do follow the recommendations, and if so, are they grateful in future years, or regretful that they did not work out their own vocational choices?

One of the more inexact testing methods devised by psychiatrists and psychologists is the stress interview, developed in the early 1900s by German psychologists, used by the German military and the British

War Office, and imported to the United States by the Office of Strategic Services, forerunner of the Central Intelligence Agency, in 1943. Freud had described anxiety as a central factor in the maintenance of both ego constancy and motivation to change in treatment. From the analyst's point of view, one of the advantages of the free-association method is that long silences and unstructured situations create anxiety, and this anxiety prompts the production of further verbalizations. For a long time psychoanalysts and psychologists have used the unstructured interview with a minimum of verbal and other cues to put pressure on patients or subjects to "open up," to be productive. Assessment testers often use the same technique. The job interview becomes a stress-test situation when the interviewer does not respond to normal social gestures of the interviewee, for in these circumstances some interviewees lose their composure and reveal what can be interpreted as their inadequacies. (Prospective psychiatric residents being interviewed for training programs and psychiatrists who apply as candidates for psychoanalytic training have felt the pressure in the unstructured interview.) Assessment testers also developed complicated situational stress programs. Sometimes subjects are pushed into a corner by techniques such as disagreeing with their positions (no matter what the positions may be) or by manufactured emergencies. The testing for industry often lasts two or three stressful days.

In the past ten years, according to Berkeley Rice, the number of corporations using assessment testing to evaluate their managers and executives has grown from a few hundred to nearly 2000. They include IBM, General Electric, Ford, General Motors, and Sears, Roebuck. An impressive list of city, state, and federal agencies, including the Department of Health, Education, and Welfare and the FBI, use assessment testing. AT&T alone has evaluated more than two hundred thousand employees in seventy assessment centers throughout the United States at costs ranging from $800 to $1500 per assessment. It processes thirty thousand employees yearly through the centers.[7] The Psychological Corporation reported in one five-year period that 90 percent of the Fortune 500 companies purchased its tests.[8] A researcher has said that "it is probably safe to say that there are more ability tests being given annually in the United States than there are people."[9]

Critics of the testing claim it is "a pseudoscientific fad whose predictive validity has never been proven." When one manager complained about the accuracy of the testing, he was advised that he would be marked as a troublemaker if he persisted. Rice says that "few of the companies that use the assessment method seem concerned about its validity." He quotes a management consultant: "People in business have been looking for years for some mechanical formula that will make their management-selection decisions for them. So they've simply accepted this thing at face value."

A variation of the practice of testing is profiling. Here, characteristics of behavior are itemized, and the person being tested is compared to a profile to see if he should be rewarded or punished because he does or does not fit into the category. If the subject meets the profile requirements of a competent executive, he may find his rise in business circles mystifyingly and gratifyingly fast. If he fits the profile of the skyjacker, he may find himself and his luggage subject to inexplicable special surveillance in airports.

Fifteen years ago a popular, well-researched study of the industry that assesses personality and fits individuals into categories, *The Brain Watchers*, estimated the industry's yearly revenue at $50 million.[10] It has grown enormously since then. One subspecialty is the marketing of easy pencil tests of personality and pathology. Schools and correctional institutions, particularly, rely on simple testing instruments of doubtful validity, and they bypass psychiatrists, psychologists, and social workers in the process. An advertising brochure comes across my desk for a new personality inventory pencil-and-paper test. "Do you need to measure differences among antisocial individuals? Do you need a test that makes sense to everyone? Do you need help in diagnosis, counseling or research with criminals or youth offenders?" The test advertised is touted as "an aid in counseling, diagnosis, and as a research tool."

Profiling and evaluating are done not only to predict the future behavior of individuals but also to classify and categorize them, and in particular to differentiate the employable from the unemployable, the desirable candidates for a position from the undesirable. Police applicants, for example, must show neither too little nor too much aggressivity, and tests and profiles are designed to evaluate their competence for the job. Irwin Perr, a psychiatrist, has described an opportunity he had as a member of a medical review board that had been set up by the New Jersey Civil Service Commission to supervise the piecemeal system of applicant screening throughout the state by providing an appeals procedure. Rejected applicants or employees terminated from state jobs, primarily policemen and firemen, had a chance to present their cases to the review board. The board found much of the psychiatric and psychologic evaluation and screening extremely deficient. One of Perr's criticisms was that "brief, nonconclusive, self-administered personality assessments are used heavily, as are vocational interest profiles . . . Some psychiatrists have relied heavily on . . . psychological testing without so specifying . . ."[11]

One of the great promises of categorizing is that problems of the future can be avoided by taking action today, that we can identify troublemakers before they have committed trouble and then negate their potential for harm. Stores use profiles and categorizing tests to ferret out potential dishonest employees and then forestall the dishonesty by not hiring the job applicant. A more humane approach is to combine predictions of future malfeasance with therapy and behavior modification programs designed to reform the malefactor who has not yet committed his malefaction. This seems particularly applicable to children, and there has been much work in spotting potential delinquents and treating them.

In 1966 Hellman and Blackman described a triad of symptoms—bed-wetting, fire-setting, and cruelty to animals—which, if found together in a child, purportedly correlated highly with a future career of crime.[12] Other researchers put forth other combinations of symptoms: Four early warnings that were said to be significant if they appeared together "excessively" or at "inappropriate" ages (although they were said to be "manifested by all children at some time") were fighting, school problems and truancy, temper tantrums, and the inability to get along with others.[13] A proposed plan to classify school children early included a battery of tests with results read out by a computer. The profile was developed by using the characteristics of Texas prisoners, and two of the predictors of future trouble were that the individual was more than averagely interested in social-service jobs, art, or music, and that he viewed other people as materialistic.[14]

A popular classification of children is "learning-disabled," which can lead to special "tracks" in school, special classes, and being sent to special schools. It can also lead to the requirement that a child take Ritalin and other behavior-altering drugs. "Learning disability" is an umbrella term that covers a number of other equally vague concepts—minimal brain damage, minimal brain dysfunction, minimal cerebral dysfunction, clumsy child syndrome, hyperkinetic syndrome, hyperactive child, and hypokinetic behavior disorder. Use of the term "minimal brain dysfunction" for learning disabilities that actually have no clinical or historical evidence of brain injury implies an organic etiology, an irreversibility, a poor prognosis. It has led school districts to require neurological examinations for admission to special education programs, resulting in unnecessary medical expenses and unreasonable demands on already overburdened pediatricians and pediatric neurologists.[15] A team of authors critical of this kind of labeling has said that without explicit criteria, estimates of the prevalence of learning disabilities have ranged as high as 20–30 percent of the total school population. "Where school districts are able to obtain additional state or federal funds for each child enrolled in a special class, there has been some tendency to assign almost any child who has been having difficulty in school to special classes for children with learning disabilities."[16]

The aim of labeling is to give children special attention so that future learning or behavior problems will be forestalled, but the actions taken can cause harm.

Many researchers have worked on tests to predict subsequent suicidal behavior for "parasuicides," people who have deliberately poisoned or injured themselves, but not fatally.[17] One problem with the identification of people at high risk for suicide, like other predictions of future deviant behavior, is that this may become a self-fulfilling prophecy. Being so labeled must immeasurably increase the risk that suicide will occur. In the short run the label may be lifesaving; it may alert hospital personnel to the fact that special precautions are needed to prevent suicide. In the long run it can be life-threatening. It tells the individual that he is on a predetermined disaster course and that long after he is out of the hospital or away from suicide precautions, the possibility or probability of suicide will remain.

Profiles and predictive diagnoses have been used widely in the criminal-justice field, with much of the research money coming from the Department of Justice and the armed forces.

A nuclear engineer lost his job after taking a group, computer-scored test that determined that he had schizophrenic tendencies. On the basis of the test he was denied security clearance. He had no previous history of mental problems, and he claims that tests performed since his dismissal confirm his mental state as normal. His employer reported the test results to other companies across the nation, and after a long period of unemployment he was only able to find a job that did not deal with nuclear projects. He sued his company and Behaviordyne, Inc., the testing company. He said, ". . . If they are going to have the test it needs to be the individual kind of test required to make that determination. You cannot have a mass-produced machine-scored test."[18]

* * *

The use of the computer adds to the ease with which categories can be constructed, people put into them, and future behavior predicted on the basis of similarities to the qualities and characteristics of others.

A way of predicting which patients will attempt to leave the hospital without permission (psychiatrists call this "elopement") has been developed as part of a state program in Missouri that combines securing information by uniform reporting on checklists with computer processing of the responses to classify and make probability assessments of all state hospital patients. By using such a program, a patient can be classified as elopement-prone and can be treated before he himself even realizes that he wants to elope. Some of the factors that indicated a high risk of elopement are sideburns, odd hairstyles, cowboy boots, heterosexual concern, general evasiveness, evasiveness with the examiner, and—the patient never wins—being ingratiating with the examiner. Factors characteristic of patients with a low risk of elopement were disorientation, motor retardation, poor memory, organic disease, and the inability to understand proverbs. The potential elopers were more likely to be single; Catholic; male; on their second or their fifth state hospital admission (but not first, third, or fourth); students or preschool; and referred by the courts. The potential nonelopers were more likely to be Protestant; widowed, divorced, or separated; housewives; referred to the hospital by a physician, or medically or emergency committed. (A single, male, Catholic patient with sideburns and cowboy boots might never understand why he has been refused ground privileges.)[19] The same automated system has been used to divide Missouri state hospital patients into categories with high and low scores for homicidal, assaultive, suicidal, persecutory, and homosexual potential.[20]

When the technique of the testing and classifying behavioral scientist is combined with the impersonality and the unchallengeability of the computer, we get an especially frightening kind of authority that can be used by agencies of government to control large numbers of people. We have seen how test results are not even evaluated by the tester. They are fed into a computer, and the computer makes a diagnosis of future dangerousness or future criminality or other behavioral deviancies. The ideal is to replace the subjective element, the individuality of the classifier, with a more knowledgeable and consistent approach by machine. Since the early 1960s behavioral scientists have been pursuing the goal of even greater use of the computer in the care of patients. Few of the researchers see the potential injustices that can occur when tests that are less than infallible and computer programs that are not as scientific as they appear are combined to categorize patients and plan for them. The problems of the confidentiality of computer assessment have been widely recognized, but the more complicated issues of the relationship of computer use to control and authority, and of procedures that would allow authority to be questioned have been generally overlooked.

The computer has been proposed as the ultimate tool to enable the clinician to make his diagnosis more definitive. In 1970 Dr. George Ulett of the University of Missouri School of Medicine said, "It will not be long before psychiatric clinicians demand computerized suggestions about their patients as they now demand laboratory reports." A computer giving data on a patient printed out three possible diagnoses from a list of a possible eight. Psychiatrists and computers agreed 60 percent of the time.[21] The time that Dr. Ulett envisioned has arrived. I recently heard a complaint from the head of a large teaching hospital. His hospital had a steady influx of patients who had been treated at another local hospital, a computerized hospital, by having their symptoms fed into a computer and by being placed on chemotherapy according to the computer's recommendation. The patients often improved enough to be discharged, but within weeks or months they were more disturbed than before, and not being in touch with any therapist whom they trusted, required a new hospitalization. The computerized therapy effort had cost the patients a great deal of money, had wasted valuable months, and had allowed the deterioration of the patients' condition and thus complicated the problem for the new hospital.

The field of mental health tabulating and processing is an expanding territory for the electronic data-processing industry. The Multi-State Information System for psychiatric patients uses IBM computers to serve terminal locations. More than 1300 state and local psychiatric facilities, which include state and private mental hospitals, psychiatric units of general hospitals, mental health centers, halfway houses, and sheltered workshops, and which admit among them at least a half-million patients per year, use basic aspects of the system. The system handles clinical and administrative information for mental health, mental retardation, alcoholism, drug abuse, and long-term nursing care. Probably well over 30 percent of the patients in state-operated mental hospitals in the United States are in facilities participating in some way in the system.[22]

The process of securing computer evaluations of patients begins with collecting data in checklisted form—a large part of the data are often secured through a self-inventory pencil-and-paper test the patient administers to himself—and transmitting it to a central computer. Automatic reports begin to issue from the computer, beginning with an Admission Note, which is a narrative report describing the checklisting and summarizing the Mental Status Examination.

One series of instruments gives appraisals of the patient's psychiatric condition. This includes a Psychiatric Anamnestic Record, which stores the following information on the computer: family history, precipitating events, previous treatments, sexuality, marriage, physical health, previous symptoms and personality traits, and childhood, adolescence, adulthood, and occupational history—all information that a clinician appreciates having but that has an entirely different quality if derived from a checklist and a computer print-out than it does when heard from the patient. (Anamnesis means the recalling of things past.)

Scaled scores have been derived from the Mental Status Examination Record by comparing print-out patient profiles to a norm group; with the mental status examination information the computer also automatically returns a "suspected diagnosis" for the clinician to consider. The Resource Directory has the capability of printing out a choice of social-service agencies to which the patient can be referred. An Automated Behavioral Rehabilitation System is under development so that "measurable objectives and interfaces," useful to devise behavior modification rewards, punishments, and objectives, can be determined by the computer.

One of the many problems with the computerized system is that it reifies and gives a spurious dignity to observations where nuances and shadings are essential, and its print-out narrative form gives this the permanence of records written on stone. One part of the Mental Status Examination Record deals with "insight and attitude toward illness." Under "motivation for working on problem" there are five choices from "very good" to "none," and there is a chance to check whether the patient desires or refuses treatment offered. Under "awareness of his contribution to difficulties," there are the same five choices, and also a chance to check whether the patient blames circumstances or blames others. Looking at the checklisted form with its scant four check marks ("none" for motivation, "refuses" for treatment, "none" for awareness of his contributions to difficulties, and "blames circumstances" for blame), one sees a bare, inadequate record that stirs up skepticism. Surely the patient must have had more flesh than this on his psychic bones. But the report as it comes out of the computer, based on this modicum of information and no more, sounds very clinical and very authoritative: "The patient has no motivation for working on his problems and he refuses treatment. He has no awareness of his contribution to any difficulties and blames circumstances for his difficulties." A distorted picture of the patient results from the forced choices and the lack of a chance for an elaborated answer. The system does allow manual notes to be added to supplement chart information, but the handwritten notes do not have the status or get the attention that the print-out does. The system forces the use of standard definitions, although these have been questioned by the leaders of psychiatry, and although in private practice nonofficial diagnoses and combination diagnoses are often used to record more aptly the clinician's impression.

The computer serves to dehumanize further the method of providing care for patients and makes a system that is not scientific or precise seem much more reliable, and much less challengeable, than less mechanical approaches. The old-fashioned hospital record at least had the virtue of allowing its inadequacies to be discovered on inspection, but there is no way to determine from the print-out how cursory and unsympathetic the examiner was or how little interest he took in his work. Even the most hurriedly assembled checklist secured by a mental health technician with no professional training, or by a foreign-trained psychiatrist who lacks English language skills and is only permitted to practice on a limited institutional license, seems like a competent evaluation when it is transcribed by the computer into an official-sounding and grammatical narrative.

Here are the workings of the Prototype Computer-Assisted Multidisciplinary Preadmission Psychiatric Assessment Unit, which the Veterans Administration has been using on an experimental basis in its hospital in Salt Lake City. Although the description reads like the result of a collaboration by Joseph Heller, Ken Kesey, and Kurt Vonnegut, Jr., it is scientific prose quoted from the *American Journal of Psychiatry.*

The prototype Psychiatric Assessment Unit is located in a newly renovated psychiatric admitting area . . . The furniture is contemporary, and bright accent colors are used throughout. Modern works of graphic art adorn the walls and plants abound. Rock and roll and other contemporary music is heard in the reception area. Free coffee and soft drinks are available.

The patient is greeted by a receptionist who enters basic identifying information into the computer system. He is then briefly interviewed by the clinical coordinator to determine whether he is able to complete the self-report testing . . . If the patient's clinical condition is such that testing is possible at intake (which is generally the case), a comprehensive evaluation process begins.

. . . The clinical coordinator administers a mental status examination, recording data on a Cathode-Ray Tube Terminal. Upon completion of this examination, the clinical rating data which have been entered into the computer are analyzed by a program (DIAGNO-II) that applies a set of decision rules to these data in order to derive a standard DSM-II diagnosis . . .

The patient is then given instructions for self-report testing, which require him to respond to multiple-choice questions presented on the Cathode-Ray Tube Terminal . . . As each test is completed, the computer analyzes the responses and prints a narrative report.

After the results of the medical history questionnaire are reviewed, a health technician performs a computer-prompted screening physical examination. The results are entered into the Cathode-Ray Tube Terminal. A computer-generated report is available as soon as the examination is completed.[23]

The system is staffed by a senior systems analyst, a programmer, a computer operator, and a half-time secretary, and the Psychiatric Assessment Unit is staffed by a psychiatric social worker, a clinical psychologist, two health technicians, and a secretary-receptionist. The psychiatrist is not an essential part of the program; he is only "on call."

Some valid reasons for utilizing the computer are obvious, among them its ability to make centralized mental health records readily available and to follow patients longitudinally over their lifetimes. But many observers have an uneasy premonition that credit data, mental health information, other kinds of disability information, job performance ratings, criminal records, and other personal information will all wind up on a computer's disks, capable of feeding each other and sharing information with each other, and to be used for purposes that at present have not been completely foreseen.

Business Week estimates that 10 percent of the population has used a psychiatrist or someone in the mental health field and says that misuses of information about such contacts are widespread. It says that information on medical insurance application forms and on request for reimbursement forms goes into an employee's record, where it stays permanently, even though the condition may have been minor or temporary. Often under individual plans and always under group insurance plans, the employer has access to health records. He administers the group plan, often submits the claims, and sometimes issues the checks for treatment. Insurance companies keep extensive health records, share them with each other, share them also with retail credit-rating services, and freely tap a computer bank of medical facts on 11 million Americans.[24]

Alan Westin, professor of public law and government at Columbia University and an authority on computer invasion of privacy, does not see computers as the weak link in the maintenance of confidentiality. Rather, he sees indiscretions and improprieties by the people who make and store the records as more important, "since most medical information is still stored on paper rather than in computers." He does feel that "as more and more sensitive information is stored in computers, as more people become aware that there are insufficiently guarded computer systems," there will be more concern about computer storage of information.[25]

* * *

When behavioral scientists can combine testing and physiological function read-outs, they can exercise great authority over their test subjects. "Lie detection" has become a common method of distinguishing criminals from noncriminals, and, although test results are not admissible in court, the method is widely used to screen applicants for police jobs and for a variety of other governmental and industrial personnel purposes. Since polygraphs record not lies but physiological stress, which may be caused by many factors besides lying, they are not accurate—one study found the accuracy to be only 70 percent. Lying is not stressful for some people, and being subjected to the polygraph test is stressful for some people who are not lying. Senator Sam Ervin once called the polygraph an instrument of "twentieth-century witchcraft,"[26] and the House Committee on Government Operations has concluded that "there is no 'lie-detector,' neither machine nor human."[27] But the use of the polygraph in government, business, and industry is steadily increasing, and the Central Intelligence Agency continues to work on polygraph improvements.[28] (Thirteen states have passed laws banning or restricting polygraph tests as a condition of employment.)[29]

The measurement of other physical responses is being used for screening and evaluation. Camera tracking of the response of the iris of the eye to verbal stimuli is being used as a new refined "lie-detector test" technique.[30] Physiological tests have been used to identify rapists. Some of the earlier and less sophisticated tests of sexual arousal in response to photographs, movies, and audio tapes containing explicit sexual material relied on such methods as "direct erection callibration," respiration, galvanic skin response, and cardiac rate (all except the first are techniques also used for lie-detection), and more recent tests have involved the measurement of nocturnal penile tumescence, sleep electroencephalogram, and eye movements in rapist and nonrapist prisoners. Modern technology has now given us a new scientific instrument to pursue these studies, the circumferential penile transducer. The researchers reported their study method in the *Archives of General Psychiatry.*

This small unobtrusive gauge encircles the penis, and as erection occurs, the increased circumference size is displayed on an oscillograph. Care was taken that the patient's penis had returned to the flaccid state or a very low steady state before proceeding to the next trial. Subjects were cautioned not to manipulate their penis during measurements, since such manipulation is easily identified on the oscillograph tracing. Results were recorded as the greatest percent of a full erection obtained during each two-minute audio description.[31]

This study used audio tapes representing only a mutually consenting and a forced sexual encounter, but other studies have included tapes of sadomasochism and other sexual situations. Sometimes the goal is only to find out more about sexual arousal, but the technique has been used to distinguish the rapist by comparing his responses to a baseline response secured from nonrapist subjects.[32]

"Psychiatry in the future may be a computerized, prophylactic science preparing individuals for their role in a highly organized, group-oriented society," says Stanley Lesse, editor of the *American Journal of Psychotherapy.* Most routine diagnoses will be performed by a "medical-technical expert" working with the computer. "In the crowded, group-oriented, highly automated world 'of the future,' it is likely that patients will not object to a more impersonal type of health science care." Computers and the regular screening of medical records will select individuals who are at risk for psychological problems and who require early therapy.[33]

The far future brings the promise of computer diagnoses and predictions with the technologist and the checklist eliminated. Electrodes applied to the scalp can at present translate unspoken thoughts or words into the activators of a computer. Unspoken word patterns—and presumably eventually feeling patterns—can be fed from the brain into the computer, with a diagnosis and a course-of-treatment print-out as the direct result.[34]

One of the problems with using the computer is that it is much more difficult to keep diagnoses from becoming fixed. The *New York Times* has described the job complications of a twenty-four-year-old Dallas construction worker when the computer read-out gave him a pregnancy rating that belonged to another patient with a similar name. He was finally returned to employment under a new contract with a clause denying him maternity benefits for nine months.[35] The *New York Times* headlined the story, "Another Victory Won in Man vs. Computer," but the mistakes on the records of mental patients tend to be more ambiguous—a statement that the patient is paranoid because he thinks public officials are conspiring against him, for example

—and the unavailability to mental patients of various kinds of resources makes it impossible for them to argue with their print-outs.

The tester never wants to give the subject the basis for his adverse report. That would detract from the authority of the tester and dissipate the Kafkaesque impenetrability that is part of his mystique and power.

In 1979 the Supereme Court upheld the power of a utility company to refuse to share with the collective bargaining representative copies of aptitude tests and test scores. All employees who had been tested had been held not eligible for changes to more skilled positions, and the positions were then given to outsiders. The union wanted to study the test and the results. The company gave the union copies of the test validation studies and a report by an outside consultant, but it refused to hand over copies of the actual test or the individual scores, on the ground that "complete confidentiality of these materials was necessary in order to insure the future integrity of the tests and to protect the privacy interests of the examinees." The National Labor Relations Board ordered the materials to be furnished to the union, and the United States Court of Appeals for the Sixth Circuit ruled that the order should be enforced, but on appeal to the Supreme Court—with the American Psychological Association joining Detroit Edison in the contention that this would threaten the confidentiality of the relationship of the tester and his client—the order was held to be erroneous and was overruled.[36]

If a patient is labeled anxious, phobic, sociopathic, withdrawn, or schizophrenic, he may never be able to establish the fact that the diagnosis is incorrect or properly belonged to someone else, or resulted from some other computer error or from improper computer programming.

Not everyone has the temperament to be a tester-classifier. If one is convinced the results will only be helpful, there is no problem, but we know there will be bad as well as good consequences. The tester plays God, and not everyone is comfortable playing God.

The psychiatrists and psychologists who are most comfortable putting people selectively into classifications become people processors. Psychiatrists who are skeptical about classifying do not get involved in legal psychiatric determinations that impose social control on patients; they ususally do not even gain enough exposure to, and expertise about, classifying to challenger classification effectively. They see themselves primarily as therapists, and they are content to let other psychiatrists exert more direct social control, although if questioned, they may often find it hard to justify the way the control is used.

When futurologists and psychologists write as they do in "Work in the Year 2001," describing new roles for workers related to increased computer use and the proliferation of a new class called "knowledge workers," they discuss whether the computer will make workers feel more alienated or less alienated.[37] They do not consider that the classification of workers into various categories will be determined by computers, so that computers will not only change the quality of work —for good and for ill—but they will also determine job assignments. In the future, determinations of status, made by diagnosis, profiling, and labeling, will be more fixed than they are today. Computer application of behavioral science principles will determine who does what in our society. What will be the behavioral science criteria to determine which person is slotted for which post? Who will determine the criteria for becoming a member of the professional technical group that determines the criteria?

Stigmatization and Discrimination

THE POWERS of psychiatrists to make diagnoses, to make predictions about future behavior, and to put people into categories can result in their placing a disadvantaged person in an even more difficult situation, forced to cope with stigma and discrimination in addition to battling with mental symptoms. People labeled mental patients lose credibility and arouse suspicion. The label leads to economic problems, involving employment, health insurance, and housing. It can lead to difficulties in social relationships. Psychiatrists have been so criticized for the errors or vagueness in their labeling procedures because the label produces a new disability, which often remains as a burden long after the symptoms that led to the label have departed.

Mental health professionals and former mental patients feel bitter about discrimination against those who are mentally ill and those who have recovered from mental illness. This discrimination makes rehabilitation difficult. Those who most need a job find the most impediments placed in their way. In *Action for Mental Health,* the report of the Joint Commission on Mental Illness and Health published in 1961, the disadvantages that stigmatization usually brings are stressed.

> The nonconformist—whether he be foreigner or "odd ball," intellectual or idiot, genius or jester, individualist or hobo, physically or mentally abnormal —pays a penalty for "being different," unless his peculiarity is considered acceptable for his particular group, or unless he lives in a place or period of particularly high tolerance or enlightenment. The socially visible characteristic of the psychotic person is that he becomes a stranger among his own people . . . It has been observed countless times that the sight or thought of major mental illness, as our culture has come to understand it, stimulates fear—fear of what an irrational person might do, fear of what we ourselves might do if we acted out our impulses in a similar manner, fear arising from the power of suggestion that we, too, might suffer a similar fate.

230

The report described the social stigma of mental illness as a real and persistent problem.[1]

The answer to the problem of rejection and stigmatization, it said, is to admit that mental patients are different and to try to come to terms with this difference in a rational way. It is not so much that the mental patient has strange symptoms—many other people in society have equally strange symptoms—but that his behavior has reached a point where "people can no longer stand it . . . It is not so much that he physically endangers them (though they may fear this); violence is more the exception than the rule among psychotic patients, popular misconceptions to the contrary. Basically, normal people are disturbed by his refusal to comply with expectations of time and place . . . The mentally ill tend to require other people to adjust to them at every point in their illness from onset to recovery."

Although this is the realistic approach—to recognize that people are characterized as mentally ill because they have shown erratic behavior that may legitimately cause fear—it has become more popular to deny the differences between psychiatric patients and medical patients, and between psychiatric patients and the mentally well. Motivated in part by the fact that so many people are in psychiatric treatment, often for minor problems, and that many of these patients are not at all disturbing, and in part by the desire to help the more severely mentally disabled regain acceptance in the community, the effort has been made to picture the mental patient as "just like everybody else," to label fear of the mentally ill as irrational. As chairperson of the President's Commission on Mental Health, Rosalynn Carter called for an end to an attitude of fear. She described a "self-feeding cycle" of fear, discrimination, and lack of understanding of mental patients and called for mental health workers to "start talking to the public" to make mental illness more acceptable, to "replace each myth about mental illness with a reassuring truth."[2]

But stigmatization and its effects do not disappear because mental health workers talk to the public, and there are not enough reassuring truths to go around. Stigma is too entrenched a phenomenon to be talked away. And some stigma is earned—mental patients are not all pleasant or cooperative—and it also serves to keep all the world from leaping on the mentally ill bandwagon, with attendant Social Security benefits, excuses for poor performance and irresponsibility, and other advantages that come with the status.

Should labels be regarded as emotionally neutral and innocuous? Edward Sagarin, a sociologist, has said that we do people a disservice when we ask them to accept their labels without shame, because the labels give only an imputed identity—alcoholic, schizophrenic, drug addict, homosexual, sadomasochist, pedophile, juvenile delinquent—which he calls a "special kind of mistaken identity." According to his argument, when we label someone a thief we do so on the basis of his actions, and we do not see his total identity as thief but only a part of his identity. But when we label someone schizophrenic or homosexual and then persuade the person that he has this identity, we are locking him into an at least partially false—or very incomplete—category, and we are giving it a changeless character.[3] A study of the attitudes in a small town indicates that fellow townspeople reject other members of the community in a direct relationship to the professionalization and specialization of the source of help, with the least rejection when help is sought from a clergyman, increasing percentages of rejection for those seeking psychiatric help from physicians and psychiatrists, and the most rejection for those who get mental hospital help.[4] A study of work supervisors shows that the knowledge that an employee is seeing a psychiatrist would be likely to rule out a promotion even if the employee is doing good work, and that a psychiatric diagnosis is considered more of a detriment than such other disabilities as obesity, heart ailments, twitches, or skin cancer.[5] A study of a large group of people that included rehabilitation workers shows that the physically ill (with the exception of tuberculosis patients), the blind, and the deaf are most acceptable; the epileptics and the cerebral palsied fall in a middle range; and the least acceptable are the tubercular, ex-convicts, the mentally retarded, alcoholics, and at the very bottom of the list, those with mental illness.[6]

The public does not feel that mental patients (at least those readily identified as such) are just like everybody else. And logic tells us that they are not like everybody else. Unless patients are recognized and designated as different, they have no claim to the benefits of their status—free or low-cost psychiatric services, special job protections, freedom from responsibility for some criminal actions, vocational and rehabilitation programs, and disability and Social Security supplemental payments. It is not reasonable to expect that mental patients and former mental patients will be treated just like everyone else for the purpose of public acceptance, but at the same time unlike everyone else for the purpose of special protections and benefits.

Patients feel the conflict between stigma and reward when they are asked to allow insurance companies to have information about them so they can be reimbursed for treatment expenses. Releasing the information may lead to stigma, but the financial reward usually makes the risk tolerable.

Studies done on the effect of brief psychiatric hospitalization on poor people who do not have the resources of family and friends show that a patient will find that after only a few days' hospitalization his job is filled, his room has been rented to another, his personal possessions have disappeared, and his life has been completely disrupted. At all socioeconomic levels, the effect of having been labeled mentally ill can be crippling or catastrophic. Says Erving Goffman, "Ex-mental patients . . . are sometimes afraid to engage in sharp interchanges with spouse or employer because of what a show of emotion might be taken as a sign of." He tells us of former mental patients securing jobs through the help of a rehabilitation service but leaving these jobs when they have a little money saved up so they can find work in a situation where their former status will not be known.[7]

The harm and potential harm done to mental patients and former mental patients is not only confined to those who have had serious illnesses, those who have been hospitalized or who have had to interrupt careers or schooling. Psychiatrists know that many people who consult them as outpatients are much less "sick" than many or most of the general population. If these people had decided not to be patients but instead to be clients or parishioners and had taken their problems to a social worker, a pastoral counselor, or a faith healer, they would have incurred no stigma. Their problems in living would not have been defined as medical and there would be no illness on their record. Some patients who want the services of a psychiatrist or a psychoanalyst pass up medical insurance benefits to which they are entitled so that their status as patient will not be on any public or corporation record. The ubiquitous questionnaires that ask, "Have you ever consulted a physician for a physical or emotional or mental condition?" do not take account of those who should have and haven't, or those who are able to answer no because they have taken their problems to an encounter group, a sensitivity-training session, an est seminar, or a consciousness-raising group, and so have escaped the discriminatory effect of seeking help.

Goffman has written about the difference between the discredited person, who is seen when he presents himself as obviously abnormal, and the discreditable person, whose differentness is not immediately apparent and is not known beforehand. The discredited individual has the task of managing the tensions caused by the reaction of others to his differentness, but the discreditable individual has a task of another nature—that of managing information about his failing. "To display or not to display; to tell or not to tell; to let on or not to let on; to lie or not to lie; and in each case, to whom, how, when, and where . . . It is not that he must face prejudice against himself, but rather that he must face unwitting acceptance of himself by individuals who are prejudiced against persons of the kind he can be revealed to be."[8]

So the mental patient or the former mental patient often passes or tries to. Some patients or ex-patients want to be accepted with full knowledge of their status, sometimes to the point of volunteering information that will surely cost them their jobs or their entrance into a licensed or regulated profession. Some would have liked to pass but had a failure of nerve when they thought of the penalties they could incur by lying on an application for federal employment or the less severe penalties that can occur for giving false information to less official questioners.

Applicants for the state of Georgia bar examination, like applicants in many other states, are required to state whether within the past ten years they have undergone treatment or consulted any doctor about the use of drugs, narcotics, or intoxicating liquors, and whether they have ever received diagnosis of amnesia, or any form of insanity, emotional disturbance, nervous or mental disorder, or received regular treatment for any of these conditions. Although there is no known instance of this information having been used to keep an applicant from taking the examination or being admitted to the Georgia bar, there are instances of denying applicants in other jurisdictions. The applicant does not like to have this information on record. He does not know what the precise use of the information will be, and he suspects that if he says he has been in treatment he will be asked to sign a release of information that will authorize his therapist to share details about his treatment with the State Board of Bar Examiners of Georgia.

There are many good arguments against this intrusive practice. It penalizes those who have sought help even though those who have not sought help may be more severe psychological risks. It penalizes those who seek help from psychologists or psychiatrists or other physicians in contrast to those who seek help from other less professional sources. It puts the treating therapist who receives the release of information form in an extremely difficult situation. He does not feel he has the right not to release information after the patient has authorized the release, but he feels he is being forced into an unprofessional stance in retailing confidences. It places the therapist at times in a position where he has to divulge information harmful to the patient—a violation of the Hippocratic injunction to "do no harm"—or alternatively, has to give a false picture of the patient to the inquirer. It raises a complicated informed-consent question: If the patient had not been coerced, or if he knew what was going to be divulged, would he have signed the release-of-information form? It blackmails the therapist into giving information, because if he refuses as a matter of policy, discretion, or conscience to give information, he may be blocking the professional progress of his patient, or at least it may lead to the inference that there is something to hide.

Most patients and ex-patients, if they feel they are not incurring the possibility of too great a penalty for lying, will not give truthful answers to questions about psychiatric treatment. Psychiatric hospitalization is more difficult to dodge because it is often a matter of public record. By concealing any or all of his mental health background, the person escapes being discredited, but he is in the uneasy position of living a lie and knowing that he is in danger of having this information discovered. Dr. Jerome Biegler, chairman of the committees on confidentiality of both the American Psychiatric Association and the American Psychoanalytic Association, testifying before a government commission on the protection of privacy, has said that people who have been treated for emotional problems should try to keep this information out of their job records. "It is common knowledge," Biegler has said, "that promising young corporate executives dare not take advantage of insurance coverage for psychotherapy lest their employers stigmatize them for having a disorder of mental health and arrest their careers."[9] But if the patient fails to reveal his psychiatric history and his deception is discovered, he can also have his career arrested.

Here are some of the discriminations that have been practiced against mental patients, with or without justifiable rationales:

• A history of past or present treatment or hospitalization, a diagnosis of homosexuality, or treatment for addiction or alcoholism has prevented employment and sometimes led to firing. Even well-functioning mild neurotics hesitate to ask for an hour off a week for therapy because of its adverse effect on careers.

• Mental patients and former mental patients have problems with professional licensure.

• They may be denied credit.

• They may have trouble renting and buying housing.

• Zoning laws are used to keep halfway houses and addict rehabilitation centers out of neighborhoods.

• A major problem for people with a history of psychiatric treatment is obtaining health insurance. Even when they are willing to waive specifically any future claim for psychiatric treatment, they are often still denied medical coverage.

• They may have difficulty securing life insurance.

• Parents, particularly mothers, who have had a history of mental illness are often deprived of their children in custody disputes.

In 1972 the regulations of the Commissioned Corps of the Public Health Service denied appointments for individuals undergoing psychotherapy. (This ruling, under a full-disclosure policy, would have disqualified 15 to 20 percent of the students at some medical schools and an even higher percentage of medical students planning to become psychiatrists.)

The question of stigmatization is intimately related to the problem of confidentiality. The United States government and its agencies have been the greatest offenders in attempts to pierce the anonymity of the patient. The government on the one hand provides the most generous insurance benefits for psychiatric care, paying forty dollars of the expense of a fifty-dollar office visit (a policy that has made Washington, D.C.–area psychiatrists the envy of their colleagues in other locations), and on the other hand it ferrets out information about past psychiatric care and uses it to disqualify job applicants.

Psychiatrists are often forced to divulge information in court. There are well-established rules concerning confidentiality and privilege, which generally have been designed to give the psychiatrist-patient relationship as much protection as possible while still making necessary information available to the court, but the amount and kind of information that can be required from a testifying psychiatrist varies greatly from one jurisdiction to another. The government is often guilty, in issues that have no relationship to a court proceeding, of trying to force out information concerning a patient's condition or confidences. At one time it justified this invasion of privacy on the ground that if courts can require such information for a trial, the same power to force psychiatrists to reveal information about a patient should belong to the government. This occurred in the 1960s and involved Peace Corps policy as it was developed by its senior consultant, Dr. Walter Menninger, and its chief psychiatrist, Dr. Joseph English. The Peace Corps was the first government agency to entrust its personnel policies to a chief psychiatrist, although other agencies had used psychiatrists to choose their personnel and decide their work assignments.

Like other federal job applicants, all applicants for the Peace Corps were required to reveal past psychiatric treatment under penalty of a jail sentence and a fine for failure to reveal the information accurately. The Peace Corps required applicants who had been in psychiatric treatment to sign releases authorizing their former psychiatrists to furnish information on their treatment to the Peace Corps. This was done under coercion; the application for the corps would not be processed unless the release was signed. Then the corps took the further step of threatening psychiatrists who did not cooperate with legal action. They were told—inaccurately—that just as courts can hold a psychiatrist in contempt for unwillingness to testify, he also risks legal punishment for failure to cooperate with a government agency. The analogy was made between doctor-patient testimonial privilege, which often must give way to court needs, and the doctor-patient confidential relationship, which, the Peace Corps said, must give way to government agency needs. Most psychiatrists were too naive or too unconcerned to fight back. They furnished the asked-for information. This bizarre policy was in effect for a number of years, and it received very little publicity. The American Psychiatric Association and the psychiatric establishment never protested the policy. When opposition finally came, it represented the courage of a few psychiatrists who refused to furnish information and refused to be intimidated by the agency's threat of legal action against them.

Menninger and English have written an article about their information-securing program that tries to put a good face on their activity. It is all, they say, in the best interest of the job applicant so that he will not be placed in a position that puts him under excessive stress. But there was no demonstration that there was a correlation between stress and job performance, and no data to show the ability of a psychiatrist to prevent emotional problems through use of the data.

Until recently the United States Civil Service Commission had a question relating to the psychiatric history of the applicant on its standard application form. The deletion of the question, at long last, affected only job seekers at the commission itself. Other government agencies were not included in the policy change.[10] But the government intrudes into the privacy of the psychiatrist-patient relationship in its efforts to be benign as well as in its attempts to be rejecting. Its generous policy of paying for the major share of employees' therapy costs involves it in demands—usually complied with—to private therapists to share information.

When someone who has had psychiatric treatment is turned down for a job or is disqualified for professional licensure, there is a gray area where one can surmise that the stigma of a psychiatric diagnosis or history has been the reason for rejection, but the applicant cannot be sure, since the rejection can possibly be justified on some other ground.

A leading case dealing with discrimination against former mental patients is *Glassman* v. *New York Medical College.*[11] Myra Lee Glassman graduated from college Phi Beta Kappa and magna cum laude and was in the ninety-ninth percentile in the Medical College Admission Test. She had placed twelfth in a statewide New York test for college graduates who demonstrated exceptional promise for medical school. Dr. Benjamin Sadock, who had evaluated her for admission to New York Medical College and recommended her rejection, conceded on the witness stand that on her Medical College Admission Test she had possibly a higher score than any of those accepted— neither he nor anyone he had talked with knew of any other applicant with a higher score. Myra had answered truthfully in her application that she had been in a mental hospital. She had spent a year between her sophomore and junior college years as a voluntary patient at Hillside Hospital in New York. The medical college claimed that she had made two suicide attempts, although Myra Lee described them not as attempts but as gestures. It established that she had interrupted her undergraduate studies for fourteen months during the time she was in psychiatric treatment.

Three psychiatrists and a psychologist who had taught her at college, all of them aware of her psychiatric history, recommended her for medical school with no reservations. They saw her as mature, well adjusted, capable of working independently, and, having surmounted her emotional problems, as "better equipped to deal with the rigors of medical school than most other applicants." Two psychiatrists and a psychologist who examined her in order to serve as witnesses at the trial of her discrimination case against New York Medical College (one of the thirteen schools that had rejected her) minimized the seriousness of the illness, describing it as "an adjustment reaction of adolescence," and described the suicide gestures as manipulative, not meant to really end her life. They pointed to a history of remarkable progress after her hospitalization, a record of brilliant college work while holding jobs to support herself. They found no evidence of any psychiatric condition that would impair current or future functioning.

Testimony at the trial showed that a faculty member who had interviewed her found her "impressive" and strongly recommended her acceptance. However, because of her history an interview with the psychiatric consultant to the Admissions Committee, Dr. Sadock, was required, and he placed a label of "latent schizophrenic" on her and recommended her rejection. During the trial he admitted that in Myra Lee's interview with him she had appeared perfectly normal and did not exhibit "any withdrawn, regressive, or bizarre behavior." Asked to explain his diagnosis, he said on the stand: ". . . The majority of people who have been in mental hospitals in a particular age group, her age group, have a diagnosis of schizophrenia, and it was on that, sir, that I made that comment . . . I did not make that comment on the basis of a history and a mental status. I am not prepared at this point to defend a diagnosis of schizophrenia in Miss Glassman . . . I trust she does not have that illness."

Myra Lee Glassman lost her case against New York Medical College. The court held that the college had denied Myra Glassman admission not because of her hospitalization, but because she had interrupted her academic career and made suicide attempts. "If the plaintiff never had been admitted to a mental hospital but had indicated that she had interrupted her career for over 14 months and that she had made two attempts at suicide, she would have been rejected by the Admissions Committee as a risk to a successful completion of her medical courses and as a practicing physician." Not past medical history, but an "aggregate of factors" was behind the rejection, said the court.[12] By the time the decision against her was announced, six months after the court hearing, Myra Lee had been accepted by a midwestern school for an unusual joint program in which she could receive medical and pharmacological degrees in five years of postgraduate study, so she did not appeal. Bruce Ennis, her lawyer, reported that after two years in the program she had earned honors in most of her courses and above-average grades in all the rest.

(The New York Medical College did not have the benefit of current research, which had not yet been published, but a study done of 116 students from the University of Michigan who in the period from 1958 to 1967 were hospitalized in acute-treatment centers in Ann Arbor because of profound emotional disturbances showed that, compared to a control group of students without an interruption in their studies, the effect of hospitalization was minimal. The study speaks of such "prejudicial policies of not admitting or readmitting students who have had or are undergoing psychotherapy, of requiring dropouts to remain away from scholastic pursuits for prescribed periods of time, or of requiring them to obtain and maintain jobs for a definite duration." The research indicated that emotional problems, even those serious enough to require hospitalization, have essentially no effect upon academic success. Similar conclusions had been reached in a study at Harvard.)[13]

There are a few signs that psychiatrists are becoming more aware of the harm they can do to patients and more careful in furnishing stigmatizing information. Blue Cross in the District of Columbia has had a policy of requiring much detail from a therapist before it would pay for mental health benefits under the Federal Employees Program. The therapist was required to answer questions about the patient's family and social life, presence of suicidal tendencies, and degree of anxiety and depression. A therapist in Maryland wrote to Blue Cross indicating he would not disclose the information for three of his patients and sent a copy of his letter to his congressman. Blue Cross had consistently maintained that the information it collected would in no circumstances be made available to outside sources. When Blue Cross answered the therapist, it sent a carbon of the letter, with the names of the three patients neatly typed in the letter, to the same congressman. Blue Cross later announced a change in its policy and withdrew the questions from insurance claims forms. This change was made after the Mental Health Law Project, a patients' advocacy legal organization with headquarters in Washington, D.C., threatened a class-action suit against Blue Cross, citing the cases of a number of people who had not entered treatment or had terminated treatment because of the threat of this intrusion into their privacy. Paul Friedman, who represented the Mental Health Law Project, said he saw a serious inconsistency between the attitude of psychiatrists who were anxious to get insurance reimbursement for their patients' fees and the same psychiatrists' attitude when other kinds of threats to confidentiality were the issue.[14]

*　　*　　*

We have embarked on a new phase of our treatment of the mentally disabled and other handicapped people. In April 1977, Joseph Califano, Jr., Secretary of Health, Education, and Welfare, signed a controversial set of regulations designed to implement the Rehabilitation Act of 1973 by banning discrimination against the handicapped by recipients of federal funds. This affects all programs supported in whole or in part by federal funds, which include federally supported schools, colleges, graduate schools, and health and welfare institutions. Programs or activities in existing facilities must be made available to the handicapped. Employers may not refuse to hire handicapped persons if reasonable accommodations can be made for them and if the handicap does not impair the ability of the job applicant. Employers may not require preemployment physical examinations and may not make preemployment inquiries about whether a person is handicapped. Colleges and universities must make reasonable modifications in academic requirements to ensure full opportunities for handicapped students. Doctors who treat Medicare or Medicaid patients must make their offices accessible to the handicapped or go to accessible facilities to treat them, even if that means making house calls. How all this applies to the mentally disabled, alcoholic, and addict population is not clear and will have to be worked out through court cases.

It is easier to see how the new regulations will be implemented as far as paraplegics, the crippled, the deaf, the blind, those suffering from heart conditions, and other physically handicapped are concerned than how psychiatric patients, alcoholics, and drug addicts will be aided. The regulations prohibit discrimination by the institutions and agencies in hiring and promotions, but in order to benefit from these, the person must both "qualify" for available employment and publicly claim the disabled status. The disclosure that one is or has been mentally ill can lead to rejection, and other reasons for the rejection can always be found. It was probably in response to the controversy caused by the inclusion, after years of debate, of the mentally ill, drug addicts, and alcoholics that Attorney General Griffin Bell advised the Department of Health, Education, and Welfare that the new regulations do not require that a person "be hired or permitted to participate in a Federally assisted program if the manifestations of his condition prevent him from effectively performing the job . . ." Bell stated that behavior that was "unduly disruptive to others" would not be covered under the new rules.[15]

The new regulations provide for a great government superstructure to ensure compliance and to investigate and hear complaints. Each recipient of federal funds must keep records and file compliance reports to show that it is not discriminating, and HEW officials are given access to these records so that they can police practices. Information must be made available to the disabled, and investigations are to be made both periodically and on the basis of complaints. A hearing procedure has been set up with such safeguards as timely notice and the right to counsel. Provisions for hearing examiners and for review of their decisions have been set up. We know discrimination is an evil; we do not yet know whether the procedures to do away with it will be workable, especially in the case of mental patients, alcoholics, and addicts.

The approach to the problem of stigmatization has been to persuade the public to be more accepting of the mentally ill and to provide governmental help against discrimination. Both of these require the patient or former patient to come forward and publicly proclaim his mental illness. But patients and former patients prefer to be less public, and they may feel that they will be getting more help when psychiatrists begin to be more selective in conferring the label of mentally ill and when better ways are devised to keep information out of records and to safeguard record keeping. Many patients will continue to want to keep their mental health histories private, to "pass."

There may be good reasons for discrimination against the mentally ill, alcoholics, and addicts. When the choice is between two job applicants, one with and one without a mental disability, there are reasons to prefer the nondisabled. Many recovered mental patients are fragile, and they may be more temperamental or less adaptable than others who have not been mentally disabled. There are valid economic reasons for not hiring the formerly mentally ill, or even those who do not show signs of maladjustment but who seek out therapy, for health insurance costs to the employer may be raised. There are few judicial precedents, statutes, regulations, or constitutional provisions that will effectively help these disabled or formerly disabled people in their employment. There are rehabilitation and vocational-training programs and welfare benefits, but they involve the full disclosure of handicapped status that Biegler sees as unwise, the acceptance of the "imputed identity" that Sagarin sees as a detriment, and the change of status from discreditable to discredited that Goffman sees as a source of further problems. The best protection for the former patient will probably continue to be not public acceptance but low visibility.

The new antidiscrimination policy applies only to those who receive federal funds. Forcing private employers to hire the disabled would raise issues of invasion of privacy and problems of enforcement. Stigmatization will continue to be a problem, and discrimination will continue to exist.

Psychiatrists can help prevent stigmatization by labeling sparingly, but it is hard to persuade psychiatrists to do less labeling. It is not until they have found someone to call "patient" that they can assume the power and authority of "doctor." The stigma of the patient is the reciprocal of the prestige of the psychiatrist.

PART THREE

HOW PSYCHIATRISTS EXERCISE THEIR POWER

Psychoanalysis and psychiatry have brought behavior within the medical model.

—WILLARD GAYLIN

Psychiatry differs from all other fields of medicine in a deplorable lack of facts on which all psychiatrists can agree.

—LUTHER KALINOWSKY AND HANNS HIPPIUS
*Pharmacological, Convulsive and
Other Somatic Treatments in Psychiatry*

The Power of Psychiatry

SINCE MENTAL PATIENTS by definition are at best less than rational and at worst completely incompetent, psychiatrists are given two entirely different kinds of powers to help deal with their disabilities. The first is the power to control, to force patients to do what the psychiatrist thinks the patient should do (or to have done what the psychiatrists thinks should be done). An entirely different kind of authority is the power to excuse patients from their obligations, to grant relief from responsibility.

Psychiatrists have other, less direct kinds of power. Even people who cannot tell the difference between a psychologist and a psychiatrist, and who would scrupulously avoid seeing either one, have had their attitudes shaped on abortion, sexuality, child rearing, treatment of criminals, drug use, and most other aspects of modern life by psychological and psychiatric opinions that filter to them through newspapers, popular psychology books, films, television commentary, and increasingly through television dramas, soap operas, and situation comedies. Newspaper editors, television writers, and film writers gather what they believe to be current psychiatric thought from their reading, and quite frequently from values transmitted to them by their own therapists, and pass these ideas on to a reading and viewing public as dogma or gospel. Although psychiatrists are split on many of these issues, they tend to take what are considered to be liberal or progressive stands on most political and social questions, and so they are more frequently cited to lend weight to arguments for, rather than against, change in many fields of social concern. (There are a number of paradoxes here. Although psychiatrists are generally members of the upper middle class who live traditional lives that are work- and family-oriented—often in that order—and are concerned with status, security, and the accumulation of material possessions, the public

245

views of many psychiatrists have been in favor of nonconformity, deviant life styles, nontraditional values, and change. Such major changes in social values as easier divorce, legalizing unrestricted abortions, and decriminalizing drug use and sexual deviancy have been spearheaded by psychiatrists. On the other hand, many psychiatrists (more so in the past than recently) have seen adherence to established social values as an indication of mental health. The same psychiatrist who encourages a family to be more permissive toward its rebellious child may be influencing his own child to follow his course into a high status professional career; coexisting with the liberalism of psychiatrists are basic values that reflect their middle-class backgrounds.)

A discussion of the uses and abuses of psychiatry must deal with the pervasive effects of psychiatry on manners, morals, ethics, and social values, but those considerations are easier to comprehend after looking at the more direct, open, and obvious interventions that psychiatrists make in people's lives.

Nothing could be more superficially benign and unthreatening than the authority of a psychiatrist to write a medical prescription so that an overworked housewife and mother will have a washing machine. A woman asks for help at a hospital emergency room. A sympathetic social worker finds that she has too many household duties and there is no one to help her. The psychiatrist who evaluates her is concerned with her sense of desperation. One of her complaints is the mountain of wash that accumulates from her four sons. The psychiatrist and social worker put their heads together and establish that the psychiatrist (or any physician) can prescribe a washing machine as a medical prescription and it can be secured through Medicaid funds. The washing machine thus becomes the psychiatric treatment.

When this example of the creative application of psychiatry was given at a conference on the needs of welfare mothers, the general feeling was that more psychiatrists should be like this, using practical methods to get real help to people in desperate need. But this kind of use of authority creates problems. If a washing machine is psychiatric treatment, what other consumer items are not just as deserving of prescription? What are the limits of the psychiatrist's authority? Are all interventions on the part of a doctor medical treatment? Why should a doctor be able to write out a prescription for a washing machine, while social workers, psychologists, mental health technicians, nurses, and other members of the treatment team, who may know this woman and her needs much more intimately than the psychiatrist but who are deprived access to prescription pads, lack the same power? Our system now declares anything done by a doctor, no matter how nonmedical (or how outlandish) to be medical treatment. The doctor makes all the difference. An orthopedic mattress bought because of a backache is not income-tax-deductible, but one bought because a doctor prescribes it is, even in the absence of a backache. A wig is tax-deductible if a psychiatrist finds a medical reason to "prescribe" it. A new term has been coined for nonmedical "medical" treatment prescribed by doctors—"psychosocial aid" or "psychosocial rehabilitation." The inclusion of psychosocial interventions as medical treatment carries its own threat. It opens the door to an expanded concept of psychiatric power in which anything can be therapy.

In contrast to a benign prescription for a washing machine, psychiatrists can assert a much more physical and punitive use of power. The punishment inflicted by therapists on self-mutilating children to modify their destructive behavior, and the physical beatings inflicted by practitioners of direct analysis[1] (John Rosen's method of dealing with regressed schizophrenic patients by physical confrontations) at first glance seem much less benign, but arguably these are just as much in the interest of the patient, and they are more typical medical interventions.

The range of psychiatric power is wide, but it is not without limit. Rosen was sued in behalf of a schizophrenic patient he had allegedly slapped in the interest of therapy, and he settled the case out of court.[2] Between the washing machine and the beating, there is a range of therapy methods that psychiatrists can advocate and in many cases can require. Patients can be forced to take drugs or have electroshock treatment. They can be put into seclusion rooms or restrained with handcuffs.

Much of the power of psychiatry relates not to prescriptions and pills and treatment of patients, but to evaluations and determinations. The psychiatrist is entrusted to make evaluations that determine committability, employability, responsibility, the capability to raise children, the ability to drive a car, and many more.

The field of commitment is full of examples of the uses and abuses of psychiatric authority. One recollection that comes back to me frequently is that of the recalcitrant patient during my residency who wanted to leave the hospital against the wishes of her family and her admitting psychiatrist. She was finally told that if she insisted on pushing to leave, the psychiatrist would be forced—this was in the days when lobotomy was still an accepted treatment method—to recommend a lobotomy.

In the 1950s and the 1960s American psychiatry became conscious that in England and other countries many fewer patients were being

247

involuntarily committed and there were many more voluntary admissions to mental hospitals. Psychiatrists began a great campaign to decrease the number of involuntary patients and increase the number of voluntary. Among the reasons that were given for this campaign was that voluntary patients related better to therapists and suffered less stigma. In the push to increase voluntary admissions, patients were told that unless they signed themselves into hospitals they would be involuntarily committed, which made the admission not at all voluntary. And when voluntary patients wanted to leave the hospital, they were told that the voluntary admissions forms they had signed authorized their detention for a certain period of days.

In some jurisdictions, after a voluntary patient submits a notice in writing that he wishes to leave the hospital, the hospital can hold him for as long as fifteen days while it decides whether it will seek to have him involuntarily committed. Until recently in most states, the hospital has been under no obligation to inform the voluntary patient that he had a right to submit a written request to be released.

Before the recent trend toward more stringent commitment laws, psychiatrists had unbridled power to commit. The commitment can be permanent or nearly permanent. Suzanne Buchannon, born with a spinal tumor and not wanted by her parents, was put in a mental hospital when she was sixteen. She tried to tell attendants she was not crazy. "A few times I got laughed at," she says. "Other times I got extra Thorazine . . . I was drugged most of the time." Twenty-three years later she was freed after she had gotten word of her situation to a mental patient rights group.[3]

Jack Smith was born in Michigan's Traverse City State Hospital. His mother had been admitted two days before his birth and died the day she gave birth. He spent his whole life in three state institutions until he was fifty-two. Released from the hospital a year ago, he is suing the state for $3 million.[4]

A striking example of the effect of the power of committing psychiatrists is the case of Anna and Michael Duzynski. In 1957 the Duzynskis came to the United States from Germany and settled in Chicago. Michael Duzynski had spent much of World War II in a Nazi concentration camp. The Duzynskis were Polish-speaking and had little English-language ability. They lived on the northwest side of Chicago, and after three years they had saved almost $5000, most of it banked, but $380 of which was in their apartment. The $380 disappeared, and they suspected that it had been taken by the janitor, who had a key to their apartment and knew they kept sums of money there. In the ensuing controversy Michael broke a window in the janitor's apartment (it was later claimed by Anna that her husband had rushed down an outside stairway to confront the janitor and had inadvertently fallen against the window). The janitor called the police and complained to them that the excited Duzynskis were insane. Examined at the Cook County Mental Health Clinic, they could not answer any of the questions asked them in English. The recommendation was for commitment, and the Duzynskis were sent to Chicago State Hospital. Six weeks later, Michael Duzynski hung himself in his hospital room. The next day Anna was released from the hospital as no longer mentally ill. When Mrs. Duzynski sued the psychiatrists who had misevaluated her, it was held that they had been acting in the service of the court in making their recommendation and were therefore protected by the immunity provided for judges, which extends to other judicial officers and agents.[5]

A long line of cases protects psychiatrists reporting to the court or testifying in court from liability for negligent examinations, on the ground that they are court officers. When psychiatrists have disobeyed a requirement of the statute that they must examine the subject in person or that they must have seen the subject recently, courts find in some cases that the doctors are protected by judicial immunity, in others that the patient was mentally ill and that the improper commitment didn't cause damage and may in fact have been beneficial.

Since the late 1960s many states have moved to raise the standard of commitment. They have done this in a number of ways. Some have raised the standard of proof necessary to secure commitment from the traditional civil law standard of "by a preponderance of the evidence" to a higher "clear and convincing proof" standard or an even higher "beyond a reasonable doubt" standard. Courts and statutes in some jurisdictions have required that the dangerousness of the patient be demonstrated by recent overt behavior, not merely by the opinion of the expert based on his understanding of intrapsychic dynamics. In a number of states the medical commitment, accomplished by the certificates of two doctors, with neither a court hearing nor an administrative procedure, has been held to be unconstitutional as a deprivation of liberty without due process of law.

But even with these protections, patients are still committed who do not meet the criteria of commitment. Virginia Hiday conducted a study of commitment procedures in North Carolina after a new statute had required recent evidence of overt dangerousness for commitment. She found that in the absence of such evidence, courts often still deferred to the judgment of the expert that commitment was necessary. The judges were unwilling to take the responsibility of overruling the judgment of the psychiatrists and psychologists and to follow the letter of the law. In her study Hiday reported that the new law had led to a considerable improvement over the old law, but that nevertheless in 20 percent of the cases she observed people were committed who did not meet the criteria of the state statute.[6]

In a similar study of court proceedings in Massachusetts, David Lelos analyzed 109 court hearings involving four hospitals in Massachusetts. For the sake of expediency and to prevent discomfort to patients, the courtroom for deciding commitment is often a designated hospital conference room. The practice saves untold hours of staff time that would be needed to transport patients to the court. The only apparent disadvantage is that these "public" hearings take place in an atmosphere of so much privacy that there is little chance to know how well they are conducted or what happens in them. Sixty-two percent of the patients had been diagnosed either as paranoid or as chronic schizophrenics. The four hospitals had commitment rates varying from 68 to 70 percent of the patients whose cases were included in the study; the average court hearing lasted nineteen minutes. (Before a new emphasis on patients' rights, many court hearings were much shorter.) The team of evaluators concluded that of the cases of patients who were committed, 58 percent met the statutory requirements of evidence of mental illness, plus behavioral and verbal evidence of danger or threat of danger based on fact rather than merely on expert opinion. The other 42 percent either had proven mental illness without factual evidence of harm (25 percent), or insufficiently proven mental illness although they had factual evidence of harm (6 percent), or no evidence of mental illness although there was factual evidence of harm (5 percent), or inadequate evidence of mental illness and only expert, not factual, evidence of harm (5 percent).[7]

Psychiatrists also have the power to refuse to admit patients to hospitals and to be immune from damage suits if the decision turns out to be wrong. Doctors can plead honest errors of clinical judgment as an excuse for not committing someone who afterward harms himself or others. Even if the psychiatrist is deficient in English-language skills, is not fully licensed and is working with only an institutional license, or has countersigned a decision not to admit made by the social worker who did the evaluation, these factors will not increase his liability to suit. Although he could be held responsible for harm if his evaluation was negligent, the courts give so much latitude to doctors to plead honest errors of clinical judgment that only the most glaring examples of negligent evaluation have been penalized.

Psychiatrists have the power to start treatment on patients who have not been adjudicated committable. When patients are committed to a psychiatric hospital, it is often on an interim or evaluatory basis, not because they have been diagnosed as mentally ill, but because there is reason to think that they might be diagnosed as mentally ill after an evaluation. Patients in this evaluatory stage have the right to protest their more permanent commitment, but medication, and particularly electroshock treatment, will decrease the ability of the patient to function effectively (repeated electroshock treatments cause loss of memory, disorientation, and apathy) and will cause the patient to lose his determination to oppose the commitment. At a private psychiatric hospital in New Jersey, when voluntary patients refused electroshock therapy, doctors saw nothing wrong in getting permission from the next of kin for the shock treatment. They then filed papers to have the patient's voluntary commitment turned into an involuntary commitment and started to administer the course of shock treatment before the court had had a chance to rule on the appropriateness of the decision. One suit against the hospital was settled out of court with a stipulation that the facts and outcome of the case would remain sealed in the court's records, which deprived other possible claimants of the chance to know that they, too, had a ground for suit.

In addition to commitment and forced therapy, psychiatrists intervene in many other personal aspects of life. We have noted that they make many employment determinations.

Adverse psychiatric reports have justified forced leaves of absence or separations from jobs, sometimes without an opportunity to know the psychiatrist's findings or to rebut the allegations on which he relied when he gave his opinion. Submitting to a psychiatric examination as well as refusing to submit to one can lead to the loss of a job.

The *Washington Post* reports that because regulations and procedural protections make it difficult to dismiss federal workers for inefficiency, stupidity, or other work deficiencies, the psychiatric examination to determine "fitness for duty" is apparently being used increasingly as a way to get rid of employees, and that critics of the system allege that sometimes personality clashes or differences regarding policy, rather than a medical condition, are the reasons for forcing the employee to undergo the examination.[8]

The power of psychiatrists is often used to ease teachers out of their jobs. It is easy to have a teacher removed for mental unfitness, but difficult to secure a removal for unsatisfactory work. A fifty-four-year-old New York teacher attempted for nine years to secure a hearing after the Medical Division of the Board of Education determined that she was "not fit at present for teaching duty." The teacher went through seven separate board-directed psychiatric evaluations and was always refused copies of the reports. Recently the United States Court of Appeals for the Second Circuit ruled that she was entitled both to know what the doctors had reported about her and to have a new hearing. The court said that the board had, by denying her access to her records, failed to provide "rudimentary fairness." During all this time she had been on involuntary leave of absence without pay.[9]

Psychiatrists are often used to screen out homosexuals or separate them from their jobs. John Gish worked as a New Jersey high-school English teacher without incident from 1965 to 1972. In 1972 he became president of the New Jersey Gay Activists Alliance. The next month the State Board of Education adopted a resolution directing him to undergo a psychiatric examination by its consulting psychiatrist, Dr. Richard Roukema, to see whether his support of homosexual rights demonstrated evidence of a deviation from normal mental health that might affect his ability to teach. To support its order to submit to examination, the board had secured Dr. Roukema's opinion that Gish's behavior carried with it a strong possibility of potential psychological harm to students. Gish protested the order to be examined. He challenged the constitutionality of the statute requiring yearly physical examinations and authorizing the board to order additional physical and psychiatric examinations when it believed an employee deviated from normal physical or mental health. The constitutionality of the law was affirmed,[10] and Gish was again ordered to be examined, this time by a "totally independent" psychiatrist, Dr. Edward Lowell. With "supportive corroboration" from both Roukema and Lowell that Gish had shown a "deviation from normal mental health that might affect his ability to teach, discipline, and associate with his students" and that a psychiatric examination to determine this would be in order, Gish was again ordered to go for the psychiatric examination.

The New Jersey Superior Court, in an opinion in 1976, pointed out "for the sake of clarity" that the reasons for requiring the psychiatric examination "do not include a single instance of any undue conduct or actions in the classroom or out of the classroom with respect to a particular student." The court relied on the "corroboration" of the psychiatrist, which dealt not with Gish specifically but with homosexuals as teachers generally, that Gish's homosexuality might affect his ability to teach. Gish was once again required to present himself for the examination or face loss of his job.[11] (Of course, if he did go for the examination, there was a good chance he would also face the loss of his job.) As of this writing Gish is still teaching while his case is being appealed.

But a psychiatric evaluation and diagnosis can also be the reason for the restoration of a job. A bill collector working for a Massachusetts utility company attacked a fellow worker and was fired. His union successfully secured his reinstatement on the ground that he had been suffering from acute schizophrenia and was not responsible for the attack, and that he had undergone psychiatric treatment and recovered to a point where, according to his psychiatrist, he could resume work under appropriate conditions. The conditions of reemployment, dictated by an arbitrator, included a weekly visit to the psychiatrist for six months, with the psychiatrist "monitoring" the patient so that company supervisors would not be "placed in the role of psychological policemen."[12]

An evaluation by a psychiatrist can entitle an assembly-line worker to workmen's compensation on the ground that the excessive speed of the assembly line caused him to become schizophrenic. Or it can enable an office worker to get compensation on the ground that her employer's excessive and steadily increasing delegation of work and responsibility had caused her mental breakdown.[13] Death benefits have been awarded to the widow of a suicide on the basis of a psychiatric opinion that the suicide was the result of an uncontrollable impulse caused by a work-related pressure.[14]

Psychiatric and psychological reports determine school admission, suspension, expulsion, and readmission. A student received failing grades at graduate school. He was notified that he could not return for the next semester. He presented to the Faculty Standings Committee a letter from his psychologist saying that his failing grades were the product of a neurosis—a neurotic fear of examinations that caused him to function poorly on them—and so should be excused. In this case the faculty committee was not swayed by the report, but therapists' letters and reports are commonly used to relieve students of an obligation to perform at required levels, and they are usually effective.

Psychiatric treatments have been made a condition of readmission to medical school. The Medical College of Pennsylvania decided to consider all scholastic failures as primarily the result of psychiatric problems. Therefore, all students who wanted to be readmitted after failure were advised to get treatment, and low-fee therapy was offered by psychiatrists associated with the medical college. The psychiatrists also helped the administration to identify students who might fail in the future unless they received psychiatric help. Reacceptance of failed students to the school depended on satisfactory completion of a course of therapy (although the psychiatrists had made the promise that no reports would be made to the school administration about progress and problems). The psychiatrists also became advisors to the medical college on applicants to the school, and they could then identify prospective students who "looked good on paper, but who by our criteria would run a greater than usual risk of failure."[15]

Psychiatrists and psychologists make determinations in other spheres of living. They have the power to keep competent people from having surgery they desire, and they can decide if people should be allowed to have life maintenance discontinued or to refuse medical treatment. With no apparent legal rationale, many surgeons require psychiatric evaluations before they will perform some kinds of elective operations on patients. When a patient wants to be surgically sterilized or wants plastic surgery, many doctors will ask for a psychiatric consultation. The consultant will disqualify the patient for the operation after a brief one-encounter evaluation on either of two grounds, both dubious legally. In some cases the psychiatrist thinks the person should not have the operation because he does not know his own mind, although there are no allegations that the patient is so mentally disordered as to be incompetent. In other cases the physician fears that this is a litigious patient, and he wants to eliminate the cause of a possible suit. One plastic surgeon has published a list of indications in applicants for surgery that raise the possibility that a psychiatric evaluation is needed. They include:

• Minimal physical defect, or a marked discrepancy between the defect and the patient's concern.
• The patient's inability to define the anatomical change desired.
• The surgeon's difficulty in communicating or establishing good emotional contact.
• The fact that the patient is a male.
• A history of previous unsuccessful cosmetic surgery.
• A history of disappointing experiences with other physicians.
• A history of psychotherapy.
• A disturbed current life situation.
• The intuitive feeling on the part of the surgeon that this patient may cause future trouble.

The psychiatrist who disqualifies a patient for an operation is taking on the function of both professional witness and judge, and the surgeon who accepts his recommendation not to perform surgery is acting as if the patient had been judged legally incompetent. (Surgeons are free *not* to do surgery. If a woman wants to be sterilized and the surgeon feels this is too early in her life for such a procedure, he can elect not to operate and refer her on. The surgeon is then taking responsibility for the refusal of the procedure, a far different situation from that of allowing the psychiatrist to veto the operation on the ground that the patient does not know her own mind.)

In addition to advising surgeons on the performing of all kinds of nonessential or discretionary surgery, psychiatrists have special authority to pass on the merits of applicants for psychosurgery. The psychosurgery patient is attempting to find a way to curb episodes of periodic violence or severe anxiety or to bring under control obsessive compulsive rituals. Because the indications for psychosurgery are debatable and the question of informed consent of a patient who presents himself with emotional problems is difficult, the psychiatrist has great leeway in determining which applicants for the procedure should be accepted and which refused.[16]

Sex-change operations are done only after psychiatric screening and approval. The transsexual hopes to affect a change that will bring his body in line with his concept of his appropriate gender, and the psychiatrist rules on whether this is a reasonable or unreasonable desire. Transsexuals differ from homosexuals and transvestites. Most homosexuals do not have a consistent or a strong desire to be a member of the other sex; they prefer their own sex and exalt it, and they avoid intimacy with the other sex. Transvestites dress as a member of the other sex, and although exhibitionistic transvestites are usually homosexual, transvestites who cross-dress in secrecy are usually not homosexual. Transsexuals both cross-dress and take homosexual sex- and love-objects, but since they see themselves as of a different sex, they see these same sex objects as being of the opposite sex. Society, which forbids homosexual marriage, allows marriage when one partner has undergone a sex-change operation. (In a support and maintenance proceeding, a court has required the husband of an anatomically changed male-to-female to pay spousal support.)[17]

Psychiatrists at one time assumed that the desire to change sex was delusional and that an operation would not lead to any real improvement in mood and feeling. On the other hand, they reported no therapeutic successes with attempts to change the gender orientation of transsexuals. The sexual surgery in 1952 in Denmark on Christine Jorgensen and her apparent adjustment to her new role cast doubt upon this formulation. Jorgensen has said recently that she has no regrets about her sex change.[18] Sex-reassignment surgery has been increasingly practiced. Courts have determined that transsexualism is an illness that may be amenable to surgical remedy.[19] A legal debate about whether it is necessary surgery to be paid for by Medicaid has been settled in some jurisdictions by a ruling that the state is compelled to pay if the court is satisfied, on the basis of psychiatric evaluation and testimony, that there is a "medical need of the surgery."[20] Some insurance companies pay for sex-change surgery if it is determined by a doctor to be necessary, but others decline to pay.[21] However, sex reassignment has been held to be a valid reason to discharge an employee; the Civil Rights Act of 1964 prohibiting sex discrimination does not prohibit this.[22]

The most disturbing legal aspect of transsexual surgery, according to Melvin Belli, is that an apparently subjective complaint is treated according to the medical direction of the patient. "The patient diagnoses his problem and prescribes the treatment . . . Thus, the surgeon is faced with removing healthy organs on demand by a possibly confused or delusional person; most gender clinics report that many applicants for surgery are actually sociopaths seeking notoriety, masochistic homosexuals, or borderline psychotics, and not true transsexuals . . ."[23]

The process of approval for the surgery is initiated by the patient, who must use certain words to secure approval, to prove he or she is a "true transsexual." He must say that he has always had the conviction that he was a female imprisoned in a man's body (or, in the case of a female seeking reassignment, a male in a female's body). Jan Morris writes, "I was three or perhaps four years old when I realized that I had been born into the wrong body, and should really be a girl. I remember the moment well, and it is the earliest memory of my life . . ."[24]

Psychiatrists have complete power over who will get sex reassignment and who will be refused, and they have been criticized for their lack of uniform standards concerning the decision for surgery. The analytically minded argue that they deal with conscious desire for castration, but that there may be a powerful contrary unconscious wish. Some of the rationales for approving surgery have been questioned. At one time it was believed that it forestalled suicide attempts, but Herschkowitz and Dickes, after reviewing the literature, have reported that from 5 to 16 percent of postoperative transsexuals attempt suicide, raising the question of whether surgery truly lessens that potential.[25] Jon Meyer, after studying twenty patients who had surgery at Johns Hopkins and twenty-one who were refused, judged that the two groups had made equally good adjustments. A common pattern for those who were operated upon was an initial phase, lasting from two to five years, of elation, often followed by "the painful realization that nothing had really changed except certain elements of body configuration."[26] Following this study, Johns Hopkins Hospital phased out its sex-change operation program.[27]

Psychiatrists who work with surgeons as part of a sex-reassignment team are supportive of the decision for surgery, and they even advise psychotherapy, and sometimes even behavior modification, to prepare for the change, to decrease the conflict, and to reenforce the characteristics of the other sex, such as feminine mannerisms in the male. However, if they anticipate a bad result, such as continued depression or conflict, regret or remorse, or a paranoid state, or even if they think the individual would not make a good representative of the other sex—would be unattractive or awkward in the new role—they turn down the application. They routinely turn down applicants on the basis of unstable personality, difficulties in social adjustment, age, criminality, a family that opposes the change, inability to hold a job, a history of any successful heterosexual performance, and inappropriate bone structure, muscular development, and distribution of body hair in the male.[28] Whether or not any of these are medical factors that should affect a surgical decision is debatable. It has been argued that the role of the psychiatrist should be as facilitator—to help the individual to a decision—and that he should not assume responsibility for a life choice or impose his concept of appropriate physique and behavior on the patient.[29] Most transsexuals seeking reassignment will be directed to an evaluating team that will tend to be sympathetic to the change. The team may, however, include considerations in its determination that represent a value judgment rather than dispassionate science, and it may arbitrarily rule out candidates for factors, such as instability, which from another point of view might seem like a reason for surgery. Few transsexuals seeking surgery will encounter psychiatrists who oppose the procedure or who think that the results of surgery are so dubious that psychotherapy, although not curative, still is a more helpful treatment.[30]

Psychiatrists have an even greater power, a true "life and death" power when they are called in to determine if someone should have renal dialysis, or should have the right to refuse life-saving surgery or to have life-maintaining procedures and devices discontinued. Terminally ill patients and patients suffering from medical conditions that cause great pain sometimes prefer death to continued treatment. Doctors concede there is a right to refuse treatment, but only if the patient is rational and knows the consequences, so the psychiatrist is called in

—often in cases where the only psychiatric problem of the patient is advanced years—to see if the patient should be allowed to make his own decisions, or if he should be kept alive or subjected to surgery against his wishes. The psychiatrist may be appointed by the court to determine if the patient is competent to make his own decision, although it is difficult to know what a psychiatrist can add to the decision by judges or lawyers, who should be able to make the determination whether someone has adequate information, and the reasoning power and ability to process the information. Judges and lawyers evaluated competency long before there were any psychiatrists; now psychiatrists are asked to do the job, and because they "understand the workings of the unconscious mind," they are presumed to be able to give a more definitive answer than a judge, or even than the patient himself.

In Tennessee, Mary Northern, a 72-year-old impoverished woman with frostbitten, gangrenous feet refused to give consent to have her feet amputated, an operation that would give her an estimated fifty-fifty chance to live. A judicial decision gave the Department of Human Services the right to decide for her, and it ordered the operation. A lawyer for Miss Northern secured a delay of the effect of the ruling so that a psychiatrist could interview her and determine whether she understood the effect of her decision. Again she was declared incompetent and unable to make her own decision. Columnist Ellen Goodman writes:

> From the low court to the most supreme, the state drew a picture of Mary Northern as a crazy lady. After all, she lived alone with six cats. She was a "spinster." She was reclusive. Her French tapestries had cobwebs, her chair was propped up with catsup bottles, her fireplace was overrun by cigarette butts.
>
> And from the low court to the most supreme, Mary Northern had only one reply: "They are not going to take my legs away from me, you understand that?"
>
> In the end, all of the courts upheld the ruling against this lady. She was judged incompetent for one basic reason: She didn't accept the operation like any "sane" person would have; she didn't choose life . . .
>
> . . . As William Curran, professor of legal medicine at Harvard Medical School, sees it, "The patient does something the surgeon considers unreasonable—like refusing some operation or treatment they think the patient should get—and the surgeon wants a psychiatric consultation."[31]

Psychiatrists have special power when they operate within total institutions. Every institution has encompassing tendencies, says Erving Goffman, but some encompass in a total way and have barriers, real or symbolic, to departure and to social intercourse with the outside world. Besides mental hospitals, Goffman classifies jails, penitentiaries, army barracks, and boarding schools, among others, as total institutions.[32] The power of the psychiatrist in the mental hospital has been described, but there are equally effective ways for psychiatrists to be used to help the management of subjects or inmates in the other kinds of total institutions.

Prison psychiatrists have unusual power over prisoners. Until recently sentence time was "tolled" while a psychiatric patient was in a hospital for the criminally insane (in spite of the fact that he would usually have more supervision and fewer privileges than in a prison), so prisoners adjudged insane would spend years in such a hospital and then be returned to prison without any credit on their sentence for hospital time.

In many states, people accused of sexual crimes or of repeated nonsexual crimes can be diagnosed as sexual psychopaths or defective delinquents by examining psychiatrists (although the psychiatrists are not diagnosing a disease condition but only stating that they see the offender as incorrigibly criminal). The definitions of sexual psychopath and defective delinquent are not in any psychiatric manual or text (psychiatry has no such categories) but originate in statutes, and even though they are legislative, they require medical doctors to apply them. Sometimes after conviction, but in some states after arraignment but before conviction and when not necessarily guilty of the charged offense, defendants are diverted from the criminal-justice system and sent to a hospital for the criminally insane, where they are kept until certified by the staff as cured, recovered, or safe to be returned to society.

Maryland, which until recently had the most broadly written defective-delinquency law, also has had the best-funded and most "therapeutic" rehabilitation program. In the 1950s a special "therapeutic institution," the closest American equivalent to the correctional hospital in Denmark at Herstedvester, was built at Patuxent. The Maryland law, unlike most state defective-delinquency laws, did not require arrest for a sexual offense or a determination of mental deficiency before selection for the program, but only a psychiatric determination of defective delinquency. (The defect referred to in the statute is not a mental defect but a moral defect, or defect of the will to lead a law-abiding life. The criteria of defective delinquency are "persistent aggravated antisocial" behavior plus low intelligence and/or emotional unbalance presenting "an actual danger to society.") At admission, at graduation from each of the four tiers of the program, and at

259

the ending of a probationary outpatient supervised status, psychiatrists made determinations. Some of these had the potential of keeping an inmate in this institution for the remainder of his life.

After twenty years of experience with prisoner rehabilitation according to this mental health model, civil libertarians advocated doing away with the program entirely. In one famous case, a prisoner, Edward McNeil, had stood on what he considered his constitutional right and had refused to cooperate with the Patuxent psychiatrists. Because they were unable to assess him and decide whether or not he qualified as a defective delinquent, this man with no history of a previous conviction was held for more than the five years of his sentence, which in practice would have been shorter with time off for good behavior. The psychiatrists apparently planned to hold him for the rest of his life if he did not cooperate. The Supreme Court refused to accept the state of Maryland's claim that the detention was therapeutic, not criminal. It ruled that McNeil should have had the due process right to remain silent about an offense while an appeal was pending, and they ordered his release.[33]

In 1978, the Maryland legislature, as the result of a seven-month study by an independent research corporation, decided what everyone had known for years—that the staff at Patuxent did not have the capability of predicting long-range future dangerousness, that the indeterminate-sentence policy affronted a concept of civil liberties and due process, that the therapy program had not been notably effective in reducing recidivism, and that defendants were not being referred to Patuxent in a fair and uniform manner. In exchange for much longer sentences and a cost-per-day nearly double that of a regular correctional institution (confinement in which, despite all its shortcomings, would have seemed preferable to most of the Patuxent inmates), the Patuxent recidivism rate was, at 69 percent, only a few percentage points lower than the 72 percent of the Maryland prisoners who went to regular criminal institutions. On the basis of these findings, the Maryland legislature revised the Patuxent legislation to abolish the "defective delinquency" diagnostic evaluation and the indeterminate sentence and to continue the institution as a specialized correctional institution with a therapeutic emphasis.[34]

The lesson of Patuxent is that an institution sponsored by liberal reformers, who saw the correctional system as bankrupt and wanted behavioral science therapeutic techniques applied so prisoners could be reformed, became in twenty-five years an institution condemned as repressive, and according to one estimate, "probably the most sued institution in the United States."[35]

Prison psychiatrists prescribe tranquilizers and order seclusion without any chance for an inmate to protest. They order inmates to hospitals for the criminally insane and accept them back as "cured" without any chance for effective protests or participation in the decision making by the inmates. They recommend parole decisions, another important kind of power.

Similarly, when a military psychiatrist makes a decision, the subject has almost no opportunity to protest. The military psychiatrist may have some regard for the patient or subject, but his main function is to consider the best interest of the armed service and to promote its smooth functioning. One military psychiatrist said he was expected to be "an officer first, a consultant second, and a physician-healer third."[36] Another said that "the primary goal of Army mental health services is to preserve the fighting strength."[37]

After they had completed their term in the service and were safely back in civilian life, some military psychiatrists have reported that they were pressured by medical staff superiors to give a psychiatric diagnosis to subjects whose major or only psychiatric symptoms were acting against the rules or expressing antimilitary attitudes.[38] When one military physician protested the way medicine was practiced in the military, he was ordered to report for a psychiatric examination.[39]

One of the great uses of military psychiatry is in the detection of malingerers, those men who report physical or mental symptoms with a view to either escaping frontline duty, evading other obligations, or securing a discharge. One problem with the detection of malingerers is that some psychiatrists who identify with the military are quick to give a diagnosis of malingering. Others with a more civilian orientation are much more ready to find that the symptoms are not being manufactured and have a basis in reality. There are even some psychiatrists who feel that the fact that someone malingers is enough to label him psychopathological. Their belief is that emotionally healthy individuals would not resort to malingering, so although they are not taken in by the deception, they fulfill the wishes of the malingerer and relieve him from duty. But usually the bias is the other way, and even military personnel with major psychiatric symptoms are returned to duty in the interest of the service.

But psychiatrists bestow benefits, too. During the Vietnam War a policy of "compassionate reassignment" kept men from overseas duty, at least temporarily, on the ground that a wife, mother, or other important relative was mentally ill.[40] The reassignment depended on the ability of the treating psychiatrist (often a civilian) to write an effective letter documenting the need for the serviceman to be at home.

Psychiatrists have always been recognized to have great power in the administration of criminal justice. Although juries are skeptical concerning psychiatric explanations in criminal trials, the testimony of a psychiatrist often has made the difference between death or life, imprisonment, psychiatric probation, or unfettered freedom.

The psychiatrist's power in the criminal-justice field sometimes receives a great deal of visibility. The battle of the experts in criminal trials with sufficient importance, and where there is enough financial support to provide a full-fledged adversarial proceeding, has been publicized in the cases of Jack Ruby, Sirhan Sirhan, and Patty Hearst, and in the determination of the competency of David Berkowitz, the "Son of Sam." In less publicized cases, defendants who are convicted often have their sentences determined by various reports, including psychiatric and psychological evaluations. Frequently the material in these reports, which may be adverse to the defendant, is not available to the defense attorney. The defendant who "has the book thrown at him" may never have a chance to learn that he was considered a potential risk on the basis of a psychiatric appraisal of dubious scientific validity, based on materials furnished to the psychiatrist that may have contained hearsay and unproven accusations that would not have been admissible in court. Some courts have not allowed the presentence report to be challenged, even though the psychiatrist's evaluation was made only on the basis of reports and documents and he had never seen the defendant.[41]

In criminal justice, the prosecution always has a stable of psychiatrists who are known to favor law and order and who can be relied on to give the best possible opposition to the defense effort to bootleg leniency into the criminal-justice process through psychiatry. The defense lawyer, on the other hand, knows which psychiatrists in the community are considered liberal and have a bias in favor of an accused and against the imposition of society's sanctions. The defense psychiatrists, if their dynamic explanations are not too farfetched and bizarre, often command more weight than the prosecution psychiatrists. The reason for this is that the prosecution relies on forensic psychiatrists who are employees of the court or of a government agency and who are often on a full-time salary basis and may earn only $30,000 or $40,000 a year. Defense attorneys secure the services of private psychiatrists, who may be university-affiliated, have a more impressive list of credentials, and be much more presentable. One has to pay dearly for such experts. Experienced forensic psychiatrists in private practice charge from $500 to $1000 a day, and they will charge for time spent conferring, studying background, evaluating, interviewing the defendant and others, writing reports, traveling, and waiting in the courtroom, as well as for their time on the stand. This kind of expert is obviously available only to defendants who are well off, and he can do a better job for a psychiatrically sophisticated defendant who can help build his own psychiatric defense than for an uneducated or unsophisticated defendant.

Having a psychiatrist in one's corner can make all the difference between prison and a coerced but relatively painless psychiatric probation. Here are some cases involving psychiatric excuses for what, without the excuse, would be a criminal action.

David Begelman, the former president of Columbia Pictures, used a psychiatric excuse when he was accused of misappropriating more than sixty thousand dollars of company funds. His misdeeds, Begelman said, were "aberrational, bearing no sense to reality. I had neurotic displays of self-destructiveness. While everyone considered me very successful, apparently subconsciously I didn't have the same high regard for myself. Therefore I was determined to do something that, if it didn't destroy me, would hurt me badly."[42]

A New York congressman who acknowledged he had solicited two young boys for sex agreed to undergo psychiatric counseling in exchange for the dropping of charges.[43]

When actor Ryan O'Neal was arrested for possession of marijuana, the court ordered him to undergo six months of psychiatric counseling, after which a determination would be made, based largely on the report of the psychiatrist, of whether or not he should be sentenced.[44] O'Neal received a favorable report and did not have to serve time.

When Mackenzie Phillips, the eighteen-year-old costar of the television program "One Day at a Time," was arrested on a disorderly conduct charge after she had been picked up semistuporous and incoherent, with traces of alcohol and Quaalude in her system, she was ordered to report to a drug treatment program for six months, after which time charges could be dropped on evidence of "satisfactory progress."[45]

When the thirteen-year-old son of Lyndon Johnson's press secretary, George Christian, shot and killed his junior-high-school teacher, the court found that his mental health was substantially impaired and that he needed hospitalization not available at Texas public facilities, so he was committed by court order to Timberlake Hospital, a private psychiatric hospital in Dallas. The cost of his care there will be borne by his family. It will go on for "at least two to four years," at $119 a day, or almost fifty thousand dollars a year.[46] A boy from a poor home would receive a different disposition.

Psychiatrists are sometimes given the power to detain in mental hospitals people who are not mentally ill. Defendants who successfully plead not guilty by reason of insanity or who are found to be sexual psychopaths or defective delinquents, are detained in a psychiatric hospital until an assurance by the psychiatrists that they are no longer insane or psychopathic and are safe to be released. Even after such a person is certified as no longer mentally ill, a judge can still require him to be detained in the hospital if it appears that he is still dangerous.[47]

Children are especially vulnerable to the power of psychiatry. In the commitment process, they have almost no rights. They can be committed at the desire of their parents as long as a psychiatrist feels the parents have a valid reason, and they have little chance to protest.[48] Once in an institution, they are powerless to oppose psychiatric decisions. Children in the custody of the juvenile court are moved from state to state, from family to family, and from family to institution on the recommendation of a psychiatrist. Psychiatrists are relied on to inform the court which of competing parents should receive custody of a child. Courts defer to psychiatrists in these kinds of dispositions, although often the psychiatric examination has been inadequate and the recommendation is ill-considered, silly, or downright wrong. Psychiatrists often recommend dispositions or give testimony that is in the interest of the agency that pays their salary, a department of human resources or a bureau of children and family services, rather than in the interest of the child. Upholding the authority of social workers and supporting agency policy takes precedence over the well-being of the subject.

In an Atlanta case, the Drummonds, white foster parents who had had the custody of a racially mixed boy, Timmy, since he was less than a month old, applied to adopt him when his mother made him available for adoption at the age of twenty-eight months. The Drummonds were considered by the Department of Family and Children Services to be qualified to raise a foster child, but they did not meet the criteria for adoptive parents, and the department did not think unsophisticated white parents could successfully raise a racially mixed child. I testified in behalf of the foster parents that taking a child away from the only parents he had ever known would be a traumatic experience. A psychiatrist for the Department of Family and Children Services was prepared to testify that children are subjected to this kind of trauma frequently and there is no evidence that it causes them psychological damage. The case was eventually lost by the foster parents on other grounds: a decision that foster parents did not have a legal standing to intervene in such a case and that race had been only one among several factors, not the sole factor, in the decision to remove the child.[49] Timmy was removed from his home, sent first to racially mixed parents, and when this did not prove satisfactory, to a black couple. We will not be able to follow his development and the effect of the changes of placement on him, because the Department of Family and Children Services, "in order to protect him," will not allow any information out about Timmy's whereabouts or his progress.

Commitment, employment decisions, control of military personnel and prisoners, adoption decisions—these are ordinary powers routinely exercised by psychiatrists. As we continue, we shall see extraordinary exercises of psychiatric powers that literally cut deeper and receive even less attention.

The Intrusive Psychiatrist

PSYCHIATRISTS INTRUDE into their patients' lives just by being psychiatrists. Patients transfer to a psychiatrist fantasies and attitudes that belong to past stages of development until the psychiatrist fills their waking lives and makes his way into their dream lives. Patients absorb the attitudes and values and follow the wishes of their psychiatrists. Psychiatrists are also capable of more open intrusions. They intrude on some patients by committing them to mental hospitals or controlling their courses of action.

Psychiatrists are sometimes even more intrusive than that. They intrude their therapeutic methods into the blood circulation of their patients by dosing them with chemicals or injecting chemicals into the blood stream, where they ultimately enter the very brain cells and bathe the nerve centers. Psychiatrists have inserted specially designed cutting needles, called leucotomes, into the frontal fibers of the brain to interrupt brain activity. They pass electrical currents through the brain to interrupt the patient's thoughts and memories. They apply electric currents to the calf or some other muscle to change the patient's characteristic stimulus response patterns. These psychiatrists invade their patients' life space by literally getting under their skin.

Surgical intervention—drilling into the skull—has been a part of psychiatry for more than 2000 years. The concept of cutting into, or cutting off, to cure behavioral disorders received a powerful impetus about 150 years ago when a surgical approach was advocated for "disordered" sexual behavior, promiscuity, excessive sexuality, and masturbation. Doctors saw these as caused by physical stimulation of the genitals, inadvertently through irritation and deliberately through self-stimulation, and saw surgery as a means of curing the problem. Simon-André Tissot's book on the relationship of masturbation to mental disease appeared in France in 1758. The range of disease entities and symptoms that were attributed to masturbation in medical journals of the second half of the nineteenth century included epilepsy, blindness, vertigo, loss of hearing, headache, irregular action of the heart, and general loss of health and strength.[1]

A popular cure for male masturbation was circumcision, and for female masturbation, clitoridectomy. Baker Brown, the author of *On the Curability of Certain Forms of Insanity, Epilepsy, Catalepsy, and Hysteria in Females,* published in 1866, advocated the removal of the clitoris as a remedy for masturbation and epilepsy.[2]

Infibulation was a nonsurgical physical method of discouraging male masturbation by placing a ring in the prepuce to make masturbation painful, and this was also accomplished through acid burns and thermoelectrocautery.[3]

When circumcision was not considered enough of a remedy, there was a more drastic method, castration. A case report in the *Medical & Surgical Reporter* in 1865 described a physician who had been confined as insane for seven years. Then he was castrated, and he soon showed evidence of being a changed man, "becoming quiet, kind, and docile" and able to return to his practice.[4] An editorial note in the *Texas Medical Practitioner* in 1898 recommends castration for epilepsy accompanied by masturbation: "Were this procedure oftener adopted for the cure of these desperate cases, many who are sent to insane asylums, soon to succumb to the effects of this habit, would live to become useful citizens."[5]

Nonsurgical remedies for masturbation were more popular. A common regimen was hard work and a simple diet. Some doctors prescribed restraining devices for the hands. If the masturbator was chaste, sexual intercourse was sometimes recommended, and some doctors advised male masturbators to acquire a mistress or patronize a house of prostitution.[6]

In the last years of the nineteenth century, Sir Francis Galton's ideas about improving the race genetically by giving financial subsidies to accelerate the breeding of hereditary genius types and by encouraging the constitutionally inferior not to procreate gave rise to the eugenics (from the Greek for "well born") movement. Sexual surgery was widely used. We now have had almost a century of experience, social acceptance, statutory authorization, and judicial support for this kind of surgical intrusion. In eugenics, sterilization was proposed not as a treatment for symptoms but as a means of social control—to prevent procreation. In the case of "defective women" (that is, women of low intelligence), it was designed to allow them to be promiscuous without having children, and as time

267

went on the eugenic sterilization that had been introduced as a method of fertility control in males eventually became largely confined to women. Many defective women were given the alternatives of remaining in an institution for the mentally retarded during their childbearing years (which was an effective "institutional sterilization") or having surgery to be made infertile and then being allowed their freedom. If they chose to be sterilized, it was not necessarily a stupid decision.

Sterilization of male defectives was carried on before there was any statutory authority for the practice. In 1889 Dr. Isaac Newton Kerlin, superintendent of the Pennsylvania Training School for Feebleminded Children at Elwyn, began to sterilize defective youths with the permission ("informed consent") of their parents. (He did not describe the procedure but it was probably removal of both testicles, castration.) Kerlin told about his sterilizations in a speech he delivered in 1892 as president of what later became the American Association of Mental Deficiency. He challenged his audience: "What state will be the first to legalize this procedure?"[7]

Dr. Harry C. Sharp developed and perfected the vasectomy in the period from 1899 to 1907, using as his experimental subjects young boy inmates of the Indiana Reformatory. At the same time the salpingectomy was being developed in France. Doctors now had effective methods of sterilizing: for males, castration and vasectomy, and for females, hysterectomy, bilateral oophorectomy, and bilateral salpingectomy.

A popular psychiatric classification of the time was "constitutional psychopathic inferior." Social deviants were assumed to have been born with a predisposition to crime and depravity. Sterilization would prevent these conditions from being passed on to posterity.

Instead of harsh terms like castration or orchiotomy or vasectomy, which convey the image of surgical intervention, the procedures were sometimes called "asexualization." In a book entitled *Mental Defectives, Their History, Treatment and Training,* Martin Barr, Isaac Kerlin's successor as superintendent at Elwyn, wrote:

> Let asexualization be once legalized, not as a penalty for crime but a remedial measure preventing crime and tending to future comfort and happiness of the defective; let the practice once become common for young children immediately upon being adjudged defective by competent authorities properly appointed, and the public mind will accept it as a matter of course in dealing with defectives; and as an effective means of race preservation it will come to be regarded just as is quarantine—simply a protection against ill.[8]

Allan Chase says, "It is hard to realize how profound the lures of the eugenics movement were to educated American professors and statesmen."[9] Theodore Roosevelt was an exponent. The Committee to Study and Report on the Best Practical Means of Cutting Off the Defective Germ-Plasm in the American Population concluded, as the result of two years of study, that at least 10 percent of Americans were by heredity socially inadequate and should not be permitted to breed.[10]

Indiana, where Sharp was at work, became in 1907 the first state to legalize eugenic sterilization. By the time he received the authority of the law, Sharp had already performed vasectomies on several hundred males at the reformatory.[11] In some of the states with early eugenic sterilization laws, the laws were later repealed or were declared unconstitutional on the ground that due process was not observed. Other statutes that provided for the eugenic sterilization of some classes of criminals were held unconstitutional as cruel and unusual punishment. In the 1920s, legislatures in two states, Michigan and Virginia, finally worked out eugenic sterilization laws that their supreme courts held were constitutional.

In 1927 the United States Supreme Court ruled in the case of *Buck* v. *Bell*[12] that the Virginia statute was constitutional. The case represents Justice Oliver Wendell Holmes at his worst, using genetic theory that even in 1927 was outdated in order to support his famous statement that "the principle that sustains compulsory vaccination is broad enough to cover cutting the Fallopian tubes." The argument was not as convincing as it appears at first glance; the penalty for refusal to be vaccinated was only a small fine, but there was no opportunity to refuse sterilization. Also, vaccination had a proven medical use, whereas eugenic sterilization had not been proven—and was not capable of being proven—to be the answer to the problem of mental deficiency. The degree of intrusiveness varies, too. Holmes ignored such considerations, saying, "Three generations of imbeciles are enough" and "It is better for all the world if, instead of waiting to execute degenerate offsprings for crime, or to let them starve for their imbecility, society can prevent those who are manifestly unfit from continuing their kind." The decision in *Buck* v. *Bell* reads like the product of a Nazi court of the Hitler period.

Holmes wrote to his young friend Harold Laski, the British political scientist, that he had just upheld "the constitutionality of an act for sterilizing feeble-minded—as to which my lad tells me the religious are astir." (The "lad" was Holmes's law clerk; Holmes had no children.) Laski wrote back that he himself was working on problems that were less interesting than "settling whether a feeble-minded Virginian is to remain virgin." He ended his letter "Sterilise all the unfit, among whom I include all fundamentalists."[13]

By 1937, ten years after *Buck* v. *Bell*, twenty states had passed eugenic sterilization laws, and twelve more states and the Commonwealth of Puerto Rico eventually passed such statutes. Some of these states have repealed their laws, and they have been declared unconstitutional in five others. In most of the states that continue to employ compulsory sterilization it is limited to residents of specifically named institutions for the female retarded or to other institutionalized patients. According to those statutes, the procedure can be done on the mentally deficient, the mentally ill, epileptics, hereditary criminals, and sex offenders. (A few states have included syphilitics.)

In the 1930s the annual number of enforced sterilizations was over 2000 a year, but since 1960 the reported rate has dropped to below 500. Most of the sterilizations at an earlier period took place in California; more recently North Carolina has been responsible for about half of the reported cases. Only a handful of states continues to use these laws, but the practice has been replaced by voluntary sterilization, which is done widely on the noninstitutionalized as well as on institution inmates. It is not too difficult for the mother of a young girl with a low IQ to get her daughter to sign a consent form. The lack of good statistics makes it impossible to determine how widespread the practice is.

Many "eugenic sterilizations" are justified on the ground that severely retarded women do not understand personal cleanliness and cannot deal with menstrual discharge, and hysterectomies rather than tubal ligations are done, but the main motive of the parents who seek to have their daughters sterilized is the fear of pregnancy. More than sixty thousand women in the United States have been compulsorily sterilized.

In recent years the use of forced sterilization (sometimes in the guise of a "voluntary sterilization" procured by such pressure as the threat of withdrawing welfare or of cutting off obstetrical care) has been extended to women who are of normal intelligence but who are considered by social workers or obstetrician-gynecologists to have had too many children or to present a threat of having illegitimate children. Cases that have come to notice include that of Nancy Hernandez, a Chicano mother of an illegitimate child, who was offered probation by a Santa Barbara judge instead of jail for a marijuana offense if she would consent to sterilization, and those of welfare recipients in South Carolina who were forced by their obstetricians to consent to future postdelivery sterilization in order to secure their services for present pregnancy.

Eugenic sterilization can be seen as a medical method of achieving a social result, and it is hard to think of it (or conceive of it) as therapy, although when Sharp developed the technique of vasectomy he thought one benefit would be an improved temperament. In contrast to eugenic sterilization, castration of men with a history of sexual offenses has been recommended as therapy, and its advocates claim it is preferable to a "more punitive" correctional approach like imprisonment. Ralph Slovenko, a law professor, writes that the general feeling is against castration as a method of dealing with sexual offenders, but that in some European countries it is considered valuable in the treatment of selected cases. Denmark, Norway, Switzerland, and Greenland provide for "voluntary" castration of people who are "impelled by abnormal sexual instincts to commit indecent offenses." Finland and Sweden authorize compulsory castration.[15] West Germany in 1970 passed a law making castration an acceptable legal method to prevent repeated offenses by "hardened sex criminals."[16]

Castration has been used at Herstedvester, Denmark's famous institution for the therapeutic rehabilitation of criminals, and some American psychiatrists have held this up as a model. Manfred Guttmacher, America's most influential forensic psychiatrist, wrote to a Denver surgeon who advocated castration: "I have visited Herstedvester, the Danish institution where castration is carried out in certain serious sex offenders. To me, it seems a more logical and more benign procedure than locking them up indefinitely."[17] George Sturup, Herstedvester's director, received the American Psychiatric Association's Isaac Ray Award for outstanding contributions to forensic psychiatry in 1965 and gave his lecture series the following year at the University of Pennsylvania. Most of his audience, which was composed largely of psychiatrists, legal psychiatrists, psychologists, and social workers, was unaware until his lectures that castration was used at this model institution.

Proponents of castration, like the advocates of psychosurgery, claim it is humanitarian because it confers freedom. A sexual offender who otherwise would have to serve a one-day-to-life term until "cured" from a condition like child molesting, for which there may not be a cure, can find castration a liberating procedure.

Castration has not been widely used in the United States, but it has its advocates and there are sporadic attempts to utilize it. At a conference on crime sponsored by the University of Colorado at Boulder in 1949, Dr. Charles Hawke, director of the State Training

School at Winfield, Kansas, read a paper describing the series of 330 feeble-minded men and boys castrated at his institution. Observers of his project, he said, had given this appraisal of the results: "Physically, the castrate is an improved organism. General health and longevity are increased . . . Contrary to general belief, castrates are not sexually incapacitated. The sex drive is admittedly reduced, but successful marriage with regular sexual performance are recorded in the study . . ."[18]

Two California judges ordered dozens of castrations in the 1940s, and a large number of castrations were performed in San Diego between the mid 1950s and 1970. Since then there have been only scattered news reports of castration in the United States, most recently in Denver in 1971 and in San Diego in 1975.

The Denver case involved a man who was apprehended for molesting a young girl and who admitted he had molested during his lifetime between 400 and 500 girls under twelve years of age. On the advice of Dr. Horace Campbell, a surgeon who was familiar with European accounts of success with castration and who had written a medical journal article advocating the procedure,[19] the judge allowed the accused to plead guilty to two charges of molesting, twelve other counts were dropped, and sentence was deferred on the condition that he voluntarily consent to surgical castration. He was castrated, and five months after the operation doctors reported that his emotional state had much improved. He no longer had outbursts of crying, he was being seen daily as an outpatient at a mental health center, and he was holding down a job. His attorney said that the castration was voluntary and "had brought about a real cure for this man." The unidentified man said that his castration had cured him and stopped his sex crimes. The president of the Colorado Psychiatric Society commented: "It will be at least a year before we can draw any conclusions. But it raises very serious ethical questions." The president of the Colorado Medical Society was not concerned with the ethical questions and did not think further consideration of the matter was needed. He said, "Considering the voluntary nature of the operation I am not at all sure the matter will be carried any further."[20]

In 1975 a San Diego judge ordered that two laborers, both forty-five years old, who were being held in the county jail, be castrated within twenty days or face indefinite terms in state prison for child molestation. On their convictions for child molestation, the two men had been sent to Patton State Hospital. They were returned to the county jail diagnosed as "incurable and dangerous to children and society." The California Penal Code provides that a convicted defendant can suggest an alternate plan for probation when faced with prison. The men, through their attorneys, had proposed their own castration. (The *Los Angeles Times* noted that the procedure was not at all novel in San Diego. The news story revealed that before 1970, when an American Civil Liberties Union law case against a San Diego judge and surgeon in a similar "free will" castration case had led to an end to the practice, there had been 370 defendants who had chosen castration.)

Superior court Judge Douglas Woodworth agreed to the castrations, but the surgeon who had tentatively agreed to do the procedures withdrew because he feared a lawsuit.[21] Commenting on the case for the *Hastings Center Report,* a biomedical ethical journal, Gerald Klerman, then professor of psychiatry at Harvard Medical School, now head of the federal Alcohol, Drug Abuse, and Mental Health Administration and the top government psychiatrist, felt that the opposition of the San Diego County Urological Society and the San Diego Medical Society had unduly influenced the surgeon to withdraw and that the societies had acted inappropriately in restricting the autonomy of the surgeon. Assuming that the procedure would be helpful and that consents were freely given, Klerman thought the men should have been allowed to choose their own fates. Said Klerman, "I suspect that we have been overly influenced by accounts of rare individuals who have maintained their sense of autonomy while incarcerated, and tend to ignore the many thousands whose capacity for autonomy and freedom has been overwhelmed by the indignity of prolonged incarceration. If this is true then I, for one, would opt to allow the prisoners the right to choose either surgical castration or pharmacological treatment over lifelong confinement."[22]

In addition to surgical castration and chemical castration, accomplished by hormone injections, sexual behavior can also be modified by direct entrance into the brain. Dr. Fritz Roeder, a West German neurosurgeon who uses a coagulation electrode to destroy part of the hypothalamus as a cure for homosexuality, feels that psychosurgery is better than the surgical or chemical approaches to the problem of the sexual deviant because, he says, it does not have some of the psychological side effects, such as depression and feelings of inferiority. Also, because this surgery theoretically operates not on the totality of sexual feelings, but specifically on homosexual feelings, he feels it raises fewer legal problems. He sees the possibility of using the procedure for the seventeen thousand persons who are indicted annually in the German Federal Republic for improper conduct with children and male juveniles.[23]

Most researchers would see chemical castration as raising the fewest legal complications, because it is a reversible procedure. West German researchers working with SH 80714, a synthetic antiandrogen, feel that the chemical approach "may make [surgical] castration absolutely unnecessary."[24]

In 1970, John Money at Johns Hopkins reported on the use of progesterone, a feminizing hormone, to cause a chemical and less-than-permanent castration. He had tried the drug, used previously for gynecological disorders and precocious puberty, in long-acting injectable form on eight male sex offenders. The action of the drug included the decrease of circulating testosterone. Psychiatrists David Barry and J. Richard Ciccone have described their use of these injections on three aggressive sexual offenders, whose plight ordinarily "would have been shrouded in therapeutic nihilism"; the men had been indicted for class B felonies and "volunteered" for the treatment as a condition of their release on bail. They reported that all three men were pleased with the result of the treatment (one noted an improvement in his acne), which led to less destructive sexual energy and a mellowing of their temperaments. Barry and Ciccone advocated more work in this field and the alerting of families and judges about this "new therapeutic opportunity" for a group previously not considered treatable as patients.[25]

Some of these methods seem very alluring to forensic psychiatrists and correctional administrators, who have the job of trying to stamp out criminal behavior. If to some of the public the castraters seem like Dr. Strangeloves, mad scientists willing to go to any length to find a scientific approach to any problem, to others of the public, to the experimenters themselves, and also to the castrates, they may seem like liberators.

Castration raises the same issues that are raised in any intrusive technique to change behavior. Is the subject giving a truly voluntary consent? Is his consent based on all the information he should know? (*The Medical-Moral Newsletter* states that cyproterone acetate, one of the antiandrogens that has been used to produce a chemical castration, is not as safe as its users claim. "As clinical experience with cyproterone acetate has accumulated, evidence that it may have serious side effects has appeared recently. The latter demands that a more cautious attitude toward this drug be taken." The same study suggests that the behavior-changing effect of cyproterone acetate may not be better than a placebo.)[26]

What are the relative weights that should be given to the right of the individual to protect the integrity of his mind and body versus the right of the state to control the individual for his own good, the good of others, or the good of society? Is freeing a defendant from an indeterminate sentence more important than protecting him from enforced therapy or particularly intrusive "voluntary" therapy? What procedural safeguards should be utilized, and how effective must the treatment be proved to be, and how free of adverse reactions, before it is forced on a person? Should the physician make the decision concerning castration on his own, or with the advice of correctional officials or the courts? Is this a medical decision? If it is, how appropriate is it for nonphysicians to participate in the decision making? If it is not, should physicians be involved?

One of the most important questions is related to the use of a technique that may be effective but also has dehumanizing aspects. Some people see castration as an opening wedge, a practice that may be useful in itself but that will serve as a paradigm for other interventions and so end up doing more harm than good. Others see no reason to prohibit a possibly effective modality merely because it may create a precedent and believe that society should deal with each new technological development on its own merits, not on the basis of how it may alter future attitudes.

*　　*　　*

It was perhaps logical that attempts to get into the organism to change feelings and actions would have begun with an attack on sexual pathology, since the cause and effect relationship of the sexual organs and sexual behavior seemed at one time to be clear-cut. But this was only one variety of feeling, and other intrusive kinds of therapy were developed with the brain as the target, with the purpose of calming schizophrenia, lifting the spirits of depression, curbing violence. The most popular of these intrusive methods is electroconvulsive therapy, which each year in the United States is administered to an estimated one hundred thousand new patients and a total of two hundred fifty thousand new and old patients.

Benjamin Franklin inadvertently received an electrical shock in 1785 and was inspired by it to recommend that it be tried as a cure for madness, but there is no evidence that his suggestion was followed.[27] Shock therapy got its start in 1927 when Manfred Sakel developed a method to put patients into a state of shock through injections of insulin. Insulin had been given for sedation and to stimulate the appetite, and when an overdose was given, the patient went into a hypoglycemic state and a coma, which was sometimes accompanied by convulsions. Sakel instituted the practice of deliberately inducing comas. This was considered a preferred method of treating schizophrenia as late as 1960, although the results of the method were always dubious, the convulsions could be very severe, and patients sometimes remained in an irreversible coma or died. The treatment was so dangerous it could only be done in a special unit of a hospital with a trained staff to monitor the patient. Some patients were given a course of 150 to 200 treatments over a period of six months or longer on a six-day-a-week basis.

Laszlo Von Meduna developed a therapy specifically designed to produce convulsions after he observed that some psychotic symptoms disappeared temporarily after a convulsion. He first used camphor in oil and later an injectable synthetic camphor preparation, Metrazol, which produced a convulsion within thirty seconds of administration. Still later, a method was developed of producing convulsions by inhaling an ether, Indoklon.

In 1938 electricity reappeared on the scene when Ugo Cerletti and Lucio Bini discovered that an alternating current sent from temple to temple for one-tenth to one-half of a second produces a strong, shaking convulsion—almost identical to the convulsion of grand mal epilepsy —during which the patient loses consciousness, and on regaining consciousness shows confusion and loss of memory for the events immediately preceding the administration of the current. With repeated convulsions, a more confused, forgetful, and regressive state is achieved.

Electroconvulsive therapy was initially advocated as a treatment for schizophrenia and neurosis. Then it was discovered that it was either useless or could be harmful in the treatment of neurosis and was usually unsuccessful in schizophrenia, but that it had a dramatic effect in restoring some patients with psychotic depression to their predepressive state of functioning. It is now considered an important treatment method—often the treatment of choice—for depressive psychosis and for two rarer conditions, mania and catatonic excitement. Particularly outside large metropolitan areas, electroconvulsive therapy is often given on an outpatient basis. It is frequently given for conditions that there is little reason to think it can help—acute schizophrenia, chronic schizophrenia, neurotic depression. It has been used for sociopathic behavior, alcoholism and, in a case in Massachusetts, given to a teenager hospitalized for smoking marijuana. It has also been given to enforce hospital discipline: An investigation of Ohio's Lima State Hospital revealed that patients were kept in line by the threat of shock and the administration of shock.[28]

Freudian therapists and other dynamic psychiatrists fought the spread of electroshock therapy because they saw it as dealing with symptoms and not psychological underlying causes. They wished to mobilize repressed anger and use abreaction, the spilling out of buried feelings, to achieve a more permanent cure. Unfortunately, severely depressed patients are often too apathetic and negativistic or out of contact to work well in verbal therapy. Also unfortunate for the psychological approach was the fact that the electric treatment did produce rapid cures for severe depressive conditions (it works much less well on less severe depression), and after a temporary eclipse of its popularity during the period when antidepressant drugs were being introduced and adopted, it has regained popularity—so much so that many patients, in particular neurotic depressives and acute schizophrenics, who would have profited from medication and verbal therapy, have their chances of recovery impaired by shock.

The degree to which electroconvulsive therapy is used varies greatly from institution to institution. A famous private psychiatric hospital, not run for profit, reported that during one year about 7.5 percent of inpatients received electroconvulsive therapy. At about the same time a proprietary (private and for-profit) hospital nearby gave electroconvulsive therapy to well over 50 percent of its patients. A study of electroconvulsive therapy in thirty-six metropolitan New York mental hospitals showed that during a recent one-year period about 4 percent of admissions received shock, but the rates varied from zero in a few hospitals that did not use shock, to less than 1 percent in six hospitals, to 40 percent in one hospital. Thirteen hospitals shocked 1–5 percent, seven shocked 6–15 percent, four shocked 16–40 percent.[29] Other private proprietary hospitals may give electroconvulsive shock to 60 or 70 percent or more of their patients. Some psychiatrists use shock as their only major treatment method.

The publication of the news that Thomas Eagleton had had two courses of electroshock therapy over a twelve-year period (in addition to one other hospitalization) led to his withdrawal as the vice-presidential nominee in 1972. At the time shock was out of favor and antidepressant medication had largely replaced it. One psychiatrist quoted on the Eagleton case described shock as a therapy "used very extensively in America" at one time, which "gradually was used less and less as other forms of therapy have been found to be more effective."[30] We have noted that shock has since made a comeback.

Although electroshock therapy has its uses, it is administered to many patients who do not have the conditions for which it is primarily recommended. Psychiatrists who favor shock, as many do, cite cases where patients at great risk of suicide or death from malnutrition, or in great distress, are "miraculously" returned to health after six or eight shocks. On the other hand, many shocked patients do not fully recover and remain partially disabled, and some successes require new courses of therapy at intervals of every few years. Patients who have received a number of shocks rarely ever again relate well to a therapist who wishes to establish a close, verbally probing relationship. At a joint meeting of the American Psychiatric Association and the International Psychiatric Association for the Advancement of Electrotherapy, advocates of electroshock recommended it for adolescents who do not respond rapidly to antipsychotics, for ongoing prophylactic treatment for recovered patients who do not have symptoms, and, in a series of six-times-weekly treatments up to a possible total of fifty shocks, for paranoid schizophrenia.[31]

One advantage in the use of this treatment as far as hospital staff is concerned is that the effect of successive shock treatments makes the patient more and more confused, regressed, compliant, and—above all—forgetful, until the patient no longer remembers that he is fighting his hospitalization and the use of electroshock treatment. If there is any question whether the patient meets the criteria for commitment, several shocks later all doubts will have disappeared as the patient becomes increasingly more disoriented and confused.

A Philadelphia judge, Lisa Richette, tells of her experience after she became depressed and voluntarily went into a New Jersey clinic. In the hospital she found many of the young women patients were receiving electric shock. They were all voluntary patients who had committed themselves, "but they were taking the shock treatments because if they didn't they could be committed involuntarily." That is the threat that doctors can hold over their patients.

Judge Richette said that she knew in the interest of her eventual cure she had to resist. "But the more I resisted, the sicker they told me I was." Within a week she told the staff she wanted to leave. She was told that even though she was a voluntary patient, the law stated that she could and would be held for seventy-two hours. "I said I'd file a writ of habeas corpus," Judge Richette said. "They allowed me to leave, and as I was leaving, they said I was psychotic." (Judge Richette attributes her cure to getting out of her system the antidepressant drugs she had taken and to getting psychological treatment—verbal therapy and assertiveness training—at a university-affiliated hospital that was not shock-oriented.)[32]

Financially, shock is very advantageous for hospitals. Many health care policies only pay for three weeks of psychiatric inpatient care (mental illness is so hard to define that insurance companies and third-party reimbursement plans are skeptical of campaigns to put psychiatric hospitalization on the same terms as other medical illness), and this is just the right period to complete a course of eight treatments. Hospitals that give electroshock treatment to almost all of their patients regardless of the diagnosis are often profitable business entities, for in addition to money received from private insurance companies, government funds pay for treatment given to Medicare, Medicaid, and other patients.

The economics of electroconvulsive therapy show why this treatment modality appeals to the venal. The electroshock machine is inexpensive. The patient who is receiving electroshock is easy to manage, sleeps a great deal, does not need much nursing care, and uses the hospital much as a hotel or motel. Blue Cross, Blue Shield, Medicare, Medicaid, and other third-party plans pay without any questioning. It is an accepted treatment modality, and if it is often given to patients whose conditions do not justify the treatment, the third-party payer is not interested in that.

Some hospitals have earned the names of "electric shock factories" or "shock mills." Neal Chayet, a lawyer who has written on mental health law, believes malpractice actions could be brought (although there are no reported cases) against "the physician who lives in an area where the local general hospital has a good psychiatric ward, but sends his patient to a shock mill instead . . ."[33]

The shaking, contorting convulsions produced by electroconvulsive therapy as it was given for many years sometimes resulted in leg fractures, spine problems, muscle sprains and tears, and other damage. In the 1950s methods of putting the patient to sleep and injecting him with muscle relaxant drugs before applying the electrodes—requiring an anesthesiologist or some other professional to "breathe for the patient"—produced a modified convulsion in which sometimes only a slight tremor of mouth or eyelid indicated that a convulsion was taking place. The development of modified shock has been one of the principal factors in its restoration to popularity. In spite of new laws in a few states restricting the use of electric shock and giving patients the opportunity to refuse it (unless the patient is ruled so incompetent that his wishes can be ignored), a psychiatric newsletter recently was able to title a story, "Electroconvulsive Therapy Is Alive and Well and Respectable."[34] Most psychiatrists agree that electric shock will produce cures of psychotic depression in patients for whom verbal therapy and antidepressant drugs have not been effective. Organized psychiatry continues to oppose any restrictions by statute, regulation, or court case on its "right" to give shock to involuntary and unwilling patients.

For many years psychiatrists reassured patients that the memory changes produced by shock therapy were transient and reversible—

not lasting more than six months—and that there was no permanent brain damage. According to the authors of one study, "there are no convincing data that would support the conclusion that this seemingly harsh form of treatment creates significant impairment of the intellectual, cognitive, or personality operations of the patient, and overall, the cost-benefit ratio for this form of treatment would appear to be well within acceptable limits."[35] Recently evidence has been presented that electroshock therapy has led to electroencephalogram changes and to changes in tests of perceptual-motor functioning for patients who have received many shocks.[36] A few professional people who have received ECT report that impaired memory is a continuing problem in technical work. One shock patient, Marilyn Rice, a former employee of the Department of Commerce in Washington, has had her experience with failure to recover her professional competence related by Berton Roueché in a *New Yorker* study entitled "As Empty as Eve," in its "Annals of Medicine." (Mrs. Rice is called "Natalie Parker" in the article, but she has since revealed her identity in the course of a series of lawsuits against her former therapists.)[37] John Friedberg, a neurologist, has called electroshock "a neurological injury."[38] He says, "Many psychiatrists are unaware that ECT causes brain damage and memory loss because numerous authorities and a leading psychiatric textbook deny the facts. Others, who know of its effects, argue that the damage is worth the interruption of unpleasant states of mind."[39]

One defender of shock therapy cites the fact that Sylvia Plath wrote *The Bell Jar* after she had received shock as proof of the proposition that shock does not decrease thinking power; he should have told the rest of the story, which includes the eventual suicide of Plath.[40] Friedberg, who believes shock always causes organic brain damage, recommends that psychiatrists be required to inform patients that shock may cause brain damage and permanent loss of memory.[41]

Ernest Hemingway received a series of eleven shock treatments at the Mayo Clinic and was sent home to Idaho cured. Three months later, almost to the day, he was back at Mayo for another series of shocks. (The very rich, who can afford the best psychiatric care and go to the Mayo Clinic at Rochester, Minnesota, or the Menninger Clinic in Topeka, Kansas, find themselves at the end of their hospitalization discharged as cured with no opportunity for follow-up treatment. Hemingway's treatment can be seriously faulted, not only for the use of electroshock but also for the discontinuity of his care.) Hemingway complained that his course of eleven shock treatments erased his memories and made it impossible for him to function as a writer. He said, "What these shock doctors don't know is about writers and such things as remorse and contrition and what they do to them . . . What is the sense of ruining my head and erasing my memory, which is my capital, and putting me out of business? It was a brilliant cure but we lost the patient. . . . They should make all psychiatrists take a course in creative writing so they'd know about writers."[42] One month after the second series was completed and he was sent home cured for the second time, Hemingway died from a self-inflicted gunshot wound. If shock interferes with intellectual functioning—or if the people who receive shock are convinced there is a detriment, whether or not it actually exists—the treatment can be the last blow in a series that makes life not worth living. Shock is a magical cure for some depressions; it has intensified the depressive quality of life for others.

Plath wrote in *The Bell Jar,*

Doctor Gordon was fitting two metal plates on either side of my head. He buckled them into place with a strap that dented my forehead, and gave me a wire to bite.

I shut my eyes.

There was a brief silence, like an indrawn breath.

Then something bent down and took hold of me and shook me like the end of the world. Whee-ee-ee-ee-ee, it shrilled, through an air crackling with blue light, and with each flash a great jolt drubbed me till I thought my bones would break and the sap fly out of me like a split plant.

I wondered what terrible thing it was that I had done.[43]

* * *

As far as psychiatrists can go, the ultimate in psychiatric intrusion is psychosurgery and its related technique, electrical stimulation of the brain. Electrical stimulation is done with the implanting of electrodes, and, unlike psychosurgery, it is reversible. Sometimes it is used as a prelude to psychosurgery to determine what part of the brain should be excised. Techniques similar to psychosurgery involve, instead of cutting, the implanting of radium and other substances to modify brain tissue. Dr. Thomas Ballantine of Massachusetts General Hospital has said, "The brain is no longer a sacred organ, excluded from surgical therapy because it supposedly houses the human soul."[44]

Psychosurgery differs from brain surgery. Brain surgery or neurosurgery is performed to remove disease tissue, cancer, and other tissues, and also abscesses and the scar tissue that is a focus of epileptogenic activity. It deals with such organic pathology as the results of traumas to the head and bleeding into the brain. Psychosurgery is also brain surgery, but it is performed not to eradicate disease but to relieve pain, to alter feelings, and to change behavior. The two kinds of surgery can be clearly distinguished, but many cases involve enough of both organic pathology and behavior change so as to fall in the gray area between the two.

The ancients practiced trepanning, the drilling of small circular holes in the skull, on their fellows, and it continues to be practiced in primitive cultures as a form of medical magic.[45] Modern psychosurgery dates from 1936, when Egas Moniz in Portugal developed the technique of lobotomy and published his *Tentatives Opératoires dans le Traitement de Certaines Psychoses.*[46] Moniz's crude surgical attack on the frontal lobe fibers of the brain earned him a Nobel Prize in 1949.

An estimated forty to fifty thousand lobotomies (or leucotomies) were done in the United States during a ten-year period, until it fell out of favor after the introduction of the phenothiazines in the 1950s. The rationale of the prefrontal lobotomy is that the frontal lobes, approximately the anterior third of the brain, do not control specific functions such as speech or vision or voluntary muscle movement but do have some nonspecific functions that affect the experiencing of anxiety and the ability to display initiative. The Moniz technique involved boring a small burr hole in the skull and cutting frontal fibers. Techniques developed by other neurosurgeons included radical lobotomies (removing a lobe of the brain) and the transorbital lobotomy, a procedure so easy to do that psychiatrists instead of brain surgeons performed the operation. It was the transorbital lobotomy, developed by psychiatrist Walter Freeman and neurosurgeon Dr. James Watts, that became so popular. We have noted in Chapter 7 how the transorbital procedure could be performed by any psychiatrist. It did not require neurosurgical training, and an electroconvulsive shock could be used to produce anesthesia.

In practice, although some patients were sufficiently improved after the operation to go home and fulfill not too complex functions (a housewife, for instance, can return to her cooking and cleaning), many other patients did not recover as promised and spent the remainder of their lives in a hospital with impaired intellectual functioning. Although a main motive was to make patients less violent, an English psychiatrist has collected examples of twenty cases of lobotomized patients who have gone on to commit murder.[47] When I was a resident in the late 1950s, a polite middle-aged woman patient, a Southerner with gracious manner and speech, stood out from the other patients. She was always impeccably dressed as if for tea or afternoon bridge, and she seemed ladylike in every way except for her complete and stunning baldness. She made and kept herself bald by meticulously plucking out every hair as it appeared. She had been lobotomized years before. Perhaps her bare skull was her message to the world that she had been stripped of her intellect and feelings.

William Arnold, a newspaper reporter who has researched the life of Frances Farmer, believes she was given a lobotomy by Freeman while she was a patient in the Western Washington State Hospital at Steilacoom.[48] Farmer, the star of Samuel Goldwyn's *Come and Get It* and of the Group Theater's stage production of *Golden Boy,* had had emotional problems that had been worsened by amphetamines and alcohol. In 1944 she was committed to Steilacoom and she remained there, with one brief interval, for five years. She was considered to be an extraordinarily difficult and uncooperative patient; Arnold believes she was being scapegoated for her outspoken liberalism and her unconventionality. Farmer has written an account, published posthumously, of the incredibly primitive conditions at the state hospital.[49] She was given electroshock, insulin, drug, and cold water immersion therapy.

Freeman made three visits as a traveling lobotomist to Steilacoom in 1947, 1948, and 1949. In his book Arnold has a picture of Freeman surrounded by a group of interested doctors and nurses, prepared with his little metal hammer to tap the leucotome through the orbit of the eye and into the frontal area of the brain of a Steilacoom patient who is strapped to a stretcher and who has undoubtedly been given an electroshock treatment for anesthesia. Freeman is dressed in a sleeveless hospital gown, and he holds the leucotome with his left hand, preparing to tap it into place with his right. He has the bearded, bespectacled face of a Viennese professor, but his hairy arms give the photograph a feel of something more primitive.[50] Freeman at one session had lobotomized thirty-five women patients who were lined up for him at Spencer State Hospital at West Virginia. On his second visit to Steilacoom, in 1948, he lobotomized thirteen women. Women were the preferred targets for the lobotomist, possibly because the goal was to get them well enough to go back to doing housework and other uncomplicated chores. While at Steilacoom he explained his treatment philosophy.

> The patients for whom this operation brings the best results are those who are tortured with self-concern, who suffer from terribly painful disabling self-consciousness, whether it expresses itself in pains in the body organs or terrible distress from feelings of persecution . . . In ordinary language, the technique severs the nerves that deliver emotional power to ideas. Along with a cure comes some loss in the patient's imaginative power. But that's what we want to do. They are sick in their imaginations . . .

Arnold believes that Farmer was given a lobotomy by Freeman during the 1948 visit to Steilacoom. He says this was probably done when Freeman and Farmer were in a remote treatment room with no witnesses present. He cites a remarkable change in personality, from fiery to docile, at this period, which allowed her to be discharged from the hospital eighteen months later, and he says that for the remaining twenty-two years she lived she showed no trace of her old vitality and rebelliousness.[51]

Farmer in her autobiography never referred to a lobotomy, although she did give details of other kinds of inhuman treatment, including gang rape, done, according to Arnold, with the connivance of hospital orderlies who were trustee inmates of McNeil Island Federal Penitentiary pressed into hospital service.[52] If she had known she had had a lobotomy, presumably she would have included it in her book. The best evidence for her having had one is only suggestive—the coincidence of Freeman's visit and Farmer's change of personality. The Farmer case raises the intriguing question of whether she could have been lobotomized without even knowing this had been done. The answer is that a lobotomy preceded by electroshock for anesthesia might be accomplished without any evidence of the procedure other than black eyes and with no memory of the operation. If she did not have access to a mirror and did not know she had black eyes, or if she did see them and did not understand their significance, she could have been lobotomized without her knowledge.

In the 1950s the lobotomy passed from popularity, leaving behind its thousands of lobotomized (or, more properly, leucotomized) patients to make their way in the world if they could. There were three reasons for the fall from popularity of the procedure. Not enough patients were sufficiently benefited to make this seem like a promising therapy, and it also eventually became apparent that lobotomized patients often displayed grossly deficient judgment. And the introduction of Thorazine made it possible to deal with symptoms pharmacologically, a less drastic and more reversible method than surgery. Freeman and a few others continued to do lobotomies on a wide scale even after the procedure had generally been abandoned. Freeman played the part of the itinerant leucotomist. At state hospitals, particularly in the South, scores of patients would be held for his next visit, and he would travel around the country (much like the traveling executioner) performing his specialty.

Most sensitive psychiatrists, and some who were not so sensitive, saw the lobotomy as crude and cruel. It had arrived on the American scene with great publicity, achieved quick popularity, and then given rise to the disillusionment that has followed the introduction of many treatment methods. Most psychiatrists were happy to see it go. But the second wave of psychosurgery was on its way. In laboratories and operating rooms at Harvard, Yale, and other impeccable institutions, new surgical techniques were being developed that would restore psychosurgery to respectability again. The new techniques were far from crude. They involved the production of minute surgical lesions at precisely specified points or the extirpation of tiny portions of the brain. The surgery was done not on the large mass of frontal fibers but on various much less accessible parts of the limbic system, that portion of the brain that rules the higher functions of emotion, self-awareness, and creativity. Stereotactic procedures enabled electrodes to be inserted and directed to any part of the brain and for surgical lesions to be made with great exactitude.[53]

Perhaps 500 experimental psychosurgical procedures are now being done each year, by about a dozen neurosurgeons. Some of the brain operations are to control violent behavior, and three doctors have been involved in the development of this aspect of psychosurgery, all at one time connected with Harvard: William Sweet, chief of neurosurgery at Massachusetts General Hospital; Vernon Mark, neurosurgery chief at Boston City Hospital; and Frank Ervin, a psychiatrist and neurologist who more recently has been on the faculty of the University of California at Los Angeles.

These three thrust themselves into controversy and prominence in 1967 when they wrote in a letter to the *Journal of the American Medical Association* that urban riots, then a great concern in major cities, might be related to "focal lesions" in the brains of the rioters that spur "senseless" assaultive and destructive behavior. There is a need, they said, for research and clinical studies to "pinpoint, diagnose, and treat those people with low violence thresholds before they contribute to further tragedies."[54]

In 1971 the California Department of Corrections drew up a proposal for a program to do complex neurological evaluations on, and to treat, violent inmates. Surgical and diagnostic procedures would be utilized to locate centers in the brain that served as a focus for outbursts of violent behavior. The program would be experimental, designed to verify that certain brain centers were the source of aggressive behavior, and it would be conducted at Vacaville, which is both a "superadjustment center" for prisoners who are difficult to control and a research center that makes use of prison "volunteers." (The California Department of Corrections has sponsored prison research using volunteers for the development of a vaccine for the plague, for work on the toxicity of organic phosphates and other chemicals, and for studies on diseases endemic in Vietnam.) Applications were made to the Law Enforcement Assistance Administration for $300,000 and to the state of California for $189,000.

The proposal had some obvious defects. The relationship between specific areas of the brain and specific behavioral attributes is much less clear than some neurologists and psychosurgeons have claimed. The program would depend on prisoners who volunteered to be subjects of surgery, and volunteering is a questionable practice in prison because the inmate's length of stay may be related to his willingness to volunteer. In spite of these facts, the plan was considered to have promise.

Governor Ronald Reagan in his January 1973 State of the State message followed up by announcing the establishment of a California research facility to be known as the Center for the Study of Reduction of Violence. The center was under the sponsorship of the University of California at Los Angeles and was headed by Louis Jolyon West, chairman of the Department of Psychiatry. The state would furnish the material—the subjects of the experiments were to be inmates from prisons, patients from mental hospitals, and residents from juvenile-detention facilities. Most of the financial backing was furnished by the Law Enforcement Assistance Administration, which was sponsoring this program on the advice of the National Institute of Mental Health.

The center, later renamed the Project on Life Threatening Behavior, was to be the first step in a program to blanket California with "violence prevention" facilities and programs that would include everything from "a network of secure settings" to a public relations campaign on television, and another campaign directed at the helping professions, to acquaint the public and psychiatrists with methods of identifying and controlling violence.[55] It was seen by some neurosurgeons as the prototype of a number of other such centers in other states, forming a nationwide network.[56]

Edward Optin, Jr., senior research psychologist at the Wright Institute in Berkeley, sat in on a discussion of the violence proposal. He objected when it was revealed that there would be psychosurgical experimentation on prisoners and possibly also experimental pharmacological castration of prisoners. Michael Shapiro and his law students from the University of Southern California waged a battle at legislative hearings and in newspaper columns that led to the abandonment of the project.

The story of this project illustrates the eagerness of the behavioral scientist to forge ahead into new areas of behavior control even though in the process there is great intrusion on individual autonomy. It also demonstrates the resistance by lawyers that has kept psychosurgery and other intrusive techniques from becoming much more widely used.

The greatest attention to psychosurgery was achieved through the famous Louis Smith case, known in lawbooks as *Kaimowitz* v. *Michigan Department of Public Health.* [57]

Dr. Jacques Gottleib and Dr. Ernst Rodin, both associated with the Lafayette Clinic, the psychiatric teaching hospital of Wayne State University, in 1970 proposed a study of methods to treat uncontrollable aggression. The Michigan State legislature appropriated $228,400 for the research project. The subjects were to be twenty-four state mental patients. The subjects were all to be nonpsychotic brain-damaged males over twenty-five with IQs over eighty, hospitalized for at least five years, who had been subjected unsuccessfully to all other known forms of treatment, who remembered their violent acts and felt remorse about them, and who were capable of understanding and deciding whether they wanted to undergo the treatment, which had as its goal their release and restoration to society.[58]

The first subject chosen was thirty-six-year-old Louis Smith, who had been a patient at Ionia State Hospital for eighteen years. When he was seventeen he had been sent to Kalamazoo State Hospital for indecent exposure, voyeurism, and stealing women's undergarments. In the hospital he murdered and then raped a student nurse. Before trial, on the advice of his lawyers, he asked to be committed to a state hospital under a criminal sexual psychopath statute that provided for the dismissal of all pending criminal charges on the medical determination of criminal psychopathy and a commitment to the state hospital. The repeal of the legislation in 1968 had led to the release of all except a few dozen of the people committed under the statute. Those who were retained, like Smith, were kept because in the opinion of the hospital staff they continued to be mentally ill and dangerous. Smith had not been violent since his commitment, but the staff pointed out he had sometimes asked to be put into isolation because he feared his violent impulses, and of course there was no way—just as in the case of the Canadian offender-patient considered earlier[59]—that his degree of dangerousness in an unstructured situation could have been predicted by his behavior in a structured situation.

When the subject of experimental psychosurgery was raised, both Louis Smith and his parents were willing and gave consent. At the time there appeared to be no other way that he could possibly satisfy the staff that he was no longer dangerous and so have an opportunity for freedom. He and his parents knew that there might be undesirable and even unforeseen side effects. Dr. Rodin explained to Smith that ten electrodes were to be implanted deep within his brain to see if abnormalities could be found that were linked with his outbursts of violent behavior, and if a focus of abnormal electrical discharge could be located, the next step would be the psychosurgery that might make freedom possible. Two committees were appointed to oversee the project. One reviewed the selection of experimental subjects and found Smith a good candidate for the procedure. The second committee, designed to guard the interests of the patient, was composed of a lawyer, a certified public accountant, and a Roman Catholic monsignor. By a vote of 2–1, with the lawyer in opposition, the committee approved the consent, and the procedure was scheduled for January 1973. Smith was transferred to the Lafayette Clinic.

Before the electrodes could be implanted, Gabe Kaimowitz, a Michigan Legal Services lawyer, brought the issue to the attention of the public through the press, and filed a suit on behalf of John Doe—a name chosen to protect Smith's identity—and twenty-three other patients who would also be made a part of the experiment. Among the contentions were that no person involuntarily detained is capable of giving an entirely voluntary consent and that the use of public funds for the project was inappropriate because psychosurgery is contrary to policy. The Michigan Department of Mental Health cancelled its appropriation for the project. The court ruled that the case could still proceed and ordered a full hearing on two issues: Can an adult detained by the state, or his guardian, after the failure of established therapies, give an informed voluntary consent to an experiment that may enhance the detainee's chances for discharge, and is it legal to conduct experimental brain surgery on a patient involuntarily detained by the Department of Mental Health?

On March 23, a three-judge panel ruled that John Doe (or Louis Smith) was being held unconstitutionally, but his release was held up pending the hearing of testimony on whether it would be safe to release him. Dr. E. Gordon Yudashkin, the director of the Michigan Department of Mental Health, testified that he did not feel he could release Smith and seventeen others originally committed under the repealed act because he considered them dangerous, but he conceded that in view of the March 23 ruling they were being held unconstitutionally. The judges were more impressed by the testimony of Dr. Andrew Watson, a legal psychiatrist from the University of Michigan, perhaps because it helped them out of a difficult legal conflict between safety of the public and individual rights. Watson testified that he had read Smith's hospital record and had interviewed him for a total of five hours and that he felt Smith was safe to be released without any psychosurgery. He testified that much of the aggressive behavior that Smith had shown in Ionia State Hospital had been the result of his frustration at being there. It was easier for Watson, who had no legal responsibility for Smith's subsequent actions, to declare him safe than for Yudashkin to do so. Yudashkin, who carried public responsibility might be civilly liable for releasing a dangerous patient who therafter caused harm, because of his job, and in addition he had attention focused on him by legislature and press.

The final decision of the Wayne County Circuit Court (by the time it was handed down Smith was released and out in the community, preparing to go to community college) was that in no case can experimental surgery be used in an attempt to eliminate antisocial behavior in involuntarily committed mental patients. According to the decision, "involuntarily confined patients cannot reason as equals with the doctors and administrators over whether they should undergo psychosurgery." The court also said that First Amendment freedoms provide that "the government has no power or right to control men's minds, thoughts and expressions. If the First Amendment protects the freedom to express ideas, it necessarily follows that it must protect the freedom to generate ideas." The court doubted the safety and efficacy of the procedure and thought the risks outweighed the possible gains.[60]

A follow-up on the Smith case: Louis Smith was arrested for stealing women's clothes from a store a few months after he was released. After he was booked he was searched and was found to be wearing nineteen pairs of women's underpants and ten slips. He entered a plea of guilty and was sentenced to thirty-two months to four years in prison. While he was in custody, Smith confessed to the crime in Kalamazoo State Hospital that had led to his hospitalization. He was tried for that murder in 1976. He pleaded not guilty by reason of insanity, but the jury found him guilty of second-degree murder, and in April 1976 he was sentenced to life imprisonment with credit for the eighteen years he had spent in institutions.[61] In 1979 the Michigan Supreme Court ruled that the murder trial violated "traditional notions of fundamental fairness" and that the designation of criminal sexual psychopath served to bar a subsequent trial.[62] (In other states, where statutes have not provided for dismissal of criminal charges on the designation of criminal or sexual psychopath, the subject can be tried after his doctors say he is cured, and this has been held not to constitute double jeopardy.)[63]

The Circuit Court of Wayne County does not carry unusual weight and the outlawing of psychosurgery in the Louis Smith case would not have been cited as a judicial precedent except for the fact that no other cases on psychosurgery have reached the courts. Other potential cases did not develop because the publicity about psychosurgery that followed the Smith case led to strict policies of performing psychosurgery only on outpatients who were adult, fully informed, and not in a position where they would be seen as easily coerced. Smith's case (or the *Kaimowitz* case as it is usually called) served as the main precedent. It was not appealed by the state so we have not had the benefit of an appellate court opinion.

Around the same time that Smith's case was being decided, a psychosurgery case involving a suburban Washington, D.C., man was reported. John Gavin, Jr., was hospitalized at seventeen after a bad reaction to LSD (lysergic acid diethylamide), and for the next few years he was able to spend only half of his time out of Virginia Western State Hospital. While home on a convalescent leave he set fire to a book on witchcraft in a mall bookstore. Gavin was returned to the hospital, and three months later he blinded himself in one eye and badly injured the other. His parents were told that drugs and other treatment had failed and psychosurgery was the only way left to halt Gavin's self-destructiveness. Psychosurgery was scheduled, but anonymous telephone calls to the *Washington Post* and the Virginia attorney general prompted an investigation. Dr. Donald Becker, neurosurgeon at the Medical College of Virginia, said that that was the first such operation he had scheduled in Virginia, and that while he was at the University of California in Los Angeles he had performed "something less than five" similar procedures. The operation was cancelled.[64]

News of other cases of psychosurgery slowly came to light:

Dr. Orlando Andy of the University of Mississippi revealed that he had done thirty or forty psychosurgical operations, most of them on children, the youngest of whom was seven. The accusation was made that Andy had not had guidelines or a proper review committee procedure, that there were no precise diagnostic criteria for patient selection, that some, or perhaps many, of his patients had no other psychiatric diagnosis except "hyperreactivity" (akin to hyperactivity) and "uncontrollability," and that most of his patients were poor, black, young, and institutionalized. Andy refused to talk to newspapermen. "I will give my reports in scientific journals and at meetings," he said.[65]

When newspapers announced that the Veterans Administration had been performing psychosurgery to modify behavior, the VA first denied that the operations had been performed, later admitted that twenty operations had been performed, and still later reduced the number to sixteen. The operations had been done between 1960 and 1971 at four hospitals. As the result of a study, the standards for the performance of "surgery of abnormal behavior" were tightened, and after the promulgation of the new standards none of the four hospitals authorized to do psychosurgery asked for permission to do further operations.[66]

In 1974 the National Commission for the Protection of Human Subjects was asked to consider psychosurgery and plan a future national policy. Its final report, issued in 1976, was unexpectedly favorable.[67] It recommended that experimental psychosurgery research be continued under carefully supervised conditions, and it advocated that the secretary of health, education, and welfare support research on psychosurgery, ensuring government funding of more surgery projects. One argument for this position is that some psychosurgery, particularly that used to relieve symptoms of pain, has produced good results. Some critics of the report thought the members of the commission had failed to differentiate sufficiently between the successes of psychosurgery to control pain and the results of psychosurgery to control violence and change behavior, which are much more equivocal.[68] The chairman of the commission, J. Kenneth Ryan of Harvard Medical School, said, "... We saw that some very sick people had been helped by it, and that it did not destroy their intelligence or rob them of feelings. Their marriages were intact. They were able to work. The operation shouldn't be banned."[69] The *Kaimowitz* decision that no prisoners and involuntarily held patients could give a valid informed consent to experimental surgery was seen as overly restrictive. The commission said, "With respect to the question of safety and efficacy, it is clear that the information presented to the court in 1973 differs significantly from that which has been presented to the Commission." It proposed that adult prisoners and mental patients be given an absolute right to refuse psychosurgery, but if they are persuaded the psychosurgery is in their best interest, they should be allowed to consent. A proxy or substituted consent could be given for children. If the operation can be shown to have a probable benefit, it could be approved for consenting, noncoerced adults, even though it is experimental psychosurgery, and for mental patients and prisoners after the experimental phase is over and it has become an accepted treatment modality.[70]

HEW announced that for the time being it will not fund psychosurgery on patients who have a limited capacity to consent—prisoners, children, committed mental patients—but at the same time it declined to formulate guidelines for when psychosurgery can be performed. It called for voluntary guidelines to be formulated and administered by a joint committee of psychiatrists and neurologists.[71]

Critics of the commission's "go-ahead" gain some consolation from the reflection that the procedures are so time-consuming and so expensive that there is little chance they will be applied in the foreseeable future on any large-scale basis. But there is the frightening aspect that if the government is encouraging this most drastic kind of behavior intervention, almost all other types of behavior control that are less drastic and more reversible would be even more immune from criticism, even better candidates for government support.

* * *

Psychosurgery represents the most irreversible and intrusive kind of psychotherapy, but it is applied to a comparatively small number of patients. Drug therapy is usually reversible, but it can be extremely intrusive, and it can be, and is, applied to great numbers of mental patients. During the last thirty years drug therapy has become important as psychiatry's main therapeutic modality. It is also important financially, as the advertising pages of psychiatric journals and newspapers that contain almost nothing but drug ads testify. A committee of the American Psychiatric Association has spent years considering the ethics of the great financial support that psychiatry receives from drug advertising, but it has never issued its opinion on the practice.

Psychiatry supports drug companies, and drug companies support psychiatry. An advertisement for one drug will occupy eight consecutive pages of one issue of a psychiatric journal. Drug companies supply funds for "educational" trips for psychiatrists and pay for lectures at the annual meeting of the American Psychiatric Association. At psychiatric meetings and conventions they provide expensive souvenir giveaways. One drug company recently reprinted 7000 copies of a current 700-page book on legal psychiatry to present to psychiatrists. Others pay for free play, musical comedy, and concert tickets for psychiatrists who attend the annual APA convention.

The popularity of psychotropic medication has contributed to the public acceptance of the chemical control of behavior and feelings, and over-the-counter sedatives and hypnotics, alcohol, and marijuana are increasingly relied on to relieve emotional discomfort.

Behavior-changing prescription drugs include the major tranquilizers, antidepressants, psychic energizers, sedatives, narcotics, and the wildly popular minor tranquilizers. One study showed that one-fifth of people sampled in Oakland, California, had taken one of the minor tranquilizers or a sedative during the preceding year, and one out of ten had used one of these medications daily for a week or more.[72] Some observers, however, would question the validity of this study, since from general experience higher figures might have been expected, and 50 million prescriptions for Valium alone (and another 20 million for Librium) were filled in a recent year.[73]

Valium, or diazepam, is the most frequently prescribed drug in the United States. More than three-fourths of its prescriptions are written by physicians who are not psychiatrists. According to Sidney Cohen, ". . . The enormous use of Valium and other anti-anxiety agents may be a consequence of a recent shift in cultural values. It may no longer be a virtue to 'tough out' noxious emotions as in the old days. Using chemicals for relief is currently an acceptable alternative for large segments of the population."[74]

A British doctor writes, "The treatment by most doctors and psychiatrists of patients with life difficulties by the single expedient of tablets encourages the population to regard physiological responses to stress as pathological processes."[75]

The possibility of using drugs to influence large segments of the population—for example, to make people tolerate situations that would otherwise seem intolerable—has been foreshadowed in *1984* and *Brave New World*. A real-life parallel, in addition to the flood of prescription drugs and over-the-counter medications, is the methadone program, which converts heroin addicts, and many nonaddicts who are only occasional heroin users, to methadone addiction and keeps them dependent on a daily dose of an extremely addicting noneuphoriant narcotic, probably more addicting than the euphoriant heroin it is meant to replace.[76] Anyone who controls the methadone supply has the potential power to exert great influence over these "chemical substance captives." Black leaders, particularly, have seen a threat in the disproportionately large number of blacks who have been encouraged or coerced to become legally addicted to methadone and are therefore dependent on the government as the source of the drug and potentially sensitive to the will of the government. They see the methadone program as a prototype of the way that the government at some future time, if the political climate were right, could control behavior and political action by the threat of cutting off supplies. Nigel Calder foresees the possibility of a totalitarian state that uses the dispensing of drugs, in addition to brainwashing and other techniques, to promote conformity; the price of the daily "trip" is obedience to the state. He cites experiments that turned peaceful rats into killer rats and killer rats into peaceful rats by pinpoint injection of drugs into the brain. "From experiments like that, to what might be literally 'brainwashing' of humans with drugs, is a long step but it would be rash to say it could never be taken. Of the existing possibilities for mind control by drugs, the very simplest of those we have noted may be the most sinister—tranquillisers in the public water supply."[77]

A more pressing concern—because this technique is now being used to create conformity and control behavior and is increasingly popular —has arisen from the development of long-acting tranquilizers. Given by injection, they can be administered with or without the consent of the patient and can control behavior for weeks, and sometimes for longer than a month. Already in use for chronic schizophrenia is a long-acting injectable phenothiazine, belonging to the family of Thorazine, Compazine, and Stelazine, which is usually injected on a once-every-second-week schedule, but in some older patients can be used as infrequently as every six weeks. One of the advantages of injectable medication is that it can be forced on unwilling patients. But the struggle and the confusion make this an unpleasant way to administer drugs, so if the frequency can be reduced to only every few weeks, the method becomes much more useful.

Richard Mayberry, a Pennsylvania prisoner undergoing psychiatric examination, writes to his lawyer about the experience.

> I was in this room about five minutes when the door opened; five attendants followed by a female nurse entered my room. The nurse had *two* hypodermic needles full of Prolixin, a powerful and dangerous tranquilizing drug. I was calm, quiet, and doing nothing that would cause them to think that I might be violent, disturbed, or in need of sedation. I told them, "Listen, I'm not violent, I'm not crazy, I'm not disturbed, and I don't want or need any dope." The head attendant was a sadist . . . He told me, "The doctor ordered that you be given this medicine." I still refused it. The attendants then grabbed me, forcibly pulled my pants and shorts down, held me immobile, while the nurse, the hateful bitch, injected one needle into each ass cheek. I was wrecked for the next two and a half weeks.[78]

Long-acting injectable tranquilizers (Prolixin is the trade name for the drug most used) have had their greatest applications in the treatment of outpatients, and they have helped significantly lower the rate of relapse in chronic schizophrenic patients, who often fail to take their medication and become delusional or hallucinatory. Coercion is introduced into the outpatient treatment situation, by telling the patient he will have to return to the hospital, or he will have his parole revoked, or some other penalty will be applied if he does not present himself for his semimonthly shots. More than any other treatment modality, the long-acting injectable drug has the greatest potential for use as a method to secure conformity.[79]

Coercive administration of oral medication has resulted from the requirement that hyperactive school children, many of them never worked up medically and with only a tentative diagnosis of hyperactivity based on value criteria, take Ritalin (methylphenidate hydrochloride), a drug that is also prescribed for minimal brain dysfunction, which is equally vaguely defined. Good statistics are lacking for the number of school children, almost all between six and twelve, who have been required to take Ritalin—often on penalty of not being allowed to continue in school—but one estimate is that about one hundred fifty thousand to two hundred thousand children are on this drug at any one time.[80] The long-acting injectables and methylphenidate both have serious side effects, as do most chemotherapy agents. One adverse effect of Prolixin is that it sometimes intensifies a depression. It can also lead to tardive dyskinesia, an unpleasant and often irreversible loss of ability to control muscular movements. Methylphenidate can cause growth-stunting, and it has many other possible adverse side effects. Some new long-acting, mood-changing injectable drugs are waiting in the wings because questions of possible carcinogenic effects have not yet been answered.[81]

Mental patients and the mentally retarded have been used frequently as subjects of experimental medicine, not only to test drugs that might benefit them but also for drugs that had no application to their condition.

In 1966 Henry Beecher published his classic paper, "Ethics and Clinical Research," which brought to public attention for the first time that medical experimentation was being done without the consent of subjects and at the risk of harm to them.[82] Following Beecher's revelations, and as the result of a developing literature on the subject of the protection of experimental subjects, federal regulations were issued requiring special protection for the mentally ill, the retarded, and children, and cases of flagrant disregard of the rights of subjects in the pursuit of pharmacological knowledge have become much less common. But instances of improper drug experimentation still persisted. In 1970 almost 200 female residents of Tennessee's Arlington Hospital and School, a facility for the mentally retarded, were put on an experimental contraceptive program of injections of Depo-Provera at three-month intervals. Depo-Provera in laboratory animals had been associated with breast tumors, some of which were malignant, and its many other side effects included the possibility of permanent sterility. Dr. James Brown, superintendent of the institution, defended the program at a Senate hearing on the ground that since the drug had some approved medical uses, it was not an experimental drug, and he continued to maintain this position in spite of the fact that the commissioner of the Food and Drug Administration had testified that its use for contraception was experimental.[83]

Many more experimental programs were planned but were halted after legislative investigation, court action, or newspaper publicity. Some of these used psychosurgery, drug experimentation, and behavior modification techniques, especially those techniques involving aversive conditioning.

*   *   *

Behavior therapy was initially proclaimed to be a method of helping people that avoided some of the intrusive aspects of the three established therapies, psychological, somatic (physical, including chemotherapy), and social. Somatic therapy was obviously intrusive, and social therapy (involving manipulation of the environment) often functioned best in a hospital that imposed great control on the patient. The psychological treatment was less obviously intrusive, but in their roles as decision makers, psychiatrists asserted enormous authority, and it had gradually become apparent to discerning mental health professionals and critics of psychiatry (although not to the general public) that the decisions lacked an objective basis. The unfairness of some of these decisions was obvious to all except the psychiatrists who made them. The psychiatrists justified these decisions on the grounds that they must be based on clinical judgment and that continued treatment would further benefit the patient. Behavior modification promised to be a new therapeutic method that was more amenable to objective standards and hence would be less oppressive.

Behavior modification is as old as man—spanking has been described as one of the most ancient and widely used behavior modification practices. Any systematic use of rewards or punishments or other conditioning stimuli to change behavior is behavior modification. It arose as a development of psychology, but it has been adopted as a therapeutic tool by psychiatrists, and this and its equally impersonal and equally mechanistic cotherapy, the drug approach, have become the major therapeutic methods. They are often used together. They are used much more extensively in institutions (including many nonpsychiatric institutions, such as prisons and juvenile homes) than either the more publicized psychological (dynamic or insight) therapy or social therapy, and behavior modification is also used in factories and business to encourage production and efficiency.

No one doubts that behavior modification can sometimes be effective; the threat of prison sentences can change behavior. The main difference between time-honored behavior modification and the scientific variety that burst upon the scene in the 1950s is the insistence on measurement of quantifiable data.

> The behaviorist carries a slide rule, charts, graphs, counters, and timers, rather than a couch. "Measure, measure, measure" is the constant demand of behaviorists, outward signs rather than inward motivation, their milieu. No one, contends the behaviorist, really knows why someone does something; all we know is that the act is done. If we really want the act done again (or not), we should forget probing for ids, egos, and primal screams, and simply evaluate the environment, determining what stimulus produced the act. Then we can reproduce (or eliminate) the stimulus.[84]

In its simpler applications behavior therapy seems unexceptionable. Chronic schizophrenics are rewarded with tokens if they keep their rooms neat, and with these tokens they can buy gum and candy or earn the privilege of seeing a movie. Retarded children on a token-economy system are encouraged to learn to brush their teeth and show good manners at meals at the risk of loss of privileges if they leave teeth unbrushed or spill their food. When it was first given wide publicity as a scientific therapy, behavior modification was seized upon avidly because much of the unfairness in the authoritarian therapist-patient relationship implicit in verbal dynamic treatment is apparently eliminated if the patient has clearly defined, measurable tasks and earns his freedom (or some other privilege) when he completes tasks or meets some preagreed conditions.

Behavior modification's rise was spectacular, and it led to a revolution in the therapeutic approach to institutionalized patients, for it presented the promise of quick, easy, and inexpensive behavior changes. More highly trained dynamic therapists are replaced by less highly trained and less well paid mental health technicians, who are competent to total up points and award privileges. The application of behavior modification can easily become a rigid and dehumanized way to care for patients. When behavior therapy is combined with chemotherapy, it becomes possible to manage a patient without making any attempt to get to know him, to form a relationship with him, or to understand the factors that led to his disturbed behavior.

Changes achieved by behavior modification have not been shown to be long-lasting. Nonconforming patients can learn to adjust their

297

behavior in order to win points and get weekend passes; the improvement in behavior is not likely to last in a less structured environment where the contingency reward and punishment system is not operating. Modification programs to cure smoking are popular, but studies indicate the relapse rate is extraordinarily high.

B. F. Skinner, the father of behavior therapy, advocates rewards rather than punishment, but it is often difficult to distinguish the two. A reward denied is a punishment. The mental patient who does not earn a weekend pass because he has not socialized on the ward sufficiently loses his reward, but he experiences the loss as a punishment.

A frequent complaint about such programs is that they infantilize the patient. The modifier is acting in a parental role, the person being modified is in a dependent role, and growth is only allowed along the conformance axis, not the independence axis or the expressive axis. When patients voice objections to the denial of rewards or the imposition of punishments, that can be a cause for further denial of rewards and imposition of punishments. Patients who earn the most points often show no basic change, but they have conformed to the expectation of the staff and are considered "good" patients.[85] (This is a counterpart to the practice in some dynamic therapy where the patient who mouths back the psychoanalytic explanation of his behavior is seen as the good patient with insight, the patient who rejects the interpretation is bad.)

Willard Gaylin has pointed out that there is a descending scale of fear reactions that is related to the level of technology involved in the application of science to behavior: The fear of psychosurgery and electrode implantation is greater than the fear of mind control by drugs, which in turn is greater than the fear of operant conditioning, "even though all three bypass rationality and choice in an effort to control human actions." Gaylin suggests that perhaps the fear might be exactly reversed, that electrode implantation and surgical ablation of brain sections as a means of political control are much more cumbersome and much less likely to be widely used than drugs or conditioning. "Drugs, brainwashing by control of television, exploitation of fears through forms of propaganda and indoctrination through the sources of education—particularly of preschool education or neonatal conditioning as suggested by Skinner—all seem more likely methods of totalitarian control."[86] The ease of widespread application would make behavior modification an overwhelming threat if only this method had been shown to have a better success record.

When instead of a reward-centered system, the emphasis is put on noxious stimuli—painful ways of sensitizing or desensitizing "reflexes"

—and the method is applied to prisoners to cause them so much pain that they will learn to reject their own criminal behavior, behavior modification becomes a brutal method of control. One of the oldest forms of behavior modification for criminals is isolation or solitary confinement, or, as prisoners call it, "the hole." Advocates of solitary confinement have found new scientific rationales for the procedure through experiments with isolation and sensory deprivation that produce in the subjects heightened responsiveness to social reinforcement and an increased desire for social contact.[87] Isolation is a painful stimulus. Other, more obviously painful stimuli involve shocking patients, causing them to fear death from suffocation, and causing them to vomit.

Even when programs with such aversive stimuli are presented to prisoners as experimental, there is often little problem in getting volunteers. Prisoners may feel that their earliest release or their eventual release depends on participation in the experiment, and they believe this even when they are assured that this is not so. Prisoners lack information on behavior modification and they lack legal advice.

Prisoners often have very little to lose. If they have a long sentence or if they are in a hospital for the criminally insane as sexual psychopaths or defective delinquents (and hence technically mental patients instead of prisoners) on a one-day-to-life sentence, their only chance of freedom may be a "cure" by some novel kind of treatment. A prisoner who raped and killed two women and wrote to doctors around the country offering himself as a subject for experimental psychosurgery was asked about his willingness to volunteer for an experiment with such an unpredictable outcome. He said, "I got life without possibility. But there is a possibility. A complete change of being. Then I might someday get out. Besides, man, look what a mess I am already."[88] Many prisoners hope for a "complete change of being." Modification programs have been carried on, or are being carried on, in many prisons; one list compiled from Congressional hearings and court cases included the federal prisons at Marion, Illinois and Springfield, Missouri, and in state prisons in California, Maryland, Connecticut, Pennsylvania, Iowa, and Ohio.[89]

At the Connecticut prison at Somers, psychologist Roger Wolfe claimed he knocked "hell out of the sexual fantasies" of convicted child molesters by administering small electric shocks to the inside of their thighs as they viewed slides of naked children. In response to charges that prisoners are unable to give a truly uncoerced consent for such experiments, he said the program "is probably more voluntary than anything else that goes on in this place. We try very hard to make sure all our patients fully understand the program—it's one of the ways we select them."[90] A similar experiment involving electric shock as an aversive stimulus was carried on at the Wisconsin prison at Fox Lake. By 1971 there had been twenty-six studies published on the use of electric shock to treat sex offenders and it had also been used to treat shoplifters, bank robbers, homicidal schizophrenics, and self-destructive retarded children.[91]

The most bizarre aversion stimulus experiments have been stopped by publicity and legal action, and researchers can no longer plan their experiments with complete freedom. But knowledge of experiments that have been planned and put into operation gives us some concept of the scientific mind at work on impersonal methods of achieving behavior change. The Special Treatment and Rehabilitation Training Program, known by the acronym START, was established by the United States Bureau of Prisons at the federal hospital at Springfield, Missouri, in 1972 to deal with prisoners whose behavior in other federal prisons had been "maladaptive." The program was designed to make the prisoner socially conforming to the "general population prison environment," and the devisers of the program thought they were doing prisoners a good turn by enabling them to earn back lost "good time" (time credited toward parole) that they had forfeited because of their past obstreperous behavior. When prisoners conformed and were polite, they were given a "Good Day" report, and when they had enough of these, their lost good time and other privileges were returned. Eventually they were transferred to another tier that had a higher "status." When a suit was brought to halt the program, three psychologists made an evaluation of it. One was adamantly opposed to it and recommended that it be closed down. One was generally approving. The third was critical of the program as it was being conducted but suggested that most of the difficulties he had with it would be removed if it were made voluntary. The program was terminated by the Bureau of Prisons before the federal court could determine whether the prisoners had a right to refuse to participate in it. Evidence was introduced in the trial seeming to substantiate prisoner claims that they had been shackled to their beds, deprived of sufficient food, and required to lie in their own excrement in order to provide an atmosphere of deprivation in which rewards would have meaning as motivations.[92]

The 1973 case of *Mackey* v. *Procunier* concerned use of a muscle-paralyzing drug, Anectine, as a noxious stimulus to condition behavior. Because the drug paralyzes muscles of respiration and the subject is then dependent on the administration of positive pressure oxygen, there is the sensation of suffocation and impending death. The United States Circuit Court of Appeals for the Ninth Circuit found that this method of modification at Vacaville was probably either cruel and unusual punishment, in violation of the Eighth Amendment, or was illegal because of a violation of due process.[93] In *Knecht* v. *Gillman*, also in 1973, an emetic, apomorphine, had been injected to cause vomiting as a punishment for violation of Iowa prison rules. This was held to be cruel and unusual punishment when given without the consent of the prisoner.[94] Prisoner-patients have complained that electroconvulsive shock therapy in prison hospital wards and in hospitals for the criminally insane has been used as a punishment; prisoners call the electroshock machine "Edison medicine." At Vacaville prisoners have complained that Prolixin was injected as a punishment.[95] One prisoner complained that the drug stayed in his system for two weeks (which it is supposed to do), preventing him from walking normally and causing a problem with inability to control his tongue and other symptoms (all of which are not infrequent side effects of Prolixin). He said prisoners called Prolixin "liquid shock therapy."[96]

These are the kinds of treatment that psychiatrists have instituted and did carry on until legal activism raised questions of constitutionality of the practices. In countries with fewer guarantees of liberty and autonomy, aversive conditioning can continue unimpeded.

Most psychiatrists do not work in institutions. They sit in pleasantly furnished offices and deal with patients who often try very hard to be cooperative, and they do not seem aware that the "helping professions" do so much that is seen by their subjects as unhelpful. Most psychiatrists, psychologists, social workers, and other workers in the field have used subtler kinds of coercion and control, sometimes over such a long period that they have become oblivious to how authoritarian their methods are. They are not aware of the intrusiveness of "other" psychiatrists—the kind that put icepicks into the brain or send shocks to the thigh. The history of psychiatry shows that its practitioners are defensive about the more ordinary kinds of intrusions that are involved in everyday therapy and blind to the plight of state hospital patients, military personnel, the retarded, and the sexual psychopaths and defective delinquents who have been the brunt of the most blatantly coercive approaches.

How Psychiatrists Usurp Authority:
Abortion and the Draft

THE EFFECT of psychiatric determinations during the last two hundred years, first in court and later also out of court, has been generally to liberalize and "humanize" social attitudes and policy. The earliest testifying psychiatrists enlarged the definition of criminal irresponsibility and made more people not responsible for actions that otherwise would have been considered criminal. Psychiatrists went on to find excuses for abrogating contracts. They developed theories by which deserting soldiers would be held sick rather than traitorous. They developed theories by which scared and frightened people could get financial damages for torts, although formerly a physical cause would have been required to recover damages. They liberalized the interpretation of workmen's compensation laws so more conditions could be included. These changes were accomplished by psychiatrists who presented "scientific" evidence to enlarge the definition of "sickness." Psychiatrists were relied on outside the courtroom to give opinions that would influence the decisions of individual administrators and for testimony in administrative hearings.

When psychiatrists found that they had this much influence, they sometimes began to give opinions that were designed to achieve a desired social end rather than to express scientific fact finding. Thomas Szasz has said that there has been a consistent bootlegging of humanistic values into the social scene through reliance on psychiatry. If capital punishment seemed like too extreme a penalty, some psychiatrists could be found to testify that a defendant had been suffering from temporary insanity, and on this basis the penalty could be circumvented. Sometimes the testifying psychiatrist would be more influenced by sympathy for the defendant or his distaste for the law under which the defendant might be executed than by psychiatric indications that there had truly been insanity. Crimes committed by juveniles are often held to be evidences of psychological disequilibrium and so to be distinguished from similar crimes that are to be punished when committed by other juveniles. Sometimes the availability of a psychiatrist makes all the difference, and sometimes the psychiatrist is not concerned with mental state but with some other factor—perhaps his belief that detention would not be in the best interest of the juvenile, or perhaps a belief that marijuana should be decriminalized and that therefore an offender should not be penalized.

Two instances in recent years, psychiatric assistance for women in securing abortions and psychiatric help in obtaining deferments for draft-eligible men, represent deviation from scientific standards by psychiatrists so that social goals could be achieved—a more liberal abortion policy and a decreased support for an unpopular war. The determinations made by psychiatrists were not medical, they were political, but they were not challenged because the social aims were so generally acceptable. The psychiatrists themselves justified their deviation from medical standards because it was in the service of a "higher morality."

Abortion, before its liberalization by the Supreme Court's decision, and draft deferment during the Vietnam War represented moral controversies. In both cases psychiatry took its stand on the liberal side of the issues and used its influence first to help people evade the law then in force and then to promote a change in the law. Abortion was the first of these issues to surface. Prior to 1967, most states had highly restrictive abortion laws. These laws sought to protect the life of the fetus, and they prohibited women from patronizing nonmedical abortionists or aborting themselves. Abortions were required to be done by physicians and only on the grounds specified in the statutes, usually to save the life or preserve the health of the mother. A few states prohibited abortion entirely, but in prosecutions for criminal abortion, courts even in these states recognized a clear threat to the life of the mother as a valid defense. In 1967, California, Colorado, and North Carolina liberalized their laws, giving additional grounds for certifying an abortion, and in succeeding years a number of other states followed. In 1973 the Supreme Court promulgated a national policy of unrestricted abortion for the first six months of pregnancy.[1]

Until the late 1940s, internists and obstetrician-gynecologists could easily certify that women with rheumatic heart disease, kidney disease, and some other illnesses needed an abortion to save or preserve their lives. When women had no medical grounds for abortion, a psychiatrist could certify that the pregnancy had made the woman so depressed that she had become a suicidal risk, and the abortion would thus "save" or "preserve" her life.

Many women had no medical grounds for abortion, and even for women with major medical problems, the introduction of antibiotics, kidney dialysis, and improved care of heart patients made it increasingly difficult to justify an abortion on strictly medical grounds. Psychiatric indications then became the main reasons for abortion.

Psychiatrists certified abortions for women who were not psychiatrically ill and did not meet the psychiatric criteria for abortion. They did this not only out of sympathy for women who wanted an abortion and had no other way to procure one legally, but also as a protest against an abortion policy they considered too restrictive. The certifications were made after only of a brief interview, on the basis of which mental illness severe enough to threaten life was imputed to women who did not have such illness. The women were pleased to be declared mentally ill. They understood that this labeling was based on convenience and that they were not considered really ill. Before the psychiatric evaluation they were often coached by their referring doctors to describe suicidal preoccupations. The obstetricians and gynecologists who referred the patients to the psychiatrists for certification were happy to have psychiatrists take responsibility for the abortion and to have the way paved for it. Psychiatrists who saw the abortion laws as too restrictive were pleased to provide this service in the interest of a liberalized abortion policy and to be able to make a political gesture for which they also received pay. Deliberate mislabeling on a wide scale was continued over a period of years, until a change in the legal system no longer made health a factor in securing abortions.

Most of the data available on psychiatric need for abortion was imprecise, but it indicated that even a woman seriously threatening suicide if she had to carry a baby to term almost never acted out this threat. Daniel Callahan, the philosopher-medical ethicist, stated that though a number of psychiatrists stressed the possibility of suicide on the basis of attempts or threats, the evidence of the actual incidence of suicide was in fact very rare, even in women who were denied abortion after threatening suicide. In 1970 Callahan wrote, "So far as I can judge from the literature, there are no data to support a view that suicide for refused abortion, or as the result of pregnancy, is significant anywhere."[2] The likelihood of a severe neurosis or of a psychosis if the pregnancy was carried to term was also remote.

In addition to traditional psychiatric factors, psychiatrists took into consideration socioeconomic factors that had not before been considered medical—the number of previous children, the wish of the patient regarding this pregnancy, whether there were other family problems, and the family's financial situation. When all these are included as health reasons for an abortion, it becomes easy for a psychiatrist who favored abortion to say that it would preserve life, and even easier for him to say that it would preserve health (in the states that broadened their criteria to include this).

Callahan, who favored a liberalized abortion policy, thought it was appropriate for psychiatrists to take all these nonpsychiatric factors into consideration in view of a "general trend in medicine to see health in the broadest possible terms." The concern of the psychiatrist, Callahan said, was to help people function in their social and cultural environment. "The judgment, for instance, whether a person should be committed to a mental institution, whether he should be given certain drugs, whether he should be given intensive or relatively relaxed treatment, will be very much determined by a psychiatrist's consideration of the broadest context of a person's life."[3] This is a position that gives the widest discretion to psychiatrists, since everything becomes a factor to be included in a psychiatric determination.

Most psychiatrists who certified abortion were not basing their decisions on a belief that they were practicing a new kind of holistic medicine. They were giving false diagnoses and prognoses out of sympathy for the plight of women who otherwise might have been forced into an illegal abortion.

Fuller Torrey, an antipsychiatric psychiatrist, believes that the widening definition of psychiatric illness will lead inexorably to "psychiatric fascism," where psychiatrists, justified by reliance on the medical model, would be given control over almost every phase of human life. He cites the abortion determinations as an example of "a social problem" that "became psychiatrized." The decision concerning abortion was left to psychiatrists, he says, and "we in turn justified our decision by value statements about the mental 'health' of the woman . . . It was all a sham, a shift of responsibility from society to psychiatrists." Torrey, like many other psychiatrists, both pro- and antiabortion, was glad when abortion reform took the decision out of the hands of the psychiatrists and made the psychiatrist honest once again, or at least took him out of this kind of dishonest psychiatric practice.[4]

Many psychiatrists did not go along with this deviation from the psychiatric tradition of a scientific and factual basis for diagnoses. Those who opposed abortion on moral grounds or because they did not want psychiatry to take on the responsibility for making such obviously nonmedical decisions did not readily certify abortion. If they did it at all, it was for the rare patient with schizophrenia, manic-depressive psychosis, or some other serious psychiatric illness that might be aggravated by the continuation of the pregnancy. But in every community the proabortion psychiatrists quickly became known, and the medical community had a sure source of certification of abortions for their patients. The typical woman who was certified for abortion by proabortion psychiatrists had never seen a psychiatrist before she consulted one to secure the abortion, and once it was granted she had no need to see one again. In the period before liberalized abortion statutes and policy, the number of legal abortions certified on medical and mental grounds rose to twenty thousand to twenty-five thousand yearly.

During the same period, there were an estimated two hundred thousand to 1 million illegal abortions done yearly in the United States, some of which resulted in infection and death. The fact that affluent patients could easily find psychiatrists to certify their abortions but ward and charity patients were usually not granted them became one of the main arguments for doing away with abortion restrictions entirely. (This was a strange social and economic phenomenon explainable only in part by the fact that teaching hospitals that took care of poorer patients had higher standards and were subject to more scrutiny than other hospitals.)

Psychiatrists promoted a change of attitude by certifying abortions and by preaching a more relaxed point of view. Some psychoanalysts saw it as a crucial decision that carried the possibility of great unconscious guilt, but many psychiatrists began to argue that the conflict involved in having an abortion had been overstated in the older psychiatric literature. These were influential factors leading to legislative and judicial action to liberalize and finally to end restrictions on abortion.

Because psychiatry is largely practiced outside public scrutiny, it had been possible for psychiatrists to promulgate their own policies. In this they were very much in the position of a district attorney who has the power to decide whether or not he considers an offense serious enough to prosecute. But the district attorney's discretionary power is not ostensibly decided on scientific grounds, not made outside public awareness, and does not usurp authority that properly belongs elsewhere in society. The usurpation of authority here was at the expense of legislatures that had devised abortion policies that psychiatrists then circumvented.

The liberalization of abortion laws was paralleled by a liberalization of psychiatric thought. In 1967 only 23 percent of responding members of the American Psychiatric Association favored abortion on demand; two years later an amazing change had taken place and 72 percent of 2041 psychiatrists surveyed approved of abortion on request.[5]

Psychiatry can be used not only to procure abortions but to shape attitudes about abortion. When Hawaiian operating-room nurses working under a liberalized state law found themselves nauseated, depressed, and made anxious by their participation in abortions, psychiatrists called these reactions neurotic—although that was a value-laden judgment—and required that the nurses go into group therapy, in which they could come to accept the fact that their reactions were inappropriate—especially so, because, in the words of one of the psychiatrists called in to deal with the problem, "what is aborted is a protoplasmic mass" and not a real live individual.[6]

When a decrease in morale on the wards where abortions were performed at the hospital of the University of Pennsylvania led to an increase in nursing turnover, two psychiatrists helped form groups so that nurses could "come to terms with their feelings." The nurses felt that the "dirty work" of saline-induced abortions was left to them, because the doctors injected the amniotic sac with saline and left the rest of the process to the nurses. Sometimes the aborted fetus had a heartbeat, and the nurses felt a conflict between their traditional role and that of assistants at abortion. They resented young unmarried mothers who were forcing them to take responsibility for "cleaning up their mess." Group therapy ventilation turned out not to be a help— in fact, the head nurse left her job after participating in nine sessions. The psychiatrists changed their tactics and got medical personnel who had a positive attitude toward the abortion procedure involved in the groups. They also made policy recommendations to improve the abortion service. They recommended that the procedure should be done earlier so that the fetus is less recognizable as a human being, and that older female nurses and male nurses be used on the abortion wards, since nurses in their twenties, who were often unmarried and childless, were too sensitive to the issues involved in abortion.[7]

Discomfort in the role of assisting at abortion, which would have been seen a decade earlier as a normal emotional reaction, had been redefined as immature and neurotic. The interest of the smooth functioning of the abortion ward had taken precedence over feelings, which, if they had not impeded hospital routine, would have been "worked with," but now had to be stamped out. By 1979 medical feeling on abortion had become so fixed in the proabortion position that medical-school graduates who opposed abortion were being denied obstetrics-gynecology residencies for their views, and applicants to some medical schools were quizzed on abortion views and were denied admission on the basis of an antiabortion position.[8]

For a period of three years, from the Supreme Court's abortion decision in 1973 until Congress passed the Hyde Amendment on the Health, Education, and Welfare Appropriation Bill in 1976,[9] psychiatrists had no need to be involved with abortion. The Hyde Amendment brought psychiatry back into the picture again by prohibiting federal funds for Medicaid abortions "except where the life of the mother would be endangered if the fetus were carried to term." The Supreme Court later ruled that when the life of the mother is not endangered, the state is not required to pay for abortion.[10] The "1978 Hyde Amendment"[11] superseded and somewhat liberalized the "1977 Hyde Amendment" and allowed federal funding for Medicaid abortion "where the life of the mother would be endangered if the fetus were carried to term" for victims of rape or incest, and when severe and long-lasting physical health damage would result from carrying the pregnancy to term. As a result of the Hyde Amendments, the psychiatrist was again in a position of authority, able to certify abortion on the ground that suicide threatened. Their certification now had a different impact: The abortion was legal without certification, but only the psychiatrist's certification could qualify it for federal funding. Now, however, so much publicity focused on abortion certification that psychiatrists were more reluctant to bend the law as they previously had.

*　　*　　*

During the Vietnam War there was an equally glaring example of psychiatric mislabeling of people as sick in order to enable them to circumvent the force of a law that they found onerous, and this involved exemption from the draft. Once again, as in the abortion process, the psychiatrist used his labeling power to confer an excuse and thus assumed authority that had never been granted to him. Like abortion certification, psychiatric deferment of draft-eligible men had a racist connotation. In both cases, minority-group members and the poor were not given the advantage of the psychiatric excuse. Sophisticated and affluent men, many of them college-educated, learned how easy it was to find a psychiatrist who would say they were neurotic and thus allow them to be deferred. Their places in draft quotas would be filled by the less sophisticated, less affluent, and less well educated, who were not as adept at circumventing the system or had less desire to be relieved of their legal obligation.

During the Vietnam War the law required every man subject to the draft to register at eighteen and the policy was to draft men nineteen and over. Beginning in 1970, a lottery system was instituted in which every nineteen-year-old male was assigned a random number based on his birthdate. The lottery system represented the decision by the government not to continue to try for a fair draft system. Henceforth, instead of equality of sacrifice, the emphasis would be on luck or fate. Under this system, a man with no deferment who was not called during his nineteenth year or a deferred man who was not called during the first year in which he was subject to the draft was home free, without further obligation.

The system produced a huge pool of draft registrants that funneled down to comparatively few drafted men. Out of a manpower pool of 27 million men there were almost 9 million enlistees and 2 million draftees. There were 2,150,000 who went to Vietnam and 46,000 who died from enemy action (of a total of 108,000 deaths). Fewer than 1 percent of all draft-age men were needed for combat duty in Vietnam at any one time.[12] The element of luck involved in the draft and the inequity of sacrifice led to widespread desire to escape the draft. Sometimes those who did not use every means to avoid being drafted, no matter how contrived, were seen as stupid or "square." More than 15 million men avoided the draft either because they were lucky in the lottery (over 4 million of these) or because they were disqualified, deferred until the risk of being drafted was over, or exempted. The variety of reasons for deferments and exemptions was broad: conscientious objection, student status, elected official, hardship, marriage, fatherhood, status as a sole surviving son, and occupational status as minister, teacher, engineer, or farmer. But the way that most men avoided the draft was to be exempted because of a physical, mental, psychiatric, or moral disqualification. More than 5 million men avoided it in this way, by failing either their preinduction or induction physical examination. Of these, there were 255,000 exemptions for psychiatric defect and 1,360,000 for mental defect.[13]

The preinduction physical examinations were done at seventy-four Armed Forces Entrance and Examination Stations throughout the country. These stations augmented their medical staffs by contracting with local doctors. The psychiatric consultants, who received sixty dollars a day, were usually traditionalists who felt assisting the military to fulfill its manpower requirements was also a fulfillment of their own patriotic duty, and they favored passing, rather than failing, inductees. But as conformist physicians, they placed a great deal of reliance on the recommendations of their fellow doctors if the inductee carried with him a medical certificate stating he should not serve.

There was another and more valid reason for the consulting psychiatrists to rely on the physician certificate that the inductee presented: A man labeled by an outside psychiatrist as neurotic and unfit for service, if drafted and later psychiatrically disabled, would be a continuing charge on the government for the remainder of his life. Less severe disability could cause inadequate performance in the service, leading to less-than-honorable discharges, dishonorable discharges, possibly court martials, assignments to rehabilitation programs, and other expensive and inefficient alternatives to satisfactory service. Consulting psychiatrists tended to disbelieve the stories of neurosis and psychiatric disability of registrants who did not have a physician certificate and to believe without reservation the word of a fellow psychiatrist that disability was present.

The knowledgeable registrant had a great advantage in attempting to manipulate the system. If he wanted to join the service, he could suppress evidence of a psychiatric disorder, and many men, particularly those from blue-collar backgrounds, where failing to serve was considered unmanly, did suppress evidence of psychiatric disorder. On the other hand, if the registrant wanted to be exempted from service, he could present a physician's certificate, even though the history of psychiatric problems may have been exaggerated or fabricated. The registrant had months to prepare his story and build up a history of psychiatric illness; the examination station consultant had only a brief interview.

Most psychiatrists did not readily certify draft-eligible men as too mentally ill to be drafted, but some who were opposed to the Vietnam War and wanted to do all they could to hamper its prosecution took action by letting draft-counseling agencies and antiwar organizations know that they would cooperate with anyone who wanted to evade the draft through a psychiatric basis for exemption. (The only problem with this gesture of opposition is that the place of the psychiatrically deferred man would be taken by someone else who did not want to take advantage of a psychiatric exemption or was not knowledgeable enough to find the path to one, and so the policy of easy psychiatric deferment did not save lives—it only meant that another person would assume the risk or hardship.)

The Selective Service System invited efforts to beat the system by listing so many grounds for exemption that a knowing inductee had a wide choice of which route he wanted to follow—being a conscientious objector, exhibiting an obscene tattoo, being in the process of having orthodontic braces fitted, having a food or bee sting allergy, having asthma, severe ingrown toenail, hemorrhoids, itchy scalp, insomnia, or hay fever, and being ugly or underweight were only a few. If none of these applied, there was always the psychiatric excuse. The Selective Service guidelines on "Psychoses, Psychoneuroses, and Personality Disorders" were vague, and broad enough to cover any enterprising registrants who wished to "go the psychiatric route." Besides a history of serious psychiatric illness, they included history of a psychoneurotic behavior that impaired school or work efficiency; a history of a brief psychoneurotic reaction within the preceding twelve months sufficiently severe to require medical attention or some brief absence from work or school; character and behavior disorders evidencing an impaired characterological capacity to adapt to the military service; overt homosexuality; other deviant sexual practices such as voyeurism, exhibitionism, and transvestism; alcohol or drug addiction; characterological disorders characterized by immaturity, instability, and personal inadequacy and dependency; and other symptomatic immaturity reactions such as bed-wetting, stammering, or stuttering. One Pennsylvania doctor said, "There's no young man so well that we can't find something to disqualify him from serving."[14] A draft counselor said, "No one is so healthy that he cannot be an army reject."[15] A researcher looking into draft exemptions wrote: "Almost anyone, at one time or another, could qualify for exemption under at least one of these."[16]

As public opinion against the Vietnam War strengthened, some doctors began to act as if they were performing a moral act by finding ways for men to evade the draft. The Medical Committee on Human Rights coached doctors in writing convincing letters to examination station doctors. One recommended method was to concentrate not on the inequity of army service for the registrant but the disadvantage to the service of drafting the registrant.[17]

Some doctors with antiwar sympathies rationalized the exaggeration of symptoms by peculiar logic. The registrant seeking help in evading the draft is a patient, they said (although most people would not see this as a doctor-patient relationship), and the problem for which he seeks medical help is not the allergy, asthma, or insomnia, which may only be marginally present, but the threat of being drafted, which is imminent and real; therefore the function of the doctor is to help the patient in every way he can to spare him the threat of the draft. An Oregon doctor, writing to the *New England Journal of Medicine*, put this position in words that are as unequivocal as they are logically and ethically dubious. Traditional medical ethics, he said, clearly set forth "the obligation of the physician to help the patient in front of him in any legal way he can."[18] These doctors represented a minority of medical opinion. Most doctors would have seen their role differently. But draft-resisting patients were drawn to draft-opposing doctors.

Draft board policy gave doctors extraordinary power. If a registrant presented a doctor's letter but the examining station doctor thought he was malingering, he would often still be rejected on the ground that a malingerer was not a good psychological risk for the armed services. Not all draft boards were as acquiescent, and the counseling of registrants eventually developed into a fine art that included the evaluation of which draft boards accepted what kinds of reasons for deferment.

Examination Station psychiatrists were suspicious of claims of homosexuality, since this was one of the popular choices for men seeking exemption, and they were often disbelieving, even when the claim was true. Many homosexuals were drafted. But claims for exemption on other psychiatric grounds, supported by a doctor's letter, tended to be believed. One army authority on medical standards said, "Even when we suspect malingering, it is impossible to prove it. The standing rule is to believe the letter brought by the examinee. If a doctor says the man has a debilitating illness, then we have no choice but to say he's out." At least one examining station gave everyone with a letter from a doctor an exemption,[19] and many others rarely questioned a letter. Most registrants preferred a physical rather than a psychiatric reason for being rejected, and the psychiatric exemptions accounted for only about 7 percent of those based on physical and psychiatric defect, but as antiwar sentiment mounted, the psychiatric exemptions increased in popularity, particularly when psychiatrists learned their recommendations were being so readily accepted.

In addition to the attempts by some psychiatrists to help men who had not been patients to avoid the draft, many psychiatrists wrote letters documenting the need for exemption for their therapy patients. The main motive for a patient's entering therapy may have been the anxiety caused by the imminence of the draft. The therapy may have been a legitimate effort to deal with the threats of separation and death caused by the draft or it may possibly have been a less legitimate effort to build up a history of treatment for a psychoneurosis in order to justify deferment. We do not know how frequently doctors wrote letters for patients in treatment—legal psychiatry operates in an atmosphere of low visibility, and we lack statistics and hard data on most subjects—but we do know that many psychiatrists wrote draft letters for a few of their patients, and some specialists in the treatment of adolescents wrote letters for many of their patients. A few analysts, conscious of the transference meaning of helping a patient remain in therapy, asked their patients to see another psychiatrist to evaluate them and write the letters. In this way they hoped to keep the transference from being "contaminated." (The suggestion to see another psychiatrist was itself contaminating, but this seemed to some classical analysts the lesser contamination.)

Like the women certified for abortion, men evaluated for draft exemption who had not been in psychiatric treatment usually did not consider themselves sick. The recommendation would sometimes be made for continuing therapy after the exemption had been secured, but both parties in this transaction knew that it would probably not be followed. Fear of induction was the "disease," and the exemption was the "cure."

One New York psychiatrist, according to *Time*, wrote as many as seventy-five letters a week, charging up to $250 for each letter, to certify men as psychiatrically unfit. Eventually examination station doctors learned to recognize her bias and to ignore her recommendations.[20] (A psychiatrist who could see seventy-five registrants and write letters for all of them at $250 per letter could earn $18,750 for a week's work.) Some psychiatrists did not accept fees for their evaluations, seeing this activity as part of their antiwar effort.

Antiwar psychiatrists felt there was no need to be objective, because the war was unjust. Peter Roemer wrote in a letter to the *American Journal of Psychiatry* that he had seen over 100 men who were looking for a way out of the draft, and he had not felt that in writing any of the letters for these men that he had any need to profess objectivity about his antiwar and antiestablishment value system. Criticizing an article that had discussed the position of the doctor writing letters for draft exemption, he said, "The authors would like to maintain that it is possible for a psychiatrist to be objective. I think this is naive . . . I do not think it is possible for one man to confront another's pressing need (in this case a letter) and not have his perceptions of that individual distorted by his feelings; certainly, his feeling about satisfying that need would distort his perceptions."[21] Peter Bourne, writing free draft exemption letters in Atlanta, was chagrined to find that some of the registrants he helped, instead of being grateful, "acted as though all doctors had a moral obligation to help them dodge the draft for nothing."[22]

Very few writers of dubious letters were challenged. When several were reported to the United States surgeon general, he was not able to decide whether there was any authority to act against them.[23] It would have been difficult for the Justice Department to prosecute physicians successfully for impeding the draft, since "clinical judgment" provides a wide scope for the decision maker, and so the doctor could always plead this was his honest clinical opinion. Local medical societies could have brought disciplinary actions such as suspension from the society, but that would not have interfered with the ability to continue to practice, and in any case there is no report that any disciplinary action was brought against any physicians for fraudulent documentation to help evade the draft.

Influenced by the growing activism of antiwar physicians, the rejection rate for the draft went from 29.9 percent in 1968[24] to 36 percent in 1969[25] to 46 percent by July 1970.[26] In Philadelphia it rose to almost 60 percent. As draft boards became less sympathetic to conscientious objector claims and as teacher and graduate student deferments were phased out, the number of medical, and particularly psychiatric, claims for deferment increased. Commented psychiatrist Benjamin Pasamanick in 1974, "During the Vietnam conflict of the last ten years a unique finding in U.S. military history was observed. For the first time rates of rejection from the armed forces were higher for white persons than for black persons. It was apparent that the white middle- and upper-class men (rejected largely, as usual, on psychiatric grounds) were able to pay for civilian psychiatric opinions that, oddly enough, coincided with the judgments of the psychiatrists on the draft boards. The black men, on the other hand, either because they were unable to pay for such independent psychiatric opinions or because they were largely unemployed and found military service the only mode of life, also had their judgments of their own psychiatric fitness coincide highly with those of the draft boards."[27]

Leslie Fiedler wrote that he had "never known a single family that had lost a son in Vietnam, or indeed, one with a son wounded, missing in action, or held prisoner of war" and that, talking to friends, he found they "all say the same."[28] In 1965, blacks accounted for 24 percent of all combat deaths.[29]

A student who was at Harvard during the time he was subject to the draft has written about his efforts to avoid being drafted. James Fallows—later President Carter's chief speech writer—wanted to secure his deferment on the grounds of being underweight. He was six feet one inch tall, and he hoped through rigid dieting to bring his weight down to less than 120 pounds. He had been advised to do this by Harvard medical students who were engaged in helping college students beat the draft. They had also advised that he try fainting spells, but he had decided that he could not fake these successfully. He was disappointed when he was put on the scales to find he weighed 122, and he persuaded the orderly to write down 120 pounds instead. Then he was sent to a final meeting with the "fatherly physician" who ruled on marginal cases. He wrote:

> I stood there in socks and underwear, arms wrapped around me in the chilly building. I knew as I looked at the doctor's face that he understood exactly what I was doing.
> "Have you ever contemplated suicide?" he asked after he finished looking over my chart. My eyes darted up to his. "Oh, suicide—yes, I've been feeling very unstable and unreliable recently." He looked at me staring until I returned my eyes to the ground. He wrote "unqualified" on my folder, turned on his heel, and left. I was overcome by a wave of relief, which for the first time revealed to me how great my terror had been, and by the beginning of the sense of shame that remains with me to this day.

Fallows wrote how, while the men from Harvard were deliberately failing their color-blindness tests, buses from the Chelsea district draft board drove up. In contrast to the Harvard contingent, these were "thick, dark-haired young men, the white proles of Boston."

> Most of them were younger than us, since they had just left high school, and it had clearly never occurred to them that there might be a way around the draft. They walked through the examination lines like so many cattle off to slaughter. I tried to avoid noticing, but the results were inescapable. While perhaps four out of five of my friends from Harvard were being deferred, just the opposite was happening to the Chelsea boys.

Fallows described how he and his friends returned to Cambridge in a high-spirited mood, but with something close to the surface that no one wanted to mention—"We knew now who would be killed . . ."[30]

In the sparse psychiatric literature dealing with the role of the psychiatrist certifying for draft exemption, the authors of one study indicated that single-interview psychiatric evaluations for draft purposes were so cursory that they tended to discredit psychiatry.[31] But the psychiatrist-authors of another study stated that a single interview lasting forty-five to sixty minutes was enough for the psychiatric determination in 93 percent (136 out of 147) of the cases they reviewed. (They recommended that all but five of the men they saw receive deferments; they said that "civilian psychiatrists have a responsibility to maintain their patients' health, which is often incompatible with military service.")[32] Other psychiatrists did not spend even forty-five minutes with the men they were evaluating, or if they did spend that time on the evaluation, they did this for legal reasons, to document the reliability of their certification, not to elicit a more accurate psychiatric story. One student tells of obtaining a letter from an antiwar psychiatrist in New York City in 1970. He visited the psychiatrist three times to have the diagnosis made, and the recommendation look professionally and conscientiously conducted, but in fact the total time spent in talking with the psychiatrist was less than fifteen minutes.[33]

With the connivance of a poorly conceived governmental policy and a legal system that would allow appeals to drag through the courts for so many years that the issue had lost its relevancy, physicians and psychiatrists had helped middle-class and educated men escape from the draft. What were the long-term social and political effects of their overzealousness? Fallows has suggested that it prolonged the war, that it permitted the opposition to Vietnam involvement to operate with less urgency than it would have if the burden of service had been more equally distributed. He says, "The more we guaranteed we would end up neither in uniform nor behind bars, the more we made sure that *our* class of people would be spared the real cost of the war. The children of the bright, good parents were spared the more immediate sort of suffering that our inferiors were undergoing. And because of that, when our parents were opposed to the war, they were opposed in a bloodless, theoretical fashion, as they might be opposed to political corruption or racism in South Africa."[34] Dr. Howard Waitzkin, who participated for two years in assisting draft resisters to secure deferments, describes the social effect as being consistent with the wishes of the armed forces, which is an explanation of why it was allowed to continue and flourish.

> The sick role is a convenient mechanism of social control for institutions like the Selective Service System. The military offers the sick role as a controllable mode of deviance for those who are unwilling to co-operate fully with the system but who will not—once granted medical exemption—actively work to overthrow the system . . . From this perspective, the sick role appears to support the institutional status quo. Physicians, often eager to satisfy the needs of individual patients, tend to expand their certification of the sick role in such institutional settings as the military draft. This apparently beneficient act on the physicians' part may result in unintended conservative and perhaps counter-revolutionary consequences for social change.[35]

The false certification of mental disability produced a guilty class of influential men who had evaded the draft, and through rationalizing this decision, found it necessary to be negativistic and destructive toward many other phases of American life as well. It kept an articulate and concerned kind of potential observer, the civilian soldier and officer who might write home and mobilize opinion, out of the fighting zone, and so let laxity, cruelty, and atrocities go unreported and uncorrected. It increased the division between social classes. It lowered respect for physicians, and especially psychiatrists, as impartial and scientific professional people. If physicians can shape their decisions in one area to accord with their political views, they can do it in other areas as well.

In one of the few public discussions of draft resistance and its relationship to medical practice, Peter Elias wrote in an article in the *New England Journal of Medicine* of his eventual disillusionment with the role he was playing, and some letters to the editor in reply provided a brief flurry of reaction. Elias reported that many physicians working with the antiwar movement or helping registrants escape the draft became unhappy as they realized two important truths that somehow had previously escaped them—that many of the men for whom they secured rejections were not opposed to the war or the draft but were motivated by selfish and personal goals, and that the benefits of the policy accrued to the advantaged and their burden was shifted to the disadvantaged.[36]

But one doctor wrote in reply to Elias to express pleasure with the role he had played in using his medical authority to circumvent the draft. Mark Sicherman said, "It has been an immensely satisfying method of protesting an immoral war and disordered governmental priorities. It has helped to alleviate my sense of powerlessness much more than the multiplicity of marches, rallies, letter-writing campaigns, tax resistances, etc., with which I have been involved. It seems to me that ceasing to participate in medical draft resistance because of its potential social consequence is analogous to believing that antiwar protests served to prolong the war."[37]

In certifying abortions and draft exemption, psychiatrists had proven how effective their interventions could be, how established social policy could be circumvented by their diagnoses and recommendations. But the certification of abortion has not been a major problem since legalization, although it still has significance as a method of securing abortions for Medicaid recipients. And the draft is gone. These particular exercises of psychiatric power have faded from the scene. But they remain symbolic of larger issues: the efficacy of psychiatry in winning exemptions from society's rules, the way that psychiatrists will lend themselves to causes that they see as just and alter their diagnostic techniques to achieve social ends, and the lack of both self-criticism and outside criticism of psychiatry or even of conceptualizing the role of psychiatry when it undertakes such social interventions.

Psychiatrists in the United States have criticized psychiatrists in totalitarian countries for being tools of the state and bending psychiatric diagnoses to serve a social purpose. They do not criticize themselves when they become tools either of the state or of movements that are in opposition to the policies of the state. Many Russian psychiatrists at least are sincere when they label a political dissident as psychiatrically ill, for they may believe that nonconformity is a symptom of diagnosable mental disease. The American psychiatrist who uses his labeling authority politically is often being deliberately dishonest.

The same potential for social usefulness in evading society's rules that was demonstrated concerning the draft and abortion is ready to show itself when other issues requiring exemptions from state policy arise. It manifests itself now in less obvious ways, as psychiatrists provide excuses for all the civil and criminal transgressions that require a letter from a psychiatrist or an opinion from a psychiatrist to help a person avoid some unpleasantness that he faces.

The same manipulations that were used against state policy on abortion and the draft are available to be used both against the state and in its service. As we shall see, an attorney general of the United States —Robert Kennedy—and a president—Richard Nixon—attempted to make use of the labeling power of psychiatrists in efforts to discredit their enemies.[38] The psychiatrists who deviate from professional standards in order to achieve humane social ends are relying on their own subjective definitions of humanity and are utilizing techniques that are also capable of being used for political purposes that may be the opposite of humane.

The Political Use of Psychiatry
Abroad and at Home

PSYCHIATRY HAS its ideological uses. Nazi Germany and contemporary Russia show two different ways it can serve the state.

Few people think of the German holocaust as having its roots in psychiatric practice for political purposes. In Germany a long history of interest in the prevention of the procreation of the "unfit" led in the 1920s and early 1930s to a program for eugenic sterilization for the "weak-minded," the "mentally ill," and criminals. After Hitler came to power this was extended to "Jews, Negroes, and Mongols" in the interest of racial purity. An estimated 2 million forced sterilizations were performed between 1935 and 1945.

This was enlarged into a program of medical and psychiatric "mercy killing," the starving of children who had psychiatric and behavioral disorders and were classified as "difficult children," along with children who had physical defects.

In 1939 a program of systematic killing of mental patients began under the sponsorship of Max de Crinis, professor of psychiatry at the University of Berlin, and more than a dozen other professors of psychiatry and departmental chairmen. Gas chambers and crematoria were set up in six psychiatric killing centers with a psychiatrist, Werner Heyde, in charge of the administration of the program.[1]

By 1941, according to a contemporary letter written by a doctor, there had been "the elimination of a few hundred thousand mental patients"; the Czech War Crimes Commission estimated the number killed in the "euthanasia program" at two hundred seventy thousand.

The psychiatric plan for the extermination of undesirables served the state so well that after two years, in late 1941, Hitler became interested in it and took the "race hygiene camps" out of the control

319

of psychiatrists to make them instruments of broader national policy of extermination. In the end 9 million people were exterminated. Simon Weisenthal has written that physicians continued to man the killing centers and to give them the aura of medical authority during the period when SS members were being trained to emulate their genocidal methods. The program followed medical procedure so exactly that selection sheets contained a space for "symptoms," except that now symptoms included such nonmedical manifestations as "member of the Communist party" or "dangerous instigator." The policy of the extermination of patients for psychiatric reasons also continued after the policy had been enlarged, and the population of German psychiatric hospitals, which had been between 300,000 and 320,000 in 1939, declined to 40,000 by 1946.[2]

There has been more awareness of the Russian use of psychiatry to enforce ideological conformity. Psychiatry has been used not to exterminate people but to extirpate their ideas. Knowledge of cruel treatment in the USSR is confined to reports about a small group of political activists and dissidents who are held in mental hospitals until they can be restored to more sane political opinions. The policy of defining mental illness on the basis of divergent political opinion serves to keep in line a much larger group who might be tempted into independent thought if there was not the threat of being labeled psychiatrically ill.

Andrei Snezhevsky is the literate and dignified dean of Soviet psychiatrists, head of the national organization of psychiatrists, director of the most important psychiatric research hospital, psychiatric adviser to the ministry of health, and editor of the major Soviet psychiatric periodical. His students head most of the other major hospitals and training centers. The fifteen thousand Soviet psychiatrists use the system of classification of psychiatric illness that Snezhevsky teaches. Snezhevsky sees many symptoms as indicative of schizophrenia. He lists three kinds of schizophrenia: continuous, periodic, and shiftlike. Some of the characteristics he lists for some schizophrenias are those used by psychiatrists in Western Europe and the United States, but others differ remarkably.

The sluggish or mild type of continuous schizophrenia, according to Snezhevsky, is destined to have a slow, steady, advancing course throughout life, but its symptoms are manifold and many people would fit under—or can easily be made to fit under—this diagnostic category. The symptoms are neurosis, self-consciousness, introspectiveness, obsessive doubts, conflicts with parental and other authorities, and "reformism." One characteristic of the paranoic type of continuous schizophrenia is a "parasitic life style." The mild subtype of shiftlike schizophrenia has such characteristics as neurosis, social conscientiousness, philosophical concerns, and self-absorption.

The playwright Tom Stoppard in his *Every Good Boy Deserves Favor* described an encounter between a Soviet psychiatrist and a sane dissident who had been hospitalized as mentally ill after he had openly defended another dissident. The psychiatrist offers the "patient" his freedom if he admits that his acts have been irrational, that he was insane. The "patient" says, "I have no symptoms. I have opinions." The doctor replies, "Your opinions are your symptoms. Your disease is dissent."[3] The play's dialogue reproduces actual encounters between dissidents and their psychiatrists, who have told them their disease is dissent and that to prove mental health they will have to disown their opinions. At the present time at least 150 and probably several thousand Russian dissidents are being held in psychiatric hospitals for the "disease" of dissent.[4]

When Soviet psychiatrists are accused of unethical practice of psychiatry in the service of the state, they defend the charge in apparent good faith. They know that psychiatry is not needed as an agent of control in a country with such total control over its citizens, and they seem surprised that they are accused of complicity to mislabel dissidents as ill. They are conforming professionals, products of a conforming society, and of conforming education and professional training, and they see themselves as unexceptional medical practitioners when they apply definitions of mental disease broader than those used in many other countries.

Soviet psychiatrists, by a process of selection, are "scientists" who believe that science must serve the state and that the laws of the natural world that the scientist discovers must substantiate the social laws laid down by the government. Pavlovian psychology became an official dogma, Walter Reich writes, because it validated the basis of the central Marxist assumption that man can be changed by changing his environment.[5] With an official psychology emphasizing the conditioning of behavior, deviant behavior can be seen as both antisocial and pathological, and nonconformity and refusal to support the body politic easily appear to be mental illness.

The world was first made aware of this view through the news stories of the fate of Pyotr Grigorenko, a former Soviet army general. In 1964 he had been given a fifteen-month sentence for his outspoken stand on human rights and had been stripped of his rank of major general and expelled from the Communist party. During eight months of this sentence he had been held in a psychiatric hospital. He was arrested again in 1969 for defending Crimean Tatars charged with anti-Soviet activity, and he was labeled schizophrenic; one of his characteristics was said to be obsessive concern with detail, a symptom of mild but progressive schizophrenia of the shiftlike variety. He was sent to a series of special hospitals over a four-year period, then transferred to an ordinary mental hospital. A statement issued by his wife on the fifth anniversary of his detention said, "As a sane man confined to mental hospitals for five years, sometimes alongside criminal lunatics, he has still maintained his spirits."[6]

Soon after the Grigorenko case came to public attention, a number of other similar instances were reported in the press. The most graphic account of abuses of civil procedural protections appeared in a book by the Medvedev brothers, *A Question of Madness,* published in 1971. Zhores, a biologist, had previously written a book detailing the rise and fall of Tofrim Lysenko, the biologist and agronomist whose views on the inheritability of acquired characteristics had become official Communist party dogma. Lysenko's theory during the agricultural scarcities of the early 1930s had promised the possibility of greater and more rapid increase in yields than traditional geneticists thought possible, and this had led to the suppression of orthodox genetics. Lysenko had done more than elevate his own theory into a party tenet; he had attacked traditional scientific and statistical methods and made those who followed them enemies of the state. Zhores Medvedev had opposed the system that had suppressed free scientific inquiry.

In May 1971 a mental hospital minibus carrying three policemen and two psychiatrists pulled up in front of Medvedev's house. With the aid of the policemen, the psychiatrists forced their way into the house. He was told, "If you refuse to talk to us, then we will be obliged to draw the appropriate conclusions." He had no history of previous psychiatric problems, but he was forcibly taken to a mental hospital for three days of examination, which were eventually stretched to six, to nine, and then further. He was diagnosed as insane on the basis of poor adaptation to social environment, obsessive reformist delusions, excessively scrupulous attention to detail in his writing as a publicist, deterioration in recent years in the quality of his scientific work, and a split personality expressed in the need to combine scientific work in his field with publicist writing."[7]

His twin brother, Roy, mobilized an international campaign to secure his release. One of the intellectuals who came to Medvedev's defense was Alexander Solzhenitsyn. He circulated a letter entitled "This is How We Live," attacking "servile psychiatrists who break their Hippocratic oath and are able to describe concern for social problems as 'mental illness,' [who] can declare a man insane for being too passionate or for his being too calm, for the brightness of his talents or for his lack of them." Solzhenitsyn warned that "this could happen tomorrow to any one of us," and continued,

If only this were the first case! But it has become fashionable, this way of settling accounts—with no pretense at seeking out guilt, when it is too shameful to state the real reason . . . It is time to understand that the imprisonment of sane persons in madhouses because they have minds of their own is *spiritual murder,* a variation on the *gas chambers* and even more cruel . . . Like the gas chambers, these crimes will *never* be forgotten, and those involved will be condemned for all time, during their life and after their death, without benefit of moratorium.[8]

Zhores was held for nineteen days in a mental hospital, after which he was given a conditional release, apparently because his brother had been so successful in publicizing the issue of use of psychiatric hospitals for political purposes. Most of the dissidents who have been detained in psychiatric hospitals have spent long years there.

In addition to ordinary psychiatric hospitals, the Soviets have a notorious Institute of Forensic Psychiatry, the Serbsky Institute, in Moscow (where Medvedev was evaluated) and twelve special psychiatric hospitals for patients who represent a "special danger for society" (like Grigorenko). Many political dissenters, after being processed through the Serbsky Institute, are sent to the special hospitals. Vladimir Bukovsky was diagnosed at the Serbsky in 1963 as being schizophrenic and was sent to the Leningrad Special Psychiatric Hospital, where he was kept fifteen months. Eventually he had three more psychiatric hospitalizations and an eight-month stay at the Serbsky. When he was rearrested in 1967, the decision was made to prosecute him criminally rather than to route him to a mental hospital, and he was sentenced to prison for three years, which he served in a labor camp.

In 1971 he gathered together case records of six dissidents who had been declared insane and held in mental hospitals, and he had these records smuggled to the West. He appealed to the World Psychiatric Association, meeting in Mexico City in 1971 for its Fifth World Congress (held every six years), to study the records and make an issue of Soviet political use of psychiatry. The World Psychiatric Association did not discuss the issue; many of its members did not want to "politicize" psychiatry. Later a group of forty-four British psychiatrists did examine the records and concluded that none of these six patients was mentally ill but that they were only exercising "fundamental freedoms—as set out in the Universal

Declaration of Human Rights and guaranteed by the Soviet Constitution."[9] In the meantime Bukovsky had been arrested again, and
he was being detained at the time the Mexico City congress, which
refused to consider his charges, convened.

In late 1971 the American Psychiatric Association, through its board
of trustees, did go on record opposing the "misuse of psychiatric facilities for the detention of persons solely on the basis of their political
dissent," but it was careful to name no countries, to express the disap-
proval generally, "no matter where it occurs." I. F. Stone, in the *New
York Review of Books,* criticized the statement as being an "innocuous
formulation" that was "a far cry from setting up a committee to study
the materials now available on the situation within the Soviet Union."
Said Stone, "The fact is that at Mexico City the undemocratic practices
customary in dealing with public complaint in the Soviet Union spread
to the psychiatric congress. The bureaucracy of the world organization
and the American Psychiatric Association in effect helped the Soviet
bureaucracy to shelve and hush protest."[10] The next month the board
of trustees finally voted to appoint a committee to study the available
documents and to make recommendations, giving as one of its reasons,
"because there are those who chose to misrepresent the APA position
statement."

The APA eventually made the issue of Soviet treatment of dissenters
a major civil-rights interest, but it took a number of years, the repeated
evidence of new cases of psychiatric abuse, and a great effort on the
part of a few members—Paul Chodoff, Walter Reich, Alfred Freeman,
and John Spiegel—before there was any important involvement in the
subject.

One complication for the APA is that, in the interest of scientific
interchange among nations, it has encouraged psychiatrists from other
countries to become members or corresponding fellows, and some
have been given the titles of distinguished fellows and honorary fellows. These members would be subject to censure and perhaps to
discipline if it could be established that they had participated in a
political use of psychiatry. In addition to Russia, countries that have
been accused of charging political dissidents with mental illness include Argentina, Brazil, Chile, Czechoslovakia, East Germany,
Greece, Iran, Laos, Peru, Portugal, Romania, South Africa, Uganda,
and Uruguay.[11]

The pressure for some action grew, however, as additional cases
involving Soviet dissenters were publicized. The case of Leonid
Plyushch, mathematician-cyberneticist, who has been accused of protesting the arrest of other dissidents and publishing his views in under-

ground publications, presented a graphic example not only of the detention and labeling practiced in Russia but also of psychiatric drugs and treatment forced on political prisoners to the point where they became tortures. Plyushch reported that he and other patients were given very large doses of neuroleptics; the drug he was given was haloperidol. He was given two series of insulin shock therapy. Plyushch writes of the effect of the treatment: "I was horrified to see how I deteriorated intellectually, morally and emotionally from day to day. My interest in political problems quickly disappeared, then my interest in scientific problems, and then my interest in my wife and children . . . My speech became jerky, abrupt. My memory deteriorated sharply . . ."[12] After almost three years in a mental hospital, Plyushch was released and allowed to emigrate.

In 1974 Vladimir Bukovsky was in Perm labor camp. For his smuggling of the 150 pages of documents detailing the case histories of six hospitalized dissidents, he had been sentenced to two years in prison and ten years at Perm. There he met Dr. Semyon Gluzman, a young Soviet psychiatrist who, after a year of practice, had protested General Grigorenko's commitment to a psychiatric hospital and had been sentenced to labor at Perm. Bukovsky and Gluzman together wrote *A Manual on Psychiatry for Dissidents,*[13] which was smuggled out of Russia.

The manual makes some of the same points that radical psychiatrists in the United States had been making for some time and that even middle-of-the-road psychiatrists have been forced to concede have some merit. Psychiatry lacks a scientific basis for its disease classification system. The basic diagnostic method is based on clinical observation and the collation of data, both of which are affected by subjectivity. The psychiatric concepts of health and sickness are arbitrary and culturally determined. The looseness of psychiatric concepts gives authority to the labeler-diagnostician.

The final advice to the dissident caught up in the mental health system who has not been able to deal with his tormentors in any other way is to dissemble, to tell the doctors he is reappraising his former unhealthy attitudes. "With all due respect for the courage of Leonid Plyushch, who is deliberately refusing to resort to any 'tactical devices' in the Dnepropetrovsk Special Psychiatric Hospital, we strongly advise you to make use of them all the same. For they, and they alone, are your only hope of salvation."

Bukovsky was exchanged in 1976 for Chilean Communist leader Luis Carvalan and is now a student at Cambridge. He has written the story of his twelve years in prisons, labor camps, and psychiatric hospitals.[14] At this writing, Gluzman is in the city prison in Perm, having been transferred there from the labor camp, and his health is said to be failing rapidly.[15]

In 1978 the American Psychiatric Association took a lead at the Sixth Annual World Congress of Psychiatry in bringing to the attention of the world the Soviet treatment of dissidents by forcing discussion and supporting the passing of a resolution against the political use of psychiatry. The congress also passed the first International Code of Psychiatric Ethics, called the Declaration of Hawaii.[16] Lest the Russians go away mad, the president of the American Psychiatric Association made it clear that he supported the resolution "with a heavy heart," knowing "that the vast number of Soviet psychiatrists are worthy colleagues and practice ethically."

*   *   *

The topic of the physician and the psychiatrist as torturer has begun to receive attention. Some commentators have suggested that the involuntary commitment of well people to mental hospitals, or of mentally ill people who are not dangerous to hospitals for dangerous criminal offenders, qualifies as torture, and this was one factor in the sponsoring in 1973 by Amnesty International of a Conference for the Abolition of Torture. The conference established a medical commission to deal with the medical ethics of torture. Physicians in many countries and psychiatrists in Portugal have been accused of applying sensory deprivation and denying sleep to prisoners in order to break them. Psychological and psychiatric techniques have improved the efficacy of brainwashing.[17] In 1975 the World Medical Assembly, meeting in Tokyo, issued a declaration on the ethical treatment of prisoners. It provided that physicians should diligently avoid abuse of their power to commit persons to mental hospitals as a means of avoiding due process of law, that medical personnel who have knowledge of torture or of plans for torture are under obligation to report this to proper authorities, and that physicians working in prisons and security camps should insist on autonomy outside the control of the institution.[18] How these principles could be applied in totalitarian countries is hard to conceptualize.

*   *   *

For three hundred years, psychiatry has had a role in controlling deviant behavior. Eccentrics, "originals," vagrants, and homeless wanderers who caused little harm but were irritating to the society they lived in were, and sometimes still are, hospitalized or deprived of legal rights. Some critics of psychiatry see this as a political use of psychiatry and see psychiatry as promoting conformity.

In addition to its role in promoting conformity, American psychiatry, starting with World War I, performed a political function in four wars by classifying and placing personnel and working to keep soldiers at the front. Its use in the criminal-justice system, and particularly its care of sexual psychopaths and defective delinquents—in the dubious category between criminals and patients—began to be seen as political in the 1950s, although at the same time that psychiatry was receiving its first major criticisms for being a political tool it was usurping additional areas of the criminal-justice field by designating more and more criminal activities as sickness or illness.

The process of "decriminalization"—called by Nicholas Kittrie "divestment" of part of its territory by the criminal law—has brought juvenile delinquents, alcoholics, and addicts out of the area of crime and into the realm of political psychiatry. The great debate on the proper rule of criminal responsibility was politically motivated in order to try to bootleg into the criminal-justice system a more humane attitude so that more people could be saved from capital punishment during a period when state legislatures were opposed to abolishing the death sentence, and associated with this was the motive of giving behavioral scientists a larger role in criminal rehabilitation. Eventually the rehabilitation concept became tarnished because it was often ineffective and it was usually only attempted halfheartedly without enough commitment of personnel and money. It was, additionally, always a justification for long sentences, since the criminal sentence was now also a form of therapy as well as a punishment and longer terms could produce greater improvement.

Critics of psychiatry have found much more that is political in psychiatry. One political problem has been the unequal distribution of psychiatric care. An apparent paradox is that minorities complain that psychiatric care is not provided for them, and at the same time that psychiatric care is repressive and used as a discriminatory agent of social control. Both complaints have merit; the paradox is only apparent. It dissolves when it is realized that what minorities need is not more psychiatric care, which might only make their lot worse, but more psychiatric care of a better quality, the kind that is sometimes available to the more affluent if they are lucky enough to find interested and competent therapists. (Even the affluent often fall into the hands of psychiatrists relying largely on treatment of symptoms—those who use as therapeutic methods primarily electroshock and chemotherapy—or of analytically oriented therapists who apply their verbal therapy in such an authoritarian way that the criterion for cure becomes the adoption of the values of the therapists. But at least the affluent have a choice of therapists. Morton Birnbaum, in particular, has denounced the two-tier system, in which an entirely different approach to psychiatry is found in state hospitals and community mental health care centers than is found in some private hospitals and some private therapeutic encounters.)[19]

Many of the indigent and many minorities may be fortunate that they do not have access to more of the poor care offered to them. No one has ever shown a correlation between the providing of additional mental health services and increased mental health, although when basic services are not provided and the most disturbed people are allowed to roam free without attention, obviously there can be much harm. (One study shows that counseled delinquent children do less well than the uncounseled.)[20]

Minorities and the poor suffer another political inequality at the hands of psychiatry. They have much less access to the psychiatric excuse. They are classified as criminal for the same kinds of acts that are excused on the grounds of mental illness or upset when committed by whites and the affluent.

Phyllis Chesler, in her *Women and Madness,*[21] makes the claim that women are oppressed by psychiatry, forced to conform to role stereotypes, and when they do not want to conform, diagnosed as mentally ill by men with a status quo orientation rather than by women, who can envision new kinds of roles for women.

Critics of psychiatry point out that white youths involved in protesting segregation in the 1960s were sometimes sent for psychiatric observation and that societal dropouts of the "beat generation" and early Vietnam protesters were labeled as mentally unstable and sometimes hospitalized. When soldiers or West Point plebes object to service practices, they can be seen as deserving psychiatric attention, as they can when they protest a war, denounce Watergate, or support amnesty.[22] Cases of the federal government's using the mental health system to immobilize or punish political dissenters are less frequent than in Russia, but they do exist. When President Woodrow Wilson was asked to intervene in favor of militant sufragettes who were on a hunger strike and had been moved to the District of Columbia jail's psychiatric ward and threatened with commitment, Wilson responded that the women's display of militancy was not only politically harmful but so unusual as to indicate instability.[23] We have already considered the case of Ezra Pound, the famous poet who was labeled mentally ill and held in St. Elizabeths Hospital for thirteen years to prevent him from being tried for his political broadcasts against the United States during World War II.[24] A striking example of the political use of psychiatry involves the psychiatric hospitalization of General Edwin Walker, which was planned by Attorney General Robert Kennedy and implemented by a government psychiatrist.

General Walker, a military hero of World War II, was in charge of the federal troops in the desegregation crisis at Little Rock, Arkansas, in 1957. In 1961 he resigned from the United States Army. He became identified with right-wing causes, was an avowed segregationist, and in September 1962 when federal troops were sent to the University of Mississippi ("Ole' Miss") at Oxford to enforce the enrollment of James Meredith, Walker was in Oxford, allegedly to aid the segregationists.[25]

After two days of disturbances at Oxford, Walker was arrested and charged with assaulting, resisting, or impeding United States marshals; conspiring to prevent discharge of duties; and inciting, assisting, and engaging in an insurrection against the authority of the United States. Walker waived a hearing and was assured he would receive a prompt trial in a United States District Court in Mississippi. He was held on $100,000 bail.

On the day that Walker was arrested in Oxford, Carl Belcher, an attorney in the Department of Justice in Washington, called Dr. Charles Smith, medical director and chief psychiatrist at the Federal Bureau of Prisons, who was also in Washington, and asked him if he would be willing to prepare a statement about the psychiatric condition of Walker.

The Department of Justice furnished Dr. Smith with some written material. There was a report by an Associated Press reporter that Walker had led a group of students armed with rocks and sticks, a transcript of testimony Walker had given before the Special Preparedness Subcommittee of the Senate Committee on Armed Services in which he described a Communist conspiracy to weaken the United States, some news clippings about Walker, and army medical records that were all at least four years old. These materials were made available to Dr. Smith in the office of Attorney General Kennedy, and Smith spent six hours there studying them. Then, without seeing the patient or even having telephone contact with Walker or his representatives, Smith composed a memorandum concerning Walker's mental health.

> Some of his reported behavior reflects sensitivity and essentially unpredictable and seemingly bizarre outbursts of the type often observed in individuals suffering with paranoid mental disorder. There are also indications in his medical history of functional and psychosomatic disorders which could be precursors of the more serious disorder which his present behavior suggests.

From this and other information available to me I believe his recent behavior has been out of keeping with that of a person of his station, background, and training, and that as such it may be indicative of an underlying mental disturbance.

The next day the memorandum was put in final affidavit form, signed by Smith, and transmitted to the United States attorney in Oxford, who was handling the government's case against Walker. He promptly filed a motion to have Walker given a psychiatric examination in a suitable mental hospital. The psychiatric examination was ordered after a hearing at which neither Walker nor his attorney was present; the only psychiatric evidence on the need for examination was Smith's affidavit. In the meantime, Walker had already been placed in a border patrol plane and flown to Springfield, Missouri, where he was admitted to the United States Medical Center for Federal Prisoners. By this time he had raised his $100,000 bail and could have been free pending indictment and trial, but as a patient in a mental hospital, according to custom, he could not be released on bail. The time period for evaluation is sixty to ninety days. If he had been found incompetent to stand trial, he would have been indefinitely, perhaps permanently, hospitalized, like Ezra Pound.

Walker's attorney characterized the commitment order as fantastic and said he had talked to Walker over a two-day period and found him "in complete possession of all mental faculties." The radical right and liberal civil-rights lawyers both saw the order to commit as political mistreatment of Walker. The Senate Judiciary Committee was asked to investigate. The American Civil Liberties Union protested the commitment for evaluation on the basis that neither Walker nor his lawyer had been present at the hearing, that there was no testimony by a psychiatrist who had examined Walker, and that there was nothing else presented at the hearing besides Smith's affidavit to indicate that Walker might be incompetent.

Walker's attorneys filed a petition for a writ of habeas corpus. The government was given five days to show that it had proper cause to keep Walker in custody without bond, but it never even attempted to prove it had a reason, and Walker was released on bond. The condition for his release, however, was that within five days he would undergo a psychiatric examination by Dr. Robert Stubblefield at the Southwest Medical Center in Dallas. Dr. Stubblefield's examination resulted in a report that Walker was competent to stand trial. But when the hearing was held to receive Stubblefield's report and to determine if Walker should stand trial, the government asked once again for Walker to be sent to the Springfield Military Hospital for a sixty- to ninety-day mental examination. It presented America's foremost forensic psychiatrist, Manfred Guttmacher, as its chief psychiatric expert. Like Smith, Guttmacher had been furnished newspaper clippings, army medical records, and all the other documents in the possession of the Department of Justice, including a new piece of evidence, a movie of a press conference held by Walker in Dallas while out on bail. Guttmacher had never personally examined Walker, but he too was willing to testify that there were grounds for suspecting mental illness and incompetency to stand trial that were strong enough to justify the sixty- to ninety-day hospital commitment. Some of the evidence relied on by Guttmacher was newspaper clippings, and cross-examination revealed that in addition to clippings describing Walker as a fomenter of violence, there were other clippings—which Guttmacher had discounted—that described him in the opposite role, that of a peacemaker attempting to keep violence from getting out of bounds. Guttmacher explained that the inconsistent news stories indicated to him that Walker had "a great deal of confusion as to just what his role was in the situation." (The lawyer cross-examining him raised another possibility—that there might be inaccuracies in the news stories.)

Walker was held competent to stand trial. The Mississippi grand jury refused to indict him, and Walker later won libel verdicts against Associated Press and the newspapers that had asserted he had led a student charge against the United States marshals. (The Supreme Court reversed a $500,000 award in favor of Walker against the Associated Press on the grounds that the mistaken newspaper account had not been inspired by malice and Walker was a public figure.)[26]

Robert Kennedy was intimately involved in this attempt to have Walker committed. Dr. Smith examined the documents from the Department of Justice's file in his office (and was served dinner in Kennedy's office while he studied them). The story is indicative of the attorney general's willingness to make a political use of psychiatry, particularly as shown by his insistence that when one effort utilizing Smith failed, another effort utilizing Guttmacher should be made.

More than 2500 complaints concerning this use of psychiatry were received by the American Medical Association. Many of the complainants were members of the radical right, but liberals interested in civil rights, who also had been affronted by the government's tactics, were represented. The AMA's Judicial Council investigated the matter and consulted several sources—three psychiatrists (whose names were never made known), its own Council of Mental Health, and the American Psychiatric Association. All agreed that Smith had not violated any of the formal Principles of Medical Ethics and that the affidavit he had given was not a "medical diagnosis." What it was exactly was never clarified. The only light on this in the judicial opinion rendered by the Judicial Council is: "Some expressed the opinion that he had given an impression or opinion based on information given to him. In this connection, it was pointed out that physicians are frequently called upon by attorneys or courts to render a professional opinion to assist the court in deciding a technical point. It is then the court's responsibility to evaluate such opinion."

Having stated without equivocation that nothing wrong had been done, the AMA Judicial Council made it clear that it should never occur again. "The Judicial Council expresses concern about possible future situations wherein a physician might be subject to political control in order to pervert his medical opinion or to be used as a tool for political purposes. The Council urges physicians to be alert to such possibilities and to refuse to give such opinions which might be used for political purposes."[27]

In the presidential campaign of 1964, when Barry Goldwater opposed the incumbent Lyndon Johnson, 2417 psychiatrists responded to a *Fact* magazine poll concerning Goldwater's mental stability. The majority stated that they saw indications of personality disturbance and instability in Goldwater, whereas Johnson was seen as being healthy and stable. In this instance, organized medicine condemned evaluation without personal examination. Donovan Ward, president of the AMA, in an official statement for his organization, said that "a physician can properly arrive at a medical opinion on the health of an individual only by following accepted clinical procedures, including personal examination of the patient."[28] (When Goldwater sued Ralph Ginzburg, publisher of *Fact,* malice was found and he was allowed to recover damages.)[29]

Whether Kennedy and other attorneys general—and the presidents they served—were aware of the use of psychiatrists and psychologists in bizarre experiments conducted by the armed forces and the Central Intelligence Agency is still in question. Starting during World War II, behavioral scientists were called in to help the armed forces and other branches of the government with a number of problems. What pressures would cause a captured serviceman to break and reveal information, and what indoctrination would help him to withstand pressure? What new nerve gases and other novel means of influencing mind and behavior could be devised as offensive weapons, and how would they be defended against if Nazi Germany or, later, Soviet Russia used such methods? Some of the contributions behavioral scientists were asked to make were innocuous and well within the limits allowed by professional ethics, such as designing training manuals that were understandable and could be easily followed. Others were strange indeed, and as time and the Cold War continued, they became more and more outlandish. We do not know if knowledge of these projects was entirely confined to the agencies that sponsored them or if higher authorities were aware of what was going on. We do know that a large number of psychiatrists and psychologists were involved in such projects over a long period of time, some aware, and many of them unaware, that the bills for their research were being paid for by the government. We also know that the greatest secrecy was maintained over decades, that few other psychiatrists and psychologists knew that these experiments were underway, and that even those involved did not grasp the large-scale involvement of psychiatry. The beginnings of these programs date back to 1943, when the Office of Stragetic Services conducted tests, apparently in some cases on unwitting subjects, to see if marijuana might be used to break down the defenses of captured enemy agents.[30]

In the immediate post–World War II period the navy began its project CHATTER, testing "truth drugs" to use in interrogation and developing drugs that could be given to American agents to prevent them from being brainwashed. The CIA project BLUEBIRD/ARTICHOKE was begun in 1950 to develop "special interrogation techniques" involving hypnosis and chemical and biological agents.[31] These programs were at their most popular during the 1950s and 1960s. CIA Director Admiral Stansfield Turner told Congress that the programs were phased out in the late 1960s, but John Marks, a former State Department intelligence officer who has written a book about the CIA's activities in mind control, asserts that a new program was started, using a cover organization headed by Dr. Edwin Land, founder of Polaroid, which continued well into the 1970s.[32] As recently as June 1977 the CIA was interested in "human testing procedures" to determine if drugs such as cocaine, mescaline, scopolamine, and LSD could increase susceptibility to hypnosis, a technique that presumably might help in eliciting information from spies.[33]

MKULTRA was the cryptonym for a major drug-testing research and development program authorized by CIA Director Allen Dulles in 1953 at the height of the Cold War. One of the early projects involved age regression under drugs, and hypnosis of two "experienced professional-type agents," who apparently had defected from Russia. Age regression was used to elicit additional memories concerning the lives of the spies before defection and to help check on the reliability of the informants.

333

MKULTRA was described in a CIA report as "research and development of chemical, biological, and radiological materials capable of employment in clandestine operations to control human behavior."[34] Another description of the program, by Dr. Sidney Gottlieb, director of the Technical Services Office of the CIA, which ran the program, was that it was designed to test surreptitious methods of administering drugs, those that could be used in interrogation and "knockout" operations and those designed to disable a victim temporarily.

The Rockefeller Commission to investigate CIA activities within the United States, in its report in 1975, described the relationship of the psychochemical experimentation to a larger program. "The drug program was a part of a much larger CIA program to study possible means for controlling human behavior. Other studies explored the effects of radiation, electric-shock, psychology, psychiatry, sociology, and harassment substances."[35]

Beginning in 1955, under an informal arrangement with the Federal Bureau of Drug Abuse Control, tests were done on "unsuspecting subjects in normal social situations." In some of the MKULTRA experiments conducted with the cooperation of the Department of Defense, drugs were administered to unknowing army personnel, civilian employees of the armed forces, mental patients, and prisoners. The concept of informed consent was not ever considered.

One of the unwitting subjects was Harold Blauer, a former army colonel and a professional tennis player who had been divorced by his wife, became depressed, and entered the New York Psychiatric Institute in December 1952. On January 8, the day before he was scheduled to be released, he was injected with a "mescaline derivative" without his permission or the permission or knowledge of his family. He died less than two and a half hours after the injection. His family sued and the government settled for $18,000.[36] (When the *Village Voice* recently tried to investigate this and alleged other instances of drug experimentation at the New York Psychiatric Institute, the reporter claimed he was faced with a coverup by officials and an "unwritten code of secrecy among . . . psychiatric researchers.")[37]

The second subject who died as the result of the experimentation was Frank Olson, an army biochemist who was surreptitiously given LSD as part of the MKULTRA program in 1953, and while under its influence, plunged to his death from a tenth-floor New York hotel window. No explanation was given to his family, and they did not learn until 1975, twenty-two years later, that his death was not a planned suicide. (In other experiments university students were given LSD.) In

1976, as the result of a suit against the government, the family was awarded $750,000.[38]

As part of Project ARTICHOKE, the CIA considered a plan to drug an important official in a foreign government while he was drinking, and then when he was in a state of altered consciousness, to program him to assassinate his head of government (the true *Manchurian Candidate* situation). A memorandum on this plan said there were operational limitations—access to the subject might be difficult and the agency would have little physical control over him—but that in spite of this the project team would undertake the problem if there were "crash conditions." The CIA has said that this and other bizarre plans were "purely hypothetical."[39]

For a number of years the CIA tried to keep information of MKULTRA and other experiments secret, even from the Senate Select Committee on Intelligence. Dr. Gottlieb told a 1975 investigation by the Select Committee that in 1973 he had followed the instruction of then CIA Director Richard Helms and destroyed the MKULTRA records.[40] In 1977 seven boxes of documents relating to MKULTRA were discovered that dealt with financial payments to eighty-six universities and other institutions. The documents had not been destroyed because they had been filed under budgetary rather than project titles.[41] Eventually 1600 pages of heavily censored documents about the project were released by the CIA.[42]

Two of the cover organizations set up by the CIA to funnel money to research projects without their knowledge that the CIA was the source were the "Society for the Investigation of Human Ecology" and the "Geshikter Foundation for Medical Research."[43] Researchers in altered-mind states found these "philanthropic foundations" were eager to support their work, and they did not know they were being supported by the CIA.

Some of the experiments were so strange that a study might be undertaken of the psychology of the experimenters. One operation, which went on for nine years, was called by CIA wits "Operation Climax." Facilities described in most newspapers as "controlled bordellos," but called by the *New York Times* "field laboratories," were maintained in New York and San Francisco. These were rented apartments with red drapes, dressing tables trimmed in black velveteen, paintings of cancan dancers, and two-way mirrors and elaborate recording equipment for spying on unwitting subjects of the experiments. The subjects were picked up by prostitutes in bars, had drugs slipped into their drinks, and were lured to the observation rooms. They were observed in order to gain data on the effect of the drugs on unsuspecting people. A magician, John Mulholland, was on the CIA payroll to teach methods of giving the drugs surreptitiously.[44]

There were many other strange projects. One experiment involved hypnotized women who were persuaded to simulate immoral, abnormal, or disloyal behavior. The conclusion was: "This activity clearly indicates that individuals under hypnosis might be compromised and blackmailed."[45] In another experiment fifteen boys from low-income families and an undisclosed ethnic background were selected by the National Health Service to be circumcised, and psychological testing was done before and after the operation to see "if the operation left any emotional after-effects" and to discover "if circumcision at a significant stage of a child's development produced anxieties such as fear of castration."[46]

Eventually, as the Cold War heated up and fears of Soviet breakthroughs became more acute, even more fanciful projects were inaugurated. A series of experiments at the Stanford Research Center concerned the ability of psychics to influence the behavior of others, to alter their emotions or health, and to knock them out at a distance or kill them by remote influence. One thirty thousand dollar study dealt with the feasibility of using psychics to transmit messages without apparatus and even of employing the minds of psychics as free-ranging spies, able to slip past embassy guards and penetrate locked files. Mulholland was employed to analyze the work of a "mystic" who said he had devised a system for sending and receiving telepathic messages.[47] Because these projects were considered potentially militarily valuable, and also because the researchers knew there would be embarrassment if Congress and the press knew the nature of the studies, they were sometimes dressed up and disguised with imposing titles. One study on using psychic power to transmit messages was named "Novel Biophysical Information Transfer Mechanisms (NBIT)."

The CIA used its own staff of trained psychologists, some of them stationed overseas, to help operations officers assess foreign nationals being recruited as agents. The psychologists administered purported intelligence tests, which were in reality disguised personality assessment tests. When they were not able to do personal interviews with the potential recruits, they gave indirect assessments based on "source material," including the interviews of others and specimens of handwriting evaluated by graphologists. On the basis of their assessments, psychologists advised on the best inducements for persuading a subject to accept covert employment. They also gave courses in psychological assessment to operations officers to help them develop their own assessment skills.[48]

The CIA was ready to enlist the power of psychiatry in any way that seemed helpful, including brainwashing or commitment to a mental hospital as "disposal methods" for "blown agents, foreign defectors who had outlived their usefulness, and defecting trainees." Erasing memory by the use of hypnosis, lysergic acid and other drugs, electroshock, and other methods of electrical stimulation of the brain were considered as possible solutions to the problem of subjects with secret information who might have to be maintained in maximum security isolation for long periods to keep them from revealing information. Experiments were performed to see how effective these techniques might be. The agency doctor who described a number of these possibilities in a memorandum also "mentioned the possible usage of the prefrontal lobotomy and stated he thought this technique could be applied to individuals his agency was no longer concerned with in the overseas areas on an experimental basis."[49]

Uri Nosenko defected from Russia in 1963 and told the CIA he had information about Lee Harvey Oswald. The CIA became convinced he was still acting for Russia and was attempting to plant false information, and it set out to break him. For three years he was held incommunicado in a concrete vault. He was watched continuously, not given adequate food, and not allowed to read or occupy himself in any way while the process of attempting to break him down—the CIA policy of "hostile interrogation"—continued. When he made a calendar out of lint to keep track of the time, it was swept away, and the next calendar was swept away too. When he managed to fashion a makeshift chess set, it was taken away from him. The CIA official in charge, the deputy director of the CIA's Soviet Branch, in a memorandum to himself, listed ways to deal with Nosenko more convenient than keeping him in his vault forever. The three options for disposal in the memorandum were to liquidate the man, to render him incapable of telling a coherent story through use of drugs in order to commit him to a mental hospital, or to commit him without having first produced mental aberration. In 1968 the CIA reversed its thinking on Nosenko and decided he was a legitimate defector. Information about Nosenko's detention only emerged ten years later when the House Select Committee on Assassinations was informed.[50]

In at least one case the CIA used commitment as a temporary expedient to handle a difficult agent. A 1952 memorandum discussing the case was made public under the Freedom of Information Act in 1979, but it was censored to suppress identifying information. A twenty-nine-year-old "ambitious, bright" leader of a small political party was "ostensibly working for independence" of an unidentified foreign country and was also working clandestinely for the CIA. The CIA was informed that he was considering selling out to another intelligence agency and arranged for him to be taken into custody by his country's police. He was held in prison for six months until he became a "nuisance," and the police of his country then asked the CIA "to take him back." The CIA, according to its memorandum, received him and put him in a mental hospital, diagnosed as "a psychopathic personality," even though he was "not a psychopathic personality." The memorandum raised the question of how to dispose of this troublesome individual: "He has now been in a hospital for several months and the hospital authorities now want to get him out since he is causing considerable trouble." The memorandum suggests that brainwashing might persuade him to be loyal to the CIA, and if that failed, "disposal is perfectly O.K."[51] The fate of the person is not known. This use of a psychiatric hospital for political convenience has never been protested.

A psychiatric threat to civil liberties in more recent times was the alliance between the National Institute of Mental Health, a branch of the Department of Health, Education, and Welfare, and the Law Enforcement Assistance Administration, a part of the Department of Justice. These two agencies worked together to find methods of behavior control that would prevent and curb violence and crime. The collaboration between the two agencies began in the late 1960s, with NIMH counseling potential recipients of grants on how to secure criminal-justice funding for "human services"—juvenile delinquency studies, forensic services on psychiatric wards, counseling and correctional programs, drug abuse programs, and experimentation in the reduction of violence. By 1974 LEAA had funded more than 350 projects that involved behavior modification, chemotherapy, or some other medical experimentation. In 1973 NIMH and LEAA entered into a formal agreement under which mental health professionals would provide technical assistance for state and local criminal-justice agencies.[52]

An experimental hospital that was designed to use behavior modification in the rehabilitation of federal prisoners was opened at Butner, North Carolina. By the time the hospital was in operation, its plan to use behavior modification techniques to rehabilitate criminals had become so controversial that its director had resigned and its therapeutic programs had been altered to eliminate the use of deprivation stimulus.[53] The Law Enforcement Assistance Administration's proposed sponsorship of a Center for the Study and Reduction of Violence at the University of California at Los Angeles led to the revelation that experimental aversive conditioning had already been funded by the state of California at Vacaville Prison and that psychosurgery was contemplated. After newspaper publicity and a California legislative investigation, it was decided not to fund the center.[54] All these projects offer evidence of the eagerness with which the government seeks medical and behavioral science help in developing ways to control behavior.

* * *

The first public act in the conspiracy we know as the Watergate cover-up was not the break-in at the Watergate but a break-in nine months earlier designed to secure psychiatric information to use against an enemy of the president. Daniel Ellsberg, originally a staunch supporter of the Vietnam War, had turned antiwar and made copies of volumes of secret Defense Department papers available to the *New York Times.* The government attempted to suppress publication, but the Supreme Court upheld the right of newspapers to print the material.

Nixon was enraged and he wanted action taken against Ellsberg that would discredit him and impair his political effectiveness. He urged Charles Colson to disseminate damaging information about Ellsberg and the people he associated with in order to show disreputable personal characteristics and lack of patriotism. Howard Hunt, hired as a White House consultant to discredit Ellsberg, asked the CIA to provide a psychological profile that could be used to hurt Ellsberg's reputation. The CIA's Office of Medical Services routinely prepared psychological profiles on world figures in order to help the government deal with them, and Fidel Castro, among other leaders, had been one of its subjects. (In 1943 the CIA's predecessor agency, the Office of Strategic Services, had had a psychiatrist, Walter Langer, prepare a secret psychological report on Adolf Hitler in which he had predicted Hitler's mental deterioration and his eventual suicide.)[55]

The CIA's chief psychiatrist, Dr. Bernard Malloy, was assigned to this project, but possibly a second CIA psychiatrist, whose name has never been revealed, did the bulk of the preparation of the report. The project was cleared with CIA Director Richard Helms, and then Malloy or his assistant, working in an office in the basement of the Executive Office Building, put together a description of Ellsberg. Malloy was told that the Ellsberg profile "was of the highest priority, even over the SALT negotiations."[56]

The finished profile described Ellsberg as motivated by "what he deemed a higher order of patriotism."[57] Hunt said in a conference with Malloy that they needed something more than that, data that would help the administration refer knowledgeably to Ellsberg's "oedipal conflicts or castration fears." He wanted conclusions drawn from Ellsberg's "rather peculiar background," experiments with drugs and sex, a "bizarre" sex life between marriages—including Swedish and Indonesian mistresses—and participation in orgies.

The Nixon staff knew from FBI reports that Ellsberg was in psychiatric or psychoanalytic treatment with Dr. Lewis Fielding, a Beverly Hills psychoanalyst. Two FBI agents appeared at Fielding's office and asked for information about Ellsberg. Fielding refused to confer further until he had had a chance to consult his lawyer. After having done so, he told the FBI that he would not violate the confidential doctor-patient relationship. On July 26, another agent was refused information by Fielding.[58] Hunt recruited a team and broke into Fielding's office.

The break-in was completely unsuccessful; the team could not locate Fielding's file on Ellsberg. Fielding reported later that the next day he found about forty pages of notes on Ellsberg on his office floor, but the burglars apparently had not recognized these for what they were.

Hunt was still determined to get his second profile, and more secret material from FBI files and from the State Department was furnished to Malloy. The second profile turned out to be almost equally useless for Hunt's purposes. It read in part:

> The loss of interest in the piano, and the subsequent concentration on a sport were associated with an automobile accident which led to his wearing a cast for a year because of a broken knee. His father was driving and his mother and sister were killed . . . It is possible that strong feelings of resentment and rage and frustration stirred up by death and personal illness or injury are associated with his apparently sudden and extreme shifts in loyalty and enthusiasm . . .
>
> His central theme for leaking the Pentagon Papers has been that "the Executive" should not alone have so much authority as to plunge the country into war and the misery and death that it brings. It is probable that the Subject is not only referring here to the various Presidents, but also to his own father whom, after all, he saw as responsible for the death of his mother and sister, injuring him to boot . . .
>
> To an important degree the leaking of the Pentagon Papers was also an act of aggression at his analyst, as well as at the President and his father . . . It is of course possible that the Subject has more documents with which he will seek to continue his odyssey of being appreciated (and disappointed) by a senior personage . . .[59]

Hunt and his associates were later assigned to the Committee for the Re-election of the President, and it was in behalf of that group that the famous Watergate break-in took place on June 17, 1972, nine months after the affair of Fielding's files.[60]

The *New York Times* in 1974 attributed to "well-placed sources" in the office of Special Prosecutor Leon Jaworski the theory that the Watergate cover-up had as a principal motive the desire not only to cover up the Watergate conspiracy but also to cover up the story of the Fielding break-in. (There was also a break-in, never shown to be by the government, at the New York office of the analyst who had Ellsberg's wife, Patricia, in treatment, and there had been an FBI request for information from her analyst.)[61] The Watergate break-in, and even its ties to the White House, might have been explained early in the game as typical campaign hijinks and no different from others on political headquarters that had occurred during election years in the past. The Fielding break-in obviously was something else. It was not campaign-connected. It emanated from the White House, not the Committee for the Re-election of the President, and it could not be justified on the ground of any threat to national security, although at one time Nixon made this claim. The Fielding incident gave force to Howard Hunt's threat to reveal his participation in "seamy things" if a solid defense were not maintained.[62]

As striking as the government's use of psychiatry in the Ellsberg case was the lack of psychiatric interest in, and response to, the news that it had taken place. The *New York Times,* in October 1976, contained news of the request of Robert Jay Lifton, a Yale University psychiatrist, for an American Psychiatric Association investigation and censure of Dr. Malloy. A member of the association wrote in to its official newspaper complaining that no news about Lifton's request had appeared in the APA publication,[63] but the whole case continued to get almost no professional attention. The matter of Malloy's conduct was referred to an appropriate APA committee, and nothing was ever heard of the matter again. (The APA has also referred to its Committee to Study Uses and Abuses of Psychiatry the matter of "Psychiatry's Role in the CIA Efforts to Control Behavior,"[64] and nothing further has been heard on this issue from the APA.)

Watergate has another connection with psychiatry. When the more famous plumbers' break-in occurred, psychiatry was used to immobilize and to discredit the one person who could have "blown the whistle" and cleared up the matter in a short time. If Washington reporters had not become convinced, by repeated statements of people close to Nixon, that Martha Mitchell was crazy, there were any number of times when her leads could have led to a determination that, as she consistently claimed, the Watergate conspiracy reached up to the highest level of the administration, that the administration was consistently using lies and deceit in its "stonewalling" effort to maintain the cover-up, and that blame was being reassigned to protect the president.

As a lonely cabinet wife, Martha Mitchell was in the habit of calling up reporters late at night, particularly the sympathetic Helen Thomas of United Press International, and giving forthright views of Washington life and politics. Sometimes she had been drinking when she made these calls.

The weekend of the Watergate break-in, Martha and John Mitchell, who had resigned as attorney general to head the Committee to Re-elect the President, were in California to raise money for the campaign and were staying at a resort motel at Newport Beach. Mitchell returned to Washington at the news that five burglars who had attempted to ransack the Democratic National Headquarters at the Watergate had been arrested. He knew that one of the arrested burglars, who had given a false name to the police, was in reality James McCord, Jr., formerly Martha's bodyguard and now chief of security for the committee. He wanted to keep Martha from this knowledge, and he wanted to prevent her from communicating with the press, so he ordered her new bodyguard, Steve King, to see that she did not receive newspapers or have any other access to news, and that she be kept isolated until he had a chance to deal with the situation. Martha was kept a prisoner for almost a week at the Newporter Inn, guarded by four bodyguards and her secretary. While Mitchell was telling the press that he was "satisfied that no senior official in the Committee to Re-elect the President had any connection" with the incident, Martha remained in ignorance that there had even been a Watergate break-in, and out of reach of the telephone. On the evening of the fourth day of her imprisonment, while King was asleep, she put a telephone call through to Helen Thomas, but King awoke, pulled the telephone out of the wall, and in the process of trying to subdue her threw her into a window, which badly cut her hand. The doctor who was called the next morning to look after the wound was told she was hysterical when she claimed she was being kept a political prisoner. He paid no attention to her protests and proceeded to inject her with a tranquilizer. The cut required emergency-room treatment and she was taken to a local hospital, where she maintained once more that she was a political prisoner and was being mistreated. Again she was seen as hysterical or drunk and was not believed. Several days later Martha was flown back to her home near Washington and kept there in seclusion.

Martha's power to hurt Nixon by insisting that something was very wrong with the administration, that its abuse of power extended to the highest levels, was nullified by reports—which one newspaper said emanated from Republicans in the highest places—that she had had a nervous breakdown and that she was untrustworthy.

When a reporter did get through to her and the story of her detention and forced treatment was printed for the first time, it was generally interpreted as another example of outrageous, untrustworthy Martha. In reality she had been uncompromisingly honest—this was one of her best qualities—but the stigma of alcoholism and mental patient were imputed to her to impair credibility. She continued during the following months to accuse the administration of a cover-up, to say that the president wanted others to "take the rap" for him and that she was afraid her husband would end up taking the blame and paying the penalty. Martha told Thomas in one interview that Mitchell had shielded Nixon in his testimony before the Senate Watergate Committee because he hoped Nixon would pay him back with executive clemency if he were to be convicted for crimes. No one except Thomas paid serious attention to the accusations.[65]

There have been many political uses of psychiatry down through the years. Most of them concern people much less prestigious than Daniel Ellsberg, Martha Mitchell, Thomas Eagleton, Ezra Pound, or General Edwin Walker. Women have been particular targets for discredit. In a well-publicized incident in 1962, two reporters, Sarah McClendon and Mary McGrory, secured the freedom of a Department of Agriculture secretary who had tried to keep her employer's files from being removed during an investigation of department irregularities and had been hospitalized on the certification of two psychiatrists that she was of unsound mind.[66] Recently, in the manner used by Wilbur Mills against Fanne Fox, and Wayne Hayes against Elizabeth Ray, Herman Talmadge used the discrediting technique by imputing mental instability to his former wife, Betty Talmadge, after she had given testimony about his financial irregularities.

One important abuse of psychiatry has been in the field of security clearance, where psychiatrists with no real scientific basis for their determinations can disqualify a government employee for employment or for advancement. Often much of the material the psychiatrist finds in the file that he uses to assist him in the evaluation is hearsay, and the applicant does not have a chance to respond to his accusers.

The government's psychiatric policy is ambivalent. It pays generously for its employees' psychiatric treatment and it passes regulations prohibiting discrimination against the mentally ill, yet it uses evidence of emotional instability—even at a very remote point in the past—as reason to reject people for employment, to fire them, or to keep them from sensitive assignments. Prospective employees for nuclear power plants, the military working on nuclear submarines or with nuclear missiles are psychiatrically screened. No one knows if the criteria the psychiatrists use are valid. If it were not for psychiatric screening, such traditional evaluation standards as personal appearance and behavior, history, record of previous mental problems, and personal and business recommendations would need to be relied on, as they were before the rise of modern psychiatry. The psychiatric screening, as crude as it is, seems reassuring to those who employ it. The screeners are naturally interested more in the safety of society than in the right of the individual to have the job, and doubts are resolved against the prospective employee unless he has unique and indispensable attributes (as in the case of some technical research).

* * *

The ultimate political power a psychiatrist can possess is to determine who is qualified to lead and to rule. Possibly psychiatrists came close to exercising this ultimate power during the last days of the Nixon administration.

In August 1974 it was apparent to everyone except Nixon and some members of his family that he would have to resign. General Alexander Haig, who had replaced H. R. Haldeman as White House chief of staff and had assumed increasing importance as the administration became unhinged during its final days, had reason to think the president might commit suicide. Woodward and Bernstein report in *The Final Days* that Haig ordered the president's doctors to deny him all pills and to take away from him the sleeping pills and tranquilizers already in his possession.[67] It is also believed that Haig had contingency plans in the event that the president, rather than resigning, would take some strange or precipitous action, try to maintain his power by force, or make irrational decisions. Haig has never revealed how incompetent the president was. When asked if he was acting president at any time, he has admitted, "I had to do things I would not have done under ordinary circumstances." He has been asked if there was ever a time when Nixon was irrational and unable to act, and his reply was: "If there were, I wouldn't tell anybody."[68] We do not know how psychiatrists would have dealt with the actual or alleged incompetency of the chief executive, but we think that during the last days of the administration the possibility that they would have to deal with it was very great.

Reporters had been aware for many years that Nixon and those around him had a "siege mentality" and that the White House saw evidence of unfriendliness—some of its perception was accurate—everywhere around. This had even been dignified with the title of the president's or the administration's "paranoia." Nixon had surprised the press and the nation in New Orleans in August 1973 when in full view of television cameras he grabbed his press secretary, Ron Ziegler, by the shoulders and issued a sharp order to him. Nixon then spun Ziegler around and gave him what was described as a "neck-popping shove" toward the press corps. The president was irritated because some members of the press were at his heels, following him into a convention hall instead of using another entrance that had been designated for them. A reporter heard the president tell Ziegler, "I don't want the press near me. You take care of it."

In a press briefing a few hours later, Deputy Press Secretary Gerald Warren acknowledged that "the past few months have been periods of pressure on the president." He also explained that the president was upset because his motorcade had been rerouted because of a reported assassination threat and he had not been able to greet the crowds that had gathered for him.

Some congressional leaders and others who saw Nixon at this time described him as increasingly haggard and tense. Presidential Counselor Melvin Laird told a reporter that "it might have been better if the President had taken a long rest" after his pneumonia the previous month."[69]

The president became more and more secluded, making himself available only to a few advisers and his family. At his rare press conferences he was sweaty and trembling, and he stuttered. There were rumors about his nocturnal piano playing at the White House, his obsessive concern with details, and his high-speed automobile dashes along California freeways. One aide recalled that during this period he passed Nixon in the hallway and heard him muttering what sounded like, "The bastards! The bastards!" His conversations rambled, and sometimes they were almost incoherent. J. Anthony Lukas writes: "Certainly, much of Nixon's behavior during his last year in office was, at the very least, unorthodox . . . One assistant compares Nixon in August 1974 to Captain Queeg, the erratic commander in Herman Wouk's *The Caine Mutiny*: "Like Queeg, he was given to sudden rages, to wild suspicions, terrible doubts about everybody.""

345

And there are other stories, stranger yet, which one is reluctant to report because they are so difficult to confirm."[70]

Haig did not have to use his contingency plans. Nixon resigned without incident, and the question of his mental stability did not become a matter for psychiatric determination. (Nixon's mental state did possibly influence Ford to pardon him. The *New York Times* and the *Washington Post* have stated that the reason for the sudden pardon was Haig's representation to the president that Nixon was in an "alarming state of health," that he was acutely depressed, and that he was a suicidal risk. According to one informant to the *New York Times,* Haig warned Ford ten days before the pardon that unless Ford moved quickly in announcing a full, unconditional pardon, instead of waiting for legal action to be taken, it might be too late to avert the "possible personal and national tragedy" of Nixon's complete physical and mental collapse.)[71]

A number of presidents in this century have had disabilities that affected, or had the potential of affecting, their ability to govern. Wilson was incapacitated by a stroke, but the extent of his disability was kept secret by a conspiracy of doctors and those closest to him. Franklin D. Roosevelt, in the months before his sudden death from a stroke, showed signs of rapid mental deterioration. Eisenhower, in addition to other health problems, had a stroke during his second term.[72] If John Kennedy had survived the Dallas shooting, he would have been brain-damaged, which was the case when Garfield was shot. The question of presidential disability has a great potential to cause disunion, and therefore the psychiatrists called in to resolve any dispute about the ability of the president would have an ultimate kind of political power.

The Psychiatrist as Social Engineer

WHEN WE THINK of seeing a psychiatrist, we think of a one-to-one relationship. Some psychiatrists deal with people in the mass—hospital psychiatrists have always been involved in setting up uniform treatment conditions for large numbers of people—but outpatient psychiatry developed as a medical specialty that focused on the individual. Particularly after the infusion of Freudian theory, with its emphasis on personal traumas and reactions to them and on the unique interchange between doctor and patient, psychiatry has been concerned with the special qualities of each person and the way he reacts in close interpersonal relationships.

But psychiatry has gradually developed the ambition of dealing with people in the aggregate. Starting with its role in soldier selection and placement, it expanded to include the categorizing and treatment of other groups—juvenile delinquents, prisoners, and other criminals, such as sexual deviants, and defective delinquents—and it developed techniques of assessing job applicants and techniques of education, in addition to other mass methods. Some psychiatrists came to believe they could be most effective when they dealt with people in groups, developing and applying principles broadly, and eventually they even came to believe that the most effective role of a psychiatrist was to make public policy or to influence those who make public policy.

Principles of mental hygiene were to be applied to the general population. Psychiatry, in its desire to deal with people in the mass, extended its borders to include not only the mentally ill and the social deviant but also normal people in stressful situations that might give rise to psychiatric symptoms (like the bereaved or the economically disadvantaged), and finally even to normal people experiencing stress that might lead to social maladjustment rather than to symptoms. After all, according to some psychiatrists, psychiatry is too good—or too powerful—to be wasted merely on sick people.[1]

Many psychiatrists came to the conclusion that the cause of psychiatric disequilibrium or dissatisfaction in living was not in the individual, which had been the emphasis in earlier psychiatry and in Freudian theory, but in the social forces that play on the individual. Some psychiatrists in recent years, for example, have reached the point where they see either poverty or racism as "the number one psychiatric problem of the nation," and the goal of the psychiatrist becomes to root out the cause of the problem. Economic and social problems had become transformed into medical problems. A new branch of psychiatry developed to deal with groups of people—social psychiatry. The psychiatrist had become a social engineer.

The introduction of effective methods of chemotherapy increased the ability of psychiatrists to apply simple treatment methods to large numbers of people. The aims of mass treatment and preventive treatment also were aided by the introduction of behaviorist psychology. Its promise was that man could be turned into a more domesticated animal, more cooperative and more peace-loving, if he could be conditioned early enough to pursue higher goals than freedom or dignity. B. F. Skinner stated that his kind of psychology had already produced experimental analyses of behavior that had led to "the improved destiny of cultural practices, in programmed instructional materials, contingency management in the classroom, behavioral modification in psychotherapy and penology, and many other fields."[2]

Somehow in the evolution of psychiatry, the psychiatrist, despite unsubstantial credentials to deal with people in the aggregate, had been accepted as an expert on group processes and on social problems, and the world had become his patient. Some psychiatrists lost interest in treating individuals entirely and were only interested in mass treatment. Psychiatrists fancifully held out the hope that eventually chemical agents could be added to drinking water at filtration plants to deal with such problems as depression or violence or antisocial attitudes. When it was discovered that there was in fact an element, lithium, in the drinking water in some parts of the world that protected people in those areas from the manic phase of manic-depressive psychosis and gave promise of modifying other behavior, including helping alcoholics control their thirst, the concept of mass treatment received a boost. When long-acting injectable tranquilizers were devised that allowed large groups of people to be kept tranquilized by a therapy that was entirely technological and impersonal, the movement became even more popular. Behavior modification techniques and chemotherapy were admirable tools for application by technologists rather than individual therapists. They were cost-efficient.

Psychiatry branched out to deal with all social issues—treatment of criminals, capital punishment, abortion, decriminalization of drug offenses, and eventually it got into areas of war and peace and international relations. Psychiatry had burst its boundaries.

The ultimate claim for psychiatry was that psychiatrists should screen and select world leaders, because social policy was too important to be left to unstable individuals who could not earn the psychiatric stamp of approval. Kenneth Clark, when he gave his presidential address in 1971 to the American Psychological Association, proposed a utopian remedy: the development of a pill that would tone down aggressive feelings and could be "force-fed" to the world's leaders. He said that we are in a survival crisis that "requires immediate mobilization of all that is positive within man to provide us with the time necessary to prevent man from destroying the human species . . ." He urged behavior scientists to come up quickly with a drug to block "the animalistic, barbaric and primitive propensities in man," one that would subordinate "these negatives to the uniquely human moral and ethical characteristics of love, kindness, empathy." By using drug "psychotechnology" within a few years the desirable goal could be reached "and with a fraction of the cost to produce the atom bomb."[3]

Clark is only one in a long line of behavioral scientists who see the solution of society's problems through direction by psychologists and psychiatrists. Of course behavioral scientists do not want to devote their energies only to world rulers. Psychiatrists want to straighten out everyone who may cause problems in society from the lowest to the highest. Emil Kraepelin, with Freud the greatest name in psychiatry, is given credit for introducing in 1880 the idea of the indeterminate sentencing of criminals, who were to be detained until a psychiatrist certified them as safe to be released. William Alanson White, the most famous and most progressive American psychiatrist of the early twentieth century, wrote: "The criminal should be sent to the reformatory to stay until cured, and he should not be allowed to re-enter the community until he can do so with safety."[4]

The obvious place to start a mass treatment approach is with children. In the dawn of psychoanalysis, when things seemed easier than they do now, psychoanalysts and psychoanalytically oriented psychiatrists thought they had the answer to emotional maladjustment. It started in children, it related to the interaction between child and parents, and it resulted from the child's lack of security. So a generation of parents who went to PTA meetings heard earnest experts tell them their children needed more security, and that the recipe for more security was more love. (Bumper stickers still promote the purposeful application of love—"Have You Hugged Your Child Today?") The parent who had love to spare but was too inhibited to express it was helped by the lectures. But most parents love their children as much as they know how, and the lecturers' injunctions often only produced self-consciousness, an artificial parent-child relationship, and guilt. Psychiatrists were perpetrating a basic fallacy, which they continue to do again and again in many ways. They had formulated a theory of individual needs related to unconscious dynamisms going on in the individual and in his reaction with his environment, and then shifted to a nondynamic common-sense and will-power approach as a way to deal with these unconscious factors. They recommended that primary-process (irrational) material be taken care of by the secondary process (rationality) without indicating some therapeutic method to effect the change.

The idea of early intervention to stem more severe childhood pathology was also attractive. Tests were designed to predict future school failure, neurosis, psychosis, maladjustment, and delinquency. Screening programs were set up to pick out the future problem. There are obvious cases of unrecognized retarded children who do not get the special schooling they need and abused children who are not recognized and are allowed to remain in violent households, but the concept of mass screening and early detection of psychopathology carries with it as much potential for abuse as it does for use.

Programs have been proposed, and some have been implemented, to identify emotional disturbance in children at a very early age. Since 1970 all four-year-old children in Sweden have been screened for medical and developmental disabilities, including a check of mental health development and a determination of emotional development.[5]

In 1970 the Department of Health, Education, and Welfare received a memorandum from the White House, signed by Nixon aide John Ehrlichman, asking the department to consider proposals put forth by New York psychiatrist Arnold Hutschnecker for mass psychological testing of children in order to predict future criminal tendencies. (Hutschnecker, before he became a psychiatrist, had been Nixon's internist.) HEW officials questioned the legality and validity of the plan,[6] and the American Psychological Association issued a statement: "The question is not that we wouldn't like to be able to predict who is going to be a criminal and who isn't; rather, it is, do we have the scientific technology to do so?"[7]

When Governor Carter's Commission to Improve Services for Mentally and Emotionally Handicapped Georgians proposed a Mental Health Improvement Plan for Georgia in 1971, one suggestion was that early childhood testing and evaluation for emotional disturbance and mental illness "be made mandatory for entrance into public schools, similar to the manner in which certain immunizations have been required . . . A public education program on the need for early detection of emotional disturbances should begin immediately . . ."[8]

Rosalynn Carter was head of a 1978 presidential Commission on Mental Health that recommended that "helping children must be the Nation's first priority in preventing mental disability," and toward this end it proposed "a periodic, comprehensive, developmental assessment" be made available to all children.[9]

Other early childhood programs have recommended screening for drug abuse, utilizing urine testing as early as the fifth grade.[10] Recently two researchers in antipsychotic drugs have suggested that use of these drugs by pregnant women may be decreasing the incidence of schizophrenia in children exposed to the drugs *in utero* (although that there is a decrease is debatable), and that use of drugs for prevention "ought to be looked into."[11]

The advocates of early screening and early intervention are obviously well intentioned. Yet experience tells us that such programs have only been helpful when they pick up obvious cases of discrete psychiatric conditions, such as retardation. They have been used for the most part, however, to identify large numbers of children as emotionally or mentally ill and have led to mass treatment programs to deal with these "problems."

One use of mass screening and early intervention has been in the attempt to identify and rehabilitate juvenile delinquents. Labeling a juvenile as delinquent and sending him into therapy always seems like a useful intervention. But recently we have begun to secure data that indicate treatment is not effective.

One recent study shows that juveniles who received no service from mental health, placement, and family agency sources had a significantly lower rate of further trouble than a matched group of children who had received help. Another study concludes that a counseling program for youth may cause stress by placing children in a conflict between the values of their lower-class families and their middle-class counselors.[12]

John Byles, author of one of these studies, comments: ". . . Most mental health services employ the medical model, which has demonstrated utility in problems of illness and disease. But there is mounting evidence that delinquency is not an illness . . ."

Disillusionment with the results of intervention plays into the hands of conservatives who want to see social-reform programs eliminated. They would like to believe that help is always ineffective, because then we could forget about offering it. Yet we know in our relations with our families and friends that we do have some power to affect others. Therapists working with individuals have the impression, even though they cannot justify it by hard data, that although many therapeutic encounters do not take, others can be extremely helpful. The adoption of an attitude of therapeutic nihilism can be a rationalization for lack of concern or plain cheapness. Many of the programs that combine goals of social reform and therapy do not represent serious therapy efforts. The hope is that, through some simple stratagem, the habits of a lifetime, established ways of thinking and behaving, and deep-seated emotional conflicts will simply disappear. One example of such a simple-minded approach is the claim that obesity can be treated by having a well-set table with nice china and appointments, with emphasis on small bites and multiple chews—the fork must be laid down between each bite or the magic does not exercise its spell. Programs almost as simplistic have been proposed for every kind of human disequilibrium, some involving suggestion and direction, some chemotherapy. The hope is that, just as cavities can be prevented by fluoridation of the water, mental and emotional problems can be cured by a simple wide-scale application.

One great effort to deal with children in the mass involved the wholesale administration of an energizing drug, Ritalin. Giving Ritalin to hyperactive school children is the closest we have come to administering chemotherapy by way of the water supply. In some areas of the country, any child who had a behavior problem or had learning difficulties was seen as hyperactive, and these children were often placed on Ritalin prescriptions without any thorough investigation of the cause of their problems, sometimes with no physical or mental examination at all. The prescriptions for Ritalin were signed by a school physician or psychiatrist, but this did not mean that the doctor saw the child.

The application of chemotherapy to childhood learning and behavior problems is not very scientific. One team of researchers say that "the hyperkinetic reaction of childhood is an ill-defined behavior disorder, often of unknown etiology," and that "although school teachers 'know' what a hyperactive child is, clinicians and researchers frequently cannot agree."[13]

Ritalin (methylphenidate hydrochloride), related to the amphetamines, was developed as a psychic energizer for adults and was widely used after it was discovered that amphetamine therapy was harmful and extremely addicting. Ritalin has fallen out of favor for adults in recent years, possibly because it is not very effective and it is habit-forming. Psychiatrists discovered that amphetamines had a paradoxical effect in some children. Instead of energizing them, it calmed them and allowed them to focus attention. Eventually Ritalin became the drug of choice for the treatment of children who were diagnosed as "hyperkinetic."

Hyperkinetic children can cause havoc in a household. They can get by with little sleep, reverse their days and nights, and be impelled into constant activity. In the classroom they can be learning problems as well as behavior problems. The concept of a drug that, like insulin, would normalize an abnormal person seemed eminently sensible. Ritalin therapy became a rage. Hundreds of thousands of school children who had learning problems or were overactive were targeted by teachers as hyperkinetic, sent for brief neurological screenings, and often diagnosed on the basis of the screenings as hyperactive (sometimes as many as 50 percent of the children sent for evaluation). Their parents were then told they could not continue in school unless they were given Ritalin twice a day.[14]

Ritalin and Dexedrine, which was also prescribed, had important side effects. They raised heart rate and blood pressure. Ritalin decreased growth both in height and weight and lowered the threshold for seizures, so children with no previously reported convulsions became convulsion-prone. Many children were kept somnolent by large doses of medication. Estimates for children on the drug at a point in time have ranged from 150,000 to 1 million;[15] recent statistics indicate there are probably 150,000 to 200,000 children on Ritalin.[16] The figures range from less than 1 percent in some rural areas to 15–20 percent in some urban areas—a commentary on the social aspect of psychiatric diagnosis.[17]

Dr. Agnes Tarr, a school board physician who prescribed the medication for many children, has defended the practice of not giving repeat examinations and neurological examinations on the ground that there was no reason for them, and she has denied that Ritalin was used to "tranquilize" the children.

"We are not trying to calm them down," Dr. Tarr says. "Who wants to calm down a normal, healthy child of that age? But they don't show as many of these frustrations, impulsive things. They conform. I hate the word conform, but they do manage to conduct themselves . . . more like the average child."[18]

Sroufe and Stewart, writing in the *New England Journal of Medi-*

353

cine, give some reasons why Ritalin programs may be harmful that were overlooked in the rush to treat classroom learning problems with chemotherapy:

The use of the drug lowers the motivation of parents and teachers to take other steps to help the child. The child may conclude that he can function only with the drug as a crutch, and this may be crucial in impairing his developing self-image. Drug treatment may provide an inappropriate solution to what are basically sociological problems; such factors as poor nutrition and lack of sufficient sleep are then masked, just as adults mask tiredness and burnout with amphetamines. Drug use conditions children to the drug culture that produces drug abuse.[19]

There have been few controlled studies of children on Ritalin. One was done by Gabrielle Weiss and her associates at Children's Hospital in Montreal. Children diagnosed as hyperactive before the era of stimulants, and therefore not treated, were compared with children at a later period who were diagnosed and treated. The results, published in 1975, surprised most investigators: There was no significant difference between the untreated group, a second group treated with a tranquilizer, and the group treated with Ritalin in terms of measures of emotional adjustment, delinquency, IQ, visual-motor coordination, or academic performance.[20]

An adult counterpart to the Ritalin program for school performance has been the methadone program for adult heroin abusers. Methadone is a synthetic opiate substitute that is taken orally. It prevents the withdrawal symptoms of the discontinuation of heroin, and it does not give heroin's euphoriant effect. It is addicting, probably more so than heroin. The withdrawal symptoms after discontinuing methadone are severe, but methadone programs are set up on the premise that the heroin user turned methadone addict may have to be maintained on methadone for life. One of methadone's main assets is that it is provided by the government and is free. No one has to steal to maintain a methadone habit, although it may be as strong as, or stronger than, a heroin habit.

In 1964 Dole and Nyswander published their study of twenty-two methadone-maintained addicts, which showed that the switch from heroin to methadone resulted in the addicts' renewed interest in themselves and a regained ability to hold jobs and engage in "constructive social activity." They recommended methadone for life to fulfill biological needs of the body that they theorized had been created by heroin use.[21]

Measured in terms of sticking with the program or keeping out of trouble with the police, the early methadone programs were great successes. In retrospect it appears that some of the success may have been due to small and intimate patient groups, interested staffs, and an individual approach to each patient. Methadone programs received massive federal support. By 1974 they had enrolled one hundred thirty-five thousand people, and the success rate had dropped. Nonaddicts were posing as addicts to get methadone to sell, large amounts of the drug were being diverted to illegal use by dishonest staff members or were unaccounted for, and—most serious—young drug users who were not true addicts (because they used street-cut heroin that was not nearly as potent as they believed it to be) were being converted to true methadone addicts.

Even when young drug-charge defendants were innocent, if they did not have a good case to present to the court, lawyers urged them to plead guilty and throw themselves on the mercy of the court in order to be diverted to a methadone program, because to lawyers this seemed like a sensible, therapeutic approach to a medical problem. Thomas Bratter, a drug center consultant, says, "Methadone maintenance gained uncritical and immediate acceptance by physicians, politicians, and the public" because methadone permitted "the illusion of a solution." For a time, before methadone maintenance was confined to government-sponsored clinics, it could be carried on by private doctors, who could make large sums of money by processing patients through for their regular doles of methadone, and even after dispensing methadone was no longer the prerogative of private physicians, for a fee doctors kept addicts supplied with such drugs as Ascodeen, Biphetamine, Demerol, Desoxyn, Dexedrine, Dilaudid, Percodan, Preludine, Quaalude, Ritalin, Seconal, and Valium.[22]

In New York City, Mayor John Lindsay advocated a policy that denied heroin users welfare benefits if they would not voluntarily enter methadone programs. No one knows how many true methadone addicts were created in the process. In Georgia, Governor Jimmy Carter promoted methadone as a cost-effective method of mass treatment.

Eventually the methadone program passed out of its great favor and was replaced by a "multifaceted approach," but one of these facets continues to be the methadone clinic.

Chemotherapy is popular in all of medicine. One medical critic says that "polypharmacy" is a way of life in the United States and that it is not uncommon for a hospitalized medical patient to be receiving eight or nine drugs simultaneously.[23] (No one understands all the complicated intereffects of these drugs working on each other.) It is particularly popular in psychiatry, where it is sometimes combined with individual therapy. In state hospitals, community mental health centers, and as practiced by welfare doctors, it is often the sole therapy, and the only contact the doctor may have with the patient is to inquire if the dose of drugs needs regulating. Sometimes there is even less doctor-patient contact. A psychiatric technician or some other paraprofessional is the patient's therapist and transmits to the doctor suggestions for changes in medication.

Psychotropic drugs have become the drugs most prescribed by nonpsychiatric physicians. Doctors have always prescribed mood-altering drugs, and laudanum, a tincture of opium, was one of the most popular Victorian-era remedies. Barbiturates and bromides were popular remedies in the first half of this century. In 1932 amphetamines were introduced as nonprescription drugs when a Benzedrine inhaler was made available in drugstores, and in 1937 the American Medical Association approved oral Benzedrine as useful in the treatment of "certain depressive psychopathic conditions" and stated further that persons under the strict supervision of a physician could take amphetamines to secure "a sense of increased energy or capacity for work, or a feeling of exhilaration."[24] But the great increase in the dispensing of psychotropic medicines in the United States occurred after the introduction of chlorpromazine (Thorazine) in the early 1950s.

This was the first drug to effectively suppress psychotic thought, and its success led to the development of other phenothiazines and related antipsychotic drugs; minor tranquilizers such as Miltown, Librium, and Valium; amphetamines and Ritalin and other energizers; antidepressants; and lithium. In time most psychiatric problems came to be treated by family doctors with a combination of approximations of dynamic therapy and directive therapy plus chemotherapy. One former patient writes:

> I have seen doctors representing most of the major schools of thought in psychiatry. I've been alternately diagnosed as schizophrenic, asocial psychopath, passive/aggressive, sociopath, a character disorder (whatever that means), and others, ad nauseum. I mention the various clinical diagnoses only to point out that despite the obvious disparities in these judgments, the method of treatment was the same in virtually every case, with each doctor.
>   I was drugged. This, then, was my treatment: sedation . . .[25]

The drugs have great usefulness. Nothing is more frightening than psychotic symptoms, and anything that can banish the symptoms of a psychosis has value. Patients who fear they are going crazy or who know they are crazy—who are delusional, hallucinating, or overcome by irrational fears, or are obsessed with the idea that they are about to fly off the handle and do some injury—are grateful for drugs that can dissipate their symptoms and alter their moods. In many cases, using a drug to deal with a crisis will help a person regain his equilibrium and no more intensive kind of treatment is needed. But the penalties of drug use are many, and they include, besides side effects, dealing with a symptom rather than an underlying problem, not allowing normal feelings to be felt and expressed and worked through, and not allowing symptoms to serve as warnings and guides.

An article on Valium (diazepam) in the *New York Times Magazine* has the title "Valiumania" and is headlined "Americans are spending almost half a billion dollars a year on a drug to relieve their anxiety —a fact that is in itself considerable cause for anxiety."[26] As many as 20 percent of medical (not psychiatric) hospital patients are receiving a psychotropic drug at any one time, and more than 20 percent of all adult Americans not confined to institutions have at least one prescription for a psychotropic drug written for them in the course of a year.[27] In 1976 in the United States doctors wrote 128 million prescriptions for hypnotic-sedatives (the barbiturates and Valium, Librium, and similar drugs). Hypnotics (sleeping pills prescribed under such names as Dalmane, Doriden, Luminal, Noctec, Placidyl, Quaalude, and Valmid) accounted for 27 million of these prescriptions, representing approximately 1 billion pills. The sedative-hypnotics were involved in 5000 confirmed drug-related deaths[28] and an unknown, but presumably much larger, number of nonconfirmed drug-related deaths. That same year the British National Health Service issued more than 75 million prescriptions for tranquilizers and antidepressants in Great Britain, an average of about 1.5 prescriptions for each man, woman, and child.[29]

Drug therapy has become the main psychiatric treatment method. The two commissions given the responsibility of recommending the future course for American psychiatry, the Joint Commission on Mental Illness and Health in 1961 and President Carter's commission in 1978, wanted more psychiatric treatment carried on by general practitioners and family doctors, and more psychiatric inpatients treated in general hospitals rather than specialized psychiatric hospitals. These doctors and hospitals rely almost exclusively on a drug approach. Many psychiatrists use drugs for most of their patients. State mental hospitals, which early in the phenothiazine era withheld drugs because of the cost, now rely on them heavily, and a frequent complaint is that patients are kept in a "chemical straitjacket," that they are overdrugged and kept in a "zombielike" condition.

The use of antipsychotic drugs revolutionized the state mental hospital system. Formerly more than half of all hospital beds were occupied by the chronically mentally ill. Now the huge state hospitals that once held ten thousand or twelve thousand patients have unused buildings and boarded-up sections, and their populations have often been reduced to 3000 patients or fewer. The wild, noisy, dangerous hospital ward has become orderly and subdued.

A study of drug therapy in four Missouri state hospitals showed that 93 percent of the patients were receiving drugs. About two-thirds of these patients were on only one drug (an antipsychotic, antianxiety, or antidepressant agent), but slightly more than one-third were on combinations of antipsychotic and antianxiety, antipsychotic and antidepressant, antianxiety and antidepressant, two antipsychotic plus an antianxiety, or two antipsychotic plus an antidepressant.[30]

The case history of a mildly retarded hyperkinetic girl shows that she was given large doses of Ritalin starting when she was nine and was treated starting at age eighteen, when she became psychotic, with Thorazine, Mellaril, Navane, Stelazine, Prolixin, Haldol, Trilafon, lithium, and Moban, as well as hypnotics for sleep and anti-Parkinsonism drugs to combat tranquilizer side effects. (She also received two courses of electroshock, for a total of thirty treatments.) Some of the adverse effects of medication, which led to the substitution of another drug, were incontinence, severe tremors, muscle spasms, motor restlessness, flailing limbs, muscle rigidity, insomnia, and vomiting. Whether her eventual recovery was due to the last drug tried, as her psychiatrist believes, or to other factors will never be know.[31]

Psychiatrists often prescribe drugs in doses far in excess of the pharmaceutical company's recommended maximum, and although this often has a therapeutic justification, it sometimes results from a refusal of the patient to live up to the psychiatrist's expectations or to capitulate to his demands.[32]

Drugs have been used as a blanket kind of approach in institutions for the mentally retarded. The number of retarded people on drugs has been estimated at 60 or 65 percent of the 200,000 who are institutionalized. In a study in Ontario, Canada, 58 percent of 2200 retarded in five institutions were receiving drug therapy, and the evaluators believed that only one-third of these were receiving sensible amounts. The other two-thirds were undermedicated, overmedicated, or unnecessarily medicated. Drug therapy was used to prevent convulsions, but it was also used for hyperactivity, excitability, aggressivity, "self-abuse," and "various psychosocial problems."[33]

A huge number of elderly patients in nursing homes are kept in a drugged state to keep them more manageable. The drugs used (very frequently Valium) cause loss of interest, disorientation, and confusion. Drugging may lead to a lack of desire to eat, and patients may slip into somnolence on their way to death. There is the opportunity for many drug interactions because the average institutionalized older person receives 6.1 drugs at any one time,[34] and most patients receive from 4 to 7. Wendell Lipscomb has written about what he calls the "spaced-out grandma syndrome": "What has happened is that a woman, usually in her 70s, has been overtreated for multiple conditions—arthritis, hypertension, periodic headaches, occasional sleeplessness, and mood swings. Each complaint is dealt with on a pragmatic basis of one symptom, one drug. Somehow, the total effect of the therapeutic cocktail is never considered."[35] The 5 percent of the elderly population who are in nursing homes are particularly the victims of overmedication. They are sedated for eccentricity, nonconformity, and irascibility. They are sedated because the staff finds them crotchety, time-consuming, or disrupting.[36] Many of them suffer from adverse and paradoxical drug reactions that are never diagnosed, and the peculiar behavior of the patient is seen as part of the aging or disease process and not recognized as a drug side effect.[37]

The most rapidly growing innovative approach in psychopharmacology is the use of long acting injectable drugs that provide for maximum control of the patient and his symptoms with minimum contact by the therapist or treatment administrator. The ultimate in impersonal and controlling treatment that can be given to large numbers of patients without any emphasis on the patient as an individual is the Prolixin clinic.

Injectable fluphenazine, marketed by Squibb Pharmaceutical Company as Prolixin Decanoate, is a long-acting injectable drug that is in the phenothiazine family and is effective in the control of psychotic symptoms. Patients whose therapy is periodic drug injections, and little or nothing more, are told to report to the Prolixin clinic at intervals of two weeks (or longer—up to six weeks or three months, if they are older or if they react more to the injection than the average patient). The proprietors of the clinic, like the proprietors of dialysis clinics and other entrepreneurial medical facilities, process large numbers of patients on a "piecework basis" and make large sums of money, almost all of it from Medicare, Medicaid, and third-party payment plans. Prolixin clinics represent an ideal way to do piecework psychiatry. The patients who are processed through the clinic do not pay for the treatment and they are unaware of the cost of their treatment or the large sums of money the clinic proprietor is making. They do not demand much in the way of care or service. The paying agent, the third-party payer, is represented by a company or a government bureaucrat who is primarily interested in seeing that patients receive the kind of care in the clinic that has a low cost per contact and the shortest possible duration, and is much less interested in the quality of psychiatric care the patients are receiving. The paying agent may in fact have little concept of good patient care.

The use of Prolixin, whether by an individual doctor, hospital, community mental health center, or specialized Prolixin clinic, is an effective way to keep psychotic symptoms controlled in patients who might neglect to take their medication. Psychiatric patients often do not take their drugs; some are irresponsible, others do not like the effects of the drugs, and some even miss the "highs" and the good feelings that accompanied their psychotic states,[38] (though most psychotic states are not accompanied by good feelings). On the other hand, there are patients who do not need drugs or for whom drug therapy is harmful rather than helpful. The Prolixin approach sweeps all these patients up and subjects them to mass treatment.

Because the amount of money allotted for state hospital treatment is progressively being reduced, economy is increasingly an important motive for the use of injectables. A small cadre of psychiatrists, nurses, and psychiatric technicians can take care of large numbers of outpatients who are maintained on Prolixin. Another advantage is that the staff can be sure that the patient has taken the drug and not flushed it down the toilet, the fate of so much psychotropic medication. (About half of all oral medicines prescribed are somehow discarded.) One advocate says that use of the drug "makes it possible to avoid depending on untrained boarding-home operators, who are unsophisticated in the techniques of patient compliance, to see that the patients take their drugs." Many patients who have not responded to other medication or to the same medicine taken orally rather than by injection have "dramatic recoveries" on the injection program, and this is explained on the ground that they had not been taking their prescribed medication.[39]

There are some disadvantages to this drug program, many of them common to all drug programs, but particularly troublesome is the fact that the drug stays in the system for long periods of time and its effects are not readily reversible. The most serious disadvantage is that some patients on phenothiazines (all phenothiazines, not merely Prolixin) develop tardive dyskinesia, a syndrome of severe gross muscular spasms. (Tardive dyskinesia is described as "a neurological syndrome characterized by slow, rhythmic, involuntary movements of the tongue, facial and limb muscles resulting in chewing motions, grimacing, cheek-puffing, lip-smacking, lip-pursing and, at times, protrusions and retractions of the tongue. In more severe forms there also may be extensions and contractions of the fingers or toes and chorea-like movements of the arms, legs and trunk."[40] It is sometimes accompanied by salivation and drooling.) Millions of patients have been treated with phenothiazines. An estimated 20 percent of those treated with large doses for long periods of time have developed tardive dyskinesia. Unless it is detected early, it is usually not reversible, and will persist for life. Some patients find their symptoms worsen when their medication is discontinued.

Tardive dyskinesia is only one of four major neurological side effects of phenothiazines. The Parkinsonism syndrome consists of symptoms like those of Parkinson's disease—a masklike face, tremor at rest, rigidity, shuffling gait, and slowness in movements. Forty to 60 percent of patients who are on Prolixin or other phenothiazines for long periods of time develop parkinsonian symptoms, and these are combatted by anti-Parkinsonism drugs such as Artane and Cogentin, which relieve the symptoms in most cases. Cogentin and other anti-Parkinsonism drugs have their own side effects, considered minor, but experienced by as many as half the patients who take them. They include dryness of the mouth, blurring of vision, mild nausea, dizziness, and nervousness. The anti-Parkinsonism drugs reduce the plasma levels of phenothiazines, so larger doses of phenothiazines are often required. Other side effects are akathisia, a restless condition in which a patient has a great urge to move about, and akinesia, a feeling of weakness and muscle fatigue. These are usually responsive to the anti-Parkinsonism drugs. Then there are other side effects such as rashes, jaundice, hypertension, and loss of sex drive.

Side effects of depot (long-acting) fluphenazines probably occur much more frequently than psychiatrists generally recognize. A recent study of outpatients on depot injections showed that 45 percent had evidence of Parkinsonism (although they were also on anti-Parkinsonism drugs), 8 percent had tardive dyskinesia, and 21 percent suffered from motor restlessness.[41]

With all these disadvantages, the advantages of Prolixin seem sufficient to constantly expand its use. It enables patients to remain out of the hospital who would have in-and-out-of-hospital careers or would need permanent hospitalization. It is cheap and impersonal, and it does not need much investment of professional skills.

There has been little consideration of the civil-libertarian aspects of Prolixin treatment. It is easy for a judge, when a patient repeatedly needs rehospitalization to control his symptoms, to "commit" the patient to outpatient therapy at a community mental health center or Prolixin clinic instead of to traditional inpatient treatment, and patients are ordered into Prolixin treatment even though they do not meet the dangerousness criterion for commitability. Patients are maintained on Prolixin long after the need for medication is over. The most comprehensive article on patient autonomy and Prolixin was written not by a psychiatrist but by a lawyer, Thomas Zander, who has asked whether Prolixin represents Big Brother by injection.[42] Zander cites two recent cases, both in Minnesota county courts of inferior jurisdiction, that have come to different conclusions. In *Re Cleo F. Lundquist,* the Ramsey County Probate Court found that Prolixin was an intrusive form of treatment with significant adverse effects and unknown long-term effects, and that it could be refused by a patient who understood she might be held in the hospital for a longer period of time if she were unmedicated.[43] In another case, the Hennepin County Probate Court ruled that since "no claim or information has come to this Court's attention that would identify or characterize Prolixin as being unusual, painful, or a hazardous substance or that its contemplated manner of use is experimental or punitive in nature," it would not interfere with the decision of doctors to use it. The court compared it with penicillin.[44]

The Prolixin clinics and the use of Prolixin in the community care system constitute a chief example of one treatment method applied indiscriminately to great numbers of patients. Squibb, in its advertising campaign, emphasizes that the use of Prolixin saves "time, money, and people."[45] Since most of the funds for Prolixin programs come from the government, and since it is primarily concerned with cost-efficiency and has little concept of a psychiatric approach that is based on a long, slow development of a therapist-patient relationship, the Prolixin approach is certain to grow.

Chemotherapy programs involving many psychotropic drugs, including Prolixin, have been extended to many nonmedical situations. They are used in the juvenile-justice system in correctional homes, reformatories, detention centers, and youth camps. They are used in prisons, and they are used in nursing homes, not for any medical indication, but merely to create a quiet atmosphere. Much of this use of chemotherapy is only remotely, if at all, under the supervision of a physician.

Yolande Bourgeois Rogers has said that forced drugging is "a widespread phenomenon affecting juvenile-detention centers and training schools, and is utilized invariably as a form of management control. A child displaying behavior which does not conform to the norm may often be subjected to forced drugging." Unqualified medical staff and nonmedical personnel sometimes dispense and administer drugs, although this is a violation of the Controlled Substances Act. Among the most used drugs are Valium, Mellaril, and Thorazine.[46] In a case against the Texas Youth Council, the authority that is in charge of incarcerated juveniles in that state, a federal court found on the basis of factual testimony that Thorazine and other behavior-altering drugs were often prescribed for juveniles, including those who had not been diagnosed as psychotic and those who had a history of previous drug abuse, "as a substitute for a more appropriate form of treatment."[47] In the fall of 1972, about half the "students" at one institution were on drugs.

Prisoners often complain that they are forcibly sedated or tranquilized, and the policy of some prisons seems to be to keep many members of the population quiet through tranquilization. A government report on the use of pain medication, tranquilizers, and mood elevators for female prisoners showed that these were given "to a large proportion of inmates." The highest rate was at the San Francisco County Jail, where 98 percent of the women inmates received such drugs. Many other institutions had a more than 50 percent rate. The study (conducted at a cost of almost three hundred thousand dollars), which investigated the conditions under which women prisoners were held, said that the "medical staff" of most of the prisons and jails surveyed reported that they frequently dispensed Librium, Valium, Triavil, Elavil, Stelazine, and Mellaril.[48] No comparable study has been done on male prisoners.

One prison physician reports that when he took over his job at a men's prison "the yard was awash in pills." All complaints of prisoners had been dealt with by dispensing tranquilizers and sedatives, particularly Thorazine. Prison health professionals know that many euphoriant drugs circulate illegally and are used as prison currency. Barbiturates, Valium, Librium, Serax, and of course narcotics are doled out reluctantly, even when a physician sees medical indications for prescribing them. (Illegal drugs, including marijuana, have such a degree of acceptance in some prisons that the authorities do not crack down on the traffic for fear of a riot.)[50]

Authorities are much more ready to dispense Thorazine and Prolixin. In normal dosages on psychotic or overwrought people they curb aggression and anxiety; in large doses and on nonpsychotic people they cause lethargy and depression and often produce such side effects as painful cramps and racing thoughts. Prisoners claim they are used as punishment and to tone down prison leaders; administrators say these drugs are "more effective and humane" than "manhandling or shackles."[51] A former California prison system inmate says, "If you speak out, say things they don't like, if you're a leader, you know—it's an unspoken threat: they'll put you on Prolixin." Another prisoner has said, "They use Prolixin more for punitive action than for medical purposes. Someone expressing anger toward the system, or anyone in it, is viewed as expressing bad attitudes and is labeled 'incorrigible.' " A California inmate who received three Prolixin injections at two week intervals while he was in the "hole," and had "lockjaw," leg cramps, restlessness, racing thoughts, and depression as side effects, says that 200 men in his prison were given Prolixin.[52]

These are some of the ways that mind-altering drugs have evolved from a medical treatment method into a mass method of behavior control.

The idea that psychotropic drugs are "too good" to be used only on the mentally ill, that they should have a place in improving the performance of people without psychiatric problems, has a seductive appeal. One of those who has advocated the use of psychotropic drugs for other aspects of personality not connected with the concept of mental illness is Arnold Mandell, cochairman of the Department of Psychiatry and distinguished professor of psychiatry, neurosciences, physiology, and pharmacology at the University of California at San Diego's School of Medicine. Mandell believes that in the medicine of the future drugs will be used for many purposes of personality engineering in people with no psychiatric "diseases," and he believes that the young psychiatric resident, "the new resident who went through the drug era of the 1960s," is already attuned to this approach and finds it hard to understand why an older generation of psychiatrists must continue to do "a complex dance of ritual obeisance" to the traditional system of diagnosing mental illness before trying to alter a person through drugs. In 1972 he was asked by Eugene Klein, the owner of the San Diego Chargers, to become the psychiatrist for the football team. He was to hang around the players, try to gauge their moods, and advise the coaching staff how to deal with them.[53] Between August 2 and November 6, 1973, Mandell wrote prescriptions for Desoxyn and other amphetamines for eleven football players. He was later investigated by the California State Board of Medical Quality Assurance and charged with overprescribing, prescribing dangerous drugs without medical indication, and gross negligence or incompetence. His defense was that the players were addicted to amphetamines and he was trying to wean them to a drug-free existence. At his hearing, two experts for the prosecution testified that his prescriptions were clearly excessive for the purpose. Psychiatric experts for his defense testified that Mandell had developed a thoughtful and careful program of drug-weaning, that other psychiatrists would have done exactly as Mandell did, and that it was proper to write prescriptions for a whole season's requirements at one time so that when he and the players related to each other they would be "interacting on problems and not on drugs."[54]

Mandell was found guilty of overprescribing but not of the other charges. He was placed on five years' probation and required to surrender his federal permit to prescribe narcotics and controlled substances. More than 100 psychiatrists and other doctors have joined the Concerned Health Professionals for Mandell, claiming that Mandell had treated without charge players who had been previously addicted and that "none of his patients was harmed." The pro-Mandell group is raising funds to support his appeal to the California Supreme Court. Among the psychiatrists who support Mandell is Bertram Brown, deputy director of the Department of Health, Education, and Welfare, who, as head of the National Institute of Mental Health, had been a leader in the community mental health center movement. Among supporting nonpsychiatrist doctors is Thomas Bryant, who was director of President's Carter's Commission on Mental Health.[55] The idea that there should be any control on how psychiatrists and other physicians prescribe and dispense has roused the psychiatric establishment to get solidly behind Mandell, who in turn is solidly behind the concept of using drugs to alter personality and behavior.

*   *   *

There are mass approaches to behavior change and behavior control that do not employ drugs, and there are also mass methods that combine drug and nondrug approaches. Behavioral scientists are working on schemes to use computers, biofeedback equipment, programmed instruction, audio cassette courses, and other technologies capable of mass application to improve mental well-being or to inculcate constructive social attitudes. The constant effort is to reduce the amount of skilled personal input and to increase the amount of evaluation and treatment that can be done by either semiprofessionals with less training, or by nonprofessionals, or by machines. Biofeedback relaxation training uses monitoring devices that tell the patient how he is responding, theoretically enabling him to become acquainted with what a state of relaxation feels like.

Biofeedback now makes normally unavailable information available to the patient, who can correlate his subjective feelings with blood pressure, muscle tension, galvanic skin response, or alpha brain waves. The physiologic responses can be communicated to the subject visually or by an auditory display. The subject is attempting to get in touch with himself, and the primary therapist is the machine. The person who monitors the machine and instructs the subject in its use is only secondarily important and is functioning as a technician rather than as a therapist. Ari Kiev has said that biofeedback is only an electronic version of the familiar behavioral therapy that goes back to Pavlov and classical conditioning, to the animal-training laboratories of Edward Thorndike,[56] who promulgated the dictum that everything that exists exists in some degree and can be measured.[57] This kind of mechanistic approach may or may not be more scientific than the dynamic psychotherapy that depends on Freudian or other formulations having to do with unconscious functioning, but it certainly is much more easily applied.

The two powerful forms of mass behavior modification, conditioning and chemotherapy, can be used together. A former inmate at the State Prison of Southern Michigan who was assigned to its Psychiatric Clinic Behavior Modification Program, has described the life of inmate-patients. During an evaluation period they are observed by nurses and mental health technicians and other specialists, who frequently see them as hostile and arrogant and who pinpoint these attitudes as targets for change. Attitudes, friendships and associations, response to stress, and other characteristics are charted. The inmate-patients are psychologically tested, and goals for change are set. The inmate-patients are assigned to work in the kitchen, and once they show they can work cheerfully there, they are assigned to school or to work as inmate-nurses.

Inmate-patients must work their way up from a C-track status to an A-track status. Reinforcing rewards include access to radios and reading materials, and punishments include confinement to a cell, failure to be promoted to the next track, or a delayed parole. To make the inmate-patients more amenable to the behavior modification program, Thorazine and other drugs are ordered. If they do not voluntarily take the drugs, inmate-patients are labeled as noncooperative and thus subject to more behavior modification. The drugs facilitate the modification program; the modification program pushes the use of the drugs.

The use of behavior-change methods for the largest possible number of people at the least possible cost is achieved when simple methods of behavior modification are entrusted to the least skilled of personnel. Correctional system employees may have estimable qualities —many of them are brave and resourceful, they do not panic in emergencies, and they deserve praise for working at underpaid jobs—but they usually are not psychologically minded. They can, however, be trained to be "behavioral technicians." This qualifies as "continuing education for line members of the staff" and thus opens the way for them to promotions and pay raises. In one program in Alabama, forty correctional officers were trained as behavioral technicians in a research program funded by the Manpower Administration of the United States Department of Labor. The range of their educational levels was from the seventh to the eleventh grade. To the satisfaction of the research team, the officers proved they could "master the basic principles of behavior modification" and could apply them to "real-life situations to influence inmate behavior." "It is clear," say the researchers, "that the bulk of the officers were capable of serving as behavioral technicians."[58] The training methods for correctional officers were incorporated into a "17-booklet Self-Instructional Training Package" so that prison workers throughout the United States could become proficient in behavior modification.

In these ways—by using drugs and behavior modification, by concentrating on symptoms and overt behavior, and by employing "therapists" who have less training—the power of psychiatry can be extended to more and more subjects.

*   *   *

Some psychiatrists have the wish for psychiatry to escape from the confines of use as a therapy into a larger public role. For these social psychiatrists the best use of psychiatry, the most efficient use, the way in which the most change will be achieved for the most patients at the least cost per patient, is not to work with the problems of individuals who identify themselves as patients but to work with the problems the social psychiatrist identifies in society. A former president of the American Psychiatric Association has said, "As I see it, our professional borders are virtually unlimited."[59]

Not all psychiatrists see themselves as social engineers and social architects. One of them has criticized "the psychiatrists' and psychologists' current popular beliefs that they are experts in anything from endocrinology to ecology, thus embracing a variety of exacting scientific disciplines about which they actually know very little." He says, "This dangerous game of 'no limits' has led psychiatrists and psychologists away from the sheer hard work of helping the mentally ill, and has allowed them the license to become politically active, experts on architecture, consultants to astronauts, students of porpoises, advisers on urban renewal and commentators, orators or authors on virtually anything."[60]

When psychiatrists speak out on social issues they are given the respect that is accorded to experts, but for many of the issues on which they have taken stands there are few psychiatric data, and only emotional bias supports their views. But many psychiatrists are intrigued by the game of no limits, and in recent years they have used their status to recommend changes in education, child rearing, child care, the law, international relations, the more effective waging of war, and the prevention of war. A psychoanalyst who is also a social scientist said at a recent conference that when dealing with such problems as child beating, psychiatrists must broaden their focus from the individual and the family and join with the social scientist in concern for the "society which is depriving children of the conditions which psychoanalysts know children need if they are to become healthy adults, and also depriving their mothers of the support the mothers need if they are to provide these conditions for their children." Psychoanalysts, he says, "have an obligation to try to ameliorate these adverse social conditions."[61] A psychologist writes that to deal with children in treatment, there must be major efforts to confront poverty and racism.[62] A sociologist declares that depression is largely a social phenomenon, caused by a particular life event in certain individuals who have been made vulnerable by social experiences.[63] Producing social change thus becomes the remedy for the depressed individual.

The social psychiatrist, if he is an activist, believes that he must involve himself in all phases of politics, from the local level to the highest level of international diplomacy. One proposal is that the psychiatrist apply his expertise to improving his community by dealing with such "issues" in local government as openness and authenticity, trust, shared influence and participation, development of people, confrontation, interpersonal competency, and change and renewal.[64]

Leading psychiatrists push for more psychiatric power in the social sphere. James Comer, in an editorial in the *American Journal of Psychiatry*, says, "As students of the effects of social and inner forces on human behavior, we are uniquely qualified to help social policymakers devise ways to make our science and technology work better for us . . ."[65]

In his presidential address to the American Psychiatric Association in 1970, Raymond Waggoner noted that district branches had already taken positions in favor of abortion, and against racism, violence, alcoholism, and drug abuse. He said, "This kind of social interest must

368

spread throughout our membership because somehow we must bring about new and more successful social mutations."[66] When the APA took a position in favor of the Equal Rights Amendment in 1974, its president, John Speigel, described—quite possibly accurately—the arguments against ERA based on psychiatric and behavioral science opinion as "without foundation" and as "hogwash" and then went on to say that passage of the amendment "clearly . . . will vastly improve the mental health of about half of our population"[67]—although this could be criticized as equally without foundation. Jack Weinberg, in his 1978 presidential address, related with pride how he and the members of the APA's Committee on Psychiatry and Foreign Affairs had visited Egypt and Israel to deal with the psychological problems that were harming the relations of the two countries.

Psychiatrists have become involved in international politics as State Department advisors. William Davidson was hired by a division of the State Department, the Arms Control and Disarmament Agency, and served that agency for two years. He later became president of a new nongovernmental organization, the Institute for Psychiatry and Foreign Affairs. Davidson concluded that psychiatrists cannot give specific answers to specific international problems. He says, "People who have tried this have gone away badly bruised and disenheartened." Instead he advocates telling world leaders how to participate in a process of dispute settlement and reconciliation. "Our contribution is to present in simple and clean language the irrational aspects of human response so that [the comprehension of] these will become a consistent part of every major policy decision."

Because they deal with intrapsychic conflict and its resolution, Davidson sees psychiatrists as having a sound professional base for participation in international affairs, but he finds that international decisions are still being made by lawyers, the military, physicists, and economists "in the complete absence" of anyone who is a specialist in conscious and unconscious behavior. He says that psychiatrists must examine this resistance to include them in the international decision making.[68]

* * *

Many psychiatrists have been eager to assume the role of evaluating the competency of high government officials and candidates for office. As long ago as 1912, Morton Prince, physician and psychologist, described Theodore Roosevelt—to the horror of Sigmund Freud—in an article in the *New York Times Magazine* as distorting reality because of his intense desire to regain the presidency. Prince accused Roosevelt, among other things, of construing support for himself as the will of the "common man" and opposition as representing "the interests."[69] He depicted Roosevelt as suffering from egomania. Freud thought the article was "absolutely inadmissible, an infringement on privacy,"[70] but eighteen years later he was persuaded to coauthor a psychobiography depicting Woodrow Wilson's pathological motives.[71] (Freud did, however, require that the book remain unpublished until all the principal characters were dead.) Many psychiatrists and psychologists have become president watchers, evaluating the capabilities of incumbents and candidates.[72] There have been psychiatric profiles, written without any direct knowledge of the "patient."[73] Sometimes the profiles have been attacks, and sometimes they have supported candidates for office.[74]

The Group for the Advancement of Psychiatry is a nonofficial organization of about 300 "socially concerned" psychiatrists that puts out position statements planning the future directions of psychiatry. It includes in its membership many of the most prominent American psychiatrists. It operates on undemocratic principles, taking in members by invitation only, meeting behind closed doors, assembling reports, and making recommendations that are not made public until their final form, when it is too late for other opinions to be included. In spite of all this and although it has no official status, its recommendations are often accepted as representing psychiatry.

In its discussion of the mental health problems of leaders, the Group for the Advancement of Psychiatry has expressed regret that psychiatric services cannot be forced upon most government officials, as they can be on career State Department employees, who are required to be psychiatrically screened, and as they can be for the military.[75] It recommends that there be more psychiatric consultation with government agencies, that important officials during the course of their annual physical examinations should also have psychiatric checkups,[76] and that a panel of qualified psychiatrists designated by the American Psychiatric Association be made available to make psychiatric recommendations at any time that the question of the competency of the president of the United States or any other high government official arises.[77] This would be a program of systematic examination of leaders and prompt psychiatric treatment of the officeholder while still in the office.

The report concludes that psychiatric screening and evaluation of high officials cannot be applied to "VIPs at the highest levels" in the present state of the art and in view of current public opinion. "Psychiatrists," it says, "must realize that their opinions about competency,

370

reliability, and judgment are not always accepted by laymen or, for that matter, at times by other psychiatrists."[78]

But many psychiatrists have gone further than GAP and have suggested that all candidates for high elective office should be screened mandatorily. Today fewer psychiatrists are willing to express this view, because psychiatric expertise has been subjected to more questioning than in the 1950s and 1960s, when the most grandiose claims were made.

Ronald Fieve, an authority on depression, asks if we should require psychiatric testing for presidential candidates and other high officials. "This idea has been debated for some time. Many people agree with it, some laugh at it, some say it sounds fantastic; others say that there is simply no way to do it because it is impossible to be objective in a psychiatric examination. Who is to say what the disqualifications should be?" If we base our test on past psychiatric illness, Fieve says, we would have eliminated Lincoln; if we base it on an interview, we would be giving the subjective opinion of the psychiatrist too much weight; if we use Rorschach and other tests, we will be utilizing instruments that are criticized because they are not sufficiently reliable. Besides, he asks, who is to say what is "normal"? If the psychiatrist tested for normality, he would be dictating to the politician—"hardly a state of affairs anyone would relish . . . Probably the greatest argument against it is the strictly practical one that even among themselves psychiatrists cannot agree on their diagnoses or on which of their colleagues is qualified."[79]

Psychiatrists may disagree on which of their colleagues are qualified to screen candidates for public office, but few doubt that they themselves are. Occasionally some psychiatrists address themselves to the problems inherent in this concept of determining the competency of leaders, the most obvious of which is the determination of the qualifications to be a qualifier. Who is to evaluate the evaluators? The difficulties in implementing such an evaluation technique are numerous, but the attraction of having the authority to certify competency for public office remains bright. Psychiatrists have had a steady increase in the amount of power they exert and their ability to extend it over larger and larger segments of the population. Many psychiatrists would enjoy extending it to the point where they would rule our rulers.

The Psychiatrist Determines Values

PSYCHIATRISTS HAVE BEEN compared to priests, shamans, and gurus. In a society that is increasingly fragmented, depersonalized, and unimpressed by authority, the psychiatrist is respected as an ultimate authority, both on issues in which he has special competence and on those in which he has none. There are no normative values—definitions of rational and irrational, healthy and pathological functioning—that have not been profoundly altered by psychiatric theory and thought. There are no relationships—parent-child, husband-wife, teacher-student, person-group, group-society—that have not changed because of psychiatric teaching. There are no precedents and traditions that have not, at the least, been challenged by psychiatric thought, and many have been superseded. Just as psychiatrists have extended their coercive authority in the past two centuries and secured more and more power to control more and more people, they have also extended the authority that depends on voluntary acquiescence and have insinuated themselves into more and more minds to alter attitudes and change perspectives.

Changes resulting from psychiatric teaching and practice have occurred gradually over a period of 200 years. Often they have met with great opposition and reaction. Yet they have continued inexorably, although often not very visibly, and we have reached a point where we have become so accustomed to the new attitudes that have been propagated by psychiatry that we accept them as givens, see them as correct, and see the old standards they replaced as rooted in error. We no longer discount many of the preachings of psychiatry on the ground that the psychiatrist is biased or has his own value system. We accept psychiatric values as true and scientific, and by doing so we have given psychiatrists their greatest authority. Changed attitudes about masturbation may in the long run affect society more than the invention of the steam engine; changed perspectives on morality influence society more than changed laws (and also often lead to changed laws).

The psychiatrist exerts his greatest authority not from without but from within. In the same way that the church and totalitarian ideologies impose their concepts on developing minds and as a result hold their subjects in thrall for life, psychiatry, by affecting attitudes, and in particular by affecting child-rearing processes, has contributed to modern-day concepts and expectations that are vastly different from those of the prepsychiatric and pre-Freudian era. Psychiatry's advocacy of permissiveness, for example, has led to altered child rearing, which in turn has led to altered children.

Psychiatry does not deserve all the credit or blame for our new values. It is only one contributor to them. There is also the question of whether psychiatry and psychoanalysis have changed society, or if an evolving society has utilized psychiatric and psychoanalytic concepts to give "scientific" rationales and imprimaturs to innovations that were already in the making—whether a process of change in society has utilized psychiatry rather than having been caused by psychiatry. We do know that such phenomena as permissiveness, the freer expression of sexual feelings, new moral standards, a greater acceptance of those sexual expressions once referred to (if they were referred to at all) as perversions, the attributing of shortcomings and unhappiness to parental fault—these and many more new attitudes—have been advanced by psychiatry and have been accepted on its authority.

The world of the psychiatric era is very different from the prepsychiatric world. The first great changes were the related concepts that care and concern were owing to people who were irrational and that such people should be excused from the consequences of their irrational acts. Earlier generations had taunted mental patients, burned them and tortured them as witches and heretics. Later they had been allowed to rot in almshouses or wander the roads as itinerant beggars. Irrational thought was feared; there was no attempt to understand it.[1] Psychiatry taught respect for patients and their infirmities and the acceptance of mental illness not as an alien visitation but as one of the many presentations of man, something that could happen to anyone, something that deserved treatment and consideration because it was not consciously willed.

From its rise in the eighteenth century, modern psychiatry has been concerned with questions of responsibility. These questions had antedated the psychiatrist by hundreds of years and had already caused endless commentary and debate. There was an early legal literature on criminal responsibility, on the civil responsibility of a mentally disordered person who injures another and whether he must pay damages, and on the ability to conceive of the effect of one's contract. The Anglo-Saxon legal system has always believed in a doctrine of individual responsibility for actions performed, making exceptions for children, the mentally incompetent, and those who did not intend the consequences of their actions. Psychiatry widened the definition of the mentally incompetent and attributed more behavior disturbances to psychopathology. As Stephen Toulmin has said, "In the field of psychiatry, the central question about human conduct in general . . . remains what it has always been, namely, *the meaning of human autonomy.*"[2]

These changed concepts of responsibility became even more influential when Freud, at the beginning of the twentieth century, set forth as one part of his theory of unconscious functioning a concept of overdetermination: Is everything determined, and do we only have the illusion of free will? When we decide to forego some temptation, might it be not a matter of our will allowing us to make the decision, but of some complex concatenation of existing circumstances destined to lead to this result? Do we then credit our will because we enjoy or require the illusion of having some control? These are the kinds of philosophical questions that Freudian psychology raised but did not answer. Nevertheless, the concept of overdetermination—that symptoms or behavior resulted from the interaction of a number of specific causes, many of which were unconscious and not subject to the influence of reason—further eroded the underpinnings of the Anglo-Saxon concept of responsibility. A law professor has stated that the psychoanalytic concept of unconscious determination has destroyed the rational basis of the common law.[3]

Many psychiatrists both before and after Freud have wanted psychiatric concepts to supersede old legal concepts more completely than they have, and psychiatric definitions of criminality to prevail. Sometimes they have wanted to put psychiatrists in a quasi-judicial position in order to apply their value system to the law, to be the determiners of what is and is not criminal. Isaac Ray was a chief spokesman for the position that psychiatrists should have a larger role in defining criminal behavior. He believed that any criminal activity of a mentally disordered person was necessarily a product of his disease (or at the least that psychiatrists were the only decision makers able to link mental disease and an act that is the "symptom" of the disease) and that the law should allow a broader definition of criminal irresponsibility, with more authority given to the psychiatrist to make judicial decisions.

Many modern psychiatrists have gone much further and have wanted to conceptualize all criminals—not merely the mentally disordered who commit crimes but all who commit crimes—as victims of their psychopathology. Karl Menninger said in 1928 that "the time will come when stealing and murder will be thought of as a symptom, indicating the presence of a disease, a personality disease, if you will . . ."[4] Benjamin Karpman, in a classic statement of this extreme position, proposed in 1949 that we treat rather than penalize all criminal defendants, not only those who are mentally disordered, because the criminal is led into his behavior by irrational impulses over which he has no control, and we have no more reason to punish an individual for his crime than "to punish an individual for breathing through his mouth because of enlarged adenoids . . ."[5] In 1955 Karpman wrote that he would fight vigorously "for the recognition of the criminal as a very sick person, much sicker than either psychosis or neurosis . . ."[6]

Freud himself never satisfactorily reconciled his concept of determination or overdetermination with his idea that most people are ultimately responsible for what they do. In him we see the paradox of the strict moralist who expected high achievement from himself and those around him, yet formulated a doctrine that has been used to excuse everything.

Freud addressed himself to this paradox in one of his last major works, *Civilization and Its Discontents,*[7] in which he proposed that neurosis is the price we pay for giving up instinctual gratification in order to achieve a culture or a common good, and that our civilization would possibly not survive because the struggle between self-control and gratification causes "a state of affairs which the individual will be unable to tolerate."[8] But he did not, as Menninger and Karpman have, excuse the criminal action on that account.

Even a psychiatrist who is a strict determinist—much stricter than Freud—might find himself in a shaky position when asked to excuse a patient who is delinquent in paying his bill on the ground that the action is out of the patient's control. (Or the psychiatrist might explain his own decision to pursue all legal remedies to get payment for the bill as being equally predetermined.) Psychiatrists are caught in a bind. Their theory tells them that people are not responsible, but in order to treat patients they must expect patients to show some degree of responsibility, at least enough to conform to the requirements of the treatment situation. An expert on alcoholism says, not very logically, that "alcoholics are no more responsible for their disease than diabetics are responsible for theirs, but both should be held responsible for their treatment."[9] To be effective in treating alcoholics, then, it follows that the physician treating them must separate in his own mind the responsibility for having the disease—the alcoholic is absolved—and the responsibility for cooperating in therapy, where he is not absolved.

Freud apparently maintained his belief that events in the present stem causally, and by implication inevitably, from roots in the past. Through the concept of unconscious thoughts and impulses, Freud thought that there could be an explanation of acts that otherwise would be inexplicable. Yet Freud could not give up his belief in free will, and he never turned his intellectual powers to a real discussion of the apparent inconsistencies of his position. We do, however, have an intimation from a 1920 case history that Freud thought that by tracing backward we could see how events are determined, but that by evaluating factors in the present we cannot project how events will be determined in the future. Discussing a case of homosexuality in an eighteen-year-old girl, Freud considered "the forces which led the girl's libido from the normal Oedipus attitude into that of homosexuality, and of the psychical paths traversed in the process." He said that "most important in this respect was the impression made by the birth of her little brother . . ." He adds,

> . . . So long as we trace the development from its final outcome backwards, the chain of events appears continuous, and we feel we have gained an insight which is completely satisfactory or even exhaustive. But if we proceed the reverse way, if we start from the premises . . . and try to follow these up to the final result, then we no longer get the impression of an inevitable sequence of events which could not have been otherwise determined. We notice at once that there might have been another result, and that we might have been just as well able to understand and explain the latter . . . Even supposing that we have a complete knowledge of the aetiological facts that decide a given result, nevertheless what we know about them is only their quality, and not their relative strength . . .[10]

Freud pointed out that the disappointments this girl had received would not necessarily lead to her homosexuality; other girls with similar disappointments do not become homosexual. But then he shifted once again to discuss special factors in this girl, factors that had been present before her Oedipal disappointment, indicating possibly that in this case, at least, the outcome was predetermined.

Freud told his patients that they had to take responsibility for the imagery and the happenings in their dreams if they wished to understand themselves better.[11] And in apologizing to a lecture audience for repeating material he had used previously, he explained why each topic had begged for inclusion and said wryly, "As you see, when one starts making excuses it turns out in the end that it was all inevitable, all the work of destiny."[12]

The ambivalences and ambiguities of this crucial question were never resolved by Freud, and psychiatrists since Freud have not resolved them. There is a basic inconsistency between psychiatry's forgiveness of criminal responsibility and its expectation of therapeutic responsibility. In spite of the lack of logic in the psychiatric position, psychiatrists popularized the positions that deviant acts were not the fault of the individual but were at least to some degree predetermined, that deviant acts were symptoms of disease and should be treated, and that they deserved understanding instead of punishment. From such concepts developed a whole ideology of a rehabilitative rather than a punitive approach to punishment. Eventually it was extended to the concept of the therapeutic state, the hoped-for or feared future in which government treats all problems of deviancy or differentness as therapeutically curable.

The therapeutic approach carries threats to liberty. In an article titled "The Humanitarian Theory of Punishment," C. S. Lewis has written that this theory replaced the traditional concept of procedurally protected, time-limited punishment with the concept of understanding and therapy for an indeterminate period, a period, as long as is necessary to secure a "cure." Lewis says that although the humanitarian theory appears to some to be mild and merciful, the "humanity" that is claimed "is a dangerous illusion and disguises the idea of cruelty and injustice without end."[13]

The psychodynamic explanation of criminal behavior allows the behavioral scientist to extend his authority to include the whole field of criminology and criminal reform, but it does much more. It changes traditional concepts of good and evil, guilt and innocence, right and wrong, responsibility and freedom from responsibility. It states not that "the devil made me do it" but, a more modern approach to disclaiming responsibility, that "my id made me do it" or "my weak ego could not keep me from doing it," and I am therefore unanswerable for any harm I have done.

A criminologist has said that "wicked people exist" and "nothing avails except to set them apart from innocent people." When this statement was repeated to Karl Menninger, he replied, "Who's wicked? *I'm* wicked, *you're* wicked, *he's* wicked. I'm utterly opposed to such a view, as a psychiatrist, as a scientist, and as a Christian—

ethically, scientifically, morally. Wickedness describes conduct, not people . . . I don't believe in such a thing as the 'criminal mind.' Everyone's mind is 'criminal'; we're all *capable* of criminal fantasies and thoughts . . ."[14] Menninger apparently believes, as did Madame de Staël, that to understand all is to forgive all. But when Freudian theory developed and in the interest of change put its emphasis on understanding, it did not contemplate that the private nonjudgmental understanding that prevailed in the therapeutic context would be applied judicially and result in a new system of legal values. The psychoanalyst attempted to be nonjudgmental, but he did not expect society also to suspend judgment.

We cannot dispense with psychodynamic formulations. They enable us to understand actions that otherwise would be beyond comprehension and to feel empathy toward people from whom, without this understanding, we would be alienated. They give us a therapeutic approach so that, at least in some cases, we can work toward rehabilitation and change. Ever since the rise of modern psychiatry we have had to consider the criminal as a troubled person as well as, or instead of, a malign person. But if we cannot get along without these new concepts, we also cannot live with them. They cause us to give up traditional concepts of retribution, the dichotomy of the upright citizens and evil doers, and deal instead in terms of therapy, in terms of the common drives and instincts and impulses which, overtly expressed or not, underlie all human behavior. They produce the blurring that comes when absolute concepts of such distinct phenomena as good and evil are first seen to have some resemblance to each other and later are merged into one image.

If psychiatry and psychoanalysis have led to a changed relationship between the individual and the legal system, it has led to much greater changes in the more personal areas of how an individual feels about himself and his society. Here Freudian psychoanalytic formulations, the "Freudian revolution," have been major influences in the alteration of values.

Freudian psychology promoted such new concepts as infantile sexuality, the ubiquity of bisexuality and perversity, the supremacy of the libido over other drives, the legitimacy of neuroticism, and the necessity for the individual to be primarily concerned with himself and his own inner perceptions and only secondarily with others. The "Freudian Left"—to use the phrase of Paul Robinson[15]—other neo-Freudians, and deviant Freudians, as well as modern anti-Freudian psychiatrict theorists, have carried the war on established values further. They have advocated new ways of thinking about the self and new ways of relating to others, and they have used psychiatric authority to promote personal and social change. Perhaps the start of the trend that led to this change can be found in Freud's attitude on masturbation, the expression of sexuality, and perversions in his "Dream Book" and his *Three Essays on the Theory of Sexuality.*[16]

Freud postulated a pleasure principle that demands that tensions be reduced or eliminated, that wishes be satisfied. The child and the primitive live by the pleasure principle, unable to delay gratification, seeking instant discharge of tensions. The pleasure principle coexists with the reality principle, which tells the older child or the adult that a greater or a more solid pleasure can be secured in the future by foregoing present gratification. *The Glossary of Psychoanalytic Terms and Concepts* of the American Psychoanalytic Association gives as an example, "when a man or woman foregoes the pleasure of a sexual affair in the interest of good marital relations."[17]

According to Freudian theory, the roots of the impulses that demand pleasure principle gratification are largely in the unconscious, whereas the reality principle is accessible to, and dominated by, reason. Freud tried to live by the reality principle—he was an earnest student, impatiently endured a lengthy engagement, gave up present pleasure to work for future accomplishment and fame—but he had the greatest sympathy for those who could not tolerate frustrations and who impulsively settled for present pleasure. We have noted that he foresaw a continuing war in all mankind between the pleasure and the reality principles and felt very possibly that the pleasure principle would prevail in the end, leading to a less structured society with a lower level of cultural achievement.

This simple concept of pleasure principle versus reality principle removed much of the stigma for those who could not conform to the demands of society. What once would have been seen as a lack of moral fiber or judged as evil was now seen as an unfortunate but natural and understandable failure to conform to the demands of adulthood, something to be deplored, perhaps, but not to be condemned. Indeed, those who tried to live too much by the reality principle, according to the early Freud, and did not have enough discharge of their tensions—in particular did not have sufficient sexual discharge—as a result built up an anxiety level that could cause neurosis. So one aspect of the reality principle was to live at least in part by the pleasure principle.

Perversions, which were seen by Freud as the unrestrained expression of the same conflicted drives and impulses that when inhibited cause neurotic symptoms, were to be resolved in the psychoanalytic process as the conflicts that they embodied were worked through. In this sense psychoanalysis was not permissive, for it required analyst and analysand to focus on every deviancy, every irrationality, and to tease out their causes and attempt to eliminate them.

But psychoanalysis was also realistic, and it conceded that in many cases these deviancies were so rooted in fixations or regressions, were so inaccessible to the curative aspect of analysis, that they would not be altered and would remain a part of the individual's repertory of behavior. Again Freud has a double message. On the one hand, analysis can cure these deviancies; the reality principle can gain control. As he put it, "Where id was, there ego shall be."[18] That is the goal of analysis, that is what it strives for. If analytic candidates cannot substantially attain this, they cannot qualify according to the selection procedure that makes a successful training analysis a requisite to be an analyst. Any successful analysis, whether training analysis or personal analysis, must require a fierce intrapsychic struggle, with the forces of regression and immaturity pitted against the forces of development and reason. On the other hand, many people cannot work through their conflicts and reach the necessary degree of control and maturity, and these people should be helped to adapt to their fates. In particular they should, through understanding of the genesis of their deviance, be helped to live with less anxiety and guilt.

In 1928, *Scientific American,* in recommending a new series of pamphlets on sex published by the National Committee for Mental Hygiene, asked a question that had been raised by the Freudian-influenced psychology and anthropology: "What are the 'average' sex practices of the human race? We had thought we knew, yet it appears we did not. We have often mistaken general impressions and traditions for fact. We must liquidate our present beliefs and remold them on a more reasonable basis. In short, if what we have thought to be abnormal in sex life now turns out to have been more the rule, must we now revise the very criterion of what actually constitutes an average normal sex life?"[19]

Although Freud himself and classical psychoanalysts preserved the distinction between normal and deviant behavior (and set up their mature selves or their ego ideals as examples of normality), many psychoanalysts have adopted a permissive view toward what was formerly considered deviancy and have accepted a wide range of normal behavior. Judd Marmor, with Robert Spitzer the chief promoter of the delisting of homosexuality as a mental disease or disorder, has said that "since value systems are always in the process of evolution and change, we must be prepared to face the possibility that some patterns of sexual behavior currently considered deviant may not always be so regarded."[20]

Most followers of Freud and those who have been influenced by Freudian theory, which includes almost everyone, have relied on this and other aspects of Freudian theory to promote a liberalization of attitudes on masturbation, other sexual expression, and sexual deviations. Before Freud, a repressive attitude promoting inhibition prevailed. Post-Freudians have seen a less repressed and less guilt-ridden sexuality as representing enlightenment and as being in the interest of mental growth and mental health. Freud saw sexual inhibitions as promoting tension, anxiety, and neurosis, and the "new psychology" was hailed in some quarters as an expression of freedom, self-actualization, and self-realization. There lies, certainly, part of the Freudian message. Freud did much to reduce guilt. But Freud was also puritanical and pessimistic, seeing id impulses as in some respects the equivalent of the theological concept of original sin, seeing an eternal war that must be waged against impulsive expressions of sexuality, and realizing that losses as well as gains are incurred with uninhibited expression of sexuality.

Freud here has another of his mixed messages. He wants to minimize guilt, he wishes parents to be less repressive toward their children, but he still sets a goal for adults in society in their sexual relations —showing mutuality, gaining pleasure from giving pleasure—that relies on control and the delay of gratification. There is still another complication here: The changed sexual attitudes favored by Freudians are not self-contained, for changed sexual attitudes influence more than the sexual sphere. Repressed children may grow up to be tense and unfulfilled but capable of high achievement, industrious, and sober. Unrepressed children may grow up carefree, volatile, interested in the moment rather than the long term, and capable of being, but often not caring to be, high achievers. Sexual mores and practices affect personality development and character. The characteristics of cultures as different as Switzerland and Tahiti may be related to attitudes about masturbation and expressions of early sexuality.

Freud's followers saw freedom from sexual guilt and sexual repression as the avenues to happiness and mental health. They did not see that they were upsetting a dynamic that had caused great pressure and much pain but also had had an important role in shaping society in nonsexual areas. From our attitudes toward sex stem our attitudes toward other aspects of living—self-control, fidelity, mutuality, thrift, expressions of aggression, desire for family, attitude toward children, and many more. (The reverse is equally true: Our attitudes toward other aspects of living shape our attitudes toward sexuality.)

Freud defined perversions as sexual activities that extend in an anatomical sense beyond the regions of the body that are designed for sexual union, or the lingering over the intermediate relations to the sexual object that should be traversed rapidly on the path toward the final sexual aim. When these displaced and preparatory activities become the desired sexual outlet, they are perversions. But if they merely become a component part of the sexual activity and the main purpose of the sexual activity is genital intercourse, then these are not perversions but instead are foreplay.[21] Here again Freud conveyed a mixed message. He appeared to give his blessing to activities that had previously been considered perverse, as long as they are not an end in themselves, but he condemned the same activities when they are an end in themselves. Similarly, bisexuality and homosexuality were seen by Freud as existing in at least a latent form in all adults and as developmental steps in the child's and adolescent's progress toward genital maturity and genital union. One result of Freud's influence has been the acceptance of perversions into the fabric of ordinary life, so that one sexual partner who does not feel comfortable in going along with some formerly perverse activity desired by the other now has the finger of blame placed upon him (or more usually her) by the marriage counselor, who sees this "straightness" as uptightness or overinhibition or a disgust with normal human processes. Conventionality was once equated with normality, and those who practiced a deviant life style ran the risk of being labeled mentally ill. Now much that was unconventional has become conventional, and the advocate of the same old established values—for example, premarital chastity—runs the risk of being labeled out of step or even "pathological." It was not Freud, but some of his followers and successors, who placed the highest value on sexual variety and categorized as old-fashioned the traditional approved forms of sexual expression and relations, but these changed attitudes are part of the Freudian revolution.

Several years ago I went to a meeting at which medical-school teachers of psychiatry discussed teaching techniques. One of the presentations was a series of films to teach future doctors to deal with sexuality more objectively and less timidly. The films were designed to desensitize the medical students to deviant (as well as normal) sexuality so they would not flinch when faced with this in their patients. Various kinds of sexual practices were portrayed in the films, with all stigma of obscenity removed because this was for a scientific purpose and in the interest of a therapeutic approach. (In addition to films of explicit sexuality that are designed to be scientific, commercial pornographic films are used in medical education to desensitize doctors to sex, sometimes in the form of "implosion therapy," in which a number of films are shown simultaneously or back to back in order to flood the viewer with stimuli and so decrease reactivity.[22] No one has done a study on the students who are exposed to the films to see if their inhibitions are released and if this helps or hinders their own expressions of sexuality.)

Besides the educational films showing masturbation and male homosexual relations, aspects of sexuality to which the medical students and psychiatric residents were believed to need desensitization, there was a film showing normal adult heterosexuality. The psychiatric educators who made the film explained that they had carefully screened applicants to eliminate exhibitionists and had found a couple with a sincere desire to demonstrate their own sexual proficiency to serve as an example to others. The naked woman on the screen was pretty, graceful, and even without clothes she was obviously intellectual. She approached her husband with appropriate solemnity. The husband was well built, muscular, bearded. They made an ideal modern emancipated couple. They started their lovemaking in the time-honored fashion, but before the film had unreeled very far they were doing all kinds of unusual things: hardly staying long enough in one position to settle down, slipping and sliding over and under each other with the suppleness of wet seals, changing from a head-to-head to a head-to-toe to a head-to-middle relationship with acrobatic ease in lovely rhythm. They were so quick and adept, sometimes it was difficult to comprehend who was doing what to whom. The activity went on for a long period of time, apparently without great excitement, but with infinite variety. Finally they became excited, and eventually the wife had a shaking climax, which the husband abetted with fingers and all else at his disposal. Then after time to recover, it was his turn, and the wife brought him to orgasm with her mouth. At the end of the film, everyone in the audience seemed delighted with this contribution to sexual enlightenment. But why had the medical educators who had produced the film decided to portray ideal heterosexuality with separate orgasms dependent on manual and oral stimulation? The question revealed my out-of-date point of view. I had been brought up in an era when a sex manual had instructed: "The ideal to be striven for is complete satisfaction of both partners, culminating in simultaneous orgasm. This cannot be achieved without study, practice, frank and open discussion between the partners and mutual aid to achieve the desired results." (This is certainly an old-fashioned manual, dating back to 1950; it is dedicated "To the Married and Those About To

Be.")[23] I was unaware that the new sex manuals say that simultaneous orgasm is not the most fulfilling sexual goal.[24] The goal is pleasure without anxiety, and the attempt to achieve mutual simultaneous orgasm is too much of a burden, too liable to lead to a feeling of failure. (One recent manual has a chapter on homosexual adjustment and another one on the "cost-benefit approach to extramarital sex.")

The psychiatric teachers pointed out to me what they seemed to imply should have been obvious—that mutual orgasm was an old-fashioned concept, not regarded as a practical goal and actually destructive if presented as a goal because it aroused feelings of guilt and inadequacy in those who could not attain it. More than that, scientific studies had shown, so I was told, that the greatest sexual pleasure comes not from any mutual sexual activity but when each partner can give complete attention to the sexual stimulation of the other. Climaxes should not be simultaneous because this prevents the ultimate in concentration, and therefore in pleasure, of first one and then the other. Traditional wisdom must give way to this modern scientific knowledge.

A recent "sex-therapy" book is based on the premise that "intercourse is not the way most women orgasm . . ."[25] A "psychotherapist" on the "Today" show, advising parents to teach children masturbation techniques and to encourage masturbation, stated that "the hand is the primary organ of sexual expression."[26] Ruth Carter Stapleton, a religio-therapist, has described masturbation as "a gift from God" and says, "The Lord wants us all to experience whole complete lives, and He offers this gift to each of us as we surrender to Him."[27] A Southern Baptist conference on family life was cancelled because a minister conducting a "one-man campaign against oral sex" objected to the keynote speaker, a Presbyterian minister who promotes oral sex in marriage. The Presbyterian promised to pray for the "sexual liberation" of the Baptists.[28] The protagonist of Saul Bellow's *Mr. Sammler's Planet* says, "It seems to me that things poor professionals once had to do for a living, performing for bachelor parties, or tourist sex-circuses on the Place Pigalle, ordinary people, housewives, filing-clerks, students, now do just to be sociable."[29]

An emphasis on personal gratification has been a characteristic of the post-Freudian sexual value, and it has led to the naming of the young as the "me generation." It is far from the concept of sexual maturity that Freud and Erik Erikson proposed, that of giving and getting pleasure through mutuality. Instead, a self-centered attempt to get the maximum for oneself was the new sexual value. This was not in response to Freudian theory, but was an extension of Freudian

384

theory by way of Wilhelm Reich, Norman O. Brown, Herbert Marcuse and others of the Freudian Left.

Classical Freudians and the Freudian Left have very different value systems regarding sexuality. Classical Freudians believe sex should be controlled in the interest of monogamy and fidelity. The Freudian Left and many others influenced by a hedonistic appeal believe in spontaneity and uninhibiting experimentation and impermanent relationships. Classical Freudians still use the word "perversions" when foreplay or "immature" expressions of sexuality become the goal instead of a method toward the goal. To some less conservative psychiatric thinkers these are not perversions but "another" type of sexual expression. Paul Goodman argued that, far from causing a threat to the survival of our civilization, removal of the blocks to instinctual gratification will lead to a more civilized state, and he saw the repression of instinctual gratification as the cause of destructive and oppressive forces in human relationships.[30]

It is debatable whether Freudian thought is as conservative and repressive as some post-Freudians and some detractors of Freud have said. Freud believed that heterosexual monogamy and living in a violence-free society were the desirable attributes that correlated with maturity and control of the id. He believed these goals could only be attained by sacrifice and discipline, but that the attempt to achieve them was well worth the effort. In this sense he was a traditionalist. But he also believed in examining all traditional values and seeing whether they were rooted in pathology or some healthy normality (defined in psychoanalytic terms), and he questioned such traditional values as religion, the assumption that traditional sexual morality was the rule rather than the exception, and the hypocritical conventions of his society. He was even more revolutionary in his technical approach and the assumptions that underlay that approach—that the mind had layers; that one can get into touch with these deeper and more primitive portions of the mind; that self-awareness leading to this new consciousness could be attained by free association and the examination of the internal stream of consciousness, dreams, and other spontaneous phenomena; and that by this kind of analytic work one could come to a new realization about the self and gain new potential for growth and development.

Freud's ideas have been used to support both the status quo and change. One answer to the paradox of Freud is to consider him both a revolutionary and a traditionalist. Possibly it was just because he was such a traditionalist that he could be such a revolutionary. James Sloan Allen comments on a book of photographs of the cozy, warm, overstuffed atmosphere of Bergasse 19, the apartment comprising residence and offices that Freud occupied for forty-seven years until he was forced to flee Vienna:

> ... The pictures tell their own story, and that concerns a bourgeois gentleman who had promised his future wife in 1882, "a little world of happiness, of silent friends and emblems of honorable humanity," where they could "pass our life in calm happiness for ourselves and earnest work of mankind." Freud fulfilled this promise with a home and offices that exuded coziness, comfort and tranquility. And although the environment seems at odds with the revolutionary ideas Freud developed there, the paradox is not baffling, for, as Peter Gay observes, who but a traditional bourgeois sensitive to rigid restraints, would know the power of restraints and the power of their enemies.[31]

But in contrast to the revolutionary nature of Freud's ideas there is always the emphasis on monogamy and heterosexuality, the acceptance of a society in which men and women played vastly different roles, the acceptance of late nineteenth-century political forms as "givens" to which the individual must make his adjustment, and the endorsement of the comfortable, class-conscious society in which servants existed to work for Herr Professors' families and in which the poor and the unsuccessful to some extent deserved their fates because they did not have the intelligence and will to circumvent their self-defeating impulses.

Followers of Frantz Fanon, Marcuse, Brown, Reich, and Erich Fromm saw Freud's message as having been applied conservatively and in the interest of repression, but they also saw that it could be interpreted entirely differently. Instead of the pessimistic conclusion that civilization causes inhibition and man must live in a state of tension between the expression of his instinctual needs and the needs of the larger society, the Freudian Left advocated a concentration on the possibility of sexual fulfillment. Reich and Marcuse linked the new sexual freedom with political values. They regarded sexual repression as one of the principal mechanisms by which the family and society impose a conservative political orientation.[32]

In time, radical Freudians would promulgate new therapies emphasizing touching, feeling, and experiencing. They would link up with psychologists to start the encounter group and sensitivity-training and consciousness-raising movements. Ultimately this would lead to such developments as Fritz Perls's involvement with the Esalen Institute, an emphasis on nonverbal therapeutic methods, and some movement of psychoanalysis and psychiatry away from the introspective, analyzing characteristic of classical psychoanalysis into a more present-oriented therapy dealing largely with feeling and awareness. In the process many traditional values were thrown overboard.

Freud would not have countenanced such deviations from his psychoanalytic method, as we know from his reaction to early deviationists, but it was his technique of psychoanalytic free association that encouraged the person-to-person, analyst-analysand encounter from which these new therapies developed. It was his theory that led to the emphasis on sexual fulfillment and gratification, and his iconoclasm that led to a questioning of all social values.

Freud did question some social values, and in spite of his own dedication to a traditional life style and family structure, he attracted around him unconventional people to whom divorce was acceptable, family structure not inviolate, and novel life styles not repugnant. Freud's first case of child analysis, the case of Little Hans, had a "happy ending" when Hans's parents divorced and each had a new and presumably more satisfactory marriage. Hans's mother had been Freud's patient, and both mother and father had been among Freud's early devoted followers. When Freud met a grown Hans in 1922 after a period of twelve years without contact, he found that he had survived the divorce and his parents' remarriages well. He was "a strapping youth" who "suffered from no troubles and inhibitions," and at the age of nineteen he lived alone and was on good terms with both his parents.[33] Early in twentieth-century psychiatry the concept became accepted that, as far as children are concerned, "a good divorce is better than a bad marriage." In time some psychiatrists would question other traditional social values—premarital chastity, marital fidelity, and exclusive heterosexuality.

Psychiatrists uphold the economic and political system as they find it, and they live and advocate upper-middle-class lives. They have whittled away at conventional morality. They have been leaders in the movement to decriminalize traffic in pornography and to promote the use of marijuana, to promote sexual experimentation, and to ban capital punishment. Some psychiatrists—a small minority—advocate homosexuality, and at least one even advocates incest. Nevertheless, the conventional lives they lead, their emphasis on the work ethic, and their advocacy of an only slightly left-of-center liberal position make them subject to the common criticism that they uphold tradition and the status quo. (The criticism would have left the early Freudians flabbergasted. They saw themselves as trailblazers.) A minority of psychiatrists are criticized on exactly the opposite ground—that they respect no conventions and are at war with tradition. Dr. Alayne

Yates, a Los Angeles pediatrician and psychiatrist who has the authority of both disciplines, advocates total sexual expression for children, with the encouragement of their parents. Masturbation should be encouraged from the time the child demonstrates interest, often in the first year of life. If early sexuality leads to increased sibling incest, there is no great harm done (Yates feels it is already "quite common . . . and relatively normal"). Father-daughter incest should be considered as sometimes beneficial (because "any kind of early pleasurable sexual experience tends to augment later sexual adjustment and enthusiasm . . .").[34]

Few psychiatrists and psychologists would take this viewpoint. Freud's views were diametrically opposed, for he saw early sexual experiences as traumatic and childhood masturbation as diminishing adult sexual potency.[35] But any value that can be expressed will be expressed and supported by some behavioral scientist, and because Yates is a behavioral scientist, her values will have more than ordinary import for some people. (So too with Freud's.) As a result we have, as Daniel Yankelovich says, "experts making value judgments in the guise of technical judgments."[36]

Not many psychiatrists are sanguine about incest, and few would want parents to encourage early sexuality. Most would emphasize instead the protection of children from excessive early stimulation. A larger number of psychiatrists—but probably still a small minority of all psychiatrists—favor a wide range of sexual experiences for adults, including selective adultery. O. Spurgeon English, a Philadelphia psychiatrist noted for his antagonism to convention and his uninhibited ways, has advocated infidelity when marriages are in the doldrums, and he states that many other behavioral scientists share his view. "It is difficult to assay at present, but many social scientists, psychiatrists, psychologists, social workers, marriage counselors, and religious leaders involved in counseling tend to conclude that the effect of adultery is often more favorable than unfavorable. Adultery seems to cause both parties to be more aware of each other's needs, more sensitive to each other's feelings, and to be more concerned about the other's happiness and emotional welfare."[37]

In time many of the social beliefs—patriotism, respect for authority, traditional morality—that were implicit in nineteenth-century society were questioned and at least partially discredited by twentieth-century psychiatry. But psychiatry acted to support other values related to the maintenance of social stratification, sexual inequality, and preservation of the economic and political advantages of the middle and upper classes.

The Psychiatrist Determines Values

Psychiatry started as a medical discipline, and it was authoritarian. It was based on the assumption that the psychiatrist was superior to the patient. Recently some few psychiatrists have questioned the paternalism that is part of all medicine and is particularly strong in psychiatry, but most psychiatrists have unquestioningly accepted a status of superiority that permits them to be directive and controlling. Psychiatrists have important class-rooted values. They are for the most part the product of the upwardly mobile lower-middle class or middle-middle class, anxious to become at home in a superior social strata, and they have unhesitatingly accepted the standards of the most affluent and the most successful in society. It is because psychiatry has so readily accepted elitist and materialistic values that critics have said that "psychiatry is the handmaiden of the status quo." In particular in its attitude toward social protest, some (but not all) kinds of political nonconformity, and the role of women, psychiatry until the last decade acted as a temporizing agent, resisting change. When parents were concerned with the desires of their children to break out of the family pattern, when a husband was concerned about the wishes of his wife to forsake the traditional female role, psychiatrists were seen as the therapeutic agents who could restore more healthy or more normal attitudes.

The battle over the changing role of women brought with it the accusation that psychiatry was opposed to that change. Some psychiatrists were tradition-bound and felt that women should play the roles they had always played—as wife and mother and keeper of the hearth —just because they had always played those roles. Other psychiatrists postulated that women had limitations and special capacities caused by biological and psychological givens that made them happier in traditional roles. Until recently only a few psychiatrists—and very recently, as the movement of women toward independence and new life styles became an irresistible force, many more—promoted a changing role for women and accepted the criticism that psychiatry was opposed to women's aspirations.

Freud, in a famous phrase, said "anatomy is destiny."[38] As this idea was carried to its utmost, it became embodied in such concepts as these: Men, because of their biological makeup, are destined to be aggressive, driving, searching; women, because of their biology, are destined to be passive, receptive, domestic. Men have a need to conquer; women have a need to nurture. Men are less interested in themselves and more interested in the outside world; women are more narcissistic, interested in adorning themselves in order to get the interest of a male, and interested less in the outside world and

389

more in what is theirs—themselves and their homes and families.

A careful reading of Freud indicates that he did not see masculinity and femininity in any such clear-cut dichotomous terms. He postulated many male qualities in normal women and many female qualities in normal men, saw them both as deriving many of their sexual characteristics from the same undifferentiated drive that at one point in development was manifested as a bisexual constitution, and felt much of what we call male and female was culturally, rather than biologically, determined. Freud says, in fact, that "to make 'active' coincide with 'masculine' and 'passive' with 'feminine' . . . seems to me to serve no useful purpose and adds nothing to our knowledge."[39] But he does go on to say what to feminists is unpardonable. He postulates much of the activity of the adolescent and mature female as a reaction to penis envy and to the wish to have a baby to compensate for what is seen as lost. (Even here he tempers what might be seen as a sexist view, because he sees a somewhat equivalent envy in men of the ability of women to be procreative, to carry and nurture a child within their bodies.)

In his personal and professional relationships, Freud was remarkably nonsexist for his time. He included many women in his social and professional circles, and if he never had much of an intellectual life with his wife, who revered him as a great man but never understood what he was about, he did have a close intellectual companionship with his sister-in-law, Minna Bernays, who spent more than forty years as a member of the Freud household. Freud included many women in his group of students and disciples, and he encouraged his daughter to follow him in a psychoanalytic career (and of all professional fields, psychoanalysis was the one that gave women equal stature earliest). But Freud himself had old-fashioned ideas about woman's role and saw the ideal woman as having the attributes of his wife—gentle, unassuming, and primarily interested in taking care of husband and family.[40] Still, he was not entirely congenial with the average woman's self-interest and absorption with family, seeing these as valuable attributes but something with which he could not quite empathize. He wrote to Marie Bonaparte, one of his disciples: "The great question that has never been answered and which I have not yet been able to answer, despite my thirty years of research into the feminine soul, is 'What does a woman want?' "[41]

Conventionally minded psychiatrists in their conventionally appointed offices, complete with bust or etching of Freud and a couch that may not be used but at least has ceremonial significance, have used or misused Freudian theory to persuade women that they should

390

not choose a single life, should be interested in having children, and should want to subordinate themselves to their husbands and children. Some of this represented unthinking acceptance of tradition and the use of Freudian theory to justify the maintenance of the status quo, a part of it undoubtedly was the result of the threat to male psychiatrists when women tried to break out into new roles, and some of it was based on a sincere appreciation of the difficult developmental tasks that children face and the need for a great amount of maternal care in the early years. When psychiatrists state, as many of them have, that they believe that day care may not be as helpful for the developing child as more personal maternal care, or that women cannot expect to combine wife-motherhood and careers without some loss in the domestic area, they are expressing values that are not necessarily incorrect. But spokespersons for women have seized on the statements of psychiatry on the role of women to denounce it as male-oriented, serving to maintain the subjugation of women, and opposed to female experimentation and change. Phyllis Chesler writes: "Clinician-theorists share the idea that women need to be mothers and that children need intensive and exclusive female mothering in order for both to be mentally 'healthy.' "[42] She continues, "Clinicians, most of whom are men, all too often treat their patients, most of whom are women, as 'wives' and 'daughters,' rather than as people; treat them as if female misery, by biological definition, exists outside the realm of what is considered human or adult. A double standard of mental health—and humanity—one for women, another for men, seems to good-naturedly and unscientifically dominate most theories—and treatments—of women and men."[43]

Chesler's thesis is that the reason more women than men are in treatment, hospitalized, and are considered psychiatrically sick is that male clinicians, using a male value system, make the determinations.

Freud postulated that women were incomplete without men. He believed that women were capable of two distinct kinds of orgasm, a clitoral orgasm, which was more easily obtained and could be achieved through masturbation, and a vaginal orgasm, which was achieved through intercourse. His "vaginal transfer" theory stated that as the female matured, the primary site of excitation shifted from the clitoris to the vagina, and that this represented the achievement of psychosexual maturity. Masters and Johnson stated that their research showed that one type of orgasm was as satisfactory as another,[44] a blow against the Freudian position. Kline-Graber and Graber, however, claim that coital orgasm is physiologically different and more satisfying than non-coital clitoral orgasm.[45] The seemingly ludicrous debate, which goes on and on, has implications that affect the militant feminist position. Are men and women dependent on each other, or can each exist without the other?

The values of psychiatrists necessarily dominate their therapeutic attitudes. Most psychiatrists are in favor of an ordered society and they evaluate many political activists as disordered. A minority of psychiatrists has favored change and revolution—Marxist psychiatrists and psychoanalysts like Wilhelm Reich and Erich Fromm, and nationalistic, terror-advocating psychiatrists like Frantz Fanon. Psychiatry can be quoted for either a traditional or a nontraditional point of view, but psychiatrists who are politically traditionalist dominate the field, and they see activists and revolutionaries as at war intrapsychically—at war with themselves psychologically. When someone commits an act of political atrocity, such as Sirhan Sirhan's murder of Robert Kennedy, the perpetrator may feel it is necessary to defend himself against the imputation of psychopathology in order to continue to maintain that the act is a valid political statement. Richard Moran, a sociologist, has argued that in the most famous case of all relating to criminal responsibility, the 1843 trial of Daniel M'Naghten (or M'Naughton) for the murder of Sir Robert Peel's private secretary, Edward Drummond, there were political factors that made it useful to see this as a bizarre psychopathological act rather than as a rational expression of a political point of view:

> At minimum, M'Naughton's alleged delusions of persecution were rooted in the political reality of his day . . .
>
> The insanity verdict was merely one of several possible explanations for how Daniel M'Naughton came to shoot Edward Drummond. The occurrence of M'Naughton's crime created extreme pressure on the Tory government to construct a theory to explain his act. The public demanded to know not only *what* happened, but more important *how* and *why* it happened. The insanity verdict served to discredit Daniel M'Naughton and the political ideas he represented by interpreting his act as the product of a diseased mind. The widespread political problems that the Tory government was experiencing throughout Britain were reduced to a personal problem plaguing Daniel M'Naughton. By regarding Daniel M'Naughton as a criminal lunatic incapable of distinguishing right from wrong, the court indicated that the explanation for this behavior would have to be sought in medical or psychiatric terms instead of political terms.[46]

When, shortly after the M'Naghten trial, John Dillon, another disgruntled partisan, threatened to shoot the chancellor of the exchequer and was taken into custody, he stated: "When I'm tried, I'll not plead insanity, but injustice."[47]

The insanity verdict, Moran says, may be the most effective way to detain and discredit those who do political acts that allow them to be brought within the category of "dangerously ill." It is easy to discount the motives of Lee Harvey Oswald, who had a history of hostility toward his mother and childhood psychiatric problems; of Leon Czolgosz, President McKinley's murderer, who "never associated with girls"; and even of John Wilkes Booth, who before he assassinated Lincoln was known as a sadistic practical joker. But such psychological references ignore social and political aspects of actions and categorize them as necessarily irrational.[48]

I have had the thought-provoking and humbling experience of having an analysand, Jeffry Galper, publish a criticism of some aspects of his three years of analysis in which he tells of his own perception of analysis as an approach to radical politics, even though he was aware that I did not see it the same way. Galper was conscious of the potential of analysis to encourage conservative values, and for him this would decrease its usefulness.

Galper wrote of his analysis with me:

For three years, ending in mid-1972, I underwent psychoanalysis. To the best of my understanding it was a fairly typical Freudian analysis. I went to four analytic sessions a week, lay on a couch, and proceeded via free association. My analyst spoke infrequently and then generally briefly, although his comments were, of course, often quite important to the progress of the analysis. I thought then, and still do, that my analyst was competent and concerned, and I feel that I was able to make reasonably good use of the analysis to understand my life better and to make more of it. The analysis continues to be an active part of my experience in that I use the self-exploratory techniques I learned in an ongoing way in my life.

The years in which I was in analysis were also the years during which I began in a systematic way to think about questions of politics, the nature of our society, and my personal relationship to the society. This process of politicization continues as a significant dimension of my life. It is leading me increasingly in a radical direction. This does not imply that my internal experience is of becoming particularly extreme, which is a connotation that the "radical" label sometimes carries. Rather, I am coming to see that our society at present is not organized to help all of us make the most of our lives. It asks us in an unreasonable way to deny or frustrate large parts of ourselves. I am coming to believe more firmly that the most reasonable alternative is a society organized on the best of anarchist and communist principles. Furthermore I am increasingly convinced that a reasonable life's work for myself and for all of us is to contribute as best we can to the achievement of that society.[49]

Galper says that in both radical and psychological circles there is a widely held assumption that psychoanalysis and radical politics are mutually exclusive. Psychoanalysis, as he experienced it, contained some very radical notions and deepened his political commitments. Among these notions were: taking people seriously, assuming that no passing thought was too trivial to be examined and no wish or fantasy too forbidden to be expressed, and not subordinating one's personal needs in the analysis to any other goal. This led to the convictions that needs do not have to be unmet, that one has a right to have one's needs met, and that this right can be satisfied through political action as well as through psychoanalytic therapy. Analysis helped Galper to see that some of his rebelliousness stemmed from anger, but that this did not have to indicate the converse—that anger was the reason for the rebelliousness. Analysis taught Galper that political activity sometimes stemmed from feelings of inadequacy or the need to confirm oneself as a person, but that the political actions could still have validity after these needs were surmounted. At the same time, he found conservative notions implicit in the process. Analysis tends to promote individualism instead of helping the analysand see his relationship to the larger world, and the analytic experience is an isolating experience that sets one apart from the rest of mankind because, Galper says, "it was undertaken alone and with the assumption, at least for the duration of the analysis, that my problems were unique to me."

> I asked the analyst on several occasions if some particular problem or other I was wrestling with was a generally shared one. His answer was to ask me about the importance to me of knowing the answer to that question. On the one hand, his response made sense. One of my jobs in the analysis was to discover the roots of my problems as I saw them, regardless of whether or not the problems were widely shared. After all, my problems were mine regardless of where they came from or how generally experienced they might be. Furthermore, on reflection, it was often the case that my question was an attempt to avoid an uncomfortable confrontation with my own contribution to my unhappiness.
>
> On the other hand, this way of proceeding was limiting. It reduced the likelihood of finding solutions in association with others since it encouraged me to take on the problems as my private issue. In so doing, it revealed a very important dilemma. An assumption inherent in the analysis, and an assumption I believe to be correct, was that my task was to deal with the problems I had, that is, the problems that were in me. However, the analytic situation encouraged me in making an unwarranted leap from seeing a manifestation of a problem in me to seeing the problem itself in me. As I mentioned before, its great attraction was in encouraging me to take myself seriously. Its great limitation was in pursuing the fallacy of individualism by

making the assumption that the only available hope for solution was contained within me. The analysis did not encourage me to develop my understanding of the need for making my struggle collective, and it did not suggest ways to do so. Rather, it supported the view that my problems were private and individual, and encouraged me to see my aloneness and difference more than my points of unity and commonality with others . . .

All therapies contain views of human nature. I came to understand that the views held by the analyst, which operated as an influence on me, were deeply conservative. His notions of what people are and, even more, what they must be, were consistent with and reinforced values supportive of the social order in its present form.[50]

The therapist who treats a patient with a political philosophy very different from his own is always under the temptation to see this as the patient's pathology. Clarence Blomquist, a Swedish psychiatrist, has recently written about his conflict in the 1950s at the start of his psychiatric career, when as an intern in a psychiatric clinic he was assigned to care for a high Swedish Communist Party official who had prospered in labor circles because of his party affiliation, but who had lately found the Communist position less and less satisfying and had become psychotically depressed. After his depression had been successfully treated with electroshock, the patient remained preoccupied with questions of conscience. Should he give up his lifetime allegiance to the Communist Party? Would others then see him, and would he see himself, as a traitor to the party? Blomquist was a staunch conservative, interested in decreasing the power and the influence of the Communist Party. As a psychiatrist he did not want his own belief system to influence his care of the patient. He decided that the proper goal of therapy would be to help the patient adjust to an inactive role in the Communist Party and avoid the stress of a break with his party. Blomquist twenty years later reevaluated his role: "Like most Western physicians I was educated in the Hippocratic tradition and believed that I should act in the patient's best interest without regard to political or economic consideration. I feared the consequences of allowing my personal preferences to affect my treatment . . ."

These were the influences that led Blomquist to choose the alternative of helping his patient become a better-adjusted passive Communist, a solution which seemed to be in the patient's interest and was his expressed desire.

I did not urge him to confront and possibly resolve—with whatever outcome for his politics—the underlying conflicts in his life. I advised him that he had done his job and was now entitled to sit at home smoking cigars while the younger generation carried on the battle.

395

In retrospect, my estimate of my own powers and my fear of using them seemed exaggerated. I now think that I should have formulated a more general goal for him, assisting him to redefine his lifestyle and leaving to fate the possibility that he might have come to share my own political attitudes. Instead, my fear of coercing him may have prevented me from truly helping him to come to terms with himself.[51]

Although this problem is found usually in a less clear-cut form, in many therapeutic situations where the therapist and the patient have opposing political views, few therapists seem aware there is a problem. Many apparently assume that their own political position is nonpathological and the patient's position is pathological. Few therapists would lean over backward as Blomquist did to protect the patient from being unduly influenced, and even fewer would be concerned enough twenty years later to question whether their scrupulous attitude had not in fact harmed the patient more than it helped him.

In 1960 a noted Freudian, Robert Waelder, wrote that except in the treatment of normal delinquents and revolutionaries, there would be few problems in a free Western society resulting from differing value systems of psychoanalyst and patient. The solution of the inner conflicts of the patient that have been brought into consciousness by the analysis will usually be in accordance with accepted moral and social standards. Waelder said that in a totalitarian society an analyst would have a conflict between his duty to a repressive and controlling state and his duty to the patient, who might by the analyst's tacit approval be encouraged to put into action his thoughts of opposition to the state. Says Waelder, "The problem has little importance in a free Western society because the inner requirements of the people's conscience are largely identical with . . . cultural requirements . . ."[52]

Since 1960, when Waelder saw little problem, a whole host of radical psychiatrists and antipsychiatrists have found major differences of values that can divide therapist and patient. There is the Freudian emphasis, noted by Galper, on resolving intrapsychic conflict instead of attributing conflict and maladjustment to the pressures of an unjust society. There are the bourgeois values that many psychiatrists accept unquestioningly as correct, though their patients may just as unquestioningly accept more militant and more revolutionary values. There is the conviction among the Freudian Left that conventional therapy promotes adjustment and not change.

Occasionally the therapist may have a much more radical perspective than his patients. Matthew Dumont, a Massachusetts social psychiatrist, states that mental health is not possible under our economic system, a system that "systematically destroys the health of the poor."

Dumont proposes a "non-capitalist vision" for psychiatrists who "cling so relentlessly to the empty hull of an expansionist society" and see themselves as "among its pilots."[53] Two radical therapists write: "One of the most vital assumptions underlying radical therapy is the goal of linking revolutionary societal transformation with personal and cultural struggles."[54]

In France, Freudo-Marxist psychoanalysts in 1968 formed the *Laboratoire Révolutionaire de Psychanalyse,* dedicated to the proposition that the authoritarian relationship between therapist and patient must be reversed, and that therapy must be devoted to the analysis of and promotion of change in family life, the work-leisure division of time, sex roles in couples relationships, and the education and rearing of children. In 1972 Gilles Deleuze and Felix Guattari published *Anti-Oedipus,*[55] which saw as a prop of capitalism the central Freudian concept that healthy maturity was a product of the resolution of the Oedipus complex. When the child resolves his or her Oedipus complex, he is shifting from adherence to the pleasure principle, the wish to possess the parent of the opposite sex, and becoming reconciled to the reality principle, that parents will remain close to each other and the child must find his own love object. These authors see Freud's ideal of the resolution of the Oedipus complex as a compelling rationale for submission to authority, an endorsement of existing society.

When patients are not being influenced by their therapists on moral positions and political philosophy, there are economic values associated with therapy that exert an influence on the patient. He is influenced to believe—perhaps correctly—that he is sick and inferior, that the therapist is well and superior, that because the therapist is well and superior he can assist the patient to an equal state of health and superiority, and that this help is worth a large sum of money. Therapists believe they have a right to live very well even when patients cannot afford to live well, and that patients should not complain when they have to suffer economically for their treatment. The life style of highly professional therapists—psychiatrists and psychologists—includes expensive suburban houses, vacation trips to exotic lands, and private schools and the best colleges for their children. The psychiatrist has an accountant, an investment portfolio, and an investment advisor. He may drive a Mercedes, which is a professional status symbol. His office is often luxurious, and he may spend several thousand dollars a year in dues to his professional organizations and in tax-deductible convention and educational trips. All this is paid for by the patient, who must learn to accept the therapist's evaluation of the worth of both the therapy and the therapist.

The therapist deludes himself that he is value-free; he prides himself on his neutrality. A standard bit of psychiatric advice to therapists is not to let personal biases and prejudices interfere with therapy, not to impose these opinions on patients. The analyst, so goes this advice (and it would hold true for other therapists as well) should differentiate two parts of his own personality. There is the private personality, which includes his personal likes and dislikes, his esthetic preferences, and his personal stand on all conventional matters, such as religion and politics, and which should be strictly kept out of the analytic situation. And there is the "universal personality," which "embodies the social, cultural and moral patterns of society achieved by generations of trial-and-error behavior . . . constituting a non-controversial, tested way of life which has provided its value, which should be introduced into the analytic situation to give the patient a model for identification and imitation."[56] Antipsychiatrists should be staggered by the implicit authoritarianism in such a statement. It presupposes that established values are noncontroversial and that psychiatrists know what these tried-and-true values are, and it assumes that the psychiatrist's own values are worth simulating. It is also based on the dubious proposition that psychiatrists can distinguish between what is personal and what is universal.

Two Toronto psychiatrists have said that the therapist both consciously and on an unconscious level believes he is "being more neutral with, and hence more unknown to," his patients than he is in actuality. In even the most neutral situation the patient picks up much information about the therapist from the location, furnishings, and decoration of his office, and from the therapist's dress and speech. In any form of ongoing therapy the patient learns a great deal about the beliefs of his therapist, beginning with the psychiatric theoretical position that is the basis of the therapy. When those who work in mental health—psychiatrists, psychiatric residents, social workers, or psychologists—go into therapy, they take into account the values that they ascribe to a potential therapist in deciding if this is the therapist they want.[57]

But more than moral, philosophical, political, economic, social, and esthetic values, it is the therapeutic values that most affect patients. The therapist may believe that his goal is to restore the patient to a preexisting state, or he may feel that the patient should do more than this and reach a better state, one that fulfills potential. The therapist may feel that unpleasant symptoms and feelings are aberrations that should be stamped out, or that they are warnings that should be heeded, or even that they are part of a creative process. He may feel that there is a sharp demarcation between well and sick, between his own emotional state and that of the patient, or he may feel that psychiatric states are a continuum and that he is not necessarily very different from, or very superior to, the patient. (There is even the possibility that the patient is better adjusted than the therapist.) Janet Gotkin has written about her therapists: "In the hospitals they treated us as less than human; they taught us to be ashamed of what we were . . . They taught us to hate ourselves and each other and to doubt our truest instincts . . ."[58]

His orientation concerning therapy determines whether a therapist will recommend long-term or short-term treatment, will use a verbal or a somatic method, will try to bring out feelings or suppress them. Whether a patient is psychoanalyzed or lobotomized depends on the therapeutic means and ends in which his therapist believes.

The whole constellation of values—personal, economic, political, philosophical, therapeutic—determines the treatment relationship. Most therapists do not examine their values. They do not see the dissonance that may exist between their own and those of their patients, and they do not recognize that a case they see as unsuccessful may represent a failure to understand and to reconcile value systems.

Because one value shared by most psychiatrists is the great worth of therapy, psychiatrists recommend treatment as a solution for more and more nonmedical problems, and they extend their authority to ever-growing numbers of people. The worth of psychotherapy is a generally agreed-on value, but there is less agreement about many others.

Behavioral scientists and members of the helping professions come in so many different sizes and styles that no uniform system of values has developed. There are permissive and traditionalist psychiatrists, conservatives and radicals, psychiatrists who attempt to be neutral, and those who try to impose themselves and their values on the patient and on society. No one can read an account of a "battle of the experts" in a criminal trial without sensing not only that can psychiatrists have diametrically different opinions, but that these opinions may stem from vastly different value systems.

In spite of a good deal of diversity, there have been general positions that can be said to represent the value system of psychiatry, and this system has been a powerful influence on individual thought and the structure of society. Its effect is sometimes "progressive," sometimes "conservative," depending on the subject involved.

In the field of personal morality it has been generally permissive and "progressive."

In the field of accountability or assumption of responsibility, it has been generally permissive and "progressive."

In the area of political thought, on the whole it has been "conservative," although at the same time that psychiatry has been encouraging adjustment and been supporting the status quo, it has, through its "progressive" values concerning moral issues—the draft, abortion, use of drugs, and sexual behavior—eroded tradition and fostered great political changes.

In the area of economics it has been very traditional and "conservative."

In the area of therapeutic orientation, it has been on the whole authoritarian, relying heavily on the medical model, which is a very "conservative" model, although some psychiatric movements have opposed medical paternalism and authoritarianism.

It is foolish for psychiatrists to claim, as they often have, that psychiatry is objective and value-free. The purpose of the therapeutic encounter is to permit one person to have enough effect on another person to change behavior and personality, and such a situation is rife with values. Those of the psychiatrist, often unexamined, will work themselves into the mind and brain of many of their patients and construct for these patients their world, and they will continue to guide the patients long after the therapy encounter has ended. The values that psychiatrists provide for their patients and for society are the most influential expressions of the great authority that psychiatry exerts.

Fifty-One Ways Psychiatrists
Exercise Authority

PSYCHIATRISTS EXERT power in so many different ways that it is difficult to keep them all in mind.

As we have seen, among the most crucial determinations they make are the decisions to commit to a mental hospital (or to persuade the patient to enter "voluntarily," with the threat of involuntary commitment often being the goad) and to release from a mental hospital.

The most publicized determinations that psychiatrists make are in the criminal-justice system, when well-known defendants (Jack Ruby, Sirhan Sirhan, Patty Hearst, David Berkowitz) are evaluated for competency to stand trial, or for criminal responsibility or diminished responsibility.

The fastest-growing field of psychiatric decision making is in civil law matters, particularly the appointment of financial guardians and the evaluations of divorcing parents to see which will receive custody.

The most pervasive decisions made by psychiatrists are their determinations of what is normal, appropriate, and healthy, and what is abnormal, inappropriate, and psychopathological.

At one point I decided to make a list of ways in which psychiatrists exercised authority. The list eventually grew to fifty-one ways, grouped under eight headings.

Commitment and the Rights of Committed Patients

1. Decisions on commitment and discharge from mental hospitals.
2. Decisions concerning "holding conditions" in mental hospi-

tals, the rights of the hospitalized patient, and the amenities offered to him.

3. Decisions concerning involuntary administration of medication, electroconvulsive treatment, and behavior modification for hospitalized patients.
4. Advising psychosurgery for violent voluntary patients (done only on an experimental basis).
5. Commitment of drug addicts and alcoholics to special programs of psychiatric treatment.
6. Decisions to institutionalize children in special schools.

Criminal-Justice and Correctional Decisions

7. Determination of criminal responsibility.
8. Determination of competency to stand trial.
9. Advising the court whether a criminal defendant should be prosecuted or whether charges should be dropped because of mental illness.
10. Advising the court on appropriate sentencing.
11. Advising the court to order outpatient therapy in lieu of prison sentencing.
12. Advising correctional systems on the type of prison and type of prison assignment for a prisoner entering the system.
13. Advising parole boards on release.
14. Diagnosing a subject as sexual psychopath or defective delinquent under appropriate statutes and by doing so, diverting him from the criminal-justice to the mental health system for a one-day-to-life term.
15. Determining whether especially dangerous mental patients and psychotic or particularly disturbed prisoners serving sentences in penal institutions are suitable for transfer to special hospitals for the criminally insane.
16. Authorization of nonphysicians (such as prison guards) to administer tranquilizers to enforce penal control.
17. Determination of whether a sexual offender should be castrated (a very rare determination, but this has been done in Colorado and California) or "chemically castrated" with hormones.
18. Psychiatric testimony under so-called guided discretion laws (as in Texas) to advise the jury whether the death penalty is appropriate after a defendant has been found guilty of first-degree murder.

19. Determining when a condemned prisoner is too insane to be subject to execution.

Civil Law Determinations

20. Determinations of the need for a financial guardian or for a guardian to make personal decisions (determinations of competency).
21. Determinations concerning the circumstances in which mental illness can be a bar to marriage or to divorce.
22. Determination of the parental rights of the mentally ill.
23. Evaluation of prospective adoptive parents to see if they are suitable.
24. Testimony in custody disputes to determine which of two divorcing parents should have custody of the child.
25. Testimony in court concerning whether a contract should be abrogated because one of the contracting parties lacked contractual capacity.
26. Testimony concerning testamentary capacity.
27. Diagnosis of traumatic neurosis or psychic damage to help make a determination in personal injury cases.

Treatment Decisions

28. Determination of whether mentally retarded women should be eugenically sterilized.
29. Evaluation for sex-change surgery.
30. Deciding when to suppress emotions by mood-changing drugs. (For example, the bereaved at funerals are often tranquilized, although this decision is more often made by a general practitioner than by a psychiatrist.)
31. Psychiatric evaluations for abortion (before the Supreme Court decision, but now done only in the case of indigent mothers seeking Medicaid support for an abortion).
32. Evaluation for such elective surgery as vasectomy or plastic surgery to see if the recipient is an appropriate subject.
33. Deciding on suitability for renal dialysis.
34. Evaluation of the competency of a terminal or nonterminal medical patient who declines further treatment (e.g., the so-called death-with-dignity cases).
35. Deciding what conditions will be treated under insurance reimbursement plans.

Classification, Excusing, and Certifying Disability

36. Placing people in educational, vocational, or personnel tracks on the basis of classifications determined by testing, evaluation, diagnosis, and profiling.
37. Providing psychiatric excuses to explain job or school delinquencies.
38. Setting up criteria for jobs; evaluating candidates for sensitive or security-related jobs.
39. Evaluation for job separation on the basis of mental instability or psychiatric problems.
40. Certification of disability for workmen's compensation and other awards; evaluation for early retirement.
41. Determining when someone is telling the truth.

Military Uses of Psychiatry

42. Evaluations of unsuitability for the draft (no longer done since the demise of the draft).
43. Evaluations for honorable and dishonorable military discharges.

Other Governmental Uses of Psychiatry

44. Determinations as to what should and should not be classified as criminal activities (such as recommendations to decriminalize homosexuality and marijuana use, and other changes in criminal law).
45. Experimentation in the interest of national security (as in the recently revealed CIA experiments during the 1950s and 1960s).
46. Development by CIA physicians of political profiles, such as those developed on Fidel Castro, Daniel Ellsberg, and others by CIA physicians.

Determining Social Norms and Promoting Social Change

47. Setting societal norms (as when psychiatrists state that premarital sex is or is not desirable, etc.).
48. Acting as agents for social change (as when psychiatrists cite poverty or racism or other social factors as causes of psychiatric illness and urge large-scale social changes).
49. Determining public attitudes by the writing of psychohistory

404

and psychobiography with particular points of view on historical and biographical data.

50. Issuing opinions on the competency of world leaders (as
    when, psychiatrists, after a poll, stated that Barry Goldwater
    was not suited to be president).

51. Making pronouncements on world issues.

PART FOUR

THE LIMITS OF PSYCHIATRIC AUTHORITY

To be good is noble, but to show others how to be good is nobler—and no trouble.

— MARK TWAIN

If I knew for a certainty that a man was coming to my house with the conscious design of doing me good, I should run for my life.

— HENRY DAVID THOREAU

The Psychiatrist Oversteps His Bounds

EVEN WHEN PSYCHIATRISTS try to be aware of their authority and its potential for abuse, and even when they go about their business in a responsible way, harm can result. Even "good" psychiatry can have bad consequences.

Much of psychiatry is not good psychiatry; it is mediocre or gray-area psychiatry. Psychiatrists are not sued or held accountable for this indifferent-to-inadequate practice—standards of care are too imprecise and the poor practice cannot ordinarily be proved to be negligent —but frequently they examine patients too superficially, commit them quickly, impose intrusive therapy too readily, detain them in institutions for overlong periods, or overmedicate and polymedicate them. The doctor who has a choice of therapies but picks electroshock because the patient's Blue Cross coverage allows for only twenty-one days of in-hospital care, and electroshock can easily be accomplished in that period, will never be criticized for his therapy choice. Patients who need a personal kind of treatment get shunted into impersonal treatment. A patient who could get along well enough without medication is lulled into insensibility with Valium or treated to the point of tardive dyskinesia with Prolixin.

Even an experienced therapist may mishandle the crucial transference aspects of the verbal therapeutic encounter, sometimes by failing to recognize the patient's positive feelings and interpreting only the anger and the hostility, sometimes by securing so much gratification from the patient's idealization of him that he allows this positive transference to continue without analysis and without an attempt to work through to a point where the patient may idealize less and be more independent. Phyllis Greenacre warned a quarter of a century ago that if an analyst takes over responsibility for making decisions for an analysand, the infantile neurosis for which the patient sought treatment may be replaced by a pathological dependence on the analyst even more powerful than the original neurosis.[1]

These are everyday ordinary violations of good psychiatric practice. Yet psychiatric society would not consider complaints about such practices worth investigating, and there would be no meaningful penalty even if the treatment could be shown to be harmful.

Even when psychiatric practice is grossly improper, the patients who are the victims of bad treatment often do not recognize it as such. Psychiatrists (for example, those who treat patients with amphetamines or create drug-dependent patients) may be particularly liked by the patients they indulge. Patients often do not realize they have been badly treated because they do not know what to expect from therapy, and those who are convinced they have received bad treatment can rarely prove this legally. The psychiatrist has a variety of easy defenses to most charges of malpractice, easier defenses than in other branches of medicine, where standards are sometimes more precise. He can assert that he was exercising his clinical judgment in a field in which experts are not at all unanimous, or that even though the psychiatric intervention caused harm, it was standard psychiatric treatment.

The therapist may advise psychoanalysis for a patient too close to decompensation to tolerate this kind of treatment, and a psychosis may develop. A therapist may make angry or ill-timed or incorrect interpretations, stir up hostility that his patient is unable to tolerate, and then angrily reject the patient, who may then fall into a suicidal depression. When patients are suicidal, sometimes the indifferent, flippant, or hostile attitude of the therapist or of the hospital staff precipitates a suicide attempt. Joseph Andriola has suggested that when seriously suicidal patients are not taken seriously or are disparaged by doctors and hospital staff, "such attitudes and the messages they convey strip the patients of any remaining shred of hope and provide him with a license for the attempted self-murder."[2] Therapists may injure patients by cutting off treatment when insurance coverage has run out and the patient cannot pay for more treatment, but they will not be held responsible, or even feel responsible, for damage to the patient.

It is common for "borderline" patients or patients with narcissistic personality disorders, who are considered not amenable to psychoanalysis or amenable only to extremely long-term analysis by particularly experienced and gifted analysts, to be selected as "control," or supervised, cases of an analyst in training, either because the case is well underway before the seriousness of the pathology becomes apparent or because of a shortage of cases with classical indications for analysis. In spite of the fact that the patient is receiving a kind of treatment that is too intensive for his condition, the analysis continues for a period of years so that the analyst in training can earn credit for the control case. The analyst in training and his supervisor are both aware that a less intensive treatment, analytically oriented psychotherapy, might be better for the patient.

Every year throughout the United States, as June 30 approaches there is a rash of poor practice. Residents in training who have been seeing their patients for a year tell them they will be leaving the clinic. The resident may not be leaving the area, but even if he remains, as a private practitioner, he will probably not be willing to see the clinic patient at a fee the patient can afford. An editorial in the *Journal of Psychiatry and Law* has said, "Given the current therapeutic modalities which foster the patient's dependence at the outset, the patient is in a most unenviable and vulnerable position at precisely the time the breach in the treatment continuity is made. This unconscionable practice is visited upon myriad numbers of patients. This procedure has been standard practice in psychiatric clinics in training centers in this country since the inception of outpatient treatment."[3] Sometimes the patient is transferred to a new therapist to repeat the process, or sometimes the case is wrapped up by hurried and mechanistic interpretations to persuade the patient that the appropriate time for termination has arrived.

None of this is provable psychiatric malpractice, and all of this is commonly done.

In other forms of medical treatment, patients are given full information before the treatment is given. This is the only way to satisfy the requirement of informed consent. Psychiatric patients enter treatment without any full concept of the treatment method and its implications. By their continued stay in treatment they give it some kind of approval, but unless they have access to more information than they possess, it is difficult to say that their consent is really informed. Should the therapist warn the patient on the first visit that there may be negative effects of psychotherapy, that the patient may end up worse rather than better? Should the patient in verbal treatment be told that there are available such alternatives as behavior modification and chemotherapy? Should patients embarking on a lengthy psychoanalysis necessarily be informed that there is short-term psychoanalytically oriented psychotherapy? Should patients be told that current studies do not prove the efficacy of one kind of treatment over another?

In particular the problem of the negative effects of psychiatric treatment is not faced. Hadley and Strupp, writing in the *Archives of General Psychiatry,* have said that if therapists want to claim that psychotherapy or psychoanalysis is a potent method of treatment, they must also admit its powerful potential for harm. They secured questionnaire responses from seventy psychiatric experts spanning a wide range of orientation. The experts were virtually unanimous in stating that there is a real problem of negative effects in psychiatric treatment. Some judged the frequency of occurrence of negative effects as only moderate, but others suggested that "negative effects in long-term outpatient psychotherapy are extremely common."[4] Patients in therapy are not informed of this, or if they raise the question, they receive false assurances. As a psychiatric resident, I heard a case presentation about a patient in the early stages of treatment. He was a novelist who was afraid that successful treatment might rob him of his ability to write. When he had raised this question with his analyst he had been given the reassuring answer, "To the extent that your creativity is the result of neurosis, there may be some loss, but your true creativity will be enhanced by the removal of neurotic blocks, inhibitions, and distortions." The answer was ingenuous but it was scarcely scientific. No one can differentiate neurotically inspired from healthy creativity, so no one knows if this answer has any validity. Certainly it represented what the patient wanted to hear and what the therapist wanted the patient to believe so that he would remain in treatment. Everyone at the case presentation seemed satisfied with the therapist's dubious solution to this patient's ambivalence toward therapy.

Although there is a body of cases involving psychiatric malpractice, with few exceptions they involve only administrative mismanagement of the patient (for example, allowing a homicidal patient a weekend visit home), technological misapplications (drug reactions or unfortunate side effects of the older, unmodified form of shock therapy), breach of confidentiality (only a few cases have been won for this injury), and sexual relations between therapist and patient. Malpractice relating to verbal therapy and the more subtle aspects of the therapist-patient relationship cannot be proved.

One study of malpractice actions against psychiatrists concludes that "the greatest single factor" in the prevention of malpractice suits is the continued "positive, cooperative relationship between therapist and patient," and that this kind of relationship allows errors in judgment to be overlooked that otherwise would be causes of malpractice actions.[5] Various authors have speculated on why therapists, in spite of all their imperfections, have comparatively few malpractice actions, and almost none relating to improper outpatient therapy. Donald Dawidoff, a lawyer who has written the only book on the malpractice of psychiatrists,[6] advances some theories: "This fact may be attributable in part to the skill of psychiatrists in handling the negative feelings of patients or to the natural reluctance of patients to open their psychiatric history to public scrutiny. The absence of any successful malpractice action may also be due to the lack of a firm doctrinal footing for such an action."[7] Other authors have suggested that although the technological application of health care may give rise to malpractice suits against psychiatrists, the office psychotherapist practices out of reach of peer review, and in addition, emotional damage is more difficult to assess than physical damage, and there are no "standards of practice for psychotherapy, and therefore no measure of the adequacy of a psychotherapist's management of a case."[8]

Bad or unforeseen results in verbal therapy are not indicated by chipped teeth or broken bones, as they are in unmodified electroshock therapy, or by agranulocytosis as a side effect from drugs. Organic and somatic therapies—shock and drugs—have led to successful lawsuits, as have some cases of improper commitment. Psychiatrists have been held responsible for suicide and homicide when their negligence in guarding the patient has been held to be a proximate cause. But the nonsomatic, nonorganic therapies are usually protected from suit because negligence is so hard to conceptualize and prove. One of the few successful cases deals with the unusual situation of the beating of a patient as part of "direct analysis" therapy.[9] Another is a California case involving "Z-therapy" (sometimes called "rage reduction"), a variation of primal-scream therapy, which involves tickling the patient until a flood of primitive emotions is released. A California court found for a Z-therapy patient and awarded her $170,000 damages after her testimony that she had been tortured, "including beating, holding and tying me down, and sticking fingers in my mouth." She claimed near-fatal kidney damage and other physical injuries.[10]

In cases involving serious matters like commitment without proper evaluation of the patient or eugenic sterilization that is secured by court order in a state that has no statute allowing the procedure, the courts have invoked such doctrines as the immunity of agents of the court, judicial immunity, or the lack of demonstrable damage to the patient in order to protect psychiatrists and court officials against suits.[11] Many extremely dubious practices—such as those experienced by Roy Schuster and Johnnie Baxstrom in hospitals for the criminally insane, and by Frances Farmer in Western Washington State Hospital at Steilacoom—have been so accepted as standard practice that patients have little basis for a suit. When an occasional case for improper commitment is won, courts often decrease the amount of damages or disallow damages entirely on review. We have noted that Kenneth Donaldson spent almost fifteen years in Florida's Chattachoochee State Hospital, although during most of this time he was "dangerous neither to himself or others," and although he had had offers of help from friends in establishing himself outside the hospital. A jury determined that the two defendant hospital psychiatrists, one of them the superintendent of the hospital, had been malicious in not allowing him his freedom soon after he came to the hospital.[12] Donaldson had his damages reduced from $38,500 to $20,000 in a review of his case. Patients have great difficulty having courts accept their cases on writs of habeas corpus when they allege they are being improperly held. They often have to fight their way through the technical aspects of the legal system (and are thrown out of court for procedural reasons), and if they win damages, they may find these eventually reduced or eliminated on some such ground as sovereign immunity or the psychiatrist's lack of malice.[13]

One of the most common abuses of psychiatry involves the confidentiality of the therapist-patient relationship. When therapists have a particularly interesting case or a particularly famous patient, they frequently discuss the case or the patient, not only in the course of their professional duties—getting another opinion from a colleague, discussing the case in a lecture to medical students or psychiatric residents—but after hours. The Group for the Advancement of Psychiatry has seen after-hour breaches of confidentiality as an important problem. "Doctors as a group tend to talk shop, even in social situations where there is a great risk of jeopardizing confidentiality. Psychiatrists are no exception. In social settings psychiatric 'gossip' about patients is to be condemned and constitutes a direct violation of the ethical responsibilities."[14]

Many psychiatrists and therapists are scrupulous in not revealing confidential information, but others are notoriously indiscreet. Sometimes confidentiality is waived or is breached in the interest of sharing an interesting case history with the scientific community, with other members of the helping professions. Even when the patient gives full consent to the disclosure of information, there is always the question of whether the patient-therapist relationship did not create some pressure on the patient, whether he was not perhaps activated by gratitude for improvement in therapy, which caused him to be willing to reveal himself publicly.

The desire of a psychiatrist to get into print with the story of her therapy over the objection of her patient gave rise to a case in which the parties were designated as Jane Doe and Dr. Joan Roe to protect their identities.

Dr. Joan Roe had practiced psychiatry for more than forty years. Jane Doe and her former husband, now dead, and possibly one of her children, had been in treatment with Dr. Roe over a long period of time. During the therapy there was a discussion of whether the patient would be comfortable if the account of the therapy were to be published in book form. Dr. Roe apparently believed it would be a contribution because the case demonstrated intrafamily dynamics and the effect of the mother's therapy on her child. At some periods in the therapy Doe agreed with her doctor that it would be a good idea to publish her case history, at other times she decided against publication. According to the testimony of Dr. Roe, when the question of consent was raised in an action for breach of privacy, the patient's consent "was there one day and not there another day. That was the nature of the illness I was treating, unreliable." Doe never gave any consent in writing to have a book about her case published. When, eight years after her treatment had ended, she learned that such a book had recently been published, she protested and had an attorney write a letter expressing her objections to any further distribution of the book. According to the court, the book reported verbatim and extensively the patient's and her husband's "thoughts, feelings, and emotions, their sexual and other fantasies and biographies, their most intimate personal relationships and the disintegration of their marriage. Interspersed among the footnotes are Roe's diagnoses of what purport to be the illnesses suffered by the patients and one of their children." Two hundred and twenty copies of the book had already been distributed. Doe was concerned because she taught in a university setting and her students, colleagues, employer, and friends were now in a position to know about her pathology and her most uncensored thoughts and fantasies. Unlike many case histories, she was easily recognizable, both because many of her acquaintances knew she had been in treatment with Dr. Roe and because of the configuration of facts, which included a divorced husband, now dead, and a disturbed child.

The case went through various stages of appeal, once as far as the United States Supreme Court.[15] Dr. Roe secured the help of the American Civil Liberties Union in fighting to lift a court restraint placed on the distribution of the book. The argument was that restraining further dissemination of the information was an interference with the First Amendment right of freedom of the press. Doe received the support of the American Psychiatric Association, which joined in submitting an *amicus curiae* brief explaining the need for confidentiality in the therapeutic relationship. Doe spent more than $50,000 in legal fees in her effort to halt the disclosure of her case history. Eventually she won $20,000 in damages from Dr. Roe and Peter Poe, Dr. Roe's psychologist-collaborator husband, but the court did not reimburse her for her attorney's fees. To do that, it would have had to find that the publication had been malicious, "morally culpable or . . . actuated by evil and reprehensible motives." It found instead that the writing and publication of the book was not malicious, willful, or wanton, but "merely stupid." The court did enjoin any further sale or distribution of the book.[16]

Some of the greatest abuses of psychiatry involve confidentiality in the area where criminal justice and psychiatry meet—the forensic examination of accused criminals—in such determinations as the "guided discretion" application of the death penalty, and in the evaluation of sexual psychopaths and defective delinquents. When the accused is told by the evaluating psychiatrist that the interview is for court purposes and will not be confidential or privileged, the warning may not be understood, and often the warning is not even given.

The exploitation of patients occurs most easily in private psychiatric practice when the patient has developed a positive or an erotic transference. Such patients are in a particularly vulnerable position, for they are in treatment because they have problems with dependency. Dynamic therapists should know that the transference has to be handled with care, that therapy is meant to be a regressive experience in which feelings related to dependency can be explored, but that patients can become overdependent and can utilize the therapeutic relationship for nontherapeutic ends. So, too, can the therapist use the situation for nontherapeutic purposes. He can secure gratification having to do with—among other violations of the Freudian principle of abstinence—financial aggrandizement, narcissistic enhancement, and sexual conquests. Patients have loaned their therapists money or left them large sums of money in their wills, and grateful patients have helped the careers of their therapists by giving money to endow chairs or support psychiatric hospitals. Sometimes patients allow themselves to be exploited by therapists who deviate from accepted psychiatric practice and appeal to their greed or perverse aspects. All of this violates the principle of abstinence, that the therapist is not to secure any special gratifications from any patient, and that his entire gratification should be the earning of an honest living and the satisfaction of feeling he is doing a difficult job well.

Psychiatrists do not talk about cases where patients are exploited. The few cases that are brought to disciplinary boards conducted by medical or psychiatric societies are usually decided in favor of the doctor, and the proceedings are not made public. A conspiracy of silence reigns, and it is only through the very small number of cases that come to court (presumably the tip of the iceberg) and an occasional glimpse, obtained through some other published report, of how therapy is sometimes conducted that we achieve any consciousness that there are unethical therapists who use patients for their own purposes.

The famous are especially vulnerable to psychiatric exploitation. Their notoriety affects the countertransference in two important ways. The therapist is so gratified by having a famous patient that he prolongs the treatment or treats the patient differently from more ordinary patients. The psychiatrist sets a high priority on the maintenance of the patient's status—as a film or a rock star, or as a concert performer—and becomes part of the exploitative pressure on the patient to maintain himself on a pinnacle of fame, even though this may be too stimulating and too exhausting a position.

Montgomery Clift, the screen star of the 1950s (who played the role of Sigmund Freud discovering the secrets of unconscious mental functioning in his last major picture), was once described by Marilyn Monroe as "the only person I know who's in worse shape than I am."[17] Clift seemed at times to have had some realization of how psychiatry was being used to bring out his worst potential, for he referred to his psychiatrist, with whom he remained in treatment for fourteen years up to the time he died from alcohol and drug abuse, as "my Mephisto."[18]

Clift was the victim of several generations of pathology. His mother, Sunny, was brought up in a foster home unaware of the identity of her parents, but with the assurance of the obstetrician who had delivered her that she was legitimate and that some of America's most distinguished blood flowed in her veins. She was grown before she learned who her parents were, and she was married and had three children —Montgomery was one of twins—before she was introduced to her family, which was indeed wealthy and distinguished. This family found the Clifts too rough to be introduced to Washington society and paid for long stays in Europe for Sunny and her children so that they could become smooth enough to be acknowledged.

Her strange upbringing had left its effects on Sunny, who has been described as a smothering, monomaniacal mother, and her children in turn suffered from her need to control them, as well as from their own strange upbringing. Clift had great difficulty in remembering his childhood and refused to discuss what he did remember. He told a journalist, "My childhood was hobgoblin—my parents traveled a lot. That's *all* I can remember."

When Monty was fifteen, Sunny found a part for him in a summer theater production and he was embarked on an acting career. He was handsome and had great acting abilities, and he had a steady succession of roles in Broadway plays. In his second film, *Red River,* made when he was twenty-eight, he became a major Hollywood star.

Two years later he consulted a New York psychiatrist, Dr. Ruth Fox, because of his excessive drinking. Fox specialized in the treatment of alcoholics. She referred him to her former psychoanalyst, Dr. William Silverberg, who she thought had a special sympathy with alcoholics.

Dr. Silverberg was a recognized leader in neo-Freudian psychoanalytic circles. He had been a cofounder, with Karen Horney, of the Association for the Advancement of Psychiatry, a liberal psychoanalytic group that broke away from the classical Freudian American Psychoanalytic Association. He believed Freud had overstressed the need to work through childhood traumas and that if he could persuade the patient to live differently, the stage would be set for a "cure."[19] Dr. Silverberg had Clift call him by the name his friends called him, Billy. Patricia Bosworth has described Silverberg: "To friends and patients alike, his rosy cheeks and cherubic smile belied an almost frosty remoteness. He had a biting sense of humor and a boundless curiosity about people, as well as a vast fund of knowledge which ranged from horse races to Beethoven to the best recipe for cheese soup." He was divorced and had two teenage sons, and he shared his office-apartment overlooking Central Park with the male secretary-companion with whom he lived for more than twenty-five years and who was a reformed alcoholic. Silverberg was not a proselytizing homosexual. He appears to have believed, with his colleague Harry Stack Sullivan, that homosexuality is a personal tragedy that can sometimes be dealt with better by confrontation than by denial or suppression. There is no evidence that he disclosed to Clift his own homosexual orientation or that he tried to convert Clift to homosexuality. But in psychiatric circles, according to Fox, Silverberg was known to be a homosexual. "It was taken for granted, but rarely discussed. I sent a great many artists-writers to Billy for consultation. They would always phone me afterwards and say, 'Why, he's one of us.' " The referral to Silverberg, when Clift, a bisexual, was obsessed with doubts about his own sexual orientation was a mistake of the first magnitude.

Clift began seeing Silverberg in a daily analysis. He soon came to hero-worship Silverberg, and apparently at Silverberg's suggestion, he became more active and aggressive, allowed his hostility to reveal itself, and initially formed closer relationships with women, particularly with Elizabeth Taylor, whom he came close to marrying. On several occasions Silverberg persuaded him to become less dependent on women, whom he allowed to manage his life, but Silverberg never tried to encourage him to be less dependent on therapy. He continued to drink throughout his fourteen years of analytic therapy. He also habitually carried in his pocket with his vitamins a variety of barbiturates—phenobarbital, Tuinal, Nembutal, and Seconal.[20] Eventually Clift gave up thoughts of marriage and heterosexuality and during his last years was involved in dangerous pickup homosexual relationships.

Clift had an arrangement not unique for film stars and similar luminaries who need the dependency of a constant analytic relationship but whose travel and work schedule makes regular therapy impossible. Clift had his analytic hour five times a week (for which he paid initially thirty dollars an hour) and he was responsible for this hour whether he was in New York and could utilize it, or whether he was in California or abroad and could not make it for months on end. The analysis went on around the year. When in the summer Silverberg went to Ogunquit, Maine, where he had a vacation house, Clift also went to Ogunquit and spent his time, except for the daily therapy session, in a motel room.

Clift's friends were worried about the relationship. Clift seemed to depend on Silverberg for advice on everything—and said his analyst was always right except when he advised him about roles—but Silverberg refused to interfere with Clift's drinking because, he said, he wanted to take an analytical and neutral stance. Finally they became convinced that Clift should be hospitalized because of his drinking, blackouts, depression, and other symptoms. Clift's personal physician, his agent, and his lawyer arranged a meeting at Silverberg's office with Clift. They told Silverberg they thought it was imperative for Clift to go into a hospital. Clift listened and said, "If Billy wants me to go I'll go." Silverberg indicated he did not want Clift to go into a hospital. Clift's father phoned Silverberg. Silverberg told him, "My dear sir, if that man gets out of my control he'll die within three months."[21]

Clift died at the age of forty-five in 1966. Silverberg, himself ill, was not informed of Clift's death on the ground that he would have been too upset.[22]

Whether Clift would have done better with better treatment is something that cannot be known. We can conclude that Silverberg did exploit Clift, that he was truly Clift's "Mephisto," and that the fourteen years of treatment were not in the interest of the patient. Silver-berg, suggests John Leonard, seems almost to have wished Clift to remain ill.[23]

The most egregious abuses of verbal psychiatry involve mishandling of the patient's transference and a lack of understanding by the thera-pist of his own countertransference, but these are not usually raised to the level of visibility. We rarely learn about such abuses.

An occasional case does surface. A 1961 English case, which has been described as the first reported case holding that transference had been mishandled, involved a psychiatrist who saw his severely disturbed patient outside the office in an on-and-off again social relationship. It was not alleged that he had been sexually intimate with the patient, but her worsened condition and attempted suicide were held by the trial and appeals courts to have resulted from negligent professional conduct.[24] A more sensational American case concerns a psychiatrist who responded to the patient's declaration of love by saying that he loved her too. He had her move to an apartment above his office, advised her to get a divorce, and told her how to handle her inheri-tance. They went on trips together, became involved in nude swim parties, and finally had sexual relations. The court, which found that the patient had been harmed by the therapy, stated that it was clear from the evidence in the case that the patient would have been harmed even if the trips "were carefully chaperoned, the swimming done with suits on, and if there had been ballroom dancing instead of sexual relations."[25]

When patients allege that they have been exploited in treatment, they are usually not believed. Most allegations by female patients of sexual seduction by male therapists are discounted. The complaints are ascribed to a sexually frustrated woman attempting to get revenge on a rejecting man, and the psychiatric patient complaining about her therapist has the additional stigma of the label "mental patient." The therapist-seduction victim has little recourse. In a case involving not seduction, but the possibly more serious claim of patient rape, F. Lee Bailey successfully defended a psychiatrist accused of injecting his patient with sodium pentothal to decrease her resistance to seduction and then having intercourse with her. Bailey offered to demonstrate in the courtroom that his own secretary with a similar injection would not be powerless to resist or scream. The woman's lawyer refused to allow the courtroom demonstration, and the jury found for the de-fendant.[26] During my psychiatric residency, my hospital admitted as patients several women, referred by psychiatrists in another city, who claimed that the referring psychiatrists had initiated a sexual relationship during therapy. There was no attempt to discover the true facts of the situation, no attempt to confront the former therapists. The fact that the inpatient therapy recommended was in a city hundreds of miles away from the home of these patients raises a suspicion that the referring doctors did not want their patients hospitalized where their stories would be made known to close colleagues. The patients were neither disbelieved nor believed. Their accusations were considered indicative of how they saw the therapeutic relationship, whether or not they had been actually seduced, and the doctors were given the benefit of a doubt based on the possibility that this was hysterical exaggeration or some other distortion. At the time we considered ourselves progressive and broad-minded because we did not outrightly disbelieve the patients, as many psychiatrists would have. From a different perspective now, I can see how frustrating and disillusioning this nonjudgmental approach to accusations of unethical professional practice must have been to the women concerned.

The intimacy of psychiatrist and patient—usually a male psychiatrist with a female patient, rarely a female psychiatrist with a male patient or a therapist with a patient of the same sex—can be justified or rationalized on the ground that patients suffer from a lack of love and need warmth, caresses, and closeness. Sandor Ferenczi, a Hungarian psychoanalyst, one of Freud's most faithful disciples until he deviated from Freud on the matter of the importance of birth trauma and then began to develop other theories of his own, eventually concluded that the main problems of his patients related to lack of love from parents, particularly maternal love (a concept now accepted by many dynamic psychiatrists), and he recast the role of the analyst to be the source of missing love in the role of the loving parent. His new technique involved kissing as therapy. Freud wrote to Ferenczi in 1931, warning him that this intimacy would lead in the case of other analysts to more openly sexual relations.

> You have not made a secret of the fact that you kiss your patients and let them kiss you; I have also heard that from a patient of my own . . .
>
> Now I am assuredly not one of those who from prudishness or from consideration of bourgeois convention would condemn little erotic gratifications of this kind. And I am also aware that in the time of the Nibelungs a kiss was a harmless greeting granted to every guest. I am further of the opinion that analysis is possible even in Soviet Russia where so far as the State is concerned there is full sexual freedom. But that does not alter the facts that we are not living in Russia and that with us a kiss signifies a certain erotic intimacy. We have hitherto in our technique held to the conclusion that patients are to be refused erotic gratifications . . .

Now picture what will be the result of publishing your technique. There is no revolutionary who is not driven out of the field by a still more radical one. A number of independent thinkers in matters of technique will say to themselves: why stop at a kiss? Certainly one gets further when one adopts "pawing" as well, which after all doesn't make a baby. And then bolder ones will come along who will go further . . .

Someday, suggested Freud, Ferenczi, gazing at the lively scene he had created, would perhaps say to himself: "may be [*sic*] after all I should have halted in my technique of motherly affection *before* the kiss."[27] But Freud predicted that his invocation of the reality principle would not prevail with Ferenczi against the gratifications of the pleasure principle, not the least of which was the pleasure of flaunting Freud's authority.[28]

For many years not much was heard about sex in therapy except for rumors that circulated in psychiatric circles and the reporting of a rare case. Various kinds of touching and feeling therapies came into prominence in the 1960s, and there were such aberrant treatment methods as nude group marathons in swimming pools. Various therapists experimented with holding and cuddling severely regressed and psychotic patients and even bottle-feeding them. The concept of touching and feeling as a treatment method gained wide acceptance, particularly for very disturbed patients who needed the sense of a protecting maternal person. The distinction was made between non-erotic touching—holding and soothing a disturbed patient—and erotic touching. A psychiatrist, using an analogy to veterinary medicine, writes: "It is my impression that the absence of touch in treating mental patients is counter-indicated by sufficient data on animal training, experimental animal behavioral studies, including primates, and also studies of humans who have been deprived in early life of adequate human physical contact."[29] A New Zealand psychologist writes that there are good and ancient reasons for a sex taboo in therapy. It is not a relationship of equals, there is the carry-over of the incest taboo, and exploitation of the patient is a real possibility. And therapy, not sex, is the business of the therapist. But he advocates touch, the earliest and most basic form of human interaction. "By forbidding touch, we as therapists cut ourselves off from a very basic way of making contact and providing comfort. In some cases it may be the only way . . ."[30]

The problem of touching is not as simple as this makes it appear. Even psychotic patients may resent having their most regressed aspects catered to. Touching can be addicting, and when it is time to phase it out, it may be impossible for the patient to get along without it. Touching and feeling can arouse fears of sexual exploitation that reach panic levels. But it can also calm panic states, and for some conditions of anguish and depression, certainly, the only possible human contact is through touch.

Anne Sexton, a poet who committed suicide, has written about the meaning of the touch of her psychiatrist, Dr. Y.

> My safe, safe psychosis is broken . . .
>
> My little illustrated armor,
> my hard, hard shell has cracked
> for Dr. Y. held my hand
> and with that touch
> my dead father rode on the Superchief
> back to me with dollar bills in his fist
> and my dead mother started to knit me a sweater
> and told me, as usual, to sit up straight,
> and my dead sister danced into the room
> to borrow something and I said
> yes, yes, yes.[31]

"Laying on of hands," has been reintegrated into the medical school and nursing curriculums;[32] touching and personal contact has been readopted as part of church worship—the "tactile liturgy."[33]

The fact that a small minority of therapists who had sexual relationships with their patients advocated this as a method of treatment surfaced in 1969 when the American Psychiatric Association expelled one of its members, James McCartney, an aging Jungian who called himself a psychoanalyst although he had had no formal psychoanalytic training, after he published a paper in *The Journal of Sex Research* advocating intercourse as therapy. In his paper entitled "Overt Transference," McCartney had said that in his forty years of practice experience he had found a large percentage of patients needed expressions of love, that about 30 percent expressed some form of overt transference, such as sitting on McCartney's lap, holding his hand, hugging or kissing him, and that about 10 percent "found it necessary to act out extremely, such as mutual undressing, genital manipulation, or coitus." Expulsions from the APA are done quietly, presumably in order to protect the guilty by keeping the expulsion from being publicized and brought to the attention of patients, and to keep it from being the source of state licensing disciplinary action—but McCartney made his name public in an "Open Letter to the APA."[34]

McCartney told his fellow APA members that during forty years of "psychoanalytic" practice he had always practiced his profession with "conscience and dignity" and with only the health of his patients in mind, and that "I can truthfully say I have never been in love with any of my patients."[35] He concluded his letter with the hope that some day he would be given a vote of confidence and reinstated in the American Psychiatric Association.

In the 1970s more and more stories came to light of sexual relationships of doctors and patients. One psychiatric wit suggested that sexual intercourse between analyst and patient might be called a form of free association.[36] An article in *New Times* comments on "pelvic therapy": "For too many psychiatrists, the laying on of hands means exactly that."[37] Some psychiatrists excused these transgressions of medical ethics as understandable in view of the pressures and strains of psychiatric practice. Some even described psychiatric practice as lonely and deficient in the interpersonal gratifications that go with other professions, and therefore susceptible to an eroticized relationship. Most psychiatrists blamed sexual encounters with patients on the seductiveness of some female patients. The rise of the women's movement produced the counterargument that the seduced female patient had been doubly exploited: She had been taken advantage of in her time of need and had then been blamed for initiating the intimacy. The victims of therapist seduction have been compared to the victims of rape because they are equally stigmatized and disbelieved, but a better analogy is to battered or sexually abused children in the care of adults who are expected to care for them, but who instead victimize them. Still another useful analogy is to incest. In all these cases, as in therapy seductions, the denials of the aggressor are often believed and the accusations of the victims ignored or disbelieved.

Whether to gratify or not gratify the patient continues to be debated among therapists, although when they talk of gratification it is not always easy to know what level of love, sex, or closeness they are discussing.

In 1973, Kardener and his associates published the first statistical study of nonerotic and erotic contact of physicians and patients. In it they reported that in a sample of 112 randomly picked psychiatrists who returned mailed questionnaires, only 30 percent said that they believed "nonerotic" hugging, kissing, and affectionate touching was never beneficial to patients, and only 45 percent said that they never engaged in nonerotic contact. Erotic behavior was defined in the study as kissing, manual and oral stimulation of the patient's genitals, manual and oral stimulation of the physician's genitals, and mutual genital stimulation. Eighty percent of the sample thought erotic behavior was never of benefit, but 20 percent thought that these practices were useful in improving sexual maladjustments or disclosing areas of sexual blocking, or that they helped make "the therapy go faster, deeper, and increases dreams."[38] Five percent of the psychiatrists—a surprisingly large number—reported they had had intercourse with patients. Psychologists and other therapists are reported to have at least as high, and possibly higher, rates of intercourse with patients. A nationwide survey showed that more than 5 percent of male Ph.D. psychologists had had intercourse with patients and more than 10 percent had had other "erotic contact." More than 7 percent of male psychologists and more than 0.5 percent of female psychologists had had intercourse with patients within three months after the termination of therapy, and 80 percent of these had had intercourse with more than one patient.[39] Linda D'Addario, a psychologist whose doctoral thesis is on "Sexual Relations Between Female Clients and Male Therapists" and who has collected victim reports of sixty-five cases, believes the incidence of sexual contact between female patient and male therapist is much higher "if you count the entire range of kinds of encounters."[40] A study of freshman medical students shows a high rate of approval for physician-patient sex (in general medical, not psychiatric, practice). Twenty-five percent of freshman medical students surveyed thought that sexual intercourse with a patient could be appropriate under the "right circumstances" if the doctor was "genuine" and "authentic."[41]

One poll showed that 19 percent of 500 psychiatrists felt there were exceptions to the rule that patient-physician sexual relations are harmful to the patient and to the therapeutic relationship, and that 70 percent of the psychiatrists knew of patients or doctors who had engaged in "physician-patient relations." Commenting on that poll, *Behavior Today* stated that the decline in the ethic concerning physician "abstinence" could not be documented "because it is almost all-pervasive," and that psychiatrists could no longer assure each other that the "offenders belonged to the horde of untrained and unqualified pseudo-therapists."[42] In spite of the growing knowledge—which became inescapable—that some therapists take sexual advantage of patients, it was not until the middle 1970s, when women's groups made sex between male therapists and female patients an issue, that this became a topic of open psychiatric discussion.

Finally, in 1976, the American Psychiatric Association held a panel on "Sex Between Therapist and Patient" at its annual meeting. Judd Marmor, president of the association, and Alan Stone expressed their alarm at the incidence of patient-therapist sex. Virginia Davidson referred to "increasing evidence that indicates therapist-patient sex may be far more prevalent than previously thought." But Stone noted that psychiatry was not prepared to deal with the problem. Licensing boards and professional associations are generally poorly equipped to act as agencies of justice, and professional associations have no power to subpoena and no expertise in investigations, and they do not have large ongoing legal staffs to protect the rights of physicians charged with unethical acts. (Stone omitted the names of all the physicians, as well as patients, in the legal case reports he cited, in order to protect the physicians "from unnecessary public attention.")[43]

The patient has little recourse. There have been very few successful suits for damages. When complaints are made, they often result in contradictory unsubstantiated statements by doctor and patient, and professional societies and licensing boards require additional evidence before they will deprive a doctor of his reputation and means of livelihood.[44] A doctor is presumably stable, and he is in a position to label his patient as paranoid or schizophrenic. When licenses are suspended, it is usually for a short period like six months, and when they are revoked, they are usually reinstituted after a short period.[45]

The first successful civil damage suit against a psychiatrist for using sex as part of the prescribed treatment was the case of *Roy* v. *Hartogs,* which was decided in 1976. In previous cases, psychiatrists had been found guilty of rape for having intercourse with drugged patients or of statutory rape for intercourse with a minor, and there had also been recovery of damages in several cases in which psychiatrists had relations with a consenting, infatuated patient, although doctor and patient recognized this was not acceptable practice. In this case, however, it was alleged that sexual relations had been a recommended part of the treatment. Julie Roy was a thirty-one-year-old depressed divorced woman working in New York who saw Dr. Renatus Hartogs on the advice of a friend. She thought there was something strange about a psychiatrist who often utilized ten-minute appointments (for which he charged ten dollars), but she became a patient. (Hartogs was the author of a psychiatric advice column that he wrote for *Cosmopolitan* magazine.)[46] Soon afterwards, she alleged, the psychiatrist, who was twice her age, induced her to have a sexual relationship as part of her "therapy," and this continued over a period of thirteen months. Then he broke off the relationship.[47]

This case, unlike a handful of other cases in which damages have been secured from seducing doctors, did not involve the patient's love or infatuation. The sex was recommended only as therapy, to help the patient over a sexual "block." The sex was not a deviation from the treatment but was the treatment. Amphetamines and mood-altering drugs were also dispensed freely. The sexual contacts and the pills were both recommended to the patient with the same promise—that they would lead to better mental health.

During the trial Hartogs maintained that the patient was suffering from a psychotic transference, that she was an incurable schizophrenic who had deluded herself into thinking that the sexual encounters had taken place. He also claimed that he was impotent. He testified, "I never had sex with this person. Never! She does not know the difference between fantasy and reality. She will never know it." In his defense his lawyer passed around photographs of a swollen benign tumor on Hartogs' right testicle that allegedly would have made sex painful.[48] But three other patients testified that he had either had sexual relations or had attempted relations with them.[49]

A jury awarded Roy $250,000 in compensatory damages because of her deteriorated psychiatric condition and the loss of opportunity for better treatment, and $100,000 in punitive damages on the ground that the malpractice had been deliberate. An appeals court found there was no basis for punitive damages and reduced the compensatory damages to $25,000.[50] (Roy received an additional $50,000 from Hartogs' insurance company, which at first had denied malpractice insurance covered sexual therapy, but later agreed to pay Roy $50,000 no matter how the case went on appeal.)[51]

The other sex-as-therapy case was decided in California in 1977. Pamela Buckingham was a twenty-six-year-old woman, depressed after surgery for cysts of the breasts, who was advised by her surgeon to go into psychiatric treatment with Dr. Robert Trahms. Dr. Trahms practiced as part of a "psychological corporation" with his wife and brother, also psychiatrists. Buckingham agreed to see Dr. Trahms for two half-hour appointments a week, at forty dollars for each appointment. After a year of therapy, Dr. Trahms suggested Buckingham join his therapy group too, and this, at twenty dollars a session, was added to the other two sessions. Marijuana was smoked as an adjunct to therapy at the group sessions, and chemotherapy—mood elevators—was also a part of the therapeutic regimen. Trahms felt that Buckingham had a "monumental hang-up" and needed to secure "a more realistic bearing about the way people really do relate in the real world of time, space and so forth . . . ."[52]

According to Buckingham, after a period of therapy that he described to her as unproductive, Dr. Trahms "said that he thought that if he had sexual intercourse with me he could help with my problems and better understand what was going on." That night Trahms came to her apartment and initiated a sexual relationship that continued in and out of the office for four months. When Buckingham performed fellatio on Trahms in his office, she was billed the usual forty dollars for the appointment.[53]

According to Buckingham, Trahms urged her to go, and went with her five or six times, to a place in San Francisco's East Bay area called Barry and Shell's. Shell is an ex-striptease artist, a topless dancer, and a masseuse, and Barry is her husband. Barry and Shell admit couples only, at a door charge of ten dollars per couple. The emphasis is on wife- (or partner-) swapping, and homosexual and group experiences are encouraged. Trahms's wife, Dr. Nancy Trahms, had located Barry and Shell's and investigated it by phone. She knew that neither Barry nor Shell were licensed sex therapists but thought that the result of Buckingham's going there with her husband would be therapeutic— "I think that many people benefit, especially patients with sexual problems, by exposure to healthier forms in a natural, relaxed setting."[54]

Trahms gave a different story. He denied under oath that he had had sexual relations with Buckingham. He said he had gone to her apartment two or three times because she was suicidal, "just to keep her alive." But he did not bill for these life-saving missions, and the progress notes he made on the case did not refer to suicidal ideation or attempts.

When Buckingham's funds ran out, she continued the group therapy, but she was forced to eliminate the individual sessions. The sexual therapy ended at this point.

Katherine Hoey was another of Dr. Trahms's patients. She was induced to use cocaine, or what she thought was cocaine—Trahms later testified it was Sudafed, a nasal decongestant, ground to a fine powder. He also influenced her to go to singles bars and to participate in orgies, and she attended the group therapy where marijuana was smoked. She loaned Trahms thousands of dollars so he could remodel a house and pay off old debts (he eventually returned the money to her).

In 1975 Buckingham and Hoey, in a joint action, sued Trahms and his corporation. The three Trahmses took the Fifth Amendment and would not even acknowledge whether Buckingham and Hoey had been patients. The attorneys for Buckingham and Hoey submitted tape recordings of therapy sessions during which patient and doctor had smoked marijuana and discussed both the sexual relationships of other patients and the sexual relationships Trahms had had with other women, including patients. Two other female patients testified against Trahms. One corroborated Buckingham's and Hoey's accounts of group therapy. The other testified that Trahms had asked to see her breasts, given her his business card, and urged her to see a real-estate developer to invest the $50,000 she had received as an insurance settlement after a car accident.

The judge who heard the case found that treatment fell below acceptable standards and awarded $304,000 in damages to Buckingham and $89,100 to Hoey. He found that the house calls and sex treatment should have been noted in the record and that the manner of sex treatment fell "outside the standard of care," and he also found that the marijuana use and borrowing of money from patients was improper.

One of the great misuses of psychiatry has been in the field of sex therapy. William Masters has said, "The sexually dysfunctional person is a pushover for seduction by an authority figure such as the psychotherapist . . . The innumerable examples of patient seduction, both heterosexual and homosexual, are a disgrace to our profession."[55] He estimates that there are between 3500 and 5000 clinics and offices offering what they call sex therapy, "but of that number perhaps 100 have adequately trained people using professional techniques."[56] In most states only the titles of psychiatrist, psychologist, and sometimes social worker are protected by law. Other therapeutic titles—psychotherapist, group therapist, marriage counselor, sex therapist, and even psychoanalyst—are not regulated by state licensing, and since there are no criteria for these titles, anyone who wishes can designate himself any of these. An investigation in New York showed that unlicensed male therapists, psychoanalysts, and marriage counselors, routinely involved women patients in a "great deal of sexual interplay" in the name of therapy.[57] The comparatively small number of approved and reputable sexual therapy centers sometimes employ prostitutes and other "paraprofessionals" (some of them housewives trained to do sex therapy) to have sex with patients who do not have their own partners. Sexual surrogates, in a technique pioneered by Masters and Johnson, represent sexual partners who are not primary therapists but who stand in for primary therapists. Psychoanalytic theorists would find it difficult to distinguish the psychological meanings to the patient of sex with the therapist and sex with a surrogate under the direction of the therapist. An article in *Human Behavior* concludes that "sex surrogate therapy is increasing as more mental health professionals learn about it and more surrogates gain training."[58] (Psychiatrists who have sexual relations with patients sometimes justify this as a form of sexual surrogate therapy.)

Some therapy gets very far afield indeed from conventional treatment, in which the rule of abstinence prevails—the rule that the therapist should not give or receive gratifications outside the scope of usual therapy interchanges. A Georgia psychiatrist was accused of conspiring with female patients to commit crimes and of giving women patients drugs in return for sex, money, and merchandise. He was convicted on nineteen drug counts, one forgery count, and two misdemeanor counts for writing bad checks. Although he went to jail and lost his license, the state employed him at Reidsville, its largest prison, as its prison psychiatrist, working under a special institutional license, while he served his sentence,[59] and after release he was appointed medical director at Reidsville.[60]

The relationship of doctor and patient can get completely out of hand. The *Miami Herald* has reported one such case, in which a psychiatrist is accused of murdering his lover-patient. The death occurred in 1975; the case has yet to come to trial. Dr. Louis Tsavaris, of Tampa, is the psychiatrist; the dead girl was Sally Burton, aged twenty-three, a legal secretary. According to Gene Miller, the *Herald* reporter, Burton's best friend told the police she was not only the patient of Dr. Tsavaris but also his girl friend. He spent two or three nights a week in her apartment but would not marry her because he had a wife and three children. Burton had become pregnant by him, and he had insisted that she have an abortion. After this they had constant fights, and Burton threatened to confront his wife.

Burton died in her apartment with Tsavaris present. He called the fire-rescue squad and said, "I have an emergency situation here. I have a girl who's apparently unconscious and I can't seem to revive her." When the squad reached Burton's apartment, she was dead.

Before the coroner, Dr. John Feegel, had had a chance to do an autopsy, Dr. Tsavaris called him at the morgue to ask about the autopsy results. Dr. Feegel asked him what he knew about the girl.

"Well, not much really," Dr. Tsavaris replied. "I hardly know her at all. She was a patient of mine about six months ago. She had a drug problem. She called me last night at my office and told me she was dizzy . . . I heard her moan. She told me to come over there."

Dr. Feegel performed the autopsy and concluded that Burton had been strangled. Tsavaris was arrested and pleaded not guilty. His lawyers claimed that office records used to build the case against him were illegally obtained, but that issue was taken to the Florida Supreme Court and lost. Three years after the first-degree murder charge, Tsavaris was not yet tried. He was out of jail on bond and practicing psychiatry, according to a news account, "as if nothing happened." In the meantime, two civil suits had been filed against him, one for retaining without payment a $10,000 diamond he had secured from his jeweler on approval, and a more serious case in which a male patient charged Tsavaris with malpractice and slander, alleging that the doctor, in group therapy, had imputed blame for the murder to him.[61]

Tsavaris is only one of nine Florida psychiatrists reported on in a series in the *Miami Herald,* "Sex and the Psychiatrists,"[62] who are accused of sexual misconduct with patients. One was identified as the adult actor in a pornographic movie with two young Tampa boys. A series of scandals involving his relations with young male patients led to a "censure" by the staff at Tampa General Hospital. He then became chief of the Children's Section at the Goldsboro, North Carolina, Cherry Hospital. Another psychiatrist was accused of seducing a patient and borrowing $20,000 from her. A seventy-seven-year-old Coral Gables psychiatrist was accused of forcing himself sexually on a patient.

Another, Dr. Edward Russario, impregnated a patient and later settled a suit for sexual malpractice for $45,000. He then lied to hospital boards by denying his guilt. He went into psychiatric treatment. At a hospital hearing to restore his privileges, his psychiatrist testified that the sexual indiscretion was "an isolated incident," only "a temporary blind spot in his personality," and he added, "I think he will be a better therapist." At a state license revocation hearing, another psychiatrist, who had never examined the complaining woman, testified for Russario, "I gained the distinct impression that Dr. Russario, much as he might think of himself as a lover, was seduced by a woman who very much needed to seduce someone." The Florida Board of Medical Examiners placed Russario on probation for three years and ordered him to remain in therapy. He continues to practice in Daytona Beach.

Dr. George Palmer, executive director of the Florida Board of Medical Examiners, saw these pending lawsuits and license revocation proceedings as not necessarily indicative of anything serious. He told a reporter, "I don't think it is a problem—according to numbers." Dr. Palmer said that in past years female patients did not file lawsuits because of sexual affairs with their therapists. "No, they didn't sue. They enjoyed it—and they didn't want to sue. I guess they sue now for a little notoriety, want to get the doctor—or get money."[63]

There is always someone around to apologize for bad practice in psychiatry. When doctors overstep their bounds and define therapy in unusually broad terms, they are defended on several counts. It is the patient who was the seducer or who wanted money or notoriety. Another defense is that these violations of standards occur so seldom that to call attention to them dignifies them too much, or that enemies of psychiatry are publicizing these few rare instances in order to discredit all psychiatrists. When Phyllis Chesler wrote a magazine article called "The Sensuous Psychiatrists" for *New York* magazine,[64] the editor of the American Psychiatric Association newspaper, *Psychiatric News,* used his own editorial columns to reply. Robert Robinson said that *New York* had "succumbed to the easy temptation in publishing" the article "by a psychologist," the "main thrust of which is that sexual intimacies between male therapists and female patients seem to be 'increasing' especially in New York and California and that the practice is bad. The barb is that the article is entitled 'The Sensuous Psychiatrists,' thereby suggesting, but by no means evidencing, that sexual exploitation of female patients is widespread." Arnold Hodas, a New York psychiatrist, wrote to protest to *New York*: ". . . A tremendous disservice was done not only to the overwhelming numbers of practicing psychiatrists who work within the highest ethical standards and with a sense of compassion for the emotional sufferings of their patients, but also to the vast population of troubled persons who, in need of psychotherapeutic help, have now been given a burden of doubt and concern grossly out of proportion to the realities of the situation."[65]

The third answer to the accusation that psychiatry has overstepped its limits is to claim that psychiatry had not previously drawn sufficiently broad limits, that this was not overstepping bounds but merely redefining standards of acceptable treatment. Eugene Levitt, a psychologist with the Indiana University School of Medicine and the Kinsey Institute, has objected to the "establishment viewpoint" that sex between patients and therapists is "never, or at least hardly ever, justified." These relationships can be therapeutic, Levitt says, providing a "transference-building mechanism," promoting "self-esteem in those with inadequate or disordered gender concepts," and breaking down "inhibitiohs and oppression of impulses."[66]

The most common attitude about therapist exploitation of patients is that the problem is not serious enough to merit much consideration or action. Most therapists condemn patient exploitation, and they see sex with patients as a blatant example of it. But many see the transgressions involving such a small percentage of therapists that the matter does not need much attention. Robinson says, "That a rare psychiatrist, and a troubled one, will succumb to the temptation of sexual relations with a patient may be presumed to be inherent in the human condition. So too will a lawyer occasionally steal, and a reporter lie."[67]

These transgressions continue not so much because a small percentage of therapists overstep bounds and exploit patients, but because all the rest of the therapists do not deal seriously with this exploitation of patients. They ignore these abuses as they ignore many other abuses of psychiatry. The large proportion of psychiatrists is not interested enough in the protection of patients or the image of psychiatry to take action against the small percentage who overstep the limits.

To clean psychiatry's house it would be necessary to define the bounds of psychiatry and clearly label what constitutes overstepping them. It would be necessary to see that all who are qualified as psychiatrists are capable of understanding these professional requirements and willing to try to live within them. It would require speaking up when there are violations so that psychiatrists would report on fellow psychiatrists, and it would mean that psychiatry would have to devise effective disciplinary mechanisms so that erring psychiatrists would be deprived of the privilege of practicing psychiatry. As of today there is little indication that psychiatry is concerned enough with the proprieties of psychiatric practice to devote time and energy to such a housecleaning effort.

The Commercialization of Psychiatry

AT SOME RECENT POINT in its development, psychiatry took a particularly materialistic turn. In addition to the traditional rewards of the therapist—the satisfaction of being in a helping profession, the interest in studying the intricacies of the mind, and the status and material security of psychiatry—it was felt there should be something more. Patients should be made to pay large fees to individuals, partnerships, corporations, and conglomerates. Psychiatry now came to be seen as a business, with a goal, like other commercial ventures, of maximizing financial reward.

Patients had always been expected to pay their own way. If they saw private practitioners or were hospitalized in private hospitals, they were expected to pay well for the care and therapy they received. Even public patients were charged what they could pay, although in the economics of mental health care this developed into a barter arrangement in which indigent patients worked on hospital farms or in hospital laundries in exchange for their care. But there is a difference between a patient being expected to pay his way and being expected to support a particularly affluent life style or, more mercenarily, being expected to yield a profit.

The change took place in the 1950s and 1960s without consideration or debate, and no one stopped to think about what these developments meant for the future practice of psychiatry. It started with Blue Cross, Blue Shield, and third-party payment plans, which made the cost of medical care no longer a factor for many patients and so encouraged physicians, including psychiatrists, to charge more. There was a rise in the standard of living of doctors and then an evolving expectation that patients should pay more to support even higher levels of living. Eventually, the way psychiatrists had traditionally related to their patients—emphasizing care and concern and only secondarily financial reward, charging reduced fees for many patients, and being content to live a middle-class existence—became much more commercially oriented, and psychiatrists and psychologists became insistent that patients support them in a truly grand manner.

There had always been some doctors who had gone into medicine to become rich, but medicine, and particularly psychiatry, had never been considered a high-paying profession. Intellectual curiosity, the idealistic goal of caring for the sick, the hope of combatting mental disease and irrationality, or the enjoyment of an authoritarian position were more important factors in attracting people to psychiatry than the hope of gain. The tradition that the psychiatrist deserved a good middle-class existence but nothing more has prevailed until recently for outpatient therapy. Helene Deutsch, a ninety-three-year-old pioneer psychoanalyst, expressed in an interview some thoughts on American psychoanalysis that could apply equally to American psychiatry. "I am not very satisfied with the psychoanalytic movement here. It is not very idealistic. It is too concerned with money. You know, here analysts are terribly expensive. You cannot believe it. My greatest fee was $30 an hour. If someone could not pay, I would do it for nothing."

Deutsch attributes the lack of idealism in American psychoanalysis partly to the character of the physicians who choose to go into analytic training. "I always put emphasis that when we take candidates, it is not so much intellectual preparation as characterological. I know the most important thing for an analyst is to have reliable character . . . In the time we started, there were people who were very much interested in analysis. Now there are people who are very much interested in money, money, how much money can they make? . . ."[1]

The new emphasis on material rewards involves all physicians, not only psychiatrists. Although many psychiatrists do remarkably well, they could be making more in other medical specialties like surgery, ophthalmology, and pathology. Except for family practice and pediatrics, psychiatry is the least profitable branch of medicine, and psychiatrists often remind each other of this state of affairs. Nevertheless, it can be extremely profitable. Psychiatrists practicing on institutional licenses, who are not qualified to practice generally, make perhaps twenty-eight thousand dollars a year, and those in state hospitals and community mental health centers may make "only" forty-four thousand dollars a year (although many of them can see patients after hours and add to their income), but many other psychiatrists make well over one hundred thousand dollars a year. Those who own their own hospitals or have Prolixin clinics not only make money as therapists but get additional profits as entrepreneurs.

Psychiatrists have also devised ways to increase their incomes by forming associations with psychologists, social workers, counselors, and pastoral counselors, with the psychiatrist receiving a portion of the fee paid to the other therapists. The scheme looks suspiciously like fee splitting, which is considered unethical in medicine, but they justify the practice—and say that the taint of unethicality or illegality has been removed from it—through the fiction that the psychiatrist is a consultant to the primary therapist. This is a particularly bad way to practice psychiatry. It lowers the stature of the cotherapist and robs him of autonomy to deal with a patient, it creates a confusing transference for the patient, and it usually involves hypocrisy and deception because there is actually little or no consultation. (If there were consultation, there would be an even worse dynamic interaction of psychiatrist, subordinate, and patient.) The great advantage of this way of practicing psychiatry is that the authority of the psychiatrist allows the treatment by his associates to qualify as medical treatment, and it becomes eligible for third-party reimbursement. The psychiatrist feels he should be rewarded for this benefit to his colleagues. He also feels justified in collecting a part of the fee because he is the referral source and turns over his excess patient load—or that part of the patient load that can only pay less than his usual fee.

Such kinds of fee splitting and remittance arrangements have been going on in psychiatry for many years. They are not discussed, and the American Psychiatric Association does nothing about them. Psychiatrists are strictly enjoined by the official *Principles of Medical Ethics with Annotations Especially Applicable to Psychiatry* not to receive kickback fees when they refer a patient to another psychiatrist or to a psychologist. "In the practice of medicine a physician should limit the source of his professional income to medical services actually rendered by him, or under his supervision, to his patients." But psychiatrists can employ other psychiatrists or psychologists or other mental health professionals and pay them salaries, and they can receive fees from members of a multidisciplinary team for "education," "administration," and "consultation." Whatever the rationale they use, some psychiatrists customarily receive a portion of the fees earned by their employees or subordinates.[2]

Even when they charge only for the therapy they themselves provide, which is the usual practice, psychiatrists can find themselves in high income brackets. Psychiatrists making well over one hundred thousand dollars a year commiserate with each other because they are not making as much as some other medical specialists. Nevertheless, compared to the psychiatrist of twenty or thirty years ago they do remarkably well.

Psychoanalysis did a great deal to foster the new commercial spirit of psychiatry. One of the first lessons the analysand learned was that no matter how expensive the treatment was, no matter how large the hourly fee, the analyst deserved this recompense for his training and skill and his best efforts. The analysand must learn to value himself sufficiently to feel he was well worth the money he was spending. Then there were special rules concerning fees in psychoanalysis: The analysand "reserved" the hour, and if he missed his hour, he was still responsible for it. The analogy was to the economics of the theater— if there is an empty seat for the performance, the person who purchased the ticket and not the play producer must take the loss. Unlike the theater ticket, however, the analytic hour could not be cancelled in advance or resold. If the analysand was going to be out of town or if he became involved in a long illness, he was still responsible for this hour. He was required to take his vacation at the same time as his analyst, or if he wanted a vacation at some other time, he had to pay for the missed hours.

Psychoanalysts justified some of the obligations they placed on patients by saying that they created an expectable environment without surprises where all contingencies had been taken care of in advance and where room for controversy was at a minimum. It gave therapy its due importance and stature. The practice of requiring patients to pay for missed hours carried over into psychotherapy. When third-party payments became common for psychotherapy, some psychiatrists adopted an ugly practice that involved a collusion between themselves and their patients, oblivious of the damage that this kind of deviance does to a therapeutic relationship. They knew that the insurance company would not pay for missed hours, since from the company's point of view no medical service had been rendered, but they believed it was essential that the missed hour be paid for. They had a variety of rationales for requiring the payment. If there were no charge, the patient would not value the hour. If there were no charge, the analyst might resent the patient, and his countertransference might interfere with therapy. Rather than have the patient dip into his own pocket to pay, the hour was billed to the insurance company as though the patient had been present.

This is only one of a number of strange financial practices that have arisen in modern materialistic psychiatry. Some psychiatrists who have patients in hospitals charge some standard sum per day for visits to the patient, and though the fee is less than an office visit because it is presumably shorter, it is still sizable, often thirty-five dollars. Psychiatrists will drop by the rooms of their patients to see them, but if the patient is asleep, they will consider the sleep too important and will not wake him. If the patient is out on the grounds or on an excursion, he will still be charged for the "visit." Even this kind of billing for phantom services has not been enough to satisfy some psychiatrists, and they have begun to charge for "administrative hours." Traditionally, psychiatrists have performed routine adminis- trative duties for their patients—written notes in a hospital chart, talked to parents or a spouse, dictated discharge summaries, written prescriptions, filled out insurance forms—without figuring out the extra time required and billing for this too. Now, since insurance companies or the government is paying the bill, the temptation to charge for these services has become too strong to resist. Relatives of hospitalized patients are sometimes told that the patient will only see the doctor four days a week but that there will be charges for five hours—the extra hour is for administrative services.

A common psychiatric practice is to postdate psychiatric pathology. Many patients who come to a psychiatrist have had symptoms for a long period of time. Often they have had previous psychiatric treat- ment. But the insurance policy may only cover conditions that were not preexisting at the time the policy was taken out, so by a conniv- ance between the patient and the therapist the condition is called a recent or a new condition so that it will be covered.

Some psychiatrists "discount" the bills of those fortunate patients who have particularly good insurance benefits. Policies may pay 80 percent of all fees after the first $100. Psychiatrists can see patients and charge them $60 an hour, and if the patient says he cannot afford the $12 portion of the fee for which he is responsible (particularly if the psychiatrist has empty hours and recommends therapy on a twice a week or three times a week basis), the therapist can assure the patient that the fee is being "discounted," that the patient need not pay his part of the fee, or he need only pay $2 or $3 or $5. The psychiatrist still makes $48, $50, or more for his "hour," which is only a part of an hour. The insurance company's purpose in the partial coverage, which is to ensure that the patient will not be encouraged to book unneces- sary appointments or stay in treatment too long, is circumvented.

The most evil financial practice of psychiatry results from insurance coverage that pays for inpatient, but not outpatient, therapy. Psychia- trists will hospitalize patients unnecessarily, when they could with support and care be carried as outpatients, so that their fees will be covered. A surprisingly large number—I would say most—of psychiatric hospitalizations can be avoided with enough attention to and support of the patient.

One of the reasons psychiatrists should not live as well as they do is that it affects the way they practice psychiatry. The organic psychiatrist who sees patients for a few minutes to prescribe a change in medication and does not try to establish a personal relationship with his patient can live in any style he likes and it will not affect the therapy. When dynamically oriented therapists are preoccupied with their patients as the source of an exceedingly high standard of living, and when they enter into a host of collusive and shady practices having to do with the financial side of treatment, they impair their therapeutic effectiveness in a number of ways. They fall short of the ideal of uncompromising honesty that Freud saw as necessary for cure, and the therapist who is dishonest cannot ask a patient to be unfearingly honest. They present themselves as shady and conniving, which gives the patient a defective model with which to identify. They develop a countertransference in which the financial status of the patient and the extent of his insurance coverage determines their feelings about the patient and his continuance in treatment.

The need for psychiatrists to justify their extravagant fees is so well recognized that it is a topic for popular humor. A cartoon in *Psychiatric News,* the American Psychiatric Association's newspaper, shows a patient lying on a couch saying, "Therapy is expensive." His therapist replies, "You must look upon it as an investment in the self, a chance for personal reflection, growth, and actualization. Unproductive behavior can be altered and human interactions bettered. Also, it's tax deductible."[3] In the cartoon "B.C." a patient stretched out on a rock asks his analyst, "How much do I owe you?" The analyst replies, "A hundred bucks." Patient: "A HUNDRED BUCKS?" Doctor: "I'm not in this business for my health, you know."[4] A Lichty cartoon shows the analysand again on the couch. The analyst tells him, "The fact that you complain about paying me 80 bucks an hour proves you're not completely nuts!"[5]

In the interest of squeezing more and more money out of the patient, psychiatrists developed the two-fold strategy of raising their fees and shortening the psychiatric "hour." Ralph Greenson, in an article with the title "The Decline and Fall of the 50-Minute Hour," noted that at one time the fifty-minute hour provided ten minutes between patients for analysts to use the telephone or jot down notes, or to use for "a variety of personal reasons." The fifty-minute hour allowed the patient to stay over a few minutes if he needed extra time for catharsis, and the analyst might extend the session a few minutes to round off an interpretation or work through something still unfinished.[6] Greenson favors the fifty-minute hour, using the term in its traditional sense —fifty minutes for each patient, appointments scheduled at hour intervals with ten minutes between patients. The fifty-minute hour is almost always now a "fifty-minute session" with no interval between patients. The couch does not have time to cool off between patients. After World War II the "production-line" method of scheduling fifty-minute appointments with no intervals or back to back, became common, and eventually this progressed in some cases to a forty-five-minute hour without an interval,[7] and recently occasionally to forty minutes.

With the decline of the fifty-minute hour with intervals between patients, says Greenson, patients were forced to pay with their time for their analyst's telephone and toilet activities. Greenson marshals all the arguments in favor of the schedule with intervals and then asks why it is disappearing.

> The primary cause, as far as I have been able to ascertain from questioning analysts and candidates alike, is money. You can squeeze more patients into your working day if there are no time gaps between patients. This is not done for the altruistic purpose of treating more of suffering humanity or for accumulating more analytic experience. It almost always comes down to financial gain . . .
>
> I believe that the decline of the 50-minute hour is symptomatic of a materialistic trend in psychoanalytic practice, at the expense of a humanistic and scientific point of view. It is obvious that taking patient after patient on an assembly-line schedule is an act of hostility, subtle and unconscious though it might be . . . It kills the pleasure in doing analytic work. Small wonder so many analysts complain of fatigue, dread Mondays, and cannot wait for Fridays.[8]

Some psychiatrists, by shrinking the fifty- or forty-five-minute hour to forty minutes and by seeing patients back to back, can realize $90 for an hour of their time. Since those with full patient loads tend to work long hours (many work ten hours a day and a half day on Saturday), they can make $5000 in a week, and even with time off for long vacations and with mounting office expenses, can find themselves in the very high income brackets.

Most psychiatrists do not maximize their incomes. They find it too fatiguing to work fifty-five hours a week, so they do not schedule every hour, and they also spend some time in their week in unpaid clinic or teaching or community work. Psychiatrists have a certain number of unfilled hours and a certain percentage of bills that they are never paid. They express envy of other doctors who can delegate responsibility and bill for injections given by nurses and electrocardiograms taken by assistants. Most psychiatrists do not share in the income of any subordinate. In spite of all this, and even though a large proportion of income will go for taxes, office expenses, investment in a retirement plan (and if this is done, an obligatory investment in a plan for secretary), and for other business expenses, such as the services of an accountant and sometimes of other management personnel, psychiatrists still are often in a vastly higher income bracket than the average patient.

Pietro Castelnuovo-Tedesco has suggested the use of the "20-minute hour." Unlike the twenty-five- or thirty-minute hour, which is sometimes employed in dynamic insight-oriented psychotherapy when patients cannot afford more, the twenty-minute hour is reserved for supportive therapy. There are one or two initial interviews to obtain a history and then a series of about ten treatment interviews, each twenty minutes long. It is necessary to limit strictly the number of sessions allowed the patient for fear that he might get into some difficult emotional area.

> One of the positive features of the Twenty-Minute Hour is its safety and essential freedom from complications. A number of the medical residents worried whether inadvertently they might trigger a serious emotional storm or bring about a worsening of the patient's condition by some ill-advised therapeutic maneuver. As it has turned out, complications of this sort are extremely unlikely, especially if the doctor confines himself to dealing with the patient's *current consciously perceived, realistic* problems, if he maintains a consistently supportive attitude, and if he avoids dealing with buried resentments or with conflictual sexual strivings of which the patient is essentially unaware but at which he may hint in the course of his conversation . . .[9]

If the patient cannot afford even twenty minutes, there is group therapy. Group therapy has its uses. It enables patients who would be inarticulate in a one-to-one therapeutic relationship to speak up and to learn from other patients. It is a socializing experience and it gives the support of group solidarity, but it does not allow the same exploration of intimate feelings and the transference relationship that are possible in one-to-one therapy. Some patients are referred to groups because the referring doctor sincerely believes this is the best treatment for the patient, others are referred because of financial exigency. A group therapist with one group scheduled for 6:30 in the evening until 8:00 and another group from 8:30 until 10:00 can handle twenty patients at twenty dollars a patient in the course of the evening and be home in time to hear the late news. Some groups that have utilized cotherapists have billed patients twenty dollars for each of the therapists.[10]

Psychiatrists locate themselves geographically where they are accessible to the affluent, and they charge very large fees and refuse to see patients who cannot pay them. Such patients are referred to community mental health care centers, where they receive a different kind of therapy. Psychiatrists congregate in expensive office locations in upper-middle-class areas. When I trained in psychiatry, there were still some few psychiatrists in training who planned to make a career in state hospital psychiatry, who were primarily interested in treating the poor. I have not seen a resident in years who was interested in state hospital employment. Community mental health care centers are so short of psychiatrists and Ph.D.-level psychologists that they use them primarily as administrative personnel, for example, to countersign decisions made by others in order to give these decisions the appearance of medical or psychological authority, and in the case of psychiatrists, to write drug prescriptions for patients whom they have never seen. Most of the work with patients in community mental health is done by social workers and semiprofessionals (many with two years or less of college). In many states the psychiatric staff of public hospitals consists largely of foreign medical-school graduates who cannot secure state licenses—sometimes because their English-language skills are deficient—and who can only secure medical employment as "institutional" physicians working in state mental hospitals on "institutional licenses." Foreign physicians secure jobs in state hospitals and are pressed into service as psychiatrists even if their training has been in internal medicine, obstetrics, or urology.

At one time the charge against psychiatrists was that they had abdicated a large share of the mental health scene to psychologists. As a result of the unavailability of psychiatrists in state hospital forensic psychiatric services, courts have been forced to relax rules against testimony by psychologists so that commitments can be ordered and so that testimony in criminal cases can be supplied to the courts. But eventually the psychologists, too, joined the flight from the indigent patient. A news item in *Psychology Today* is titled "Psychologists Practice Where the Money Is." It gives the result of a study showing that most mental health professionals—psychologists, psychiatrists, and social workers—are located in affluent urban states, in larger cities, and in university towns. The three professions were found to be distributed "in strikingly similar ways."[11] Nicholas Cummings, president-elect of the American Psychological Association, says that most people who live in poor areas are not covered by outpatient reimbursement schemes, and "psychologists will go where the reimbursement is."[12]

One psychologist recently commented on the apparent unfairness of life. Psychologists who make only forty thousand dollars a year running psychiatric wards in hospitals, filling up the gap caused by a shortage of hospital-based and academic psychiatrists, resent the salary differential that enables a psychiatrist to earn one hundred thousand dollars or one hundred fifty thousand dollars for the same work.[13]

*   *   *

There are many ways that treating a patient can be made more profitable, but the most obvious is to earn from the patient in two capacities, as a therapist and as an owner or part-owner of the hospital that houses him.

In earlier times, care of the mentally ill in England was performed by religious orders as a good work. Quakers in the seventeenth century began a tradition of operating nonprofit mental hospitals. But contemporaneously with this development, English physicians began to open their homes as "private madhouses" or "houses for lunatics," and by the end of the eighteenth century there was a well-developed "trade in lunatics." The private entrepreneurs dominated the field until the middle of the nineteenth century, when state hospitals, and later teaching hospitals, gained the reputation of being better facilities for patient care. In the first half of this century private hospitals fell into a state of disrepute. They were often run by down-at-heel psychiatrists who were willing to take care of alcoholics and administer electroshock and sequester the troublesome. In the 1950s and 1960s the philosophy of the Eisenhower-Kennedy-Johnson era glorified the capability of the private sector in many areas, including health care, and large sums of federal funds became available to subsidize care in private hospitals. Third-party reimbursement plans also provided a ready source of funds for private (but usually not for state hospital) care. The for-profit hospital was restored to respectability, and individual proprietors, partnerships, corporations, and conglomerates all participated in this money-making medical activity. The for-profit hospitals did not have the fixed overheads of the older state hospitals, and they could undersell university and teaching hospitals by utilizing less well trained personnel, eliminating free and low-cost care for the indigent, and dispensing with training and research programs, which put great financial drains on institutions. The for-profit hospitals send patients who have no insurance benefits or who have used up their benefits to the state hospitals or to the long-suffering nonprofit institutions, increasing the deficits of the nonprofit sector and giving further proof of the "greater efficiency" of the proprietary hospitals.

The patient in the for-profit hospital now was required not only to pay for his care but to provide something extra so that the stock of the corporation that ran the hospital would show a growth trend, and so that the price/earnings ratio of the stock would justify an increase in the value of the stock and the stockholders could net a long-term capital gain. Just as efficiently as pigs were processed in Kansas City to extract every last bit of profit from their carcasses, mental patients were processed in some of these new hospitals in order that the hospital could show a larger profit each year.

There were even franchise hospitals—just like motels and fast-food restaurants—where the parent corporation would come and build a hospital, give instructions on running it, and furnish a "turn-key" entry into the hospital business.

The newest financial wrinkle is the extended treatment clinic or primary medication clinic, where outpatients are regularly given their doses of injectable long-acting tranquilizers on a piecework basis at so much a head. These are patterned on the profitable abortion and renal dialysis clinics.

Turning a profit from mental patients was a natural extension of other government programs. The first area to be exploited by private entrepreneurs who saw an opportunity for making profits by providing services was the education of veterans of World War II. The educational benefits of the G.I. Bill led to the expansion and opening of all kinds of trade and vocational schools—electronics, radio and television, modeling, air conditioning, or art—to provide proprietary education.

The aging members of the population became the next market for for-profit services. Private nursing homes became a booming field. Members of Congress, including Congressman (now Speaker) Thomas "Tip" O'Neill, became partners, sometimes with very small investments, in nursing-home schemes. (O'Neill, who invested only $5000 to become a partner in a nursing home, has said he withdrew his investment in the firm in 1972. He was listed as a partner during the life of a Small Business Administration loan, an apparent violation of federal law, according to a Boston newspaper.)[14] *Time* heralded the nursing-home boom in its news of investment: "Gold in Geriatrics."[15]

It soon became obvious that there could also be a profit from children, that day care, education, and the care of the retarded could bring the same kind of financial rewards. Activities that formerly were performed by volunteers, charities, church groups, or those who tried to be helpful without regard to economic gain are now undertaken routinely by professionals. Day care and early education attracted entrepreneurs, who built up chains through takeovers of established programs. One article on this growing phenomenon was called "Kentucky Fried Children."[16] The title is not farfetched. The Hospital Corporation of America, one of the most successful of the investor-owned hospital chains, was founded in 1968 by two Nashville physicians together with Jack Massey, who had headed the Kentucky Fried Chicken Corporation.[17] In only nine years it grew large enough to recruit the retired chairman of the Prudential Insurance Company of America, the country's largest life insurance company, as its chairman.[18]

The same push toward profit invaded the traditional nonprofit hospital. Amitai Etzioni has written that "many *medical* services with not-for-profit hospitals are provided strictly on a for-profit basis. Profit is made ... in a wholesale way: chiefs of service, especially in anesthesiology and pathology, contract with the hospital to provide all the services required of their specialty for a lump sum, perhaps a million dollars a year. They then retain staff from their pocket and keep the difference, whether it be one hundred, two hundred—or two hundred thousand—dollars."[19]

The field of health care was eventually seen as a prime investment opportunity. Health care became "America's fastest-growing industry." The emphasis on care of patients for a profit was bound to spread to mental health care, although this was a field of medicine where charitable or other nonprofit care and state-supported free care had long traditions.

There were many commercial angles. Some private psychiatric hospitals line their corridors with signed prints by important artists and build an art collection that is deductible as a business expense on the theory that this is a necessary part of the environment for the patient. Mental health corporations pay for fringe benefits, trips and excursions, elaborate public-image-promoting cocktail parties at the time of annual conventions. They provide cars for company officers.

For-profit hospitals and other for-profit providers of services have become so popular that John Gardner, the founder of Common Cause, has felt it necessary to form a new group to "insure the survival of the nonprofit sector." He sees the traditional providers of nonprofit care threatened by government encroachment and tax policy. Gardner says, "Ever since colonial days, foreign visitors have commented on the extraordinary impulse of Americans to form voluntary groups and invent nongovernmental institutions to serve community purposes." Now, he says, nonprofit institutions "are in trouble."[20] Government tax policies increasingly discourage philanthropic giving by small donors, who have in the past provided 80 percent of the support to nonprofit institutions, by encouraging the standard, rather than the itemized, deduction. At the same time, government policies allow large tax write-offs for private for-profit institutions, give large sums to them in grants and contracts, and provide them with huge third-party reimbursement compensations.

The step to the franchise hospital was a natural one for psychiatry. Nursing homes and child care provided examples. In 1967 a group of District of Columbia psychiatrists headed by Leon Yochelson, the professor and chairman of the Department of Psychiatry at the George Washington University School of Medicine, opened a new private hospital, the Psychiatric Institute of Washington. It had no connection with the government, but since it was in the District of Columbia, most of the payment for patient care came from funds that were thereby diverted from support of public facilities. Two years later the same group started the Psychiatric Institute of America "to help answer the need for mental health care on a national scale" by providing "clinical and management expertise." PIA soon showed itself to be a growth company in a growth industry. According to its brochure, published in 1977, "The PIA network now consists of 11 hospitals with more than 500 psychiatrists and 1300 employees. Since 1972 PIA has been experiencing an annual growth rate in excess of 40% ... There is a strong and growing demand for the comprehensive mental health care that PIA provides. Investor-owned hospitals account for 25% of the growth in this fast-growing field. 42% of all hospital beds are psychiatric beds and PIA is now the largest supplier of private mental health services in the country."[21]

The government gave advice in helping PIA develop—for PIA's profit—special programs in drug abuse, prisoner rehabilitation, developmental schools, and adolescent services.

PIA runs a day and residential special educational facility for children and adolescents from age seven to eighteen in the District of Columbia. It runs another Developmental School and Psychiatric Day Treatment Center for Adolescents through its Montgomery County Day Treatment Center. It conducts group psychotherapy, group counseling, and group work-training programs, and its affiliated hospitals run similar programs throughout the country.

PIA was employed by the government of the U.S. Virgin Islands to develop a comprehensive mental health program for the territory, including an inpatient facility, clinics, emergency and home care, and special consultation services for schools, courts, and other agencies. There is no phase of psychiatry that PIA has not been willing to explore with a profit in mind. One new project is in the treatment of alcoholism, a field with a potential of 10 million patients. It describes itself as expanding its business in three ways: acquiring new hospitals, establishing hospitals in partnership with local psychiatrists, and managing hospitals owned by others and providing mental health services for them on a contractual basis.[22] Its senior vice president was formerly with the Internal Revenue Service. Its executive vice president was formerly an associate with the financial firm of Lazard Frères and earlier had a management position with Procter and Gamble. It has a psychiatrist-president, Dr. Edward Fleming, and a twelve-man management team that includes a vice president for financial services, a vice president for provider reimbursement and tax planning, and a vice president of development.

The language of business permeates the brochures and reports of PIA. It says of its acquisition strategy that it is in a good position to accomplish this because of its "strong financial position and its access to capital markets." Announcing an addition to an existing hospital, it describes this as a modern "plant" of 160 beds. In its publications PIA speaks of "the hospital business."

A 1976 report to stockholders showed PIA had total assets of $5,-672,000, compared to $5,121,000 a year earlier, and stockholders' equity, after subtracting long-term liabilities and subordinated debentures, of $2,546,000, a rise of more than $500,000 from $2,060,000 in one year.[23]

PIA is only one of a number of for-profit corporations that have invaded the mental health field. E. Fuller Torrey says, "There's money to be made in madness, and big business knows it."[24] Other corporations that have become involved in the delivery of mental health care include the Hospital Corporation of America, American Medicorp, Community Psychiatric Centers, National Medical Care, American Health Services, and Hospital Affiliates. Hospital Corporation of America (mainly in nonpsychiatric hospitals), after growing by more than 25 percent per year in recent years, projects a continuing growth rate of 20 percent a year. It advertises in the *Wall Street Journal* that it is "the fastest growing company in health care, the nation's largest industry."[25] Community Psychiatric Centers has a growth curve that most corporations would envy: Its earnings per share of common stock were 30 cents in 1969, 40 cents in 1970, 49 cents in 1971, 65 cents in 1972, 84 cents in 1973, $1.01 in 1974, $1.27 in 1975, $1.51 in 1976, $2.34 in 1977, and a remarkable $3.30 in 1978. In 1978, Community Psychiatric Centers was listed on the New York Stock Exchange with the trading symbol CMY. (Besides inpatient psychiatric services, Community Psychiatric Centers also is a leader nationwide in providing dialysis.)[26]

The new for-profit institutions claim they undersell old established programs. Old hospitals have antiquated facilities that raise their cost per patient. The new facility will draw patients away from established facilities, creating underutilization and higher costs per day for public and for nonprofit hospitals, and causing them to operate at even greater deficits. This does not concern the entrepreneur. He does not deal with the overall effect of his innovation on the community or on the total of health expenditure. He is only interested in seeing that a large proportion of the health care budget comes his way. He does not provide training facilities, money for research (unless he thinks this will add to the image of his corporation), or free services to the poor. He is in a good position to demonstrate to state and federal officials that he can deliver a product through his franchise operation at a lower cost per day per patient, and so more and more government dollars go in his direction. (Torrey points out that some not-for-profit hospitals with superior reputations—Hartford's The Institute for Living, Baltimore's Sheppard and Enoch Pratt Hospital—continue to charge much less than the for-profit hospitals like the Carrier Clinic of New Jersey and the Psychiatric Institute of Washington.)

The conglomerate has entered the field of mental health. The Purolator Company, best known for oil filters and as operator of an armored-car service, owns the Carrier Clinic, a 255-bed psychiatric hospital. Has it been a profitable venture for the corporation? "Excellent," says Jack Milne, Purolator's vice president for corporate communications: Carrier generates $9 million a year in revenues and "its earning growth has been extraordinary."

Torrey quotes *Barron's*: "The specialized, free-standing private psychiatric hospital constitutes the smallest—but fastest growing—part of the nation's mental health care delivery system . . . Now the care of people who suffer acute psychic breakdowns can be quick, effective —and profitable."[27] News of hospitals is found in the *Wall Street Journal* and on the financial pages of other daily newspapers. A typical headline reads "Investor-Owned Hospitals Grow."[28] A newspaper carries in its "Securities" column the story "Care for Retarded: New Investment Field."[29]

Although a recent lawsuit against Excepticon, Inc., a for-profit corporation that operates centers for the mentally retarded in Kentucky, claimed that in a 300-bed facility there were inadequate staffing, insufficient programming, and risk for the residents of the possibility of physical injury and harm,[30] neighboring Tennessee has under study the feasibility of hiring private management services to operate all state mental institutions, in order to free the state of all custodial responsibility for the care of patients.[31]

The for-profit hospitals and other entrepreneurs have recently found still another field in which to invest. Ever since the rise of the community mental health system, the emphasis has been on short-term hospital care with supportive services in the community. Many patients are released from hospitals while they still have florid symptoms, and halfway houses and transitional homes have been started to take care of them. Chronic patients need extended care facilities. States are reluctant to appropriate start-up funds for these kinds of "less restrictive alternatives" to total hospital care. They prefer to see private individuals, partnerships, corporations, and conglomerates buy or rent property and take care of the patients on a contract basis. This is a potentially large area for for-profit psychiatry.

Entrepreneurs tout these programs with the argument that the cost is significantly lower than inpatient care. The saving to the state is less than first appears because the fixed costs of existing state services continue with fewer patients, raising the cost per patient. And once more, this gives ammunition to the argument that private services can provide care at a cheaper rate.

There are no figures available on how much of the mental health dollar accrues to for-profit hospitals, but the diversion is occurring at an accelerating rate. Since federal money has become so important in health care, for-profit hospitals maintain lobbyists for their own interests. In this atmosphere of government regulations and government financing, more personal Washington connections are extremely important in order to get grants, get federal subsidies for programs and grants, and to have fees set at the highest possible rates.

A by-product of the traffic in health care is the business of supplying information to health care providers. Newsletters and news services have sprung up to tell purveyors of health care about pending changes in policies and regulations, new laws that are being drafted and introduced, and availability of funds.

*   *   *

With the pressure to maximize material gain in medicine and psychiatry, a number of fraudulent practices arose. These were more flagrant than charging psychiatric patients for missed or administrative hours, or discounting fees. Some of these fraudulent psychiatric practices were detailed in an article in the *American Journal of Psychiatry* by

449

O. B. Towery and Steven Sharfstein, both National Institute of Mental Health psychiatrists.

- Psychiatrists bill for patients never in treatment.

- They bill for multiple services to members of the same family on the same day. This practice is known as "ganging." A family is urged to bring the patient for his treatment, and bills are submitted for family therapy or for individual therapy for each member of the family.

- They refer patients to colleagues for unneeded testing and rehabilitation services in the expectation that they will be rewarded by future referrals of other patients. This is known as "ping-ponging."

- They charge for services by paraprofessionals or medical students or others not eligible for reimbursement.

- They offer or receive kickbacks. (For instance, a therapist refers patients to a psychologist for psychological testing and receives a percentage of the fee.)

- They bill more than one third party—for example, both Medicare and Medicaid—for the same service.

- They make excessive profits from a legitimate treatment. (As an example, a therapist charges each person in a ten-person group the standard fee for an individual session and collects $450 for each hour of group therapy.)

- They steer patients to a particular pharmacist, who renders gifts and favors in return.

- They prescribe indiscriminately. This is one of the most profitable and most fraudulent stratagems of psychiatrists (and other doctors dealing with psychiatric patients), who secure great financial reward by distributing drugs indiscriminately for a fee. A psychiatrist will freely write prescriptions for Valium or phenobarbital for anyone who walks into his office, with no attempt to treat the patient. The patients include those the psychiatrist knows will resell the pills on the street for a profit.[32]

Indiscriminate prescribing is often encouraged by government mental health policy. Dr. William Triebel, the director of a methadone clinic in New York, received eight hundred fifty-seven thousand dollars in Medicaid payments in 1974. Seven other operators of methadone clinics each received from one hundred thirty-one thousand dollars to six hundred eighty-eight thousand dollars in Medicaid funds. The *Village Voice* commented: "And that is only from Medicaid. Clinics with non-Medicaid patient populations gross much more. The distribution of methadone . . . has created a new class of millionaires . . ."[33] For-profit methadone clinics have now been phased out, but the Department of Health, Education, and Welfare is encouraging private entrepreneurs to explore other aspects of the field of health care.

Much indiscriminate prescribing is fraudulent. Physicians accept fees for writing prescriptions for patients who cannot possibly be helped and may be badly hurt by drugs such as Ritalin, Quaalude, Seconal, Biphetamine, Percodan, Desoxyn, Valium, Preludine, Demerol, Dexedrine, Dilaudid, and Nembutal.[34]

The term "scrip doctors" is used to describe California doctors who prescribe large amounts of dangerous drugs freely and who particularly prescribe for young people and addicts. Most doctors who prescribe drugs freely on prescription are not trained as psychiatrists, although they are fulfilling a psychiatric function in "treating" the drug-dependent population. Medi-Cal, a $3.2 billion Medicaid program in California, is charged with promoting drug abuse by supplying millions of addictive pills each year that foster addiction in patients and are also resold to supply street addicts. This drug-dispensing practice has become known as the "Medi-Cal connection." Many of the prescriptions are issued to patients who have forged or false Medi-Cal cards.[35] One California doctor was charged with manslaughter after prescribing 5400 tablets of Ascodeen for a patient who died from an overdose. (This is a habit-forming combination of aspirin and codeine recommended for arthritis victims with severe pain.) Another doctor allegedly wrote 420 Ritalin prescriptions in a nine-day period for a total of 24,720 tablets. Another doctor wrote for one patient 640 prescriptions for Quaalude over a three-month period.[36]

The wholesale writing of prescriptions for Medicaid patients supports a host of addicts and is the mechanism through which great quantities of drugs are resold illegally on the street, but it is only one phase of the fraudulent prescribing of dangerous substances. Many prescriptions are written for affluent patients who pay $15 or $20 for a visit to the doctor, much more than the Medicaid fee. The Drug Enforcement Administration describes cases of doctors who charge a patient $20 for a prescription and see 200 prescription patients in one day—a $4000-a-day business.[37]

Health care has become so profitable that more and more fraud is inevitable. So far, no Mafia or mob involvement in mental health care has come to light, but organized crime is known to have invested in the nursing-home industry and it is readily conceivable that it can spread into the fast-growing field of for-profit mental health care.

Most psychiatrists do not deal in drugs, bill two parties for the same service, or practice ganging or ping-ponging. If they indulge in some

451

materialistic practices that seem to them to be mildly fraudulent, like charging insurance companies for missed hours or discounting fees, they are able to rationalize this or to keep this out of their minds. They practice psychiatry with a feeling of rectitude. They resent charges that psychiatry is materialistic. They pay no attention to the grossly fraudulent practices of some of their colleagues because they say those psychiatrists represent only a small proportion of the profession, and they allow the practices to continue and to grow. When a critic attacks fraud or materialism in psychiatry, they counterattack on the ground that the critic is antipsychiatric.

* * *

All these money-making activities relate to therapy or purported therapy, but psychiatry and psychology have other applications that are unabashedly commercial and that have no pretense of serving any therapeutic goal. Psychiatry and psychology deal with feelings, choices, and preferences, including those that determine consumer purchases. Psychiatrists, and in particular psychologists, sell themselves and their services to commerce and industry and are increasingly using their techniques to measure and to influence political attitudes.

Psychiatrists and psychologists are engaged in studies to determine consumer preferences and to help market new products. They consult on advertisements. The advertising industry has a term, "psychographics," for the technique of dividing consumers into markets on the basis of their psychological attributes and then tailoring advertisements, and even devising new products, to appeal to specific markets.[38] A firm called MPI Sensory Testing, which has among its clients Pepsico, Campbell Soup, and Chesebrough-Pond's, combines computer techniques with the sensory-measuring techniques of academic psychology to "psych out the consumers' taste for everything from table sauce to blue jeans to political candidates."[39] A psychologist studies corporate life and becomes a confidential adviser to heads of corporations, counseling them on how to keep their top management people from leaving and how to be more forcible corporate leaders.[40] Psychiatrists and psychologists counsel political candidates on how to market their "merchandise" and what images they should convey. An expert on body language coaches candidates in hand and body movements to indicate decisiveness, openness, and friendliness.

One of the great themes of world literature is that certain gifts can be used in the service of others, but not for self-aggrandizement and self-enrichment, for when the gift is perverted to a mercenary or a selfish use, it becomes a force for evil instead of good. If psychiatry is such a gift, many of its practitioners have not learned the lesson. They are increasingly on the lookout for new commercial angles. Vance Packard[41] and Martin Gross[42] have documented the industrial uses of psychiatry and psychology, and since their books appeared there have been many new examples. One of these is a service to assist the management of professional sports teams. A psychologist claims that thirteen National Football League teams and thirteen big league baseball teams have been customers for his service, which is to analyze the psyches of athletes in order to "scout the inner man" and see how personality traits match up with those of winning performers.[43]

Popular psychological techniques are being used in the service of litigants, and in particular to help defendants in criminal cases. Two lawyers and a psychologist, going under the name of The Team Defense Project, offer a two-day $200 seminar for lawyers on "Innovative Psychological Concepts Applied to the Law." The aim of the seminar is to teach lawyers how to employ "interdisciplinary techniques" so they can use the law uniquely, make an effective defense or offense, find and utilize experts successfully, and select an optimal jury. The psychologist in this effort is described as a "juristic psychologist," specializing in jury selection and in conducting public opinion surveys to be used as legal evidence. The seminar plans to present "sound psychological bases for legal strategy," to analyse "into procedure . . . that which Darrow knew by instinct . . ."[44]

A "science" of preparing "social profiles" has been developed, and these are used in selecting juries in order to win a better chance of an acquittal for the defendant. This practice received wide publicity after the trial of Angela Davis, when her counsel said this technique had been helpful in securing a jury disposed to acquit her. The "science" of using social profiles and computer technology to decide which jurors to challenge and which to accept is probably less effective than its advocates believe, and it is enormously expensive in terms of the cost of investigating the characteristics of all members of a jury pool,[45] but it can be profitable for the behavioral scientist and at the same time satisfy a need for social activism. It is sometimes justified on the ground that it equalizes "the advantage" that the prosecution has in jury trials.[46] One of the first to question the use of this jury manipulation technique was Amitai Etzioni, who says, "Clearly, the average defendant cannot avail himself of such aid and therefore, the net effect of the new technique, as is so often the case with a new technology, will be to give a leg up to the wealthy or those who command a dedicated following."[47]

In addition to jury selection, there is a field for commercial psychology and psychiatry in the coaching of legal witnesses. Hypnosis is the technique that is favored, both to help witnesses recover material that may have been forgotten and to assist in coaching witnesses so that their testimony will stand up on cross-examination. The Los Angeles Police Department has been using hypnosis since 1970 to hypnotize witnesses and victims to "aid" the criminal-justice process.[48] Authorities on hypnotism, criticizing this use, have stated that suggestible hypnotized subjects may "recall" a hypnotically induced memory as real although it was "produced," and as a result hypnotized witnesses may "remember too much." But courts in some jurisdictions nevertheless allow hypnotically coached testimony.[49]

The commercial and industrial applications of psychiatry and psychology are innumerable. A psychologist counsels shopping-center clerks on how to size up potential customers in order to persuade them to maximize the dollar amounts of their purchase. Television viewers, linked by electrodes to a monitoring machine, show by their brain-wave tracings how they react to test commercials. Eye-tracking and voice-print analysis are used to test commercials, too.[50] The Equitable Life Assurance Company's "in-house psychologist" has pioneered an innovation in corporation psychology, a biofeedback laboratory to protect employees from stress by training them in relaxation. The International Meditation Society is on contract with 120 business companies to conduct classes.[51]

Another commercial use of psychiatry is in selling psychiatry. There is the Mental Health Practitioners Book Club to distribute books on family and marital therapy, alcoholism, counseling children, care of the aging, assertiveness training, and more. There is the Psychotherapy and Social Science Book Club, with scores of titles every month advertised in an elaborate free monthly magazine that runs to sixty-four pages.

Self-help and self-love books proliferate, many of which, like Robert Ringer's *Winning Through Intimidation* and *Looking Out for Number One,*[52] Michael Korda's *Power!* and *Success!*[53] and Wayne Dyer's *Your Erroneous Zones*[54] make it to positions high up on the bestseller lists. Dr. Joyce Brothers' *How To Get Whatever You Want Out of Life* promises that you can secure this with "a pencil, a piece of paper, and sixty seconds a day."[55] The Psychology Today Book Club promotes Wayne Dyer's *Pulling Your Own Strings,* Carlos Castaneda's *The Second Ring of Power,* Katinka Matson's *The Psychology Today Omnibook of Personal Development,* and *Self-Creation.* (*Self-Creation* provides "the one key principle that will show you what you are, how you became that way, how you can change.")

The market for psychological self-help books is inexhaustible, proving perhaps that previous books of the same genre did not accomplish their goal. Most of them borrow concepts of a dynamic psyche from Freud and explain problems and symptoms on the basis of the unconscious—guilt, will to fail, or whatever—but then proceed to the assumption that conscious effort or will is enough to change the habits and perceptions of a lifetime and to dissipate the symptoms. Silvano Arieti has said that such how-to books have little effect beyond instant gratification, and "they may have a negative long-range effect by fostering an attitude of complacency or by inducing us to accept a thin layer of reality or relation at the expense of understanding and genuine sensitivity."[56] But media publicity is readily available for such books, and their authors are out on the trail, visible on television and audible on radio, boosting book sales on promotional tours.

There are a variety of new techniques of help, self-help, and gratification on sale. The *Brain/Mind Bulletin* ("The Publication You've Needed All Along!") informs its readers about new theories and practical applications in "the physics of consciousness, psychology, drugs, perception, meditation, biofeedback, parapsychology, acupuncture, pain, hypnosis, learning, psychiatry, creativity, dreams, memory, and humanistic medicine."[57] Publications and tapes can be bought that cover all phases of human nature and human potential. Nightingale-Conant Corporation, "the Human Resources Company," sells a series of tapes on personal management by objectives. (Prisons and youth detention centers are prime customers for such self-help programs.) Lansford Publishing Company's catalogue of audio-visual products lists forty-six programs in psychology, from Group Brainstorming to Accelerating Personal Achievement, that can be bought for from $15.95 to $195.95.[58]

Aggressivity training is a popular commercial application of psychology-psychiatry. The American Management Association has a three-day course called "Assertiveness Training for Managers," which for $490 ($425 for members) teaches "how to be pushy without being overbearing." Says the *Wall Street Journal*, "At an increasing number of companies, taking courses such as this has become part of managerial life."[59] Pitney Bowes and Gulf Oil use transactional analysis consultants to train personnel how to respond to customers.[60]

Perhaps the most lucrative application of pop psychology is the Werner Erhard est seminar. At the start of 1978 there were one hundred thirty-two thousand people who had graduated from est training, and the number was growing at a rate of about fifty thousand a year.[61] The training is taken on two weekends for $250 (more recently $300), yielding a total of over $33 million since the start of the program, with a current yearly gross (for the basic course alone, excluding "graduate" courses) of $15 million. Four recent books with such titles as *EST: 60*

455

Hours That Transform Your Life and *EST: 4 Days to Make Your Life Work* extol the seminar, and celebrities like Valerie Harper, Dick Gregory, Diana Ross, and John Denver publicly endorse the method.[62]

Other, more psychologically oriented entrepreneurial uses of psychiatry and the behavioral sciences involve hypnotism, now undergoing a revival of popularity; biofeedback training to deal with a variety of physical and mental problems; and specialized symptomatic clinics relating to smoking, compulsive gambling, obesity, and a variety of other human foibles.

A Soviet psychiatrist comments, "The question is, how do Americans, so famous for their pragmatism and common sense, fall into such crudely laid traps? How is it that those who are accustomed to saving every cent, freely give away their dollars to aggressive charlatans?"[63]

In addition to the obvious exploitation involved in commercial applications of behavioral sciences, there is another objection to it. It dilutes and cheapens the principles of the disciplines involved and makes them less credible and less capable of providing help in times of need. Joyce Brothers tells readers of travel news in the *New York Times* how to survive the postvacation blahs. (Plan a little treat for the middle of the first week back.)[64] Dr. Richard Kohl tells readers of the *New York Times* why they prefer to return to the same resort year after year. ("People feel uneasy about going to a strange place and leaving the safety and security of home . . .")[65] Dr. Fredrick Koenig tells readers of the *National Enquirer* how to cope with the fears of everyday living. (Accept the fact that life is a risk—and stop worrying . . .)[66]

Every commercial exploitation of psychiatry, large or small, detracts from an integrity that psychiatry needs if it is to have meaning, and it trivializes it. Freud, when he was approached to give his authorization to a movie with a psychoanalytic theme, refused, saying, "We do not want to give our consent to anything insipid."[67]

When it becomes commercial, psychiatry dwindles down to a treatment of symptoms and exploitation of techniques, a pretense of interpersonality that achieves only impersonality, a pretense of helping another that helps only the self. Many psychiatrists do not approve the commercialism of psychiatry. They follow a code that prohibits fraud and personal publicity and the other concomitants of the new materialistic psychiatry. But almost no psychiatrists speak out against it. They turn their eyes away to avoid the sight of the money tree being shaken, and if they become aware of it, they hold their tongues. In the absence of a protest from the psychiatrists who do not exploit psychiatry, those who do, flourish.

456

The Brave New World of Psychiatry

PSYCHIATRY HAS DEVELOPED a number of methods—verbal therapy, chemotherapy, other somatic therapies, and behavior modification are the chief categories—to change man's thoughts and feelings and to control his behavior, but these at their best are less than completely effective. Scientists continue to work to refine existing methods and to develop new techniques to gain greater control over thought, feelings, and behavior. The transfer of learning from worm to worm, the transplanting of monkeys' heads, the study of the contraction of the iris of the eye, a science of interpreting voice patterns to quantify such a characteristic as sincerity, these are the kinds of research that our Dr. Frankensteins, Dr. Arrowsmiths, and Dr. Strangeloves, with motives that range from the idealistic to the megalomaniacal, pursue in the interest of greater effectiveness.

Psychiatry is still a new science. The discoveries of useful chemotherapy agents and of the method of verbal therapy are less than a century old. Somatic treatments like psychosurgery and electroshock therapy are only half a century old. Behavior modification and aversive conditioning have been used widely only for two decades. We can anticipate that there will be developments to refine all these means of treatments, and that in addition, innovative scientists will develop new techniques of treatment and control that will give psychiatrists increased power.

Talking of even newer ways of controlling thoughts and feelings seems farfetched when the methods we now use already sound like the fulfillment of the most unlikely predictions of George Orwell, Aldous Huxley, and Anthony Burgess. In *1984, Brave New World,* and *A Clockwork Orange* we have a foretaste of a science-dominated world in which man will be controlled through the application of drugs, educational or brainwashing indoctrination techniques, and behavioral modification. The prediction of a population lulled into conformity by drugs has been at least partially fulfilled. The use of precise stereotactic surgery on the brain has outdistanced the imagination of the novelist, and such innovations as treating criminals with hormones to control their violence are not something predicted for the future but a description of what is going on in the present. Some of the wilder aversive conditioning approaches to control of criminal behavior have only been curbed by the eternal vigilance of civil-libertarian lawyers. Certainly nothing in the futuristic predictions of novelists is any more bizarre or outlandish than the concept of forcing people, by the threat of imprisonment if they are on parole or probation, or by the threat of psychiatric commitment, to present themselves at biweekly intervals to be injected with a long-acting tranquilizer and so to have their thoughts, actions, and sexual appetites quelled.

In the laboratory there are even more powerful tools of thought and behavior control that are being perfected. Some of them may not prove to be effective. Some of them may be curtailed by legal action. Nevertheless a culture that is increasingly depersonalized, fragmented, and pragmatic will inevitably turn to new methods of thought and behavior control to deal with any number of its problems, ranging from social maladjustment to criminal behavior.

One of the most "promising" lines of research has to do with the possibility of the transfer of learning. Primitive societies have always had a belief in the transfer of learning. Cannibals have tried to gain the strength and the courage of their adversaries by eating their hearts, brains, livers, or testicles. If learning and memories are contained in, or encoded on, some physical substance, it could be transferred from one individual to another, or synthesized so that learning and memories could be supplied by pills or injections. In the 1960s researchers at the University of Michigan claimed that by grinding up trained planarians (primitive flatworms) and feeding them to untrained planarians, they had incorporated the learned responses of the trained into the behavior patterns of the untrained. Later, extracts of the brains of rats who had been trained to fear the dark by being conditioned with electric shocks were injected into untrained rats, and apparently these rats were also made fearful of the dark. The 15-amino acid polypeptide, called scotophobin because it caused fear of the dark, was later said to produce the same dark-avoidance response when injected into untrained rats, mice, goldfish, and cockroaches.[1] Dr. Georges Ungar of Baylor University has said that when the complete memory code is deciphered it may be possible to "devise custom-made molecules to achieve a desired effect in a child who cannot learn easily."[2]

Much of the learning-transfer research has been questioned. In some cases results have not been duplicated by other researchers and in others the experiment design has been criticized. Avram Goldstein, a pharmacologist at Stanford University, raises the question of whether what had been transferred was a fear of the dark or was instead an unspecific fear related to the stress of the electric shock conditioning. But he said, "If this material . . . is truly capable of specifically transferring learned behavior to untrained recipient animals, the discovery certainly ranks among the most fundamental in modern biology."[3]

Even if specific learned responses cannot be transferred, there is the possibility that the ability to learn can be greatly augmented by increasing the substances in the brain associated with learning and memory. Psychological as well as nutritional and chemical approaches are being used experimentally to expand the size of the brain's cortex. Professor Holger Hyden of the University of Göteborg has reported that ribonucleic acid in rat brains increases by as much as 35 percent when the animals are learning difficult tasks.[4] Researchers at the University of California have found that rats living for as few as four days in an "enriched environment," with enough toys and objects of stimulation, develop brains measurably larger than less stimulated rats. The quantity of protein in the diet at crucial stages of development—during the second half of the intrauterine period when the central nervous system is developing rapidly and during the first six months of life when the brain's glial cells are increasing most rapidly—affects brain size and learning ability of experimental animals. A team of psychopharmacologists and other scientists seeking a cure for neurological disorders have succeeded in the grafting of the functioning part of the brain of one rat onto the damaged brain of another and have reported growth of the graft in the "new" brain.[5]

Maya Pines, reporting on experiments to shape the infant brain, says, "Within a few decades, we will know how nutrition, chemistry, activity, environmental variety and other factors interact to shape the infant's brain at specific periods in its development . . . When more is learned about the mosaic of differential maturation in the brain, and about critical periods in brain development, we will know how to intervene and when—not only to prevent subnormality, but to produce more intelligent and stabler human beings. Physicians will then find themselves involved in far more than traditional medicine. In

459

addition, they will have to prescribe vital components for the enrichment of the infant's environment."[6]

The world of the future may be as concerned with making people lose their memories as in making them remember more. We already have powerful agents to erase memories (one of the main results of electroshock therapy is the selective loss of memory) or to cause memories to lose their emotional force, which is the effect of some chemotherapy. George Orwell envisioned a world in which a ruling class of technologists could require history to conform to every change in governmental policy. The process currently goes on in all the school systems of the world, most notably in totalitarian countries, but it only works efficiently on the unlearned, who do not have learning to erase. Unlearning could create a more malleable population. A new drug, lorazepam, given before surgery, is alleged to create a reliable controlled form of amnesia so that all memories of the surgery and events immediately preceding it vanish from the mind.[7]

A promising field of neuroendocrinological research has to do with ways of augmenting pleasure. Enhanced pleasure could serve as the most powerful reward of behavior-reinforcing schemes. In the 1960s researchers discovered that when electrodes were put in the pleasure center of the brains of rats and the rats were allowed to stimulate these areas by slight shocks, they lost interest in everything else. They chose stimulating their own pleasure centers over receiving food, water, and sexual opportunity, preferring to spend their time pressing the stimulation bar as frequently as 8000 times an hour.

In addition to electrical stimulation, the brain can give pleasure by manufacturing its own opiatelike hormones. A team of Scottish researchers isolated from beta-lipotropin two peptides that acted like morphine in giving pain relief. Named enkephalins, these were the first natural pain-relieving molecules to be found in the brain and body, and they opened a whole new line of scientific research into internally generated, rather than externally supplied, pleasure-giving and relief of pain. The researcher who finds the way to call upon this brain function at will, perhaps by stimulating its production through an ingested drug or enzyme, will have a most powerful means of rewarding behavior.[8]

Morphine, Demerol, methadone, and the amino acid chain of the enkephalins all attach to the same receptor sites in the brain. It has been suggested that the enkephalins may be related to feelings of pleasure just as opiates are related to feelings of euphoria, and that there may be a correlation between low enkephalin levels and a susceptibility to depression.[9]

460

In 1976 Choh Hao Li, discoverer of the pituitary growth hormone, reported the isolation of a natural opiate manufactured by the pituitary, beta-endorphin, which was said to be twenty to forty times more potent than morphine when injected into the brain and three to four times more potent when administered intravenously. Beta-endorphin promised to be useful in the treatment of morphine withdrawal,[10] but it is of more interest as a naturally occurring opioid substance that has more efficacy than other similar agents. (He had previously isolated a pituitary hormone fragment, beta-MSH, which may have application in helping the mentally retarded to comprehend and work better and the senile to remember better.)[11] Recently, Nathan Kline has reported success in using beta-endorphin to treat schizophrenia intractable to antipsychotic drugs.[12] One fascination that enkephalins and endorphins have for researchers is that they bring together three different fields of research that increasingly are seen as interrelated—pain relief, drug addiction, and mental illness.

Hormones are released in the bloodstream and affect the internal environment, whereas pheromones are combinations of aliphatic acids that convey their messages at a distance, exerting specific effects on the behavior or the physiology of another of the same species. One of the first pheromones to be isolated is emitted by the female silkworm to turn on the male's copulatory efforts and is so sensitizing that only one-trillionth of a gram is needed to activate the male.

The study of pheromones is bringing us information on the attraction that people have for other people, their antipathies, and their sexual arousal patterns. It opens the way to a further understanding of the early interaction of mother and infant. Smell has always been considered the human sense that is least utilized, one hypothesis being that smell became less useful as man raised himself to a bipedal posture. In comparison to animals, which choose their friends and their mates on the basis of smell, man seems to react only to the most obvious smells of his environment. There remains the possibility that human odors and biochemical cues affect human relationships more than we realize and that biological family closeness, possibly in the first hours of life, may be forged by the action of pheromones.

Pheromones were first studied as sexual attractants and aphrodisiacs in the lives of moths and butterflies, but they are now known to act in many species to warn off competing males or territorial invaders, to mark trails toward food and shelter, to denote group pecking orders, and to announce danger. In addition to affecting overt behavior, pheromones also influence deep endocrine processes. The odor of a strange male mouse will block pregnancy in a newly impregnated female. (Hippocrates had noted that in the human female the sense of smell can lead to a miscarriage.)[13]

British researchers were the first to show the action of pheromones in the higher primates. They demonstrated that male monkeys habitually lost interest in ovariectomized females, but that they stopped differentiating between receptive and unreceptive sex partners if their nostrils were plugged and their nasal nerve supply severed. In the 1960s Richard Michael isolated the chemical that signaled the sexual condition of the female to the male and named it "copulin." In 1974, Michael and his group, now at Emory University, reported that he had found a sex-attractant pheromone in human vaginal secretions and that taking oral contraceptives can disrupt its production.

A psychoanalyst has pointed out that the axilla is also covered with coarse hair and produces secretions and an odor that can act as a sexual attractant, and indeed, the skin itself has been called "the principal organ of sexual attraction."[14] Jane Rosenzweig has identified as the elements of the human sexually related pheromonal system the axillary and pubic apocrine glands, hair tufts, vaginal glands, prepuce, labia, and smegma. Rosenzweig says that such practices as circumcision, the use of antiperspirants, and axillary shaving are promoted by the human awareness that various parts of the body have a specific capacity to arouse.[15] Human pheromones are only beginning to be studied. Do modern living practices, which make the elimination of bodily odors a social necessity, alter the forces of sexual attraction?

Perhaps an even more important topic for the future of the race relates to the effect of pheromones on mother-infant interaction. We know that, in other species, when mother and infant are separated from each other in certain critical periods of infant development they can never again establish a strong affectional bond. The separation of infants and mothers by modern obstetrical practice may lead to an impaired mother-child relationship. Perhaps someday adoptive mothers and fathers will be painted with pheromones in order to bond their children more closely to them. We already know that nursing babies at the age of six weeks will respond to the mother's odors (absorbed on pads worn inside brassieres), but not to a strange mother's odor, although at two weeks they are much less selective. Pheromones can be created synthetically. In the future we may be able to manipulate the pheromonal system to attract, repel, calm, excite, and affect many other responses.

A number of other pharmacological, surgical, and electrical approaches to the brain are being studied, and research reports are constantly announcing new discoveries. In the field of drug research, physostigmine is being used to improve memory.[16] Researchers are working on drugs to improve creativity and productivity that will be less addicting and harmful than the amphetamines,[17] and a new antianxiety drug has been developed that does not affect the central nervous system and is said to enhance performance.[18] Since drugs are so profitable and pharmaceutical companies have such hopes of huge financial rewards from new discoveries, drug research is the best-financed area of psychiatric research.

The use of antianxiety drugs will have negative as well as positive effects. Jeffrey Gray, writing in *Human Nature,* says that in his own research antianxiety agents had therapeutic benefit, but they also lessened the ability of an animal to notice change in its environment and to respond to new events, and they prevented animals from learning to persist when faced with an adverse and unpredictable environment.[19] Other experiments show that mind-altering drugs in laboratory animals can cause them to lose interest in earning rewards.[20] Researchers consider lack of ambition, insensitivity to environment, and disregard of danger to be drawbacks that are attached to the use of some psychotropic drugs. But from another point of view—from the position of a government that wished to keep a population docile and conforming—these might be seen as desirable effects, and drugs might be produced that promoted these characteristics. In any case, the fact that there is potential profit from these new drugs and that they promise relief from anxiety, fear, depression, psychotic thinking, and all other unpleasant affects will keep this research popular.

Human aggression is receiving particular research consideration, for chemotherapeutic methods to control aggression would be useful to criminologists and penologists as well as psychiatrists. A study on navy volunteers showed that those with the lowest aggression test scores had the highest levels of serotinin in their cerebrospinal fluid and those with the highest aggression scores had the highest levels of norepinephrine.[21] A long-time study at the National Institute of Mental Health concerns the way stimulation of the brain is either inhibited or intensified. Some people, known as reducers, decrease the magnitude or intensity of stimuli and others, augmenters, intensify stimuli.[22] Finding the mechanisms and agents that produce these shifts could lead to the application of techniques to make people more or less reactive. Other new research ranges from ways of facilitating the indoctrination of ideas to neurosurgery on primate fetuses and consenting human adults.

Some of the newest fields of research interest are brain regeneration[23] after physical injury and the differentiation of the functions of the left and the right sides of the brain.[24] Regeneration opens the prospect of increasing brain size and capacity. Lateralization studies have an implied promise of improving both the creativity that has been associated with the nondominant side of the brain and the more logical thinking that has been associated with the dominant side.

David Goodman, a psychobiologist, has written that a division in the brain more significant than right and left, or longitudinal, splitting is its latitudinal splitting into the frontal cortex and the posterior cortex. Two levels of intelligence are postulated: One is logical, linear, and verbal; the other relates to foresight, self-regulation, and adult social sense. Goodman thinks we can exploit the potential of the brain to think in a more adult fashion.[25] Among the possible practical applications of the longitudinal right-and-left hemisphere studies of the brain is that of making electroconvulsive therapy more effective by shocking only one side of the brain. Some studies found shocking the dominant side more effective, some the nondominant side, but in any case researchers will continue to try to increase the effectiveness of therapies by more specifically localizing the sites of the treatment.[26]

Something else to think about is the marriage of electronics and the circuitry of the brain. In 1970 a team of researchers at Yale Medical School headed by José Delgado announced the achievement of two-way radio communication between a computer and the brain of a chimpanzee. The experiment had implications for diagnosis and also for the eventual development of brain pacemakers to monitor areas of the brain's electrical activity by remote computer. Delgado raised the possibility that this someday could be the treatment for epilepsy. Electrical activity in the brain that could lead to convulsive attacks would be directed and corrected by computer while the patient continued normal activities. Another possible development would be direct communication from brain to brain.[27]

Adam Reed, a Rockefeller University scientist, has said that "ideally, the computer of the future should be an electronic extension of the brain, functioning in parallel with some of the existing brain structures and using the same program and data languages." Reed says he is talking about the "ultimate technology of the indefinite future," but he adds that there is nothing in the present state of knowledge to make such a brain-connected computer impossible and that it could be developed within the next half-century. The computer would share with the brain "the informational processes which we think of as our minds," helping the mind to function faster and more reliably, and it would have an almost infinite memory storage capacity with incomparably greater reliability than unaided memory. The computer adjunct

464

of the brain would make contact with the brain's neurons for both input and output without interfering with their normal operations. "Finally," Reed says, "the user's terminal and preferably the entire computer should be implantable in a convenient position under the user's scalp." Reed admits it is conceivable that the technology could be misused, "that thoughts could be injected into a person's mind with such a system." He believes that it is essential that people be able to use computer thoughts for their own purposes, rather than have thoughts "imposed on them by the political structure . . ."[28] and adds that if there were abuses, "those who work in the field would simply shut off the availability of that technology." The brain-computer hookup would be a "great thing to have," he says, "as long as it was under one's personal control."[29] His suggestion for a future time when such a technology is abused is practical but not hopeful: "If the political system changes and massive abuses appear likely, that would be the time to disappear from society." Commenting on Reed's proposal, John McCarthy, a computer expert, said, "If fully successfully done, this would constitute a complete evolutionary jump in the species. Fundamentally, it's something that can't be suppressed."[30]

A Stanford Research Institute neurophysiologist and electrical engineer, Lawrence Pinneo, has demonstrated that a computer, by translating the electroencephalogram tracings of brain waves, can react to the demands of a subject expressed not in words but in thoughts. He has taught his computer to recognize with 60 percent accuracy the brain-wave patterns for seven different commands—up, down, left, right, slow, fast, and stop—and to directly control a dot on a TV screen to follow these commands. Reporting on Pinneo's experiments, *Time* says,

> He foresees the day when computers will be able to recognize the smallest units in the English language—the 40-odd basic sounds (or phonemes) out of which all words or verbalized thoughts can be constructed. Such skills could be put to many practical uses. The pilot of a high-speed plane or spacecraft, for instance, could simply order by thought alone some vital flight information for an all-purpose cockpit display. There would be no need to search for the right dials or switches on a crowded instrument panel.
>
> Pinneo does not worry that mind-reading computers might be abused by Big Brotherly governments or overly zealous police trying to ferret out the innermost thoughts of citizens. Rather than a menace, he says, they could be a highly civilizing influence. In the future, Pinneo speculates, technology may well be sufficiently advanced to feed information from the computer directly back into the brain. People with problems, for example, might don mind-reading helmets ("thinking caps") that let the computer help them

untangle everything from complex tax returns to matrimonial messes. Adds Pinneo: "When the person takes this thing off, he might feel pretty damn dumb."[31]

A dream of behavioral scientists is accurate diagnosis of abnormal mental states and accurate testing of intelligence. If information about the brain or its capacity can be secured by a direct print-out, rather than through such intervening steps as observed or described symptoms or by performance on tests, it could be much more reliable and much easier to obtain. (It also could give much more authority to the diagnoser or the tester, whose evaluation of the subject would now become incontestable.) The method of measuring intelligence and diagnosing illness by recording electrical impulses generated by the brain has been called "brain gauging." A Canadian psychologist has developed a machine that he claims measures a child's intelligence by the speed with which the brain responds to light. A California study of navy personnel is attempting to correlate their brain-wave responses, evoked by light and other stimuli, with their performance in the service. One research project explores the differences between the signals emanating from the two hemispheres of the brain as a gauge of intelligence, while still another use of brain gauging studies the effect of drugs by measuring changes in response times.[32]

A research team at New York Medical College's Brain Research Laboratory has invented a new brain test called the Quantitative Electrophysiological Battery. Electrical potential from the brain is fed from a forest of electrodes placed over the scalp into a computer, which processes eighty-five thousand readings from each individual and compares them to average readings in the population from which the subject comes. With this technique, it would be possible to have mass screening—like X-ray programs to detect cases of tuberculosis—for brain disease, mental defect, and organically caused learning dysfunctions.[33]

Brain gauging could be used to open or close doors to higher education and vocational or professional training. It could even be applied to family life. Eugenic-minded scientists have revived the old concepts that only certain people should be encouraged, or even allowed, to have children. (One proposal is to add a contraceptive to drinking water to render the whole population sterile with only those approved by the state furnished with the antidote.)[34] In the future we may test potential parents by a Quantitative Electrophysiological Battery or some other brain-gauging method to see if they should be allowed to have children.

466

Research developments hold out the promise of greater ability to prevent crime, fraud, and lying, and to control the physical movement of people such as paroled criminals under surveillance.

A system called "electronic rehabilitation" was proposed by Ralph Schwitzgebel a decade ago. This system would weld small transmitters to the arms of parolees to report on all their movements. Schwitzgebel later suggested that in addition to location monitoring, there could be remote monitoring of voice, blood pressure, brain waves, and other physiological activity. The electronic system could be developed so that it not only reported on the offender but also transmitted signals to him that could activate behavior modification devices worn on his body. Schwitzgebel noted that a small portable shock apparatus with electrodes attached to the wrist had been used to help inhibit a patient's addiction to Demerol, and he described other similar developments: a cigarette case that shocks the user whenever he opens it, a device that emits a musical tone to tell the wearer when his posture is sagging, and a device worn on the head that administers a small amount of direct current to the forehead of a patient to reduce depression. Schwitzgebel said, "Gradually, a new field of study may be emerging, variously known as behavioral engineering or behavioral instrumentation, that focuses upon the use of electromechanical devices for the modification of behavior . . . As can be seen, new developments in monitoring and intervention systems are occurring rapidly and are greatly increasing communication capabilities within the offender's natural environment."[35]

Two criminologists have proposed a sophisticated and updated version of Schwitzgebel's proposal to keep paroled criminals under surveillance by implanting electrodes in their brain and monitoring their movements and physiological processes. With this new device, a wired-up parolee whose read-out indicates he is in a jewelry store or bank with a rapid respiration rate, increased adrenalin flow, and muscle tension would be called to the attention of the police or parole officials. A further development of this scenario would be to have the computer transmit an electrical impulse to the subject, causing him to forget or abandon his plan to rob.[36]

One of the present uses of behavioral science technology is the detection of lies. The polygraph is a half-century-old device that is used by the government and many businesses and is increasingly accepted as evidence by courts. Many newer techniques raise the possibility of more accurate and more effective methods of lie detection that do not even involve the subject's knowledge that he is being tested.

Many prospective employees are screened by preemployment polygraph tests, and from three hundred thousand to five hundred thousand tests yearly are done on job applicants, employees suspected of theft, and as routine "revaccination" quizzing of employees as a deterrent to future theft.[37] The questions asked in preemployment testing usually involve such areas as the applicant's health, education, financial affairs, and use of drugs.[38] Sodium pentothal and other "truth serums" have been used to uncover deception, to recover memories, and to facilitate therapy.

Now a new battery of truth-testing devices is being developed to increase the effectiveness of lie detection. The psychological stress evaluator has the advantage of requiring no cooperation from the subject. Its inventor, Allan Bell, has said that it "is the first lie detector that can be used on a dead man." The psychological stress evaluator detects lies—or more accurately, measures stress—by recording the intensity of muscle tension connected with speaking, and a tape recording of the voice is enough basis for the testing. The evaluator was developed in the late 1960s when a small electronics company headed by Bell, a retired army intelligence officer, was commissioned to measure the stress that people showed in responding to poll interviews. Bell saw odors and the voice as the two obvious methods of approach to the problem, but he discarded the idea of testing by odors because they are so numerous, are contaminated by other odors, and are quickly dispelled.[39] (Nevertheless, detecting and deciphering chemical signals may someday be a major method of analyzing behavior.)

Bell picked out the voice as an easily observed indication of tension. All muscles in use, including those controlling the vocal cords, vibrate slightly. The vibration is called the "muscle microtremor." When a subject is under stress or is consciously striving to think, the tremor is suppressed. Tapes of voices played through a small portable PSE machine plot the amount of stress by its inverse relationship to the microtremor. Bell tested the device by analyzing the voices of contestants on "To Tell the Truth" who all claimed to be the real subject. From the suppression of the microtremor when the contestant said, "My name is . . . ," Bell claimed he achieved 95 percent accuracy in picking out the false contestants.[40] The method was soon applied to crime detection. It is now used routinely in some jurisdictions to confirm the stories of criminal defendants. By 1975, a few years after its introduction, more than 700 PSE machines had been sold at $4200 each. One early study of PSE, or voice-stress, analysis, done by the Land Warfare Laboratory of the Department of Defense, indicated that the machines were only 33 percent accurate (a result about the same as chance), in comparison to 76 percent accuracy for the polygraph, but Bell disputes this.[41] He claims that his machine can facilitate psychotherapy by graphing responses to stress words and says, "We can do six months' worth of psychoanalysis in ten minutes."[42]

Some of the objections to PSE are that it can be utilized without the knowledge of the subject and that it can be used in conjunction with wiretapping. It can also be the basis for the denial of employment without the job seeker ever knowing that his voice was analyzed for sincerity or other attributes. (Although these are cited as drawbacks, others would call them advantages.)

Voice-stress analysis indicated that Nixon was lying or showing great stress when he said no one at the White House was involved in Watergate, and again when he said he would turn over all relevant tape recordings and material regarding his discussion of Watergate to the House Judiciary Committee. Voice-stress analysis of the Carter-Ford debates showed that Carter was either less truthful or under more stress than Ford. (Ford's campaign director decided not to publicize the result for fear of introducing a new and unproven element into political campaigning.)[43] Former CIA computer specialist George O'Toole has written a book asserting that Lee Harvey Oswald was innocent of any killing. His belief is based partly on a voice analysis of Oswald's statement, "I didn't kill anybody, no sir."[44] The Hagoth Corporation advertises to executives that for $1500 they can buy a voice-stress analyzer that can be connected to telephones or used independently, which indicates by displays of red and green lights when a speaker is under stress. According to the advertisement, the machine "is used in situations where money is in jeopardy, and where a business decision is called for. In a complex negotiation, it can give you the edge."[45]

Cynthia Kasabian, a *Wall Street Journal* reporter, has noted that Hagoth's president cannot produce any independent test data that prove the effectiveness of his device, and that when she prepared a list of ten questions about her personal life in order for him to determine the truth of her answers, he misjudged six. (She gives an example: to the question "Do you live near your brother?" her answer was yes. The green lights on the Hagoth analyzer indicated a truthful answer. Kasabian has no brother.)[46]

But whether or not these particular voice-analysis methods work in detecting lies or indicating sincerity, the search will go on to improve methods to test for truthfulness with and without the cooperation of the subject, and even without his knowledge. The stakes are high, and not only law enforcement agencies but the security operations of department stores, jewelry and other retail stores, trucking firms, banks, and investment houses provide a great market for any lie detection device. (Tiffany and Company gives preemployment polygraphs to all its employees. The firm that does the testing reports a 40-percent turndown rate, usually because of unacceptable answers concerning gambling, drinking habits, or a history of theft.)[47]

Some of the newer methods of discovering deceit or ascertaining emotional reactions need the cooperation of the subject, others do not. Some are alleged by their developers to give a direct read-out on the brain instead of reporting on secondary phenomena such as perspiration, heart rate, and blood pressure.

Measuring the pupil of the eye is one new approach. Lying is said to cause an increase in the size of the pupil. Pupillary measurement also detects emotional response, pleasant stimuli causing expansion, and unpleasant stimuli, contraction.

Dr. Frederick Davidson has developed a lie detection technique that depends on pupil size and other functions of the eye such as changes in the color of the retina and changes in focus. Davidson reads the eye by using the ophthalmologist's retinoscope. The color of the retina at times varies from red to white to yellow, with red indicating emotionally charged perception, white nonemotionally charged perception, and yellow "true disinterest." After the Kent State killings Davidson was employed to use his technique to screen applicants for campus police jobs.[48]

Israeli scientists are working on a microwave respiration monitor to determine truthfulness from a distance and without the knowledge of the subject, and Israeli police have used the device. A microwave detects otherwise imperceptible movements of the stomach, the theory being that lying increases respiration, which increases stomach movements. A congressional committee report says, "The device offers the possibility of widespread, random, remote and surreptitious 'truth verification' at border crossings, airports, and police lineups."[49]

Penile plethysmography—the determination of increased blood volume in the penis by using various types of penile circumference and volumetric gauges—has been used to detect the emotional responses of sexual criminals to various kinds of sexual stimulation. (They have also been used in aversive conditioning programs to indicate when the aversive stimulus should be applied.) Thermography, the detection of minute temperature changes in the penis, is also used to measure sexual responsivity.[50] (Sexual response is not hard to detect, but the scientist's task is to find some means to quantify the response.)

One of the discoverers of a new method of lie detection is a journalism professor, Roger Bennett, who claims that split-second facial expressions, which he calls "micromomentaries," occur at the precise moment when a person tells a lie, and that psychopathic liars who can outwit a polygraph are unmasked by his method. Bennett videotapes his subjects and studies the tape for bizarre expressions—and especially for rapid eye movements—that are allegedly produced by subconscious conflict.

Bennett said that when he publicly announced his method, he was besieged by requests from such diverse institutions as Sears, Roebuck and the United States Treasury Department to teach his technique. He plans, however, to reserve his method for use by the news media.[51]

A proposed method of controlling criminal behavior offers lie detection to monitor behavior as an alternative to incarceration. Convicted defendants who chose monitored parole instead of prison would have to present themselves for periodic checks to see if they had committed further illegal acts and if they were conforming to the conditions of probation. A polygrapher who advocates this scheme says it could revolutionize the criminal-justice approach. Obviously, in the absence of civil liberties protections, it also could be applied to control behavior in noncriminal populations.[52]

Honest citizens who have nothing to fear applaud the use of lie detection techniques. The prospect of a world free of lies—without industrial and business theft, with more effective administration of the criminal-justice system, and with the guilty punished and the innocent vindicated—seems like a great improvement over the present deceit-ridden state of society. But lie detectors can be used in harmful ways. A preemployment screening program that is 70 percent accurate will do an injustice to 30 percent of job applicants. More important, the use of detection techniques represents a new invasion into the citizen's fast-diminishing area of personal privacy. More important still, the detection techniques can be used not only in the service of law and order and the smooth functioning of business, but they can also be used by totalitarian states to stamp out dissent and by political torturers to ferret out secrets. We know enough about how other countries use psychiatry politically to ensure conformity, and even as an adjunct of torture, to realize that these powerful new tools will have repressive uses.

Even when used benignly in a free country, lie detection creates an atmosphere of coerced, rather than freely chosen, honesty, and this may make a difference in character formation and the philosophy and value systems of those who are watched. The employee who spends a lifetime being honest because his voice patterns will give him away if he deceives—because Big Brotherism is operating—will develop personality characteristics different from the employee who resolves a conflict in favor of honesty on the basis of his own decision. Surveillance leads to the passive acceptance of the values of those who have the technology to survey or, in psychoanalytic terms, to the externalization of the superego that now is applied from outside, not integrated into the psyche.

The future will bring other means of control. The computer will be teamed with behavioral approaches in the interest of a smoothly functioning society and to produce conformity. Computers are now used to track and profile, to test and diagnose, and to predict drug responses and a propensity to violence and other deviant behavior.

But computers are also being studied for their therapeutic applications. Kenneth Colby, a UCLA psychologist, has spent thirteen years developing methods for computers to act as therapists. In a time of short supply of therapists, the computer therapist could take care of the more chronic and the less troubled patients so that human therapists could concentrate on the patients who need or would benefit from help most. Colby says a computer could operate for one or two dollars an hour, would be available at any time of day or night, would never get bored or angry with a patient, and would never disremember or distort what had been said. A computer, says Colby, has no moral judgments and no superior social status to intimidate a patient. Massachusetts Institute of Technology Professor Joseph Weizenbaum sees this use of computers as threatening. Weizenbaum says, "Computers are machines, they're nonliving objects, and so by their very nature they are incapable of ever having a human experience . . . When a computer says 'I UNDERSTAND,' that's a lie and a deception and an impossibility, and it shouldn't be a basis for psychotherapy." But Colby points out that the computer programs are written by humans on the basis of human experience. Says one upholder of Colby's position, "You can't argue that a computer therapist is the best possible solution, because the best solution would be to interact with a living, warm, and understanding therapist. But you can argue that it is better . . . to interact with a program written by a caring therapist than to interact with no one at all."[53]

The University of Missouri has pioneered in the use of computers to assess patients, produce their diagnoses, predict whether they will attempt suicide or run away, and plan their treatment. The university's Dr. Ulett has recommended using computers to process treatment data in order to obtain predictions of probable response.[54] The computer thus can serve as an authority for therapists to lean on or can be a therapist itself.

Those who advocate the computer as a therapist are usually advocates of directive and rational therapy—an exploration of alternatives so that the patient can pick his best option. They see a computer as more capable than a conventional therapist of presenting all possible choices. Those who fear the computer see therapy as a process—resembling the maturing process the patient failed to complete successfully with his parents—where the decisions made are not as important as achieving methods of reaching, and taking responsibility for, decisions. The two views of therapy are incompatible. The therapist may use both methods with the same patient, but to the extent that he is rational and directive, he denies the chance for the analysis of defenses, which is an integral part of dynamic therapy. Neither school stops to clarify the basic differences in concept that lead to such divergent views on the future of therapy and the place for computer therapy.

Not all the strange new directions of psychiatry will prove to be effective and practicable. We can assume that the psychiatry of the future will not represent a direct development from the research of the present. Research now going on of which we are ignorant and developments that have not yet been conceptualized will have their effects on the future of psychiatry. We cannot make precise predictions about psychiatry's "brave new world" but we do know that there will be one and that it will be technologically oriented, concerned with control of behavior, and replete with potential threats and invasions of individual rights. Peter Breggin, an antipsychiatric psychiatrist, has envisioned the psychiatry of the year 2212 in his novel *After the Good War.* [55] He sees a society controlled by psychiatrists. Untoward and antisocial thoughts and deeds are corrected by a variety of behavior technologies ranging from group therapy and Skinnerian behavior modification to lobotomy and electronic stimulation of the pleasure site in the brain. My own scenario would call for an equally pervasive but much more subtle kind of imposed psychiatric authority, involving much reliance on conformity and much prescription of drugs, and with psychiatric values superseding traditional values, but possibly with restrained use of such gross techniques as lobotomy or electrical stimulation of the brain. Both Breggin and I share with Dr. André Bourguignon the feeling that society is tending toward a "psychiatrocracy," [56] a state in which psychiatry has expanded to fill the roles of police, judges, educators, social workers, and eventually politicians. While the psychiatrocracy develops, the American Psychiatric Association remains a passive onlooker. Its Task Force on Social Issues in 1971 stated that psychiatry should have a role in assessing such developments as transsexual operations, electronic control of behavior, and other aspects of human experimentation, but it added that what that role should be "remains elusive."[57]

Because its function has been defined so loosely and broadly, psychiatry will continue to encompass more and more of the problems of living. This trend will be accentuated by proposed economic alterations in the health care delivery system. The community mental health care system, the provider of second-tier (less than optimal) services for great numbers of people, will be expanded and will be funded more heavily, according to the recommendations of the Carter Commission and the policy of the Department of Health, Education, and Welfare and its branch, the National Institute of Mental Health. Medicaid benefits for mental health care will be increased.[58]

The greatest shaper of future psychiatry—and a change that is ardently recommended by the American Psychiatric Association and the American Psychoanalytic Association—will be full coverage for all psychiatric services under national health insurance. The American Psychiatric Association claims that it only advocates equal coverage with other medical conditions, not unlimited coverage, but under any broad insurance plan this would be the same as unlimited coverage. Psychiatrists and psychoanalysts are also asking for complete coverage for all mental health care under private third-party reimbursement schemes. Because of psychiatry's lack of definitions and the elastic demand for services, this would give psychiatry an expanded role in the national life.[59]

We do not know what waits for us down the road in terms of specific applications of psychiatry. We can see a general trend toward its greater use as an agent of conformity and an ameliorator of distress, rather than as an agent of individual growth. We can see a declining interest in Freud's concept of psychiatry as a means of understanding intrapsychic processes in order to promote maturity, and a heightened emphasis in psychiatry on mere symptomatic relief. We know that psychiatry is becoming more and more impersonal and that the development of the community mental health care system signified a government policy to work for symptomatic treatment for large groups of people with vaguely defined problems, rather than to attempt to secure a more complete kind of treatment for fewer people with more clearly defined symptoms. We know that biological rather than psychological approaches will be stressed[60] as therapy but that, paradoxically, the definition of therapy will be increasingly broadened to in-

474

clude environmental manipulations as treatment. The psychiatrist will rely on drugs, but he will also make heavy use of his prescriptions of supplemental financial support, vocational rehabilitation, and structured living situations.[61]

Psychiatrists have described the "managerial revolution" in psychiatry and have called it a true revolution. Control over policies affecting the organization of care has passed from practitioners to a coalition of governmental-insurance-accrediting reviewers who are distant from patient care. The subject matter of psychiatry has been redefined to concentrate on the medical and minimize the intrapsychical and the interpersonal. In addition, the emphasis has shifted from dealing with the problem of mental illness to dealing with the problem of delivery of care and to formulating evaluating programs, and therapy has been redesigned to conform to ideals of rapid treatment and patient mobility. This kind of managerial revolution has led to the delivery of a product by the assembly-line characteristic of high volume. It is a stereotyped product with minimal variation. The patient experiences repeated brief contacts rather than a more intensive effort. This results in an increasing workload that falls on less highly trained paraprofessionals. The future developments of psychiatry may or may not emphasize transfer of learning or erasing of memories. They may or may not be concerned with increased efficiency of indoctrination or with greatly expanded use of electronics and skilled technologies like psychosurgery. But they certainly will be concerned with government policy making, greater use of chemotherapy, wide application of the computer, and extending the psychiatric net so that more patients are encompassed within it; and all these will lead to an enlarged and more impersonal practice of psychiatry.

We do not know all the specific methods it will use, but we can clearly see psychiatry's direction, and we know that in the future it will wield more authority than it has in the past and will have more power to control thoughts and actions than it does in the present. The marriage of technology and a politicized mental health establishment will produce new potential for psychiatric power.

The Silent Psychiatrist and the Limits of Psychiatric Authority

. . . Observe the smallest action, seeming simple,
With mistrust
Inquire if a thing be necessary
Especially if it is common
We particularly ask you—
When a thing continually occurs—
Not on that account to find it natural
Let nothing be called natural
In an age of bloody confusion
Ordered disorder, planned caprice,
And dehumanized humanity, lest all things
Be held unalterable!

—BERTOLT BRECHT
The Exception and the Rule

PSYCHIATRISTS DO NOT LIKE to be told they possess too much power and that there is not enough surveillance of them as they go about using this power. I have been criticized by forensic psychiatrists— several of the most reputable and most thoughtful in the field—for saying that psychiatrists have too much power and that they have not done enough to conceptualize the extent of their power and to devise ways to keep it within limits. When I raised the issue in public of the power of the psychiatrist in the commitment process,[1] I was told by a discussant that I had misconceptualized the issue: Psychiatrists do not commit. Protested commitment is a judicial process (in most states), so goes this argument, and all the psychiatrist does is act as an expert witness, stating the reasons he believes commitment would be proper. If the court wishes to commit, this becomes the court's decision, not the psychiatrist's. I have been told, concerning criminal cases,

476

that juries so often disagree with psychiatric testimony that, far from being powerful, psychiatrists and forensic psychiatrists are professionally among the most impotent members of society.[2]

Sociologists who have produced data showing that psychiatrists have overpredicted dangerousness and a law professor who tried to alert psychiatrists to the abuse of diagnostic evaluation procedures in the Texas "guided discretion" death cases have remarked that psychiatrists are either unconcerned with what their critics say or resist hearing it. Psychiatry, which spends so much of its time forcing people defined as patients to confront their own deficiencies, does not care to examine its own deficiencies. Judge David Bazelon has attacked psychiatry and the American Psychiatric Association for "studiously avoiding the examination of the possible misuse of psychiatry" and said that this appears to be "a profession that wishes to judge but not be judged, to examine but not be examined."[3]

At one time I decided to write a book called *The Silent Psychiatrist.* I had become concerned with the idea that major abuses and injustices were being inflicted in the name of psychiatry and that very few psychiatrists seemed to care. I had become aware through the law case reports that crossed my desk that psychiatrists had more power than they realized, and I was disappointed at the lack of interest psychiatrists showed in learning about judicial decisions that were critical to them and in studying in their residency programs and courses of continuing medical education the social effects of behavioral science interventions. As time went on I collected more and more instances of arbitrary and unscientific uses of psychiatric authority—both because the authority of psychiatry continued to grow and because I was becoming more aware of it—and I was constantly faced with the puzzle of why psychiatrists allowed the abuses to continue. Why was so little being done? Why did so few psychiatrists care?

When one begins to see that psychiatry is less scientific than it purports to be, and when more and more instances of psychiatric blindness and obtuseness and cruelty become apparent, this can soon progress to a full-blown "emperor's new clothes" syndrome. But unlike the conclusion of the story, the crowd does not join in and confess that it, too, had been aware of the emperor's nudity but had been persuaded its perception was wrong, or that it had been too duped or too afraid to speak out but now is willing to admit what it saw (or did not see). On the contrary, the silence of the mental health profession, with only a few notable exceptions, and of the public at large has remained deafening.

The discerning psychiatrist, who is part of that small minority of psychiatrists that does become concerned about the abuse of psychiatric authority, pays a penalty for his sensitivity. He not only becomes aware of the fallibilities of other psychiatrists, but he begins to question how he uses his own authority, the basis of his professional stance. At some point in his development he goes through a crisis when he doubts his own therapeutic ability and questions the theories that underlie his methods. Allen Wheelis has written of the "vocational hazards" of psychoanalysis. The young practitioner reluctantly comes to the conclusion that his discipline "is not what it is represented to be, and he begins to be troubled by a vague sense of fraudulence." From there he can retreat into dogma and abolish his doubts by fiat, and eventually he may become a serious defender of orthodoxy. He may continue to question and to doubt, and he may become a rebel. He may, even if he is "unusually gifted and skillful . . . have the good fortune to be expelled from the ranks and thereby achieve martyrdom." Or he may reach a nadir in which he has lost all of the tenets of professional faith, retaining "only the belief that it is possible for one person to help another." From this point there is the chance of recovery, in the process of which he will salvage much of his belief but retain skepticism and an openness to change.[4]

At the point where psychiatrists question their own authority and lose a sense of their own omnipotence, the ideas of Thomas Szasz and R. D. Laing become comprehensible. Their conceptualizations of the misapplication and the overuses of psychiatric authority not only offer the possibility of a less authoritarian and more creative approach to psychiatry, but also give the reassurance that others see imperfections in the system, too. Their presence relieves the dread feeling of being alone in one's views. But the problem is not as simple as Szasz and Laing make it out to be, because the nihilism and the egalitarianism they preach deprive the psychiatrist of the ability to help a number of patients, patients who need or demand control. Some of the authoritarianism that is so rampant in modern psychiatry is thrust upon the psychiatrist, who might prefer to play a less responsible role. And the concepts of Szasz and Laing have been picked up by the most antipsychiatric lawyers and sociologists and used to attack psychiatry in an all-inclusive way. Psychiatrists do not believe that mental illness is a myth. Most psychiatrists, often even when they are sensitive to psychiatric abuses, see value in therapy and want to be therapeutic. They find value in Freud's concepts of the unconscious mind and the stages of psychosexual development, Sullivan's concept of interpersonal relationships, and Klein's concept of the mother-child relationship in the infantile pre-Oedipal period. Whether or not the frame-

478

work of ideas they use in therapy is completely scientific and justifies the subjugation of the patient to a therapist, the concepts remain important. They allow for the psychological influences that obviously affect thoughts, feelings, and behavior, and they deserve to have some application in a therapeutic process.

Psychiatrists also see the need to medicate some patients, even in cases where the patient does not feel he needs medication, although they may feel that in general there is too much medication imposed on patients. They see the need for involuntary commitment of patients who do not feel they need to be hospitalized, even though they may feel that too many patients are hospitalized for too long periods of time.

The problem for the discerning psychiatrist, then, is to preserve enough of this belief in his ability to help that he can continue to work intimately with people caught up in powerful struggles, but not to be so enamored of his authority that he relies too heavily on it or proclaims it to be more scientific than it is. The discerning psychiatrist must acknowledge that society has given him too much authority, and he has to begin to define the limits of his authority.

Most psychiatrists do not try to limit their own authority. This book is full of examples of psychiatrists who exercised more authority than their professional expertise warranted and were only stopped from continuing abuses, if they were stopped at all, by the efforts of lawyers and other opponents of psychiatry. Other psychiatrists who do acknowledge the problem have remained strangely passive, tending to be unconcerned with issues outside the narrow confines of their clinical practices or their research, seeing psychiatric abuses as society's or someone else's problem, but not psychiatry's problem or their own. Only a few psychiatrists have spoken out about psychiatric injustice and threats to liberties.

In the interest of a book about psychiatric abuses, I started a file folder with examples of cases that might have been expected to arouse psychiatrists' indignation, but had not. There were cases about individuals—people improperly committed who spent lifetimes in mental hospitals or patients subjected to electroshock as punishment. There were many cases of patients who were properly committed to mental hospitals but improperly retained there long after they should have been released.

Besides individual cases, the file contained examples of widespread general abuses that had affected groups of people—eugenic sterilization, lobotomy, the plight of the patient in the old-fashioned state hospital, the lack of psychiatric services in prisons, the failure of the community mental health care system to provide follow-up care for patients released from hospitals, and the use of psychiatry by the Central Intelligence Agency.

The projected book never got written. A book that did nothing but remind psychiatrists of their shortcomings would meet resistance, and the title "The Silent Psychiatrist" has no impact since psychiatrists are expected to be silent. Instead I began to expand my concern to the larger problems of why psychiatrists abuse authority, what the source of psychiatric power is, how it developed, and what should be done. A more comprehensive book, this book, was the result. But the raw data documenting the abuses of psychiatry still deserve attention—this book details a number of instances—and the silent psychiatrist needs to be prodded into action by the specifics of psychiatric abuse.

Let me give one final example of the abuse of psychiatric authority. When a Virginia prison inmate was turned down for parole in 1976, he became "highly emotional," and he was transferred to the prison wing of Central State Hospital. He was given Prolixin, and he continued to be given Prolixin when he was returned to prison, administered now by other prisoners assigned as aides. He developed tremors, slipped into a stupor, and for six months lay in the prison hospital essentially without medical treatment. He developed enormous bedsores, which became infected and maggot-infested. His hip and arm joints became immobilized, and his hip joints had to be removed surgically. He is permanently paralyzed. (In January 1979, a federal district judge approved a $518,000 damage award for him.)[5]

This is the kind of case that concerns lawyers more than psychiatrists. Psychiatrists do not attend seminars dealing with injustice to patients. If they attend seminars on confidentiality or psychiatric malpractice, they do this for a practical concern, because they are threatened by the prospect of malpractice actions in their own practices.

Why are psychiatrists so little interested in correcting abuses and defining the limits of their power, a topic of great interest to lawyers? Some of the reasons lie in the difference between the medical model and other models of professional relating, the differences between medical education and other kinds of professional training, and the personality characteristics of psychiatrists, which are possibly very different from those of other professionals.

The medical model is authoritarian. Law, in some of its aspects, is just the contrary, emphasizing protection from authority. Because law and psychiatry are so different, training is very different. Legal education tries to promote analytic ability and constant questioning, whereas medical education emphasizes the respectful acceptance of what the lecturer presents as scientific fact. Lawyers are not insulted when they are challenged to give the basis of their opinions, but psychiatrists often appear incensed when their conclusions are questioned or rejected.

But the differences between physicians and lawyers come from more than their education—the two disciplines are so dissimilar that very different kinds of people are drawn into them. There is a physician's personality and a lawyer's personality. Psychiatrists are not entirely typical of the physician personality, for they tend to have more ambivalences and more flexibility or greater broad-mindedness, and studies show they are less conservative. Nevertheless, they are very different from lawyers. Like their fellow physicians, and unlike lawyers and social scientists, they do not see mental patients' rights as being as important as their therapeutic needs.

Although some psychiatrists feel that the training for their field should be oriented more to the study of the humanities than to laboratory science, students good in the humanities are systematically screened out of the pool of successful medical-school applicants. Psychiatrists must come from the pool of medical students, and medical schools select their students specially. Students who have a high aptitude for medical school, as shown by the Medical College Admission Test, but who have not done outstandingly in undergraduate sciences, are eliminated. Many of the students who are accepted have a negative image of psychiatry, so there is only a small number of interested and capable medical students from which to draw all future psychiatrists. Medical students who are not very capable and not psychologically minded find it easy to secure a psychiatric residency. (One study shows that only a small percentage of physicians in practice who were surveyed ever considered psychiatry as a career option, and only one-half would agree to psychiatric treatment for themselves if it was recommended.)[6] Medical school itself, with its expense, its long hours, and its night assignments, does nothing to ameliorate the narrowness or the driving quality of students. By the time they graduate they feel they have invested so much in medical education that they are justified in building a practice to maximize financial return. Their enormous investment in education demands a high return.[7]

Two major results of the system of entry into psychiatry are that psychologically minded people have been selectively diverted from psychiatry and that nonpsychologically minded people have taken over much of psychiatry, and even much of psychoanalysis. Many psychiatrists, and a number of psychoanalysts, are medical-school graduates who needed some field of medicine in which to specialize and found psychiatry least displeasing. In contrast, many people who have been refused entry into medicine, and consequently into psychiatry and psychoanalysis, have had high motivation to be therapists. (Some of these do become nonphysician therapists, but many are lost to the field.)

Ten years ago John Medelman, who had flunked out of medical school in his sophomore year, wrote an article for *Harper's* entitled "Why I Am Not a Psychiatrist." Medelman had a long-time interest in psychiatry, and his work in a mental hospital, in spite of its disillusioning aspects, convinced him that psychiatry was his mission. But he found the preclinical years of medical school very unsatisfying, and he did not do well. He wrote: "We spent hundreds of hours with the struts and pulleys of the dead, hours the prospective psychiatrist should spend with the concepts and troubles of the living."

In some dim and utopian future, Medelman predicts, psychiatric residents "might hear lectures by lawyers as well as doctors, and observe the seedy unhappiness of a courtroom instead of memorizing the muscles of the foot; they might hear about the monetary problems of state mental hospitals instead of trying to find whether they have pentose or fructose in their test tubes; and they might exchange lectures on tumor pathology for lectures on social anthropology and theories of ethics."[8]

In time, many of those refused entry into psychiatry learned that they could, through psychology, social work, counseling, and pastoral counseling, also become therapists with responsibility for patients, but they received a very different training from that of psychiatrists and psychoanalysts—and care of patients became a fragmented field.

Many of the excesses and the deviations in modern psychiatry represent the clash of the medically trained and the rebellious splinter groups, the members of which were not allowed to join psychiatry and so decided if they could not join it to beat it. The medically trained psychiatrist-psychoanalyst continues to dominate the field, set standards, and exercise authority most completely, but many others practice very different psychiatry.

Part of the solution to the problem of the abuse of psychiatric power is to have a better class of psychiatrists who practice psychiatry because of its potential to help patients achieve stability and independence, not because it may produce a high standard of living or give the pleasure of exerting authority. But psychiatry is emphasizing symptomatic relief secured through medication, and it is becoming more biological, more anxious to identify with the rest of medicine, less interested in its psychological roots. We cannot expect the medically oriented psychiatrist to become interested in defining and limiting his authority. Until a new, less authoritarian breed of psychiatrists emerges, psychiatry will continue to exert too much power over too many people, gaining authority from its two antecedents, medicine and Freudian psychology, and providing care that either emphasizes the medical aspect of psychiatry or is a watered-down version of verbal therapy.

When mental patients did begin to receive help belatedly in the 1960s in the recognition and protection of some basic procedural and substantive rights, their protectors were not psychiatrists, but lawyers who had cast the psychiatrists in the role of the oppressors and had allied themselves with sociologists, who provided the documentation of psychiatric abuse. With very little funding but with a great deal of brilliance and much zeal, a small group of young lawyers who specialized in mental patient advocacy—the "mental health bar"—began to wage and to win important cases in which the rights of mental patients were defined: to have procedural safeguards during the commitment process, to have a time limit on a holding for incompetency to stand trial, and to have improved conditions at mental hospitals and institutions for the retarded. At first psychiatrists fought even the most rudimentary reforms, which they saw as an attack on their authority. But in recent years the American Psychiatric Association in a few cases has joined the opposition to participate in the legal attack on other psychiatrists.

The new legal activism brings its own problems. It makes life more difficult for psychiatrists, particularly for those who worked at understaffed and underfunded state institutions and now have to spend much more time in legal activities and to practice their psychiatry, in some cases, under the supervision of judges and lawyers. The new emphasis is not on locking up all mental patients until they are assuredly safe to be released, but instead involves risk-taking. The mental patient is compared to a criminal defendant who is presumed innocent until proven guilty, and he must be proven guilty by a high standard of proof, "clear and convincing evidence." This means that some patients are allowed out of hospitals to kill themselves or others, that many patients are released too early into communities that lack support systems for them, and that other patients never get the hospitalization that might have helped them. But even though legal activism complicates psychiatric practice and causes some harm, the fact that psychiatrists have shown so little interest in straightening up their own house makes it a necessity.

It has only been since the 1960s that a comparatively few psychiatrists have joined the lawyers and sociologists who feel that psychiatry has overrun its bounds and that it must define its area of competency, set the limits of its authority, and begin a policy of restraint.

Any effective curbing of psychiatric abuse must involve institutional methods—legal restraints, peer review, and the disciplining of erring psychiatrists. (It is much easier to plan institutional methods than it is to produce a change in psychiatrists, although it is less efficacious.) In providing these controls, psychiatry must listen more to advice from the critics of psychiatry among lawyers, sociologists, and the lay public and in the media. Psychiatrists cannot continue to dismiss all its critics as antipsychiatric. Simple reforms, like periodic reviews for long-term committed patients or a limited detention period for those held incompetent to stand trial, have been only recently instituted, and this happened because courts have listened to the critics of psychiatry whom psychiatrists refused to hear. Other simple and obvious reforms come to mind. Patients need legal help to protect their rights. Any attempt to deprive them of legal help should be seen as a violation of human rights. (And the most effective deprivation is to allow for help but never let the patient know it is available.) Some states in recent years—New Jersey, Michigan, and a few other jurisdictions—have funded programs to provide legal help for mental patients.

Patients should be held in security institutions only as long as they need to be held, for many chronic patients can survive in less restrictive settings. On the other hand, the concept of deinstitutionalization and the prospect that this will save the state money should not justify allowing patients to go without effective help. More checks are needed to see that hospitalization is provided appropriately and for appropriate periods of time.

Indefinite or indeterminate quasi-criminal detainments, as when exhibitionists or child molesters are held until the staff certifies them as cured, should be abolished. Patients should be held only if they meet the criterion for civil commitment, which is mental illness plus danger, and they should not have to wait until a nonexistent cure is conferred or until a staff makes an arbitrary decision that they are safe to be released.

Psychiatrists working in institutional settings must decide where their primary loyalty lies—to the state that pays their salaries or to the ostensible patient, and the patient should not be misled concerning the confidentiality of his communications or the dual role that his therapist plays.

Commitment and detention decisions should not be made in an atmosphere of obscurity. Lawyers and the press and the public are not allowed at the staff conferences where important decisions regarding the fate of patients are made. Someone representing the outside world must have access to the decision-making process.

The adversary process should be encouraged, contrary to the recommendations of many psychiatrists who would like to have their testimony considered impartial and to act as advisors to judges rather than witnesses. The adversary system should be used to open the opinions of psychiatric experts to challenge. The use of pretrial reports and posttrial dispositional recommendations should be considered suspect when it gives the psychiatrist a power to influence that cannot be challenged through the adversary process.

The kind of pretrial diversion and psychiatric probation that places criminal defendants in "therapeutic communities" and in methadone maintenance programs should be recognized as conferring great power to coerce on the therapist. The practice of sentencing well-to-do defendants to outpatient "psychiatric probation" should be considered suspect because it discriminates against poor defendants and often leads to a peculiar kind of therapy in which the patient cannot express himself for fear of the reaction it will arouse in the therapist who reports on his progress to the probation office or the courts.

When psychiatric reports are used in the making of important decisions—whether a mother's parental rights should be terminated, which of two divorcing parents should have custody of a child, whether a defendant is incompetent to stand trial—the basis of the evaluation and its limitations should be clearly spelled out. Courts regularly accept recommendations as authoritative in which only a conclusion is reached and the reasoning that led to the conclusion is omitted.

The basic reform should be to provide patients with real, not theoretical, procedural rights. When survivors such as Kenneth Donaldson and Roy Schuster finally win their freedom, their histories usually indicate repeated denial by the courts of a full exercise of rights. Psychiatrists have antipathy to procedural safeguards because they create an atmosphere of legalism that complicates practice, but they are nevertheless necessary.

Psychiatry could be doing much more than it is on its own to define its limits and cure its abuses. Psychiatry has never attempted to use effective disciplinary measures against psychiatrists who overstep their bounds. When evidence of wrongdoing by psychiatrists comes to light, as, for example, in the stories of Central Intelligence Agency psychiatrists who planned and carried out bizarre experiments, the offenders should be publicly identified, prosecuted if appropriate, and in any event professionally disciplined. Professional disciplining and license revocation should be applied to psychiatrists who victimize their private patients.

Psychiatry has never mounted an effort to eliminate long-standing abuses in state hospitals such as inadequate staffing, use of irregularly licensed (and often non-English-speaking) physicians to serve as psychiatrists, deficiencies of funding, and lack of aftercare. The overworked state hospital psychiatrist has been left to wrestle with these problems. He often becomes defensive because he realizes he is doing all that he can and he feels society does not recognize the difficulty of the job it has entrusted to him. Private practice psychiatrists, who are the majority, think of these as someone else's problems.

But institutional reforms are only a partial answer, and sometimes they are less than that and are merely another aspect of the problem. Imposing institutional systems of safeguards and reviews creates several more layers of a new bureaucracy. So we have advocacy, mental health information services, patients' rights committees, ombudsmen to protect patients' legal rights. We have peer review and evaluation committees and cost accountancy to assess the quality and efficiency of psychiatric care. Much of the mental health dollar is increasingly being diverted from psychiatric care to protection of patients' rights and to evaluation. The criteria used to judge the care of patients are often misleadingly materialistic—number of cases processed, number of patient contacts, cost per contact per patient—and the important aspects of psychiatry, such hard-to-measure attributes of the psychiatric relationship as trust of patient for therapist, empathy of therapist with patient, and therapist integrity are impossible to measure. My one-time department chief at a suburban Philadelphia hospital who ordered electroshock therapy too quickly for too many patients might have done very well on a cost/efficiency basis or on an evaluation based on achievement of rapid "cures," but most of the patients he shocked so quickly deserved a longer and better-considered approach to their problems, although it would have been more expensive and less "justifiable." Institutional safeguards are only part of the answer, and they need to be evaluated themselves lest they become a detriment to the care of patients. The cycle can go on indefinitely as we seek ways to evaluate the evaluators and the evaluations of the evaluators. Contact with patients is easily lost.

Many critics of psychiatry have taken pleasure in the increasing exposure of psychiatric abuses and the bad press that psychiatry is receiving. But in spite of the criticism, psychiatry does not wither

486

away; instead it continues to prosper. The shortcomings of psychiatry are becoming more easy to recognize, but the needs that impel people to seek psychiatric help continue to grow. Other sources of authority —the church, the law, education—continue to lose prestige, and people in trouble turn to psychiatry in spite of the criticisms it has received. There are enough people in pain and in trouble to keep psychiatry growing, and the criticism that it has not used its great authority well does not lead to major changes.

Jerome Frank says psychiatry is "the healthy invalid," apparently in a parlous condition, but in reality "about to enter a period of vigorous health . . . Human social behavior now looms as the greatest potential cause of disability and death . . . There will be no dearth of individuals seeking psychiatric help."[9] An article in *Clinical Psychiatry News* says that the status of psychiatry gains while other specialties decline.[10] One reason for the increased status of psychiatry, according to the article, is the increasing identification of psychiatry with biological medicine.

Psychiatry is said to have grown "exponentially in recent years."[11] Bertram Brown, when he was director of the National Institute of Mental Health, predicted a shortage of ten thousand psychiatrists by 1982. He said that criticisms of psychiatric services had not caused any decline in the demand for psychiatric services, that psychiatry should continue to grow until the mid-1980s, and that it will put more emphasis on biological psychiatry.[12] Alan Stone, president of the American Psychiatric Association, has said that psychiatry is advancing in spite of criticisms.[13] The Health Resources Administration of the Department of Health, Education, and Welfare estimates that by 1990 psychiatry will need a huge influx of new workers. In 1975 there were twenty-six thousand psychiatrists, twenty-three thousand psychologists, twenty-three thousand psychiatric social workers, and thirty-nine thousand psychiatric nurses—a total of one hundred eleven thousand. The estimate is that by 1990 we will need a total of one hundred eighty-nine thousand—fifteen thousand additional psychiatrists, sixteen thousand more psychologists, sixteen thousand more social workers, and thirty-one thousand more nurses.[14]

There are enough uses of psychiatry, both good and bad, and enough demand so that it will continue to grow and to prosper. Sometimes this will be for good reasons—because it helps people reach self-understanding and gives them greater ability to control their lives. Sometimes it will be for bad reasons, such as the need for authorities on whom to rely, the enjoyment of power by psychiatrists, the development of the concept of mental health as a political right, or increased funding for psychiatry and increasing money-making possibilities in mental health.

Psychiatry today is continually growing, although its functions are not adequately defined or limited. The only curb on it is cumbersome legalistic supervision, which hinders as well as helps. In this situation the individual will have to maintain his own guard against the encroachment of psychiatric power. He must see the potential threat as well as the potential source of help in psychiatry, and he must refuse to buy authority on the claim that it is authority. "How are mothers and fathers to make sense of what the experts are advising this season?" asks Walter Goodman. "Well, one thing they can do is listen with respectful skepticism. They may have a lot to learn, but so do the experts."[15] The advice applies to all areas of psychiatry. We must have respectful skepticism toward all the members of the vast army of the "helping professions" who advise us, create the climate of our thinking, and impose their values on us.

When an individual cannot depend on himself any longer and needs a psychiatrist, he is admitting that he cannot take responsibility for his own thoughts, and perhaps not for his own actions, that he needs help in the managing of his life. Seeing a psychiatrist is both an abdication of responsibility—the admission that someone more responsible must share the burden—and a responsible decision—the recognition that the burden cannot be carried alone and must be shared. But in the ultimate analysis, everyone must depend on himself for his own salvation, with the help of others or without, and the authority of psychiatrists must be resisted if it does not meet the needs of the patient. The decisions and interpretations the psychiatrist furnishes act on the individual, and the individual accepts them at his own peril, hoping that they will bring relief, but knowing that may not necessarily be correct.

Good psychotherapy is an engagement of two people that leaves both changed. If only the patient changes, the therapy has been a failure. Therapists must be ready to accept the opposition and the hostility of their patients and to try as objectively as they can to see how much of it is merited. (The requirement of a personal analysis for the analyst is an attempt to ensure his objectivity, although sometimes it just causes him to become doctrinaire.) The most common mistake in psychiatric therapy is the discounting of the opinion of the patient because the patient is "sick" and the therapist is "well."

The patient who challenges the therapist continually can be exasperating. He is obviously, at least in part, using disputatiousness to keep the therapist at arm's length and to make him ineffectual. At some stage in treatment he may benefit from the relaxation of disbelief and the experiencing of regression with its idealization of the therapist and its dependency. But the decisions made in the therapist's office affect the life of the patient more than the therapist, and the patient has the responsibility of seeing that these decisions are not foisted upon him. He must take this much responsibility for his own "cure."

Hospital patients are in a disadvantaged position when they try to resist authority. Since they are presumably in the hospital because they have evidenced irrationality, they cannot be expected to work well together to defend against excessive authority. And when they become more rational and leave the hospital they lose interest in patients' rights.

Nevertheless, if anyone is to guard against the excessive powers of psychiatry, it must be the patient on whom the psychiatrist is imposing his values, the hospitalized patient who is being committed after too cursory an examination, the parent whose child is being required to take drugs for schooltime "hyperactivity," the employee who is being promoted or denied promotion on the basis of dubious psychological testing, the executive required to attend an adjustment seminar to equip him to function better on the higher rungs of the corporate ladder. Individuals, particularly patients, cannot defend themselves alone; they need legal help. But they will never get legal help until they can specify how they are being adversely affected by powers that psychiatrists improperly assume. They must at least call attention to their situation.

Psychiatrists have been happy to exert their authority without giving an opportunity for it to be challenged. They insist on making their decisions in obscurity where the process of decision making can go on free from questioning. They continue to want to define limits for their patients and clients without defining their own. The force of the psychiatrist-patient interaction is too powerful, the controls that psychiatrists sometimes are required to impose on patients are too encompassing for this power to be exercised without scrutiny and with only a few safeguards. Every exercise of psychiatric authority demands scrutiny. If the patient's dreams or slips of the tongue or associations are worth attention, so too are the psychiatrist's methods and values. If psychiatric authority is left unscrutinized and undefined, psychiatry will have had a paradoxical effect. It will have represented itself as promoting autonomy and maturity, but it will be working in the interest of immaturity, because this is the way it maintains a superior status.

The assumption of powers by psychiatry can be pathological, as pathological as any of the symptoms that psychiatry tries to change or suppress in patients. Patients must force psychiatrists to grow by resisting excessive authority. They must demand that psychiatry use its powers thoughtfully and well. The patient must do this in the interest of a better psychiatry and also in the interest of his own health.

Bertolt Brecht has described our need to protect ourselves from the power of others, the vigilance we must exercise, the solution we must provide:

> . . . You have heard and you have seen
> You have seen what is common, what continually occurs
> But we ask you:
> Even if it's not very strange, find it estranging
> Even if it is usual, find it hard to explain
> What here is common should astonish you
> What here's the rule, recognize as an abuse
> And where you have recognized an abuse
> Provide a remedy![16]

NOTES / INDEX

Notes

INTRODUCTION

1. H.D. [Hilda Doolittle], *Tribute to Freud* (New York: Pantheon, 1956), pp. 17–18.
2. *Kaimowitz* v. *Michigan Department of Mental Health,* Civil No. 73-19434-AW unreported (Cir. Ct. Wayne County, Mich., July 10, 1973), *summarized* at 42 U.S.L.W. 2063, reprinted in Alexander Brooks, *Law, Psychiatry and the Mental Health System* (Boston: Little, Brown, 1974), pp. 902–24.
3. *Baxstrom* v. *Herold,* 383 U.S. 107 (1966).
4. *Painter* v. *Bannister,* 140 N.W.2d 152 (Iowa, 1966).

CHAPTER 1

1. Stanley Lesse, "Caveat Emptor?—The Cornucopia of Current Psychotherapies," *American Journal of Psychotherapy* 33 (July 1979): 329.
2. For a description of the varied backgrounds of mental health personnel at one community mental health center, see E. Mansell Pattison et al., "A Code of Ethics for a Community Mental Health Program," *Hospital & Community Psychiatry* 27 (1976): 30.
3. In a published paper, I made much the same distinction between two kinds of authority possessed by psychiatrists, but I called voluntarily accorded authority the "implicit" power of psychiatrists and coercive authority the "explicit" authority of psychiatrists. "The Limits of Psychiatric Authority," *International Journal of Law and Psychiatry* 1, No. 2 (1978): 183–204. I now find those terms confusing and prefer the use of the terms "voluntary" and "coercive."
4. Martin Gross, *The Psychological Society* (New York: Random House, 1978), pp. 9, 17.

CHAPTER 2

1. The Wolf-man, "Memoirs of Wolf-man, 1909–1911," *Bulletin of the Phila-delphia Association for Psychoanalysis* 19 (1969): 195.
2. Quentin Bell, *Virginia Woolf: A Biography* (New York: Harcourt Brace Jovanovich, Harvest Books, 1972), 1: 44–45.
3. Ibid., p. 90.
4. Virginia Woolf, *The Flight of the Mind* (London: Hogarth Press, 1975), 1: 148.
5. Ibid., p. 159.
6. Ibid., p. 175.
7. Ibid., p. 428.
8. Woolf's biographers have seen Leonard as selfless, except for Roger Poole, who pictures him as insistent on emphasizing Virginia's earlier illness, rather than current life situations, to explain the recurrence of her symptoms, and engaged in a lifelong conspiracy with doctors against her. Roger Poole, *The Unknown Virginia Woolf* (Cambridge: At the University Press, 1978).
9. Bell, *Virginia Woolf,* 2: 5.
10. Ibid., pp. 6–7.
11. Ibid., p. 8.
12. Ibid., p. 89.
13. Leonard Woolf, *Downhill All the Way* (New York: Harcourt, Brace & World, 1967), p. 51.
14. Virginia Woolf, *Mrs. Dalloway* (New York: Harcourt, Brace & Co., 1949), p. 149.
15. Hannah Green, *I Never Promised You a Rose Garden* (New York: Holt, Rinehart and Winston, 1964).
16. Janet and Paul Gotkin, *Too Much Anger, Too Many Tears* (New York: Quadrangle/The New York Times Book Co., 1975), p. 384.
17. Ibid., p. 382.

CHAPTER 3

1. Nigel Walker, *Crime and Insanity in England* (Edinburgh: University Press, 1968), 1: 15–19, 219–20.
2. Ibid., pp. 25–26.
3. Ibid., pp. 24–25.
4. Ibid., p. 63.
5. *R.* v. *Hadfield,* 27 St. Tr. 1281 (1800).
6. Isaac Ray, *A Treatise on the Medical Jurisprudence of Insanity* (1838; reprint ed., Cambridge, Mass.: Harvard University Press, 1962).
7. *McDonald* v. *United States,* 312 F.2d 847 (D.C. Cir. 1962); *Washington* v. *United States,* 390 F.2d 444 (D.C. Cir. 1967).
8. *New York Times,* Nov. 19, 1978; John Kifner in *New York Times,* Jan. 14, 1979.
9. Robert Jones, "Observations on Psychiatry and the Law in Canada," in

494

Forensic Psychiatry and Child Psychiatry, ed. D. Ewen Cameron, International Psychiatry Clinics (Boston: Little, Brown, 1965), p. 87.

10. William Blackstone, *Commentaries on the Laws of England* (Oxford: Clarendon Press, 1759, Vol. 4; facsimile reprint, London: Dawsons of Pall Mall, 1966), pp. 388–89.

11. See Henry Weihofen, "A Question of Justice: Trial or Execution of an Insane Defendant," *American Bar Association Journal* 37 (1951):651.

12. *United States* v. *Barnes,* 175 F. Supp. 60 (S.D. Cal. 1959).

13. *Competency to Stand Trial and Mental Illness,* Laboratory of Community Psychiatry, Harvard Medical School (New York: Jason Aronson, 1974), p. v.

14. Henry Davidson, *Forensic Psychiatry* (New York: Ronald Press, 1952).

15. R. Crawford Morris and Alan Moritz, *Doctor and Patient and the Law* (Saint Louis: C. V. Mosby, 1971).

16. *Jackson* v. *Indiana,* 406 U.S. 715 (1972).

17. *Hardy* v. *Barbour,* 304 S.W.2d 21 (Mo., 1957).

18. *In re Strittmater's Estate,* 140 N.J. Eq. 94, 53 A.2d 205 (Ct. Err. & App. 1947). See Ronald Leifer, "The Competence of the Psychiatrist to Assist in the Determination of Incompetency: A Skeptical Inquiry into the Courtroom Functions of Psychiatrists," *Syracuse Law Review* 14 (1963): 564.

CHAPTER 4

1. Sigmund Freud, *The Interpretation of Dreams,* Standard Edition (London: Hogarth Press, 1958), Vols. 4 and 5.

2. Jacques Mousseau, "Freud in Perspective: A Conversation with Henri J. Ellenberger," *Psychology Today,* March 1973, p. 53.

3. The President's Commission on Mental Health, Report to the President (Washington, D.C.: Government Printing Office, 1978), 1:8. The report also described, in addition to the 88 million with mental disorders, or who are not disordered but who are in a category characterized by intense suffering and the need for assistance, a large number of Americans who suffer from serious emotional problems associated with other conditions —10 million who have alcohol-related problems, an unspecified number with drug-related problems, more than 200,000 cases yearly of child abuse, 2 million children with severe learning disabilities, and 40 million physically handicapped, "many of whom suffer serious emotional consequences because of their disabilities." Rosalynn Carter, who was a chairperson of the commission, uses a figure that is more conservative— "20,000,000 to 30,000,000 Americans who need mental health care and one family in four . . . affected"—but that still represents three to five times the number of those (6.7 million) currently receiving specialized mental health services. Dennis Breo in *Chicago Tribune,* May 17, 1979. See also Chapter 9.

4. "Guidelines for Peer Review of Psychoanalysis Submitted to NIMH," *Newsletter of the American Psychoanalytic Association,* April 1978, p. 7.

5. Sigmund Freud, "Recommendations on Analytic Technique," Standard Edition (London: Hogarth Press, 1958), 12: 128–29.
6. Robert Waelder, *Basic Theory of Psychoanalysis* (New York: International Universities Press, 1960), pp. 25–26.
7. Philip Rieff, *The Triumph of the Therapeutic* (New York: Harper & Row, 1956).
8. Hermann Rorschach, *Psychodiagnostik* (Bern: E. Bircher, 1921).
9. The concept has been expressed frequently in talks and addresses by Willard Gaylin: "Psychoanalysis and psychiatry have brought behavior within the medical model."

CHAPTER 5

1. Esther Fischer-Homberger, "Germany and Austria," in *World History of Psychiatry,* ed. John G. Howells (New York: Brunner/Mazel, 1975), p. 282.
2. Sigmund Freud, "Memorandum on the Electrical Treatment of War Neurotics," Standard Edition (London: Hogarth Press, 1955), 17:211–15.
3. P. M. Ashburn, *A History of the Medical Department of the United States Army* (Boston: Houghton Mifflin, 1929), p. 313.
4. Emil Kraepelin, *Lectures on Clinical Psychiatry* (London: Balliere, Tindall and Cox, 1904; facsimile reprint, New York: Hafner, 1968), Ch. 39.
5. Samuel Yochelson and Stanton Samenow, *The Criminal Personality,* 2 vols. (New York: Jason Aronson, 1976 and 1977); Norval Morris, *The Future of Imprisonment* (Chicago: University of Chicago Press, 1974); Ernest van den Haag, *Punishing Criminals* (New York: Basic Books, 1975).
6. Bernard Glueck, *Studies in Forensic Psychiatry* (Boston: Little, Brown, 1916), pp. 264–65.
7. Mitchell Shields, "The Criminal Mind," *Atlanta Journal and Constitution Magazine,* Feb. 4, 1979, p. 18.
8. Justine Wise Polier, *The Rule of Law and the Role of Psychiatry* (Baltimore: Johns Hopkins Press, 1968), p. 71.
9. Morris Ploscowe, *Sex and the Law* (New York: Prentice-Hall, 1951), p. 226.
10. *Jackson* v. *Indiana,* 406 U.S. 715 (1972).
11. *Commonwealth* v. *Dooley,* 232 A.2d 45 (1967).
12. *In re Maddox,* 88 N.W.2d 470 (1958).
13. Karl Menninger, *The Human Mind,* 3d ed. (New York: Knopf, 1945), pp. 448–49.
14. Manfred Guttmacher and Henry Weihofen, *Psychiatry and the Law* (New York: W. W. Norton, 1952), pp. vii–viii.
15. Ibid., pp. 10–11, 106, 252, 254.
16. Ibid., p. 297.
17. Ibid., p. 106.
18. Quoted with other similar claims for psychiatry in Michael Hakeem, "A Critique to the Psychiatric Approach to Crime and Correction," *Law and Contemporary Problems* (Duke University School of Law) 23 (1958): 655–59.

19. Benjamin Karpman, "Criminal Insanity and the Law," *Journal of Criminal Law and Criminal Police Science* 39 (1949): 584–604.
20. *Durham* v. *United States,* 214 F.2d 862 (D.C. Cir. 1954).
21. "Judge Bazelon Honored," *American Journal of Psychiatry* 114 (1957): 565.
22. Abe Fortas, "Implications of Durham's Case," *American Journal of Psychiatry* 113 (1957): 581.
23. William O. Douglas, *Law and Psychiatry* (New York: The William Alanson White Institute of Psychiatry, Psychoanalysis and Psychology, 1956), p. 6.

CHAPTER 6

1. The account of Schuster's detention is based on the cases cited below, stenographer's minutes of hearing at Dannemora State Hospital, May 1, 1963, in *Schuster* v. *Herold,* No. 3699 (Supr. Ct., Clinton Co., 1963), the hearing transcript and the supplementary argument concerning Dr. William Carson's testimony prepared by Schuster for *Schuster* v. *Herold,* No. 65-Civ-408 (2nd Cir. 1965), the transcription of the proceedings of that case, and tapes of my conversation with Schuster, June 17, 1977.
2. Conversation with Schuster, June 6, 1977.
3. Ibid.
4. Hearing transcript, *Schuster* v. *Herold,* 410 F. 2d 1071 (2d Cir. 1969), pp. 29–30.
5. Hearing at Dannemora State Hospital, 1963, p. 26.
6. Ibid., p. 28.
7. Ibid., pp. 35–36.
8. Ibid., pp. 9–10.
9. *Baxstrom* v. *Herold,* 383 U.S. 107 (1966).
10. The Steadman studies include, among many other publications, "Follow-Up on Baxstrom Patients Returned to Hospitals for the Criminally Insane," *American Journal of Psychiatry* 130 (1973): 317–19, and "Some Evidence on the Inadequacy of the Concept and Determination of Dangerousness in Law and Psychiatry," *The Journal of Public Law* 1, No. 4 (1973): 409–26.
11. *Schuster* v. *Herold,* 410 F.2d 1071 (2nd Cir. 1969).
12. *Dennison* v. *New York,* 267 N.Y.S.2d (Ct. Cl. 1960).
13. *Dennison* v. *New York,* 280 N.Y.S.2d 31 (3rd Dept. 1967).
14. *Schuster* v. *Herold,* 410 F.2d, *cert. denied* 396 U.S. 847 (1969).
15. *Schuster* v. *Herold,* 440 F.2d 1335 (1971).
16. Minutes of May 6, 1972, Parole Board Hearing, IIS-440467, GH. CF.-17722, quoted in *Schuster* v. *Vincent,* 524 F.2d 153 (2nd Cir. 1975) at 157.
17. *Schuster* v. *Vincent,* 342 N.Y.S.2d 18 (Supr. Ct., Dutchess Co., 1972).
18. Ibid.
19. *Schuster* v. *Vincent,* 344 N.Y.S.2d 735 (1973).
20. *Schuster* v. *Vincent,* 353 N.Y.S.2d 969 (1974).

21. *Schuster* v. *Vincent,* Memorandum and Order, 74 Civ. 1705 at 5 (S.D. N.Y. March 27, 1975).
22. *Schuster* v. *Vincent,* 524 F.2d 153 (1975).
23. Kenneth Donaldson, *Insanity Inside Out* (New York: Crown, 1976).
24. *Kaimowitz* v. *Michigan Dept. of Mental Health,* Civil No. 73-19434-AW unreported (Cir. Ct., Wayne Co., Mich., July 10, 1973), reproduced in Alexander Brooks, *Law, Psychiatry and the Mental Health System* (Boston: Little, Brown, 1974), pp. 902–24).
25. Acel Moore and Wendell Rawls, Jr., in *Philadelphia Inquirer,* June 27, 1976.
26. *Mackey* v. *Procunier,* 477 F.2d 877 (9th Cir. 1973).
27. *Cullins* v. *Crouse,* 348 F.2d 887 (Kans., 1965).

CHAPTER 7

1. Gregory Zilboorg, *A History of Medical Psychology* (New York: W. W. Norton, 1941), pp. 299–362, 548, 550.
2. Wilhelm Griesinger, *Mental Pathology and Therapeutics* (London: New Sydenham Society, 1867; facsimile reprint, New York: Hafner, 1965), p. 473.
3. Ibid., p. 470.
4. Ibid., pp. 470–82.
5. William Salter, *A Textbook of Pharmacology* (Philadelphia: W. B. Saunders, 1952), pp. 210–11.
6. Emil Kraepelin, *Lectures in Clinical Psychiatry* (London: Balliere, Tindall and Cox, 1904; facsimile reprint, New York: Hafner, 1968), p. 268.
7. Salter, A Textbook of Pharmacology, p. 218.
8. Hannah Green, *I Never Promised You a Rose Garden* (New York: Holt, Rinehart and Winston, 1964).
9. Jonas Robitscher, "Eugenic Sterilization: A Biomedical Intervention," in *Eugenic Sterilization,* ed. Jonas Robitscher (Springfield, Ill.: Charles C. Thomas, 1973).
10. *Buck* v. *Bell,* 274 U.S. 200 (1927).
11. *Stump* v. *Sparkman,* 435 U.S. 349 (1978).
12. "APA Task Force Report Calls ECT a Valuable Treatment For Some Affective Disorders," *Hospital & Community Psychiatry,* Feb. 1979, p. 144.
13. There is a more thorough treatment of psychosurgery, eugenic sterilization, electroconvulsive therapy, and other "intrusive" treatment methods in Chapter 16.
14. John Howells and M. Livia Osborn, "Great Britain," in *World History of Psychiatry,* ed. John Howells (New York: Brunner/Mazel, 1975), p. 201.
15. One manufacturer advertises a "full line of feedback, monitoring, and data acquisition" machines for "electromyographic, electroencephalographic, electrodermal, and temperature feedback." Autogenic Systems, Program of the Annual Meeting of the American Psychiatric Association, Toronto, 1977, p. xxix. See a further discussion in Chapter 13.

16. Martin Gross, *The Psychological Society* (New York: Random House, 1978), p. 282. This is less than the "two hundred more or less varieties of treatment procedures: of Stanley Lesse's estimate, see Chapter 1, note 1, but Lesse includes somatic and other nonverbal therapies.
17. Brochure for The Art of Successful Therapy, Course No. 616, American Institute, Inc., offered at Marriott Motor Hotel, Atlanta, Georgia, Feb. 17–20, 1977, and Riviera Hotel, Las Vegas, Nevada, March 3–6, 1977.
18. Harvey Rosenstock, "The 'Contra' Strategy with Adamant Adolescents," *Behavioral Medicine*, Sept. 1978, pp. 43–44.
19. Sarah Cash in *Atlanta Journal and Constitution*, Dec. 7, 1975.

CHAPTER 8

1. Anthony Crosland, quoted in Colin Welch, "Crosland Reconsidered," *Encounter*, Jan. 1979, p. 85.
2. Ramsey Clark, *Crime in America* (New York: Simon and Schuster, 1970), pp. 266–67.
3. Manfred Guttmacher, *The Role of Psychiatry in Law* (Springfield, Ill.: Charles C. Thomas, 1968), pp. 154–55.
4. Henry Davidson, *Forensic Psychiatry*, 2d ed. (New York: Ronald Press, 1965), p. 237.
5. Paul Hoch and Joseph Zubin, eds., *Psychiatry and the Law* (New York: Grune & Stratton, 1955).
6. George Dession, "Deviation and Community Sanctions," in *Psychiatry and the Law*, ed. Hoch and Zubin, p. 6.
7. Harold Lasswell, "Legislative Policy, Conformity and Psychiatry," in *Psychiatry and the Law*, ed. Hoch and Zubin, pp. 13–40.
8. Lawrence Freedman, "Conformity and Nonconformity," in *Psychiatry and the Law*, ed. Hoch and Zubin, p. 43.
9. Ibid., p. 48.
10. Michael Hakeem, "A Critique of the Psychiatric Approach to Crime and Corrections," *Law and Contemporary Problems* 23 (1958):650.
11. *Durham* v. *United States*, 214 F.2d 862 (D.C. Cir. 1954).
12. Raoul Berger, *Government by Judiciary* (Cambridge, Mass.: Harvard University Press, 1978).
13. Morton Birnbaum, "The Right to Treatment," *American Bar Association Journal* 46 (1960):499.
14. *Rouse* v. *Cameron*, 373 F.2d 451 (D.C. Cir. 1966).
15. *Lake* v. *Cameron*, 364 F.2d 657 (D.C. Cir. 1966).
16. *United States* v. *Hiss*, Criminal No. C128-402 (D.C. S.D. N.Y., Nov. 17, 1949); 88 F. Supp. 559 (D.C. N.Y. 1950); 185 F.2d 822 (2d Cir. 1950). Excerpts from Binger's testimony are found in William Curran, *Law and Medicine* (Boston: Little, Brown, 1960), pp. 577–82, and in Richard Allen, Elyce Ferster, and Jesse Rubin, *Readings in Law and Psychiatry* (Baltimore: Johns Hopkins Press, 1968), pp. 132–35.
17. Curran, *Law and Medicine*, p. 577.
18. G. S. Fraser, *Ezra Pound* (New York: Grove Press, 1961), p. 1.

19. The story of Pound's detention is based on the account by Charles Norman, *The Case of Ezra Pound* (New York: Funk & Wagnalls, 1968). This book reprints the testimony of the four psychiatrists in the 1946 hearing.

20. Charles Olson, "Kavka and Pound," in *Blue Jolts*, ed. Charles Steir (Washington, D.C.: New Republic Books, 1978), pp. 56–60.

21. See A. Louis McGarry, "Competency for Trial and Due Process and the State Hospital," *American Journal of Psychiatry* 122 (1965): 623–31.

22. *Jackson* v. *Indiana,* 406 U.S. 715 (1972).

23. Frank Lindman and Donald McIntyre, eds. *The Mentally Disabled and the Law,* 1st ed. (Chicago: University of Chicago Press, 1961); 2d ed., Samuel Brakel and Ronald Rock, eds. (Chicago: University of Chicago Press, 1971).

24. Thomas Szasz, *The Myth of Mental Illness* (New York: Hoeber Medical Division, Harper & Row, 1961).

25. Erving Goffman, *Asylums* (Garden City, N.Y.: Doubleday, Anchor Books, 1961).

26. Manfred Guttmacher, "Critique of Views of Thomas Szasz on Legal Psychiatry," *Archives of General Psychiatry* 10 (1964): 238–45.

27. For the Walker case, see Chapter 18.

28. Thomas Szasz, *Ideology and Insanity* (Garden City, N.Y.: Anchor Books, Doubleday, 1972), pp. 30, 111.

29. R. D. Laing, *The Politics of Experience* (New York: Pantheon Books, 1967).

30. E. Fuller Torrey in *Washington Post,* Oct. 13, 1974.

31. E. Fuller Torrey, *The Death of Psychiatry* (Radnor, Pa.: Chilton Book Co., 1974).

32. J. Herbert Fill, "An Epidemic of Madness: The Confessions of a Perpetrator," *Human Behavior,* March 1974, pp. 40–47.

33. Lee Coleman, "Toward the Divorce of Psychiatry and Law," *Virginia Law Weekly, Dicta* 27, No. 10 (1974): 1.

34. Peter Breggin, "Psychiatry and Psychotherapy as Political Processes," *American Journal of Psychotherapy* 29 (1975): 369–82.

35. D. L. Rosenhan, "On Being Sane in Insane Places," *Science,* Jan. 19, 1973, pp. 250–58.

36. Bruce Ennis, *Prisoners of Psychiatry* (New York: Harcourt Brace Jovanovich, 1972); Henry Steadman and Joseph Cocozza, "We Can't Predict Who Is Dangerous," *Psychology Today,* Jan. 1975, p. 12. See also Daniel Oran, "Judges and Psychiatrists Lock Up Too Many People," *Psychology Today,* Aug. 1973, p. 20; Annette Ehrlich and Fred Abraham-Magdamo, "Caution: Mental Health May Be Hazardous," *Human Behavior,* Sept. 1974, p. 64; Theodore Sarbin, "Schizophrenia is a Myth, Born of Metaphor, Meaningless," *Psychology Today,* June 1972, p. 18; James Hardisty, "Mental Illness: A Legal Fiction," *Washington Law Review* 48 (1973): 735; Carol Wade Offir, "Civil Rights and the Mentally Ill; Revolution in Bedlam," *Psychology Today,* Oct. 1974, pp. 60–72.

37. Kenneth Donaldson, *Insanity Inside Out* (New York: Crown, 1976).

38. Janet and Paul Gotkin, *Too Much Anger, Too Many Tears* (New York: Quadrangle/The New York Times Book Co., 1975).
39. Anthony Brandt, *Reality Police* (New York: William Morrow, 1975).
40. John Talbott, "Radical Psychiatry: An Examination of the Issues," *American Journal of Psychiatry* 131: No. 2 (1974):121–28.
41. Judy Freespirit, "Open Letter to My Former Shrink," *Issues in Radical Therapy*, Jan. 15, 1973, pp. 13–14.
42. Marilyn Rice, "The Rice Papers," *Madness Network News*, April 1975, p. 4.
43. "Drugs Replace Guns in Prisons," *Issues in Radical Therapy*, Summer 1974, p. 29.
44. Nicholas Kittrie, *The Right to Be Different: Deviance and Enforced Therapy* (Baltimore: Johns Hopkins Press, 1971).
45. Mary Jane Ward, *The Snake Pit* (New York: Random House, 1946).
46. Ken Kesey, *One Flew Over the Cuckoo's Nest* (New York: Viking Press, 1962).
47. Bertram Brown, quoted in "Criticisms Haven't Reduced Psychiatric Service Demand," *Clinical Psychiatry News*, Aug. 3, 1975, p. 3.

CHAPTER 9

1. For the year 1972–73, for example, Mississippi spent $9.99, South Carolina $11.18, and Virginia $14.06 per day per patient. National Institute of Mental Health statistics, 1972–73, reported in *Mental Health Scope*, Nov. 20, 1974, pp. 1, 4.
2. Harry Solomon, "Presidential Address," *American Journal of Psychiatry*, 115 (1958): 1–9, 7.
3. U.S., Congress, Senate, Committee on the Judiciary, testimony of Robert Kennedy, *Constitutional Rights of the Mentally Ill*, Hearings before the Subcommittee on Constitutional Rights, 87th Cong., 1st sess., 401, 1961.
4. U.S., Congress, House, Mental Health Study Act of 1955, Pub. L. 182, 84th Cong., Ch. 417, 1st sess., H.J. Res. 256.
5. The psychiatric members included such members of the psychiatric establishment as Kenneth Appel and Lauren Smith of Philadelphia, Leo Bartemeier of Baltimore, Francis Braceland of Hartford, and Walter Barton of Boston (later executive director of the American Psychiatric Association).
6. Report of the Joint Commission on Mental Illness and Health, *Action for Mental Health* (New York: Basic Books, 1961).
7. Ibid., p. xi.
8. Ibid., p. xvi.
9. Ibid., p. x.
10. Ibid., p. xii.
11. Ibid., pp. xii–xiii.
12. Ibid., p. xii.
13. Ibid., p. xvii.

14. Ibid., p. xiv.
15. Ibid., p. xxiii.
16. Morton Wagenfield and Stanley Robin, "Boundary Busting in the Role of the Community Mental Health Worker," *Journal of Health and Social Behavior* 17 (1976): 111–21.
17. Franklin Chu and Sharland Trotter, Ralph Nader's Study Group Report on the National Institute of Mental Health, *The Madness Establishment* (New York: Grossman, 1974), pp. 203, 205, 206.
18. H. Richard Lamb and Alexander Rogawski, "Supplemental Security Income and the Sick Role," *American Journal of Psychiatry* 135 (1978): 1221–24.
19. Letter of Stanford Ross, commissioner of Social Security, July 15, 1979.
20. *New York Times*, Sept. 2, 1979.
21. Jerry Henisz, Hilda Flynn, and Michael Levine, "Clients and Patients of Mental Health Services," *Archives of General Psychiatry* 34 (1977): 1345–48.
22. William Crosby, "Lead-Contaminated Health Foods," *Journal of the American Medical Association* 237 (1977): 2627–29.
23. Irving Rosen, letter to editor, "Is Psychiatry Doing the Job," *American Journal of Psychiatry* 133 (1976): 1347–48.
24. *Duchesne* v. *Sugarman*, No. 76-7475 (2nd Cir., Sept. 12, 1977); *Clearinghouse Review*, Nov. 1977, p. 658.
25. Report of The Governor's Commission to Improve Services for Mentally and Emotionally Handicapped Georgians, *Helping Troubled Georgians Solve Their Problems: A Mental Health Improvement Plan for Georgia*, Atlanta, Oct. 29, 1971 (mimeographed).
26. The President's Commission on Mental Health *Report to the President* (Washington, D.C.: Government Printing Office, 1978), Vol. 1.
27. Daniel Greenberg, "Washington Report," *New England Journal of Medicine* 298 (1978): 1211–12.
28. See Chapter Four, note 3.
29. "Recommendations of Commission Funded in 1980 Budget," *Mental Health Reports*, Jan. 24, 1979, p. 1.
30. "CMHCs Emerging in Strengthened Form from Budgetary Armageddon," *Behavior Today*, Jan. 22, 1979, p. 1.
31. "House, Senate Vote NIMH Money Bills," *Mental Health Scope*, July 30, 1979, p. 1.
32. François Bondy, "European Diary: God's Own Testament," *Encounter*, Sept. 1979, p. 56.
33. Teresa Kurzman-Seppala, "A Minnesota Primer on the Prevention of Chemical Use Problems," *Contemporary Drug Problems* 6 (Spring 1977): 86.
34. "Mental Health Commission Proposals Carry Immense Potential Impact," *Behavior Today*, May 15, 1978, p. 1.
35. Gene Hoffman, *From Inside the Glass Doors* (Brooklyn, N.Y.: The Turning Press, 1977).

CHAPTER 10

1. *A Psychiatric Glossary*, 4th ed., Subcommittee of the Committee on Public Information, American Psychiatric Association (Washington, D.C.: American Psychiatric Association, 1973).
2. Robert Campbell, quoted in "Pasnau Becomes Speaker; Lipsett Elected for 1980," *Psychiatric News*, June 15, 1979, pp. 1, 6; The President's Commission on Mental Health, *Report to the President* (Washington, D.C.: Government Printing Office, 1978), 1:8.
3. Robert Neville, "Environments of the Mind," in *Philosophy and Medicine*, ed. H. T. Engelhardt and S. F. Spicker (Boston: D. Reidel, 1978), 4:169.
4. Thomas Hackett, "The Psychiatrist: In the Mainstream or on the Banks of Medicine?" *American Journal of Psychiatry* 134 (1977): 432–34.
5. Gerald Grob, *The State and the Mentally Ill* (Chapel Hill: University of North Carolina, 1966), pp. 356–57.
6. Thomas Szasz, *Ideology and Insanity* (Garden City, N.Y.: Doubleday, 1972), Ch. 7.
7. *Washington* v. *United States*, 390 F.2d 444 (D.C. Cir. 1967).
8. Transcript of Proceedings, *Edmondson* v. *United States*, Civil No. 15, 911-1 (W.D. Mo. March 31, 1967), pp. 125–56.
9. "What's a Traumatic Experience Worth in Court?" *Medical Economics*, June 22, 1970, p. 42.
10. "Nymphomania," *Psychiatric News*, July 1, 1970, p. 19.
11. *Philadelphia Inquirer*, July 18, 1970.
12. *Philadelphia Inquirer*, June 9, 1971.
13. *Robinson* v. *California*, 370 U.S. 660 (1962).
14. *Powell* v. *Texas*, 392 U.S. 514 (1969). This is one of the strange decisions of the Supreme Court, like the decision in the *Bakke* case, in which the Court lines up 4-4 and the ninth member of the Court agrees with one faction on some aspect of the case, the other faction on another aspect of the case, and the result is a straddling decision that does not really answer the legal questions at issue.
15. Thomas Dawber, "Unproved Hypotheses," *New England Journal of Medicine*, 299 (1978):455.
16. " 'Addictive' Process Seen In Prostitution Study," *Psychiatric News*, Sept. 2, 1977, p. 2.
17. See Otto Rank, *The Trauma of Birth* (New York: Brunner, 1952), p. 212.
18. "IRS Rules on Alcoholism as a Sickness," *Mental Health Scope*, March 10, 1976, p. 3.
19. The regulations to 29 U.S.C. §794 appear in Federal Register 42:22672–702 (May 4, 1977), *to be codified in* 45 C.F.R. Part 84. They have also been printed in *Mental Disability Law Reporter* 1, No. 5, Part II (March-April 1977).
20. See Opinion of Attorney General, April 12, 1977, Department of Justice, Washington, D.C. (mimeographed) pp. 16–17.

21. D. L. Davies, "Is Alcoholism Really a Disease?" *Contemporary Drug Problems,* Summer 1974, pp. 197–212.
22. Vern Bullough, "Is Homosexuality an Illness?" *Humanist,* Nov./Dec. 1974, pp. 27–30.
23. F. Gordon Pleune, "All Dis-Ease Is Not Disease: A Consideration of Psycho-Analysis, Psychotherapy, and Psycho-Social Engineering," *International Journal of Psychoanalysis* 46 (July 1965): 358–66.
24. Thomas Szasz, "Bad Habits Are Not Diseases," *Lancet,* July 8, 1972, pp. 83–84.
25. Paul Kaunitz, "On the Other Hand," *Medical World News,* Nov. 8, 1974, p. 124.
26. Kenneth Altshuler, interviewed on "Daniel Foster, M.D.," Public Broadcasting System, June 15, 1978.

CHAPTER 11

1. Brian Clark, quoted in Mel Gussow in *New York Times,* July 30, 1978.
2. Joseph Heller, *Catch-22* (1961); paperback edition (New York: Dell, 1970). See Chapter 15.
3. Lewis Wolberg, *The Technique of Psychotherapy,* 2d ed. (New York: Grune & Stratton, 1967), p. 467.
4. *Addington* v. *Texas,* 99 S. Ct. 1804 (1979).
5. Opinion of Gordon Claridge in "News Briefs," *Mental Health Scope,* Nov. 15, 1972, p. 6.
6. Michael Alan Taylor and Richard Abrams, "The Prevalence of Schizophrenia: A Reassessment Using Modern Diagnostic Criteria," *American Journal of Psychiatry* 135 (1978): 945–48.
7. Nolan Lewis and Zigmunt Piotrowski, "Clinical Diagnosis of Manic-Depressive Psychosis," in *Depression,* ed. Paul Hoch and Joseph Zubin (New York: Grune & Stratton, 1954), p. 37; *Proceedings of the American Psychopathological Association* 42 (1952): 25–38.
8. Emil Kraepelin, *Lectures on Clinical Psychiatry* (London: Balliere, Tindall and Cox, 1904; facsimile reprint, New York: Hafner, 1968), Ch. 39.
9. American Psychiatric Association, *Diagnostic and Statistical Manual of Mental Disorders* (Washington, D.C.: American Psychiatric Association), 1st ed. (1952), 2d ed. (1968).
10. "DSM-III Approved. Will take Effect 1980," *Psychiatric News,* July 20, 1979, p. 1.
11. Alexander Brooks, *Law, Psychiatry and the Mental Health System* (Boston: Little, Brown, 1974), p. 49.
12. *Durham* v. *United States,* 214 F.2d 862 (D.C. Cir. 1954).
13. Testimony of Dr. Addison Duval, *Leach* v. *Overholser,* 257 F.2d 667 (D.C. Cir. 1957).
14. Brooks, *Law, Psychiatry and the Mental Health System,* fn. 12.
15. *Blocker* v. *United States,* 274 F.2d 572 (D.C. Cir. 1959).
16. *Blocker* v. *United States,* 288 F.2d 853 (D.C. Cir. 1961).

17. Randy Von Beitel, "The Criminalization of Private Homosexual Acts: A Jurisprudential Case Study of a Decision by the Texas Bar Penal Code Revisions Committee," *Human Rights* 6 (1977): 23, fn. 1.
18. Sigmund Freud, "Some Neurotic Mechanisms in Jealousy, Paranoia, and Homosexuality," Standard Edition (London: Hogarth Press, 1955), 18: 230–32.
19. Charles Socarides, *The Overt Homosexual* (New York: Grune & Stratton, 1968), p. 64.
20. The history of the movement in the American Psychiatric Association to declassify homosexuality is derived largely from Malcolm Spector, "Legitimizing Homosexuality," *Society,* July/Aug. 1977, pp. 52–56.
21. Robert Spitzer, "Open Letter to Jonas Robitscher," *Journal of Psychiatry and Law* 5, No. 4 (Winter 1977): 596.
22. Spector, "Legitimizing Homosexuality," fn. 21.
23. "U.S. Rejects Spiegel's Appeal for Homosexual Aliens' Rights," *Psychiatric News,* Sept. 4, 1974, p. 7; *New York Times,* Aug. 15, 1979.
24. *Chicago Tribune,* May 18, 1979.
25. "Can the Sane Be Distinguished from the Insane?" *Mental Health Scope,* Dec. 3, 1975, p. 7.
26. Bruce J. Ennis and Thomas R. Litwack, "Psychiatry and the Presumption of Expertise: Flipping Coins in the Courtroom," *California Law Review* 62 (1974): 741.
27. "Sick Again?" *Time,* Feb. 20, 1978, p. 102; "Time Magazine Admits Error in Sex Article," *Psychiatric News,* July 7, 1978
28. Joel Greenberg, "How Accurate Is Psychiatry?" *Science News,* July 9, 1977, pp. 28–29.
29. Alex Kaplan, "The Conference on Improvements in Psychiatric Classification and Terminology (DSM-III)—A Report," *Newsletter of the American Psychoanalytic Association,* Oct. 1976, pp. 1, 5.
30. "Axes IV & V Made Optimal in DSM-III," *Psychiatric News,* Nov. 17, 1978, p. 1.
31. Ibid., p. 14.
32. "Trustees to Draft DSM-III Criticisms," *Psychiatric News,* May 18, 1979, p. 1.
33. Robert Spitzer, in *Newsletter of the American Psychoanalytic Association,* Dec. 1976, p. 3.
34. "AAPL and DSM-II," *Newsletter of the American Academy of Psychiatry and the Law* 1, No. 2 (Summer 1976): 11.
35. "Draft of DSM-III Classification, Oct. 4, 1976," American Psychiatric Association.
36. "Current DSM-III Outline," *Psychiatric News,* Nov. 17, 1978, pp. 15–17.
37. Alfred Freedman, Harold Kaplan, and Benjamin Sadock, *Modern Synopsis of Comprehensive Textbook of Psychiatry,* 2nd ed. (Baltimore: Williams & Wilkins, 1976), pp. 758–59.
38. Ibid., p. 407.
39. Greenberg, "How Accurate Is Psychiatry?"

40. Lorrin Koran, "Controversy in Medicine and Psychiatry," *American Journal of Psychiatry* 132 (1975): 1065.
41. "Psychiatric Diagnosis Hit by UCLA Psychiatrist," *Mental Health Scope,* Oct. 14, 1974, pp. 4–5.
42. Daniel Goleman, "Who's Mentally Ill?" *Psychology Today,* Jan. 1978, p. 34.
43. George Albee, letter to editor, *APA Monitor,* Feb. 1977, p. 2.
44. Goleman, "Who's Mentally Ill?" p. 41.
45. John Spiegel, "Presidential Address: Psychiatry—A High-Risk Profession," *American Journal of Psychiatry* 132 (1975): 697.

CHAPTER 12

1. Jonas Rappeport, *The Clinical Valuation of the Dangerousness of the Mentally Ill* (Springfield, Ill.: Charles C. Thomas, 1967), Ch. 9.
2. Arthur Zitrin et al., "Crime and Violence among Mental Patients, *American Journal of Psychiatry* 133 (1976): 142–49; James Mullen, "Factors of Deviant Behavior in Mental Patients," *North Carolina Journal of Mental Health* 8, No. 6 (1977): 14–20; Larry Sosowsky, "Crime and Violence among Mental Patients Reconsidered in View of the New Legal Relationship between the State and the Mentally Ill," *American Journal of Psychiatry* 135 (1978): 33–42; John Lagos, Kenneth Perlmutter, and Herbert Saexinger, "Fear of the Mentally Ill: Empirical Support for the Common Man's Response," *American Journal of Psychiatry* 134 (1977): 1134–37.
3. *Atlanta Journal and Constitution,* Sept. 7, 1975.
4. *Atlanta Constitution,* July 17, 1976.
5. *Atlanta Constitution,* Feb. 23, 1976.
6. Darold Treffert, "The Practical Limits of Patients' Rights," in *Psychiatrists and the Legal Process,* ed. Richard Bonnie (New York: Psychiatric Annals, 1977), pp. 227–30.
7. Henry Steadman, "Follow-Up on Baxstrom Patients Returned to Hospitals for the Criminally Insane," *American Journal of Psychiatry* 130 (1973): 317–19.
8. Abraham Blumberg, *Criminal Justice* (Chicago: Quadrangle Books, 1967), p. 137.
9. Mark Pogrebin and John Stratton, "Legal and Human Rights of Mentally Ill Prisoners," *Corrective & Social Psychiatry* 20, No. 1 (1974): 3–9.
10. Mark Pogrebin, "Is the Use of a Psychiatric Facility for Parole Evaluation Justifiable?" *International Journal of Offender Therapy* 19, No. 3 (1974): 270–74.
11. Albert Deutsch, *The Mentally Ill in America,* 2d ed. (New York: Columbia University Press, 1949), pp. 419–20.
12. James Boswell, *Life of Johnson,* ed. George Birkbeck Hill, rev. L. F. Powell (Oxford: Oxford University Press, 1934), II, p. 73.
13. *O'Connor* v. *Donaldson,* 422 U.S. 563 (1975). See Kenneth Donaldson, *Insanity Inside Out* (New York: Crown, 1976), pp. 94, 150, 180, 192, 222,

246–47, 257, 272, 286, 304, 319, and 337; testimony of Dr. Walter Fox, p. 308.

14. *Matter of Josiah Oakes,* 8 *Law Reporter* 123 (Mass. Supr. Ct., 1845), discussed in *The Mentally Disabled and the Law,* 2d ed., Samuel Brakel and Ronald Rock, eds. (Chicago: University of Chicago Press, 1971), pp. 6–7, fn. 3.

15. Virginia Aldigé Hiday, "Reformed Commitment Procedures: An Empirical Study in the Courtroom," *Law and Society Review* 11 (1977): 651–66.

16. Alan Stone, *Mental Health and Law: A System in Transition* (Washington, D.C.: Department of Health, Education, and Welfare Publication, 1975), p. 37.

17. *Addington* v. *Texas,* 99 S. Ct. 1804 (1979).

18. *Millard* v. *Harris,* 406 F.2d 964 (D.C. Cir. 1968).

19. Bruce Tefft, Andreas Pederson, and Harounton Babigian, "Patterns of Death Among Suicide Attempters, a Psychiatric Population, and a General Population," *Archives of General Psychiatry* 34 (1977): 1155–61.

20. *Mayock* v. *Martin,* 245 A.2d 574 (1968).

21. Matt. 5:29–30. There are similar injunctions in Matt. 18:8–9, and Mark 9:43–49, where the enjoinder includes foot as well as hand and eye, and where the right side is not specified.

22. *Mayock* v. *Martin.*

23. *Furman* v. *Georgia,* 408 U.S. 238 (1972).

24. Art. 37.071 (b), *Texas Code of Criminal Procedure Supp.,* 1976–77.

25. John Bloom, "Killers and Shrinks," *Texas Monthly,* July 1978, p. 64. Other Texas death cases in which the question of the reliability of psychiatric testimony has been raised in an appeal include: *Gholson* v. *State,* 542 S.W.2d 395, 400–1 (1976); *Livingston* v. *State,* 542 S.W.2d 655, 661–62 (1976); *Moore* v. *State,* 542 S.W.2d 664, 675–76 (1976); *Collins* v. *State,* 548 S.W.2d 368, 377 (1976), *cert. denied,* 430 U.S. 959 (1977); *Battie* v. *State,* 551 S.W.2d 401, 406–7 (1977); *Granviel* v. *State,* 552 S.W.2d 107, 114–16 (1976), *cert. denied,* 431 U.S. 933 (1977); *Shippy* v. *State,* 556 S.W.2d 246, 254–55 (1977), *cert. denied,* 434 U.S. 935 (1977); *Chambers* v. *State,* 568 S.W.2d 313 (1978), *cert. denied,* 99 S. Ct. 1264 (1979); *Von Byrd* v. *State,* 569 S.W.2d 883 (1978). Smith's case was one of the first to question use of psychiatric testimony to support the death penalty. Grigson's testimony was at issue in five of these cases, as well as in the *Smith* case.

26. Robert Jones, "Observations on Psychiatry and the Law in Canada," in *Forensic Psychiatry and Child Psychiatry,* ed. D. Ewen Cameron, International Psychiatry Clinics (Boston: Little, Brown, 1965), p. 87; previously quoted in Ch. 3, fn. 9.

27. Edward Colbach, University of Oregon, unpublished manuscript.

28. Bloom, "Killers and Shrinks," pp. 64–65; George Dix, "Participation by Mental Health Professionals in Capital Murder Sentencing," *International Journal of Law and Psychiatry* 1 (1978): 287.

29. Bloom, "Killers and Shrinks," p. 68.

30. Psychiatric Testimony at Penalty Hearing in *Smith* v. *State*, 540 S.W.2d 693 (Tex. Cr. 1976), transcript, pp. 2791–2821.
31. Bloom, "Killers and Shrinks," p. 68.
32. Ibid. Also see John Bloom, "Doctor for the Prosecution," *American Lawyer*, Nov. 1979, pp. 25–26.
33. George Dix, "The Death Penalty, 'Dangerousness,' Psychiatric Testimony, and Professional Ethics," *American Journal of Criminal Law* 5 (1976): 151, 154.
34. Alan Stone, "To Let Live or Die," *Psychiatric News*, Oct. 1, 1976, p. 1.
35. *Smith* v. *State*, 445 F. Supp. 647 (N.D. Tex. 1977).
36. *Livingston* v. *State*, 542 S.W.2d 655 (Tex. Crim. App. 1976), *cert. denied*, 431 U.S. 933 (1977).
37. See Motion for Leave to File Brief *Amicus Curiae* and Brief *Amicus Curiae* for the American Psychiatric Association, *Smith* v. *State*, No. 78-1839 (C.C.A. 5, 1978).
38. American Psychiatric Association, *Amicus Curiae* brief, *Tarasoff* v. *Regents of University of California*, 551 P.2d 334 (Cal. 1976).
39. William McCord and Joan McCord, *Psychopathy and Delinquency* (New York: Grune & Stratton, 1956).
40. See Chapter 11.
41. Chip Barker, "I Decide Who Goes to the Mental Hospital," *CoEvolution* 18 (Summer 1978): 52–55.
42. Jane Bryan Quinn in *Philadelphia Inquirer*, Aug. 19, 1978; *Science*, April 28, 1978, p. 419.
43. Oliver Wendell Holmes, Jr., dissenting opinion in *Abrams* v. *United States*, 250 U.S. 616 (1919) at 630.

CHAPTER 13

1. H. J. Eysenck, "The Case of Sir Cyril Burt," *Encounter*, Jan. 1977, pp. 19–24.
2. Francis Galton, *Hereditary Genius* (New York: Appleton, 1871).
3. Francis Galton, "Hereditary Improvement," *Fraser's Magazine*, January 1873, p. 129, quoted in Allan Chase, *The Legacy of Malthus: The Social Costs of the New Scientific Racism* (New York: Knopf, 1977), p. 100.
4. *Brown* v. *Board of Education*, 347 U.S. 483 (1954).
5. David Musto, "Whatever Happened to 'Community Mental Health'?" *The Public Interest* 39 (Spring 1975): 53–79.
6. Martin Gross, *The Brain Watchers* (New York: Random House, 1962), p. 47.
7. Berkeley Rice, "Measuring Executive Muscle," *Psychology Today*, Dec. 1978, p. 95; Barbara Lovenheim in *New York Times*, Jan. 21, 1979.
8. "Employment Discrimination and Title VII of the Civil Rights Act of 1964," *Harvard Law Review* 84 (1971): 1109, 1120.
9. Ibid.
10. Gross, *The Brain Watchers*.

11. Irwin Perr, "Psychiatric Screening of Civil Service Candidates with Particular Reference to Police Applicants," *Journal of Forensic Sciences* 20 (1975): 176; Perr, "A Review of Rejected Police Candidates," *Journal of Forensic Sciences* 20 (1975): 714–18. The appeals to the Civil Service Medical Review Board led to the overruling of most of the challenged evaluations.

12. Daniel Hellman and Nathan Blackman, "Eneuresis, Firesetting and Cruelty to Animals: A Triad Predictive of Adult Crime," *American Journal of Psychiatry* 122 (1966): 1431–35.

13. Blair Justice, Rita Justice, and Irwin Kraft, "Early Warning Signs of Violence: Is a Triad Enough?" *American Journal of Psychiatry* 131 (1974): 457–59.

14. *Atlanta Constitution,* Sept. 20, 1972.

15. The use of Ritalin and amphetamines in the treatment of hyperactive children is discussed in more detail in Chapter 19.

16. Joseph Wepman et al., "Learning Disabilities," in *Issues in the Classification of Children,* ed. Nicholas Hobbs (San Francisco: Jossey-Bass, 1975), pp. 301–3.

17. Dorothy Buglass and John Horton, "A Scale for Predicting Subsequent Suicidal Behavior," *British Journal of Psychiatry* 124 (1974): 573–78; Avery Weisman and J. William Worden, "Risk-Rescue Rating in Suicide Assessment," *Archives of General Psychiatry* 26 (1972): 553–60.

18. *Atlanta Journal,* June 13, 1979.

19. Harold Altman et al., "Prediction of Unauthorized Absence," *American Journal of Psychiatry* 128 (1972): 1460–63.

20. Harold Altman et al., "Demographic and Mental Status Profiles—Patients with Homicidal, Assaultive, Suicidal, Persecution and Homosexual Ideation," *Psychiatric Quarterly* 45 (1971): 57–64.

21. ". . . And Computerized Psychiatry," *Medical World News,* June 19, 1970, p. 11.

22. "The Multi-State Information System for Psychiatric Patients," International Business Machines, New York, undated; "Multi-State Information System: Brief Description 1977," Rockland Research Institute, Orangeburg, N.Y. (mimeographed).

23. Thomas Williams, James Johnson, and Eugene Bliss, "A Computer-Assisted Psychiatric Assessment Unit," *American Journal of Psychiatry* 132 (1975): 1074–75.

24. "Psychiatric Records May Be Used against You," *Business Week,* Aug. 23, 1976, p. 73.

25. "A Threat That Won't Go Away," *Impact,* May 23, 1977, p. 4.

26. *New York Times,* June 24, 1971.

27. House Committee on Government Operations, "Use of Polygraph as 'Lie Detectors' by the Federal Government," H. Report 89–198, 89th Cong., 1st sess., 1968, p. 1.

28. Clarissa Wittenberg, "CIA Chief Reveals Behavioral Experiments," *Psychiatric News,* Sept. 2, 1977, p. 14.

29. *New York Times,* Aug. 28, 1977.
30. See Chapter 24 for a further discussion.
31. Gene Abel, et al., "The Component of Rapists' Sexual Arousal," *Archives of General Psychiatry* 34 (1977): 898.
32. *Atlanta Constitution,* Dec. 15, 1975.
33. Stanley Lesse, "The Medical Machine versus Today's Superspecialist—A Study in Anachronization," *American Journal of Psychotherapy* 24 (July 1970): 377–79.
34. "Psychiatry Newsletter," *Psychiatry Digest,* Sept. 1975, p. 11.
35. *New York Times,* Aug. 19, 1977.
36. *Detroit Edison* v. *National Labor Relations Board* 560 F.2d 722 (C.C.A.6, 1977); 440 U.S. 301 (1979).
37. William Abbott, "Work in the Year 2001," *The Futurist,* Feb. 1977, pp. 25–31; Herbert Simon, "What Computers Mean for Man and Society," *Science,* March 18, 1977, pp. 1186–91.

CHAPTER 14

1. Joint Commission on Mental Illness and Health, *Action for Mental Health* (New York: Basic Books, 1961), pp. 59–60.
2. *Atlanta Constitution,* Aug. 26, 1977.
3. Edward Sagarin, "The High Personal Cost of Wearing a Label," *Psychology Today,* March 1976, p. 25.
4. Derek Phillips, "Rejection: A Possible Consequence of Seeking Help for Mental Disorders," *American Sociological Review* 28 (1963): 963–72.
5. Study by Gerald Melchiode, Hahnemann Medical College and Hospitals, reported by Arthur Snider in *Atlanta Journal and Constitution,* May 18, 1975.
6. John Tringo, "The Hierarchy of Preference toward Disability Groups," *Journal of Special Education* 4, No. 3 (Summer 1970): 295–306.
7. Erving Goffman, *Stigma* (Englewood Cliffs, N.J.: Prentice-Hall, 1963), pp. 15–94.
8. Ibid., p. 42.
9. "Keep a Low Emotional Profile," *Business Week,* Aug. 23, 1976, p. 73.
10. "Psychiatric History Question Removed from Govt. Application," *Mental Health Scope,* June 7, 1974, p. 6.
11. *Glassman* v. *New York Medical College,* 64 Misc.2d 466, 315 N.Y.S. 1 (1970).
12. Bruce Ennis, *Prisoners of Psychiatry* (New York: Harcourt Brace Jovanovich, 1972), pp. 162–76.
13. Melvin Reinhart et al., "Evaluation of Academic Performance in a Neuropsychiatric Hospitalized Population," *Archives of General Psychiatry* 26 (1972): 68–70; Armand Nicholi, Jr., "Harvard Dropouts: Some Psychiatric Findings," *American Journal of Psychiatry* 124 (1967): 651–58.
14. "Blue Cross to Withdraw Sensitive Queries From Form," *Psychiatric News,* July 1, 1977, p. 1; "Blue Cross/Blue Shield Gives in on a Privacy Issue," *Behavior Today,* July 4, 1977, p. 5.

15. Lawrence Mosher, "The High Cost of Aiding the Handicapped," *National Observer,* May 16, 1977, p. 3; Nancy Hicks in *New York Times,* May 1, 1977.

CHAPTER 15

1. John Rosen, *Direct Psychoanalysis,* 2 vols. (New York: Grune & Stratton, 1953).
2. *Hammer* v. *Rosen,* 181 N.Y.S.2d 805 (N.Y., Supr. Ct., App. Div., 1st Dept., 1959); 165 N.E.2d 756 (N.Y. Ct. App., 1960).
3. *Atlanta Journal,* Sept. 5, 1978.
4. *New York Times,* March 11, 1979.
5. *Duzynski* v. *Nosal,* 324 F.2d 924 (USCA 7, 1963); some of the factual description of the case is derived from Nicholas Kittrie, *The Right to Be Different: Deviance and Enforced Therapy* (Baltimore: Johns Hopkins Press, 1971), pp. 83–84.
6. Virginia Adigé Hiday, "Reformed Commitment Procedures: An Empirical Study in the Courtroom," *Law and Society Review* 11 (1977): 651–66.
7. David Lelos, "Courtroom Observation Study of Civil Commitment," in A. Louis McGarry et al., *Civil Commitment and Social Policy,* Final Report of the Laboratory of Community Psychiatry, Harvard Medical School (Boston: Laboratory of Community Psychiatry, Harvard Medical School, 1978).
8. Kathy Sawyer in *Washington Post,* Dec. 28, 1978.
9. Arnold Lubasch in *New York Times,* Feb. 25, 1979.
10. *Kochman* v. *Keansburg Board of Education,* 305 A.2d 807 (N.J., Supr. Ct., Cen. Div., 1973).
11. *Gish* v. *Board of Education,* 366 A.2d 1337 (N.J., Supr. Ct., App. Div., 1977).
12. *Wall Street Journal,* Aug. 17, 1976.
13. *Carter* v. *General Motors,* 106 N.W.2d 105 (Mich., 1960); *Fireman's Fund Insurance Co.* v. *Industrial Commission,* 579 P.2d 555 (Ariz., 1978).
14. *Trombley* v. *State,* 115 N.W. 561 (Mich., 1962).
15. Barry Schwartz and Lawrence Snow, "On Getting Kicked Out of Medical School," *American Journal of Psychotherapy* 28 (1974):574–83.
16. For a further discussion of psychosurgery, see Chapter 16.
17. *M.T.* v. *J.T.,* 355 A.2d 204 (N.J., 1976).
18. *Atlanta Journal,* Feb. 23, 1979.
19. *J.D.* v. *Lockner,* 146 Cal. Rptr. 229 (Cal., 1978).
20. *Rush* v. *Parham,* 440 F. Supp. 383 (N.D. Ga., 1977).
21. *The Star* (Washington, D.C.), Nov. 9, 1976.
22. *Voyles* v. *Ralph K. Davies Medical Center,* 403 F. Supp. 456 (N.D. Cal. 1975); *Holloway* v. *Arthur Andersen and Co.,* 566 F.2d 659 (9th Cir. 1977).
23. Melvin Belli, "Transsexual Surgery: A New Tort?" *Journal of the American Medical Association,* 239 (1978): 2143–48.
24. Jan Morris, *Conundrum* (New York: Harcourt Brace Jovanovich), p. 3.

25. Samuel Herschkowitz and Robert Dickes, "Suicide Attempts in a Female-to-Male Transsexual," *American Journal of Psychiatry* 135 (1978): 368–69.
26. "Sex Changes and the Real World," *Science News*, May 4, 1977, p. 312; "Transsexual Surgery Candidates Evaluated—and Followed Up," *Frontiers of Psychiatry*, Sept. 1, 1977, p. 3.
27. "Sex Change Operations of Dubious Value," *Science*, 205 (1979): 1235. Meyer's study indicated that psychotherapy was as helpful as sex-change surgery in producing emotional adjustment.
28. Jan Walinder et al., "Prognostic Factors in the Assessment of Male Transsexuals for Sex Reassignment," *British Journal of Psychiatry* 132 (1978): 16–20.
29. Deborah Heller Feinbloom and Michael Sherwood, "Counseling Issues with Transsexuals," *Psychiatric Opinion* 14, No. 1 (1977): 33–37.
30. Charles Socarides, "Transsexualism and the First Law of Medicine," *Psychiatric Opinion*, 14, No. 1 (1977): 20–24; Martha Kirkpatrick and Claude Friedmann, "Treatment of Requests for Sex-Change Surgery with Psychotherapy," *American Journal of Psychiatry* 133 (1976): 1194–96.
31. *Atlanta Constitution*, Jan. 26, 1976; *Atlanta Constitution*, May 2, 1978; Ellen Goodman in *Atlanta Journal and Constitution*, March 5, 1978. The case is *Northern* v. *State*, 575 S.W.2d 946 (Supr. Ct. Tennessee, 1978). In this case, the doctors, having won the right to amputate, decided not to, and the patient continued with her legs intact, but without the legal power to control the doctors, until her death three months after her admission.
32. Erving Goffman, *Asylums* (Garden City, N.Y.: Doubleday, Anchor Books, 1961), pp. 4–5.
33. *McNeil* v. *Director, Patuxent Institution,* 407 U.S. 245 (1972).
34. Margaret McDonald, "Patuxent: Change Looms," *Psychiatric News*, Feb. 3, 1978, p. 1. The recidivism rate of Patuxent's discharged patients has been a matter of controversy. Some studies have shown low recidivism rates, but they have been challenged on the ground, among others, that only minimal-risk patients were included in these studies. "Patuxent Claims Success as Controversy Rolls," *Psychiatric News*, May 2, 1973, p. 1.
35. Jonas Rappeport, Editor's Commentary, *Bulletin of the American Academy of Psychiatry and the Law,* 5, No. 2 (1977): v.
36. Stephen Shanfield, "The Military Psychiatrist: Themes of Separation and Dislocation," *Psychiatric Annals* 8 (May 1978): 85.
37. Edward Colbach and Matthew Parrish, "Army Mental Health Activities in Vietnam: 1965–1970," *Bulletin of the Menninger Clinic* (1970): 341, quoted in Henry Friedman, "Military Psychiatry: Limitations of the Current Preventive Approach," *Archives of General Psychiatry*, 26 (1972): 118–23.
38. Roland Atkinson, "Ineffective Personnel in Military Service: A Critique of Concepts and Rehabilitation Practices from a Psychiatric Viewpoint," *American Journal of Psychiatry* 127 (1971): 1612–18.

39. "Psychiatric Test Blocked for Navy MD," *American Medical News*, Oct. 3, 1977, p. 11.
40. Edward Colbach, "Psychiatric Criteria for Compassionate Reassignment in the Army," *American Journal of Psychiatry* 127 (1970): 508–10.
41. See *Commonwealth* v. *Childs*, 360 N.E.2d 312 (Supr. Jud. Ct. Mass., 1977).
42. David Begelman, quoted in "The Power of Psychiatrists Must Be Curbed," *People*, March 6, 1978, p. 35.
43. *New York Times*, Nov. 9, 1978.
44. *Atlanta Constitution*, March 10, 1976.
45. *Atlanta Journal and Constitution*, Feb. 5, 1978.
46. *Tulsa World*, June 3, 1978; *Atlanta Constitution*, June 7, 1978.
47. *Application of Miller*, 342 N.Y.S.2d 315 (Monroe Cty., 1972).
48. *J.L. and J.R.* v. *Parham*, 47 U.S.L.W. 4740 (1979).
49. *Drummond* v. *Fulton Cty. Dept. of Family and Children's Services*, 563 F.2d 1200 (5th Cir. 1977), *cert. denied*, 434 U.S. 881 (1978).

CHAPTER 16

1. H. Tristram Engelhardt, Jr., "The Disease of Masturbation: Values and the Concept of Disease," *Bulletin of the History of Medicine* 48 (1974): 234–48.
2. Baker Brown, *On the Curability of Certain Forms of Insanity, Epilepsy, Catalepsy, and Hysteria in Females* (London: Hardwicke, 1866).
3. Engelhardt, "Disease of Masturbation," p. 244.
4. J. H. Marshall, "Insanity Cured by Castration," *Medical and Surgical Reporter* 13 (1865): 363–64, cited in Engelhardt, "Disease of Masturbation."
5. R. D. Potts, "Castration for Masturbation, With Report of a Case," *Texas Medical Practitioner* 11 (1898): 8; J. B. Shelmire, editorial note, ibid., p. 9, cited in Engelhardt, "Disease of Masturbation."
6. Engelhardt, "Disease of Masturbation," p. 245.
7. The date for the first sterilizations is sometimes given as 1889, sometimes as 1892, and another version of Kerlin's remarks is: "Whose state shall be the first to legalize oophorectomy and orchotomia for the relief and cure of radical depravity?" See Julius Paul, "State Eugenic Sterilization History: A Brief Overview" in *Eugenic Sterilization*, ed. Jonas Robitscher (Springfield, Ill.: Charles C. Thomas, 1973), pp. 28–29 and fn. 2, pp. 35–36.
8. Ibid., fn. 3, p. 36, quoting Martin Barr, *Mental Defectives, Their History, Treatment and Training* (Philadelphia: P. Blakiston's Son, 1904), p. 191.
9. Allan Chase, testimony on the regulations applicable to sterilizations funded by the Department of Health, Education, and Welfare, Washington, D.C., Jan. 17, 1978 (New York: Center for Epidemiology and Health Econometrics, 1978), p. 19.
10. Allan Chase, *The Legacy of Malthus: The Social Costs of the New Scientific Racism* (New York: Knopf, 1977), p. 127.

11. Albert Deutsch, *The Mentally Ill in America,* 2d ed. (New York: Columbia University Press, 1949), p. 370.
12. *Buck* v. *Bell,* 274 U.S. 200 (1927).
13. Oliver Wendell Holmes, Jr., to Harold Laski, April 25, 1927; Laski to Holmes, March 7, 1927. *Holmes-Laski Letters,* ed. Mark DeWolfe Howe (Cambridge, Mass.: Harvard University Press, 1953), 2: 937–41.
14. *Sparkman* v. *McFarlin,* 552 F.2d 172 (7th Cir. 1977); *reversed sub nom, Stump* v. *Sparkman,* 435 U.S. 349 (1978).
15. Ralph Slovenko, "Sexual Behavior and the Law: A Panoramic View," in *Sexual Behavior and the Law,* ed. R. Slovenko (Springfield, Ill.: Charles C. Thomas, 1965), p. 104.
16. International Comments, "Anti-Androgen for Sex Offenders," *Journal of the American Medical Association,* 219 (1972): 230.
17. Manfred Guttmacher, quoted in Horace Campbell, "The Violent Sex Offender," *Rocky Mountain Medical Journal* 64 (June 1967): 40–43, 41.
18. Hawke's study is reported by Campbell, ibid., pp. 40–41.
19. Ibid., pp. 40–43.
20. *Psychiatric News,* June 7, 1972, p. 12; *Atlanta Constitution,* April 8, 1972.
21. *Los Angeles Times,* March 9, 1975.
22. Gerald Klerman, "Case Study: Can Convicts Consent to Castration?" *Hastings Center Report,* Oct. 1975, p. 18.
23. *Psychiatric News,* Oct. 20, 1971, p. 30.
24. International Comments, "Anti-Androgen for Sex Offenders."
25. David Barry and J. Richard Ciccone, "Use of Depo-Provera in the Treatment of Aggressive Sexual Offenders: Preliminary Report of Three Cases," *Bulletin of the American Academy of Psychiatry and Law* 3 (1975): 179–84.
26. "Sex Offenders: Should They Be Incarcerated or Castrated?" *The Medical-Moral Newsletter,* undated issue, 1976, p. 4.
27. Franklin letter of April 29, 1785, quoted in letter by Walter Ford, "Franklin and ECT," *Psychiatric News,* July 21, 1978, p. 12, from *Connecticut Journal of Public Safety,* June 1956.
28. Jerry Flint in *New York Times,* Nov. 27, 1971.
29. Gregory Asnis, Max Fink, and Sire Saferstein, "ECT in Metropolitan New York Hospitals: A Survey of Practice," *American Journal of Psychiatry* 135 (1978): 479–82.
30. Stewart Ted Ginsberg, quoted by Jeff Nesmith in *Atlanta Constitution,* July 28, 1972.
31. "ECT and Memory Loss: The Debate Goes On," Journal of the *American Medical Association,* 242 (1979): 2690.
32. Dianne Gordon in *Philadelphia Bulletin,* Oct. 6, 1978.
33. Neal Chayet, "Should You Sign That Commitment Order?" *Medical Economics,* Nov. 22, 1971, pp. 130, 144.
34. "Electroconvulsive Therapy Is Alive and Well and Respectable," *Frontiers of Psychiatry,* Feb. 15, 1977, p. 1.
35. John Exner and Luis Murillo, "A Long-Term Follow-Up of Schizophrenics

Treated with Regressive ECT," *Diseases of the Nervous System,* March 1977, pp. 162–68.

36. Donald Templer, Carol Ruff, and Gloria Armstrong, "Cognitive Functioning and Degree of Psychosis in Schizophrenia Given Many Electroconvulsive Treatments," *British Journal of Psychiatry* 123 (1973): 441–43; Herbert Goldman, Frank Gomer, and Donald Templer, "Long-Term Effects of Electroconvulsive Therapy upon Memory and Perceptual-Motor Performance," *Journal of Clinical Psychology* 28 (1972): 32–34.

37. Berton Roueché, Annals of Medicine, "As Empty as Eve," *The New Yorker,* Sept. 9, 1974, p. 84.

38. John Friedberg, "ECT as a Neurological Injury," *Medical Opinion,* Jan./Feb. 1977, pp. 16–19.

39. "Shock Treatment Is a Brain Disease, Says Neurologist," *Behavior Today,* June 28, 1976, p. 5.

40. David Avery, "The Case for 'Shock' Therapy," *Psychology Today,* Aug. 1977, p. 104.

41. John Friedberg, "Let's Stop Blasting the Brain," *Psychology Today,* Aug. 1975, p. 18.

42. Ernest Hemingway, quoted ibid.; also see A. E. Hotchner, *Papa Hemingway* (New York: Random House, 1955), pp. 279–80.

43. Sylvia Plath, *The Bell Jar* (New York: Harper & Row, 1971), pp. 160–61, quoted in *Blue Jolts,* ed. Charles Steir (Washington, D.C.: New Republic Books, 1978), p. xv.

44. H. Thomas Ballantine, Jr., quoted in "Psychosurgery Returns," *Time,* April 3, 1972, p. 50.

45. Frederick Redlich and Daniel X. Freedman, *The Theory and Practice of Psychiatry* (New York: Basic Books, 1966), p. 338.

46. Egas Moniz, *Tentatives Opératoires dans le Traitement de Certaines Psychoses* (Paris: Masson, 1936).

47. Patrick McGrath, Physician Superintendent, Broadmoor Hospital, to Jonas Robitscher, June 14, 1973.

48. William Arnold, *Shadowland* (New York: McGraw-Hill, 1978).

49. Frances Farmer, *Will There Really Be a Morning?* (New York: Dell, 1972).

50. Ibid., p. 138.

51. Ibid., pp. 9–12, 219–23, 227.

52. Arnold, *Shadowland,* p. 198. Farmer merely says that there were rapes that "claimed every inmate" but does not allege this was arranged by orderlies. Farmer, p. 260.

53. The description of the state of psychosurgery is based on Constance Holden, "Psychosurgery: Legitimate Therapy or Laundered Lobotomy," *Science,* March 16, 1973, pp. 1109–12.

54. Letter quoted in Holden, ibid.

55. Ibid., pp. 683–84.

56. Lee Coleman, "Perspectives on the Medical Research of Violence," *American Journal of Orthopsychiatry* 44 (Oct. 1974): 683–84.

57. *Kaimowitz* v. *Michigan Department of Mental Health,* Civil No. 73-

19434-AW unreported (Cir. Ct. Wayne Co., Mich., July 10, 1973), summarized at 42 U.S.L.W. 2063, reprinted in Alexander Brooks, *Law, Psychiatry and the Mental Health System* (Boston: Little, Brown, 1974), pp. 902–24.

58. Holden, "Psychosurgery," p. 1110.

59. See Chapter 6.

60. See *Kaimowitz* v. *Michigan Department of Mental Health,* note 56.

61. [Ralph Slovenko], "Whatever Happened to John Doe?" *Hastings Center Report,* April 1977, p. 12.

62. *Detroit Free Press,* Feb. 6, 1979; *State* v. *Smith,* 275 N.W.2d 466 (Mich., 1979).

63. A majority of the sexual psychopath statutes allow a subsequent criminal trial and sentence after a finding of, and hospitalization for, sexual psychopathy, in spite of the obvious argument that this seems like double jeopardy. See Samuel Brakel and Ronald Rock, eds., *The Mentally Disabled and the Law,* 2d ed. (Chicago: University of Chicago Press, 1971), p. 346. An additional hazard for the hospitalized "quasi criminals" is that they may be housed in a minimum security facility where patients frequently "elope" (absent themselves without leave) and where escape is easy, and they may be subjected to conditions and to treatments that inspire elopement, but the escape from the hospital can constitute an additional felony deserving of prosecution. *State* v. *Ewing,* 518 S.W.2d 643 (Mo., 1975).

64. *Washington Post,* March 27, 1973.

65. Jim Hampton, *National Observer,* March 25, 1972; "Surgery Stalled in 2 States, Considered in a Third," *Mental Health Scope,* April 20, 1973, p. 2.

66. VA Circular 10-72-246, Oct. 20, 1972.

67. Barbara Culliton, "Psychosurgery: National Commission Issues Surprisingly Favorable Report," *Science,* Oct. 15, 1976, pp. 299–301.

68. George Annas, "The Attempted Revival of Psychosurgery," *Medicolegal News,* Summer 1977, p. 3.

69. Culliton, "Psychosurgery," p. 291.

70. "Protection of Human Subjects: Use of Psychosurgery in Practice and Research: Report and Recommendation for Public Comment," *Federal Register,* 42, No. 99, 26318–32 (May 23, 1977).

71. "U.S. Curbs on Psychosurgery Rejected," *American Medical News,* Dec. 1, 1978, p. 1; "New Group Regulates Psychosurgery in U.S.," *Legal Aspects of Medical Practice,* Feb. 1979, p. 19.

72. E. H. Uhlenhuth, Mitchell Balter, and Ronald Lipman, "Minor Tranquilizers," *Archives of General Psychiatry,* 35 (1978): 650–55.

73. Gilbert Cant, "Valiumania," *New York Times Magazine,* Feb. 1, 1976, p. 34.

74. Sidney Cohen, "Valium: Its Use and Abuse," *Drug Abuse and Alcoholism Newsletter,* May 1976.

75. A. A. Freed, quoted from the *British Journal of Medicine* in *Modern Medicine,* March 1, 1977, p. 27.

76. For a fuller discussion of the methadone program, see Chapter 19.
77. Nigel Calder, *The Mind of Man* (New York: Viking Press, 1970), pp. 74–75.
78. Richard Mayberry, quoted in Michael Bomstein, "The Forcible Administration of Drugs to Prisoners and Mental Patients," *Clearinghouse Review*, Oct. 1975, p. 379.
79. The use of injectable tranquilization is discussed further in Chapter 19.
80. See Chapter 19.
81. Peter Quitkin et al., "Long-Acting Oral vs. Injectable Antipsychotic Drugs in Schizophrenics," *Archives of General Psychiatry*, July 1978, pp. 889–97. See Chapter 19 for a further discussion of Ritalin and mass drug administration.
82. Henry Beecher, "Ethics and Clinical Research," *New England Journal of Medicine* 274 (1966): 1354–60.
83. U.S., Congress, Senate, Committee on Labor and Public Welfare, *Quality of Health Care—Human Experimentation, Hearings* before the Subcommittee on Health, 93rd Cong., 1st sess., pt. 1, p. 94.
84. Richard Singer, "Consent of the Unfree: Medical Experimentation and Behavior Modification in the Closed Institution," Part I, *Law and Human Behavior* 1 (1977): 25.
85. Peter Zeldow, "Some Antitherapeutic Effects of the Token Economy: A Case in Point," *Psychiatry*, Nov. 1976, pp. 316–24.
86. Willard Gaylin, Sounding Board, "The Frankenstein Factor," *New England Journal of Medicine*, 297 (1977): 665.
87. Peter Suedfeld and Chunilal Roy, "Using Social Isolation to Change the Behavior of Disruptive Inmates," *International Journal of Offender Therapy* 19, No. 1 (1975): 90–99.
88. Nick DiSpoldo, "A Prisoner's View of Behavior Modification," reprinted from the *New York Times*, in Alex Gordon, "Behavior: Conditioning the Convict's Response," *Physician's World*, Oct. 1974, p. 63.
89. Gordon, "Behavior," p. 61.
90. Ibid., p. 62.
91. Richard Singer, "Consent of the Unfree," p. 37.
92. Singer, "Consent of the Unfree," fns. 139 and 142.
93. *Mackey* v. *Procunier*, 477 F.2d 877 (9th Cir. 1973).
94. *Knecht* v. *Gillman*, 488 F.2d 1137 (8th Cir. 1973).
95. Dr. Philip Shapiro quoted in Jessica Mitford, *Kind and Usual Punishment* (New York: Knopf, 1973), p. 130.
96. California prisoner quoted in Werbner, "Gabriel's Judgment," *Venceremos*, Nov. 1971, p. 20, cited in Singer, "Consent of the Unfree," p. 39.

CHAPTER 17

1. *Roe* v. *Wade*, 410 U.S. 113 (1973), and *Doe* v. *Bolton*, 410 U.S. 179 (1973).
2. Daniel Callahan, *Abortion: Law, Choice and Morality* (New York: Macmillan, 1970), p. 62.
3. Ibid., p. 64.

4. E. Fuller Torrey, *The Death of Psychiatry* (Radnor, Pa.: Chilton Book Co., 1974), pp. 105–6.
5. Eric Pfeiffer, *Archives of General Psychiatry* 23 (1970): 405.
6. Walter Char and John McDermott, "Abortions and Acute Identity Crisis in Nurses," *American Journal of Psychiatry* 128 (1972): 952–57.
7. Kenneth Kessler and Theodore Weiss, "Ward Staff Problems with Abortions," *International Journal of Psychiatry in Medicine* 5, No. 2 (1974): 97–103.
8. Chris Connell in *Atlanta Journal*, Jan. 3, 1979.
9. §209, Pub. L. 94–439 (1976).
10. *Beal* v. *Doe*, 432 U.S. 438 (1977) and *Maher* v. *Roe*, 432 U.S. 464 (1977).
11. Superseding rider to Pub. L. 95–205 (1977).
12. Lawrence Baskir and William Strauss, *Chance and Circumstance: The Draft, the War and the Vietnam Generation* (New York: Vintage Books, 1978), p. 14.
13. Ibid., Fig. 1 (p. 5), Fig. 2 (pp. 30–31).
14. William Mandell, "The Institutionalization of Draft Resistance," *Philadelphia Magazine*, Sept. 1970, pp. 96, 178.
15. David Suttler, quoted in "Physical Disqualification for Armed Forces," *Modern Medicine*, Oct. 5, 1970, pp. 77, 84.
16. David Ingram, "Psychiatric Deferment from the Military," Villanova University School of Law, 1970 (unpublished).
17. Mandell, "Institutionalization of Draft Resistance," p. 182.
18. Craig Leman, "Letters to Editor," *New England Journal of Medicine*, 288 (1973): 1305–6.
19. Baskir and Strauss, *Chance and Circumstance*, p. 47.
20. "Draft-Defying Doctors," *Time*, Nov. 16, 1970, p. 67.
21. Peter A. Roemer, "Letters to the Editor," *American Journal of Psychiatry* 127 (1971): 1236–37.
22. Baskir and Strauss, *Chance and Circumstance*, p. 49.
23. *Time*, Nov. 16, 1970.
24. Ibid.
25. "Physical Disqualification for Armed Forces," *Modern Medicine*, Oct. 5, 1970, p. 81.
26. *Time*, Nov. 16, 1970.
27. Benjamin Pasamanick, "Letters to the Editor," *American Journal of Psychiatry* 131 (Jan. 1974): 107.
28. Leslie Fiedler, "Who Really Died in Vietnam?" *Saturday Review*, Nov. 18, 1972, p. 41.
29. Baskir and Strauss, *Chance and Circumstance*, p. 8.
30. James Fallows, "Vietnam—the Class War," *National Observer*, Feb. 21, 1976, p. 14.
31. Ira Frank and Frederick Hoedemaker, "The Civilian Psychiatrist and the Draft," *American Journal of Psychiatry* 127 (1970): 497–503.
32. Robert Liberman, Stephen Sonnenberg, and Melvin Stern, "Psychiatric

Evaluations for Young Men Facing the Draft: A Report of 147 Cases," *American Journal of Psychiatry* 128 (1971): 147–52.

33. Personal account of exempted registrant.
34. Fallows, "Vietnam."
35. Howard Waitzkin, "Letters to the Editor," *New England Journal of Medicine*, 288 (1973): 1306.
36. Peter Elias, "Medical Draft Resistance," *New England Journal of Medicine* 288 (1973): 399–402.
37. Mark J. Sicherman, "Letters to the Editor," *New England Journal of Medicine*, 288 (1973): 1306.
38. The General Walker and Daniel Ellsberg cases are described in Chapter 18.

CHAPTER 18

1. Frederic Wertham, *A Sign for Cain* (New York: Macmillan, 1966), p. 170. Wertham's account of the Nazi killing of mental patients has not received adequate attention by psychiatrists.
2. Peter Breggin, "The Psychiatric Holocaust," *Penthouse,* Jan. 1979, p. 81.
3. Quoted in Edwin Wilson in *Wall Street Journal,* July 18, 1978.
4. Accurate figures for this practice are difficult to secure. Peter Reddaway, a political scientist who has done much investigation of this topic, estimated in 1972 that about 150 cases were known to him personally but that the total number was probably much higher. Peter Reddaway, letter to editor, *Time,* Feb. 28, 1972, p. E2. In a book coauthored by Reddaway that was published in 1977, more than 200 documented cases are cited. Sidney Bloch and Peter Reddaway, *Psychiatric Terror: How Soviet Psychiatry is Used to Suppress Dissent* (New York: Basic Books, 1977). Some researchers have estimated the number as high as 8000, which is a figure issued in 1974 by the International Committee for the Defense of Human Rights in the Soviet Union and also the figure of Dr. Norman Hirt, a Canadian psychiatrist who did research over a period of years on treatment of Soviet dissenters; but Clayton Yeo, a political scientist who has worked for Amnesty International, believes the Hirt figure is exaggerated on the basis of the data he presents. Vladimir Bukovsky, a dissident who was hospitalized, estimated in 1977 that there were probably at least 2000 political dissidents in mental hospitals. Vladimir Bukovsky, interview with E. Fuller Torrey, "The Serbsky Treatment," *Psychology Today,* June 1977, pp. 38, 41. Marina Voikhanskaya, a Soviet psychiatrist who protested the use of psychiatry and was allowed to emigrate in 1975, placed the figure as between 700 and 1000, *Honolulu Advertiser,* Aug. 30, 1977, B-1. See "Soviet Asylums/House the Sane?" *Atlanta Journal and Constitution,* Oct. 20, 1974, 20-C; Clayton Yeo, "Psychiatry, The Law and Dissent in the Soviet Union," *The Review International Commission of Jurists,* Nos. 12–15, 1974–75, pp. 34–41.

5. Walter Reich, review of *Psychiatry and Psychology in the USSR*, Samuel Corson and Elizabeth Corson, eds., *Psychiatry* 41 (1978): 218.
6. Christopher Wren in *New York Times*, May 12, 1974.
7. Alan Dershowitz, review of *A Question of Madness, New York Times Book Review*, Nov. 28, 1971, p. 4.
8. Solzhenitsyn, quoted in Zhores Medvedev and Roy Medvedev, *A Question of Madness* (New York: Knopf, 1977), pp. 135–36.
9. "APA to Study Alleged Political Commitments," *Psychiatric News*, April 5, 1972, p. 5.
10. I. F. Stone, "Betrayal by Psychiatry," *New York Review of Books*, Feb. 10, 1972, pp. 7, 12.
11. E. Fuller Torrey, "Not Just a Soviet Problem," *Psychology Today*, June 1977, p. 44; *Atlanta Constitution*, May 16, 1974.
12. "Soviet Union: The *Psukhushka* Horror," *Time*, Feb. 16, 1976, p. 26; "Freed Soviet Dissenter Tells of Psychiatric Abuse," *Psychiatric News*, May 7, 1976, p. 3; U.S., Congress, House, Committee on International Relations, statement of Leonid Plyushch, *Psychiatric Abuse of Political Prisoners in the Soviet Union, Hearing* before the Subcommittee on International Organizations, 94th Cong., 2d sess., March 30, 1976, p. 7.
13. Vladimir Bukovsky and Semyon Gluzman, *A Manual on Psychiatry for Dissidents* (London: Working Group on the Internment of Dissenters in Mental Hospitals, 1976); reprinted (Washington, D.C.: United States Committee Against the Political Misuse of Psychiatry, 1977).
14. Vladimir Bukovsky, *To Build A Castle—My Life as a Dissenter* (New York: Viking Press, 1979).
15. Harvey Fireside, letter to editor, "Soviet Dissidents," *Psychiatric News*, Feb. 16, 1979, p. 2.
16. "The Declaration of Hawaii," *Psychiatric News*, Oct. 7, 1978, p. 23.
17. Albert Jonsen and Leonard Sagan, "Torture and the Ethics of Medicine," *Man and Medicine* 3 (1978): 33–49, 37.
18. Leonard Sagan and Albert Jonsen, "Medical Ethics and Torture," *New England Journal of Medicine*, 294 (1976): 1427–30; ibid., pp. 33–53.
19. Morton Birnbaum, "The Right to Treatment: Some Comments on its Development," in *Medical, Moral and Legal Issues in Mental Health Care*, ed. Frank Ayd (Baltimore: Williams & Wilkins, 1974), pp. 135 ff.
20. "Thirty-Year Follow Up: Counseling Fails," *Science News*, Nov. 26, 1977, p. 357.
21. Phyllis Chesler, *Women and Madness* (Garden City, N.Y.: Doubleday, 1972).
22. Martin Ferrand, "Political Hospitalization," *Psychiatric News*, March 1, 1972, p. 2; *Atlanta Constitution*, Aug. 24, 1973; *Atlanta Constitution*, March 30, 1973; James Feron in *New York Times*, May 11, 1976.
23. Janice Law Trecker, "The Suffrage Prisoners," *American Scholar*, Summer 1972, pp. 409–23.
24. See Chapter 8.
25. The account of the General Walker case is based in part on Thomas Szasz,

"The Case of Mr. Edwin A. Walker," in his *Psychiatric Justice* (New York: Macmillan, 1965).

26. *Associated Press* v. *Walker,* 388 U.S. 130 (1967), *reh. denied,* 389 U.S. 889; 418 S.W.2d 379 (Tex. Civ. App. 1967).

27. Opinion of Judicial Council, American Medical Association: "General Walker and Dr. Smith," *Journal of the American Medical Association* 185 (1963): 36.

28. Donovan Ward, quoted in "Evaluation of Goldwater Irresponsible, AMA Says," *AMA News,* Oct. 12, 1964, p. 1.

29. *Goldwater* v. *Ginzburg,* 414 F.2d 324 (2d Cir. 1969), *cert. denied,* 396 U.S. 1049 (1970).

30. *Atlanta Journal and Constitution,* Sept. 5, 1977.

31. *Atlanta Constitution,* Sept. 2, 1977.

32. Bill Richards in *Washington Post,* Jan. 29, 1979; John Marks, *The Search for the "Manchurian Candidate": The CIA and Mind Control* (New York: Times Books, 1979).

33. Richard Moran, "Biomedical Research and the Politics of Crime Control," in *Contemporary Crises* 2 (1978): 351–52.

34. *Atlanta Constitution,* July 21, 1977.

35. Commission on CIA Activities Within the United States, *Report to the President, June 1975* (Washington, D.C.: Government Printing Office, 1975), p. 226.

36. Howard Kohn and Mark Porter, "Justice Department Apologizes in Burger Drug Case," *The Rolling Stone,* June 16, 1977, p. 34.

37. Joseph Treaster in *New York Times,* Aug. 3, 1976; Treaster in *New York Times,* Sept. 4, 1975; Treaster in *New York Times,* Aug. 14, 1975; "Psychiatry and Drugs: A Strafing Run by the *Village Voice*," *Behavior Today,* Sept. 18, 1978, p. 41.

38. Nicholas Horrock in *New York Times,* July 17, 1977.

39. *Atlanta Journal and Constitution,* Jan. 14, 1979.

40. Ibid.

41. *Atlanta Constitution,* Aug. 4, 1977.

42. *Atlanta Constitution,* Sept. 2, 1977.

43. Nicholas Horrock in *New York Times,* Aug. 3, 1977.

44. Joseph Treaster in *New York Times,* Aug. 3, 1977.

45. *Atlanta Journal and Constitution,* Feb. 19, 1978.

46. "C.I.A. Researched Psychic Impact of Child Circumcision, Editor Reveals . . . ," *Behavior Today,* Oct. 24, 1977, p. 4.

47. Treaster, *New York Times,* Aug. 3, 1977.

48. U.S., Congress, Senate, Committee on Human Resources, testimony of Admiral Stanfield Turner, Director of Central Intelligence, *Project MKULTRA, The CIA's Program of Research in Behavioral Modification, Joint Hearing,* 95th Cong., 1st sess., Aug. 3, 1977 (Washington, D.C.: Government Printing Office, 1977), pp. 17–18.

49. *Atlanta Journal and Constitution,* Jan. 14, 1979.

50. *Atlanta Journal and Constitution,* Sept. 16, 1978.

51. *Washington Post,* Jan. 23, 1979.

52. Jeffrey Gillenkirk, "LEAA and NIMH-Collaboration since 1968," *Psychiatric News,* April 17, 1974, p. 1.
53. Robert Levinson and Donald Deppe, "Optional Programming: A Model Structure for the Correctional Institution at Butner," *Federal Probation,* June 1976, pp. 37–44.
54. Jeffrey Gillenkirk, "Violence Control Project Tests LEAA's MH Plans," *Psychiatric News,* May 1, 1974, p. 1.
55. Walter C. Langer, *The Mind of Adolf Hitler* (New York: Basic Books, 1972).
56. *New York Times,* Sept. 26, 1973.
57. Congressional Quarterly, *Watergate: Chronology of a Crisis* (Washington, D.C.: Congressional Quarterly, 1974), p. 262, referring to *New York Times,* Aug. 3, 1973.
58. J. Anthony Lukas, *Nightmare: The Underside of the Nixon Years* (New York: Viking Press, 1976), pp. 92–93.
59. Ibid., pp. 103–4.
60. Barry Sussman, *The Great Cover-Up: Nixon and the Scandal of Watergate* (New York: Thomas Y. Crowell, 1974), pp. 212–7.
61. *Watergate: Chronology of a Crisis,* p. 663; Lukas, *Nightmare,* pp. 101–2.
62. *Facts on File, Watergate and the White House,* vol. 3 (New York: Facts on File, 1974), p. 56, quoting *New York Times,* March 3, 1974.
63. Paul Lowinger, letter to editor, "Full Information," *Psychiatric News,* Nov. 19, 1976, p. 2.
64. Actions of American Psychiatric Association Board of Trustees, Dec. 1977, p. 27.
65. The material on Martha Mitchell is based on Jonas Robitscher, "Stigmatization and Stonewalling: The Ordeal of Martha Mitchell," *Journal of Psychohistory* 6 (1979): 393–408.
66. *Congressional Record,* May 14, 1962, pp. 8343–44; May 17, 1962, pp. 8717–22; May 21, 1962, pp. 8755–56; Sarah McClendon, *My Eight Presidents* (New York: Wyden Books, 1978), pp. 144–46.
67. Bob Woodward and Carl Bernstein, *The Final Days* (New York: Avon, 1977), pp. 447–48.
68. High Sidey, "A Loyalist's Departure," *Time,* Sept. 30, 1974, p. 31.
69. *Watergate: Chronology of a Crisis,* p. 285.
70. Lukas, *Nightmare,* p. 562.
71. Everett Holles in *New York Times,* Sept. 7, 1974; Philip Shabecoff in *New York Times,* Dec. 19, 1975.
72. These and other illnesses of prominent political leaders are described in Group for the Advancement of Psychiatry, *The VIP with Psychiatric Impairment* 8, Report No. 83 (New York: GAP Publications, 1973).

CHAPTER 19

1. "Therapy is too good to be limited to the sick," from Erving and Miriam Polster, in *Gestalt Therapy Integrated* (New York: Vintage Books, 1973), p. xi.

2. B. F. Skinner, *Reflections on Behaviorism and Society* (Englewood Cliffs, N.J.: Prentice-Hall, 1978), pp. 77, 82.
3. Kenneth Clark, presidential address to American Psychological Association, "The Pathos of Power: A Psychological Perspective," *American Psychologist* 26 (1971): 1047–57.
4. William Alanson White quoted in "Mental Health Librarians," *Hospital & Community Psychiatry* 28 (1977): 52.
5. "Swedish Program to Screen 4-Year-Olds," International Comments, *Journal of the American Medical Association,* 235 (1976): 1062.
6. "Future Criminals," *Behavior Today,* April 13, 1970, p. 4.
7. "Future Criminals," *Behavior Today,* April 20, 1970, p. 6.
8. Report of The Governor's Commission to Improve Services for Mentally and Emotionally Handicapped Georgians, *Helping Troubled Georgians Solve Their Problems: A Mental Health Improvement Plan for Georgia,* Atlanta, Oct. 29, 1971 (mimeographed), pp. 48–49.
9. The President's Commission on Mental Health, *Report to the President* (Washington, D.C.: General Printing Office, 1978), 1:52.
10. *Atlanta Constitution,* July 26, 1972.
11. "Clues to Preventing Schizophrenia," *Science News,* March 24, 1979, p. 182.
12. Dorothy Trainor, "Psychiatry Said Useless in Delinquency Problems," *Psychiatric News,* Nov. 5, 1977, p. 13; "Early Criminals: Hands-Off Vs. Intervention," *Human Behavior,* July 1978, pp. 40–41.
13. L. M. Greenberg, M. A. Deem, and S. McMahon, "Effects of Dextroamphetamine, Chlorpromazine, and Hydroxyzine on Behavior and Performance in Hyperactive Children," *American Journal of Psychiatry* 129 (1972): 532–39.
14. *Atlanta Constitution,* Feb. 28, 1978.
15. Alan Sroufe and Mark Stewart, "Treating Problem Children with Stimulant Drugs," *New England Journal of Medicine,* 289 (1973): 407; "Hyperkinesis and Drugs," *Human Behavior,* Aug. 1973, p. 33; "Classroom Pushers," *Time,* Feb. 26, 1973, p. 65; Peter Schrag and Diane Divoky, *The Myth of the Hyperactive Child* (New York: Pantheon, 1975); Peter Schrag in *New York Times,* Oct. 19, 1975.
16. ". . . Berkeley Study Finds Few Children Hyperactive—and Fewer Drugges," *Behavior Today,* Oct. 9, 1978, p. 1; Joseph Bell, "The Family That Fought Back," *McCall's,* May 1977, p. 28.
17. "Use of Therapeutic Drugs in Elementary Schools," *Behavior Today,* April 26, 1976, p. 5.
18. Bell, "The Family That Fought Back," p. 40.
19. Sroufe and Stewart, "Treating Problem Children," pp. 410–11.
20. This and other studies skeptical of Ritalin's efficacy are summarized in "Childhood Hyperactivity: A New Look at Treatment and Causes," *Science,* Feb. 3, 1978, pp. 515–17.
21. "Sounding Board: The Crisis in Methadone Maintenance," *New England Journal of Medicine* 296 (1977): 1000.
22. "California Launches Crackdown on 'Scrip Doctors' Who Aid Ad-

dicts," *American Medical News,* March 27, 1978, p. 3. See Chapter 23.

23. Dr. Irving Leopold, quoted in "Problem: Too Many Drugs," Medical News, *Journal of the American Medical Association* 236 (1976): 339.

24. Lester Grinspoon and James Bakalar, "The Amphetamines: Medical Uses and Health Hazards," *Psychiatric Annals* 7 (Aug. 1977): 381, 382.

25. Murray Kane, "Crazy . . . Or Criminal?" *Madness Network News* 5 (Winter 1979): 2.

26. Gilbert Cant, "Valiumania," *New York Times Magazine,* Feb. 1, 1976, p. 34.

27. Richard Gottlieb, Theordone Nappi, and James Strain, "The Physician's Knowledge of Psychotropic Drugs: Preliminary Results," *American Journal of Psychiatry* 135 (1978): 29.

28. National Institute on Drug Abuse, *Sedative-Hypnotic Drugs: Risks and Benefits* (Washington, D.C.: DHEW Publication No. (ADM) 78–952, 1977), reported in *FDA Drug Bulletin,* Jan.—Feb. 1978, pp. 5, 6.

29. John Lister, "By the London Post: Operation Dump," *New England Journal of Medicine* 299 (1978): 707.

30. Aaron Mason, Vincent Serviano, and Robert DeBurger, "Patterns of Antipsychotic Drug Use in Four Southeastern State Hospitals," *Diseases of the Nervous System,* July 1977, pp. 541–45.

31. Domeena Renshaw, "Mentally Retarded, Hyperkinetic and Psychotic," *Diseases of the Nervous System,* July 1977, pp. 575–76.

32. Joseph DiGiacomo and Richard Cornfield, "Implications of Increased Dosage of Neuroleptic Medications during Psychotherapy," *American Journal of Psychiatry* 136 (1979): 824–26.

33. Jun-bi Tu, paper given at 1977 annual meeting of the Canadian Psychiatric Association, reported in "Psychiatrists Said Ignoring Mental Problems of Retarded," *Psychiatric News,* Nov. 4, 1977, pp. 20, 21.

34. Joel Greenberg, "The Aging of Sleep," *Science News,* July 1, 1978, p. 11.

35. "Geriatric Drug Abuse Said Virtually Ignored Problem," *Psychiatric News,* April 1976, p. 1.

36. Sidney Cohen, quoted, ibid.

37. The discussion on use of chemotherapy in nursing homes is based on "Drugs in Nursing Homes," *The Nursing Home Law Letter,* Feb. 7, 1977 (Los Angeles: National Senior Citizens Law Center).

38. Theodore Van Putten, Evelyn Crumpton, and Coralee Yale, "Drug Refusal in Schizophrenia and the Wish to Be Crazy," *Archives of General Psychiatry* 33 (1976): 1443–46.

39. David Owens, "The Use of Fluphenazines in a Continuing-Care Program," *Hospital & Community Psychiatry* 29 (1978): 115–18.

40. "Ethical and Legal Dilemmas Posed by Tardive Dyskinesia," *Medical-Moral Newsletter,* Oct. 1977, p. 1.

41. David Sherman and J. Donald Easton, letter to editor, "Involuntary Jaw Movements in Elderly Patients," *Journal of the American Medical Association* 237 (1977): 1690; Mark Amdur, letter, ibid., pp. 1690–91; José Chalis-

sery et al., "Iatrogenic Morbidity in Patients Taking Depot Fluphenazine," *American Journal of Psychiatry* 136 (1979): 867–977.

42. Thomas Zander, "Prolixin Decanoate: Big Brother by Injection?" *Journal of Psychiatry and Law* 5, No. 1 (1977): 55–75.
43. *Re Cleo F. Lundquist,* No. 140151 (1976), Ramsey County (Minn.) Probate Court.
44. *In the Matter of Fussa,* No. 66110 (1976), Hennepin County (Minn.) Probate Court.
45. Zander, "Prolixin Decanoate," p. 66, fn. 1.
46. Yolande Bourgeois Rogers, "The Involuntary Drugging of Juveniles in State Institutions," *Clearinghouse Review,* Nov. 1977, pp. 623–29.
47. *Morales* v. *Turman,* 383 F. Supp. 53 (U.S. D.C. E.D., Texas, 1974), 103–4.
48. *Atlanta Constitution,* Aug. 8, 1977.
49. Robert Freeman, M.D., "One M.D. Who's Seen Prison Life From Both Sides of the Bars," *American Medical News,* June 9, 1978, p. 15.
50. John Turner in *Atlanta Journal,* Oct. 3, 1978.
51. Research Department, International Secretariat, Amnesty International, Summary of Allegations of Medical and Psychiatric Ill-Treatment in United States Prisons (1974), p. 2.
52. Zander, "Prolixin Decanoate," pp. 67–68.
53. Robert Lipsyte in *New York Times,* June 27, 1976.
54. "Amphetamines and the San Diego Chargers: Mandell 'Guilty' of Excessive Prescribing," *U.S. Journal,* Dec. 1977, p. 3.
55. "Psychiatrists Organize to Aid Mandell Fight," *Psychiatric News,* Feb. 17, 1978.
56. Ari Kiev, "BFT: Psychiatry Goes 'Electronic'," *Drug Therapy,* June 1976, pp. 169–70.
57. Raymond Cattell, "The Nature and Measurement of Anxiety," in *Theories of Personality,* ed. Gardner Lindzey and Calvin Hall (New York: John Wiley, 1965), p. 357.
58. Robert Smith et al., "The Correctional Officer as a Behavioral Technician," *Criminal Justice and Behavior* 3 (1976): 345–60.
59. Howard Rome in "The Psychiatrist, The APA, and Social Issues: A Symposium," *American Journal of Psychiatry* 128 (1971): 686.
60. Peter Goode, letter to editor, *Psychiatric Opinion* 9, No. 1 (1972): 34, 35.
61. Leon Ferber and Justin Krent, reporters, "Open Forum: The Role of the Psychoanalyst in a Changing Society," *International Journal of Psycho-Analysis* 57 (1976): 445.
62. Louis Fairchild, "Some Retrospective Impressions of Psychiatric Programs for Treating Children," *Hospital & Community Psychiatry* 28 (1977): 772–73.
63. Dorothy Trainor, "Depression Called Largely a Social Phenomenon," *Psychiatric News,* May 19, 1978, p. 49.
64. William Eddy and Robert Saunder, "Applied Behavioral Science in Urban Administrative Political System," *Mental Health Digest,* May 1972, pp. 31–34.

65. James Comer, "Nero and Rome: Psychiatry and Survival," *American Journal of Psychiatry* 131 (1974): 1386–87.

66. Raymond Waggoner, Sr., "The Presidential Address: Cultural Dissonance and Psychiatry," *American Journal of Psychiatry* 127 (1970): pp. 1–8.

67. "APA Backs ERA," *Behavior Today*, June 3, 1974, p. 155.

68. "Psychiatrist Finds Resistance to His Aid in Foreign Policy," *Frontiers of Clinical Psychiatry*, Dec. 1, 1970, p. 3.

69. Morton Prince, "Roosevelt as Analyzed by the New Psychology," *New York Times*, March 24, 1912, (Sunday) Magazine Section, Part VI, 1–2.

70. William McGuire, ed., *The Freud/Jung Letters* (Princeton, N.J.: Bollingen Series 94, Princeton University Press, 1974), p. 500.

71. Sigmund Freud and William Bullitt, *Thomas Woodrow Wilson: A Psychological Study* (Boston: Houghton Mifflin, 1967).

72. Leslie Bennetts in *Philadelphia Evening Bulletin*, Sept. 24, 1976; "Measuring Presidents," *Time*, Aug. 3, 1970, p. 52; "Nixon the Extremist," *Behavior Today*, Aug. 3, 1970, p. 1.

73. Eli Chesen, *President Nixon's Psychiatric Profile* (New York: Peter H. Wyden, 1973); David Abrahamsen, *Nixon v. Nixon* (New York: Farrar, Straus and Giroux, 1977); Richard Liebert, "Nixon and the Enemy Within," review of *Nixon v. Nixon* by David Abrahamsen, *Psychology Today*, March 1977, p. 68.

74. Robert Coles, "Jimmy Carter: Agrarian Rebel?" *The New Republic*, June 26, 1976, pp. 14–19; "The Psychiatrist Who Is a Top Carter Aide: An Interview," *Behavior Today*, Oct. 11, 1976, pp. 4–5.

75. Group for the Advancement of Psychiatry, *The VIP With Psychiatric Impairment* 8, Report No. 83 (New York: GAP Publications, 1973) p. 154.

76. Ibid., pp. 187, 188.

77. Ibid., p. 199.

78. Ibid., p. 176.

79. Ronald Fieve, *Moodswing* (New York: William Morrow, 1975), pp. 156–57.

CHAPTER 20

1. Some recent historians of psychiatry say that traditional historians have overstated the reliance in the Middle Ages on a demonological rather than a naturalistic theory of the cause of mental illness: See Jerome Kroll, "A Reappraisal of Psychiatry in the Middle Ages," *Archives of General Psychiatry* 29 (1973): 276–83; Richard Neugebauer, "Medieval and Early Modern Theories of Mental Illness," *Archives of General Psychiatry* 36 (1979): 477–83.

2. Stephen Toulmin, "Introductory Note: The Multiple Aspects of Mental Health and Mental Disorder," *Journal of Medicine and Philosophy* 2 (1977): 194.

3. James Monahan, quoted in A. Louis McGarry, "Who Shall Go Free?" *Psychiatric Opinion* 5, No. 6 (1968): 19.

4. Karl Menninger, "Medicolegal Proposals of the American Psychiatric Association," *Journal of Criminal Law & Criminology* 19 (1928): 367, 373.

5. Benjamin Karpman, "Criminality, Insanity and the Law," *Journal of Criminal Law and Criminal Police Science* 39 (1949): 586–604.
6. Benjamin Karpman, "Criminal Psychodynamics: A Platform," *Archives of Criminal Psychodynamics* 1 (1955): 96.
7. Sigmund Freud, *Civilization and Its Discontents*, Standard Edition (London: Hogarth Press, 1961), 21:145.
8. Ibid.
9. Maxwell Weisman quoted in "Alcoholics Should Be Responsible for Sticking to Therapy," *Clinical Psychiatry News*, May 1976, p. 1.
10. Sigmund Freud, "The Psychogenesis of a Case of Homosexuality in a Woman," Standard Edition (London: Hogarth Press, 1957), 18:167–68.
11. Sigmund Freud, "Moral Responsibility for the Content of Dreams," Standard Edition (London: Hogarth Press, 1961), 19:133. In the same work Freud appears to be saying that the legal psychiatric concept of lack of criminal responsibility based on a separation of the "knowledge" of the id from the ego is dubious because the ego developed out of the id and forms with it a single biological unit, which explained the fact that the individual in obsessional neurosis indicates that his ego takes responsibility for the contents of the id "of which it knows nothing." He says, "The physician will leave it to the jurist to construct for social purposes a responsibility that is artificially limited to the metapsychological ego. It is notorious that the greatest difficulties are encountered by the attempts to derive from such a construction practical consequences which are not in contradiction to human feelings." P. 134.
12. Sigmund Freud, *New Introductory Lectures on Psycho-Analysis*, Standard Edition (London: Hogarth Press, 1964), 22:113.
13. C. S. Lewis, "The Humanitarian Theory of Punishment," *Res Judicatae*, (Melbourne University Law Review) 6 (1953): 224.
14. Karl Menninger in response to statement of James Q. Wilson, quoted in Daniel Goleman, "Proud to Be a Bleeding Heart," *Psychology Today*, June 1976, pp. 81, 82, 83.
15. Paul Robinson, *The Freudian Left* (New York: Harper & Row, 1969).
16. Sigmund Freud, *The Interpretation of Dreams*, Standard Edition, Vols. 4 and 5; *Three Essays on the Theory of Sexuality*, Standard Edition, Vol. 7 (London: The Hogarth Press, 1953).
17. Burness Moore and Bernard Fine, eds., *A Glossary of Psychoanalytic Terms and Concepts*, 2d ed. (New York: The American Psychoanalytic Association, 1968), p. 85.
18. Sigmund Freud, *New Introductory Lectures*, 22:80.
19. "50 and 100 Years Ago," *Scientific American*, Feb. 1978, pp. 12, 14.
20. Judd Marmor, "'Normal' and 'Deviant' Sexual Behavior," *Journal of the American Medical Association*, 217 (1971): 165–70.
21. Freud, *New Introductory Lectures*, 22:149.
22. The *New York Times* reported in a 1977 article: "Pornographic films, always a staple of fraternity parties, were first used in classrooms several years ago as part of the education of doctors. Their use quickly moved into other spheres such as psychology and nursing, and then into undergradu-

ate biology programs . . . [This is] part of a recent national trend toward more college courses in sexuality, accompanied by greater use of explicit films." Richard Flaste in *New York Times,* Sept. 27, 1977.

23. S. A. Lewin and John Gilmore, *Sex Without Fear* (New York: Medical Research Press, 1950), p. 45. A recent study contrasts marriage sex manuals published prior to 1969 and recent manuals dealing with marriage and sex. The earlier books saw marital sex in terms of a "work ideology"; the more recent books extol a "fun morality" as a "nonpuritan ethic." Dennis Brissett and Lionel Lewis, "The Big Toe, Armpits, and Natural Perfume: Notes on the Production of Sexual Ecstasy," *Society,* Jan./Feb. 1979, pp. 63–73.

24. Barry McCarthy, *What You Still Don't Know About Male Sexuality* (Scranton, Pa.: Crowell, 1977).

25. Sherry Hite, endorsing Leon and Shirley Zussman, *Getting Together,* advertisement of The Atlantic Literary Institute, 1979.

26. Eleanor Hamilton, "Today" show, National Broadcasting Company, Nov. 24, 1978.

27. Ruth Carter Stapleton in *Atlanta Journal,* Jan. 23, 1979.

28. *Atlanta Journal and Constitution,* Dec. 2, 1978.

29. Saul Bellow, *Mr. Sammler's Planet* (New York: Viking Press, 1970), p. 159.

30. William Merrill Downer, "A Psychological Justification of Anarchism: The Case of Paul Goodman," *The Psychohistory Review* 7, No. 3 (Winter 1979): 37.

31. James Sloan Allen, review of *Bergasse 19: Sigmund Freud's Home and Offices, Vienna 1938; The Photographs of Edmund Engleman, New Republic,* Nov. 13, 1978, pp. 33–34.

32. Robinson, *The Freudian Left,* p. 5.

33. Sigmund Freud, *Analysis of a Phobia in a Five-Year-Old Boy* [The Case of Little Hans], Standard Edition (London: Hogarth Press, 1955), 10:148.

34. Philip Nobile in *San Francisco Chronicle,* May 15, 1978, p. 21.

35. Sigmund Freud, "Contributions to a Discussion on Masturbation," Standard Edition (London: Hogarth Press, 1958), 12:252.

36. Daniel Yankelovich, in a talk at Aspen Institute, Aspen, Colorado, July 8, 1978.

37. O. Spurgeon English, "Viewpoints: What Impact Does Adultery Generally Have on a Marriage?" *Medical Aspects of Human Sexuality,* Oct. 1975, pp. 127, 133. A more cautious and conventional attitude on infidelity is expressed in H. S. Strean, "Extramarital Affair: Psychoanalytic View," *Psychoanalytic Review* 63 (1976): 101–13.

38. Freud originally used this phrase in another context, the connection of the sexual and of the excremental; see Sigmund Freud, "On the Universal Tendency to Debasement in the Sphere of Love," Standard Edition (London: Hogarth Press, 1957), 11:177–90, 189. In "The Dissolution of the Oedipus Complex," Standard Edition (London: Hogarth Press, 1961), 19:171–79, 178, he applies it to the girl who feels she has been deprived of a penis.

39. Freud, *New Introductory Lectures,* 22:115.

40. Ernest Jones, *The Life and Work of Sigmund Freud* (New York: Basic Books, 1953), 1:153; 2:421.
41. Ibid.
42. Phyllis Chesler, *Women and Madness* (Garden City, N.Y.: Doubleday, 1972), p. 73.
43. Ibid., p. xxi.
44. William Masters and Virginia Johnson, *Human Sexual Response* (Boston: Little, Brown, 1966).
45. Georgia Kline-Graber and Benjamin Graber, *Woman's Orgasm: A Guide to Sexual Satisfaction* (Indianapolis: Bobbs-Merrill, 1977).
46. Richard Moran, "Awaiting the Crown's Pleasure: The Case of Daniel M'Naughton," *Criminology* 15, No. 1 (1977): 22–23.
47. "Threatened Assassination of the Chancellor of the Exchequer," *Illustrated London News,* March 7, 1843, p. 173.
48. Richard Moran, review of *Social Structure and Assassination,* by Doris Wilkinson, in *Journal of Criminal Law and Criminology* 68 (1977): 465.
49. Jeffry Galper, "Personal Politics and Psychoanalysis," *Social Policy* 4 (Nov./Dec. 1973), p. 35.
50. Ibid., pp. 39, 40–41.
51. Clarence Blomquist, "Is a Crisis of Conscience a Medical Problem?" *Hastings Center Report,* June 1976, p. 26.
52. Robert Waelder, *Principles of Psychoanalytic Therapy* (New York: International Universities Press, 1960), pp. 244–45.
53. Matthew Dumont, "Is Mental Health Possible under Our Economic System—No!" *Psychiatric Opinion* 14, No. 3 (1977):9, 33, 44.
54. Carol Boggs and William Caspary, "Therapy and Revolutionary Change," *Issues in Radical Therapy,* Spring 1977, p. 4.
55. Gilles Deleuze and Felix Guattari, *Anti-Oedipus: Capitalism and Schizophrenia,* trans. Robert Hurley, Helen Lane, and Mark Seem (New York: Viking Press, 1977).
56. Henry Greenbaum, "Opinion: Ethics, The Quality of Life, and Psychoanalysis," *The Academy Forum* (The American Academy of Psychoanalysis) 22 (Autumn 1978): 1, 19.
57. Stanley Greben and Stanley Lesser, "The Question of Neutrality in Psychotherapy," *American Journal of Psychotherapy* 30 (1976): 627, 630.
58. Janet and Paul Gotkin, *Too Much Anger, Too Many Tears* (New York: Quadrangle/The New York Times Book Co., 1975), p. 386.

CHAPTER 22

1. Phyllis Greenacre, "The Role of the Transference: Practical Considerations in Relation to Psychoanalytic Therapy," *Journal of the American Psychoanalytic Association* 2 (1954): 671–84.
2. Joseph Andriola, "Brief Communications: A Note on the Possible Iatrogenesis of Suicide," *Psychiatry* 35 (1973): 213–218.
3. Gerald Epstein and Howard Nashel, "Editor's Page," *Journal of Psychia-*

try & Law, Summer 1977, pp. 163–64. For an account of the reactions of patients to a forced break in treatment see James Krainin, "A Last Day," *Voices,* Summer 1972, pp. 54–57.

4. Suzanne Hadley and Hans Strupp, "Contemporary Views of Negative Effects in Psychotherapy," *Archives of General Psychiatry* 33 (1976): 1291–1302.

5. Kenneth Pope, N. Henry Simpson, and Myron Weiner, "Malpractice in Outpatient Psychotherapy," *American Journal of Psychotherapy* 32 (1978): 593.

6. Donald Dawidoff, *The Malpractice of Psychiatrists* (Springfield, Ill.: Charles C. Thomas, 1973).

7. Donald Dawidoff, "The Malpractice of Psychiatrists," *Duke Law Journal* No. 3 (Summer 1966): 696–716.

8. Pope, Simpson, and Weiner, "Malpractice," p. 593.

9. *Hammer* v. *Rosen,* 181 N.Y.S.2d 805 (1959), *modified,* 165 N.E.2d 756 (1960).

10. "Ticklish Treatment," *Newsweek,* July 30, 1973, pp. 74–75; "Rage Reduction Suit," *Psychiatric News,* Dec. 6, 1972.

11. *Stump* v. *Sparkman,* 435 U.S. 349 (1978).

12. *O'Connor* v. *Donaldson,* 422 U.S. 563 (1975), consent judgment ratified Federal District Court for Northern District of Florida, Feb. 4, 1977.

13. For example, see *Bartlett* v. *State,* 383 N.Y.S.2d 30 (N.Y. Supr. Ct., App. Div., 14th Dept., 1975), where a patient at New York's Willard State Hospital for thirty-seven years was only allowed to bring an action against the state of New York, after a court of claims had originally dismissed the suit, on his showing that he received little or no treatment during his hospitalization (there were only thirty-seven entries in his record showing personal contact with physicians), and after a court had determined that he probably should have been released to outpatient status shortly after his original commitment.

14. Group for the Advancement of Psychiatry, *Confidentiality and Privileged Communication in the Practice of Psychiatry* 4, Report No. 45 (New York: GAP Publications, 1960), p. 105.

15. *Doe* v. *Roe,* 420 U.S. 307 (1975).

16. "Judge Awards Patient Damages in Novel Ruling," *New York Law Journal,* November 25, 1977, p. 1; *Doe* v. *Roe,* 324 N.Y.S.2d 71 (1971): *cert. dismissed,* 420 U.S. 307 (1975).

17. Patricia Bosworth, *Montgomery Clift* (New York: Harcourt Brace Jovanovich, 1978), p. 330.

18. The account of Montgomery Clift's life and therapy is from Bosworth and from Robert LaGuardia, *Monty: A Biography of Montgomery Clift* (New York: Arbor House, 1977).

19. LaGuardia, *Monty,* p. 94.

20. Bosworth, *Montgomery Clift,* p. 206.

21. Ibid., pp. 388, 389.

22. Ibid., p. 231.

23. John Leonard, review of *Montgomery Clift* by Patricia Bosworth, *New York Times*, Feb. 23, 1978.
24. *Landau* v. *Werner*, 105 Sol. J. 1008 (1961), aff'g. 105 Sol. J. 257 (1961).
25. *Zipkin* v. *Freeman*, 436 S.W.2d 753, 761 (Supr. Ct. Mo., 1969).
26. Evan McLeod Wylie, "For the Defense . . . ," *This Week*, Sept. 11, 1966, pp. 4–5.
27. Letter from Freud to Ferenczi, Dec. 13, 1931, in Ernest Jones, *The Life and Work of Sigmund Freud* (New York: Basic Books, 1957), 3:163–64.
28. Ibid., p. 165.
29. Irwin Rothman, "Animals and People," *Medical Affairs* (Univ. of Pa.), March 1968, p. 51.
30. Jules Older, "Four Taboos That May Limit the Success of Psychotherapy," *Psychiatry* 40 (1977): 198.
31. Anne Sexton, *Words for Dr. Y.* (Boston, Houghton Mifflin, 1978), p. 31.
32. *Atlanta Journal and Constitution*, Nov. 24, 1977.
33. "Let Us Touch," *Time*, Aug. 2, 1968, p. 54.
34. James McCartney, "Overt Transference," *Journal of Sex Research* 2 (1966): 227–37; James McCartney, "Open Letter to the APA," *American Journal of Psychiatry* 126 (1969): 577–78.
35. McCartney, "Open Letter to the APA," p. 577.
36. Robert Jay Lifton, *Psychobirds* (Taftsville, Vt.: Countryman Press, 1978), unpaged.
37. Jonathan Black, "Pelvic Therapy," *New Times*, Dec. 11, 1978, p. 52.
38. Sheldon Kardener, Marielle Fuller, and Ivan Mensh, "A Survey of Physicians' Attitudes and Practices Regarding Erotic and Nonerotic Contact with Patients," *American Journal of Psychiatry* 130 (1973): 1077–81.
39. Jean Holroyd and Annette Brodsky, "Psychologists' Attitudes and Practices Regarding Erotic and Nonerotic Physical Contact with Patients," *American Psychologist*, Oct. 1977, pp. 843–49.
40. Linda D'Addario, quoted in Noel Osmont in San Diego (Cal.) *Union*, Feb. 18, 1978.
41. N. Wagner, presentation at Western Workshop of the Center for the Study of Sex Education in Medicine, Santa Barbara, Cal., 1972, quoted in Kardener, Fuller, and Mensh, "A Survey of Physicians' Attitudes," p. 1080.
42. "Nearly 20 Percent of Polled Psychiatrists See 'Exceptions' to Patient-Sex Tabu . . . ," *Behavior Today*, March 13, 1978, pp. 5–6.
43. Alan Stone, "The Legal Implications of Sexual Activity between Psychiatrist and Patient," *American Journal of Psychiatry* 133 (1976): 1140, 1138.
44. *McWilliams* v. *Haveliwala*, 403 N.Y.S.2d 103 (N.Y. Supr. Ct., App. Div., 2nd Dept., 1978).
45. *Ross* v. *State*, 342 S.2d 1023 (D.C. App., Fla., 1977); *Atlanta Constitution*, Dec. 1, 1975.
46. "Love Thy Analyst," *Time*, March 24, 1975, p. 76.
47. Lucy Freeman and Julie Roy, *Betrayal* (Briarcliff Manor, N.Y.: Stein and Day, 1976).

48. Black, "Pelvic Therapy," p. 55.
49. Stone, "Legal Implications," p. 1139.
50. Ibid., pp. 1139, 1140.
51. "Court Lowers Sex Case Award," *Medical World News,* March 8, 1978, p. 9.
52. *Buckingham and Hoey* v. *Trahms* (App. Dept. Super. Ct., San Francisco, Cal., 1977), deposition of Robert Trahms, M.D., June 10, 1977, reported by Lorna Cunkle in *Pacific Sun,* Sept. 9, 1977.
53. The account of *Buckingham* v. *Trahms* is from Cunkle in *Pacific Sun,* Sept. 9, 1977; the testimony of Buckingham concerning the start of the sexual relationship is on pp. 5 and 6.
54. Ibid., p. 5.
55. "Masters Blasts 'Innumerable' Patient 'Rapes'," *Medical Tribune,* June 11, 1975, p. 1.
56. *Atlanta Constitution,* March 6, 1976.
57. "Sexual Misconduct Laid to Unlicensed New York 'Therapists'," *Psychiatric News,* January 17, 1973, p. 9.
58. Marilyn Elias, "Stand-In for Eros," *Human Behavior,* March 1977, p. 23.
59. Alexis Scott Reeves, *Atlanta Constitution,* March 5, 1976.
60. Charles Seabrook, *Atlanta Journal,* April 12, 1979.
61. The stories of Tsavaris and other Florida doctors are from the series by Gene Miller, "Sex and the Psychiatrists," *Miami Herald,* June 4–7, 1978. The series documents the ineffectuality of the state licensing board in enforcing professional standards.
62. Ibid.
63. Ibid., June 7, 1978.
64. Phyllis Chesler, "The Sensuous Psychiatrists," *New York,* June 19, 1972, pp. 52–61.
65. Robert Robinson, "In the Public Eye: Psychiatry in the Mass Media," *Psychiatric News,* July 19, 1972, p. 4; letter of Arnold Hodas to *New York* quoted, ibid.
66. "Physicians Who Have Sex with Patients Held in Need of Therapy," *Clinical Psychiatry News,* August 1977, pp. 1, 33.
67. Robinson, "In the Public Eye."

CHAPTER 23

1. Suzanne Gordon, "Helene Deutsch and the Legacy of Freud," *New York Times Magazine,* July 30, 1978, 23–25, 25.
2. *The Principles of Medical Ethics with Annotations Especially Applicable to Psychiatry* (Washington, D.C.: American Psychiatric Association, 1973), revision of May 1975, states: "An arrangement in which a psychiatrist provides supervision or administration to other physicians or nonmedical persons for a percentage of their fees or gross income is not acceptable; this would constitute fee-splitting. In a team of practitioners, or a multi-

disciplinary team, it is ethical for the psychiatrist to receive income for administration, research, education or consultation. This should be based upon a mutually agreed upon and set fee or salary . . ."

3. Lions, "Dr. Fogg," *Psychiatric News,* Jan. 21, 1977.
4. Hart, "B.C.," *Atlanta Constitution,* May 10, 1977.
5. Lichty, "Grin and Bear It," *Field Enterprises,* Nov. 9, 1978.
6. Ralph Greenson, "The Decline and Fall of the 50-Minute Hour," *Journal of the American Psychoanalytic Association* 22 (1974): 787.
7. Ibid., p. 787.
8. Ibid., pp. 789, 790.
9. Pietro Castelnuovo-Tedesco, "The Twenty-Minute Hour: A Technic of Brief Psychotherapy," *Southern Medicine,* Oct. 1976, pp. 33–37.
10. Martin Allen, "Peer Review of Group Therapy: Washington, D.C., 1972–1977," *American Journal of Psychiatry* 135 (1979): 446.
11. "Psychologists Practice Where the Money Is," *Psychology Today,* June 1978, p. 35, reporting on findings of James Richards and Gary Gottfredson, "Geographic Distribution of U.S. Psychologists: A Human Ecological Analysis," *American Psychologist,* Jan. 1978, pp. 1–9.
12. Nicholas Cummings, quoted in "Psychologists and Urban Affluence," *Science News,* March 4, 1978, p. 134.
13. Unnamed American Psychological Association source, "News Roundup," *Behavior Today,* Oct. 16, 1978, p. 7.
14. *Atlanta Constitution,* Oct. 23, 1978.
15. "Gold in Geriatrics," *Time,* June 6, 1969, p. 103.
16. Joseph Featherstone, "Kentucky Fried Children," *New Republic,* Sept. 12, 1970, pp. 12–16.
17. Philip Shabecoff in *Atlanta Journal and Constitution,* Sept 3, 1978.
18. Ibid.
19. Amitai Etzioni, "Public Affairs: Defrocking Sacred Cows," *Human Behavior,* July 1978, p. 16.
20. *New York Times,* Dec. 3, 1978.
21. Psychiatric Institute of America, brochure, 1977.
22. Ibid.
23. Quarterly Stockholders Report, for the period ending Dec. 31, 1976, Psychiatric Institute of America.
24. E. Fuller Torrey, "A Merger of Oil Filters and Ids," *Psychology Today,* May 1979, p. 120.
25. Advertisement for Hospital Corporation of America, *Wall Street Journal,* Oct. 11, 1974; Shabecoff, "Private Hospital Chain."
26. Advertisement for Community Psychiatric Centers, *Wall Street Journal,* July 10, 1978; and *Moody's Industrial News Report* 50, No. 88 (1979): 2567. The figures have not been adjusted for the two-for-one stock split of July 1978.
27. Torrey, "A Merger of Oil Filters."
28. *Atlanta Journal and Constitution,* Oct. 21, 1973.
29. Paul Troop in *Atlanta Journal and Constitution,* March 19, 1978.

30. *Kentucky Association for Retarded Citizens* v. *Conn.* No. C-77-0048P (W.D. Ky., filed June 2, 1977), reported in *Clearinghouse Review*, Aug. 1977, p. 398.
31. Joe Hatcher in *Atlanta Journal and Constitution*, Jan. 2, 1977.
32. O. B. Towery and Steven Sharfstein, "Fraud and Abuse in Psychiatric Practice," *American Journal of Psychiatry* 135 (1978): 92–94.
33. Doug Garr, "How M.D.s Gross Methadone Millions," *Village Voice*, Nov. 24, 1975, pp. 9, 10.
34. "California Launches Crackdown on 'Scrip Doctors' Who Aid Addicts," *American Medical News*, March 27, 1978, p. 3.
35. "California Health Chief To Tackle 'Medi-Cal Connection'," *American Medical News*, Nov. 17, 1978, p. 9.
36. "California Launches Crackdown."
37. Ronald Buzzeo, quoted by Marsha May in *National Enquirer*, May 16, 1978, p. 43.
38. John Peterson, "Psychographics: Ads That Try to Get inside Your Head," *National Observer*, Feb. 26, 1977, p. 15.
39. Berkeley Rice, "Cooking with Psychophysics," *Psychology Today*, Oct. 1978, pp. 80, 122.
40. John Cunniff in *Atlanta Journal*, Nov. 5, 1978.
41. Vance Packard, *The Waste Makers* (New York: McKay, 1960); *The Pyramid Climbers* (New York: McGraw-Hill, 1962).
42. Martin Gross, *The Brain Watchers* (New York: Random House, 1962).
43. Charlie Roberts in *Atlanta Constitution*, March 2, 1973; Bill Bruns, "Psychologist in the Lineup," *Human Behavior*, June 1973, p. 8.
44. Flyer for June 25–27, 1977, Atlanta Seminar, The Team Defense Project.
45. Gilda Mariani, "Peremptory Challenge—Divining Rod for a Sympathetic Jury?" *Catholic Lawyer*, Winter 1975, pp. 56–81; "Jury Selection: Social Scientists Gamble in an Already Loaded Game," *Science*, Sept. 20, 1974, p. 1033. Cases besides the Angela Davis trial that have utilized jury surveying include the Harrisburg Eight, the Camden trial of radical Catholics for draft-record destruction, a series of trials arising out of the Indian takeover of Wounded Knee, a civil-damages suit on behalf of the survivors of the Buffalo Creek dam disaster, the trial of Daniel Ellsberg and Anthony Russo, the trial of John Mitchell and Maurice Sans, the Attica trials, and the Gainesville, Florida, trial of Vietnam Veterans Against the War.
46. Howard Moore, Jr., "Redressing the Balance," *Trial*, Nov./Dec. 1974, p. 29.
47. Amitai Etzioni, "Creating an Imbalance," *Trial*, Nov./Dec. 1974, pp. 28, 30.
48. "Investigative Hypnosis," *Human Behavior*, April 1978, p. 36.
49. "Hypnotized Witnesses May Remember Too Much," *American Bar Association Journal* 64 (1978): 187.
50. John Cooney in *Wall Street Journal*, April 12, 1979.
51. Kathy Slobogin, "Stress," *New York Times Magazine*, Nov. 20, 1977, pp. 48, 50; *Wall Street Journal*, Nov. 17, 1977, p. 1.

52. Robert Ringer, *Winning Through Intimidation* (New York: Fawcett Crest, 1978); *Looking Out for Number One* (New York: Funk & Wagnalls, 1977).

53. Michael Korda, *Power!* (New York: Random House, 1975); *Success!* (New York: Random House, 1977).

54. Wayne Dyer, *Your Erroneous Zones* (New York: Funk & Wagnalls, 1976).

55. Advertisement for Joyce Brothers, *How to Get Whatever You Want Out of Life* in *New York Times Book Review*, Jan. 21, 1979, p. 44.

56. Silvano Arieti, "How to Read How-To Books," *Psychology Today*, Oct. 1977, pp. 142, 148.

57. Flyer, *Brain/Mind Bulletin* (Los Angeles: Interface Press).

58. Catalogue, Lansford Publishing Company, San Jose, Cal., 1979).

59. Roger Ricklefs in *Wall Street Journal*, Sept. 19, 1977.

60. Labor Letter; *Wall Street Journal*, Jan. 9, 1979.

61. Flyer for est Community Guest Seminar, Atlanta, Ga., Oct. 23, 1978.

62. Carl Frederick, *EST: Playing the Game the New Way* (New York: Delacorte Press, 1976); Adelaide Bry, *EST: 60 Hours That Transform Your Life* (New York: Harper & Row, 1976); William Greene, *EST: 4 Days to Make Your Life Work* (New York: Pocket Books, 1976); Robert Hargrove, *EST: Making Life Work* (New York: Dell Publishing Co., undated); Harper, Gregory, Ross, and Denver quoted in advertisement for W. W. Bartley III, *Werner Erhard* (New York: Clarkson N. Potter, Inc., 1978).

63. Melor Sturua, "The Quest for Identity," *Impact* (supplement to *American Medical News*), Nov. 24, 1978, p. 6.

64. Joyce Brothers, quoted in Barbara Dubivsky in *New York Times*, Sept. 5, 1976.

65. Richard Kohl, quoted in Florence Isaacs in *New York Times*, May 1, 1977.

66. Arline Brecher in *National Enquirer*, March 3, 1977, p. 43.

67. Hilda Abraham and Ernst Freud, eds., *The Letters of Sigmund Freud and Karl Abraham* (New York: Basic Books, 1965), p. 384.

CHAPTER 24

1. "Fish Tests Bolster Memory-Chemistry Link," *Medical Tribune*, Dec. 12, 1973, p. 19.

2. Ibid.

3. "Another Assault on Memory Transfer," *Science News*, March 24, 1973, p. 180.

4. "Where the Memory Is," *Newsweek*, Aug. 23, 1965, p. 70.

5. "Animal Brain Grafts Survive," *Science News*, May 12, 1979, p. 308.

6. Maya Pines, "Shaping the Infant Brain," *Physician's World*, Dec. 1973, pp. 45–48.

7. "Erasing the Painful Memories of Surgery," *Medical World News*, Nov. 8, 1974, p. 27.

8. Joan Arehart-Treichel, "Brain Peptides and Psychopharmacology," *Science News*, Sept. 25, 1976, pp. 202–3; Solomon Snyder, "The Opiate Re-

cepter and Morphine-Like Peptides in the Brain," *American Journal of Psychiatry* 135 (1978): 645–52.

9. Sidney Cohen, "Internal Opioid-Like Compounds," *Drug Abuse and Alcoholism Newsletter*, Sept. 1977, p. 1.

10. "Natural Opiate in Pituitary Promises 'Very Exciting' Uses," *Medical Tribune*, December 8, 1976, p. 5.

11. Joan Arehart-Treichel, "Brain Peptides and Psychopharmacology."

12. "Brain Peptides as Psychiatric Drugs," *Science News*, Sept. 17, 1977, p. 182.

13. "Smells: 'Surer Than Sounds or Sights'," *Medical World News*, Sept. 13, 1974, pp. 36C–36D.

14. Benjamin Brody, "The Sexual Significance of the Axillae," *Psychiatry* 38 (1975): 278–89, and William Montagna, quoted by Brody, p. 278.

15. "Are Deodorants Suppressing Humans' Sexually Arousing Aromas?" *Clinical Psychiatry News*, May 1976, p. 31.

16. "Physostigmine: Improvement of Long-Term Memory Processes in Normal Humans," *Science*, July 21, 1978, pp. 272–74.

17. Richard Saltus in *Atlanta Journal and Constitution*, July 10, 1977.

18. "A Drug That De-Fuses Stage Fright," *Science*, Dec. 3, 1977, p. 376.

19. Jeffrey Gray, "Anxiety," *Human Nature*, July 1978, p. 42.

20. "Neuroleptic-Induced 'Anhedonia' in Rats: Pimozide Blocks Reward Quality of Food," *Science*, July 21, 1978, pp. 262–64.

21. "Human Aggression Linked to Chemical Balance," *Science News*, June 3, 1978, p. 356.

22. Monte Buchsbaum, "The Sensoriat in the Brain," *Psychology Today*, May 1978, p. 96.

23. "Can the Brain Repair Itself?" *Mental Health Scope*, Dec. 3, 1975, pp. 2–3.

24. Daniel Goleman, "Split-Brain Psychology: Fad of the Year," *Psychology Today*, Oct. 1977, p. 89.

25. David Goodman, "Learning From Lobotomy," *Human Behavior*, Jan. 1978, pp. 44–49.

26. David Galin, "Implications for Psychiatry of Left and Right Cerebral Specialization," *Archives of General Psychiatry* 31 (1974): 579.

27. "A Radio Links Chimp's Brain And Computer," *Medical Tribune*, Oct. 5, 1970, p. 3.

28. Brian Sullivan in *Miami Herald*, Feb. 23, 1976.

29. "A Computer under Your Hat," *Science News*, Feb. 28, 1976, p. 133.

30. Sullivan, *Miami Herald*, Feb. 23, 1976.

31. "Mind-Reading Computer," *Time*, July 1, 1974, p. 67.

32. Patricia McBroom in *Atlanta Journal and Constitution*, Aug. 27, 1972.

33. Daniel Goleman, "A New Computer Test of the Brain," *Psychology Today*, May 1976, p. 44.

34. Roger McIntire, "Parenthood Training or Mandatory Birth Control: Take Your Choice," *Psychology Today*, Oct. 1973, p. 34.

35. Ralph Schwitzgebel, *Development and Legal Regulation of Coercive Be-*

havior Modification Techniques With Offenders (Chevy Chase, Md.: National Institute of Mental Health, Center for Studies of Crime and Delinquency, 1971), pp. 15–21.

36. Barton Ingraham and Gerald Smith, quoted in Elliot Valenstein, "Science-Fiction Fantasy and the Brain," *Psychology Today,* July 1978, p. 29.

37. Robert Ferguson, Jr., *The Scientific Informer* (Springfield, Ill.: Charles C. Thomas, 1971), p. 130.

38. News Briefs, *Mental Health Scope,* Sept. 19, 1972, p. 7.

39. Constance Holden, "Lie Detectors: PSE Gains Audience Despite Critics' Doubts," *Science,* Oct. 24, 1975, pp. 359–62.

40. Ibid., p. 360.

41. Ibid.

42. Ibid., pp. 361, 362.

43. Lyn Martin in *Atlanta Constitution,* Nov. 18, 1976; *Atlanta Journal and Constitution,* Nov. 7, 1976.

44. Holden, "Lie Detectors," p. 360.

45. Advertisement, Hagoth Corporation, "Truth Has a Price Tag," *Sky* (magazine of Delta Airlines), Sept. 1978.

46. Cynthia Kasabian in *Wall Street Journal,* Aug. 6, 1978.

47. Anna Quindlen in *New York Times,* Aug. 19, 1977.

48. U.S., Congress, House, Committee on Government Operations, *The Use of Polygraphs and Similar Devices by Federal Agencies,* H. Rept. 94-795, 94th Cong., 2d sess., 1976, p. 7.

49. Ibid.

50. Gene Abel et al., "The Components of Rapists' Sexual Arousal," *Archives of General Psychiatry* 34 (1977): 895–903; R. C. Rosen, "The Use of Penile Plethysmography in a Medicolegal Examination," *Journal of Forensic Sciences* 22 (1977): 791–94.

51. *New York Times,* Sept. 25, 1977.

52. K. Michael Schmidt, George Soloman, and Herbert Johnson, "Artificial Conscience: New Approach to Rehabilitation of Selected Criminal Offenders in Integration of Polygraph into Forensic Behavior-Sciences," *Corrective and Social Psychiatry* 23 (1977): 93–100, summarized in "Novel Probation: Choosing the Lie Detector over Jail," *Human Behavior,* Sept. 1978, p. 66.

53. Kenneth Colby, Joseph Weizenbaum, and Margaret Boden, quoted in George Alexander, "Terminal Therapy," *Psychology Today,* Sept. 1978, p. 50.

54. "Computerize Lab Results . . . ," *Medical World News,* June 19, 1970, p. 11.

55. Peter Breggin, *After the Good War* (New York: Stein and Day, 1973).

56. "Trend toward 'Psychiatrocracy' Can Be Reversed," *Clinical Psychiatry News,* Feb. 1977, p. 42.

57. "Official Actions," American Psychiatric Association, *American Journal of Psychiatry* 128 (1971): p. 393.

58. Margaret McDonald, "Area II Succeeds in Changing Medicaid," *Psychiatric News,* Dec. 1, 1978, p. 1.
59. Robert Gibson, "Equal MH Coverage? Yes!!" Daniel Patterson, "Unlimited MH Coverage? No!!" *Psychiatric News,* March 17, 1978, pp. 5 and 6; letter of Alex Kaplan to members of the American Psychoanalytic Association, Nov. 9, 1978.
60. Lee Weiss, "The Resurgence of Biological Psychiatry: New Promise or False Hope for a Troubled Profession," *Perspectives in Biology and Medicine,* Summer 1977, pp. 573–85.
61. Richard Lamb, "Rehabilitation in Community Mental Health," *Community Mental Health Review* 2, No. 4 (1977): 1.

CHAPTER 25

1. Jonas Robitscher, "The Uses and Abuses of Psychiatry (The 1976 Isaac Ray Lectures)," *Journal of Psychiatry and Law* 5, No. 3 (Fall 1977):333–404.
2. "Tanay Rebuts Robitscher," *Newsletter of the American Academy of Psychiatry and the Law* 4 (Jan. 1979): 12.
3. "Bazelon Says Psychiatry Resists Self-Scrutiny," *Psychiatric News,* Aug. 15, 1973, p. 1.
4. Allen Wheelis, "The Vocational Hazard of Psychoanalysis," in *The Quest for Identity* (W. W. Norton, 1958), pp. 231–35.
5. Linda Greenhouse in *New York Times,* Jan. 6, 1979; "Leaving Prison in a Wheelchair," *Institutions, Etc.* 2 (Jan. 1979): 18–19.
6. "Decline of Psychiatric Residents Subject of Probe," *Psychiatric News,* June 15, 1979, p. 28.
7. "The Doctors' Lot," *New Republic,* April 22, 1978, p. 8.
8. John Medelman, "Why I Am Not a Psychiatrist," *Harper's,* Feb. 1967, pp. 46–49.
9. Jerome Frank, "Psychiatry, the Healthy Invalid," *American Journal of Psychiatry* 134 (1977): 1354.
10. Donald Light, Jr., quoted in "Status of Psychiatry Gains While Other Specialties Decline," *Clinical Psychiatry News,* June 1977, pp. 1, 54.
11. Group for the Advancement of Psychiatry, *Problems of Psychiatric Leadership* 8, Report No. 90 (New York: Group for the Advancement of Psychiatry, 1974), p. 934.
12. Bertram Brown, "Life of Psychiatry," *American Journal of Psychiatry* 133 (1976): 489–95; "Criticisms Haven't Reduced Psychiatric Service Demand," *Clinical Psychiatry News,* Aug. 1975, p. 3.
13. "Stone Sees Psychiatry Advancing Despite Criticism," *Psychiatric News,* June 3, 1977, p. 24.
14. "More Psychiatrists, Psychologists, Needed Over Next 12 Years," *Mental Health Scope,* March 31, 1978, p. 1.
15. Walter Goodman in *New York Times,* March 8, 1979.
16. Bertolt Brecht, *The Exception and the Rule,* trans. Eric Bentley, in *The Jewish Wife and Other Plays* (New York: Grove Press, 1965), p. 143.

Index

Abortion, psychiatric assistance in securing, 303–8
Abstinence, principle of therapist, 416, 425, 429–30
Accountability, psychiatrist's, 409
Action for Mental Health, 230–31
Addiction: as illness, 149, 151, 154–156; prostitution as, 158; Methadone programs and, 293, 354–55, 460; prescription writing and support of, 451. *See also* Drugs/chemotherapy
Addington v. *Texas,* 192
Adebimpe, Victor, 181
After the Good War (Breggin), 473
Aggression: Freud on, 30; experimental psychosurgery to treat uncontrollable, 287–90; research on, 463. *See also* Violence
Aggressivity training, 455
Albee, George, 182–83
Alcoholism: treatment of, 92, 418; as illness, 149, 151, 154, 156–58, 160; profit in treatment of, 447
Alexander, Franz, 34, 84
Allen, James S., 385–86
American Medical Association, 331–32, 356
American Psychiatric Association: president of, on state hospitals, 119, 122; on nomenclature, 147, 167–68, 169–83; on mental health/illness range, 161; on homosexuality, 161, 169, 170–77; on predicting dangerousness, 206; drug companies' support of, 292; on abortion, 307; on Soviet treatment of dissenters, 324, 326; on government's use of psychiatry (Ellsberg; CIA), 341; president

of, on social uses of psychiatry, 367, 368–69; on Equal Rights Amendment, 369; and psychiatric screening and evaluation of U.S. president and other high government officials, 370–71; on need for confidentiality in therapeutic relationship, 416; on sex between therapist and patient, 423–24, 425–26; on social issues, 473–74; on insurance coverage for psychiatric services, 474; on psychiatric abuses, 483
American Psychoanalytic Association, 379
American Psychological Association, 349, 350
Amphetamines, 83, 356, 426, 463; Ritalin related to, 352–53, 354
Analysis. *See* Freud, Sigmund; Psychiatry; Psychoanalysis; Therapy; Treatment/therapy
Analytic school of psychiatry, 5, 6–7
Andriola, Joseph, 410
Andy, Orlando, 290
Anectine, 300–301
Antabuse, 92
Anthropological view. *See* Cultural aspects
Anti-Oedipus (Deleuze and Guattari), 397
Antipsychiatrists, 18, 109–16, 397, 398, 473
Antipsychotic / antidepressant / antianxiety drugs. *See* Drugs/chemotherapy
Anxiety: Freud on, 31, 217, 379–80; testing of (stress interview), 216–17; drugs in treatment of (*see* Drugs/chemotherapy)
Apomorphine, 301

Predictions (*cont.*)
227; technology of, 350. *See also* Testing
Prescriptions: authority to write, 246–47; indiscriminate writing of, 450–41
Presidential leadership. *See* Leadership
Primal-scream therapy, 94
Prince, Morton, 369–70
Prisons: power of psychiatrists in, 42–54, 259–61, 402–3; token economies in, 92–93; testing in, 211, 218; experimental psychosurgery in, 285–86, 301; other experimental programs in, 299–301, 366–67; forced drugging in, 362–64; employees of, 366–67. *See also* Hospitals
Privacy, invasions of personal, 471–72. *See also* Confidentiality issue; Intrusiveness
Private/personal personality, of therapist, 398
Pro bono publico, 190
Procedural safeguards: for prisoners, 42–54; therapeutic purpose of detention versus, 184; basic right of habeas corpus and, 189–91, 330, 414. *See also* Civil liberties; Commitment; Indeterminate sentences
Profiling, uses of classificatory tests in, 218
Projective techniques, 36, 211
Prolixin, 294, 295, 301, 359–64, 480
Prosecution-minded psychiatrists, 24–25, 262
Prostitution, as addictive disease, 158
Prototype Computer-Assisted Multidisciplinary Preadmission Psychiatric Assessment Unit, 224–25
Psychiatric Anamnestic Record, 223
Psychiatric Institute of America (PIA), 446–47
Psychiatric reports/evaluations: uses of, 35 (*see also* Commitment); criticisms of, 45–46; errors of clinical judgment in, 250; for U.S. presidents and other high government officials, 346, 349, 370–71
Psychiatrists: education/training of, 5–6, 119, 382–84, 410–11, 480–82; as universal experts, 37–38, 368–69; criticized as eccentric or peculiar, 98–99; double agent aspect of, 111; in community mental health centers, 127; inconsistencies of, 147; and changes in values, 245–46, 302–3, 372–400; status quo orientation of, 328, 387, 389; as social engineers,

347–71; as politically traditionalist, 392; the silence of, 476–90
Psychiatrocracy, 473–74
Psychiatry: role and uses of, 5, 39 (*see also* Criminal justice system; Mental illness); schools of, 5–6; reliance of the law on, 19–28, 43–44, 152–53, 158–61; Freud's influence on, 29–31, 35–36 (*see also* Freud, Sigmund; Freudian concepts); criticisms of, 97–99, 110–16, 145–146, 327–28, 482–84, 487; politicalization of, 106–12, 117–41, 319–46, 349, 369, 370–71; demand for, 116, 487 (*see also* Mental health care); drug companies support of and by, 292 (*see also* Drugs/-chemotherapy); no limits attitude of social, 367–69; future directions of, 370–71, 457–75; teaching of, 382–84 (*see also* Education/training); value system of, 399–400; abuses of, 409–33; commercialization of, 434–56; managerial revolution in, 475; reforms to correct abuses of, 484–86
Psychiatry and the Law, 101
Psychics, CIA experiments with, 336
Psychic trauma, Freud on, 30–31
Psychoanalysis, origin of, 29–30; length of treatment required by, 32–33; scientific validity of, 33–34; concepts of, used by nonanalysts, 34–35; medical affiliation of, 35–36; homosexuality theories of, 172; psychiatry's dissociation from, 179; deviations from classical, 386–87; radical politics and, 393–95; commercial aspects of, 437
Psychobiography, 369–70
Psychodiagnostik (Rorschach), 36
Psychological Society, The (Gross), 9, 94
Psychological stress evaluator (PSE), 468–69
Psychopharmacology. *See* Drugs/chemotherapy
Psychosexual development, Freud's stages of, 30–31, 32
Psychosis: of V. Woolf, 12–15; as reparative process, 112; diagnosis of, 113–14; in state hospitals, 119; as disease, 159; drugs in treatment of, 91, 356–57, 358, 360
Psychosocial intervention. *See* Social control
Psychosurgery, 87–89, 273, 281–92, 299–301
Psychotherapy. *See* Freud, Sigmund; Patient-therapist relationship; Psychiatry; Psychoanalysis; Therapy; Treatment/therapy

555